6/78

D0992411

Computer Storage Systems and Technology

Computer Storage Systems and Technology

Richard E. Matick

International Business Machines
Yorktown Heights, New York

A Wiley-Interscience Publication
JOHN WILEY & SONS
New York • London • Sydney • Toronto

Library of Congress Cataloging in Publication Data

Matick, Richard E.   1933–
    Computer storage systems and technology.

    "A Wiley-Interscience publication."
    Bibliography: p.
    Includes index.
    1. Computer storage devices.   2. File organiza-
tion (Computer science)   3. Data structures
(Computer science)   I. Title.

TK7895.M4M37   621.3819′533   77-5812
ISBN 0-471-57629-8

Printed in the United States of America

10 9 8 7 6 5 4 3 2 1

To my mother and father,
Barbara and Michael Matick,
who made it all possible
and to my wife, Doris,
and our children, Lisa and Jill,
who made it all realizable

Preface

Since the inception of the modern computer in the late 1940s, computing systems have continually grown in complexity, both in hardware and in the associated systems programming. This complexity is by and large due to two factors: first, the tradeoffs in cost/performance versus size for various memory technologies, and second, the way human beings organize and use data. If technology could produce an infinitely fast, infinitely large, random access memory at a low cost, many of the problems faced by systems designers would disappear. There would be no need for memory hierarchies, virtual systems, or storage management. In addition, technology could be aimed at producing only one type of memory (i.e., random access), rather than a seemingly infinite variety of memory designs, each with its own advantages and disadvantages. Unfortunately it is not possible to make this ideal random access memory, and there will always be a spectrum of memory systems having varying cost/performance characteristics and different sizes. Thus memory presents an interesting and difficult challenge to designers, not only technologically but from the entire perspective of a memory–storage system.

This book, which confronts the challenge just noted, has grown out of a series of courses taught at the University of Colorado at Boulder, Stanford University, and various IBM locations. The students' backgrounds have ranged from sophomores, juniors, seniors, and graduate students, to engineers, programmers, physicists, metallurgists, and others. As a result, the book is organized as a textbook, although it is intended also for self-study and as a reference for those working in this or related areas. This book requires general familiarity with computers, preferably some courses on programming, computer logic, and introductory computer science or computer architecture. Certain sections assume some physics, device, or circuit background, although those not so oriented should be able to grasp the essential points with little difficulty.

The book is written in terms of the fundamentals as nearly as possible. In many cases, the fundamentals had to be articulated, if not discovered, since there appear to have been no previous attempts to establish the fundamental requirements for storage devices, organization, writing, retrieval, and so on. Thus after having worked in the field for more than 15 years, I realized that the area has never received a comprehensive fundamental treatment, and I have attempted to rectify the situation.

This book has two main purposes: first, to bring together all related aspects of computer storage systems and technology in one volume, and second, to relate the various aspects of data structure and usage to the hardware design and tradeoffs. There are several reasons for undertaking this task; first, if one wishes to learn about computer memory and storage, it is necessary to search through countless books, papers, and scattered literature. Even then many significant gaps exist. In addition, there are sharp distinctions drawn in practice between main memory, storage, mass storage, data structuring and file organization, memory hierarchy, virtual systems, and other aspects of a complex system. In the past, these distinctions also established the boundaries between technologies (i.e., magnetic cores, magnetic disks, tapes, etc.). However these boundaries are becoming less clear, particularly in the new advanced technologies being considered for memory and storage. It is not certain, for instance, whether an advanced technology such as magnetic bubbles is useful strictly for storage or memory, or whether it is applicable at some point in between within the file gap. Even less advanced technologies such as transistorized integrated circuits are currently used in memory and are being studied for large backup storage. Furthermore, the size of main memory in use on third and fourth generation systems today exceeds that of "storage" used on older first and second generation systems. Thus these boundaries are not only arbitrary and unnecessary, but they promote misunderstanding of the overall problems, such as similarity and tradeoffs between memory technologies and the relationship between the way in which people use data and the possible means of storing and retrieving data usefully and economically. When all these topics are covered in one volume, the hardware designer can better understand not only other technologies but also the relationship of the overall systems and programming problems to the technology at hand. In a like manner, the systems or machine level applications programmer can acquire a deeper understanding and broader perspective of the various technology tradeoffs and how they relate to data storage and retrieval requirements.

The major technology problem in computing systems today lies mainly in providing large, fast, inexpensive storage. The CPU itself is no longer the major problem, since there are ways to achieve faster logic; but the directions for memory and storage are less clear. Much of what systems programmers do is a result of the large discrepancies between speed, size, and cost of the various storage technologies. Programming systems expend considerable effort to bridge and smooth the gaps that technology has not been able to eliminate at a competitive cost; that is, it is cheaper to bridge gaps with programming and system architecture rather than new intermediate technologies. How long or how far this can be done is an important question that is not considered in this book; only the marketplace can provide an answer.

This book is interdisciplinary to the extent that it deals with the various disciplines that are directly related to storage. It is a further aim to permit the scientist to acquire a fundamental understanding of memory, to be better able to see where new inventions, discoveries, or understanding may be useful in this field, which needs new ideas continuously.

Chapter 1 presents a brief history of memory storage technology to show the speed gap between the CPU and main memory, how we arrived at the present state of the art, and why storage systems are important. The various memory systems and cost/performance gaps are covered briefly, to show a very wide range. Several sections are devoted to relationships between the main memory and CPU (e.g., the connection between CPU and memory clocking period in terms of an instruction execution period). A study of the size of main memory versus the speed of the CPU has revealed some important relationships and "universal constants" that have not previously been recognized. The effects of limited storage capacity on the problem size is treated in a separate section. Some current requirements for storage both in scientific and commercial data processing are included, as well as some future hardware needs for weather forecasting. An important question often asked but hitherto not answered is, With the advent of large-scale integration of memory devices, why can't we just make the entire storage system a random access memory? A fundamental treatment of this question in terms of the size of random access memory relative to the number of logic gates in the central processor is presented in a separate section, along with the concept of the one level store. A brief discussion of the human memory system reveals a number of very interesting relationships to a computer memory hierarchy. Chapter 1 thus places the entire storage area into perspective and sets the stage for the remainder of the book.

Chapter 2 presents the fundamental device and system requirements for storing and retrieving information as well as the fundamental differences and similarities between storage systems of various types (random access, sequential, etc.). The important engineering fundamentals that are applicable on a general scale to memory design are included in the areas of magnetism and magnetic circuits, semiconductor technology, superconductivity (including the Josephson effect), and certain electrical properties of array conductors. There is a separate section on the "ultimate" limits on storage density.

Chapter 3 focuses on the principles of operation, characteristics, and design of the major cells and devices that have been implemented in either commercial or experimental random access memories. Included are ferrite cores, thin films, junction and field effect transistors, superconducting cells, ferroelectric cells, and read-only memory devices. Important design parameter and tradeoffs are presented.

Chapter 4 covers random access memory systems with particular emphasis on the advantages and disadvantages of various types of organization. It discusses design principles, important parameters, and organization methods, as well as limitations of magnetic cores, thin films, and transistor and other memories. A section on associative memory is included.

Chapter 5, which is devoted to magnetic recording principles, serves as a stepping stone to Chapters 6 and 7. Chapter 5 covers the basic principles associated with all digital magnetic recording techniques, as well as materials and systems parameters. Chapter 6 consists mainly of a discussion of magnetic tape and related systems; Chapter 7 covers disks, drums, and related systems. Although a significant amount of technology is worked into these two chapters, the basic problems of addressing and retrieving information, including the amount of "stored addressing" information, are considered in detail. The importance of this factor is often overlooked, yet it represents a fundamental tradeoff in achieving low cost at the expense of nonlocal, nonrandom access of data.

Chapter 8 reviews file organization techniques and the major difficulties as related to storage systems (e.g., disks and tapes). The reader is led through several fundamental examples to explore the various ways a given file might be organized, with the tradeoffs in terms of storage space, access time, and ability to insert and delete records.

Chapter 9 is a fundamental discussion of memory hierarchy systems and storage system architecture. Particular attention is given to virtual memory, including cache, showing the tradeoffs in buffer size, page size, and replacement algorithms, in addition to the design concepts that are possible. Examples of commercial systems are discussed in terms of the fundamental requirements. This chapter is unlike any other book dealing with virtual memory and should be of interest to memory system designers as well as to systems programmers.

This book was originally written by pulling together all the aspects of memory and storage that I considered important. In addition to more details and other topics, this included a chapter on advanced concepts for shift register storage, including magnetic bubbles, charge coupled semiconductor devices, beam-addressed storage, and dynamic reordering for improved access time. Unfortunately, this would have resulted in an enormous book with additional delays and hence were removed. A brief discussion of shift register storage with numerous references can be found in Matick (1975).

An earnest attempt has been made to keep this book at a fundamental level and dissociated from any particular computer organization or design. However this is not always possible, and specific examples sometimes relate to one type of organization. When this occurs, the type of organization assumed is specifically indicated to prevent any misconceptions from arising. This fundamental approach avoids the common pitfall of introducing a subject by describing the typical commercial implementation. Rather—the fundamental requirements for any system or part of a system are first established; then typical examples are described in terms of implementing the fundamentals. This is a major departure from the approach of other books dealing with related subjects.

RICHARD E. MATICK

Peekskill, New York

April 1977

Acknowledgments

Many persons have contributed to this book in various ways, and their efforts are most sincerely appreciated.

I am especially indebted to Ralph Gomory, IBM Vice-President and Director of Research, for providing me the opportunity for a teaching sabbatical in 1972–1973. It was during this time that I formulated the basic subject matter of this book and decided how it was to be organized. No less a debt of gratitude is due to William Turner, who in early 1972, having learned of my impending teaching sabbatical, planted the idea of a book.

Frank Barnes, Chairman of the Department of Electrical Engineering, University of Colorado, Boulder, gave me the opportunity to teach two courses on which much of this book is based. My first students, Barbara Langdon, Tom Burrows, Ching Tuan, Kent Weldon, Clarence Ellis, Doug Johnson, Van Norred, Lee Warc, Paul Williams, and Ted Hommel, deserve special thanks for their interest and suggestions. There were many subsequent students at Stanford University, IBM, and elsewhere, too numerous to include.

The enthusiasm of one student, Hjalmer Ottesen of IBM Boulder, who continued the courses I had initiated at IBM and the University of Colorado was a source of inspiration to me.

The typing assistance of Barbara Juliano over the past three years has been above and beyond the call of duty. Without her skill and dedication, this effort would have been formidable. The drafting skills of Sally Bradford, who did most of the complex drawings, has substantially aided in communicating such a complex subject. The understanding and willingness to help on the part of Linda Callahan, Louis Kristianson, Mary LaMarre, Bob Monahon, and many others is sincerely appreciated.

An internal company text on magnetic recording by Jim Smith has been of considerable value in certain parts of Chapter 5. Countless individuals have helped over the years, and I acknowledge these efforts as being the small epsilons whose summation amounts to a large value.

I hope that this book can serve as an example for future books dealing with memory and storage, in terms of demonstrating a more fundamental approach, as well as inclusion of all aspects of memory systems.

My wife, Doris, and our children, Lisa and Jill, have been most sympathetic during this rather long and tedious undertaking.

R. E. M.

Contents

Chapter 8   File Organization and Data Structure   508

Chapter 9   Memory Hierarchies and Virtual Memory Systems   532

1

Introduction to Memory and Storage

1.1 INTRODUCTION: CPU–MAIN MEMORY SPEED GAP

Modern computing systems consist basically of four hardware components shown in Fig. 1.1-1: the central processing unit (CPU), the main memory, the secondary storage (e.g., disks, tapes, and drums), and the input/output equipment that interfaces with humans. This book is concerned primarily with the memory and secondary storage systems, although certain aspects of the CPU are included out of necessity.

Since the beginning of the modern computer era in the late 1940s and early 1950s, the need for larger storage capabilities has become increasingly apparent. For example, the size of main storage directly addressed from a computing system has increased from a few thousand words of typically 10 to 36 bits per word in the early and mid-1950s to well over several million bytes in use on many systems today. The magnitude and characteristics of such storage needs have changed considerably over the years, although three requirements have remained paramount—larger capacity, higher speed, and lower cost. The major factors responsible for these trends can be characterized in terms of two fundamental laws.

1. *Law of Expanding Computer Power*. Problems expand to fill the power of the CPU allowed for their execution.
2. *Law of Expanding Storage*. Problems expand to fill the storage allowed for their completion.

These two laws are interrelated in a variable manner, as will become evident later. For specific cases, however, the need for CPU power is motivated primarily by the complexity of scientific, engineering, and mathematical problems, whereas the need for larger storage is due mainly to the vast amount of data stored in data processing and data based applications. These laws merely reflect the fact that the complexity of nature and society still greatly exceeds our ability to understand and model the real world. With respect to the first law, for instance, in the early days of computing, the range of problems that could be solved was quite limited, as was the accuracy of the results. A major impetus for computer development came from military

1

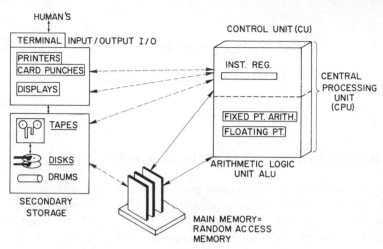

FIGURE 1.1-1   General computer organization.

and scientific needs (e.g., calculating artillery trajectories; physicists' attempts to solve complex nuclear reactions for atomic bombs). Hence modern computers evolved from these basic motivations of scientific calculations.* Since experiments are extremely complex, expensive, and difficult, the more one knows (i.e., can calculate) beforehand, the more meaningful and fruitful will be the design, implementation, and interpretation of the experiment. However to solve even relatively small scientific problems requires considerable computation speed and storage, and the demands on the computer increase rapidly for modest increases in problem complexity (see Sections 1.6 and 1.8). Thus larger and faster computers furnish a better means to solve increasingly complex scientific or engineering problems with accuracy and in a reasonable amount of time.

   With respect to the second law, the ability of users to find applications for large storage is at least as good or better than the ability of technological advances to provide it, at an acceptable cost, of course. The result of these two laws has been an ever-increasing gap between the CPU and main memory speed. Such a gap did not exist in early computers. For instance, the first large scientific computer, the IBM 704, had a basic machine (CPU) cycle time† of 12 μsec and a main memory cycle time of also 12 μsec for 32K words maximum. The CPU cycle time was dictated by the main memory

* Excellent reviews of this early history and scientific needs are given in Bethe (1970) and Goldstine (1970).
† Logic delay was 250 nsec per stage, or several microseconds to perform a simple function if run at fastest speed.

cycle time, and the basic logic and memory device speeds were comparable. As technology progressed, logic speed increased greatly while memory speed (at reasonable costs) increased much less, relative to logic, until there existed a large gap measured in orders of magnitude between logic delay and memory cycle time. For example, the logic delay on an IBM model 195 is 5 nsec per stage, a basic machine cycle time of 54 nsec and a main memory (magnetic cores) of 0.5 μsec cycle time*; a CDC 7600 computer has a basic cycle time of 27.5 nsec and a main memory of 0.275 μsec. Faster main memories in the range of 0.2 μsec have been built from other technologies such as plated wires and magnetic thin films, but this equipment is still rather expensive. Thus CPU cycle times and logic delays have improved dramatically while main memory has improved at a much slower rate, leaving a significant gap. This discrepancy in speed can be seen in Table 1.1-1, which lists some of the important parameters for several of the larger commercial computers. A comparison of the two columns "main memory cycle time" and "CPU cycle time" (defined in Section 1.4) clearly shows the latter improving much more than the former. This difficulty with main memory can be seen even more dramatically by plotting main memory cycle time versus year as in Fig. 1.1-2, which indicates that main memory cycle time has bottomed out. The continually increasing gap between the CPU and main memory speed is shown in Fig. 1.1-3. The interleaving of memory modules, as well as many of the newer architectural concepts such as cache memory, virtual memory, and memory hierarchy, is due primarily to this large speed gap (see Section 9.1). It is, of course, possible to increase further the speed of main memory, but difficulties arise in two ways: first, it is necessary to go to new technologies, which are more expensive; second, the size of main memory required on a given system has increased dramatically (see Table 1.1-1, and Fig. 1.5-3), which in itself tends to increase the cycle time just by increasing the array delay. Furthermore, even if the cost per bit remained constant, the large size means that the total cost (total number of bits × cost/bit) is increasing with each new system. Technology is faced with the need to decrease the cost per bit while increasing the speed—a rather formidable task.

As a result of the greater demand for storage capacity and speed, and the inability of main memory technology to maintain the rapid pace, direct access disks and drums have stepped in, along with new systems concepts to help bridge the gaps. Thus it seems that the need for large storage with reasonable characteristics is open ended, the supply never being able to satisfy the demand. This has been the trend in the past, and it will continue

---

* The gap between logic and main memory is bridged by a small cache memory paged out of main memory; see Section 9.11.

TABLE 1.1-1   Parameters of Various Large Computing Systems Versus Year (K = 1000, K′ = 1024)

Computer	Year Delivered	Main Memory Capacity	A Word Size (bits)	Main Memory Cycle Time (μsec)	B CPU Cycle Time (μsec)
Eniac	1946	20 numbers— flip-flops	40 bits/no.		0.2 msec
		104 numbers— resistors	(4 bits/digit)		
Univac I	1951	1000 words Hg delay line	91	400 max circulation time	0.4 but serial
IBM 650 (drum main)	1954	1–2K words	60 5 bits/digit	4.8 msec rotation (0.094 msec word)	7.8 μsec/pulse but serial by digit
RCA BIZMAC (core main)	1955	4K′ char.	7 bits/char.	20 μsec access 50–80 cycle[a]	50–80[a]
IBM 704	1955	4–32K′ words	36[b]	12	12
IBM 7090	1960	32K′ words	36[b]	2.2	2.2
IBM 7030 STRETCH	1961	16–256K′ words	64	2.1	0.6 [5]
CDC 6600	1964	32–128K′ words	60[c]	1.0	0.1
Univac 1108	1965	64–256K′ words	36[b]	0.75	0.125
IBM 360/75	1965	256–1024K′ bytes	64[d]	0.75	0.195
RCA Spectra 70/55	1966	64–512K′ bytes	32	0.84	
IBM 360/85	1969	512–4096K′ bytes +16–32K′ cache	64[d]	0.96 (0.08 cache)	0.08
CDC 7600	1969	64–512K′ words	60[c]	0.275	0.0275 [6]
IBM 360/195	1971	1–4M′ bytes +32K′ cache	64[d]	0.81 (core) 0.054 (cache) 0.162 (effective) [7]	0.054
Burroughs B7700	1972	128–1024K′ words	48 (word oriented)	1.5	0.0625
Univac 1110	1972	131K′–1024K′ words 32–256K′ plated wire	36[b]	1.5 (core) 0.52 write 0.38 read plated wire	0.075
IBM 370/168	1973	1–8M′ bytes +16K′ cache	32–64	~0.32 0.08 cache	0.08
Amdahl 470V/6	1975	1–8M′ bytes +16K′ cache	32 [8]	0.2 [8] 0.032 cache	0.032
Cray I	1976	1M′ words	64	0.05	0.0125 (pipelined)

[1]   Kolsky (1967).
[2]   Freeman and Ragland (1970).
[3]   Knight (1966).
[4]   Knight (1968).

[5]   Buchholz (1962).
[6]   Elrod (1970).
[7]   Murphey and Wade (1970).
[8]   Electronics (1972).

Address size (bits)	A/B Bits Processed per CPU cycle (bits/μsec)	C Memory Size (millions of characters)	C/M_1 M Char./MIPS	M_1 Average MIPS (approximate)		M_2 Average MIPS (3, 4)	
				MIPS	Ref.	Scientific	Commerical
						7.5×10^{-6}	45×10^{-6}
		0.016	0.8	0.02	1		
20 (4 decimal digits)						0.11×10^{-3}	0.29×10^{-3}
15	3	0.05	0.5	0.1	1	0.011	0.004
15	16.4	0.2	1.0	0.2	1	0.097	0.045
18	120	0.8	1.3	0.6	1	0.37	0.63
18	600	0.65 (max)	0.55	1.2		7.02	4.09
18	288					2.1^e	2.1^e
24	328	0.26–1	0.26–1 0.6 avg.	1.0	2	3.6	1.44
16						1.34	1.22
24	800	0.5–4	0.1–1.3 0.7 avg	3			
30	2182	2.6 (max)	0.52	5			
24	1185	1–4	0.2–0.8 0.5 avg	5			
20	770						
24	480						
24	400–800	1–8	~ 1	~ 2–3^a			
24	1000	1–8	~ 0.75	~ 3–5^a			
	5120	5	~ 0.4			~ 20–25^a	$\ll 25^a$

^{a} Estimate based on available information.
^{b} 1 char. = 6 bits + parity.
^{c} 1 char. = 12 bits + parity.
^{d} 1 char. = 8 bits + parity.
^{e} 1108-II.

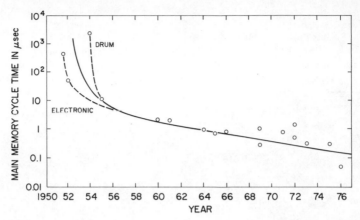

FIGURE 1.1-2   Main memory cycle time versus year (from Table 1.1-1).

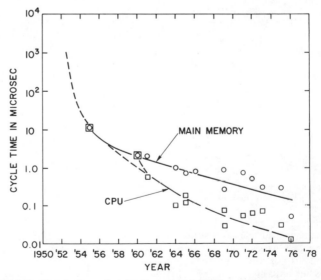

FIGURE 1.1-3   Comparison of main memory and CPU cycle times for large systems.

for the foreseeable future. This trend, coupled with the above-mentioned gap between CPU and memory cycle times, has placed memory and storage in the limelight. The emphasis will likely become even more severe in future computing systems.

1.2 HISTORICAL SURVEY OF STORAGE SYSTEMS

The numerous books and papers on the history of computers, deal primarily either with the history of the motivation and means by which calculators evolved to electronic computers, or with the speed of the calculating capabilities (i.e., how fast to add or multiply two numbers). The storage systems associated with these machines are often ignored or briefly mentioned, giving a somewhat lopsided view of computer history. In the very earliest calculators of the 1930s, the raw arithmetic speed was indeed the major problem for large computations, with storage being easily handled by punching cards; the situation changed dramatically, however, when the arithmetic speeds reached the millisecond range. Indeed, the first electronic calculations were plagued by storage limitations, and evolution of storage systems has played a major role in the evolution of computer speed and architecture. Our review of the history of storage systems in this section supplements other works on computer history. Some of the same ground must be covered, but the emphasis is on storage systems. No attempt is made to be complete: only the developments judged by the author to be highlights are included.

For the history of computers themselves, there are several good sources that contain innumerable references (Fernbach and Taub, 1970; Goldstine, 1972; Levy, 1968; Nisenoff, 1966; Pomerene, 1972; Randell, 1973; Rosen, 1969). Excellent reviews of hardware characteristics of early computers (logic and memory) are contained in Smith (1959), and Stifler (1950).

All mathematical computations, either mental, mechanical, or electronic, require a storage system of some kind, whether the numbers be written (stored) on paper, remembered in our brain, counted on the mechanical cogs of a gear, punched as holes in paper, or translated into electronic circuitry. The minimum storage requirements of any computing or calculating system are as follows:

1. An internal storage capability for temporarily holding the numbers to be processed, the intermediate results, and final answer.
2. External storage for recording input numbers to be processed.
3. External storage for permanent recording of answers for further use.

(In some cases 1 and 3 or 2 and 3 may be the same media.)

The power of a computer or calculator depends to a large extent on the size and speed of its associated storage capabilities, both internal and external. As shown in Section 1.1, the speed of early computers was generally dictated by the speed of main memory. In addition, in the very first computers in the 1940s and early 1950s the organization of the CPU (i.e., parallel or serial) was also dictated by the mode of operation of the memory. Since all the early memories were serial delay lines, Williams tubes, and magnetic drums, the first computers were serial (e.g., ENIAC, EDVAC, BINAC, UNIVAC, EDSAC, and SEAC). The first parallel machines were the Institute for Advanced Study machine at Princeton (1952) and the Whirlwind at MIT. In fact, the choice of main memory was the critical decision, the CPU then following the memory design. Thus it is not surprising that the development of storage capabilities has played and continues to play a significant role in the development of calculators and computers.

The early mechanical systems, such as Pascal's arithmetic machine (1642) used cogs on a wheel to store decimal numbers, add, and carry. The output (answer) appeared on numeral indicators above the wheels. Thus the internal storage was mechanical position of a cog on a wheel, and external storage was either pencil and paper, or the user's brain. Numerous mechanical systems were devised along similar principles, some to do multiplication and division as well as sums, such as the Leibnitz calculator of 1694, and even the two famous Babbage machines, the difference engine (1822) and analytical engine, which were never completed. Though the latter was mechanical, it differed in that it was to handle all mathematical computations, operate from instructions stored on punched cards that were to be read in sequence, contain internal mechanical storage of 1000 numbers of 50 digits each for storing intermediate results that could be used over again, and have capabilities for printing the output results (i.e., hard copy external storage). These concepts were unique, ahead of their time, and a precursor to many ideas of modern computers except for the concept of a stored program with address modification. Unfortunately, mechanical technology was not sufficiently advanced, so the analytical engine was never built.

A significant advance in technology came about in 1890 with the introduction of the Hollerith electrical tabulator (Martin, 1891). The purely mechanical systems were now replaced by an electromechanical system. The internal storage was still mechanical (i.e., position of a dial), but it was activated electrically. The external input storage was paper cards, written by punching holes in appropriate places. This concept was borrowed from the famous Jacquard weaving loom of 1812, which used punched cards to store the weave pattern. In this early loom the sensing, or reading of the cards was mechanical, needles either passed through (punched) or did not pass through (unpunched) appropriate positions on the card. In the Hollerith machine, the mechanical sensing was replaced by much faster electrical sensing. The cards were "read" or counted by small wires that passed through the holes and made electrical contact on the other side, thus electrically activating the counter dials. The output indicators, which were also the internal storage, were the dials with two arms to count from 0 to 9999 per dial. The external output storage was pencil and paper—the dial numbers were copied. Later versions added an electrical typewriter for printing, thus providing automatic external storage on paper.

The first Hollerith machines were counters, tabulators, and sorters, activated by electromechanical devices and requiring considerable human manipulation for operation. Nevertheless, the concept of "punched card" processing of statistical and business data was established by these machines, became well known, and was even used for scientific purposes, as in the tabulation of the positions of the moon by Comrie as early as 1928 (Comrie, 1928, 1932). Later versions included multiplying capability (still electromechanical) and were used for astronomical calculations by W. J. Eckert (1940) at Columbia University, for ballistic calculations at Aberdeen Proving Ground in early 1940s, and at Los Alamos in 1943 to calculate the amount of implosive compression one could achieve for fissionable material in atomic bombs. These later machines still required considerable human manipulation, and the storage remained punched cards and ink on paper (printers).

Between the earlier and later versions of the Hollerith-type machines came the first major attempt at analog computation. In 1927 Bush, Gage, and Stewart of MIT introduced a mechanical analog device to solve certain first-order differential equations in electrical networks. Various improvements through the 1930s and early 1940s led to the differential analyzer, which could solve more complex second-order differential equations; all machines were mechanical, being coupled mechanical integrators. Internal storage was analog and was represented simply by the rotational position of a wheel, gear, or shaft. External storage was a recorded wave form on a chart for input with a manual curve following device; output storage was printed numbers obtained from the angular position (analog) of the readout wheels. The latter provided mechanical analog-to-digital conversion. Thus there was essentially no storage as we know it today. These machines were rather cumbersome and difficult to "program"—each problem required substantial redoing of the mechanical interconnections. Nevertheless differential analyzers were used at the Moore School of Engineering (University of Pennsylvania) for engineering calculations and at Aberdeen for ballsitic calculations, the latter subsequently augmented by the addition of the previously mentioned Hollerith (IBM) punched card calculators in 1942.

The concept of general purpose digital storage could hardly have been recognized at this time, since all computers were still mechanical or electrically activated mechanical devices. Thus it was reasonable for storage to be in the same mode. In addition, analog calculators were often employed in special applications for various reasons, and these devices circumvent the large storage that otherwise would be required for a discrete value system. For instance, the aiming of an antiaircraft gun requires azimuth and vertical positioning on a continuous or near continuous basis as calculated from tracking sensors. Such calculations are now done digitally, but the first firing Directors were analog. Among other things, tracking information must be multiplied by $\cos \theta$; where θ is the azimuth angle. The function $\cos \theta$ was stored as a wire-wound potentiometer resistance on a card with the value of resistance from a fixed point varying as $\cos \theta$ (see Loevell, 1947). In essence, these served as stored function tables and would be equivalent to a library subroutine in digital computers. Such storage for directories was used for the M9 and other large guns during World War II.

All machines up to this time were mechanical in both the calculator and storage technologies and required substantial human manipulation, that is, they were not automatic, hence were extremely slow both in time per calculation and in number of sequential calculations per unit time. The first calculator to incorporate both electromechanical technology in the form of relays, and the automated sequencing concepts of Babbage (still not stored program) was H. Aiken's Mark 1, Automatic Sequence Controlled Calculator.* The external input storage was paper tape for instructions and paper cards for necessary data tables, and so on; any constants needed in the calculation could be internally stored with up to 60 constants of 24 columns (i.e., 1474 switches) entered by dial switches on the panel. Thus the program, rather than being stored in main memory as is done today, was stored externally as holes in paper tape; instructions were read in one at a time, then executed immediately. As such, there could be no branching or address modification as is required for a general purpose computer. The internal storage was 2204 counter positions, which included 72 counters of 24 positions each (23 digits plus sign) for storing intermediate results of complex computation with the additional positions used for addition, subtraction, and accumulation. The external output storage was either punched cards or electric typewriters. In essence, this machine was nothing more than an automated calculator. Although this calculator was a substantial improvement over previous systems, performing full (23 digit and sign) division in 15.3 sec and full multiplication in 5.7 sec; it nevertheless was rather slow and not very attractive for the more advanced problems envisioned by physicists, such as nuclear diffusion or detailed hydrodynamic calculations

---

* This device, built in conjunction with IBM and finished in January 1943, was turned over to Harvard on August 7, 1944.

of shock waves associated with nuclear bombs and reactor design. Thus uses for larger, faster machines became apparent, and work quickly proceeded along these lines.

The next major technological advance was made by J. P. Eckert and J. Mauchly at the Moore School of Engineering. They replaced electromechanical devices with completely electrical devices, namely, electronic vacuum tubes. The tubes were connected as flip-flop circuits in much the same manner as transistored flip-flops are used even today; thus they replaced the "on-off" status of relays and switches with an "on-off" electronic switch, operating several orders of magnitude faster. Even though this flip-flop storage circuit was first described by Eccles and Jordan in 1919 (see Appendix 1-A) and subsequently used in numerous ways, the first large scale application to calculators was embodied in the ENIAC (electronic numerical integrator and calculator), completed in 1946 for the army (Goldstine and Goldstine, 1946; Brainerd, 1948). The Eniac used vacuum tubes for storing 20 numbers of 10 decimal digits or 40 numbers of 5 digits in the accumulator. In addition, there was a capability for separately storing constants or independent variables in a resistor matrix called a function table. It had a capacity of 104 numbers or about 4K bits (i.e., 4 bits/decimal digit, 10 digits/number).* This was essentially a read-only memory, since the writing was performed externally by means of switches on the panel. Because of the limited read/write storage capacity, it was necessary to store the intermediate results for any calculation on punched cards. The speed of calculation was thus dictated by the speed of punching, which was 0.6 sec per card (2 to 4 numbers per card) and 0.3 sec for reading. A simple calculation demonstrates that larger main storage could not be built from vacuum tube technology. Typical storage sizes desired would be in excess of 1000 words with 40 bits per word. The classical Eccles–Jordan flip-flop used in the Eniac requires a minimum of 2 tubes/bit.† Thus a 1000 word memory would require

$$1000 \text{ words} \times 40 \text{ bits/word} \times 2 \text{ tubes/bit} = 80K \text{ tubes}$$

a rather sizable number. Further development—say, to a 5000 word memory —would require 0.4×10^6 tubes; this is over 20 times that in the Eniac and is a totally unreasonable number.‡ Thus alternative technologies were not just desirable but necessary before computers could become useful and practical.

---

* Three such tables were available.
† The storage was serial, not random; if a random access memory were to be constructed, a minimum of 4 tubes/bit would be required (see Section 3.8), at least doubling the tube count.
‡ The Eniac used a total of about 18K vacuum tubes, 1500 relays, hundreds of thousands of resistors, capacitors, and inductors, and consumed nearly 200 kW. Increasing these by a factor of 20 was out of the question.

The Eniac still was not a stored program computer. All so-called computers up to this time were calculators in this sense that the program was "wired in" and had to be changed by engineers each time a new calculation was to be done, or instructions were read and executed sequentially, one at a time (i.e., no stored program and no address modification). The stored program concept was suggested by John von Neumann in 1945 for a proposed new computer as a successor to Eniac, the EDVAC (electronic discrete variable automatic calculator).* Although the first proposed stored program computer, it was not the first to be built. The first computer as we think of them today—that is, stored program with address modification—was built at Cambridge University, England. Known as EDSAC (electronic delay storage automatic calculator), it was first operated in May 1949, before Edvac. Both the Edvac and the earlier Edsac stored program computer used ultrasonic delay lines for main storage. The Edsac memory consisted of hollow tubes filled with mercury and sealed with quartz crystals (transducers) on each end. Each tube could store 576 bits or 32 numbers of 16 binary bits plus one sign and one space = 18 bits/number or 16 numbers of 34 binary bits plus one sign and one space = 36 bits/number, the latter representing about 10 decimal digits. There were 32 such tubes in the memory, for a total of 18,432 bits, giving either 1024 words of 18 bits/word or 512 words of 36 bits/word, a rather sizable memory for its time. Total circulation time was 1.1 msec for each 576 bit tube, with a pulse or bit repetition interval of 1.9 μsec per bit.† The first commercial electronic computer, Univac I in 1951, also used mercury delay lines for storage.

One of the first main memory technologies to operate at electronic speeds was the cathode ray tube (CRT), the so-called Williams tube. A small research version was first operated successfully at Manchester University, England, in June 1948 (Kilburn et al., 1953; Williams and Kilburn, 1949). This memory stored binary bits as represented by stored charge on the phosphor surface of a cathode ray tube, which was a modified, ordinary TV tube. This technology is quite fascinating and provided a great impetus to realization of all electronic digital computers. However it was short-lived because of reliability, cost and technical problems. We summarize only the overall operating characteristics here.

An early version of the Williams tube could store a maximum of 32 numbers of 32 bits (called digits then) per number. The bits were scanned serially in a raster scan, much as a TV tube is scanned even today. Thus this system was serially accessed across the tube, or 32 bits of a number,

---

* Edvac construction was started first at the Moore School of Engineering but was delayed and completed after EDSAC.

† This main memory was backed by 4608 words of magnetic drum storage.

although access to any given line (number) on the tube was random. Hence the memory was random access to a number (word) but serial by bit. One tube could store $32 \times 32 = 1024$ bits. This early version was subsequently modified to store 40 bits/number or 1280 bits/tube. The latter version was also run at double density (2560 bits/tube), but reliability problems forced a reduction back to the original value. The first digital computer to use such storage, the "miniature machine" at the University of Manchester, used two such tubes for a total main memory of $2 \times 2560 = 5120$ bits. This system was scanned at a rate of 10 μsec/bit or 320 μsec/32 bit word, with a random access time to any word measured in microseconds (value not published). This miniature machine also introduced one of the first magnetic drums storing 47 tracks of 2560 bits/track. The concept of a rotating drum had been proposed earlier by Atanasoff in 1940 but used charge stored on rotating capacitors rather than magnetic recording. Though introducing one of the first workable drums, the miniature machine was built primarily as a test vehicle to determine feasibility of the CRT storage concept. The machine had only a token computing circuit for subtraction and crude input/output facilities. The experiment proved successful, and in late 1949 a new machine was started which was to be a full-scale digital computer.

The new machine at Manchester used eight Williams tubes at a density of 1280 bits/tube for a main memory of 10,240 bits. An improved magnetic drum was also developed which consisted of a 6 in. diameter, 8.5 in. long cylinder plated with nickel (the magnetic medium) with a linear density of about 136 bits per inch (bpi). The original version which contain 47 tracks (5.5 tracks/inch—tpi) with 2560 bits/track, was increased to 256 physical (512 logical) tracks (30 tpi) with one read and one write head per track. Each physical track stored twice as many bits as a single Williams tube, the latter being 1280 bits/tube in its final form; hence each physical track is divided into two logical tracks for paging into a Williams tube. Thus the total storage capacity of the drum was 655,360 bits, although only 112 tracks or about 280,000 bits were implemented, still a rather sizable amount. However the access time was rather slow, being 15.6 msec average (31.2 msec/rev, or 1920 rpm) compared to the microsecond access time of the CRT store, hence the latter served as main memory and the drum as intermediate storage, being placed into main when necessary. Nevertheless magnetic technology later led to the demise of the cathode ray tube; for example, IBM 701 first used a CRT, but later versions used cores for main memory.

Both the miniature machine and the improved Manchester machine had a "B tube," a special CRT that served for address modification such as is used in iterative loops. Hence these machines were in essence, general purpose computers similar to today's models. The concept of a stored program with address modification, together with the knowledge gained in the early and mid-1940s that large complex problems were amenable to calculations, formed a major stimulus to the search for large, fast storage media. Thus began the modern history of computer storage technology.

In the late 1940s and early 1950s, numerous computers (stored program variety) were built, but usually they were one or several of a kind, built under contract for special use. The first real production, full-sized computer was the IBM 650 magnetic drum system (Hamilton and Kubic, 1954), introduced in 1954.* It featured a 4 in. diameter drum 14 in. long, plated with nickel-cobalt and spinning at 12,500 rpm or 4.8 msec/rev. The latter speed represented a significant improvement in access time of about 6.5 times over early systems. This, coupled with the 1 + 1 addressing (where an instruction stores, in addition to its own operand address, the address of the next instruction), greatly improved the overall speed of drum-oriented systems. The drum served as main memory, storing all data, instructions, subroutines, and so on. The external input storage was punched cards that were read into the drum. Likewise, external output storage was cards or electric typewriter written from the drum. The drum could store a total of 120K bits of useful memory, consisting of 2000 words (1000 words on smaller model), 5 bits/digit in the bi-quinary code used, and 12 digits/word (i.e., 60 bits/word). The linear density was 50 bpi. The 2K words are stored in bands of 50 words/band along the cylinder circumference, requiring a total of 40 bands along the cylinder axis. Since the 5 bits of each digit are in parallel along the cylinder axis, whereas the successive digits of a word are in series along the circumference, a total of 40 bands times 5 bits/band requires 200 read/write heads, one for each track. A band is thus 5 bits wide (i.e., 5 tracks wide × 600 bits long, or 600 bits/track). In addition, there are 20 additional tracks for clocking and buffer storage. Thus access to any of 2K words could be obtained in a maximum of one revolution of 4.8 msec, and 2.4 msec average. This represented a great improvement not only in speed and size, but also in reliability compared to the Williams tube and previous drums.

Even before the early 1950s, many had recognized that storage was an important and fruitful area. As a result, much research and development activity was started in several directions, pursuing device concepts and the underlying technologies that appeared promising. The use of the two magnetic states of an ordinary torroid without a square BH loop for the binary "1" and "0" had long been recognized. Since such a nonthreshold device cannot be coincidently selected by itself, alternate schemes such as the use of

---

* The Univac (1951), which was the first commercial computer, and the IBM 701 (1953) were earlier machines but were not volume machines as was the IBM 650; the 701 sold only 20 machines, whereas more than 2000 of the 650s were manufactured. The 701 use a cathode ray storage tube that was rather unreliable and was replaced by core memory in a latter model. The Univac used mercury delay lines similar to the design of the Edsac.

a diode selection matrix (Section 4.10) to coincidently select a magnetic toroid were proposed at various times (Eckert, 1953). The concept of coincident selection was proposed as early as 1947 for storing information in a three-dimensional array of low pressure gas, glow discharge tubes (Forrester, 1947). However the use of square *BH* loop magnetic toroids as a coincidently selected storage was not proposed until 1949.* Subsequent development was undertaken in many laboratories around the world to produce materials and devices with the desired characteristics. Several years were required not only to find the proper devices, but also to incorporate them into a workable, economically attractive memory system. This technology came to fruition in the summer of 1953, and an operable full-scale model of the first coincident selection magnetic core memory of 2048 words developed at MIT (memory test computer) (Smith, 1959) was subsequently installed on the Whirlwind computer. The scheme proved highly feasible, and commercial systems started using core memories such as the RCA BIZMAC (probably the first commercial core memory sytem) and a modified IBM 701, which became the 704, both of 1955 vintage. Simultaneous with the development of the magnetic core memory in the late 1940s and early 1950s, a seemingly infinite variety of devices and systems were proposed for digital storage. Though much too numerous and involved to include here, they ranged from alternate implementations of the mercury delay line (e.g., piezoelectric delay lines) and alternate cathode ray tubes (e.g., holding-beam, barrier-grid) to new matrix memories using neon bulbs with resistors, neon-capacitor, capacitor-diode, optical memories, as well as rotating diodes to replace drums, and many others. In any case the coincident selection magnetic memory provided what seemed to be the best balance between size, speed, cost, availability or practicality, reliability, and potential for further improvements. Thus this technology gained a stronghold on main memory that was felt by many to be only a temporary situation. Prior to the first magnetic core memory, considerable development had already been underway in technologies that were to replace magnetic cores. Even at the time of their debut, magnetic cores were felt to be too cumbersome to make and "wire" in an array (see Chapter 3). It was already recognized that they were slow devices, they were large structures,† and they would never lend

* Court interference case, document "Brief for Forrester on Final Hearing" Interference #88269, *Jay W. Forrester* vs. *Jan A. Rajchman*, p. 18 claims that Forrester invented the concept at least as early as May–June 1949. First technical publication is Forrester (1951).

Jan Rajchman patent was filed on September 30, 1950, and first technical publication was Rajchman (1953). Interference was settled out of court. Forrester is generally accredited for the *x-y* selection scheme and Rajchman for the inhibit concept. Other patent interferences are still in progress.

† Magnetic cores were 0.034/0.054 in. ID/OD by 0.016 in. height in the model of Rajchman (1953). Early commercial systems used 0.080 and 0.090 in. OD cores.

themselves to automation, let alone planar processing via photolithography, which was an emerging technology at the time. Thus many technologies were pursued which held promise to avoid the fabrication and speed limitations of cores.

Ferroelectric devices, the electric analog of square looped magnetic device, were felt to hold more promise for low cost, automated planar processing in addition to the capability for very small devices with attendant large densities, and, hopefully high speed. Considerable research was carried out on ferroelectric devices starting in the early 1950s, continuing but tapering off into the 1960s, and even today smatterings of ferroelectric device work reappear.

Work with ferroelectrics quickly encountered serious materials problems: lack of a well-defined switching threshold (coercive force), fatigue of the switchable stored charge, inherently slow switching mechanism, and others. It was felt by many scientists that these problems could be overcome by finding a suitable material, thus much effort was devoted to ferroelectric materials and switching processes. As a result, considerable scientific knowledge has been accumulated, but no suitable material has ever been found. Unfortunately, this could not have been known beforehand, since there is no theory nor any fundamental principles saying such a material cannot exist.

While ferroelectrics were being seriously studied, Dudley Buck (1956) proposed the superconducting "cryotron" as a computer memory device that presumably had all the advantages of ferroelectrics but none of the disadvantages. One major drawback was the need for a low temperature environment of $4°K$. Cryotron devices received much attention, and development work continued well into the 1960s, but the low temperature requirement was felt to be a major obstacle by many, and other alternatives to magnetic cores were sought. The concept of using thin magnetic films with open flux paths appeared in the mid to late 1950s and offered all the advantages of planar processing, small devices, operated at room temperature; it used the phenomenon of magnetism, which was reasonably well known, so it was thought. Thus in the late 1950s there were several phenomena—ferroelectricity, superconductivity, and open flux path magnetics—incorporated into countless device structures, all aimed at replacing magnetic cores. The scientific and engineering world was ablaze with activity in basic and applied research as well as engineering development centered around these ideas. This enthusiasm had one major effect that although not seen at the time, was self-defeating. The competition and impending threat to magnetic cores acted as a pacesetter and spurred those doing core research to take their technology to its limits. As a result, none of the other technologies have made any serious inroads into the domain of main memory, which has been and continues to be dominated by cores. However cores have been pushed to their limits (see Chapter 3) and are being replaced by a latecomer, namely, large-scale integrated semiconductor memories.

Some of this history is not only interesting but enlightening from a scientific point of view; we now attempt to highlight some of the important developments concerning the problems associated with magnetic cores versus those with cryotrons, and thin magnetic films. Chapter 3 presents the detailed characteristics of these devices.

In the mid-1950s it was "well known" that switching in ferrite cores occurred by the slow process of domain wall motion. Thin magnetic films had been sufficiently studied and were known to be capable of a much faster switching process, namely, coherent rotation, where the entire film switched as a unit magnetic moment if properly driven, or by domain wall motion if not properly driven, and by a third process of nonuniform rotation under an "in-between driving field." Since thin films could be properly driven, resulting in uniform rotation, they possessed inherently faster switching properties by orders of magnitude. The switching properties of magnetic structures had been studied theoretically, and the conclusion seemed inescapable that ferrites could not switch by rotation, whereas thin films could. This prompted numerous investigators to look more closely at the switching behavior of ferrites, and it was subsequently found that ferrites could switch faster than previously expected, by the process of nonuniform rotation (see Section 3.2). This was a significant discovery, and the directions were made clear—faster ferrite memories were possible but required significant reduction in core diameter, since large driving fields are required for fast switching. As a result, ferrite cores have continually decreased in size with inside–outside diameters (in.) ranging from 0.080–0.120 to 0.050–0.080, 0.030–0.050, 0.019–0.030, 0.013–0.020, and even experimental arrays of 0.006–0.012.

The array speed has continually become faster also, but it has reached a limit of about 500 nsec cycle time for arrays of reasonable size (i.e., 4K word modules).* While these studies were going on, work was simultaneously proceeding on cryotrons. A very unfortunate state of affairs existed. Though it was known that cryotrons switch by the process of superconducting domain nucleation and boundary growth, a process very much akin to magnetic domain wall motion, it was nevertheless implicitly assumed that cryotron memory elements possessed fast switching characteristics. This seemed reasonable because devices of the first type possessed a circuit L/R time constant that was rather large (in the range of 50 μsec). Various devices

---

* The CDC 7600 has a core memory of 275 nsec cycle time, but most commercial systems are 0.5 μsec or slower.

were invented to improve this fundamental limit. In the devices with small L/R, however, the switching mechanism within the storage medium itself was basically slow, although this was not conclusively shown until 1962 when measurements were finally made (Brennemann et al., 1963). The measurements were one of several death blows given to this type of cryotron device. Others are detailed in Chapters 2 and 3 and include need for critical control of the superconducting material properties (hence poor yield) and marginal operating characteristics; need for terminated transmission lines in large arrays, which dissipate substantial energy (an undesirable condition at 4°K, since this requires larger refrigeration); and difficulty in building cryotron selection (decode) trees to work with large arrays. Thus in the early to mid-1960s it became apparent that the fast-switching cryotron was not suitable for memory, and work quickly fell off in this area, leaving thin films as the major competitor to cores.

In fact thin film memories had already been introduced in a commercial system. The Univac 1107, which became operational in 1962, contains only 128 words (36 bits/word) with an access time of 0.3 μsec and was backed up with 65K' of core memory (1.8 μsec). Thus although films offered potential improvement in speed, the high cost, hence small memory size, left room for improvement, and much research and development work continued around the world. Improvements were made and additional commercial systems using thin film memories appeared such as the Burroughs B7500 (announced (1967) with a read access time of 300 nsec (write cycle time about 500 nsec) and the B8500, using a 100 nsec scratch-pad thin film memory backed by 500 nsec core; also IBM introduced in 1968 a 120 nsec cycle time thin film memory in the S360 model 95, which was short-lived. While improvements were made in films, significant advances also occurred in cores; not only did the cycle time of the latter improve to 400 nsec and even 275 nsec in some cases (e.g., CDC 7600), but the price dropped to as low as 0.5 ¢/bit in the early 1970s. In the meantime thin film memories at reasonable sizes could not be made with cycle times below 100 nsec; rather, values of 120 to 300 nsec were more reasonable. This was not much improvement over cores, and the higher cost could not be justified. Some of the major problems with thin films were severe array fabrication tolerances and large devices, hence low density with long delays. In addition, the memories were disturb sensitive (i.e., lost information on repeated half-select pulsing because of large, self-demagnetizing forces along the edges) and they had large drive currents, low sense signals, and usually destructive read-out, as well. Even with planar fabrication, the device tolerances were sufficiently critical that fabrication over a reasonable array was expensive. Though the magnetic film itself could be switched fast, the device produced very small signals and tended to be large (0.010 to 0.03 in. diameter spots), giving long lines with long delays that added to those of the complex cricuitry, gave a system with only a factor of 2 or 3 improvements in speed over cores instead of the orders of magnitude originally predicted. This latter was due to the fact that core systems achieved faster speeds than originally expected and films achieved lower speeds than expected. It is possible to reduce the size of thin films to reduce line length delay as well as reduce the required driving currents, but unfortunately the films become disturb sensitive. The disturb sensitivity can be eliminated by using ferrite "keepers" to partially close the otherwise open flux path. This flux closure further reduces the drive currents to 100 mA or less and makes the devices compatible with integrated circuits. However the structure begins to look more like a core memory with small air gaps cut into the cores. The fabrication costs increase, the signals are quite small and noise is large, requiring sophisticated amplifiers and discriminators. While nondestructive read-out is possible, destructive read-out is more feasible, with an attendant increase in cycle time or slower speed. Thus in the late 1960s it began to become evident that thin films were not the technology to replace cores; and additional interest was revived in the older concept of plated wires as a way to batch fabricated closed flux structures. This concept in terms of plated rods was experimented with at least as early as 1958 (Meier, 1958) and appeared in commercial systems such as the NCR 315 rod memory introduced in 1965, plated wire memory in the Univac 9000 series starting in 1967, the NCR Century Series announced in 1968, in a large system, the Univac 1110 introduced in 1970, and others. These technologies had the ever-present disadvantages of low density, incompatibility (fabricationwise) with peripheral circuits, low speed, and high cost resulting from the only semiautomated or partial batch fabricated production procedure. By this time (late 1960s) great strides had been made in semiconductor technology and the late-comer, integrated circuits, suddenly stepped in and offered the potential to circumvent the shortcomings of magnetic cores, thin films, plated wires, and all other contenders. Integrated circuits offered extremely high density, far beyond anything imaginable with thin magnetic films, while still requiring very modest driving signals with very large sense signals; there was no disturb sensitivity, and read-out was nondestructive. The net result was that integrated circuit memories began to appear in the late 1960s: the first mass-produced commercial IC memory was the IBM 64 bit/chip bipolar buffer memory introduced in 1968 (see Section 4.9). Initially quite expensive, the devices gradually decreased in cost until in the early 1970s they started to replace magnetic cores. The major step in this direction was provided in 1970 by IBM with its announcement of bipolar main memories for system 370 model 145, and by the Data General Supernova SC. The metal-oxide semiconductor (MOS) field effect transistor (FET) was recognized to have potential for lower cost than bipolar transistors and was announced for main memory by IBM in 1972 for the S370 models 158 and 168. Subsequently many commercial systems have appeared using MOS chips for main memory: the Burroughs B1700, the Univac model 9480, the Honeywell model 6025, and many others. By the end of 1972 it was estimated that semiconductors accounted for 17% of the main memory market, plated wires 4%, and cores the remaining 79%. Thus after many years of refinement and billions of cores strung on wires, ferrite core technology was finally being displaced by a device (the transistor) and a technology (integrated circuits) that did not even exist when the first core memory was envisioned in 1948.

Secondary Storage Evolution

Identification of the first magnetic tape, drum, and disk systems is difficult, since many parallel efforts, usually experimental, were undertaken in the late 1940s and early 1950s. The IBM 701, announced in 1952 and installed in 1953, made use of magnetic tapes and drums (Buchholz, 1953; Frizzell, 1953) in addition to the electrostatic storage tube. The National Bureau of Standards systems Standard Western Automatic Computer (SWAC) also used a drum memory to back up a Williams tube main memory and the Standard Eastern Automatic Computer (SEAC) used a magnetic tape to back up 512 words of delay line storage (Huskey, 1953; Greenwald, 1953). The vacuum tape column invented in 1949 (IBM) was an important factor in allowing tape storage to achieve prominence. This technique, which controls the reeling and unreeling of the tape from the two spindles and prevents it from snapping, continued in use for many years. The first commercial tape system was employed in the Univac I, first operated in 1951, and the first commercial drum was that used in the IBM 701. The Univac I tape was made of steel ribbon and recorded at 25 bpi. The oxide-coated, nonmetallic half-inch tape, which was the forefather of current tape, was introduced by IBM with the 701 computer. Each tape consisted of an 8 in. reel, 1200 ft long and 0.5 in. wide, recorded at 100 bits per linear inch using NRZ coding and a seven-track system. Drums were used for main memory in some early computers; but with the introduction of cores in 1955, drums, tapes, and subsequently disks, were relegated to the position of cheaper, slower, secondary storage and have dominated that area ever since.

In the early systems, magnetic drums were used primarily because of the overall mechanical stability of the rotating drum, which allowed better control of the separation between the read/write heads and the surface. This separation is all-important in determining the density (see Chapter 5), and typical values in the early systems were in the range of 100 bpi by 10 to 30 tpi. The limited surface area provided by a cylinder greatly restricted the total storage capacity available on one surface. Numerous ideas were advanced for using a

TABLE 1.2-1   Disk and Drum Recording Densities Versus Year

Year	Model	Maximum Storage Density bits/in^2	Maximum Linear Density bpi	Track Density tpi
Drums[a]				
1948	Manchester miniature	750	136	5.5[b]
1951	Manchester new	4100	136	30[b]
1954	IBM 650	700	50	14[b]
Disks (IBM)				
1956	IBM 350	2,000	100	20
1960	IBM 1405	8,000	200	40
1961	IBM 1301	25,000	500	50
1963	IBM 1311	50,000	1000	50
1964	IBM 2311	110,000	1100	100
1965	IBM 2314	220,000	2200	100
1970	IBM 3330	808,000	4040	200

[a] Many drums were introduced in the early and mid 1950s (see Weik, 1955).
[b] Estimate based on information available.

series of thin magnetic disks that would provide greater surface area, hence greater capacity, if the same density could be achieved. Furthermore, since the read/write heads are a major part of the overall cost, it was also recognized that sharing the heads among many disks was essential (see, e.g., Rabinow, 1952). However the mechanical stability of a rotating thin disk is substantially inferior to that of a more massive drum; hence there would be a need for a larger head to disk separation and lower density, thus compromising the advantage of larger surface area. Controlling this separation is further complicated if a movable head is used, but the latter is essential for low cost. This dilemma was solved by IBM with the announcement in 1956 of the RAMAC disk system, using one head to service a group of disks mounted on a common shaft. The significant innovation was the "air cushion" or "air bearing," which can maintain the head at a fixed distance above the surface even for surface fluctuation as large as 100 times the nominal spacing. This permitted densities comparable to drums* but with much larger capacity and lower cost (one head). The air cushion was provided by pressurized air fed into a hole in the head, directed toward the disk surface where it spread out in

* Densities of 100 bpi × 20 tpi on first RAMAC, storing 40M bits on 100 surfaces per system, with access time of about 0.5 sec to any record on any disk.

TABLE 1.2-2 Chronology of Implementation of Major Storage Technologies

Date of Major System Operating[a]	Storage Technology	System Identification or Implementor	Module Size	Speed	Comments
BC	Mud tablets; ink on papyrus	Malasians; Egyptians and Greeks		Minutes	
1623	Mechanical positions; cogs on wheels	Schickard's semiautomatic calculator			Probably first mechanical calculator; not extant
1642	Mechanical positions; cogs on wheels	Pascal's calculator	10 digits/wheel 8 wheels	Seconds	First mechanical calculator still extant
1812	Punched cards	Jacquard weaving loom			First use of punched card storage
1890	Electromechanical dials, punched cards	Hollerith census machine	40 dials, 10K decimal digits per dial	Seconds per card (operator dependent)	First electrical calculator; mechanical storage electrically activated;
1940	Capacitors on rotating durm	Atanasoff		1 rev/sec	Precursor to other circulating types of memory
1942	Electrical resistance on cards (analog)	Western Electric electrical director			Analog storage of functions

Year	Technology	System	Specifications	Performance	Description
1943, 1944	Electromechanical relays, punched tapes (papers)	Mark I IBM—Harvard U	Internal counter, 2204 positions		First fully automatic calculator
1946	Vacuum tube flip-flop Resistor array	ENIAC (University of Pennsylvania)	20, 10 decimal digit numbers 4K bits (100 numbers)		First large-scale electronic storage
1948	Cathode ray (Williams) tube, magnetic drum	Manchester University (England) miniature machine (not full computer)	CRT (1) 1024 bits, (2) 1280 bits; drum 120K bits		First CRT storage; one of the earliest operational drums
1949	Mercury delay lines	EDSAC (Cambridge University, England)	576 bits/tube 18K bits total	1.1 msec circulation time	First fully operational delay line memory
1951	Magnetic tape (commercial)	UNIVAC I	1.44M bits max 1500 ft, 128 char./in.	100 in./sec	First commercial tape (and computer)
1953	Magnetic cores (coincident selection)	MIT memory test computer		20 μsec access	First operational core memory
1955	Magnetic cores (coincident selection)	RCA BIZMAC			First commercial core memory
1956	Magnetic disk, movable heads	IBM 350 RAMAC	40M bits on 100 surfaces	0.5 sec access	First commercial movable head system
1962	Thin magnetic films	UNIVAC 1107	128 words 36 bits/word (scratch-pad memory)	0.3 μsec	First commercial thin film memory

TABLE 1.2-2 *(Continued)*

Date of Major System Operating[a]	Storage Technology	System Identification or Implementor	Module Size	Speed	Comments
1965	Plated rods	NCR 315			First commercial system
1968 FCS	Transistor (bipolar), integrated circuits	IBM buffer memory S360/M85, M25	512 words 18 bits/word 64 bits/chip	60 nsec cycle	First mass-produced integrated circuit memory; First cache memory (M85)
1971 FCS	Transistor (bipolar) main memory	IBM main memory S370 M145	128 bits/chip	0.54 μsec cycle	First integrated circuit main memory
1973 FCS (announced 1972)	MOS FET	IBM main memory S370/M158, M168	1024 bits/chip		First mass-produced MOS memory

[a] FCS = first customer shipment.

a thin cushion. By maintaining constant air pressure and constant tension of the head toward the surface, an accurate spacing can be maintained. Around 1960 another significant innovation was introduced—the self-lubricating bearing. The pressurized air was removed and the head was "flown" on a thin layer of air that follows the rotating disk (see Chapter 6). This allowed even greater densities to be achieved, as indicated in Table 1.2-1.* These innovations, with attendant increases in density, improved disks enough to promote them to the status of major backup systems to main memory, with tapes serving more an archival function and as backup to disks. Drums are used mainly when access times faster than those of disks are critical. The disk concept became extremely popular in 1962–1963, and by 1967 many commercial systems appeared.† In the meantime many believed that the ultimate limits of magnetic recording were fast approaching, primarily because of the severe mechanical spacings and tolerances required (measured in microinches). Thus many alternate technologies to replace magnetic recording were actively sought through the 1960s and still in the 1970s.‡ The situation was very much like that previously described with respect to alternative technologies for replacing magnetic cores. These new technologies have similarly acted as pacesetters, and magnetic recording has been pushed to ever higher densities: by late 1970s, a density of 10^8 to 10^9 bits/in.^{2} is anticipated. Of course some ultimate limits will be forthcoming eventually (see Section 5.7). When, and which technologies will then step in, remains for future historians to record.

Extensive summaries of operational computing systems can be found in the series of surveys by Weik (1955, 1957, 1961, 1964). A historical summary of the major storage technologies, with dates of initial implementation is given in Table 1.2-2. There are, needless to say, many events, proposals, and inventors bypassed by such a summary. A more complete review of general computer history is provided in the previously cited references.

1.3 MEMORY SYSTEMS AND COST/PERFORMANCE GAPS

Despite frequent debate and much speculation about what kind of storage is needed for practical computers, it should be understood that with few exceptions,§ the fundamental requirements for computer applications

---

* For additional historical perspective, see Hoagland, (1967, 1972).

† For a review of the disk and drum systems available at various times, see the series of articles in the Technology Profile section of *Modern Data*, December 1968, February 1969, May 1969, January 1971, February 1971, March 1971.

‡ For a review of the more notable ones in the late 1960–early 1970 period, see Matick, (1972).

§ Small associative memories are useful in "paged" memory hierarchies—see Section 9.13.

of all types can be reduced to large, random access, writable, high speed (both read and write) memory systems, at very low cost. Although the size of main memory attached to computing systems has greatly increased in capacity, along with a substantial decrease in cost per bit, the storage requirements for most systems still are so large that the use of main memory technology only is much too expensive. The appearance of a variety of hardware as well as software systems, storage allocation, data management, buffering, paging, and so on, resulted simply because in most cases, the tradeoffs between cost, speed, and size can be made more attractive by combining various hardware systems coupled with these special features. Thus technology and systems requirements have together produced a variety of memory types. The definitions are somewhat arbitrary, but five classes are readily identifiable and frequently encountered in practice, namely: (1) random access, (2) direct access, (3) sequential, (4) associative, (5) read only (postable and nonpostable).

We describe each type, then give some rules of thumb for the access time and the cost of various systems relative to one another.

1. *Random Access Storage* (*RAS*). A memory for which any location (word, bit, byte, record) of relatively small size has a unique, physically wired-in addressing mechanism and is retrieved in one memory cycle time interval; that is, time to retrieve any given location is made to be the same for all locations.
2. *Direct Access Storage* (*DAS*). A memory (storage) system for which any location (word, record, etc.) is not physically wired in and addressing is accomplished by a combination of direct access to reach a general vicinity and minimal sequential searching, counting, or waiting to find final location. The access time depends on the physical location of the record at any given time, thus access time can vary considerably both from record to record, and to a given record when accessed at a different time. Since addressing is not "wired in," the storage media must contain a certain amount of information to assist in the location of the desired data—this is referred to as *stored addressing information* (SAI) throughout the book.
3. *Sequential Access Storage* (*SAS*). A memory for which the stored words or records do not have a unique address and are stored and retrieved entirely sequentially. Stored addressing information in the form of simple inter-record gaps (IRG) is used to separate records and assist in retrieval. Access time varies with record being accessed (as with direct access); however sequential accessing may require searching of every record in the memory before the correct one is located.

4. *Associative* (*Content Addressable*) *Memory* (*AM*). A random access type of memory that in addition to having a wired-in addressing mechanism has wired-in logic, which enables one to compare desired bit locations for a specified match, and do this for all words simultaneously on one memory cycle time. Thus the specific address of a desired word need not be known, only a portion of its contents. All words (can be more than one) that match the specified bit locations have their addresses stored and can then be addressed on subsequent memory cycles.

5. *Read-Only Memory* (*ROM*). A memory that has permanently stored information programmed during the manufacturing process: it can only be read and it never can be destroyed. There are several variations. Postable or programmable ROM is one for which the stored information need not be written in during the manufacturing process but can be written at any time, even while the system is in use (i.e., can be posted at any time). Once written, however, the media cannot be erased and rewritten (i.e., read only after written). Another variation is a fast read, slow write memory, for which writing is an order of magnitude slower than reading. In one such case, the writing is done much as in RAS but very slowly, to permit use of low cost devices—this is more nearly like RAS. Another version of slow write is a changeable substrate—for example, magnets on a card, wires, or metal plates (capacitors) punched with holes. These memories are programmable at any time but require considerable time (minutes to hours) to change.

In addition to the above-mentioned types, there is another, frequently referred to as "cache" memory. This small, fast, random access memory, built mainly for speed, at large cost, falls at one end of the memory hierarchy (Chapter 9).

The primary reason for the large variety of memories is cost, and cost is related to the memory access time (time to find a given location). A short access time (fast memory) can only be obtained at a high cost, conversely, inexpensive memories have slower access times. Approximate rules of thumb for cost and access time comparisons of specific types of memory and storage are as follows (B = bytes):

Cost or price

$$\text{cache } \text{¢}/B = 10 \times \text{main } \text{¢}/B = 10^4 \times \text{disk } \text{¢}/B = 10^7 \times \text{tape } \text{¢}/B$$

(off line)

$$\text{gap} \approx 10^3 \qquad\qquad \approx 10^5 \times \text{tape } \text{¢}/B$$

(on line)

(1.3-1)

Access time

$$\text{cache } T_c = 10^{-1} \text{ main } T_m = 10^{-6} \text{ disk } T_D = 10^{-9} \text{ tape } T_t \qquad (1.3\text{-}2)$$

$$\text{gap} \approx 10^5 \qquad\qquad \text{gap} \approx 10^3$$

We see some large gaps between main and disk and disk and tape. These large gaps in cost (1.3-1) can be brought about only by large gaps in access time as indicated in (1.3-2). The access time is sacrificed to achieve economy. This is an inherent characteristic that can be understood only by considering the physical system requirements for storing and retrieving information. This is covered in Section 2.2, where it is shown that addressing small pieces of information very fast calls for large numbers of transducers (decoders, drivers, sense amplifiers) and therefore is expensive. The cost can be lowered by sharing transducers, which necessitates a slower system. Thus we face continually the tradeoffs between cost and speed which, along with size, provide a spectrum of memory systems.

1.4 RELATIONSHIP BETWEEN MAIN MEMORY AND PROCESSOR CLOCKING PERIODS

We wish to consider the main memory cycle time and how it relates to other cycle or delay times within the processor. In particular, we want to compare main memory cycle time first to the CPU cycle time, and second to the logic circuit delay per stage.

The cycle time of main memory is a well-defined quantity (Section 2.5). There is no ambiguity regardless of the hardware or organization used to implement it because only two operations are ever performed—namely, read or write—and one takes the worst case reference period as the cycle time. Even though the pulse period of the clock provided by the storage control unit (Section 4.2) that paces the sequential operations through one memory cycle may vary with technology and organization, the cycle time definition remains unchanged. The processor clock pulses are used in a very similar manner to pace the operations and data flow through the computer. We might attempt to define the CPU cycle time as the worst case delay from some given operation but the question is, Which operation? The CPU must perform many functions rather than just two as the memory does. To decide which operation to select for CPU cycle time, let us look at all the operations required in a simple program execution. The example chosen consists of two arrays of numbers A_k and B_k, which are added termwise to produce a third array C_k. The machine language program is given in Table 1.4-1A. First $A1$ is entered into the accumulator, then $B1$ is added to $A1$ and the result is stored in $C1$. A similar procedure repeats for adding $B2$ to $A2$, and so on. To simplify

TABLE 1.4-1   Termwise Addition of Two Arrays A_k and B_k to Produce Array C_k

A. Machine Language Program

Instruction Number	Operation	Operand (Address)
1	Enter in Accumulator	$A1$
2	Add to Accumulator	$B1$
3	Store Accumulator in	$C1$
4	Enter in Accumulator	$A2$
5	Add to Accumulator	$B2$
6	Store Accumulator in	$C2$
	etc.	

B. Computer Logical Operations		Overlapped Operations
I	Fetch inst. 101	$1\ \tau_M$
	Decode	$1\ \tau_{CPU}$
	Instruction says	
E	Fetch $A1$ from main	$1\ \tau_M$
	Place $A1$ in accumulator	$1\ \tau_{CPU}$
I	Fetch inst. 102	$1\ \tau_M$
	Decode	$1\ \tau_{CPU}$
	Instruction says	
E	Fetch $B1$ from main	$1\ \tau_M$
	Add $B1$ to accumulator	$\alpha\ \tau_{CPU}$
I	Fetch inst. 103	$1\ \tau_M$
	Decode	$1\ \tau_{CPU}$
E	Write accumulator contents into main at $C1$	τ_M
I	Fetch inst. 104	$1\ \tau_M$
	Decode	$1\ \tau_{CPU}$
	etc.	

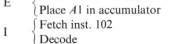
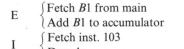

C. Sequential Time Events with Overlapped Operations

A	Fetch inst. 100	$1\ \tau_M$	ΔT_1
B	Decode inst. 100: Fetch inst. 101	τ_M or τ_{CPU}	ΔT_2
C	Fetch $A1$ from main: Decode inst. 101	τ_M or τ_{CPU}	ΔT_3
D	Place $A1$ in accumulator: Fetch inst. 102	τ_M or τ_{CPU}	ΔT_4
E	Fetch $B1$ from main: Decode inst. 102	τ_M or τ_{CPU}	ΔT_5
F	Add $B1$ to $A1$: Fetch inst. 103	τ_M or $\alpha\ \tau_{CPU}$	ΔT_6
G	Store accumulator in $C1$: Decode inst. 103	τ_M or τ_{CPU}	ΔT_7
	etc.		

the discussion, we assume that no branching or other interrupts occur for a long time. To perform this computation, the instructions must be stored in main memory, fetched in proper order, decoded, and executed. Thus all computations can be broken into two basic parts, the instruction or I cycle, which fetches and decodes an instruction, followed by an execution or E cycle, at which time the fetched instruction is executed. The logical steps required to process the machine language program of Table 1.4-1A appear in Table 1.4-1B. Instructions are stored in main memory starting at a fixed or known address. This address is contained in the instruction counter. Each time an instruction is fetched, the instruction counter is incremented by 1 (or other fixed increment) to provide the address of the next sequential instruction. It is assumed the instructions are stored in contiguous memory addresses starting at address 101. The first system cycle in Table 1.4-1B fetches instruction 1 from address 101. This requires one memory cycle time τ_M as shown. The second system cycle decodes that instruction. This is assumed to require at least one CPU cycle time τ_{CPU}, where the latter has not yet been defined. These two together constitute the first I cycle. The first E cycle starts, in accordance with instruction 1, with the fetching of $A1$ from main, requiring one τ_M. The data $A1$ is then transferred from the memory to the accumulator and is assumed to require one τ_{CPU} at most.* The second I cycle fetches and decodes the second instruction as shown. The second E cycle first fetches $B1$ from main, requiring one τ_M; next $B1$ is added to $A1$ in the accumulator. This latter operation is assumed to require $\alpha\tau_{CPU}$, where $\alpha \geq 1$. The third I cycle fetches and decodes instruction 3 and the third E cycle stores the result in main memory at location $C1$. The process repeats itself for $A2$ and $B2$, and so on. Note that as long as the instructions are sequential (i.e., no branching or other interrupts), the fetching and decoding of instruction 2 can be overlapped—done in parallel—with the decoding of instruction 1 and fetching of $A1$, respectively. Similarly for other I cycles. In fact, as long as sequential instructions are executed, all I cycles can be overlapped with previous E cycles as shown. As a result, the logical system operations of Table 1.4-1B reduce to the sequential time events in Table 1.4-1C. A τ_M and a τ_{CPU} always occur in pairs, as is necessary for overlapping (i.e., two memory operations cannot be overlapped in this case). Each of these sequential events requires a total time ΔT, which is the larger of either τ_M or τ_{CPU} in most cases, and the larger of τ_M or $\alpha\tau_{CPU}$ in some cases. The total processing time of n sequential events is obviously the sum of the individual times or

$$T_n = \sum_{j=1}^{n} \Delta T_j \qquad (1.4\text{-}1)$$

* In some cases, this transfer can be done as part of the memory cycle but not always.

To keep T_n as small as possible, it is obvious that all ΔT's should be as small as possible, which requires

$$\tau_{CPU} \approx \tau_M \qquad (1.4\text{-}2)$$

$$\alpha = 1 \qquad (1.4\text{-}3)$$

If τ_M is much less than τ_{CPU}, the processing is limited by the CPU speed. Since in most cases τ_M is much larger than τ_{CPU}, the speed is limited by the main memory cycle time. Hence a cache (Sections 9.10 and 9.11) can be used to increase the overall speed in such cases. The value of α depends on the operation being executed as well as the complexity, hence cost, of the logic hardware devoted to performing each operation. In actual systems, the value of α can be made 1 for simple operations, and reasonably small (< 10) for other complex operations, such as multiply. Special designs are required for $\alpha > 1$, however, and this is expensive. One example is given by Conti et al. (1968).

So far we have discussed the CPU cycle time τ_{CPU} in the abstract, assuming that it is at least long enough to decode any instruction. It can be seen from Table 1.4-1C that τ_{CPU} appears singly, associated with instruction decoding or data movement, more frequently than it appears with an α multiplier for an operation execution. Hence it would seem reasonable to make τ_{CPU} approximately the time to decode an instruction, provided this does not force α to be large for all operation executions (i.e., as long as α can be small for most operations). Assuming this to be the case, the next question is, What is τ_{CPU} in terms of the basic logic circuit delay per stage?

Both the CPU and main memory are paced through the various necessary sequential operations by some underlying timing mechanism, usually a clocking pulse train. The period of the pulse train is often different for the two, but fundamentally it need not be. The main memory cycle time thus consists of a larger number of smaller pulse periods.* In a like manner, the CPU cycle time consists of a large number of small pulse periods as follows. The logical structure of all synchronous computers consists of a large network of combinatorial logic stages such as those shown in Fig. 1.4-1. The inputs to such a net consist of various inputs i from other logic nets including control circuits plus a clock pulse CP. When all the logic inputs are available, the application of clock pulse triggers a series of combinatorial events within the net; no further inputs are required. After a certain delay time, the results of this logic appear at the output terminals, which are connected to other combinatorial nets as shown.

In the operation of sequential steps of subsequent combinatorial nets, a second clock pulse cannot be provided until all inputs are available. This

---

* Some semiconductor memory chips have built-in delays and timing requiring very little external clocking.

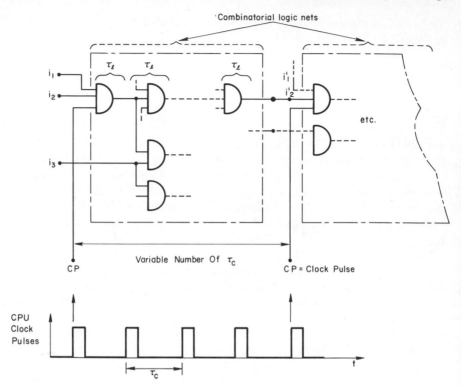

FIGURE 1.4-1 Relationship between basic machine cycle time and combinatorial networks in a synchronous computer.

means that we must wait for the time delay of the slowest previous combinatorial net within the sequential chain. In many cases, when previous nets are fast all inputs are available before the clock pulse is applied; hence additional delay is encountered. This is the penalty paid for synchronous operation.* In any computer, the number of logic stage delays within any given combinatorial net varies depending on the function performed. In addition, this number also varies from one computer to another, depending on the architecture of the system (i.e., amount of pipelining or parallelism). However some very approximate rules of thumb 'for high performance systems are that fundamentally, neglecting clock skewing and other practical problems,

---

* Asynchronous operation is possible in which subsequent stages are triggered when the inputs are available; however the control and design of such machines becomes too complex to be practical. All large computers run synchronously.

the CPU clocking period τ_c is roughly equal to the logic delay per stage τ_l or

$$\tau_c \approx \tau_l \qquad (1.4\text{-}4)$$

and the CPU cycle time τ_{CPU} is roughly 10 logic delays or

$$\tau_{CPU} \approx 10\tau_l \approx 10\tau_c \qquad (1.4\text{-}5)$$

where τ_l is the average logic circuit (such as an AND or NOR) delay per stage with typical loading, τ_{CPU} represents the basic arithmetic logic unit (ALU) or CPU cycle time, and τ_c is the smallest clocking period within the CPU that paces the various combinatorial nets. The actual number in (1.4-5) can vary from slightly less than 10 in highly parallel machines to 20 or more in other systems. On small systems designed for lower cost, the relationships become nebulous.

From the foregoing discussion, one might conclude that if $\tau_l \equiv \tau_c$, every combinatorial net must have one logic delay. This is not necessarily the case, since as indicated in Fig. 1.4-1, not every pulse from the CPU clock need be used for a sequential combination of nets. Other combinatorial nets are clocked by the intervening pulses to perform, say, the entire instruction decoding. Several combinatorial nets in overlapped sequence may be needed to complete the decoding with the total elapsed time given approximately by (1.4-5).

Depending on circuit technology and logic complexity, most simple operation executions can be performed with the same time period; thus $\alpha = 1$ or at least is small for most operations.

As previously discussed with reference to Table 1.4-1, a balance system would ideally satisfy (1.4-2), namely

$$\tau_M = \tau_{CPU} \qquad (1.4\text{-}6)$$

or substituting (1.4-5)

$$\tau_M \approx 10\tau_l \qquad (1.4\text{-}7)$$

Then for a logic technology with $\tau_l = 5$ nsec/stage, we would like a memory and machine cycle time of about 50 nsec. This is approximately the case for the IBM 370/195, in which the cache (Section 9.11) takes the place of main memory for speed. Note also from (1.4-3) that for a well-balanced system, we should also have $\alpha = 1$. This condittition seldom occurs on modern systems, but it indicates one direction for improvement.

The major conclusions concerning memory versus CPU speed are summarized by (1.4-6) and (1.4-7). These present the ideal case in which no branching or other interrupts occur in the sequential processing of an instruction stream. Such interrupts must eventually occur, and when they do, the conclusions just stated are still valid. However the requirement for new, additional considerations for processing efficiency leads to additional complexity in the overall CPU architecture. Nevertheless, it is still desirable to have main memory cycle time equal to that of the CPU cycle time.

1.5 SIZE AND SPEED OF MAIN MEMORY VERSUS CPU CAPABILITIES

We are interested in exploring two rather basic questions: How do the size and the speed of main memory relate to CPU capabilities? Though exact relationships do not exist, there are definite trends, and these coupled with statistical averages can give a significant perspective on computer architecture.

Usually for any given piece of data in a computer, one wishes to perform only a few, limited manipulations (add or multiply with another number, divide, etc.). This is a fundamental fact and leads to the concept of instructions executed per byte of data, called I/B, which has a reasonably narrow range of values for each class of problem. Assuming this to be true for the moment, it would be extremely uneconomical to tie a very fast CPU to a very small, and/or slow main memory: this would keep the CPU idle most of the time because there are not enough data available to work on (small size), or because the memory store and fetch times consume most of the available time (low speed). Likewise, it would not be very economical to tie a very large and/or fast main memory to a very small, slow CPU because just the reverse effect would occur—the CPU would be busy most of the time while the memory remained idle (i.e., the same CPU performance could be obtained with a smaller, slower memory and data transfers from secondary storage). A more balanced system is desirable because both the CPU and the main memory are expensive. Thus, just from general arguments, it is reasonable to expect that as the processing speed of a computer increases, both the size and the speed of memory available to the processor should also increase if a balanced system is to be maintained. This is, in fact, the case, as we see shortly. Before we can proceed it is necessary to understand three basic concepts.

1. Million instructions per second (MIPS) rating, which expresses the CPU speed and capabilities.
2. Instructions executed per byte of data (I/B), which expresses the fundamental amount of mathematical manipulation required by various classes of data.
3. Main memory storage capacity per MIPS (M char./MIPS), which expresses the amount of memory data running at approximately the same clock cycle as the CPU, needed for each CPU instruction performed.

The following are only approximations, but they can serve as rules of thumb; it would be a major breakthrough if some fundamental expressions could be uncovered for them, but unfortunately no such relationships have been found. Thus the science of computer usage proceeds by way of statistical averages or approximations. We now discuss the three concepts just enumerated and then use them to relate the size and speed of memory to the CPU capabilities.

1.5.1 MIPS

The inherent capability of a CPU is not determined by the speed of the basic logic circuits or clock cycle time alone, but also by the complexity of the logic, the number of parallel functions and data paths, and the built-in hardware for time-consuming multiply and floating point operations, and so on. Thus overall speed can be improved by logic complexity in addition to raw circuit speed. Nevertheless, economics of design results in any given computer requiring different amounts of time to perform the different functions (add, multiply, move logical, compare logical, etc.).

As explained in the previous section, instruction execution cycles are paced by the basic CPU cycle time (i.e., add may require 2 cycles, full word mulitply may require 10 cycles, etc.). Furthermore, not only does each instruction require varying numbers of machine cycles for a given computer, but the ratio for similar instructions can vary from one computer to another. Thus one might suspect large discrepancies in the number of machine cycles required by different computers to perform a given computation. Even if the computers have equal cycle times, computation times can differ significantly. How can one hope to provide an accurate measure of machine performance? The answer lies in statistical averages—one machine may perform poorly compared to a second computer on one problem but may do much better on another. It has been found that if a wide variation of job mixes is taken, the variations in performance tend to balance out, leaving a reasonably fair measure of computer performance. This measure has come to be known as the MIPS rating—the number of instructions (in millions) executed per second, defined as follows. If a computer can perform m instructions labeled

$$I_1, I_2, I_3, \ldots, I_m \tag{1.5-1}$$

and the time to perform each is, respectively

$$t_1, t_2, t_3, \ldots, t_m \tag{1.5-2}$$

the total number of instructions performed for a given job stream is simply the sum of the number of times $n_1, n_2, \ldots,$ that each instruction is performed, or total instructions executed is

$$I_t = n_1 + n_2 + \cdots + n_m \text{ instructions} \tag{1.5-3}$$

The total elapsed time is then

$$T_t = n_1 t_1 + n_2 t_2 + \cdots + n_m t_m \tag{1.5-5}$$

Thus the IPS rating for this job stream is

$$\text{IPS} = \frac{n_1 + n_2 + \cdots + n_m}{n_1 t_1 + n_2 t_2 + \cdots + n_m t_m} \text{ instructions/second} \tag{1.5-6}$$

and

$$\text{MIPS} = \text{IPS} \times 10^{-6} \tag{1.5-7}$$

where n through n_m are the number of instructions of each type I_1 through I_m executed.

To compare CPU processing speeds for two different computers using the MIPS concept, it is necessary to specify the actual instruction set I through I_m to be evaluated. To do this, one often resorts to the notion of "kernels," which are nothing more than typical operations required for data processing. In scientific processing, a kernel could be a matrix multiplication, a square root evaluation, a finite difference solution to a differential equation, or any one of many others. For commercial processing, some typical kernels are editing a decimal field (e.g., print checks, statements with all appropriate dollar signs and decimal points), logical or numerical comparison of two fields of equal character length, character (alphanumeric) movement from one field location into another, and sorting. Such comparisons of individual problems on two separate computers can be useful if one knows that these are the types of kernel that will run most often. The kernel evaluation can be by direct execution of the problem; or, when many time-consuming kernels are considered, one can dynamically trace and analyze the actual job, selecting a small number of job steps that contain an instruction execution frequency mix closely matching the job as a whole. Thus in effect a large number of jobs can be simulated within a short period of time, giving an accurate estimate of internal performance.*

Evaluation by the kernel trace technique requires considerable preparation and evaluation, which can be expensive and is not feasible in many cases. Evaluations based on one or few kernels are not realistic since this case seldom obtains; computers of any reasonable size are eventually called on to execute a wide variety of kernels. In addition, the user is interested in the *total* time required to execute the problem, which, of necessity, includes all input/output to peripheral storage, printers, readers, and so on. A more useful evaluation, which is gaining in popularity, is that of "benchmark"

* Murphey and Wade (1970) make extensive use of this technique to evaluate relative performance of the IBM 360/195.

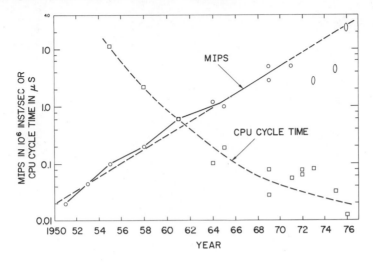

FIGURE 1.5-1   Approximate MIPS rating and CPU cycle time versus year for large systems.

problem runs. In this approach, actual problems are run from beginning to end and the CPU, I/O, and other elapsed times of interest are recorded. This evaluation includes all aspects of the computation process including the programming; therefore the program should be done by a person high skilled in the language used. The MIPS rating for various computers over the years is given in Table 1.1-1 and Fig. 1.5-1 plots the larger systems from column M_1. The latter shows a very substantial increase, with the straight line approximation being given by

$$\log(\text{MIPS}) = -1.7 + 0.12x \qquad (1.5\text{-}8)$$

where x is measured in years from 1950 (i.e., $x = 20$ for 1970). This curve shows an improvement by a factor of about 300 times from 1950 to 1970. The CPU cycle time in Fig. 1.5-1 exhibits a similar decrease over the years; as would be expected to achieve such increases in MIPS.

It could be argued that the MIPS rating is not very useful for comparing computers because it varies from problem to problem, being just a gross average. Intuitively, it would seem that a more fundamental measure could be derived, but numerous attempts* have been generally unsuccessful. One measure of machine hardware performance and complexity is the number of bits processed per CPU cycle time given in column A/B in Table 1.1-1, and

---

* See Sharpe (1969) for summary of various measures of CPU effectiveness.

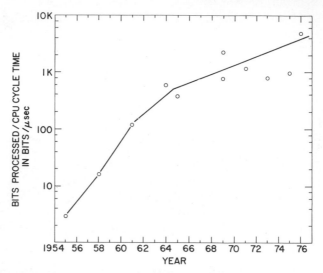

FIGURE 1.5-2   Bits processed per CPU cycle time versus year for large systems.

plotted in Fig. 1.5-2 versus year. This curve shows an improvement by a factor of about 10^3 times from 1955 to 1971, suggesting that large systems have improved more than is indicated by the MIPS curve of Fig. 1.5-1.

1.5.2 I/B—Instructions Executed per byte of Data and the Speed of Main Memory

Some approximations to the speed of main memory required for a CPU of a given MIPS rating could be obtained, if we knew the amount of data required for each instruction executed. If such a relationship exists, a product of this relation with the MIPS would give the required data rate of main memory, or its cycle time. Intuitively, it seems reasonable to suppose that there is some such relationship between the number of bits of data that are processed and the number of bits of instruction required to tell the computer what to do with the data. The relationship need not be exact, in fact we would expect to find the number of bits of instruction per bit of processed data to be higher for scientific calculations than for commercial data processing. This discrepancy results because in scientific calculations, considerably more manipulation is required of each piece of data (e.g., one parameter in a set of simultaneous equations can have a significant effect on many parts of the problem). In commercial data processing, this extensive interrelation seldom exists, a change in one employee's weekly salary, for example, has no effect on others' wages. Such relationships do exist and can be used to evaluate the speed and capacity of the storage required for a given system. Two ratios can be defined, one that is more applicable to complex mathematical calculations, and the other for specifying the input/output requirements of a system. The first ratio expresses the average number of instruction executions required in the CPU to process a given amount of alphanumeric data. It is convenient to work with bytes of data B. Thus the ratio becomes

$$\frac{I}{B} = \frac{\text{number of CPU instructions executed}}{\text{number of bytes data processed}} \qquad (1.5\text{-}9)$$

where I is the total number of instruction executions required by the processor to complete the calculation and is *not* the number of instructions in the program. Because of looping, branching, and so on, I is much larger than the program instruction count. If the foregoing ratio is known, it can be used to determine the speed of main memory in relation to that of the CPU, as will be seen. The I/B given by (1.5-9) expresses primarily the complexity of the mathematical problem. Though the built-in logical complexity of the CPU can change the total number of instructions required to manipulate those data, the number does not vary greatly for reasonably large computers.

To evaluate the overall throughput of a system, one needs a measure of the input/output requirements of various classes of problem. For this, a modified form of the I/B ratio is required—namely, the average number of instruction executions performed by the CPU for each byte of data B_{sp} transferred from secondary (disk) to primary (main) storage or

$$\frac{I}{B_{sp}} = \frac{\text{number of CPU instructions executed}}{\text{number of bytes transferred}} \qquad (1.5\text{-}10)$$

where I is as previously defined. If the information transferred is only alphanumeric data, such as a segment of a matrix in a large scientific calculation, and if all the data are processed, B_{sp} is essentially the same as previously and the two ratios become equal. In many cases, however, the information transferred consists of both program instruction and alphanumeric data or

$$B_{sp} = I_p + B$$

where I_p = program instructions (bytes)
B = alphanumeric data

In most cases, however, the total instructions executed for a job stream is much larger than I_p, $I \gg I_p$, and the two ratios given by (1.5-9) and (1.5-10) are nearly equal. In fact, the difference is generally much smaller than the uncertainty in either ratio. For example, suppose $I/B_{sp} = 4$ and $I = 100 I_p$. Then the ratio of I/B can easily be calculated by substituting these numerical values in (1.5-10) or

$$\frac{I}{B_{sp}} = \frac{I}{I_p + B} = \frac{I}{0.01 I + B} = 4$$

TABLE 1.5-1   Instructions Executed per Byte of Information Transferred, for Various Problem Types

I/B Average Over Many Jobs	Problem Type
8	Scientific: Fortran and others
4	Commercial: Cobol and others
1–2	Interactive terminal systems (e.g., administrative, information reservation systems)

Solving the foregoing gives

$$\frac{I}{B} = 4.2 \tag{1.5-11}$$

The difference for the assumed conditions is 5 %, which is considerably smaller than the uncertainty in either ratio as we soon see. In all subsequent analysis, we assume these ratios to be equivalent.

Values for the I/B ratio have been determined by a number of investigators. Brooks (1969) says that "in many different machine designs one finds the instruction flow in bits to be $\frac{1}{4}$ to 1 times the data flow in bits."[*] Unfortunately, that study provides no measurements to show the conditions under which the numbers are valid. A number of more recent studies supply useful ranges for these ratios. Gibson (1970) has shown that the I/B_{sp} on a particular benchmark job stream varied from 1 to 30, with the range of 1 to 10 being more common; 8 was an average for the job analyzed. The I/B_{sp} is near unity for data processing and near 8 for scientific calculations, but both depend, of course, on the particular job details. Yeh (1971) measured wide variations of I/B for individual jobs, but the results indicate that a range of 1 to 10 is a reasonable average for many job streams. Some approximate values of I/B_{sp} for several problem types are given in Table 1.5-1. One could argue that the measurements are only for computer systems of certain types (IBM 360), thus are not applicable in general. However Brooks indicates that the ratio varies little for machines of different designs, suggesting the existence of some fundamental relations between data bits and the information bits required for processing the data. For hydrodynamic calculations such as weather predictions, the I/B ratio (1.5-9) varies from about 4 to 40 for simple to complex problems respectively (see Section 1.8).

---

[*] If we used Brooks' numbers and converted to a 32 bit instruction and 8 bit bytes of data, we would get $I/B = \frac{1}{16}$ to $\frac{1}{4}$, which is somewhat lower than the numbers measured more recently.

Assuming the range of I/B ratios to be correct, if we know the IPS rating of the CPU, the approximate speed of main memory is given by

$$\text{cycle time}\left(\frac{\text{seconds}}{\text{byte}}\right) = \frac{1}{\text{speed (bytes/second)}} = \frac{I/B}{\text{IPS}} \quad (1.5\text{-}12)$$

For a given IPS rating, as I/B increases, the required memory cycle time increases (slower speed) as expected, since more CPU cycles or more instructions are needed for each memory cycle. Table 1.5-1 indicates some significant variations in the performance of computers used for purely scientific versus commercial data processing. This is primarily because scientific problems tend to be more ordered or organized than other types. We see some of this in Section 1.8.

A natural question that frequently arises is, What kind of computer should one build for general purposes—a science-oriented or business-oriented computer? This is, of course, very difficult to answer, but when looking at the computer types available, a very important point should be borne in mind; namely, of all the computer computations performed each year, scientific-engineering computation comprises to a very crude estimate, about 20% or less of the total. The actual amount of scientific calculation increases dramatically each year, but so does the amount of commercial and other nonscientific data processing. Needless to say, it is difficult to attach a specific number to the percentage of scientific processing, since not only is judgment often required in classifying many computations, but collection of meaningful, representative data is extremely difficult. However a good rule of thumb for judging capabilities or versatility of a system for scientific versus commercial computing is

$$\text{scientific computation} \gtrsim 20\% \text{ total processing} \quad (1.5\text{-}13)$$

1.5.3 Characters of Memory per IPS and the Size of Main Memory

We have already argued that to maintain a balanced system, the size of main memory should increase as the CPU capabilities increase. Figure 1.5-1 shows the CPU capabilities versus year, indicating rapid improvement for large systems. Therefore we would expect the average size of memory attached to these to display a similar trend. This is indeed the case, as is shown in Fig. 1.5-3, where the typical sizes have increased by about 300 times from 1950 to 1970, which is the same factor of improvement in MIPS. The relationship between memory size and MIPS can be more easily seen by plotting the ratio of number of characters of memory per IPS versus year as in Fig. 1.5-4 from column C/M_1 in Table 1.1-1. The values fluctuate only

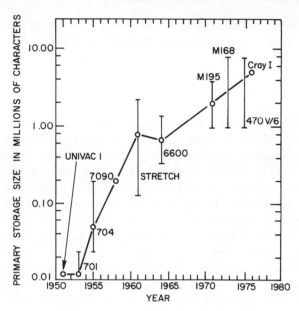

FIGURE 1.5-3 Growth of computer storage versus year for large systems.

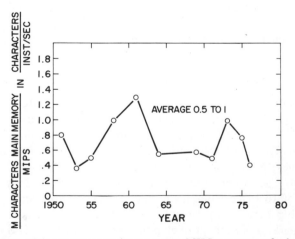

FIGURE 1.5-4 Main memory capacity per system MIPS versus year for large systems.

slightly (linear scale), with an average value of approximately between 0.5 and 1. Thus, as a rule of thumb, we can say a large computer requires

$$\frac{M \text{ char.}}{MIPS} \sim 0.5 \text{ to } 1 \tag{1.5-14}$$

If we know the MIPS rating of a large computer, the approximate size of memory can easily be obtained as

$$\text{size of main memory (M char.)} = \frac{M \text{ char.}}{MIPS} \times MIPS \tag{1.5-15}$$

$$\approx (0.5 \text{ to } 1) \times MIPS \tag{1.5-16}$$

Let us now use these approximations to determine for a given computer MIPS rating and typical average I/B ratio, the size and speed of main memory expected for that CPU. Let us use 5 MIPS for the CPU and typical problem mix of $I/B = 4$. From (1.5-12) and (1.5-16) this would require a memory of

$$\text{cycle time} = \frac{4}{5 \times 10^6} = 0.8 \times 10^{-6} \text{ sec} = 0.8 \ \mu\text{sec}$$

$$\text{size} = (0.5 \text{ to } 1) \times 5 \sim 2.5 \text{ to } 5M \text{ bytes}$$

If $I/B = 1$, the cycle time requirement becomes 0.2 μsec, and the size is unaffected. These values are quite typical of the size and speed of main memory on the 5 MIPS machine of Table 1.1-1. We use these concepts in Section 1.8.

If we assume that the current trends will continue in the future, some estimates of the size and speed of main memory of future years can be deduced within the limits of extrapolation. If we assume that the straight line of MIPS versus year shown in Fig. 1.5-1 continues, a machine of 80 MIPS should be available by the early 1980s. If again we use $I/B = 4$ and 1, allowing M char./ MIPS = 1, we require a memory of

$$\text{size} = 1 \frac{M \text{ char.}}{MIPS} \times 80 \text{ MIPS} = 80M \text{ char.}$$

$$\approx 10^9 \text{ bits}$$

and

$$\text{cycle time} \bigg|_{I/B=4} = \frac{4}{80 \times 10^6} = 50 \text{ nsec}$$

$$\text{cycle time} \bigg|_{I/B=1} = \frac{1}{80 \times 10^6} = 12.5 \text{ nsec}$$

Both these are about an order of magnitude improvement over 1970 values.

1.6   EFFECTS OF STORAGE CAPACITY ON PROBLEM SIZE

Although practically speaking the size of a problem amenable to computer solution has always depended on the computer storage capacity, from a fundamental point of view, the storage capacity places no restrictions on the size of the problem solvable. This is true only because the actual storage capacity of any computer can be made nearly infinite by the use of, say, disks, punched cards, punched or magnetic tape, or typed pages. The drawback, hence the practical problem, is of course one of speed: since the latter storage media, being rather slow, may require years to complete a given computation, they would be uneconomical or impractical. Nevertheless the lack of any fundamental limit is an important point because it permits the use of a memory hierarchy to solve problems of large size. Let us now examine some of the practical limits imposed on problem solution.

The type of problem we consider are scientific and related situations having a mathematical formulation, such as a finite difference representation to a partial differential equation that requires considerable storage and many computations. We see here and in Section 1.8 that both the memory and storage requirements and the raw processing speed of the CPU (i.e., MIPS) are bottlenecks in such problems, the latter being more serious in most cases. Of course, if the MIPS were to be increased, the memory and storage speeds would also have to be increased, to maintain a balanced system. These problems should be distinguished from those of data processing (information retrieval, payroll calculations, etc.), in which usually few calculations are performed and the major problems often consist of having sufficient file storage capacity, with adequate access time. Section 1.8 demonstrates that large files are often associated with data processing. The difficulties usually center around the capability of the device to find one or few records from a large file, do some rather simple processing, and return the material to the file in revised form. Such processing most often does not tax the CPU speed of large systems but rather is I/O bound because of the large quantity of data that must be searched.

Most large problems require storage exceeding that of main memory. For instance, many scientific problems require the use of a grid or mesh to represent the geometry of interest. Each grid point requires a certain number of variables, the exact number depending on the type and complexity of the problem. In weather calculations, a very sophisticated model may have 30 variables, whereas calculating the potential distribution in a corona discharge at steady state involves only one variable, namely, the voltage at each point. The size of the grid depends of course on whether the problem is one, two, or three dimensional. For most 2D and 3D problems that have several variables per grid point, the product of the total grid points times the number of variables exceeds the number of words available in main memory; hence secondary storage is required for solution. The grid size depends not only on the dimensionality of the problem but also on whether it is a boundary value problem, an initial value problem, or a combination of boundary value with a transient solution. Problems of the latter type are usually the most complex, requiring large storage capacity (e.g., nuclear transport in a reactor, worldwide weather model). Main is then backed up with secondary storage, to permit the total storage capacity of a large machine to be extended to quite a large value. Hence the storage capacity, if we count all storage media, is not the limiting factor in the size of problem that can be solved. In nearly all mathematical computations it turns out that the limitations on problem size are the speed of CPU and the access time and data rate of secondary storage. The nature of mathematical computations make it possible to break problems into relatively small pieces, for storage and solution in segments, with perhaps many iterations on each segment. The art of solving large scientific problems consists of two main parts: (1) arranging the computational algorithm to ensure that the CPU works as fast and efficiently as possible; (2) segmenting or partitioning the data transfer between main and secondary storage, to allow the computation to proceed as efficiently as possible, as if only main memory were used for storage.

Many interesting problems that have practical applications and strain the power of modern computers fall into the general class of the "many body problem." When many particles interact over both long- and short-range distances, the change in the parameters of one particle (i.e., position, velocity, temperature, etc.) affects many other particles, giving a complex system of interactions. Such problems require solution both at the particle level, often within a few particle diameters, as well as at the macroscopic level of the entire system or collection of particles. Examples are plasma physics (thermonuclear reactions), fluid or continuum mechanics, potential distribution in charge fields (corona discharges, transistor and other solid state structures), nuclear physics, weather simulation, and reaction chemistry. The particles may be charged or uncharged electrons, ions, atoms, or water or air particles, where interactions at the particle level are decisive in determining the ultimate behavior. The overall system may be a transistor, a nuclear reactor, or the earth's surface. The wide range of interactions (long- and short-range) and the large number of variables are the two major factors that compound the problem, taxing the speed and storage capacity of computers. We consider the weather simulation problem in some detail in Section 1.8; for now let us discuss in a very general way the storage capacity required for such problems.

Suppose our system of interest consists of a cube of any size and we wish to analyze the behavior within. If the problem consists of a simple electrostatic potential problem with no charged particles, and if the fields vary smoothly and not very rapidly over the volume, dividing the cube into 1000 smaller cells (i.e., 10 cells on each side) is reasonable. If there is only one variable, the voltage (potential), using a finite difference approximation over 1000 grid points would hardly tax the storage of any computer. We might find in such a solution that the field is a little more gross than we would wish (e.g., near some sharp boundaries such as the cube corners), and we may need a finer mesh, say $32 \times 32 \times 32 = 32K'$. With one variable, this still is well within the storage capacity of most computers, although the computation time may be getting long, depending on the problem complexity. Suppose now that the cube contains a plasma of 10^{12} to 10^{18} electrons and ions, as in real cases. For a 3D solution, we must store at least the three position coordinates and three velocity components, or six parameters for each particle, requiring a storage of up to 6×10^{18} (one word for each parameter). In addition, there are three components for each of the following: electric fields, magnetic field, and current vectors. We need go no further—the storage requirement exceeds that of any system. Such problems must then be simplified if computer solution is to be feasible. Problems involving plasmas and fluid flow can exhibit turbulence and instability that require examination of the behavior closer to the particle level, hence on a much finer mesh than $10 \times 10 \times 10$. To obtain detailed results, a mesh of 256 on each side would be desirable. For such a grid and, say, only 64×10^6 particles, the storage requirement* would be as follows: each grid point would need nine variables or words (three each for electric field, magnetic field, and current), and each particle would require six words (three position and three velocity), for a total storage requirement of

$$\text{grid} \qquad 256^3 \times 9 = 1.51 \times 10^8 \text{ words} \qquad (1.6\text{-}1)$$

$$\text{particles} \qquad 64 \times 10^6 \times 6 = 3.84 \times 10^8 \text{ words} \qquad (1.6\text{-}2)$$

or total exceeding 500 M words. Though rather large, this capacity is possible with high density, high speed disk storage paged into main memory. There are two problems: first, just the actual computation time is still rather long and expensive; second, the segmentation problem becomes complex and can reduce the CPU computational efficiency, resulting in additional time and expense to solve the problem. One can either reduce the number of cells and particles, or solve a 2D instead of 3D problem (i.e., assume uniformity in one dimension). This is what is done in practice, and some typical values for 3D are $32 \times 32 \times 32$ grid with up to 10^6 particles; thus the parameter storage requirement (exclusive of program and other

---

* See Fernbach and Taub, (1970) for interesting discussions of many such applications.

details) becomes

$$\text{grid} \qquad 32^3 \times 9 = 0.295 \times 10^6 \qquad (1.6\text{-}3)$$

$$\text{particles} \qquad 6 \times 10^6 \qquad (1.6\text{-}4)$$

or about 6.3M words.

In 2D, 128 $\times$ 128 cells with 10^5 particles is reasonable (requiring only two components):

$$\text{grid} \qquad 128^2 \times 6 = 16{,}384 \qquad (1.6\text{-}5)$$

$$\text{particles} \qquad 4 \times 10^5 \qquad (1.6\text{-}6)$$

or about 4.2×10^5 words, a considerable reduction.

The various types of large problems differ in detail, but the numbers are very similar. Real problems are always 3D ultimately, and detailed analysis requires very fine meshes for all complex problems. A subdivision into 10 units per side is generally too coarse, 32 is reasonable, and 256 more desirable. Each grid point for any complex problem will have at least six variables, and often several times that. As the model becomes more sophisticated, the number of variables increases beyond that solvable, hence simplifications are made to keep the problem reasonable. Thus computer analysis of seemingly different types of problem use similar grid spacings and comparable numbers of parameters, hence have comparable storage requirements.

Large scientific calculations are expensive because they tend to require considerable computer time. To minimize the cost for a given system, it is desirable to keep the CPU busy as much as possible. A high CPU efficiency not only reduces cost but produces the solution more quickly. To achieve this, it is usually necessary to break the problem into segments close to the natural block length of data that can be processed without interruption. The average natural block length tends to be relatively small, whereas the total amount of data to be processed is large. This requires a large number of segments and transfers from secondary storage to main memory. To achieve a high CPU utilization, it is necessary to transfer the proper segments at the proper time, to ensure that any given segment is present in main memory when needed. To understand this segmentation problem, let us do a simplified analysis of a large computing system, solving a large scientific problem using a disk overlaid into main memory. We assume that the problem contains many bytes of data, each of which must be processed once for each iteration. A CPU of 5 MIPS with 256K bytes of main memory available for data is to be used. The problem can be broken into segments of B_s bytes/segment, with the blocks relatively independent of one another. Once main memory is full of segments, then, all succeeding processing requires transfer out of one segment and transfer in of a new segment. It is *assumed* that the CPU *cannot* address main memory during this data transfer time.* Thus once steady state has been reached, the computation consists of CPU processing of B_s bytes, data transfer-out, data transfer-in, CPU processing, and so on. Let us calculate the CPU utilization for different values of segment size B_s. To do this, we need other information about the average number of instructions executed per byte of data and the disk access and transfer times. For these, we assume instructions executed per byte of data, $I/B = 5$:

$$\text{disk system: total access time (average)} = T_a \text{ msec}$$
$$\text{data rate} = D_r \text{ in M bits/sec}$$

Using the above assumptions, first calculate the length of time the CPU will work on the B_s byte segment of data assumed to be already in main memory. Since the machine can process 5 MIPS, the B_s bytes can keep this CPU busy for a time

$$T_b = B_s \frac{\text{bytes}}{\text{segment}} \times \frac{5 \text{ inst.}}{\text{byte}} \times \frac{\text{sec}}{5 \times 10^6 \text{ inst.}} = B_s \times 10^{-3} \text{ msec/segment}$$

$$(1.6\text{-}7)$$

After processing this entire segment, the CPU must wait for a new segment to be found and transferred into main memory and for an old segment to be removed. The average wait time for each is access time plus transfer time. For our system, average access time is T_a msec, whereas for B_s bytes, the latter is

$$T_{\text{transfer}} = B_s \text{ bytes} \times \frac{8 \text{ bits}}{\text{byte}} \times \frac{\text{sec}}{D_r \text{ M bits}} = \frac{8B_s}{D_r} \times 10^{-3} \text{ msec/segment}$$

$$(1.6\text{-}8)$$

The total transfer time per segment is $T_a + T_{\text{transfer}}$, and two such transfers are required before the CPU can be busy again. Hence the total waiting time is twice the above or

$$T_w = 2\left(T_a + \frac{8B_s}{D_r} \times 10^{-3}\right)\text{msec} \qquad (1.6\text{-}9)$$

The CPU utilization is then CPU processing time divided by the total time interval or

$$\text{CPU utilization} = \frac{T_b}{T_b + T_w} = \frac{B_s \times 10^{-3}}{B_s \times 10^{-3} + 2T_a + (16B_s/D_r) \times 10^{-3}}$$

$$(1.6\text{-}10)$$

---

* This simplifying assumption is considered more fully in Section 9.2.

where B_s is the segment size in bytes and D_r is the disk data rate (Mbytes/sec). To keep the CPU utilization large, we want B_s and D_r to be large and T_a small; D_r and T_a are fixed by the hardware, and improving them generally means higher cost. The value of B_s is fixed by the problem—it may or may not be variable. Let us calculate the CPU utilization for $B_s = 16K$ bytes $D_r = 2(\text{Mbits/sec})$ and $T_a = 30$ msec. Substituting these into (1.6-10) gives

$$\text{CPU utilization} = \frac{16}{16 + 60 + 128} = 0.08 \qquad (1.6\text{-}11)$$

or 8 %, which is quite low. If the disk system is improved so that $T_a = 1$ msec and $D_r = 16$, we have

$$\text{CPU utilization} = \frac{16}{16 + 2 + 16} \approx 0.5 \qquad (1.6\text{-}12)$$

or nearly 50 %, a much better value. If the disk cannot be made better, some improvement can be obtained by using larger segments to eliminate many of the disk accesses T_a. For instance, using $T_a = 30$ msec and $D_r = 2$ but letting B_s be the full size of main memory or 256K bytes gives

$$\text{CPU utilization} = \frac{256}{256 + 60 + 8(256)} \approx 0.11 \qquad (1.6\text{-}13)$$

or 11 %, which is somewhat better than the previous 8 %. The use of such a large segment may or may not be possible, depending on the details of the problem. Thus for such a simple computing system, the two major factors that really limit problem size are the speed of the CPU and the speed and efficiency of secondary storage. The first factor has led to the development of numerous sophisticated techniques to speed up computation, including sparse matrix computations and fast Fourier transforms, which are applicable in a large variety of physical problems, hence are very general techniques; the second factor has led to the development of numerous segmentation or partitioning techniques to permit efficient overlaying of disk to main memory while still maintaining high CPU (computational) utilization. Unfortunately, the latter techniques are unique for each problem, thus not generally applicable. The essential point is that such segmentation is possible, although it is expensive because it requires considerable programming. Nevertheless segmentation of problems has become an essential part of computer solutions to large problems and is widely used in many areas.

Virtual memory systems (Chapter 9) with many disk drives and additional I/O hardware sometimes simplify the processing of large problems. However the large page tables and supervisory program can consume large amounts of main memory, possibly offsetting the gain. For extremely large problems, fine tuning is necessary for all systems.

1.7 STORAGE REQUIREMENTS FOR COMMERCIAL AND RELATED DATA PROCESSING

The amount of storage required for any purpose depends on the amount and type of data to be stored. It was customary in bygone years to store archives on paper; that is, books were shelved in various housings. Retrieving information from such archives is a research task in itself, requiring much time and patience. The U.S. National Archives (Rosenkrantz, 1971), for instance, contains 20 million cubic feet of records (mostly paper). Such records are growing at the rate of more than 10% per year, which not only is becoming unwieldy but impairs official and legal business and makes the machinery of government very inefficient. Thus it makes sense to automate such documents whenever possible. Various methods have been used—for example, microfilm, which is a valuable medium for certain types of data. However films are not easily machine processed, and magnetic tape has found widespread applications for high density storage of archived information, since tape is machine processable, stores a large amount of data, and can be changed or updated relatively quickly compared to films. For instance, a standard 2400 ft reel of tape recorded at 800 bpi using a 0.6 in. interrecord gap and 8 tracks (plus parity), and storing records of 1K byte each, can hold a total of 16.2M bytes or 1.3×10^8 bits of data. (Note: The interrecord gaps account for nearly 50% or the tape—larger records sizes would give more data per reel.) Assuming a printed page of 100 characters per line and 50 lines per page (a rather dense page), the reel of tape described is equivalent to more than 3200 such pages. An average typed page is somewhat smaller, in the range of 3000 characters per page, which would make a tape reel equivalent to 5400 pages. This represents a considerable saving in space as well as time for retrieval. A 3200 page document (standard bond paper) would normally occupy roughly 8.5×11 in. per sheet by 8 in. deep, compared to a standard reel of tape for which the protective case is $11\frac{5}{8}$ in. diameter and $1\frac{3}{8}$ in. thick (0.5 in. for the tape, remainder for the containing reel and case). As for speed, newer tape drives can go as high as 250 in./sec, allowing the entire reel (3200 pages) to be sequentially scanned in 115 sec, or less than 2 min. Needless to say, the manual searching of a 3200 page paper document would require orders of magnitude longer is most cases. Thus it is not surprising that 13% of the National Archives had already been recorded on magnetic tape by 1971.

An example of a vital governmental function that requires large storage capacity is the collection of vital statistics. For example, the U.S. 1970 Census consists of 10 files stored on 2K reels of magnetic tape.* Using the previous

---

* Such files are public information and can be obtained for a fee. Each of the 10 files is organized in a specific way (e.g., by profession, by income). The Census Bureau has available about 200 different files for public use.

figure of 1.3×10^8 bits/reel, these 10 census files alone require 2.6×10^{11} bits (i.e., approaching a trillion bit file). If we postulate a more complete information file containing a number of pertinent records about each person in the world, the capacity becomes considerably greater. Suppose we store the equivalent of 10 dense pages of 5K characters per page for each person, or a total of about 50K characters per person; then for the approximately 3×10^9 people in the world, we would require a file of 15×10^{13} bytes, or about 10^{15} bits using 8 bits per character. This enormous file would call for some new technologies, since more than 10^7 reels of tape would be required, an unwieldy number.

In 1971 the Social Security Administration tape library (Fraher, 1971) contained nearly 200K reels or approximately 2.6×10^{13} bits of information (using previous figures for real capacity). In addition, the processing on these files required at that time 13 IBM 360/M65 computers working round the clock, nearly six days a week. Since the activity on such files is inherently low (e.g., a request to update one person's record out of many thousands), the system tended to be limited by the sequential search speed of the tape drives, leading to various techniques to circumvent this restriction.

The average annual growth rate of government files has been in the range of about 10% per year and is expected to remain or increase. Within the approximately 5000 computer installations of the federal government as of 1971, there were about 5M reels of tape on active inventory*. Note that 5M reels is equivalent to 6.5×10^{14} bits. A compound growth rate of 10% per year will double its amount every 7.5 years, leading to a staggering amount of stored data within the government alone. This growth will no doubt be even further compounded by the many new and urgent emerging governmental needs for data storage, including those due to the trend toward socialized medicine with all its accounting implications, the establishment of national criminal data files, the monitoring for ecological purposes of pollution of waterways, air, foods, and so on, the compilation of weather data for prediction (see Section 1.8), stored historical records, and many others. Significant problems are associated with magnetic tape for archives and retrieval, but tapes are a thoroughly entrenched technology, as indicated, and could be displaced only by another technology or system demonstrating considerable compatibility.

Although the government has perhaps some of the largest requirements for data storage, private enterprise also finds some rather significant applications. Two typical commercial applications with large storage requirements are summarized below.

United Airline's (Kirkpatrick, 1971) message switching, flight planning

---

* Though only 5M reels were active, the government buys about 1M reels each year. Tapes wear out and are replaced; some are used for temporary storage, copies, and so on.

and monitoring, aircraft routing, maintenance and status, and parts inventory control are handled by a general purpose, medium volume, on-line system with off-line capabilities.* This system serviced 1490 remote CRT terminals and 560 printers in a conversational mode, with 2 sec response time to CRTs. It handled a peak load of 40K calls/hr (11 calls/sec), each generating one or more system tasks. This large number of calls, coupled with the large number of CRT terminals and 2 sec response time, required a mass storage system with fast response time. As a result, magnetic drums in a type of mass store hierarchy were used, providing

10^7 bit drums, 4.3 msec access time (average);

10^8 bit drums, 17 msec access time (average);

10^9 bit drums, 92 msec access time (average)

An interesting feature of this system is that the data base was directly word addressable to any of the 10^9 words (36 bits/word), unlike most storage systems, bringing benefits as well as disadvantages. The advantages are less exposure to parity failures and alleviation of the necessity for fast data rates between main memory and storage. Future needs for such systems include capability to address the smallest practical byte on the storage device (i.e., small record) and fast access time for a responsive conversational system. Chapters 5, 6, and 7 reveal that the tradeoffs in storage systems (disks, tapes) tend to favor the use of large record sizes and high data rates for more efficient utilization of storage space. In practice, most often the structure and use of a file is compatible with large record sizes, but this is not always the case.

The IBM Advanced Information System AAS† is a terminal-oriented, customer order-entry system. When placing an order, a customer may wish to know the delivery data as well as all possible options, configurations, price, and so on, and these can be obtained at the terminal. This system at the time of inception contained more than 20M data records, 27M index records, 2.5 billion bytes of data, and just under 0.4 billion bytes of indexes. The indexes and data were on 150 disk packs (IBM 2316) with a maximum of 29.1M bytes each, or a maximum of nearly 4.4 billion bytes (assuming 100% storage media utilization). Only 3 billion of the maximum possible 4.4 billion bytes were used. Two points are to be noted: first, 100% storage media utilization is impossible; second, a large amount of stored addressing information is required for all file systems (i.e., $\approx 0.4/2.5$ or 15%, in this case).

---

* In addition, United has a special purpose, high volume, on-line flight reservation system as do other airlines.

† System went live in May 1968; first publication by J. H. Wimbrow (1971).

This necessity for stored addressing information is a very fundamental point of growing concern, since it represents an additional cost in the implementation of any file (see Chapters 6, 7, and 8).

1.8 STORAGE REQUIREMENTS FOR SCIENTIFIC DATA PROCESSING

The Parkinson-type law of storage expansion (Section 1.1) is applicable to both commercial and scientific data processing, but it has a certain justification in the latter. Assuming that we know the fundamentals or correct model, a large, complex scientific problem can be solved more and more accurately as the size of the memory becomes larger. This is simply because all numerical solutions are an approximation, and as the memory becomes larger, we can more closely approximate the actual problem. Several classes of problem in science make use of large data processing and storage capabilities of modern computers. Some of these classes depend more on the shear raw processing speed of the CPU and are not limited by the storage capabilities of computers, whereas other problems require both. We now examine these several classes and investigate the limiting factors and implications on computer storage.

The classes of scientific problems include at least the following problems, for which

1. The fundamentals are well known but are extremely complex except for trivial cases (exact models).
2. Some or most of the fundamentals are sufficiently well known to allow reasonable attempts at computer modeling of complex problems — progress requires continual improvement of model and larger and faster computers (approximate models).
3. Neither the fundamentals nor accurate models are well known; rather, models are hypothesized and continually improved by computer simulation, requiring larger and faster computers for testing and comparison (hypothesized models).
4. Data collection and initial processing (real time or off-line) are the only requirements.

CLASS 1.   EXACT MODELS

One notable example for class 1 is that of Schrödinger's equations for chemical physics. The equation for a single electron is not very complex (Sproull, 1956), and we would not expect this to tax the power of large computers. This is, in fact, the case when there are no interactions from other electrons. However when several atoms are present, each with many electrons, these all have mutual interactions, and a "many body" problem results. With multiple nuclei and electrons, the problem expands rapidly, requiring a large computer for solution. Large problems of this type must be segmented (Section 1.6) because of the storage limitations, and this approach appears to be quite feasible. The major problems are the CPU speed and data transfer rate from disk to memory. The difficulty arises because even for problems of moderate size, the storage and computations required are large. For instance, for a calculation of the shape of the potential well for the hydrogen bridge in the DNA structure,* which includes 9 carbon, 8 nitrogen, 2 oxygen, and 10 hydrogen atoms, or total of 136 electrons, it is necessary to compute more than 2×10^9 integrals for each point in the curve (potential vs. distance). Storing each of these integrals during the iterative process would require 64 bits $\times 2.4 \times 10^9 = 1.55 \times 10^{11}$ bits (64 bits = double precision). This large storage requirement would necessitate the use of tapes, and given medium density tapes at, say, 1.3×10^8 bits/tape (Section 1.7), more than 10^3 tapes would be required, which is unreasonable and unworkable; higher density tapes could reduce this amount to a few hundred. Clearly some contraction of storage requirements is needed, and in fact special techniques were developed in this case, requiring two tapes for solution. Nevertheless the entire computation still required 8 days on an IBM model 195, indicating the complexity of such numerical calculations. Some of the numerous other scientific problems that also fall into this category were covered in Section 1.6.

CLASS 2.   APPROXIMATE MODELS

Weather prediction problems fall mainly into class 2. Attempts to numerically calculate and predict weather date back more than half a century (Richardson, 1922), but early attempts were unsuccessful, primarily because of the lack of large capacity, high speed computers. Consequently the modern history of weather prediction has followed closely the history of computers. No attempt is made to review this history nor the details of weather prediction models. Kolsky (1967) gives an excellent review of the history, physics, models, and computing speed requirements for weather prediction, but little information about memory and storage requirements is available in the literature. We concentrate primarily on the latter. However the processing speed of the CPU and the weather model used have a significant bearing on the storage requirements—thus the essential details of weather prediction must be included for a complete understanding of the storage problems.

The basic physical equations for expressing the detailed local interaction of

---

* Part of a study to determine the role of proton tunneling in spontaneous mutations in genetic code (Clementi et al., 1971).

the physical quantities involved in determining weather are a set of nonlinear partial differential equations in both time and space, and they must be solved from the initial conditions, stepping forward in time, as well as matching difficult boundary conditions (e.g., at the surface—oceans, mountains of irregular slope, etc.). The model is represented by a varying number of differential equations depending on the complexity of the model. In the system of differential equations in use at NCAR (National Center for Atmospheric Research) (Kasahara, 1970) four independent variables specify grid point (latitude, longitude, height, and time). There are also at least eight dependent variables, including the three components of wind velocity, pressure, specific humidity, air density, water vapor density, and temperature, plus at least four driving functions, namely, rate of heating of air per unit mass, longitudinal and latitudinal components of frictional force of air particles per unit volume, condensation rate of water vapor per unit mass, and rate of change of water vapor per unit mass due to vertical and horizontal diffusion of water vapor. These equations relating the various parameters are expressed in a system of finite difference equations that can number 15 or more. In addition, the initial values of pressure, air density, and wind velocities at time $t = 0$ must be inserted, and a very complex set of boundary conditions must be matched. Solution of these equations under realistic conditions, for a significant portion of the earth's surface, constitutes the current problem. Nonfinite difference techniques do exist (e.g., calculation in spatial frequency domain via Fourier transforms rather than real time); the most promising technique, however, appears to be the straightforward representation of differentials by finite difference approximations and subsequent numerical solution by what amounts to trial and error. Thus this technique is used in all subsequent analysis.

Actual weather forecasting currently done makes use of simple models compared to the more advanced experimental models; hence the former are tailored to current computer capabilities. If we consider the more advanced models such as that in use at NCAR, the model consists essentially of dividing the earth into an angular grid with a fixed number of latitude and longitude degrees between points as in Fig. 1.8-1, given by α and β degrees, respectively (usually $\alpha = \beta$), and grid spacing expressed in degrees. Obviously the actual spacing between grid points in meters or miles will vary, being larger at the equator and smaller near the poles. Grid points are taken for each longitude point on a given latitude circle (e.g., equator) around the entire sphere or 360°. Thus longitudinal subscripts encompass 360°. The number of such concentric circles can extend only from one pole to the other or 180°, thus latitude subscripts encompass only 180°. Since weather is not confined to the earth's surface, a finite distance into the atmosphere and under the surface must also be covered. Thus the atmosphere

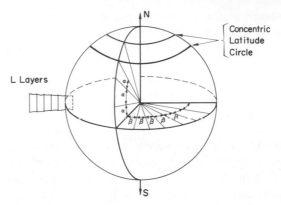

FIGURE 1.8-1   Coordinate system and grid spacing used in global weather calculations.

and surface are divided into layers, and each layer assumed to have uniform parameters at any given grid point and time. For this type of calculation, the amount of storage required can be determined as follows.

For the finite difference approximation, seven adjacent lines (concentric circles) of latitude represent the second derivative in space and the first derivative in time. Each latitude circle has $360/\beta$ grid points and each grid point has L layers (some of which can be beneath the surface). Each point within the $(360/\beta)L$ matrix contains a certain number of physical parameters (air velocity, temperature, etc.). Although the accuracy of the overall model depends on several factors,* the amount of storage space needed depends to a significant extent on the total size of the grid and the number of variables per grid point. Each grid point must have a minimum of four variables, the two components of horizontal wind velocity (third component can be calculated from conservation of momentum), temperature, and humidity (or related parameter). More accurate models include variables to represent clouds, radiation, and so on, and can range from 8 variables for current models to 30 variables for future models. Thus we allow the number of variables N_v to range between 8 and 30. If we assume that each variable (floating point

---

* The accuracy of various models depends on several factors: the number of parameters used to represent local conditions (e.g., allowances for clouds, vegetation cover, radiation and absorption characteristics of different soils and water, etc., approximations within the equations themselves—some physical laws apply only within very small dimensions, such as condensation of water applicable to raindrops, and dissipation of kinetic energy through frictional forces accomplished by air particles rubbing against themselves and other surfaces (both these require dimensions measured in millimeters), whereas the calculations are done over ranges of hundreds of kilometers; the size of the grid spacing, which determines the accuracy of the finite difference approximation to the actual differential equation; the handling of difficult boundary conditions such as mountain ranges, oceans with varying temperature and other properties.

number) in main storage requires one word, the total number of words required in main storage at any one time is

$$W_m = \frac{360}{\beta} \times C \times L \times N_v \tag{1.8-1}$$

where C = number of adjacent latitude circles for finite difference approximation

W_m = number of main memory words

L = number of layers

N_v = number of variables

β = longitude grid spacing (degrees)

Whereas main storage need hold only C latitude circles, the external storage must hold the entire globe data points or all the latitude circles. This requires $180/\alpha$ such circles; thus the total number of external storage words required is

$$W_s = \frac{360}{\beta} \times \frac{180}{\alpha} \times L \times N_v \tag{1.8-2}$$

where W_s = number of external storage words

α = latitude grid spacing (degrees)

and β, L, and N_v are as in (1.8-1). Some typical values in use are

$$\alpha = \beta = 5° \qquad L = 6 \qquad N_v = 14 \qquad C = 7$$

Substituting these numbers into (1.8-1) and (1.8-2) for main and external storage gives

$$W_m = 72 \times 7 \times 6 \times 14 = 42{,}336 \text{ words} \tag{1.8-3}$$

$$W_s = 72 \times 36 \times 6 \times 14 = 217{,}728 \text{ words} \tag{1.8-4}$$

These values represent the minimum requirements on the computing system for such a problem. We have neglected the actual program instructions themselves (which would reside in main memory), the operating system (also in main memory), plus some "fine" points in the calculations (the latter increase the above numbers by a very small amount and can be neglected here). The instructions (i.e., code for such a problem) might require 10 to 12K words and a like value for the operating system, thus a main memory of about 65K words; at 60 bits/word this is a main memory of 3.9M bits, a sizable amount. For external storage, the size is about $60 \times 220\text{K} = 13.2\text{M}$ bits, again a sizable amount. It should be further noted that a 5° grid is very coarse; for example, at 40.5°N latitude (New York City

$= 40.5$), $5°$ corresponds to 265 miles separation between grid points (assuming earth's diameter at 8K miles). Thus this spacing is useful for large cyclonic-type predictions but certainly would not give a picture for local conditions. A grid spacing of $1°$ (i.e., 53 miles at $40.5°$ latitude) would be more desirable.

For future calculations of this nature, let us consider the computing system needs in terms of the next major step from current models. Assume $\alpha = \beta = 1°$ grid spacing, $L = 18$ layers, and $N_v = 30$ variables. Using $C = 7$, (1.8-1) and (1.8-2) give for future requirements

$$W_m = 360 \times 7 \times 18 \times 30 \quad = 1.3608\text{M words} \tag{1.8-5}$$
$$= 81.6\text{M bits}$$

$$W_s = 360 \times 180 \times 18 \times 30 = 34.992\text{M words} \tag{1.8-6}$$
$$= 2.1 \times 10^9 \text{ bits}$$

These numbers, though somewhat large, are certainly not unreasonable. Systems are already available with main memories of 4M bytes and disk storage of 800M bytes per system or larger. The major question is one of large cost for such memory systems.

Thus the storage system needed for a rather sophisticated weather prediction on a $1°$ grid is quite reasonable. Now let us estimate the MIPS rating one might need to do the same sophisticated problem of $\alpha = \beta = 1°$, $N_v = 30$, $L = 18$. Assume that we wish to do a 5 day forecast and complete the computation in a maximum of 10 hr computer time. How many MIPS should the computer have? The data points required (words) per time step are given by (1.8-6) or about 35M words. Assume a very sophisticated program so that $I/B = 40$.* The number of instructions per time step is

$$\frac{I}{\Delta t} = \frac{I}{B} \times W_s \times 5 \text{ bytes/word}$$

Substituting these values gives

$$\frac{I}{\Delta t} = 40 \times 35 \times 10^6 \times 5 = 7 \times 10^9 \text{ inst./time step}$$

---

* Kolsky (1967, p. 594) has pointed out that for a large number of hydrodynamic problems, the number of instructions executed per grid point per unit time step ranges from 300 for uncomplicated models to about 3000 for very complex programs. An estimate of the I/B ratio can be obtained by using the previous numbers for representing grid variables, namely, one 60 bit word per variable and 14 variables per grid point. In this system, 60 bits = 5 bytes (12 bits per byte in CDC system in use at NCAR) or $5 \times 14 = 70$ bytes per grid point, so the I/B ratio is estimated to range from

$$I/B = 300/70 \text{ to } 3000/70 \approx 4 \text{ to } 40.$$

A $1°$ grid will require a time step $\Delta t = 2$ min, or $30 \times 24 = 720$ time steps per day, giving $5 \times 720 = 3600$ time steps in 5 days. To do the 5 day forecast requires

$$7 \times 10^9 \frac{I}{\Delta t} \times 3600\Delta t = 25.2 \times 10^{12} \text{ inst.}$$

If this forecast is to be computed in 10 hr, these 25.2×10^{12} instructions must be executed in 10 hr (36,000 sec); thus the speed of the computer must be

$$\text{inst./real time} = \frac{25.2 \times 10^{12}}{3.6 \times 10^4} = 7 \times 10^8 \text{ inst./sec}$$

$$= 700 \text{ MIPS}$$

This is nearly an order of magnitude larger than that projected for MIPS in the early 1980s. Thus we must be content with more gross weather calculations for larger grids and less sophisticated models. Here we have an example in which the size of storage systems, though presenting numerous problems, is not the limiting factor; rather, the raw computing power of the CPU, which includes the memory cycle time, limits the use of more sophisticated models. These rather strenuous computational requirements have motivated researchers to look for better, more accurate models in simpler forms, as well as more efficient techniques for solving present physical models.

CLASS 3.   HYPOTHESIZED MODELS

This area encompasses an enormous variety of fields including economics, urban planning, world models, forest growth, water runoff, pollution, psychology, and many others. In this area, rather than just solving already known fundamentals for complex parameters, the computer allows us to discover fundamental relationships by permitting more accurate models to be devised continually, showing which parameters are most important. The computer requirements can become rather demanding, nevertheless the major problems tend to be the synthesis of the mathematical model and understanding of which factors need be considered, as well as methods of solution. Storage capacity seldom is of much concern, although in practice, the models definitely tend to expand to fill the size of storage allotted for solution.

Each problem has its own storage and computing requirements, making generalizations quite difficult. Examples of such problems can be found in many references (Hamilton and Nance, 1971; Laska, 1972; Cushman, 1971; Tomkins and Messick, 1963) and are not included here.

CLASS 4.   DATA COLLECTION AND PROCESSING

The amount of raw data generated during a scientific experiment is very large in several major applications, requiring large storage capability. A linear accelerator facility at Los Alamos (Anderson, 1970; Worlton, 1971) produces a proton beam with energies of up to 800 MeV directed into graphite or copper targets to produce secondary meson beam emission. A single experiment can generate up to 5×10^{10} bits of data. The data are processed and subsequently reduced to about 5×10^9 bits, which are retained in a file for a year. Since only about 10 such experiments are performed each year, the total bulk storage for such applications is thus in the range of 10^{11} bits. If such data were stored on magnetic tape, and assuming 10^8 bits/reel, then about 10^3 reels, 50 to 100 reels per experiment would be required. This is not unreasonable, yet access to individual pieces of data is much too slow. An access time of about 1 sec to any piece of archieval data is desirable, thus eliminating tape. In this particular application, an IBM-1360 Photo Digital Storage System was used.*

Another type of data collection and processing application is that of image storage and transmission. High resolution photographs are used in space exploration to record pictures of other planets as well as for exploring the earth's surface in earth resources studies. Such pictures are taken either by camera or scanned with a TV monitor, then digitized for transmission to earth. For instance, the photographs from Mariner VI and VII contain about 10^7 bits, photographs from Lunar Orbiter have more than 10^8 bits, and high resolution aerial photographs of the earth can contain about 10^{10} bits (Murray and Davis, 1970). These numbers are based on a standard 23×23 cm frame, 200 lines/mm lens resolution (over entire frame), and a 5 bit gray scale (32 gray levels) per point. Clearly such digitized images can consume large quantities of data. A reasonably high resolution photo of about 10^8 bits would require about 1 reel of tape per photo (assuming 10^8 bits/reel). Since photos numbering in the hundreds, thousands, and millions are collected as scientific data from various sources, the storage requirements become quite large.

Even relatively low resolution photos of scientific data often require large storage: for instance, up to 1967 TIROS satellites had transmitted more than a half-million photographs of cloud cover for the study of the earth's atmosphere. Original pictures are 500×500 array elements, the brightness of each element represented by a 6 bit number. The resolution is such that the final pictures in digital form require only $250 \times 250 \times 5$ bits or 0.3125M bits per photo (Arking, 1967). A half-million photos would then require storage in the amount of

$$0.3125 \times 10^6 \times 0.5 \times 10^6 \approx 1.5 \times 10^{11} \text{ bits}$$

* This system can store 10^{12} bits on-line: the device consists of 32 photosensitive silver halide chips in a box. Each chip can store 4.7×10^6 bits, thus giving $32 \times 4.7M = 1.5 \times 10^8$ bits/box.

Such a file would occupy about 1000 reels of tape (using 1.3×10^8 bits per reel.) Although high density tapes can reduce this by a factor of 8, and further increases in density are anticipated with time, the amount of storage needed tends to increase also with time; thus the improvements will likely just match the expansion (again fulfillment of the law of storage expansion, Section 1.1). In any case, this section has shown quantitatively the sizes of storage required in various scientific calculation, indicating that capacities of 10^{12} to 10^{15} bits are not unreasonable. The Ampex Terabit Memory (delivery July 1972) and the IBM 3850 Mass Storage System (available in 1975) are applicable to such large requirements. The IBM system can store up to 472 billion bytes or nearly 4×10^{12} bits in the full system. The basic storage unit consists of a cartridge containing 770 in. of tape approximately 4 in. wide. Tracks are recorded at an angle, as in Fig. 6.7-1. Each cartridge can hold 50M bytes of data, and a full system can hold up to 9440 cartridges.

1.9 LIMITS ON RANDOM ACCESS MEMORY SIZE: ONE–LEVEL STORE CONCEPT

Throughout this chapter it has been emphasized that the speed and capacity of main memory is a primary limitation on computer processing. If we could make random access memory arbitrarily large, arbitrarily fast, and reasonably cheap, we could do away with all the secondary storage. The concept of making present systems appear as a "one-level store" (discussed later), even though there are several storage levels, would then reduce to a "pure" one-level store in concept and actuality. Since large-scale integrated circuit memories are reducing cost and increasing the capacity, we may expect to see the cost of main memory begin to approach that of secondary store. Therefore, let us ask the question, Why not make all the storage random access?

The answer is ultimately "high cost," but it is not obvious how and why this is so. To gain some perspective, let us perform a rather simple engineering analysis on a very large random access, semiconductor memory system. We will see that for large memories, the decoding logic gates required to address the individual words and bits exceeds the logic gates* within the CPU by many orders of magnitude. Thus the size of main memory must grow in some proportion to the size (number of logic gates) of the CPU for an economical balance. The speed of the memory module is also an important factor in limiting the size, but for our analysis, we neglect the speed considerations. We assume that our devices and technology provide adequate speed for any size, and we simply count the logic gates needed for decoding.

* A logic gate is a complete logic circuit (AND, NOR, etc.).

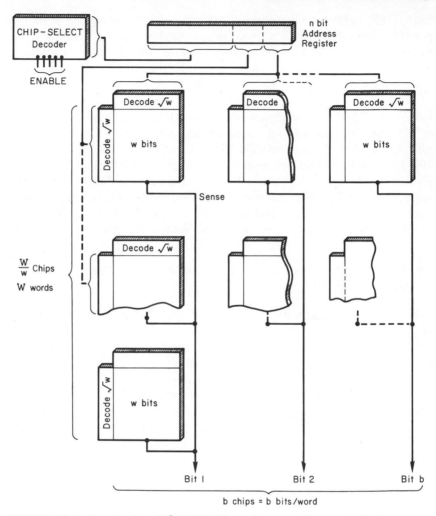

FIGURE 1.9-1 Organization of $2\frac{1}{2}$D, 1 bit/chip random access, integrated circuit memory.

We assume that our technology provides integrated circuit chips with a maximum w bits per chip (Fig. 1.9-1). The memory system is organized as one bit per chip, identical to that in Fig. 4.9-3.* Other chip organizations could be used but would not change the results. For a "square" chip array, there will be $w^{1/2}$ word lines and $w^{1/2}$ bit/sense lines on each chip. Decoding logic gates must then be present on-chip to select one world line and one bit/sense

* See Section 4.9 for a discussion of integrated circuit memory organization.

line. This requires a minimum of $w^{1/2}$ gates for word decoding and $w^{1/2}$ for bit/sense decoding, assuming that a one-level decoder can be used. Since a two-level decoder increases the logic gate count only slightly, we assume one-level decoding. Thus each chip has a minimum of $2w^{1/2}$ logic gates for decoding. We wish to organize these chips into a large memory of W words $\times\ b$ bits/word. We can achieve this by using an array of b chips in one direction to achieve the word length, and W/w chips in the other dimension to achieve the required number of words, as shown. A chip-select decoder also is required, but the number of logic gates for this function is approximately equal to W/w. This is negligible compared to the gates required on the chips and is ignored. That is, the size of the basic storage module (BSM) is unimportant in the final analysis.

Let us now count the total number of logic gates needed for the entire memory. The array of chips consists of

$$\text{total number of chips} = \frac{W}{w} b \qquad (1.9\text{-}1)$$

The minimum number of decoding logic gates per chips is

$$\text{decoding gates/chip} = 2w^{1/2} \qquad (1.9\text{-}2)$$

Thus the minimum number of decoding gates required for the entire memory is the product of (1.9-1) and (1.9-2) or

$$\text{total decoding gates} = \frac{W}{w} b 2w^{1/2} = \frac{2Wb}{w^{1/2}} \qquad (1.9\text{-}3)$$

This expression becomes more meaningful when typical numbers are substituted. We have shown in previous sections that a storage of 10^{15} bits is not unreasonable in the near future. Suppose we attempt to implement this size as 10^{13} words $\times\ 10^2$ bits/word, giving

$$W = 10^{13} \qquad \text{and} \qquad b = 10^2 \qquad (1.9\text{-}4)$$

A reasonable value of w, the bits per chip, can be easily estimated. Current levels of integration are in the range of 4K to 16K bits/chip and several times that is possible. Hence 10^5 bits/chip appears reasonable for the near future and about 10 times that for the distant future, or

$$w = 10^5 \text{ bits/chip} \qquad \text{(near term)} \qquad (1.9\text{-}5)$$

$$w \approx 10^6 \text{ bits/chip} \qquad \text{(future)} \qquad (1.9\text{-}6)$$

Substituting these two values for w, and (1.9-4) into (1.9-3) gives

$$\text{total decoding gates } (w = 10^5) \approx 6 \times 10^{12}$$
$$\text{total decoding gates } (w = 10^6) \approx 3 \times 10^{12}$$

The number is quite large, in the range of 10^{13} gates for both levels of integration. We would have to increase w very dramatically to reduce the gates, since (1.9-3) varies as the square root of w.

The magnitude of the above number of required gates is quite enormous. Very large scale computers have CPU logic circuit counts measured in the 10^6 circuit range,* but computers with 10^5 circuits are more typical. A further comparison can be obtained by making a very crude estimate of all the logic gates in existence throughout the world. In the early 1970s there were very approximately 10^5 computers of various kinds, small, medium, large. Let us assume an average of 50K circuits per CPU and 50K circuits for the peripheral controllers and other logic functions. Thus 10^5 circuits average per computer and 10^5 computers yields the total gates in the world as roughly 10^{10} gates in the early 1970s. This is 2 to 3 orders of magnitude smaller than the gates required to decode our 10^{15} bit memory. Even if our estimate of the world population of logic gates is low by a factor of 10 or 100, the conclusion is inescapable. Since the CPU logic gates are no different in principle from those used for decoding, the costs will be similar. It seems clear that to maintain a balance of cost between CPU and memory, the memory size can only increase in some proportion to the CPU size. Figure 1.5-4 shows that this has tended to be the case in commercial systems, and now we begin to see some of the underlying reasons. It should be pointed out again that other factors (e.g., speed vs. cost and levels of integration) that ultimately must be included have been neglected for simplicity.

The logic circuit count was based on the use of a $2\frac{1}{2}$D memory organization. Such an organization lends itself readily to the use of extremely simple, very dense, hence inexpensive two-terminal cells, which is most desirable for such large numbers (i.e., 10^{15} bits). The decoding logic gates and interconnections are considerably more complex than a cell array by orders of magnitude. These logic gates could be reduced in number by the use of a 3D organization. However this requires a much more complex, three-terminal memory cell (see Chapter 4). Since this complexity must be duplicated at every bit cell, the array cost increases very rapidly. Hence this approach does not necessarily provide any advantage and in fact could be worse.

It should be clear from the foregoing example that random access to a very large number of locations (words or bytes) is out of the question just from circuit count considerations. One way to circumvent the difficulty is to make the words much longer in bit length, hence reduce the number of physical locations that must be selected at random. Further cost savings can be obtained by sharing of the circuits and transducers as much as possible to

---

* The Illiac IV System (Bouknight et al., 1972) has a total of nearly 0.8×10^6 logic switching circuits in one quadrant, or in the range of 3×10^6 for the full system.

keep the "per bit" cost down, since the number of bits is quite large. This is precisely what is done in practice, and although it results in a nonrandom access memory, it can lead to a substantial cost savings, as shown in (1.3-1). Of course this saving can be obtained only by sacrificing something else—namely, access time, as shown in (1.3-2).

One-Level Store Concept

The foregoing discussion demonstrates that a physical, one-level store of large size is not feasible. In fact, most computers make use of a main memory far smaller than the random access addressing capability of the CPU. Typical computers have address registers ranging from about 12 to 16 bits for minicomputers and 24 to 32 for medium and large size, general purpose systems. IBM System 360 uses a standard 24 bit address (32 bits on special models of M67). This range of address lengths allows direct CPU addressing of

$$2^{16} = 65,536 = 64\text{K}' \tag{1.9-7}$$

$$2^{24} = 16,777\ 216 = 16\text{M}' \approx 16.7 \times 10^6 \tag{1.9-8}$$

$$2^{32} = 4,294,967,296 \approx 4.3 \times 10^9 \tag{1.9-9}$$

words or bytes* for 16, 24, and 32 bit address lengths, respectively.

Typical systems thus have the capability to directly address a maximum of 16M' bytes or about 10^8 bits but typically have less than a few million bytes of main memory. Anything larger than this must be stored elsewhere. Hence all such computing systems employ at least two modes of addressing, one for the random access memory (Chapter 4) and another mode for the secondary storage such as tapes (Chapter 6) or drums and disks (Chapter 7). The formats for each are different and greatly complicate the use and allocation of storage, as discussed in Chapters 6 through 9. A system incorporating the one-level store concept has only one mode of addressing, namely, random access addressing, thus the CPU logical address must be large enough to address the entire store. Our analysis postulated a random access memory of 10^{13} words as the sole storage attached to a computer; this would require a total CPU logical address of nearly 44 bits. Such a system is a one-level store of the purest form, both in its addressing means and in storage implementation. However we also saw that the use of one-storage technology would not be very economical, hence would undoubtedly lead to the use of a complex storage hierarchy. However if we maintain the CPU logical addressing at, say 44 bits, and specify that 1.7×10^{13}† separately

---

* 1 byte = 8 bits + parity is used here; K' = 1024 M' = 1,048,576 = (K')^2.
† $2^{44} = 1.75921856 \times 10^{13}$.

addressable words or bytes is the maximum that can ever be attached to the system, no matter what form it may take, the system would still appear to the user as a one-level store, even though the underlying storage consisted of a hierarchy of storage systems. The hierarchy can be made to appear this way by the use of a large virtual memory system with an effective logical address of 44 bits. The major question is whether such a large system could be efficient, and more specifically, whether the cost/performance ratio would be attractive. No such large, one-level store system has yet been built. All computers to date have some form of removable secondary storage, hence at least two methods of addressing.

1.10   THE HUMAN LINK AND HUMAN MEMORY

The ultimate goal of all computer computations is to produce, eventually some change in the human mind. Whether this change be a new conception of the atomic structure of nature or the universe, or even just a larger numerical value on our paycheck, the information eventually is stored in our organic brains. In fact, considerable effort and hardware is expended within a computing system to link the computational process ultimately to the human brain (Fig. 1.10-1). The computer works at very high speed, processing large quantities of data, and it makes relatively few errors. On the other hand, the human mind is very slow and makes many errors when processing large quantities of numerical data, for instance. Thus there is a significant gap in this link between the ever-increasing power of computers and the unchanging capabilities of the human mind. Considerable work remains to be done in bridging this gap; we need better techniques to condense and display data, as well as better understanding of the process of learning within the human mind. Rather than attempting to bridge this gap, let us concentrate on the speed and capacity of human memory.

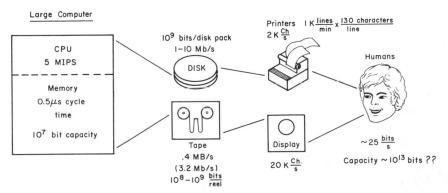

FIGURE 1.10-1   Computational capacity gap from computer to human brain.

Despite considerable advances in the general understanding of the human mind made during the past 20 years, there are few if any established fundamentals, and little in the way of hard scientific data. For example, the mechanisms or processes by which any of the four fundamental requirements for any storage system (presented in Section 2.2) are accomplished in the human memory are totally unknown. Scientific debates continue over fundamental questions such as those relating to the storage medium. Without this knowledge, the method of implementation of the other requirements can hardly be known. Furthermore, without the medium, it is impossible to specify the general character of the storage cell (Section 2.3). We do not even know whether the basic storage cell is binary or otherwise, whether the addressing mechanism is random access, direct, sequential, associative, or "other." There is some evidence that all four access mechanisms are present, but it is not clear whether they are separately accessed systems as in a computer, or just a more complex cell and array structure that can operate in different modes. Nor do we know the capacity or speed of the human brain. Some crude estimates of the latter two parameters can be made, as we shall see. Often contradictory results arise because of different initial assumptions, all of which may seem reasonable. These disparities only further point to a lack of fundamental understanding of various processes and concepts.

Let us first consider the capacity of the human brain. The basic structural component of the central nervous system (brain, brain stem, and spinal cord) is the neuron (Katz, 1966). One theory postulates that memory is a result of the circuit connection of these neurons. It is estimated that there are roughly 10^{10} neurons in the brain and on an average, 10^3 interconnections or synapses between them. If we assume that each synapse stores one bit of information, probably a bad assumption, we arrive at a capacity of 10^{13} bits, a rather tenuous value. The value of 10^{10} neurons itself is a crude estimate obtained by measuring the average distance between cells on microscopic slices of brain tissue. From such measurements, the density for various regions of the brain can be obtained. An estimate of the total volume of each region multiplied by the density yields the total number of neurons. Needless to say, the estimate is only approximate. Since the basic storage cell is unknown, an even greater uncertainty arises in connection with the factor by which the number of neurons is multiplied. Nevertheless, let us use 10^{13} bits as the capacity and analyze the consequence on learning rate. If we assume that 10^{13} bits are filled to capacity in one's lifetime, then using 65 years as a lifetime, or about 2×19^9 sec,* we must store information at the rate of

$$\frac{10^{13} \text{ bits}}{2 \times 10^9 \text{ sec}} = 5K \text{ bits/sec}$$

* 1 year $= 31.5 \times 10^6$ sec, 65 years $= 2.04 \times 10^9$ sec.

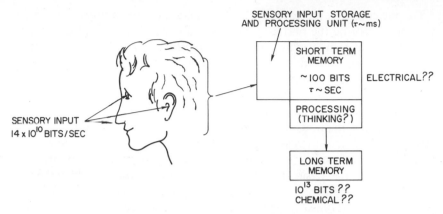

FIGURE 1.10-2   Memory hierarchy of the human brain.

If the assumptions are true, this rate must exist, on an average, for every second (awake, asleep, etc.) of our lives. Various studies indicate that the input and output rate capacity of humans is orders of magnitude smaller, in the range of 25 to 100 bits/sec. These, however, ignore the possibility that after the information is inputted, some processing may be done internally, perhaps generating and storing large quantities of new information. This process may, in fact, be what "thinking" really is. Since we know nothing about thinking, let us look first at the general organization of memory and afterward consider the input/output rates of humans.

It is reasonably well established that humans have at least a two-level hierarchy consisting of a short-term memory and a long-term memory (Fig. 1.10-2). Information is processed as it is received and is stored temporarily in short-term memory.

In addition, there is a sensory information storage and processing unit. This function can retain sensory data such as images for a fraction of a second. Some processing takes place, relevant information is stored in short-term memory, which retains information, depending on the complexity and structure, for a time interval measured in seconds. Important information is further processed and stored in long-term memory, which has a retention time of days, years, sometimes a lifetime. The writing time constant of short-term memory is much shorter than what would be expected if it were basically chemical. This is in contrast to the rather long time required for writing in long-term memory. The latter is theorized as being chemical, whereas short-term memory is thought to be electrical (Lindsay and Norman, 1972, Chs. 8, 9, 10). However there are still many contradictions and unexplained phenomena. For instance, short-term events of a strong emotional character can be stored for a lifetime. Other factors thus appear to be important, leading ultimately to the basic motivations of life itself. The only conclusions possible are that there appear to be various memory systems at work, perhaps a continuum, perhaps discrete; but the fundamentals remain to be discovered.

Let us look at the capacity and input rate of the human brain. Studies of the various tasks performed by human beings indicate that the channel capacity, which includes both our processing and storing functions, is about 25 bits/sec. As a check, we speak or understand an average of about 3 mono-syllable words per second. The information capacity of monosyllable English words is roughly 10 bits/word, giving a rate of about 30 bits/sec. The information content of 10 bits/word is estimated as follows. There are, very roughly, 1000 common English monosyllables. If we measure information in binary bits, 1000 separate distinguishable entities requires 10 bits (i.e., $2^{10} = 1024$). We can arrive at a similar answer by using a different measure of the information content of words. There are 26 letters in our alphabet plus a space for word separation; thus the information required to decode one out of 27 is $\log_2 27 = 4.75$ bits. Since the average English-language text uses approximately 4.5 to 5 letters per word plus a space, counting the space as one letter, we arrive at an average of

$$3 \text{ words/sec} \times 6 \times 4.75 \text{ bits/word} = 85 \text{ bits/sec}$$

which is about the same as previously. These numbers, however, are the bits required in the address register for decoding (i.e., accessing). For the storage itself, an important question is, How are data stored? If each character is stored separately, a large number of bits is necessary. The number of characters in use is considerably larger than 26; in fact, it is closer to 128. Recognizing each such character requires a minimum of about $\log_2 128 = 7$ bits/char.* This would give a much larger bit count need for storing than for accessing, as would be expected in a computer. Carrying the analysis further, the human brain can certainly recognize more than 128 characters, but the method by which this is done is not known. It could be a subroutine-like processing, pure storage, or a combination of these. Until we know more about the information content of input data and methods of organization and storage, these questions cannot be answered. John von Neumann (1958) estimated that the human memory capacity was in the range of 10^{20} bits, based mainly on the assumption that all input information in one's lifetime is stored and that about 10^{20} bits are received in lifetime. He estimated that the sensory system receives information at the rate of 14×10^{10} bits/sec. However it seems clear now that not all the input information received by the sensor input storage and processing unit of Fig. 1.10-2 is actually

---

* For further information on various aspects of learning and communications, see Miller (1967).

perceived. That which is perceived is processed and stored in short-term memory; only a small portion ever reaches long-term memory.

Thus we know very little about the fundamental structure or organization of the human brain. The similarity to computer memories is most remarkable. An understanding of the fundamental principle of computer memory organization, storage, and retrieval, applied to the human brain, may prove useful in uncovering the totally unknown principle of the latter. Likewise, a better understanding of the human memory may indicate new approaches to the structure and organization of computer memories. Billions of years of evolution has produced a memory system of high efficiency for the necessary function of life. Since these functions demand storage and retrieval of information, we can anticipate that much could be learned from the structure of our little-understood memory system.

APPENDIX 1-A: ECCLES–JORDAN FLIP-FLOP CIRCUIT

One version of the classical Eccles–Jordan flip-flop circuit appears in Fig. A1-1. Either current i_0 or i_1 ("0" or "1") flows, but not both; hence either tube V_0 or V_1 conducts.

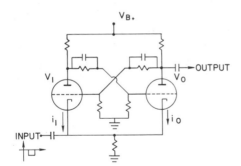

FIGURE A1-1 Classical Eccles–Jordan flip-flop circuit with serial input and output.

Application of successive pulses to the input line cause alternate switching between "0" and "1" states, giving output pulses at one-half the repetition rate of the input. Thus such circuits in tandem are useful for binary counters. Since only one functional input terminal is available, no coincident selection is possible with such a circuit without significant modification (i.e., minimum of two functional, independent, terminals required). Many variations of this circuit are possible (inputs to grids, pentodes), and many were used in early computers to provide insensitivity to variations in tube and circuit parameters, fast switching, minimization of loading effects from other interconnected flip-flops, and other features.

2   Fundamental Principles for Memory and Storage

2.1   INTRODUCTION

The storage and retrieval of information proceeds in accordance with certain fundamental requirements dictated by the overall memory system. These in turn dictate additional fundamental requirements of the physical medium (storage device) in terms of the laws of physics, to enable one to store and retrieve the desired information. Numerous phenomena of nature fulfill the requirements to serve as storage devices, but only certain ones have attractive overall features, making them serious candidates. This chapter gives these system requirements for all types of storage, as well as the fundamental requirements for binary storage media and cells. These basic system and device requirements demonstrate in a very general way why random access memory is more complex to implement but easier to use than nonrandom access memory:

The basic principles of magnetism and magnetic circuits, needed in subsequent chapters, are covered here, as well as some fundamentals of integrated circuit technologies and superconductors. A number of important engineering relationships with respect to static and dynamic electromagnetic fields are derived which are used later.

The subject of the ultimate limits on storage capacity which one can expect to ever achieve has evoked continued concern for a number of years. A section at the end of the chapter provides a summary and some general conclusions. A more specific treatment with respect to ultimate limits in magnetic recording is given in Chapter 5; Chapters 6 and 7 contain sections specific to practical density limits in tapes and disks.

2.2   FUNDAMENTAL SYSTEM REQUIREMENTS FOR STORING AND RETRIEVING INFORMATION

Before we can specify the fundamental requirements of a storage system, we must state the purpose or function of such a system. All computer storage systems have essentially one purpose, to service the CPU or other processing part of the computer. The two services provided are to store (write) and to fetch (read) information as requested. To do this, the storage system must wait for specific orders from the CPU concerning which function is to be accomplished (read or write) and where (CPU logical address). Furthermore, the CPU must provide the data to be stored for a write operation, or a place for the data to go after a read operation. *Throughout this book, except where noted, we assume that the CPU logical address is already available and the memory system merely references the requested word.* This word may be an instruction, a piece of data, or the address increment of another word. We are seldom concerned with the use of the word referenced in storage or with the generation of the CPU logical address. This Section treats the fundamentals of how the storage system perform its service for the CPU.

In virtual memory systems, the CPU logical address is not the final address of the desired word; hence considerable additional functions are necessary to reference the desired word. Some of these functions are part of the virtual *memory* system and some are part of the virtual *processing* system. Since the amount in each is a design tradeoff, we must broaden our concept of memory system to be able to understand virtual memories. This is done in Chapter 9.

To service the CPU, a considerable amount of control is necessary, irrespective of whether the storage is random or nonrandom access. Storage systems therefore usually have two functional parts called the storage control unit and the storage unit (Fig. 2.2-1). The control unit essentially takes the operation (read or write) and address from the CPU and sees to it

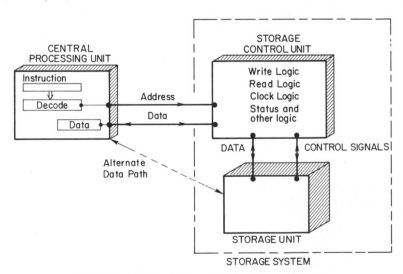

FIGURE 2.2-1 General organization of storage systems.

that all the necessary gating and timing signals are provided to the storage unit. It also signals back to the CPU when data are available after a read operation or that a new read or write cycle may be initiated. Data to and from the CPU usually go through the storage control unit, but not always. For disks, tapes, and related nonrandom access storage, the data always go through the control unit for various reasons. The control unit for such cases is usually quite complex, being a medium sized, special purpose computer. This computer plays a key role in providing part of the addressing mechanism described later.

For random access memory, if the CPU logic hardware is compatible with the memory circuitry, the data can go directly between the memory and CPU as shown by the "alternate data" path in Fig. 2.2-1. The timing of this movement is still gated by the control unit. For random access memory the control unit is generally not as complex as that for nonrandom access storage. One important difference is that the addressing mechanism is "wired in," hence requires no special assistance. Section 4.2 discusses these control units for random access memory in more detail. Sections 6.8 and 7.11 cover control units for tapes and disks.

In general, the more simple the storage unit, the more complex must be the storage control unit. The reverse is also true: the more complex the storage unit, the less complex the control unit. However simpler systems such as tapes or disks are still cheaper per bit than random access cores or semi-conductors, even when the control unit is included in the cost. In addition, for nonrandom storage, one control unit can service several storage units (e.g., several disks), further reducing the cost per bit.

In view of the foregoing, all memory systems must be able to store information and subsequently find and retrieve it, all on command from the CPU. To achieve this, a storage system must have the following basic requirements:

1. Medium for storing energy.
2. Energy source for writing the information—that is, "write" transducers (word and bit).
3. Energy sources and sensors to read—that is, read and sense transducers.
4. Information addressing capability—that is, address selection mechanism for reading and writing.

Item 4 includes some coincidence mechanisms within the system (not necessarily within the device) to bring the necessary energy to the proper position on the medium for writing, and likewise, a coincidence mechanism for associating the sensed information with the proper location during reading. In random access memory this coincidence must be contained within the device, whereas in nonrandom access storage, it is commonly contained within the system—for example, in the coincidence of an electrical signal with mechanical position (e.g., disks, tapes). In many cases, the "write" energy source serves as the "read" energy sources as well, leaving only sense transducers for item 3. Nevertheless a "read" energy source remains a basic requirement.

The differences among all forms of memory systems hardware lie only in the manner in which the four requirements are implemented and more specifically, in the number of "transducers" needed to accomplish these functions. Here "transducer" denotes any type of device (e.g., magnetic head, laser, transistor circuits) that generates the necessary energies for reading and writing, senses stored energy, and generates a sense signal, or provides the decoding for address selection. We now consider some of the similarities and differences among various memory systems based on the four requirements just enumerated.

In all storage systems in use today (with the possible exception of holographic systems, which are mainly experimental), a discrete quantity (e.g., magnetic moments, current, conduction paths) is stored; thus the physical or mechanistic storage attributes of the medium are not a distinguishing feature separating main memory from other storage. In fact, the same physical phenomenon can be, and has been, used for both. For example, the magnetic phenomenon of magnetic recording systems is identical in principle, although different in detail, from that used in ferrite cores, flat film, and plated wire main memories. With few exceptions, however, main memory systems use discrete, physically isolated devices to store a bit, whereas mass storage uses a continuous medium and the isolation is provided by the writing process. This difference of discrete versus continuous media is not a fundamental difference but rather arises because discrete devices greatly ease the problems of noise and interaction in high speed main memory, thus allowing a better engineering design. The fundamental difference between main memory and other storage lies in our second, third, and fourth requirements, namely, in the writing, sensing, and addressing mechanisms.

To achieve a high speed main memory system, each bit location must be electrically "wired" to be able to receive (writing) and send (sensing) energy locally. The storage medium is stationary with all writing and reading transducers hard-wired to the memory. Thus the read/write transducers cannot be shared but rather are on constant alert to serve the bits designated in the hard-wired design. This is essential in providing high speed reading and writing. Since these transducers are expensive, they account for a substantial part of the memory cost, considered in detail in Chapter 4.

In contrast to this, the read/write transducers in nonrandom storage systems are generally shared over a large number of bits, greatly reducing the cost per bit. This is precisely what is done in disk, tape, drums, and other related storage systems, where as a rule one read/write head assembly (sometimes having groups of heads, e.g., nine) is used to reduce cost, and the storage medium is moved (no hard-wiring) to provide access to large areas of storage. This results in substantial cost savings, but also greatly increased access time. The degradation in access time for mass storage is primarily a result of the mechanical nature of the task of moving the medium (and the slider head assembly in disk technology). If it were possible to design mechanical systems with time constants comparable to electronic systems, the access time limitation could be reduced. This does not appear to be possible. Electronic shift register storage such as magnetic bubbles and charge coupled semiconductors appear necessary to achieve this improvement.

The sharing of transducers in nonrandom storage requires that the addressing mechanism *not* be "wired" into the storage unit. But since the storage system must still be able to retrieve an address specified by the CPU, some other mechanism must be provided within the storage system. This is generally done by the control unit in conjunction with additional information stored within the storage medium, referred to as *stored addressing information* throughout this book. Logical functions, part of which can be built into the control unit and part included in the user's program, serve to operate on this stored address information to determine the correct location of the referenced data space. Thus the reduced cost achieved by sharing transducers is offset partly by the consumption of storage space for the stored address information and partly by the additional complexity in the control unit and programming logic. Nevertheless, a net cost savings is obtained. The *use of stored addressing information is fundamentally important in all nonrandom storage.* It is discussed in considerable detail for tapes and disks in Sections 6.5 and 7.6, respectively.

The four system requirements are represented schematically in Fig. 2.2-2 for random and nonrandom access storage units. The control units for the latter are specified only indirectly as the logic and motion control functions. Thus writing, reading, and addressing mechanisms of random and non-random storage differ fundamentally. Random storage is directly addressed out of the address register, immediately into the "dedicated" writing (decoders) and reading (sense amplifier) transducers. A specific location (byte or word) can be directly addressed as desired. With nonrandom storage, addressing must wait until the media and transducers are in proper coincidence before any transactions can take place, giving inherently slow access time because of the longer mechanical time constants compared to electrical time constants. From these simple considerations of sharing transducers, it becomes apparent that nonrandom storage is cheaper than main memory, indicating a variety of storage systems are likely to be around for some time.

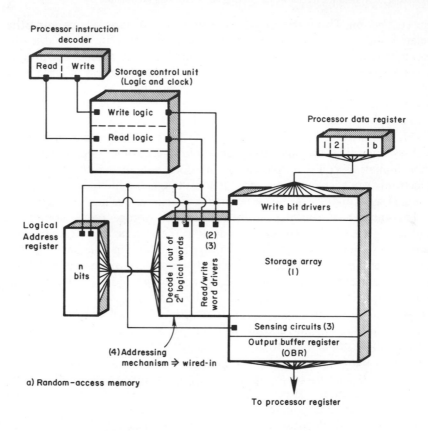

Processor instruction
decoder

Read ¦ Write

Storage control unit
(Logic and clock)

Write logic

Read logic

Processor data register

1 ¦ 2 ¦ b

Logical
Address
register

n
bits

Decode 1 out of
2^n logical words

(2)
(3)

Read/write
word drivers

Write bit drivers

Storage array
(1)

Sensing circuits (3)

Output buffer register
(OBR)

(4) Addressing
mechanism ⇒ wired-in

a) Random-access memory

To processor register

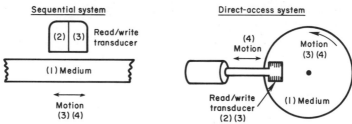

Sequential system

(2) (3)   Read/write
transducer

(1) Medium

Motion
(3) (4)

Direct-access system

(4)
Motion

Motion
(3) (4)

Read/write
transducer
(2) (3)

(1) Medium

b) Nonrandom-access storage
  Writing   – coincidence of motion and electrical pulse
  Reading   – medium motion + logic
  Addressing
  mechanism – stored addressing information + logic + motion

FIGURE 2.2-2 Differences in writing, reading, and addressing mechanisms for random and nonrandom access systems.

2.3 FUNDAMENTAL REQUIREMENTS FOR A REVERSIBLE BINARY STORAGE MEDIUM

To construct a binary memory system of any type, it is first necessary to have a storage medium (requirement 1 in Section 2.2) to store energy in terms of some discrete physical quantity (magnetic moment, circulating current, etc.), which is a symbolic representation of the two binary states of a bit of information. To accomplish this, a potential media for binary storage must have at least (a) two stable (or semistable) energy states separated by a high energy barrier, as in Fig. 2.3-1, (b) capability of switching between these two stable states an infinite number of times by the application of external energy, (c) capability for sensing the two energy states with an external energy source, and (d) energy losses during writing for reliable storage.

It should be pointed out that there is another case which is more applicable to mechanical storage, that is, punched cards, ordinary pencil writing, thermoplastic recording, microgrove (phonograph records), and so on. The characteristic potential well is given by Fig. 2.3-2, in which the "1" and "0" states are not separated by restoring forces as in Fig. 2.3-1 but rather are separated by the slowness of Brownian motion for the particular medium. Given sufficient time, the information would, in principle, destroy itself through simple Brownian motion of the particles. In practice, other factors (chemical deterioration, mechanical wear, etc.), are more significant and faster acting than Brownian motion. We do not consider storage media of these types.

The two energy states in requirement a do not necessarily have to be stable for an infinite time; in fact it is only necessary that they remain stable with time constants much larger than the time needed to "refresh" or rewrite the information. Many such storage systems have been built this way, including the Williams tube (Section 1.2) and the very popular one-device semiconductor cell (Sections 3.9 and 4.9).

The energy losses in requirement d are necessary during the writing process and not at steady state. Some devices (e.g., transistor flip-flop cells) also dissipate energy at steady state, but this is not a fundamental requirement. For the bistable device characterized by Fig. 2.3-1, several arguments can

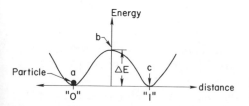

FIGURE 2.3-1 Bistable potential well for storing binary information.

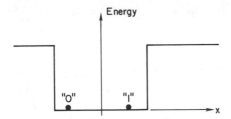

FIGURE 2.3-2 Storage device character-istic using one potential well.

be used to demonstrate the need for dissipation during writing, to achieve reliable storage of the intended information (Landauer, 1961, 1962). One argument proceeds from elementary physics as follows. Suppose that our binary information is represented by a small particle that is initially in the "0" state (left-hand potential well) and we wish to set it into the "1" state reliably. If there are no losses, we can supply a force toward the right that supplies just enough potential energy ΔE to overcome the barrier plus an infinitesimal (and assumed negligible compared to ΔE) amount of kinetic energy to the right, to ensure that the particle will enter the potential well on the right. Obviously the particle will roll down into the well, up the steep right-hand side, and back down into the well, starting up the hill represented by the energy barrier ΔE. If there are no losses and the initial kinetic energy was negligible, the particle will end up exactly at point b. It can then, with equal probability, fall toward point a or c; indeed, it can continue oscillating indefinitely if the losses are truly zero. If the particle is to remain in potential well c, there must be some small losses to prevent returning to point b. Obviously any small amount of loss will suffice, provided the initial energy input was exactly equal to ΔE and the initial kinetic energy was negligible. However such a delicate balance of energy could conceivably make for an unreliable device, since the particle might fall back to point a because of minor imperfections or variations in physical parameters (ΔE) or applied forces. Thus a margin of safety is desired, and the amount of dissipation required increases as the excess energy input is increased. A similar situation results if the particle is initially in the "1" state, (but we do not know it) and we wish to end with the particle in the "1" state. If we again apply an amount of energy exactly equal to ΔE and there are no losses, the particle will be forced up the steep right-hand side and when released will oscillate between the two wells. Again any losses will prevent this, giving a stored "1." But once more the reliability and margins of safety enter. The minimum amount of energy dissipation required has not been amenable to calculation from first princi-ples. However current devices are orders of magnitude away from foreseeable lower limits.

Many physical phenomena satisfy our four media requirements for

TABLE 2.3-1   Examples of Phenomena Used for Storage in Various Memory Systems

Energy Storing Parameter	Memory System Implementation
Magnetic moment **M**	Cores, thin films, plated wires, all magnetic recording, magnetooptic beam addressed memory, magnetic bubbles
Displacement **D** or charge Q	Ferroelectrics, FET memories, MNOS, surface waves, cathode ray tube
Circulating current **J**	Flip-flop cells, cryotrons
Atomic structure	Switchable resistors
Physical structure	Punched cards, tape, and so on.

storage, but few are attractive. Some of the more notable phenomena are summarized in Table 2.3-1.

To implement a storage medium that satisfies a through d, into a storage system, the system requirements 2, 3, and 4 in Section 2.2 must be fulfilled. These three requirements of the system can be fashioned around the medium in numerous ways, and the different ways chosen represent another fundamental distinction between various memory systems. In random access memory, a considerable amount of the four system requirements is contained within the medium or basic storage cell itself, whereas in nonrandom access memory, very little is contained within the medium or cell, hence must be provided by other parts of the system. Thus for random access, the cell is rather complex, more difficult to fabricate, and more costly. This cost, added to the substantial "stand-by" transducers needed, yields an expensive array that is also fast and easily addressed. This complexity is duplicated many times within each cell and is spread over a large array. Although the array is more complex internally, from an external point of view it is quite simple, requiring very little external components for actual operation. On the other hand, nonrandom access cells are relatively simple, hence cheap, but the remainder of the system must be more complex. This complexity is not duplicated, however, and the cost per bit can be reduced by having the additional complexity serve many inexpensive cells or bits.

2.4 ADDITIONAL REQUIREMENTS FOR RANDOM ACCESS MEMORY CELLS

The basic requirements for a storage system (Section 2.2) and for a storage medium (Section 2.3) are the minima and did not specify the means of accessing, but only that the information be writable and subsequently retrievable. For random access systems, the information addressing requirement of random access to any small area of storage (e.g., a word), places additional constraints on the memory cell. The number and severity of these additional constraints varies with the complexity of the memory organization; a 3D organization (Chapter 4) requires more from the basic memory cell than does the 2D or certain types of $2\frac{1}{2}$D organizations. For a cell used in a 2D organization, the additional requirements to those of Section 2.3 are as follows:

a. A well-defined threshold for coincident writing.

b. insensitivity to write disturbs on unselected cells.

c. Two separate functional terminals (ports) for coincident writing of words and noncoincident reading of bits.

For a random access cell used in 3D organization, the additional requirements to those of Section 2.3 are as follows:

a′. A well-defined threshold for coincident writing *and* reading.

b′. Insensitivity to write disturbs *and* read disturbs on unselected bits.

c′. *Three* separate functional terms (ports) for coincident reading and coincident writing.

Thus the designations 3D and 2D seem reasonable, being related to the minimum number of functional terminals required in the cell. For $2\frac{1}{2}$D organization, either a two- or three-terminal cell can be used, resulting in two types of $2\frac{1}{2}$D organization. The designation of $2\frac{1}{2}$D is less obvious but results from the fact that $2\frac{1}{2}$D is between 2D and 3D organization. The necessity for these requirements can be understood only by considering the details of the various organizations. This is done in Chapter 4, and we shall accept the requirements here without further justification.

In addition to the necessary requirements, a number of other desirable, but fundamentally unnecessary characteristics can help produce a practical, economical random access memory system. Some of these desirable characteristics are as follows:

1. Large energy output for sensing.
2. One-device structure per stored bit of information.
3. Nondestructive read-out capability.
4. Low energy losses during storing and sensing (so most of input energy is stored and eventually sensed).

All these desirable but nonessential characteristics have been and are considered in the actual design of storage systems. All are growing in importance as packing density becomes larger and speed increases. High packing density greatly impedes the cooling of the array, and the energy dissipation per device must be kept low to prevent excessive local heating deep down in the array structure. Furthermore, to get high density requires the smallest possible structure per bit, and since many structures are limited by the capabilities of photolithography, the fewer devices per bit, the denser the array can be. Reduction in size itself will help increase speed, but having to rewrite information after it is read can cause nearly a doubling of cycle time in some cases. However if an increase in density is possible with a destructive read-out cell, the relative merits of requirements 2 and 3 call for specific consideration. For the one-device semiconductor cell (Section 3.10), the former is more important than nondestructive read-out.

As often happens in engineering, one encounters conflicting demands or requirements, and optimum design is a compromise. Such a conflict is inherent in all storage devices and arises from the conflict between the fundamental need for a barrier with losses for reliable storage and the practical need to keep the losses low. To the memory hardware designer, losses in the storage medium are a nuisance and at times impose a serious limitation on the storage density, as mentioned earlier. Thus in practice one attempts to reduce the losses, either switching, quiescent, or both, to the smallest value possible. Unfortunately, as was shown in Section 2.3, the losses cannot be reduced to zero, since the ability to store a reliable, stable, reproducible binary state requires the existence of some finite losses within the storage device. It should be understood that the fundamentally necessary amount of heat generation for storage is orders of magnitude smaller than that present in actual storage devices, thus considerable improvement is still possible. The essential point is that the dissipation can be reduced but not totally eliminated, rather, it is necessary and desirable as far as storing information is concerned, while at the same time being undesirable from a practical point of view. Some of the questions and considerations relating to the ultimate storage density are discussed in Section 2.14.

2.5 STORAGE SYSTEM PARAMETERS

In any storage system, the most important parameters are the size or capacity of a given module, access time to find any desired piece of stored information, data rate at which the stored information can be read out, once found, the cycle time (i.e., how frequently the system can be referenced), and the cost to implement all these functions.

The capacity is simply the maximum number of bits, bytes, or words that can be assembled in one basic storage module that is totally self-contained (e.g., 4K bytes of core memory, 29M bytes on a disk pack). Access time can vary, depending on definition—the definition used here is different for random and nonrandom access storage. For random access memory, the access time is the time span from the instant a request is gated out of the CPU address register until the desired information appears in the output buffer register or proper location in memory, where it can be further processed. For nonrandom access memory, the access time is the time span from the instant an instruction is decoded, asking for nonrandom access memory, until the desired information is found (but not read). Before the information can be further processed, it must be transferred, usually serially or in part serially to another location within the computer (usually to main memory). The time required to transfer the information equals the product of the data rate and the size of the information being transferred. Thus access time is a different quantity for random and nonrandom access memory. In fact, it is the access time that distinguishes the two, as is evident by the definitions in Section 1.3. Access time is made constant on random access memory, whereas on nonrandom storage, access time can vary quite substantially depending on the location of information being sought and the current position of the storage system relative to that information. Data rate is the rate (usually bits/sec, bytes/sec, or words/sec), at which data can be read out of a storage device. Data rate is usually associated with nonrandom access memory, where information is stored and read serially. Since an entire word is read out of random access memory in parallel, data rate has no significance and is applicable only to nonrandom, serial storage. Data rate is a constant for a given time, but obviously the data transfer time depends on the length of the data.

Cycle time is the inverse of the rate at which a random access memory can be referenced, or in other words, the inverse of the maximum number of references per unit time. For instance, a random access memory with a 1 μsec cycle time can be referenced (read, write, or any combination) at a maximum rate of $1/10^{-6} = 10^6$ references/sec. Cycle time does not necessarily equal the access time (usually does not) for various reasons. If a random access memory works in the destructive read-out mode, the information must be regenerated before another access can be made, causing a wide disparity between access and cycle time. Even if nondestructive read-out is used, there are quite often transients that must be allowed to die out; drivers or sense amplifiers must recover from large transients that drive them into saturation; ringing (i.e., multiple pulse reflections on the array lines), must be allowed to die out, and so on. Furthermore, since any word or combination of words can be accessed in sequence, the cycle time must allow for the worst case, such as referencing the word with the smallest internal delay followed by the word with the largest delay, and vice versa. Cycle time is applicable primarily to random access storage and has little meaning with respect to nonrandom serial storage.

2.6 MAGNETIC CIRCUITS AND SELF–DEMAGNETIZATION EFFECTS

2.6.1 Magnetic Circuits and BH Loop

By far the most widespread and commonly used phenomenon for random and nonrandom access memory media has been magnetism. Ferromagnetism is a property that arises from the fact that the atoms of certain materials exhibit spontaneous magnetization in the absence of any external fields; that is, the atoms have a net magnetic moment. Certain intrinsic material characteristics of many materials can be made to be nearly ideal for memory applications. However the geometrical configuration of the cell, which determines the magnetic circuit, can have a very large effect on the overall characteristics, as we shall see shortly.

One very important magnetic property for memory applications is the material hysteresis or BH loop where B is the magnetic flux density, which is the stored quantity, and H is the magnetizing force. This intrinsic property can be measured by using a closed magnetic circuit such as the toroid in Fig. 2.6-1 with two windings. We can "see" this loop if we apply a slowly varying current in one winding, integrate the sense voltage, and apply these two signals to the x and y deflection inputs of an oscilloscope. Here H is proportional to i through Ampere's circuital law

$$\int H \cdot dl = Ni \qquad (2.6\text{-}1)$$

and the flux density B is proportional to $\int V \cdot dt$ because

$$V = N \frac{d\phi}{dt} \propto \frac{dB}{dt}$$

where the total flux $\phi = BA$ and A = cross-sectional area.

Ideally, for memory applications, materials should have a "square" BH loop, meaning nearly vertical sides and horizontal top meeting at a $90°$ (square) angle. No material has a truly "square" loop, but some come reasonably close (see Sections 3.4 and 5.2). The H field required to reverse the magnetic state from $+B_r$ to $-B_r$ is the coercive force H_c and this is the internal agent that keeps the toroid magnetized.

For this simple case, there was no self-demagnetizing field due to the idealized "closed flux" magnetic structures. In many memory applications such as thin films and magnetic recording, the magnetic circuit is an "open flux" structure for which self-demagnetization plays a *major* role. The self-demagnetizing field is always in a direction opposite to the flux density

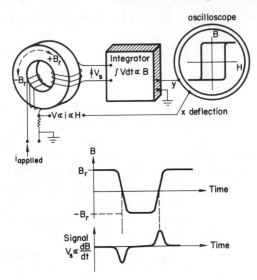

FIGURE 2.6-1   Measurement of *BH* loop of an ideal, square loop magnetic toroid.

inside the medium and has a value proportional to a geometrical factor D, and the actual flux density as in (2.6-6). For such a structure in any given magnetization state B with no externally applied field, the total internal field acting on the magnetization, in the direction of B is

$$H_{\text{int}} = H_c - H_D \tag{2.6-2}$$

Effect of Self-Demagnetizing Field on BH Loop

Let us determine the *BH* loop of some general, open flux structure with a self-demagnetizing factor D and ideal square loop intrinsic material characteristics. Let us assume that the structure is at negative saturation $-B_r$ and is able to remain at this state in the absence of any applied field. From (2.6-6), there will be a self-demagnetizing field present which is in a direction opposite to B_r or, since B_r is assumed to be negative, the demagnetizing field is in the positive H direction on the *BH* loop axes. The intrinsic coercive field H_c is in the direction B_r or negative H direction, hence opposes the demagnetizing field. As long as H_c is larger in magnitude than H_D, the net field is negative, holding the structure in negative saturation. If we now apply a positive external field H_{ex}, the total internal field becomes

$$H_{\text{int}} = H_{\text{ex}} + H_D - H_c \tag{2.6-3}$$

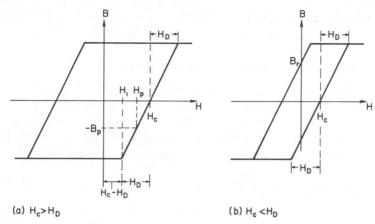

(a) $H_c > H_D$ (b) $H_c < H_D$

FIGURE 2.6-2   Effect of self-magnetizing field on a material with an intrinsically square *BH* loop.

The structure will remain at $-B_r$ with H_D a constant until the total internal field becomes 0. Equating (2.6-3) to zero and solving for this point gives

$$H_{ex} = H_c - H_D \qquad (2.6\text{-}4)$$

This represents the point H_1 in Fig. 2.6-2. Any further increases in the applied field will cause the magnetization to start reversing or B to start decreasing, which, from (2.6-6), will result in a decrease of the magnitude of the self-demagnetizing field. For any given applied field, a sufficient amount of magnetization will reverse to exactly balance the increase in applied field to satisfy (2.6-4). At any given external field H_p in Fig. 2.6-2a, the corresponding flux density B_p can be found by substituting (2.6-6) in (2.6-4) to get

$$H_p = H_c - D B_p \qquad (2.6\text{-}5)$$

This curve of B_p versus H_p is a straight line passing through H_c at $B_p = 0$, and it has a slope of B_r / H_D, where H_D is the maximum self-demagnetizing field for the maximum residual flux density. Obviously the *BH* loop must be symmetrical in the opposite direction, as shown. The net effect of the self-demagnetizing field is to shear the otherwise "square" *BH* loop by an amount equal to H_D. In fact the *BH* loop can be used to measure H_D if the intrinsic material characteristics are known. If the intrinsic *BH* loop is somewhat slanted, H_D will obviously add to it.

It is possible for H_D to be larger than H_c. In such cases, of course, the material must be partially demagnetized at zero applied fields, as in Fig. 2.6-2b. These self-demagnetizing effects are so important in magnetic structures that various analytical equations have been derived for numerous cases. A few simple but useful cases are given below.

2.6.2 Self-Demagnetizing Factors for Various Geometries

The self-demagnetizing field for solid magnetic bodies with uniform residual magnetization or for such a body placed in an initially uniform magnetic field is a constant throughout the volume only for ellipsoids of revolution. For all other bodies, the self-demagnetizing field varies throughout the volume; hence a fixed value for self-demagnetizing is necessarily an average value of considerable ambiguity.

The self-demagnetizing field is given by

$$H_D = -DB \tag{2.6-6}$$

where H_D = self-demagnetizing field (Oe)
       D = demagnetizing factor (Oe/G)
       B = flux density (gauss, G)

In some cases, the demagnetizing factor is written as

$$H_D = -NI \tag{2.6-7}$$

where H_D = self-demagnetizing field (Oe)
       I = magnetization (emu/cc)
       N = demagnetizing factor (Oe cc/emu).

and D and N are related by

$$D = \frac{N}{4\pi} \tag{2.6-8}$$

since

$$B = 4\pi I + H \approx 4\pi I \tag{2.6-9}$$

The approximation is valid because the total H field is negligible inside the magnetic material.

For a three-dimensional ellipsoid of revolution in the xyz plane with semi axes a, b, c, respectively, the demagnetizing factors along these axes are labeled D_a, D_b, and D_c, respectively. It is a fundamental fact that for all ellipsoids of revolution

$$D_a + D_b + D_c = 1 \tag{2.6-10}$$

or

$$N_a + N_b + N_c = 4\pi \tag{2.6-11}$$

For the special case of a sphere, all the self-demagnetizing factors must be equal along any diameter, and the magnitude of the demagnetizing field is

$$H_D \,(\text{Oe}) = \tfrac{1}{3} B_r \,(\text{G}) \tag{2.6-12}$$

Demagnetizing factors have been analytically derived for numerous cases of ellipsoids of revolution and rectangles (Bozorth and Chapin, 1942; Brown, 1962; Osborne, 1945; Stoner, 1945). For a very thin, circular disk (oblate spheroid) magnetized in the film plane, the complex equation for self-demagnetization reduces to approximately

$$H_D = \frac{0.1}{32} \frac{T}{d} B \tag{2.6-13}$$

where H_D = self-demagnetizing factor (Oe)
$\quad T$ = thickness (kÅ)
$\quad d$ = diameter (in.)
$\quad B$ = residual flux density (kG)

This formula can be used to approximate H_D at the center, but not the edges, of a real, nonellipsoidal film as shown in Section 3.3.

An infinite sheet of finite thickness t, with sinusoidal magnetization variation in one direction, is treated in Wallace (1951). For a wavelength of λ and thickness t, the maximum in-plane component is

$$H_D(\text{max}) = -B_m(1 - e^{-\pi t/\lambda}) \tag{2.6-14}$$

where B_m = amplitude of sinusoidal function
$\quad t$ = sheet thickness
$\quad \lambda$ = sinusoidal wavelength

This expression is used in Section 6.2 for estimating the required material coercive force in typical magnetic recording.

For a solid bar with a rectangular cross section, the self-demagnetizing field varies throughout its volume. An analytical treatment requires some assumptions about the magnetization within the bar and the definition of self-demagnetizing field. Such bars of infinite width are treated in Brown (1962) and include normalized tables for various cases.

It should be clearly understood that self-demagnetizing fields arise *only* because magnetic poles are formed somewhere in the structure. These poles produce the self-demagnetizing field. In all the foregoing cases, the geometry of the magnetic circuit and the magnetization is known or assumed. The poles are assumed to exist in a very thin layer at the edges of the solid. In magnetic recording, the medium is continuous, and magnetic poles, which represent the stored information, are spread over a finite volume. If we know the total pole distribution, we can always find the self-demagnetizing field at any point. However we seldom know this pole distribution, and finding it provides the self-demagnetizing field. In fact, the length of the pole distribution along the medium is the length of the recorded bit (linear density) and is related to the material coercive force by means of the all-important self-demagnetizing field, as detailed in Section 5.8. Determination of this field is somewhat different. The functional form of the pole density distribution is assumed, and the self-demagnetizing field is obtained from a field integration over the pole volume.

2.7 MAGNETIC SWITCHING MODES AND SWITCHING CONSTANT

In nonrandom access memory functions such as magnetic recording, the speed with which the medium magnetization reverses states is usually *not* an important parameter. The *BH* loop and self-demagnetizing effects are of prime importance, as discussed in Sections 5.2, 5.3, and 5.8. In high speed random access memory, however, the magnetization switching speed is the most significant parameter, in addition to the *BH* loop. The dynamics of the switching process are quite complex and require analyses at the microscopic level to determine how individual magnetic moments interact. As a result, the memory designer seeks other, more macroscopic views of switching phenomena. One widely used method of expressing the high speed switching characteristics of memory devices is in terms of the so-called switching curve. All magnetic devices exhibit some form of a characteristic switching curve of the general shape presented in Fig. 2.7-1, where τ_s is the time to reverse the flux density from $+B_r$ to $-B_r$, or vice versa, under a given set of excitation conditions. These conditions are usually a pulse with rise time much less than

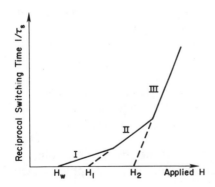

FIGURE 2.7-1 General idealized switching curve for magnetic devices showing three distinct regions.

τ_s and pulse width much greater than τ_s. The curve generally consists of three nearly straight line portions, hence three distinct regions. These three regions result from the different types of switching mechanisms involved, namely;

Region I. domain wall motion; slow.

Region II. Nonuniform or incoherent rotation; medium speed.

Region III. Uniform or coherent rotation; fast.

The inverse slopes of the line segment portions define the switching constant given by

$$S_w = \frac{H - H_t}{1/\tau_s} = \tau_s(H - H_t) \qquad (2.7\text{-}1)$$

where τ_s = switching time as defined above

H = applied field

H_t = threshold field, extrapolated to zero, for that line segment region (i.e., either H_w, H_1, or H_2)

For each of the three switching regions, we then have a linear equation of the form

$$\frac{1}{\tau_s} = \frac{1}{S_w}(H - H_t) \qquad (2.7\text{-}2)$$

where the appropriate values of S_w and H_t must be used. These parameters are determined experimentally.

For nearly all magnetic structures, some microscopic domains of reverse magnetization exist at boundaries or defects. As such, it is only necessary to apply a field capable of moving the walls of these domains to initiate low speed switching. Hence the threshold for region I is H_w, the threshold for domain wall motion. In ideal magnetic structures where the self-demagnetizing field is zero, H_w is essentially the low frequency coercive force H_c. This is essentially true for toroidal ferrite cores. The distinction between the two is discussed more fully later. Obviously H_1 and H_2 are the threshold fields for the onset of incoherent and coherent rotation, respectively. Within any given region, the quantity $H - H_t$ is referred to as the "excess field," the amount of overdrive in excess of the required threshold to switch the magnetization. The larger the excess field, the faster will be the switching or the smaller will be τ_s for the same amount of flux switched. Thus the speed of switching can be increased by overdrive. This is true for ferrite cores as well as for thin film devices, as Chapter 3 reveals.

In the high field region, the switching constant S_w of ferrites and thin Permalloy films are roughly in the range of 0.2 and 0.02 Oe-μsec, respectively.

Thus although films have potentially a 10 times faster switching capability, as shown even more specifically in Section 3.2 and 3.3, other problems erode this advantage.

2.8 INTEGRATED SEMICONDUCTOR TECHNOLOGIES FOR MEMORY

It is beyond the scope of this book to describe either transistor physics or the details of fabrication of semiconductor devices. Many excellent references are devoted to these subjects, including Camenzind (1968), Carr and Mize (1972), Integrated Circuit Engineering (1966), Luecke et al., (1973), and Warner (1965). Rather, the more important features of semiconductor technology—those which are most pertinent to memory design and fabrication—are summarized.

The two major types of structure used in integrated circuits are the junction transistor and the insulated gate field effect transistor (IG FET). Other semiconductor devices such as charged coupled devices are coming into use, but the basic fabrication processes are not much different. Typically, other devices require a reordering of the fundamental processing steps with some small changes, having advantages and disadvantages. Hence we concentrate on junction and field effect transistor processing technology. The approach is to understand the basic requirements of the technology and the steps essential to the achievement of these. The infinite variety of fabrication procedures then can better be understood in terms of the few goals being sought. We first provide an overview in terms of density related to physical dimensions and some of the implications for integrated circuits. Then the fundamental processing sets the stage for subsequent separate discussions of the junction transistor and n-channel, insulated gate FET device. Finally, all these accumulated fundamentals are used to compare the junction transistor and FET device size to show the inherent density advantage of the latter.

2.8.1 Overview of Planar Technology and Masking Limitations

Before the advent of printed circuit techniques, all electrical circuits consisted of discrete components such as tubes, transistors, resistors, and capacitors, interconnected with wire. The components were very large and bulky, and the wires were relatively small. The need for speed and density in computer circuits (both logic and memory) led to the use of printed circuit boards to lower the cost and simplify the interconnection of discrete components. The components were still relatively large compared to the wire, hence the density was still low. It was recognized that substantial improvements were possible if planar processing of semiconductor devices could be made economical.

The planar fabrication of discrete transistors and hybrid packaging techniques (Davis, 1964, Warner, 1965, Ch. 5) in the late 1950s and early 1960s were major steps in that direction. The eventual fully integrated planar semiconductor processing that came shortly thereafter (Hogan, 1964; *Proc, IEEE,* 1964; Kilby, 1976) allowed a very substantial increase in density and reduction in cost. The planar process has continually evolved: to understand the evolution and the current limits on density improvements, we must digress for a moment.

In the design of any device, the physical dimensions are very important in determining the overall characteristics. Other physical and metallurgical parameters are also important, but the density is ultimately related to the dimensions that can be achieved. Any given processing technology at a given time is capable of producing a minimum line width depending on the lithographic and processing sophistication. Given a minimum line width, the device designer may make the circuit devices larger than the minimum line width and reserve the minimum line width for the interconnecting wires. This was done in discrete planar transistor fabrication and early integrated circuits. In such cases, the designer has freedom in both the lateral and vertical profiles to optimize the device and circuit operation. If, on the other hand, all devices are designed as close to the minimum line width as possible, to improve density, the vertical profile becomes more important in optimizing the devices and circuits. In other words, as the lateral dimensions become more restricted, the vertical dimensions become more important (c.g., see FET process).

If the vertical dimension of each layer becomes too large and the lateral dimensions too small, some significant problems arise. First, via holes, necessary for interconnecting between various layers, may become impossible to fill, as in Fig. 2.8-1a. As the aluminum is deposited, the top edges build up and may eventually create a bridge across the hole. The bridge may eventually break away or remain, but in either case no contact is provided between layers. Even if a complete bridge does form, the steep edges will make the metal lines very thin or irregular, which can lead to electromigration or gradual mechanical breakage. Another problem enters any attempts to achieve minimum or accurate dimensions. Lateral etching of any given layer proceeds at very nearly the same rate as vertical etching, giving an opening that is much wider at the top, and wider than the minimum mask line width, as in Fig. 2.8-1b. A similar effect occurs for diffusions through a mask: the lateral diffusion generally proceeds at roughly half the rate of vertical diffusion. Other effects cause holes to etch away at the interfaces between layers. Most of these undesirable effects can be minimized by keeping the lateral dimensions much greater than the vertical dimensions.

In early monolithic planar semiconductor processes, the minimum lateral

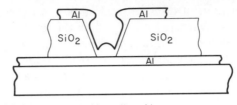

(a) Via hole and side wall problem

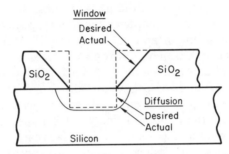

(b) Lateral etching and diffusion problem

FIGURE 2.8-1   Three-dimensional character of photolithographic processing when minimum line width becomes comparable to vertical dimensions.

line widths were generally in the range of several mils, gradually evolving to 0.2 mil as an industry standard in the early to mid-1970s. Since typical vertical layers were 0.1 mil thick or smaller, the minimum lateral dimensions were much larger than the vertical dimensions. The early integrated circuits used devices that were not restricted to minimum line widths; thus both the lateral and vertical dimensions were variable for optimization. It was recognized that better density could be achieved by restricting all devices to minimum line widths wherever possible. At or above a minimum photo-lithographic line width of 5 μ (0.2 mil), the vertical dimensions are still small enough that the topology problems of Fig. 2.8-1 are not severe. However, as the line width decreases much below 5 μ to, say, 1.25 μ while devices are designed to minimum line widths, the need for design freedom in the vertical dimension forces a very irregular topology that then requires special process-ing techniques. The full recessed oxide (ROX) process is one technique that can be used in both junction and field effect transistor technology to provide more freedom in the vertical profile while attempting to minimize the irregular surface topology. The reverse sputtering technique is a method used to replanarize a surface after each (or several) steps to avoid the problems illustrated in Fig. 2.8-1. Reactive ion etching is another processing tool that can give very steep sides with narrow holes, avoiding some of the under-etching problems associated with chemical etching.

The vertical dimensions of the devices can be reduced somewhat to compensate for the reduced lateral dimensions, but generally they cannot be reduced by the same proportions. For instance, the aluminum interconnecting lines cannot be made too thin; otherwise the series resistance as well as electromigration become serious problems. Diffusion depths are already near their minimum values and cannot be changed by orders of magnitude. The result is that the vertical profile has become a significant factor in limiting device density in terms of achieving smaller absolute dimensions.

A related problem imposing important restrictions on device density at all line widths is that of the lithographic mask line width dimension and alignment tolerances. Both photo and E-beam lithography are used, but the problems are the same in principle. Hence we consider the lithography problems in terms of several photographic masks that must be overlaid and aligned on subsequent steps. A fundamental problem arising in the fabrication of all devices is that of maintaining a certain minimum separation between the edges of two overlaid masks when both line width tolerances and alignment tolerances are important. The minimum separation may be necessary for restricting breakdown voltage, leakage current, and so on. The minimum separation must be maintained under the worst case conditions, which requires adding the line width and mask alignment tolerance many times. This makes the overall line widths on subsequent masks much larger than is desirable, but the condition is unavoidable. To see how this arises, assume a lithographic process with minimum line width of $W_m \pm \Delta W$, where W_m is the nominal value and ΔW is the absolute tolerance on any line width. The basic problem is encountered when locating edges of a line and placing other edges at a minimum spacing from this first edge under worst case conditions. Let us attempt to do this with three separate masks.

The first mask, (mask I in Fig. 2.8-2) contains a line of nominal width W_m. It is assumed that this mask does *not* require any alignment but rather its centerline $\mathfrak{C}_1$ provides the alignment mark for subsequent masks. We are interested in, say, only the right-hand edge A of this line and subsequent lines. The first mask edge can be situated at A or A', where both are a distance $\Delta W/2$ from the nominal position $L_1 = W_m/2$.* A second edge of nominal distance L_2 from $\mathfrak{C}_1$ is to be located at the minimum spacing of S_m with respect to the first edge, under worst case conditions. The centerline of mask II, namely, $\mathfrak{C}_{II}$, can be aligned to $\mathfrak{C}_1$ within only a tolerance of $\pm A_x$, as shown. The worst case occurs when mask I is its largest value, placing edge I at point

---

* Photolithographic tolerances are given in terms of absolute tolerance on total line width or $\pm \Delta(W/2)$ on each edge.

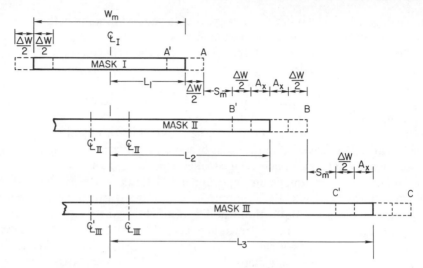

FIGURE 2.8-2   Effect of lithographic tolerances and minimum edge separation on line width.

A, while mask II is its smallest value simultaneous with the centerline shifted toward the left at point $\mathcal{C}'_{II}$ thereby placing edge II at B'. The minimum distance must now be maintained between A and B', making the nominal value of L_2 equal to

$$L_2 = L_1 + \frac{\Delta W}{2} + S_m + \frac{\Delta W}{2} + A_x \tag{2.8-1}$$

If there were no tolerances, so that ΔW and A_x were zero, L_2 would be equal to just L_1 plus the minimum separation S_m. The alignment tolerance only enters once, added to $\Delta W/2$ of the second mask. This is the case because mask I was assumed to require no alignment. Hence the first $\Delta W/2$ term does not have A_x added to it.

If we now attempt to place a third edge on mask III at a minimum spacing with respect to edge II, a similar situation arises, but the alignment tolerance enters twice, once with each edge tolerance of $\Delta W/2$. The worst case occurs when mask II is as large as possible and is aligned to the right at $\mathcal{C}_{II}$ with its edge at B, while mask III is as small as possible and is aligned to the left at $\mathcal{C}'_{III}$ with its edge at C'. The nominal mask dimension L_3 is now (adding terms from left to right)

$$L_3 = L_2 + \left(\frac{\Delta W}{2} + A_x\right) + S_m + \left(\frac{\Delta W}{2} + A_x\right) \tag{2.8-2}$$

or

$$L_3 - L_2 = S_m + 2\left(\frac{\Delta W}{2} + A_x\right) \qquad (2.8\text{-}3)$$

Note that now each $\Delta W/2$ term has the alignment tolerance A_x added to it because each mask required alignment. Also note that between the nominal value of L_2 and L_3 given by (2.8-3), two values of $\Delta W/2 + A_x$ were required. These fundamental rules for adding lithographic tolerances, as expressed by (2.8-1) and (2.8-3), are used later to compare device sizes. These tolerances can have a very significant effect. For instance, suppose the tolerances and minimum spacing are of equal magnitude and are 20% of the minimum line width (not an unreasonable case), or

$$\Delta W = A_x = S_m = 0.2W_m \qquad (2.8\text{-}4)$$

Let us see what the length of L_3 must be, assuming mask II has minimum line width or $2L_2 = W_m$. Substituting this into (2.8-4) gives

$$\Delta W = A_x = S_m = 0.4L_2 \qquad (2.8\text{-}5)$$

Substituting this into (2.8-2) gives

$$L_3 = L_2 + 4(0.4L_2) = 2.6L_2 \qquad (2.8\text{-}6)$$

This is quite a large increase in physical dimension. Each subsequent mask that requires alignment and critical separation will likewise experience a large tolerance effect. Even though we might start with a narrow line, the device structure can become quite large. For high density as needed in memory, it is therefore necessary to control tolerances, or to pick structures that minimize the tolerance effects. The latter is more practical and is achieved with FET devices, as shown by the comparison of the junction versus field effect transistor device size example given later.

   Much of the complexity evident in the technology is due primarily to these problems. Of course other factors enter—scaling the device parameters, lowering the power dissipation, and so on. However the dimensions in terms of lateral and vertical profile are always significant. This becomes evident in our discussion of the various processing technologies; here often complex steps are introduced to provide more freedom in the vertical direction because of restrictions in the lateral dimensions, or complex steps are taken to control the lateral masking tolerance problem (e.g., see Section 2.9.2).

2.8.2   Planar Silicon Process: Fundamental Requirements and Processing Sequences

Discrete transistors of the preplanar and planar processing eras were often made of germanium as well as silicon. Germanium is particularly attractive for high speed because its average electron-hole mobility for typical cases is at least three times larger than that of silicon. However, the advent of fully integrated circuits in the early 1960s led to the demise of germanium technology, despite its potential for higher speed. The major difficulty is that unlike silicon, germanium does not form an oxide. Hence the processes required to obtain insulators and diffusion masks are more complex and expensive for germanium. A valiant attempt was made to develop a germanium integrated circuit process in the 1960s (Reisman, 1969), but the advances in silicon technology and the advent of the n-channel, insulated gate FET made the more complex germanium technology unattractive. Because silicon dominates the semiconductor industry for memory and logic, we concentrate on this process.

Any technology must be capable of providing all the passive as well as active devices needed for circuit operation. The general field covering all electronics requires all the well-known devices (resistors, capacitors, inductors, transformers, linear and switching active devices, etc.). Some of these, such as inductors and transformers, are difficult to make in planar integrated technology; hence we find elaborate or unusual schemes. Fortunately digital memory (and logic) circuits, except for power supplies, most often require only transistors, resistors, and capacitors; occasionally diodes are desirable, mostly in junction transistor circuits. Power supplies are still typically made from discrete, bulky components with partial integration of limited portions, such as the regulator circuit. Except for decoupling capacitors and occasionally regulators, the power supplies are external to the memory. Hence we need concern ourselves only with these four basic components: *transistor, resistors, capacitors, and diodes.*

To fabricate these components, a planar process for semiconductor memory circuits basically requires only *dopants, insulators,* and *conductors, selectively arranged* on a silicon wafer. In essence we must be able to vary the conductivity by very large values and within very small, selective areas. Thus the fundamental requirements become

1. Semiconductor doping processes (moderate, variable conductivity).
2. Insulating (low conductivity) process to provide a good dielectric between conducting regions.
3. Conductor (high conductivity) fabrication process for low resistance interconnections.
4. Selection process to provide device delineation and selection of area for each of the above three processes.

To reduce cost, it is desirable to supply these requirements as simply as possible and with as much parallel processing as feasible. The practical methods by which these can be achieved, however, result in considerable complexity. In a planar process, the selection of areas for a change in conductivity is done through windows within the surface to be processed. These windows are obtained by a suitable lithographic mask. *Each* of the *three* materials and related processes (i.e., doping, insulating, conductor fabrication), requires a selective window or masking means. Thus fundamentally three *process masks* are required. Ideally we would like one photosensitive or E-beam-sensitive material that could serve as a mask for all three conductivity processes. Unfortunately, this is not yet possible. The available photosensitive or E-beam-sensitive resist materials can be used for the insulator and conductor process masks, but not for the diffusion mask. Doping processes require high temperature during typical thermal diffusion (1000 to 1200°C) or a moderately high temperature anneal (300 to 500°C) afterward as in ion implantation. As a result, the diffusion process mask, as well as all previous processes, must be capable of withstanding these temperatures. Fortunately in silicon technology the low conductivity insulating material silicon dioxide (SiO_2) can also be used as the diffusion mask. This helps offset the need for a separate diffusion process mask but does not eliminate the requirement for additional steps. The basic sequences of events in selectively changing the conductivity of planar regions can be more easily visualized in terms of the following process sequences.

Diffusion Sequence

1. Deposit thick layer of SiO_2; cover with layer of photoresist.
2. Prepare windows in resist via light through a photomask, or E-beam pattern generator, and a selective resist etchant (developer).
3. Prepare windows in SiO_2. Use selective SiO_2 etchant (hydrofluoric acid) through resist windows to obtain windows in SiO_2.
4. Diffuse through SiO_2 windows.

Insulator or Conductor Sequence

1. Deposit insulator or conductor; cover with resist.
2. Prepare windows on resist as previously.
3. Use selective etchant to remove unwanted insulator or conductor (i.e., open windows).

A *process sequence* thus typically consists of a deposition of a material, followed by a masking and etching step. The diffusion sequence adds a third, namely "diffuse dopant" step. It can be seen that the diffusion sequence is more complex than the other two; hence the number of diffusion sequences should be minimized whenever possible. The fabrication of various circuits consists essentially of an alternating series of the three process sequences, as we shall see. The implementation of these may require many additional and intermediate steps, such as clean the surface, strip resist, rinse etchant, and anneal in inert atmosphere. The total number of such elementary processing steps to produce junction transistor circuits can be in the range of 150, a quite sizable number. Fabrication of FET devices typically require 25 to 50 such elementary steps, making them more attractive for low cost.

Ohmic contact must be made to various devices to complete the circuit. This is usually accomplished by depositing a metal such as aluminum directly on a portion of a diffused area. A metal-semiconductor layer will form a diode unless special precautions are taken. If the region for contact is heavily doped n^+, ohmic contact is obtained. Metal on a lightly doped, n^- region can form a Schottky barrier diode, which is very desirable in some memory cells (Section 3.9). For a given unit of junction area, a Schottky diode can give a much lower forward resistance than an equal area FET, and resistance about equal to or lower than a *pn* junction diode. Cells using such diodes are covered in Chapter 3, but we do not discuss the fabrication of Schottky diodes any further.

2.8.3 Junction Transistor Technology and Circuit Layout

This technology is so well known and well documented that only the essential steps needed in Section 2.10 for comparisons with FET device size are presented here. The four basic components of memory cells are transistors, resistors, diodes, and capacitors. In this technology, capacitors are usually obtained from the depletion capacitance of a reversed biased diode, making the fabrication procedure redundant for a diode and capacitor. Hence we outline the fabrication of a series resistor, a diode, and an *npn* transistor as in Fig. 2.8-3. Simplified schematics of the cross-sectional and top views of the fabricated circuit appear in Fig. 2.8-4. The basic procedure in terms of the process sequence defined previously and other additional steps is as follows (refer to Fig. 2.8-4).

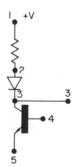

FIGURE 2.8-3 Schematic of junction transistor circuit for planar fabrication.

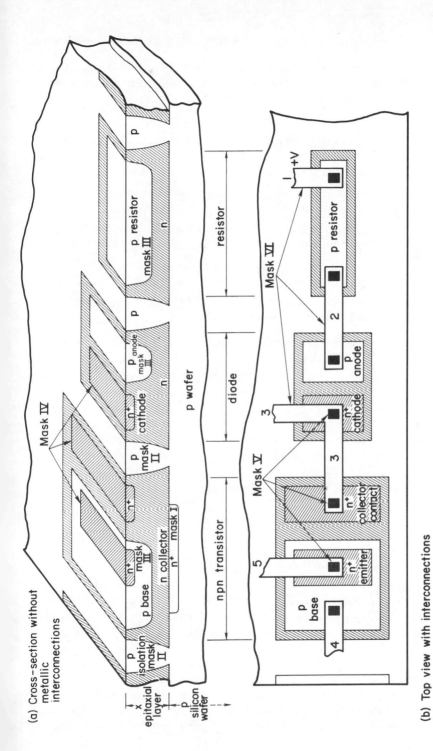

(a) Cross-section without metallic interconnections

(b) Top view with interconnections

FIGURE 2.8-4   Planar layout of junction transistor circuit of Fig. 2.8-3 showing double diffusion and isolation.

99

1. Diffusion sequence on p silicon wafer (mask I) provides low resistance n^+ subcollector to reduce high resistance of the subsequent collector region.

2. Epitaxial layer of n silicon several microns thick, grown on wafer provides collector region and layer for remaining structure.

3. Diffusion sequence (p type) for device isolation (mask II): deep diffusion through epitaxial layer to original silicon wafer provides an isolated n island for each of the three devices.

4. Diffusion sequence (p type, moderate depth) into each of the three isolated islands (mask III) provides transistor base, diode anode, and resistor.

5. Diffusion sequence, shallow n^+ type (mask IV) provides transistor emitters, collector ohmic contact, and diode cathode.

6. Insulator sequence, SiO_2 (mask V) provides windows for subsequent contact and circuit connections.

7. Conductor sequence, aluminum (mask VI) provides contact and circuit interconnections as in Fig. 2.8-4b.

Some notable consequences of the technology just summarized that affect memory density deserve emphasis. The p-isolation diffusion must proceed through a deep epitaxial layer, giving a very large surface opening because of lateral etching. Since each circuit element requires isolation, the isolation consumes a large portion of the area, giving low density. A double diffusion of the n^+ emitter into the p base is required, with a very well-controlled separation between emitter and collector—this requires stringent fabrication controls and special processes. Six masks and four diffusion sequences are necessary.

In the circuit of Fig. 2.8-4 we could reduce the overall length by sharing the n^+ collector contact with the n^+ cathode of the diode, thereby eliminating the small p-isolation area between transistor and diode as well as part of the metal interconnections. A similar saving could be obtained with the p anode of the diode and the p resistor. The saving in area would be small but desirable and is possible in some circuits. However in most digital circuits a resistor is connected directly to the collector of the transistor. In such a case no sharing of diffused regions is possible. Usually all devices must be completely isolated and must have external metal interconnections. This distinct disadvantage over FET technology, where internal connections are possible, has led to the appearance of new junction transistor structures such as "merged transistor" circuits aimed at circumventing the internal connection problem as well as the large power dissipation.

The above fabrication procedure produced an npn transistor. Obviously a pnp can be made by reversing polarities of the wafer, dopants and so on. However there are difficulties associated with pnp fabrication that are completely analogous to those of an n-channel FET. Any silicon surface oxidized with SiO_2 tends to accumulate positive charges at the interface. For an n-silicon surface, these positive charges increase the electron-carrier concentration, making the surface more difficult to invert, hence preventing leakage across the surface. With a p surface, however, the positive charge depletes the hole-carrier concentration and in fact can invert the surface, making it conductive, identical to an FET channel. These positive charges can be reduced but require more careful process control. Hence the rule is to fabricate devices with n-type material between critical paths. In Fig. 2.8-4a the collector is n: suppose all polarities were reversed so that the isolation, wafer, and base are n while the collector is p, and the collector contact and emitter are p^+. A p surface now separates the base from collector contact. If accumulated positive surface charge inverts this surface, the base either can be shorted or can have large leakage to the collector contact, making the device unworkable. Other such leakage paths can also occur. This problem can be eliminated by better process control or by making npn transistors. As a result, most integrated circuits use the latter type.

The topology problem discussed in the overview becomes a very serious problem in this technology as the line widths approach 1 μ. The recessed oxide process described in Sec. 2.9.1 for FET devices has also been used in junction transistor technology to improve surface planarity.

2.9 INSULATED GATE FIELD EFFECT TRANSISTOR TECHNOLOGY

There are two choices of FET devices: the n-channel and the p-channel types. The n-channel device has a distinct performance advantage over the other type because of the greater mobility—about 1300 cm^2/V-sec for electrons in an n-channel versus 500 cm^2/V-sec for the holes in a p-channel. This allows the n-channel device to be faster for the same geometry, or alternately, permits a smaller device for the same power and speed. For this reason, we limit all our discussions to n-channel devices, which dominate memory applications.

The mid-1960s witnessed the advent of the first practical and commercial metal oxide silicon (MOS) FET devices. The first such devices and those for many succeeding years were all p-channel because of some initial fabrication problems with n-channel structures. In the processing of both p- and n-channel devices, positive charges become trapped within the interface between the silicon and SiO_2 gate oxide surface. For an n-channel device, these positive charges reduce the threshold to the point where the device is either "on" or *nearly* "on". Hence it is no longer a useful enhancement mode device but rather is a depletion mode device. The same positive charges are trapped in a p-channel device; but being of the same polarity, they *increase* the threshold. The latter effect often makes the p-channel device threshold larger than desirable, but there are special techniques to reduce it somewhat, although the voltages remain incompatible with those used for junction transistors. The most serious problem resulting from the near-zero threshold on n-channel devices is the ineffectiveness of the thick oxide in isolating neighboring devices. As a result, early n-channel devices had intolerable leakage over unwanted paths because the silicon surface between devices had zero threshold. A comparable p-channel device, with increased threshold, presents no such isolation problems; hence the FET technology was introduced by way of p-channel devices.

In the early history of the MOS FET, the entire industry committed itself to the p-channel device except IBM Research Division, which launched a major effort to develop the n-channel device. It was largely through this effort that the n-channel came into its own. It was found that by maintaining reasonably clean conditions to minimize positive ion accumulation at the interface, followed by adequate annealing in forming gas, the trapped charge could be reduced to a workable level. The charge in the interface is due not only to free ions such as sodium, which are present in the processing chemicals, but also to the exposed charge resulting from the change in silicon concentration, hence structure, at the $Si–SiO_2$ interface. These incomplete bonds are apparently completed by the diffused hydrogen during annealing. The process is complex and is not entirely understood. In any case, the threshold can be controlled relatively easily. The major problem becomes that of controlling the variation or spread in thresholds over the chip area. In fabrication of p-channel devices, it is desirable to keep the thresholds low, which calls for reduction of the interface charge, and to keep the threshold spreads low, which requires well-controlled processes. As a result, the p- and n-channel processes do not differ greatly, thus giving the n-channel a distinct advantage. Nearly all books and survey articles published before 1975 given the incorrect information that n-channel devices are not practical, or assign them second place to the p-channel. This is no longer the case, and since the n-channel is more desirable, we concentrate on it.

A major limitation on FET device speed is the parasitic capacitances from gate to source/drain overlap and source-substrate depletion capacitance, the former being more important. The amount of these unwanted capacitances varics with thc fabrication tcchnology. As would bc cxpcctcd, the simpler, cheaper processes give more unwanted parasitics, and the processes that reduce these are more complex and costly. The former is the standard commercial process used in the early 1970s. The parasitic capacitance resulting from gate to source/drain overlap can be reduced by the "self-aligned gate" process, and the unwanted portions of the depletion capacitances can be reduced somewhat by the recessed oxide or related processes. The reduced depletion capacitance is only a side effect, since the recessed oxide process is introduced mainly to allow thick oxide to be placed between devices without severely distorting the planar surface topology; that is, it provides freedom in the vertical profile without seriously compromising the lateral dimensions. Since there are as many variations within these processes as there are inventors, we discuss the essential features of one standard process, one self-aligned gate process, and one recessed oxide process. All devices are basically enhancement mode, n-channel (induced), insulated gate FETs.

Fundamental Fabrication Problem in All Insulated Gate FETs

The source and drain of IG FET devices are identical; the difference is set by the circuit and voltage connections. The resistance of the channel region between any two n^+ regions is modulated by the application of an electric field. A high electric field will cause large current flow and low channel resistance. Since the n^+ regions of neighboring devices are mutually indistinguishable, some means must be provided to isolate neighboring devices. One could imagine a separate deep diffusion or etching as used in junction transistor processing, but this requires an additional mask, complicates the processing, decreases the density, and may not be possible in certain cases. A better way is to recognize that the devices are operated with fixed voltages, that the electric field between two metal plates decreases as the separation or dielectric thickness increases, and that the electric field between a gate conductor and a channel must reach a certain threshold before significant conduction can occur. With these fundamentals in mind, we quickly come to the conclusion that for a given voltage, a thin oxide separating a conducting gate from two n^+ regions will yield a large electric field to turn "on" the channel between these two regions, whereas interconnecting conductors separated by a very thick oxide from neighboring n^+ regions will yield a very small electric field that can be kept below threshold. Thus the use of *thick oxide between devices will provide self-isolation without additional processing.* However the processing must provide both thick and thin oxide over various regions of a wafer; hence either irregularities in the surface topology *or* variations in the vertical profile at selected regions of the wafer are a fundamental requirement. As the lateral dimensions become smaller, this need for freedom in the vertical dimensions produces a more complex process than if only one thickness of insulation were needed. This should be kept in mind in the following discussions.

---

* As FETs become smaller, a separate metal or polysilicon " field shield " is often used to provide additional isolation, depending on the exact technologies.

2.9.1   Standard Induced *n*-Channel FET Process

An outline of the processing steps in terms of an alternating series of the three basic process sequences described earlier is as follows.

A. *Diffusion Sequence.* Prepares source and drain diffusion mask followed by n^+ diffusion.

B. *Insulator Sequence.* Thick insulation to cover exposed source and drain, followed by window openings for gate.

C. *Insulator Sequence.* Thin insulation for gate oxide followed by annealing and window openings to source and drain.

D. *Conductor Sequence.* Metallization of source and drain windows and entire surface, followed by etching (windows) to provide interconnections.

   In more detail, these steps are as follows.

Diffusion Sequence

A wafer of silicon about 0.01 in. thick, doped to a resistivity of about 1 to 10 Ω-cm is first covered with about 4 to 5 kÅ of thermally grown silicon dioxide (quartz) followed by a thin layer of photoresist as in Fig. 2.9-1*a*. The silicon dioxide serves as the diffusion mask in Fig. 2.9-1*c* and also provides part of the thick oxide dielectric needed to isolate neighboring devices. The first photolithographic mask delineates the source and drain windows (Fig. 2.9-1*b*). The photoresist exposed to ultraviolet light is polymerized while that shielded by the mask is subsequently dissolved away by a selective etchant (developer).* This exposes the silicon dioxide over these window areas. The exposed SiO_2 regions are then etched away with hydrofluoric acid (a selective etchant for quartz) leaving exposed the silicon wafer surface within only the windows (Fig. 2.9-1*c*). The required n^+-doped source and drain are obtained by diffusing phosphorus into the windows at high temperature via phosphorus oxychloride in nitrogen. The lateral diffusion makes the source and drain wider than the original windows, as shown.

Insulator Sequence

The windows are now filled in with about 4 to 6 kÅ of silicon dioxide, making the previous layer about 8 to 10 kÅ thick and leaving some irregular topology on the surface (Fig. 2.9-1*d*). A layer of photoresist and mask II are used to delineate the gate region (Fig. 2.9-1*e*). Exposure and etching of the resist and the SiO_2 leaves a window down to the silicon surface. Since it is necessary for the gate region to extend from the edge of the drain to the edge

---

* This describes the positive resist process. The exact inverse is also possible with negative photoresist material.

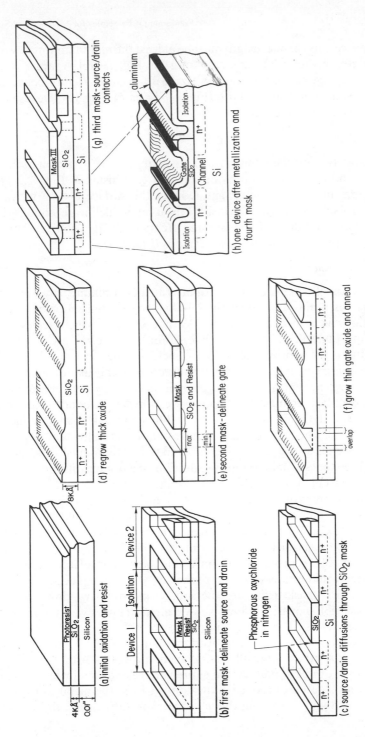

FIGURE 2.9-1 Standard *n*-channel FET process steps.

(a) initial oxidation and resist

(b) first mask - delineate source and drain

(c) source/drain diffusions through SiO₂ mask

(d) regrow thick oxide

(e) second mask - delineate gate

(f) grow thin gate oxide and anneal

(g) third mask - source/drain contacts

(h) one device after metallization and fourth mask

105

of the source, this channel length must be at least the minimum window opening expected because of tolerances ("min" in Fig. 2.9-1e). A larger window representing the maximum window size will produce overlap between the gate and source or drain or both (Fig. 2.9-1e or f). This is the cause of the parasitic gate overlap capacitance.

Insulator Sequence

An accurately controlled, thin gate oxide of about 1 kÅ is grown in the gate window (and elsewhere) to provide the thin gate insulator (Fig. 2.9-1f). A subsequent anneal in forming gas reduces the surface charge within the thin oxide–silicon interface. Mask II is used to delineate contact holes to the source and drain. Exposure and etching provides holes through the SiO_2 down to the surface of the n^+ regions (Fig. 2.9-1g).

Conductor Sequence

Metallization of the entire wafer by sputtering of aluminum provides contact to all sources, drains, and gates (Fig. 2.9-1h). The personalization of the circuit connections is provided by mask IV (not shown), which separates the aluminum connections between source, drain, and gate of a given device but interconnects the appropriate regions of neighboring devices.

Many intermediate steps as well as subsequent excapsulation are required, but the foregoing represent the major operations. Only one level of metal is used, and only four masks. Silicon oxide, which is a good insulator and compatible with the silicon, serves as the diffusion mask as well as thick and thin dielectric. The total process requires about 25 individual steps but is relatively simple and inexpensive compared to junction transistors, requiring two to three times as many steps in addition to a double diffusion.

It is important to note that two insulator sequences were required in succession because of the need for both a thick and thin oxide. *If* only *one thickness* of oxide was needed, at least one mask step could be eliminated and the gate could be made self-aligned to the source and drain regions. This could be done, at least in principle, as follows. Assume that the oxide step in Fig. 2.9-1a provides the only thickness of insulator needed. The second step could be metallization of the entire oxide in place of the photoresist. The first mask delineates the source and drain windows as in Fig. 2.9-2 (mask not shown; windows shown after etching away the metal and SiO_2 under layers). The source and drain are diffused into the windows to provide self-aligned regions. The overlap is due only to the lateral diffusion that exists to some extent in all "self-aligned" processes. After the diffusions, a photoresist can be applied to the entire surface and small windows can be opened with a second mask to allow contact from the metal to the source and drain without disturbing the gate metal. A subsequent, third masking

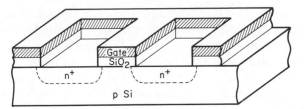

FIGURE 2.9-2   FET process assuming that only one thin layer of insulator is required.

operation can provide the personalization. One major difficulty associated with this process is that diffusion requires high temperatures (around 1000°C). Since the metal is applied before diffusion, it must withstand such high temperatures. Aluminum vaporizes at these temperatures; clearly a refractory metal such as molybdenum is required. This imposes other problems, but assuming they are not severe, the major point remains that this simplified, self-aligned process is possible only if one thickness of oxide is required. The natural question is, What other technique besides the use of thick oxide are available for device isolation? One obvious approach is to use a non-conducting substrate to support the wafer and etch out the semiconductor between the devices. A thick wafer (Fig. 2.8-1) would require an enormous hole, making this unattractive. A more reasonable way is to grow a thin silicon crystal epitaxially on a nonconducting substrate such as a spinel. After processing with one thickness of oxide, the silicon can be etched away between devices for isolation. In addition, if the etching is done on the outside edges of the source and drain, the unwanted depletion capacitance can be partially reduced. Such schemes are possible (Cushman, 1971; Luisi, 1969) but are not yet economically attractive. This method is very similar to the deep isolation diffusion performed in an epitaxial layer for isolating junction transistors.

Resistors (FET Technology)

It is possible to use diffused regions for resistance as in junction transistor technology. For most FET circuits, however, a depletion mode FET with the gate tied to the source provides better load resistance. The depletion load device is obtained by adjusting the threshold through the use of different gate insulating materials that have different work functions or by doping the gate region. Most of the fabrication steps of depletion mode devices are identical to those of enhancement mode devices, thus can be done simultaneously, except for the gate fabrication. The depletion devices typically introduce an additional mask and more steps.

In conventional technology, this technique of masking depletion mode load devices is unattractive. A simpler method is to make an ordinary enhancement mode device and connect the gate either to a separate bias voltage or to the positive voltage on the drain. The former approach has certain circuit performance advantages and is commonly used, despite a requirement for additional interconnecting lines and a separate voltage source. The latter scheme has serious circuit performance disadvantages. The more advanced ion implantation technology with self-aligned gates is aimed at higher speed. Depletion load devices are easier to fabricate in this technology and can give faster charging time; hence they are preferred.

Capacitors:

A thin oxide above a silicon wafer provides a very good MOS capacitor. The details of capacitor fabrication vary, depending on use of the device and its position within the circuit, but the principles remain the same. One example is the storage capacitor of the so-called one-device memory cell of Section 3.10.

Diodes

Diode fabrication in FET technology introduces additional complexity. A junction diode would require double diffusion and contacts to both areas. This compromises not only the fabrication simplicity of FET circuits, but also the density, which is of prime importance in memory. A simpler way to make a diode is to use a metal-semiconductor Schottky barrier, as described previously. If a metal such as aluminum is evaporated on to a lightly doped n^- region, a Schottky barrier diode is formed. However for FET devices we want highly conductive n^+ source and drain regions to minimize the source and drain internal series resistance. The devices will work with n^- source and drains, but memory arrays using diffused regions as conductors would be restricted to small array sizes because of the large resistance per unit length. Thus we must introduce additional processing steps to provide both n^+ and n^- regions, or use an alternative scheme for low resistance array wiring. Either way complicates the processing. Though diodes can be used to reduce the complexity of some cells (see Section 3.9), the saving is offset by greater process complexity.

2.9.2 Self-Aligned Gate Process Using Thick Oxide Isolation

Considerable improvements in density and speed can be obtained by making the source and drain self-aligned to the edge of the gate. Of the numerous methods that have been selected for attempts to accomplish this in a economical and practical way, some use high temperatures, and other use ion implantation. All the techniques are essentially the same as that described in conjunction with Fig. 2.9-2, the gate region is formed first and acts as the

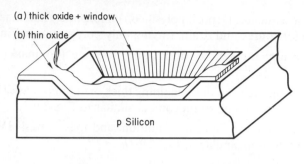

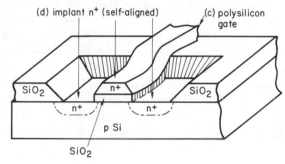

FIGURE 2.9-3   Schematic of essential steps in self-aligned gate, n-channel FET.

window through which the source and drain regions are defined adjacent to the gate. With the arrangement of Fig. 2.9-2, however, we need a gate conductor that can withstand the subsequent high temperature processing, and we need a method of isolating neighboring devices. If we retain the concept of using a thick oxide for the latter, we must provide a method for introducing it, as well as the high temperature gate. The thick oxide is easily provided by adding another step. A common gate electrode is amorphous silicon, which can be deposited in thin layers and easily withstands high temperatures. This electrode acts as the mask during subsequent diffusion or implantation of the source and drain. As a result it is heavily doped with n^+ ions, which makes it a good conductor as desired. The remaining processes step are much the same as the previous, non-self-aligned process.

The self-aligned gate process sequence is as follows:

a. Insulator sequence provides thick oxide for part of isolation, large window via mask I for source-gate-drain (a in Fig. 2.9-3).

b. Deposit insulator. Thin oxide for gate dielectric (no windows) (b in Fig. 2.9-3).

c. Conductor sequence. Deposit polysilicon (amorphous) and mask windows (mask II) for source and drain, leaving only polygate (*c* in Fig. 2.9-3).

d. Diffuse or implant source, drain, and polygate (no mask) (*d* in Fig. 2.9-3).

e. Insulator sequence provides remaining thick oxide, and mask III provides windows for source and drain contact similar to Fig. 2.9-1*g*.

f. Conductor sequence. Deposit aluminum and mask (mask IV) windows for interconnection similar to Fig. 2.9-1*h*.

Although this process sequence requires only four masks, like the standard process with non-self-aligned gates, we now need two additional depositions, one insulator and one conductor (polygate). Thus the process is somewhat more complex. An additional layer of silicon nitride (Si_3N_4) is sometimes used between the gate oxide and polysilicon as a means of lowering the threshold (Vadasz, 1968). This technique must be used with caution, since the interface can act as a trap for hot electrons injected from the channel. Any trapped charges will act as a fixed bias on the gates, which increases the threshold. This effect becomes more severe in small devices, where the electrons reach saturation velocity in the channel region.

2.9.3 Recessed Oxide (ROX) for Thick Oxides

As all devices become very small, the surface topology constitutes a serious problem as detailed previously. The use of a thick oxide in any silicon technology (e.g., for FET device isolation) can produce such steep side walls or deep holes that fabrication is rendered impossible. Therefore, a method is desired that can provide a thick oxide while not creating serious step changes in surface topology. One common technique is the use of recessed oxide. When SiO_2 is grown on a silicon surface at high temperatures, the oxidation proceeds *into* the silicon surface at nearly the same rate as the SiO_2 grows above the surface. Thus when thermal oxidation is used, part of the thick insulator is always recessed into the wafer (Fig. 2.9-4*a*). The total oxide insulation thickness is then about twice the height of the surface hill. The surface can be planarized by etching the silicon to a little more than one-half the desired oxide thickness before thermal oxidation as in Fig. 2.9-4*b*. The subsequent growth of oxide for a controlled thickness results in a planar surface as desired. This process is referred to as full ROX. The thickness ratio in typical cases is about 40% in silicon and 60% above.

It should be apparent that this ROX process can be used for surface planarization in junction transistor technology as well as for FETs. A disadvantage of the ROX process is that typically there are always other areas on the surface that have silicon dioxide in contact with the silicon

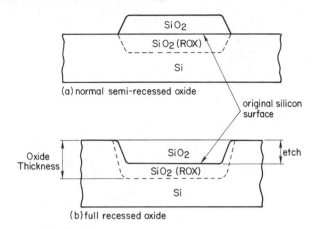

FIGURE 2.9-4 Surface planarization using recessed oxide.

prior to the ROX step. For instance, a gate oxide of an FET device, or a thin oxide for a subsequent diffusion or contact hole in junction devices, may have been formed previously. We do not want this oxide to grow into the silicon during the ROX step; hence a blocking mask (e.g., a very thin layer of Si_3N_4) must be imposed on the silicon surface before the all-silicon dioxide deposition to prevent this undesired undergrowth. This necessitates additional steps in the process and can also create surface state problems in FET's. The latter can cause threshold shifts and/or leakage, which are undesirable. Highly sophisticated processing becomes more essential.

2.9.4   FET Circuit Layout: Example

In addition to the smaller devices possible with FET, the circuit interconnections are easier than those with junction transistor circuits. In FETs, the source and drain diffusion are indistinguishable except from the circuit connection. Hence when two FET devices are connected in series with the source of one to the drain of another, or in parallel with, say, several drains in parallel, one diffusion can serve multiple functions. As an example, consider a simple two-input NOR gate (Fig. 2.9-5) that could serve as the on-chip decoders of a memory array.* The load is a depletion mode FET device obtained by connecting the gate to the drain of an ordinary enhancement mode device. The logic is determined by the active devices 1 and 2. It is obvious that the drains D_1 and D_2 are in parallel and sources S_1 and S_2 are likewise in parallel; also S_3 is in series with D_1, D_2. Reasonable circuit

* A one-input NOR would be half a flip-flop circuit.

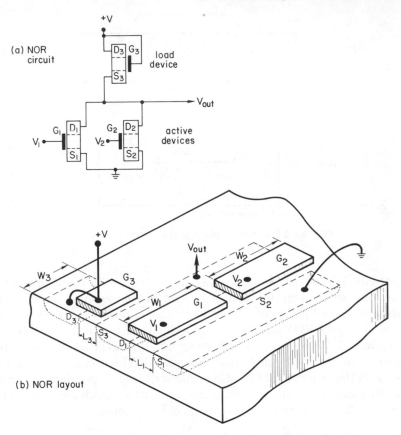

FIGURE 2.9-5 Example of FET NOR circuit layout showing internal circuit connections and varying device widths (oxide not shown).

operation can be obtained with devices having width-to-length ratios of $W_1/L_1 = W_2/L_2 = 4$ and $W_3/L_3 = 2$. Such a circuit can be laid out with internal source and drain interconnections given in Fig. 2.9-5b. The final metallization is excluded (except gates) to show the sharing of diffusions. This concept is important in reducing circuit size not only in the decoding logic gates, but also in the memory cells. A similar sharing can be accomplished with the MOS flip-flop circuits of Section 3.8. Figure 3.10-3 gives an example of one diffusion serving as the source for many devices and as the common bit/sense line.

A certain amount of such internal circuit interconnection can be achieved with junction transistor technology but not as effectively, as previously indicated. Quite often a *p* region must be connected to an *n* region. For instance, in Fig. 2.8-4, if the diode is not present and the resistor is connected to the collector, a p region must be connected to an n^+ region, requiring an external interconnection. Thus FET structures have several features that lead to higher density.

2.10   JUNCTION TRANSISTOR VERSUS FET DEVICE SIZE

The FET memory cells for similar photolithographic line widths and similar circuits are nearly always much smaller than those of junction transistor cells. The difference depends, of course, on the actual cell being compared. For the flip-flop cells of Figs. 3.8-3 and 3.8-4 the difference in cell areas depends very significantly on the value of load resistor, hence power of the junction transistor circuit. For low power dissipation this resistor must be very large in value, which makes it physically large, consuming a substantial area. The FET can achieve a low power dissipation with a small load device.

It would be very useful if we could make a fundamental comparison of the absolute density advantage of FETs. However there are too many variables which cannot be specified. For instance, the circuit configuration of a "very small" junction transistor cell would differ somewhat from the circuit of a "very small" FET cell, and new or improved cells are always evolving. It is possible, fortunately, to do a meaningful density comparison of one aspect of the two technologies. Section 2.8 indicated that lithographic mask and alignment tolerances can yield a significant increase in device dimensions. We further saw that junction transistors require double diffusions, deep device isolation diffusions, and usually external metal interconnections, whereas the MOS FET (Section 2.9) is much simpler. The more complex processing coupled with the lithographic tolerances makes junction transistor inherently larger than FET devices. To see how this comes about, let us compare the lateral dimension required for the active device in a circuit consisting of a load resistor in series with a switching transistor (Fig. 2.10-1). This is a typical structure appearing in many memory and logic cells. The junction transistor requires an isolated resistor with external

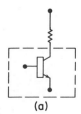
(a)

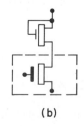
(b)

FIGURE 2.10-1 Schematic of circuit configuration and device portion used in density comparison. (*a*) Junction transistor with resistor load. (*b*) MOS FET with depletion mode FET load.

connections, whereas the FET uses an induced depletion mode FET as a load that can have an internal connection as in Fig. 2.9-5. We compare only the active device sizes, as indicated by the dashed boxes in Fig. 2.10-1. Hence we do not have to lay out the load, but only allow whatever isolation or connection spacing is necessary. For the junction transistor, we must provide complete isolation on all sides, as was done in Fig. 2.8-4. A simplified, idealized layout of the transistor portion of Fig. 2.8-4, allowing for mask line width, alignment, and minimum separation S_m between edges appears in Fig. 2.10-2a. The lateral etching and lateral diffusion considerations are neglected or can be assumed to be lumped in the mask tolerances. However all edge definitions are assumed to have the same mask line width tolerance $\pm \Delta W_m/2$, which does not allow for the different lateral spreads that can result from different diffusion depths. One exception is the deep p-isolation diffusion, which is *assumed* to give a final surface opening of $2W_m$. Since the buried n^+ subcollector in Fig. 2.8-4 is assumed to be much narrower than the distance between isolation,* we can neglect its masking tolerances and start directly with the p isolation as mask I. This isolation diffusion mask I is assumed to provide the alignment mask and requires no alignment. Thus the tolerance is only $\Delta W/2$ without the mask alignment term A_x, similar to edge A in Fig. 2.8-2. All subsequent edge definitions require a tolerance of $\Delta W/2 + A_x$ similar to edge B or C in Fig. 2.8-2. The minimum line width is used on mask IV to define the metal contact to the collector, emitter, and base as shown. For simplicity, all separations between adjacent edges are assumed to have the same minimum value S_m. The minimum nominal transistor cell width is the sum of all the dimensions indicated in Fig. 2.10-2a or

$$W_J = 5W_m + 2\frac{\Delta W}{2} + 10S_m + 18\left(\frac{\Delta W}{2} + A_x\right) \qquad (2.10\text{-}1)$$

$$= 5W_m + 10S_m + 10\Delta W + 18A_x \qquad (2.10\text{-}2)$$

If we assume that the line width tolerance, alignment, and minimum separation are all the same and equal to 20% of the minimum line width or, assuming

$$\Delta W = S_m = A_x = 0.2W_m \qquad (2.10\text{-}3)$$

substitution into (2.10-2) gives

$$W_J = 5W_m + 38\Delta W \qquad (2.10\text{-}4)$$

$$= 12.6W_m \qquad (2.10\text{-}5)$$

---

* In more sophisticated structures, this subcollector cannot be neglected.

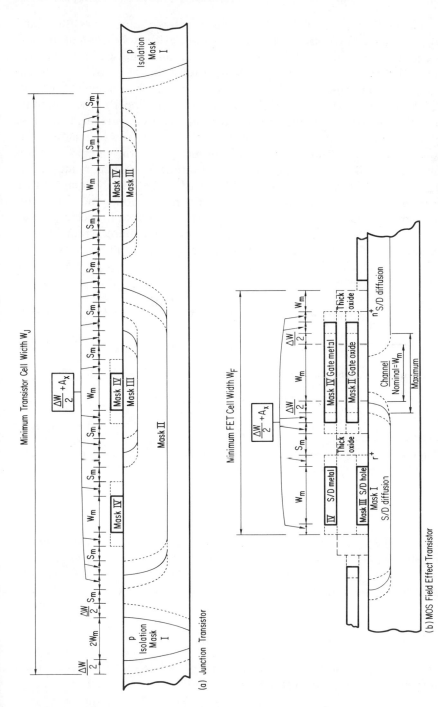

FIGURE 2.10-2 Comparison of junction and field effect transistor cell widths using similar photolithographic ground rules.

115

In a similar manner, the FET is laid out with the same assumptions and ground rules as previously. The source of one device is the drain of the next device as in Fig. 2.10-2b. The nominal minimum line width defines the nominal channel length of mask I. Mask I is assumed to provide the alignment mark, hence only has tolerance of $\Delta W/2$ *without* the alignment tolerance A_x. To ensure that the channel always turns on properly, the minimum possible gate window on mask II, and the minimum size gate metal on mask IV, must equal the maximum possible size of channel length as shown. The exact opposite conditions can and will occur: that is, the channel length is minimum at $W_m - \Delta W$, and the gate electrode is at maximum size of $W_m + 2(\Delta W/2) + 4(\Delta W/2 + A_x) = W_m + 3\Delta W + 4A_x$. The gate metal then overlaps undesirably on the source and drain diffusions, and this is the fundamental source of the large gate overlap capacitance in such a process.

The cell width is the distance from the center of one source-drain diffusion to the center of the next such diffusion—or, in principle, and easier to portray —from one edge to the corresponding edge as shown. This gives a nominal cell size of

$$W_F = 2W_m + 2\frac{\Delta W}{2} + 2S_m + 6\left(\frac{\Delta W}{2} + A_x\right) \qquad (2.10\text{-}6)$$

$$= 2W_m + 2S_m + 4\Delta W + 6A_x \qquad (2.10\text{-}7)$$

If, as before, we assume the equality of (2.10-3), the above becomes

$$W_F = 2W_m + 12\Delta W \qquad (2.10\text{-}8)$$

$$= 4.4W_m \qquad (2.10\text{-}9)$$

The ratio between the lateral width of the junction and FET device, given by (2.10-5) and (2.10-9) with all attendant assumptions, is thus

$$\frac{W_J}{W_F} = \frac{12.6}{4.4} = 2.9 \approx 3 \qquad (2.10\text{-}10)$$

Thus FETs have a fundamental advantage in one dimension of approximately a factor of 3. We have purposely neglected the other dimension in the analysis. The "width" of the devices* into the paper is a variable that determines the power dissipation, as well as other circuit parameters. Typically this dimension is also smaller for FET devices, giving another factor of 2 or 3. Thus the surface density advantage of FET devices can be a factor of roughly 5 to 10 times better.

---

* The FET channel is typically referred to as a "length" and the variable dimension into the paper of Fig. 2.10-2 is typically called the device "width."

To compare cell density, one must include the remainder of the circuit. The large resistors typically required for junction transistor circuits can give FETs another factor of 3 or more advantage. This "circuit" disadvantage of junction transistors has received significant attention. The relatively new "merged transistor" circuit concept and corresponding technology (Berger and Wudmann, 1975) is an attempt to circumvent this problem by eliminating the load resistors, using merged diffusions on adjacent devices to reduce both the amount of isolation area and the number of metal interconnections required per cell.

2.11 SUPERCONDUCTIVITY FUNDAMENTALS

Superconductors have four basic properties that make them attractive as random access storage media.

1. A direct current circulating in a superconducting loop will remain flowing indefinitely if left unperturbed; that is, it can store information and will not lose it if power is lost (provided 4°K temperature bath can be maintained with a reservoir).

2. Superconductors are totally lossless (perfect conductors) under static conditions, while carrying direct current (i.e., no standby power dissipation). This is a corollary of property 1.

3. Only two different superconducting materials (e.g., tin and lead) and insulation (e.g., oxide) are needed to make all computer logical and storage functions.

4. A superconductor can be switched to a normal resistance state by the application of a relatively small field or current with the normal-to-superconducting resistance ratio being infinite.

Properties 1 and 2 are quite attractive for an operational system. Quiescent power dissipation is zero and actual switching losses are extremely small, giving a low average power dissipation system. In addition, since the connecting wires between storage cells are also made of superconductors, the signal attenuation and phase (pulse) distortion normally encountered in large arrays can be greatly reduced, since even at high frequencies superconductors have small (but not zero) losses. Property 3 lends itself to large-scale planar fabrication, hence low cost. Property 4 makes the phenomenon attractive for computer logic and memory cells (Section 3.11).

To understand a single superconductoring memory device, as well as many devices in a system with decoding, terminations, and so on, it is essential to know a few of the fundamental properties of superconductors, including (*a*) resistance as a function of temperature, (*b*) resistance as a function of frequency, (c) Meissner effect, (d) critical current density, critical magnetic field, and switching, (e) superconducting current penetration depth versus temperature, (f) superposition of fields and currents of multiple superconductors, (g) coherence length, (h) superconducting tunneling (Josephson) phenomena, and (i) current density penetration and critical field as a function of conductor thickness.

We summarize, without proof, only some of the important properties necessary for other chapters. See Matick (1969, Ch. 6) and Newhouse (1964) for more details.

2.11.1 Resistance as a Function of Temperature

Below a certain critical temperature T_c, superconductors lose all apparent dc resistance. Measurements have shown that the maximum resistivity must be less than 10^{-23} Ω-cm; which is 1.7×10^{-17} times smaller than that of copper at 25°C. Circulating currents that have been established experimentally in superconductors have continued to flow for years with no measurable deterioration. Thus for practical devices, we may assume the dc resistivity to be identically zero.

2.11.2 Resistance as a Function of Frequency

The current flow in a superconductor is carried by electrons of two types—the ordinary or normal electrons, and paired or superconducting electrons. The former produce the usual type of conduction losses; the latter do not. Normal electrons require some electric field to accelerate them and produce collisions (resistance). Since there can be no electric field in a superconductor at dc, the normal electron flow is zero. When a time varying voltage or current is applied, however, the time varying superelectrons produce a small electric field, but no losses in themselves. This small electric field in the direction of current flow accelerates the normal electrons and produces losses. The electric field produced by the time varying supercurrent increases approximately as the square root of the frequency. This field is extremely small at low frequencies and begins to become noticeable only above roughly 10^9 Hz. For most computer applications with pulse rise times of greater than 0.1 nsec, the pulse frequency spectrum just barely extends into this range; thus the ac losses in such superconductors are generally negligible unless higher frequencies are used.

2.11.3 Meissner Effect

A magnetic field is excluded from the usual type I superconductors of interest here. To understand this, suppose a strip of tin at any temperature above the critical temperature T_c is placed in a constant magnetic field as in Fig. 2.11-1a.

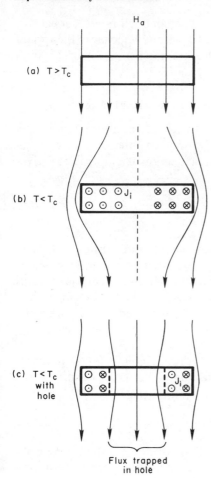

H_a

(a) $T > T_c$

(b) $T < T_c$

J_i

(c) $T < T_c$
     with
     hole

J_i

Flux trapped
in hole

FIGURE 2.11-1 Strip of tin in a constant magnetic field at various temperatures.

After some initial transients, the field penetrates the tin as shown. If the temperature is now lowered to below T_c, supercurrents are induced within the tin. These supercurrents give rise to a magnetic field that cancels the applied field within the tin, and the total field appears as in Fig. 2.11-1b. The magnetic field is excluded from the tin, except for a very narrow region on the surface where the supercurrents flow. This is known as the penetration depth and is typically in the range of 500 Å for most common superconductors. If the tin strip originally had a hole in it as in Fig. 2.11-1c, the magnetic field is excluded from the tin, but it is possible for some of the flux to get trapped in the hole as illustrated. The hole can be microscopic in size, and many such holes might make it appear on a macroscopic level that the flux is not excluded from

the tin, which is a false impression. Thus superconductors are perfect dia-
magnets, having an induced magnet moment equal and opposite to the applied
magnetic field. These penetration and flux trapping phenomena are very
important in some random access storage cells.

2.11.4   Critical Current Density, Critical Magnetic Field, and Switching

Superconductors at a given temperature switch to the normal resistance
state whenever the *total current density* within the interior exceeds some
critical value. This critical current density as a function of temperature is given
by

$$J_{cr} = J_0\left[1 - \left(\frac{T}{T_c}\right)^2\right] \tag{2.11-1}$$

where T_c is the critical temperature in the absence of any current and J_0 is the
critical current density at absolute zero. The currents flowing in any superconductor can be those applied directly by some external current source, those
induced by a magnetic field via the Meissner effect, or the vector sum of these
two. The condition is that J_{cr} must be the total current density, however
obtained. This critical current depends only on the temperature as indicated
previously, and on the superconducting material.

Because of the existence of a typically small superconducting penetration
depth (Section 2.11.5), the supercurrents flow on the surface. The surface then
has a magnetic field that is exactly equal to the surface current density or

$$H = J \text{ A/m} \tag{2.11-2}$$

As a result of this direct relationship, it is possible to use the concept of a
critical magnetic field rather than a critical current for switching to normal
resistance. By making use of (2.11-2) in (2.11-1) we arrive at a critical field
concept given by

$$H_{cr} = H_0\left(1 - \frac{T}{T_c}\right)^2 \tag{2.11-3}$$

where H_0 is the critical field at absolute zero. Some values of H_0 are given in
Table 2.11-1.

Since a magnetic field impressed on a superconductor always induces
supercurrents, it makes no difference whether we use the concept of critical
current density or of critical field, as long as the total, maximum component
of either can be evaluated. In most experiments the applied H field is more
easily determined, whereas the current density, which is quite variable, is
seldom measurable. Hence the critical field tends to be more commonly used.

TABLE 2.11-1   Important Parameters of Some Common Superconductors

Material	T_c (°K)	Critical Field $(T = 0°K)$ H_0 (Oe)	Penetration Depth λ_0 (10^{-10} m)	Coherence Length ξ (10^{-10} m)
Aluminum	1.196	99	500	16,000
Cadmium	0.56	30	1300	
Indium	3.407	293	640	4400
Lead	7.175	802.6	390	
Molybdenum	0.92	98		
Niobium	9.25	1944		
Tin	3.74	305	510	2300
Zinc	0.91	53		
Zirconium	0.55			
Nb_3Sn	18.07	$> 10^5$		

This equivalence is valid *only* for a superconductor in the superconducting state. For instance, for a small superconducting sample with an applied field H_a, the induced currents are equivalent. But when H_a exceeds the critical field, the sample becomes normal, and the supercurrents that now produce $I^2 R_n$ joule losses, will die out. The magnetic field now becomes the sole agent maintaining the sample in the normal state; that is, the field prevents the coherence coupling of the Cooper electron pairs, which are necessary for superconductivity. Thus in the nonsuperconducting state, the maximum magnetic field at any point is the important quantity.

The equivalence between the applied field and the induced currents in a superconductor begins to break down when the penetration depth becomes comparable to the superconductor thickness (see Section 2.11.8).

Most practical devices include both an externally applied current and an external magnetic field. While the sample is in the superconducting state, we may consider either the total maximum current density or the magnetic field created by these two external sources. When either exceeds the critical value, that part of the superconductor becomes normal. The currents and field then readjust themselves to the new situation. Typically, the critical condition is exceeded in the remainder of the sample, and the entire sample becomes normal. This processing is interesting and important to understand, at least in concept. Consider a long, wide, thin superconducting strip above a ground plane as in Fig. 2.11-2. A current i_g applied down the length of the

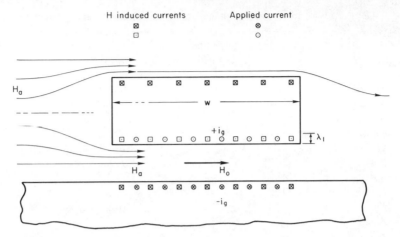

FIGURE 2.11-2 Cross sections of long, thin, wide superconductor with externally applied H field and current.

strip and returning in the ground plane will penetrate into both superconductors only a distance λ_1. Ideally the volume and surface current densities are

$$\text{volume} \qquad J = \frac{i_g}{\lambda w} \quad \text{A/m}^2 \qquad (2.11\text{-}4)$$

$$\text{surface} \qquad J_s = \frac{i_g}{w} \quad \text{A/m} \qquad (2.11\text{-}5)$$

If a magnetic field is applied with polarity as shown, the induced supercurrents add to the applied current on the bottom surface of the strip as well as the top of the ground plane. Concentrating on the strip, if the combination of these two currents or fields exceeds the critical condition, the bottom region of thickness λ will become normal. The H field can now penetrate that region. For this field to continue to be excluded from the remainder of the superconductors, supercurrents must now flow in a new penetration depth region λ_2 (Fig. 2.11-3). However since the induced currents or fields are the same as

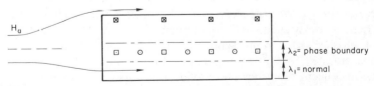

FIGURE 2.11-3 Superconductor switching to normal state by motion of phase boundary.

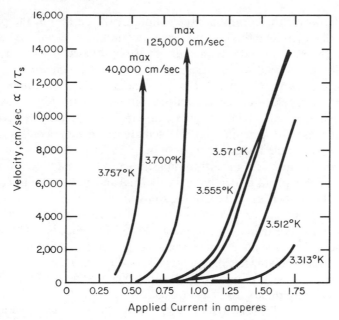

FIGURE 2.11-4 Velocity of superconducting—normal phase boundary versus applied current for a tin film 1μ thick and 5 mm wide, $T_c = 3.87°$K, normal resistance per unit length $R_n/l = 7 \times 10^{-3}$ Ω/mm. After Cherry and Gittleman (1960).

previously, this region λ_2 also goes normal. In fact, a superconducting–normal phase transition region propagates upward through the strip. This boundary is much like a magnetic domain wall in some respects because it propagates with a mobility, hence a velocity, that is proportional to the excess field or overdrive. This phase boundary velocity as a function of fast rise time driving current is plotted in Fig. 2.11-4 for a tin film 1 μ thick. For any given sample, the time for the phase boundary to move across the entire film is inversely proportional to the velocity, hence the vertical scale is proportional to $1/\tau_s$. We cannot specify the proportionality exactly, since like magnetic domains, superconductors typically switch by nucleation of several normal domains that propagate at a velocity determined by the current. Note the similarity of these switching curves with magnetic switching curves of Figs. 2.7-1, 3.2-3 and 3.3-13. However there is *no* "fast" mechanism in super-conductors analogous to rotational switching in magnetics.

After the entire strip has switched, the behavior of the superconductor depends on the external source supplying the strip current i_g as well as the thermal properties of the strip in liquid helium. Suppose i_g is supplied by a stiff current source. Once the entire sample becomes normal, a resistance R_n

appears. However the current source maintains the current at the previous value; ideally, therefore, this current in conjunction with H_a will maintain the sample in the normal state. If the current was provided by, say, a voltage source with an internal source resistance equal to R_n, then when the entire sample becomes normal, i_g will fall to $i_g/2$. Assuming that the sample remains at constant temperature, the critical conditions are no longer exceeded, causing switching back to the superconducting state. Once this occurs, the current increases to i_g again, and an oscillatory, unstable condition could exist. However, joule losses in the form of $i_g{}^2 R_n$ normally heat the sample, lowering the critical field or current density so that it may remain normal. The exact state depends critically on the thermal and electrical time constants as well as the properties of the driving source.

The critical current or field phenomenon is used to control the state of all superconducting switching and memory devices, hence is of fundamental importance. The critical current or field can be reached by combinations of fields or currents flowing in closely coupled conductors. Thus several separate conductors (terminals) under separate control can be used to switch or not switch a superconductor to the normal resistance state. This is the basic property found in all superconducting storage and logic devices (Section 3.11). The fundamental manner of combining field or currents for various typical conductor arrangements is given in Section 2.11.6.

2.11.5 Superconducting Current Penetration Depth λ Versus Temperature

This penetration phenomenon occurs under dc or ac conditions. The electrical behavior of the effect is identical to that of classical penetration or skin depth of an electromagnetic wave into a normal conductor, with one difference: the latter occurs only for ac operation and varies with frequency, whereas superconducting penetration depth is independent of frequency. There is a very slight, usually negligible dependence on magnetic field and strong dependence on temperature given by

$$\lambda = \lambda_0 \left[1 - \left(\frac{T}{T_c} \right)^4 \right]^{-1/2} \tag{2.11-6}$$

where λ_0 is the penetration depth at absolute zero and is about 500 Å for a number of materials (see Table 2.11-1).

2.11.6 Superposition of Field and Currents of Multiple Superconductors

A memory cell must have at least two isolated functional terminals (Sections 2.4 and 4.2). In superconducting cells, this typically requires the superposition of fields or currents of overlapping conductors. The principles underlying this

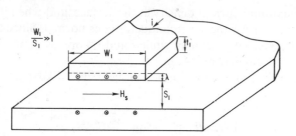

FIGURE 2.11-5 Ideal superconducting strip line above a superconducting ground plane.

superposition are essential for comprehending device behavior. The fundamental criterion for switching of a superconductor to the normal resistance state is that the maximum current density or magnetic field must exceed some fixed threshold J_{cr} or H_{cr} given in Section 2.11.4. We consider various ways in which these critical conditions can be exceeded, first by current in a single conductor, then by current in various multiple conductor arrangements.

Assume a single, ideal superconducting line of width W_1 and thickness t_1 located a distance S_1 above an infinite superconducting ground plane, as in Fig. 2.11-5. For simplicity, we assume $W_1/S_1 \gg 1$; thus when a current is applied in the line as shown, the dc magnetic field is uniform between and zero everywhere else. We also assume the superconducting penetration depth λ to be much smaller that the conductor thickness. When a direct current is applied in the conductor with return path in the ground plane, the current flows on the surfaces as shown. This direct current in a superconductor is very much like a high frequency skin depth penetration in an ordinary conductor. The current density is governed by the equation [see Matick, 1969]

$$\nabla^2 J = \frac{J}{\lambda^2} \tag{2.11-7}$$

which for a thick conductor is very nearly

$$J = J_s e^{-z/\lambda} \quad \text{A/cm}^2 \tag{2.11-8}$$

where J_s is the maximum current density at the surface and can be obtained by noting that the total applied current is

$$i = W_1 \int_0^\infty J_{s1} e^{-z/\lambda}\, dz = J_{s1}\lambda W_1 \tag{2.11-9}$$

or

$$J_{s1} = \frac{i_1}{\lambda W_1} \quad \text{A/m}^2 \tag{2.11-10}$$

This is the maximum current density at the surface, and when it exceeds the critical current density, the superconductor goes normal. Since total current is the variable external parameter while λ and W_1 are given, we can calculate J_1 when these parameters are given.

We could also express the surface H field in a like manner by using Ampère's law

$$\oint H_s \cdot dl = i \qquad \text{or} \qquad H_s W_1 = i \tag{2.11-11}$$

where H_s is the surface field at each conductor. If we equate (2.11-10) to (2.11-11) we find

$$H_s = J_s \lambda \quad \text{A/m} \tag{2.11-12}$$

The important point is that both the maximum surface current density and the field are linearly related to the applied current and to each other.

Suppose we now place a second conductor of width W_2 a distance S_2 above the first conductor as in Fig. 2.11-6, with an applied current i_2. We again

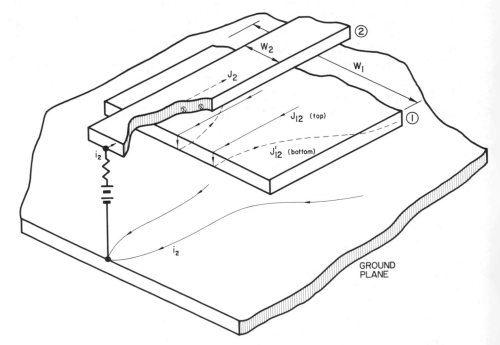

FIGURE 2.11-6   Two superconducting strip lines above a superconducting ground plane.

assume $W_2/S_2 \gg 1$, giving uniform fields and allowing edge effects to be neglected. The field H_2 produced by this current will be, from (2.11-11)

$$H_2 = \frac{i_2}{W_2} \tag{2.11-13}$$

Since this field must be excluded from the lower superconductor, a supercurrent will be induced on the top and bottom surfaces of conductor 1. On the top surface, this field must be excluded by an opposite polarity current density of amplitude

$$J_{12} = \frac{H_2}{\lambda} \tag{2.11-14}$$

Substituting (2.11-13) gives the current density in conductor 1, produced by a current in conductor 2, as

$$J_{12}\bigg|_{\text{top 1}} = \frac{i_2}{\lambda W_2} \quad \text{A/m}^2 \tag{2.11-15a}$$

Thus an image current of equal amplitude and opposite polarity is induced, just as in the ground plane of Fig. 2.11-5. On the bottom surface of conductor 1, the situation is more complex but fundamentally important. The same total current must flow on the top and bottom surface of conductor 1, although the current density can be different. Assume thin conductors but with thickness greater than 2λ, also $W_2 < W_1$, and conductor 2 longer than 1, as in Fig. 2.11-6. At the front edge of conductor 1, the induced current must loop around from the top to the bottom surface so the current density will be the same at this edge. As the current flows along the length of the bottom surface, however, it spreads out as shown. At a distance along the bottom of conductor 2 that is approximately equal to W_1, the current is nearly uniformly distributed over the width W_1, giving a smaller current density of value

$$J'_{12}\bigg|_{\text{bottom 1}} = \frac{i_2}{\lambda W_1} \tag{2.11-15b}$$

For superconducting devices that are switched from the superconducting to the normal state, the maximum current density is of importance in determining the critical point. Hence if we are attempting to switch conductor 1, the maximum current density occurs at the front edge, given by (2.11-15a). If we now apply a separate current in conductor 1, as was done in Fig. 2.11-5, the induced current density J_{12} will add directly to the applied current on the bottom surface of superconductor 1. The maximum current density at the surface is the sum of (2.11-15a) and (2.11-10).

$$J_{max} = J_{s1} + J_{12}$$

$$= \frac{i_1}{\lambda W_1} + \frac{i_2}{\lambda W_2} = \frac{1}{\lambda}\left(\frac{i_1}{W_1} + \frac{i_2}{W_2}\right) \qquad (2.11\text{-}16)$$

When this value exceeds the critical current density, superconductor 1 goes normal. The value of J_{max} can be measured by applying only i_1 and increasing its amplitude until switching occurs at some value I_{max}.

$$J_{max} = \frac{I_{max}}{\lambda W_1} \qquad (2.11\text{-}17)$$

If the critical field is known, it can be used instead. For instance, from (2.11-12) we have

$$J_{max} = \frac{H_{max}}{\lambda} \qquad (2.11\text{-}18)$$

Substituting this into (2.11-16) gives

$$H_{max} = \frac{i_1}{W_1} + \frac{i_2}{W_2} \qquad (2.11\text{-}19)$$

Since J and H are equivalent, either can be used. Note in these expressions that if $W_1 = W_2$, the currents in *separate* conductors add as if they were applied in the *same* conductor. This is an important fundamental point in memory device design. Also, for equal currents $i_1 = i_2$, the effect of one or the other can be made stronger by decreasing the respective conductor width. This increases the current density and H field for a given value of i.

The spreading of the current on the bottom of conductor 1 does not affect the critical point for switching, but it does affect the time required for switching. For instance, for an in-line cryotron (e.g., Fig. 3.11-1), the critical condition is exceeded only at the front (and back) edge of 1 and the superconducting–normal phase boundary must propagate inward along the length of 1, from each edge. Thus the spreading of current is undesirable in this case, but sometimes it can be used to advantage. For instance, Josephson cryotrons do not switch from the normal to superconducting state; in addition, it is the H field or current density flowing at the junction site that is important. If a Josephson junction is located at the front edge of conductor 1 in Fig. 2.11-6, the current density induced by i_2 is the maximum value. If, however, the junction is located far enough away from the front or back edge, the induced current density is a minimum. In forming logic circuits, several control lines similar to conductor 2 would be used. The manner in which their individual current densities add affects the logic function characteristics. Using control lines that induce their maximum current density on the junction can produce an OR, whereas the minimum current density case produces an AND (see Herrell, 1974, for an example). These principles are important in memory device design.

The currents in the above two conductors were applied in the same direction and therefore add. Obviously if they were applied in opposite directions, they would subtract. In a like manner, if the two conductors were oriented at 90° to each other (cross-film) their individual current densities would be the same as before but would be oriented at 90°. Hence vector addition would be required, giving the maximum value as

$$
J_{\substack{max \\ (orthogonal)}} = \frac{1}{\lambda} \left[\left(\frac{i_1}{W_1} \right)^2 + \left(\frac{i_2}{W_2} \right)^2 \right]^{1/2}
\tag{2.11-20}
$$

or

$$
H_{\substack{max \\ (orthogonal)}} = \left[\left(\frac{i_1}{W_1} \right)^2 + \left(\frac{i_2}{W_2} \right)^2 \right]^{1/2}
\tag{2.11-21}
$$

These principles are used for memory devices and cells in Chapter 3.

2.11.7 Coherence Length

This concept arises from the Bardeen-Cooper-Schrieffer (BCS) theory, according to which the superconducting state is characterized by the formation of electron pairs that are coupled over relatively long distances, the coherence length ξ. This distance is on the order of 1 μ (Table 2.11-1), which is very large compared to the electron mean free path in ordinary metals (about 0.01 μ) or to the superconducting penetration depth (0.05 μ). This parameter is of fundamental importance in Josephson tunneling, which is the basis of the tunneling cryotron.

2.11.8 Superconducting Tunneling Phenomena

The well-known phenomenon of tunneling of electrons through a barrier is the basic mechanism in the tunnel diode. Tunneling occurs at room temperature in semiconductors separated by a junction barrier. Superconducting tunneling, while similar in some respects, is nevertheless quite different, occurring only at low temperatures and in superconductors separated by a thin insulating barrier. To understand this effect, let us start with two superconducting lead plates, separated by some distance d (e.g., a dielectric) to form a junction. Let us then vary only two parameters—namely, the separation d and the ambient temperature T—while looking at the current through

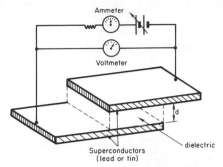

Superconductors
(lead or tin)   dielectric

FIGURE 2.11-7   Two superconducting plates separated by a dielectric of variable thickness d.

the junction and the voltage across the junction as in Fig. 2.11-7. If we keep the junction of lead-dielectric-lead at room temperature with d large, say, in the millimeter range, no dc current can flow. Thus as we increase the supply voltage V_B, a momentary charging current flows of value $I = C(dV_B/dt)$ only, to charge the capacitance of the plates and provide a voltage equal to V_B, but no dc current flows. Thus the full supply voltage appears across the junction with $I - V$ characteristic as given in Fig. 2.11-8a. If the separation d is reduced to the region where quantum mechanical tunneling can occur (50–100 Å) while still at room temperature, the junction will have a linear $I - V$ characteristic as shown in Fig. 2.11-8b. The slope (effective resistance) varies strongly with separation d; in fact, at any given voltage, the current varies exponentially with d as given by quantum mechanics

$$I = \frac{V_B}{R} e^{-\eta d} \tag{2.11-22}$$

where V_B/R is the maximum current that would flow if $d = 0$ (ohmic contact), $e^{-\eta d}$ is the fraction of the maximum that actually crosses (probability of a crossing), and η is a constant depending on the barrier height and the applied voltage (Beam, 1965).

If the temperature is now lowered such that the lead plates become superconducting (i.e., below 7°K), while maintaining a separation of $d \sim 50$ Å, the $I - V$ characteristics of Fig. 2.11-8c reveal that a different phenomenon is present, namely, a "gap" with low current and suddenly a jump to a larger current, where the junction becomes essentially a normal resistance (Giaever and Megerle, 1961). As the current is increased further, the $I - V$ characteristic is a straight line extrapolating to zero, with a resistance value equal to the normal resistance. If the plate separation is now further decreased to about 30 Å, everything else remaining the same, an additional phenomenon is observed (Fig. 2.11-8d) as the current is increased from zero, there is a region over which no voltage drop appears across the junction, but a finite current

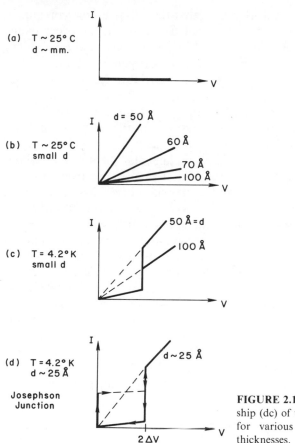

(a) T ~ 25° C
     d ~ mm.

(b) T ~ 25° C
     small d

(c) T = 4.2° K
     small d

(d) T = 4.2° K
     d ~ 25 Å

Josephson
Junction

FIGURE 2.11-8 Current-voltage relationship (dc) of two metal plates of Fig. 2.11-7 for various temperatures and dielectric thicknesses.

flows (i.e., the junction is acting as a superconductor). If the current exceeds a certain maximum value I_m, the device switches as shown to a voltage drop of $2\Delta V$, in other words, the junction has become normal. This effect, unlike most scientific discoveries, was predicted from BCS theory by Josephson (1962, 1964, 1965), and the experimental confirmation followed. Thus a junction with a very small separation d can behave in some respects very much like an ordinary superconductor. However two very important differences relative to computing devices are as follows: (1) the junction switching speed is very fast $\gtrsim 30$ psec, and (2) if any part of the junction goes "normal," the entire junction goes normal; that is, switching speed does *not depend on the excess field or overdrive, like usual superconductors* or magnetic devices. These differences provide attractive features for high speed devices (Matisoo, 1967).

The basic phenomenon at work here is that the effective superconducting coherence length of the lead-dielectric-lead barrier is on the order of the dielectric thickness. Hence two electrons on either side of the boundary can act as a pair, as though the dielectric were a superconductor, which it now becomes in essence. Paired electrons can tunnel through the thin barrier without any voltage drop (i.e., zero voltage state). When the critical current density or magnetic field is exceeded, the pair tunneling is suppressed. Since the barrier is so thin, individual electrons can still tunnel through the barrier, but only with a voltage drop equal to $2\Delta/e$ (where Δ is the energy gap of the superconductor). In terms of fundamental theory of superconductivity, the zero voltage state corresponds to paired electrons (Cooper pairs) in the two superconductors on the two sides of the barrier having a constant phase difference; thus the electrons can tunnel as a unit. The phase is that of the Ginzberg-Landau wave function. When the critical current is exceeded, the phase difference between these paired electrons on opposite sides of the barrier changes with time, which means that pair tunneling is no longer possible but only single particle tunneling. A typical I versus V characteristic is plotted in Fig. 2.11-9. For given materials and oxide thickness, the critical current density is fixed, but the actual critical current of a junction will vary with the surface area. This is true only as long as the Josephson penetration depth discussed below is comparable to the length l of a junction. When the junction length becomes much larger, the current becomes independent of l as will become evident later. The critical gate current I_{max} at which switching occurs from the zero voltage condition to 2

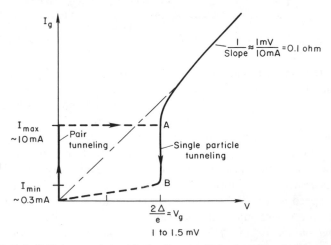

FIGURE 2.11-9   *I-V* characteristics of a 1 mil × 1 mil tin–tin oxide–tin Josephson junction at 4°K.

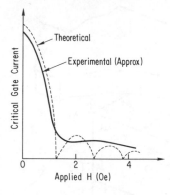

FIGURE 2.11-10 Critical "zero voltage" gate current versus applied field for short ($l < \lambda_J$) Josephson junction (approximate typical values).

times the gap voltage (i.e., from pair to single particle tunneling) can be varied by the application of a magnetic field in the plane of the oxide junction. Figure 2.11-10 demonstrates both the theoretical and experimental dependence for a very short junction ($l < \lambda_J$). This theoretical functional dependence is a $\sin \theta/\theta$ curve or, more specifically,

$$J_{max} = \frac{J_1 \sin \pi(H_a/H_0)}{\pi(H_a/H_0)} \qquad A/m^2 \qquad (2.11\text{-}23)$$

where H_a is the applied field, H_0 is the critical field at zero current, and J_1 is the intrinsic Josephson current density, which depends only on the conductor-oxide materials (work function) and oxide thickness. The significant point is that the application of a field in the range of 1 Oe is capable of "switching" the junction. This field value is quite attractive because it can easily be generated by relatively small currents in narrow conductors. For instance, from (2.12-14), for a conductor width of $W = 0.001$ in., a field of 1 Oe is produced by a current of approximately $I = 10^{-3}/0.5 = 2$ mA. These properties and principles are used in Section 3.11 to obtain practical memory devices and cells.

The intrinsic Josephson current density J_1 can be varied from approximately 10 to 5000 A/cm² by suitable choice of materials, oxide thickness, and fabrication. Since this current density depends exponentially on the oxide thickness similar to that of (2.11-22), special fabrication techniques are required to ensure uniform and reproducible results. Thus a wide range of junction properties can be obtained by varying the lateral and/or vertical dimensions.

Switching of a Josephson junction occurs when the maximum current density or H field is exceeded in any part of the junction. The applied gate current and any currents induced by an external H field add, just as they do in usual superconductors. However the geometry is somewhat different

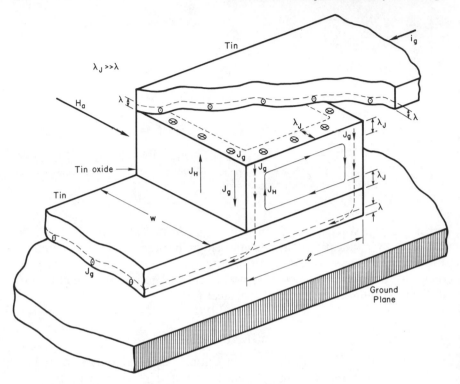

FIGURE 2.11-11   Applied and induced currents in Josephson junction showing Josephson penetration depth.

and must be taken into consideration. In Fig. 2.11-11 a basic junction of width w and length l is located a small distance above a ground plane. A small current applied in the top gate conductor tunnels through the oxide barrier with no voltage drop and out the bottom gate conductor. The current in the metallic superconductors flows on the bottom surfaces of both because of the proximity of the ground plane. This shallow skin region is the usual penetration depth λ (typically ≈ 500 Å). Within the thin oxide, the current penetrates inward from the edges by a distance equal to the Josephson penetration depth λ_J given by

$$\lambda_J - \left[\frac{\phi_0}{2\pi\mu_0(\lambda_1 + \lambda_2 + t)J_1} \right]^{1/2} \text{ m} \qquad (2.11\text{-}24)$$

in RMKS, where $\phi_0 = 2.07 \times 10^{-15}$ V-sec (flux quantum $h/2e$), $\mu_0 = 4\pi \times 10^{-7}$ H/m, λ_1 and λ_2 are the penetration depths in the top and bottom gate conductors, respectively, t is the oxide thickness (m), and $J_1(A/m^2)$ is the intrinsic critical Josephson current density, which is fixed for a given junction. Typically λ_J is about 0.01 to 0.1 mm (10 to 100 μ); thus $\lambda_J \gg \lambda$. An applied in-plane field H_a will induce circulating supercurrents J_H within the oxide as shown.

An important difference between Josephson and other typical super-conductor devices is the self-field created on the oxide by the gate current. As the gate current flows along the bottom surface of the upper superconductor, an in-plane H field is created on the oxide (not shown in 2.11-11). The bottom conductor does not produce such a field because the currents flow on the lower surface, adjacent to the bottom superconducting ground plane. The self-field of the gate current induces a circulating current similar to J_H induced by the applied field (not shown separately). For the critical condition in the junction, there are now three quantities to consider rather than two. These are the external magnetic field, the self-field on the oxide generated by the gate current, and the gate current itself in the oxide. The self-field of the gate current causes a redistribution of the current density in the upper gate conductor, and the effect is important for scaling of these devices. Consider a cross section along the axial length of the junction with *only* gate current applied as in Fig. 2.11-12. Initially the vertical z component of gate current density through the oxide attempts to distribute itself symmetrically along the length of the junction with maxima near the two edges $x = 0$ and $x = l$ (Fig. 2.11-12b). This transport current produces a magnetic field H_g on the oxide with polarity as shown. Since the oxide acts as a superconductor and excludes this field, a current density J_i is induced. The vertical component J_{iz} appears in Fig. 2.11-12c, along the junction length. This induced current is of the opposite polarity and exactly cancels J_g in the region near $x = 0$. Near the region $x = l$ these two currents are in the same direction and there-fore add. The total vertical component of current density across the oxide is as in Fig. 2.11-12d, crowding in a region approximately $2\lambda_J$ wide. Obviously this crowding near the right edge is only valid for $2\lambda_J$ somewhat smaller than l, the actual condition being approximately $3\lambda_J < l$. If λ_J is equal to or larger than l, the current density along the junction length will be nearly uniform. For the long junction case shown, the total oxide current density can be approximated roughly by

$$J_g = \frac{i_g}{2\lambda_J w} \quad \text{A/m}^2 \qquad (2.11\text{-}25)$$

where w is the width as in Fig. 2.11-11. This assumes that the current density is constant over the region of $2\lambda_J$ in Fig. 2.11-12, which is an obvious approxi-mation. The factor of 2 is reasonable for some cases but varies as the ratio of λ_J/l changes. For such long junctions, the curve of J_{max} versus H is no

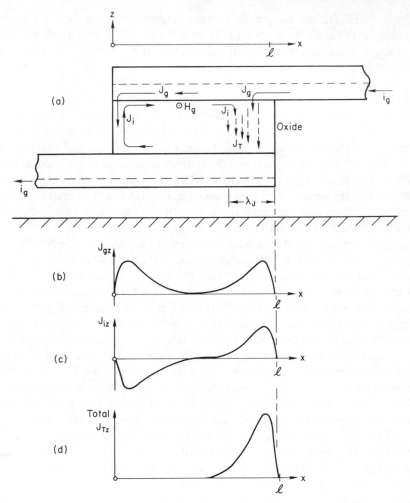

FIGURE 2.11-12   Redistribution of gate current density in a long ($3\lambda_J < l$) Josephson junction due to self-field of gate current.

longer the $\sin\theta/\theta$ function of Fig. 2.11-10 but rather becomes a straight line of the form

$$J_{\max} = J_1\left(1 - \frac{H_a}{H_0}\right) \qquad (2.11\text{-}26)$$

where H_0 is the critical field in the absence of gate current and J_1 is the intrinsic junction Josephson current. Substituting (2.11-25) into (2.11-26) gives the critical switching relationship

$$i_{max}\bigg|_{l>3\lambda_J} = 2\lambda_J w J_1\left(1 - \frac{H_a}{H_0}\right) \tag{2.11-27}$$

For short junctions with $l < \lambda_J$, the uniformity of the current density permits us to write

$$J_{max} = \frac{i_{max}}{lw} \tag{2.11-28}$$

where J_{max} versus H is the $\sin\theta/\theta$ function of Fig. 2.11-10 given by (2.11-23). Substituting (2.11-28) into this expression gives

$$i_{max}\bigg|_{l<\lambda_J} = J_1 wl \frac{\sin(\pi H_a/H_0)}{\pi H_a/H_0} \tag{2.11-24}$$

This represents the critical condition for a short junction.

Note there is no superconductor–normal phase boundary, therefore *no dependence* of the switching speed on overdrive, and this junction does *not* have a switching curve like Fig. 2.11-4 for an ordinary superconductor. The switching speed of such isolated, unloaded devices has been measured to be about 30 psec, the limits of measuring speed. Estimates project the single device speed to be possible as small as 5 psec.

2.11.9 Current Density Penetration and Critical Field as a Function of Conductor Thickness

This very important consideration in the design of memory cells was a major contributor to the demise of early superconducting devices (in line and crossed-field cryotrons). The observed phenomenon was that the external in-plane field required to switch a superconductor to the normal state was often much larger than that predicted from simple theory. For practical devices (e.g., cryotrons of Section 3.11), this meant that currents larger than predicted were required in the control lines. This significantly reduces the gain in a logic cell to less than unity and is extremely undesirable. In memory cells, gain is not important. In coincidently selected cells, however, this effect can be important because of the ratio of half-select currents and the amount of overdrive, just as in thin magnetic films and ferrites.

This effect of increasing control current results from thickness variation of any real conductor. Ideally, a thin film conductor should have the cross section of Fig. 2.11-13a. Depending on the fabrication process used, however, the cross section will be quite different, as in Fig. 2.11-13b for a subtractive etching process. If the penumbra gradually tail off as shown, there will be

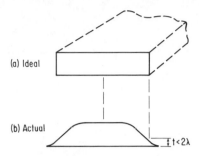

(a) Ideal

(b) Actual

$t < 2\lambda$

FIGURE 2.11-13 Cross section of any conductor obtained by photolithographic (subtractive) etching process.

an edge region for which the metal thickness is less than twice the superconducting penetration depth. These regions are more difficult to switch because the *current density* induced by an external field is smaller in the thinner regions than in the thicker regions. As a result, the critical current density is exceeded first in the thicker regions, and a small, superconducting region remains, still giving zero resistance. In essence, the thin regions "appear" to have a larger critical field for switching. In reality, the critical current density remains the same, but the ability of an external field to induce additional current in a superconductor depends on the film thickness. The induced current density for a given external field decreases as the conductor thickness decreases. Thus a larger external field is required to induce the same critical current in a thin conductor.

To understand this effect, we must look at the dc penetration of an H field into a superconductor from both sides. This requires an exact mathematical analysis based on the London and Maxwell equations. The final result is presented in terms of simple curves of current density versus thickness and field, which are easily understood.

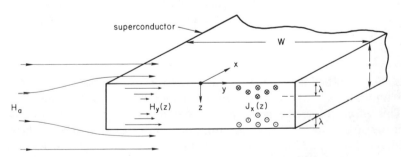

FIGURE 2.11-14 Geometry and coordinate system for determining penetration in a thin superconductor.

We start with a very wide, thin superconductor lying in the xy plane with coordinates as in Fig. 2.11-14. A uniform dc magnetic field H_a is applied externally in the y direction over the entire superconductor, as shown. This magnetic field penetrates a small distance λ into the superconductor on both sides. The induced supercurrent density J_{sc} within these two surface regions is a function of the distance z into the conductor, with a positive x polarity on the top surface and a negative x polarity on the bottom, as illustrated. When the thickness t becomes comparable to the penetration depth λ, these two surface currents begin to cancel each other, thereby giving a smaller value of current density at $z = 0$ and $z = T$. A large H_a is then required to produce the critical current density, which will switch the superconductor to the normal state. Assuming the superconductor to be very wide with $W \gg t$, we can neglect the small nonuniform field and current at the corners of the cross section. Then it can be demonstrated that the supercurrent density is given by

$$J_{sc}(z) = \frac{H_1}{\lambda} e^{-z/\lambda} - \frac{H_2}{\lambda} e^{z/\lambda} \qquad (2.11\text{-}30)$$

with H_1 and H_2 given by

$$H_1 = \frac{H_a(1 - e^{t/\lambda})}{e^{-t/\lambda} - e^{t/\lambda}} \qquad (2.11\text{-}31)$$

$$H_2 = \frac{H_a(1 - e^{-t/\lambda})}{e^{t/\lambda} - e^{-t/\lambda}} \qquad (2.11\text{-}32)$$

It should be noted that for a very thick conductor, or one for which λ is very small, the surface current (sheet) density is

$$J_{surf} = \lambda J_{sc} = H_a \qquad (2.11\text{-}33)$$

In other words, for a thick conductor the maximum sheet surface current density is obtained and equals H_a: that is, the field is totally excluded beyond the distance λ. As the thickness decreases and becomes comparable to λ, the field need not be totally excluded, and the peak surface current density decreases. Figure 2.11-15 plots the normalized current density $\lambda J_{sc}/H_a$ versus z for a thick ($\lambda/t = 0.1$) and a thin ($\lambda = t$) superconductor. For the thick case, the current density is indeed maximum at the two surfaces and falls off rapidly with z. For a thin superconductor, the peak density is much less, and the current density falls off less rapidly with distance. We would have to increase the value of the external field H_a by approximately a factor of 2 at $\lambda = t$ to get the surface current density back to its peak value. Thus this peak surface density at $z = 0$ (or $z = t$) gives rise to the "apparent"

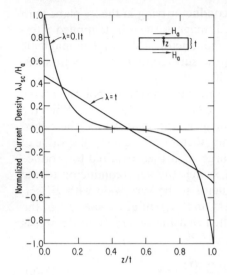

FIGURE 2.11-15 Normalized supercurrent density versus distance into conductor, induced by H_a applied on both surfaces for two ratios of thickness to penetration depth.

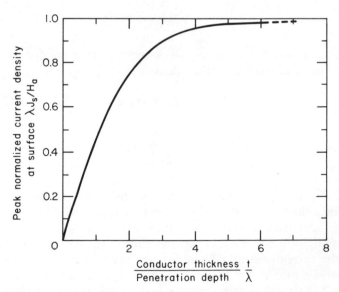

FIGURE 2.11-16 Peak normalized supercurrent density at $z = 0$ or t versus conductor thickness to penetration depth ratio.

increase in the critical threshold field. This *peak surface current density* as a function of conductor thickness is plotted in normalized form in Fig. 2.11-16. It can be seen that the thickness must become less than roughly 3λ before penetration effects become significant.

2.12 STATIC FIELDS OF CONDUCTORS

For simple cases, which occur frequently, the static magnetic field of current carrying conductors can be found from Ampére's law

$$\oint H \cdot dl = NI \quad \text{RMKS} \quad (2.12\text{-}1)$$

where H = magnetizing force (A-turns/m)
  dl = elemental path length (m)
  N = number of turns
  I = current (A)

We use these to find the magnetic field of several cases that are needed elsewhere in this book.

2.12.1 Single Circular Wire in Linear Medium

An infinitely long circular wire of diameter D, located far away from the current return path conductor or any other current carrying conductors, produces a field pattern of concentric circles (Fig. 2.12-1). The amplitude of the circumferential field component at any distance r from the center is obtained directly from (2.12-1) as

$$H = \frac{B}{\mu} = \frac{I}{2\pi r} \quad \text{RMKS} \quad (2.12\text{-}2)$$

where μ is the permeability of the linear medium.
  A more easily remembered form in terms of commonly used units is

$$H = \frac{0.1575I}{2r} \approx \frac{0.16I}{2r} \quad (2.12\text{-}3)$$

where r (in.) is the radial distance to the point in question, H is in oersteds, and I is in amperes. Note that the field intensity is independent of the wire diameter but, rather, depends only on the total current enclosed. This is important in core and other magnetic devices.

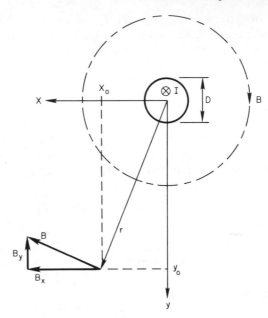

FIGURE 2.12-1   Single current-carrying wire in linear medium.

2.12.2   Sensitivity Function of Single Infinite Wire in Linear Medium

In the above example, we obtained only the circumferential component of the field. In analyzing magnetic recording heads, we make use of the x component of the field along a plane some distance y_0 below the wire, as in Fig. 2.12-1. The total field is given by (2.12-2). The horizontal component is given by

$$B_x = B \sin \theta \tag{2.12-4}$$

But

$$\sin \theta = \frac{y_0}{r} \quad \text{and} \quad r^2 = x_0{}^2 + y_0{}^2 \tag{2.12-5}$$

Substituting these into (2.12-3) gives the final result

$$H_x = \frac{I}{2\pi} \frac{y_0}{x_0{}^2 + y_0{}^2} \tag{2.12-6}$$

This relation, known as the sensitivity function of a single wire, is used in Chapter 5.

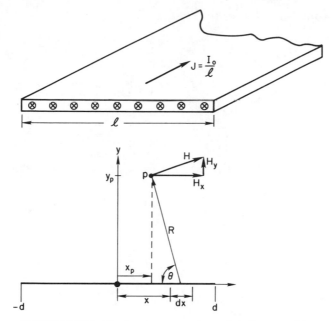

FIGURE 2.12-2 Single current-carrying strip in linear medium.

2.12.3 Magentic Field and Sensitivity Function of a Single Strip Conductor Carrying Uniform Current

An infinitely long, very thin strip conductor of width $l = 2d$ is assumed to carry a uniform current I_0 as in Fig. 2.12-2a. The linear current density or current per unit width is obviously $J - I_0/2d$. We wish to find the x and y components of magnetic field produced by this strip line for any general point p at position x_p, y_p. The strip line can be divided into elemental line currents of width dx, each such element carrying a current

$$I = J \, dx \qquad (2.12\text{-}7)$$

The field at any point must be the sum of the individual contributions from each element. Since the conductor is assumed to be very long, we can use the field from each element as that of an infinite wire given by (2.12-2) or

$$dH_p = \frac{B}{\mu} = \frac{I}{2\pi R} \qquad \text{RMKS} \qquad (2.12\text{-}8)$$

where I is the current in that element and R is the radial distance from wire to P. Summation of these elemental field components over all current elements from $-d$ to d gives the final result

$$H_x = \frac{J}{2\pi}\left[\tan^{-1}\left(\frac{d+x_p}{y_p}\right) - \tan^{-1}\left(\frac{x_p - d}{y_p}\right)\right] \qquad (2.12\text{-}9)$$

$$\equiv \frac{J}{2\pi}\left[\tan^{-1}\left(\frac{d+x_p}{y_p}\right) + \tan^{-1}\left(\frac{d - x_p}{y_p}\right)\right] \qquad (2.12\text{-}10)$$

$$H_y = \frac{J}{4\pi}\ln\left[\frac{(d - x_p)^2 + y_p^{\,2}}{(d + x_p)^2 + y_p^{\,2}}\right] \qquad \text{RMKS} \qquad (2.12\text{-}11)$$

When the width of the strip reduces to zero or a single conductor, the field components reduce to

$$H_x\bigg|_{\text{single wire}} = \frac{I}{2\pi}\frac{y_p}{x_p^{\,2} + y_p^{\,2}} \qquad (2.12\text{-}12)$$

$$H_y\bigg|_{\text{single wire}} = \frac{I}{2\pi}\frac{(-x_p)}{x_p^{\,2} + y_p^{\,2}} \qquad (2.12\text{-}13)$$

Equation 2.12-12 is identical to (2.12-6), as it should be.

2.12.4   Magnetic Field of Parallel Strip Line Conductors

Two wide strip conductors of width W, having a very close separation S so that $W/S \gg 1$, and carrying equal currents in opposite directions, produce a very nearly uniform magnetic field of

$$H \approx \frac{0.5I}{W} \qquad (2.12\text{-}14)$$

where H is in oersteds, I in amperes, and W in inches. The same field is obtained if one conductor is a ground plane as in Fig. 2.11-5, provided $W/S \gg 1$.

2.13   SENSE SIGNALS ON LONG SENSE LINES

In addition to the common attenuation problem associated with all signal propagation, sense signals induced in one local portion of an otherwise long sense wire have other properties that need consideration. The basic concern is whether the signal appears as a series or parallel generator across the transmission line and the resulting affect on its discrimination by the sense amplifier and latch (OBR).

In many memory arrays the sense line may be electrically long, and singals from random access cells might be generated at any point along the line.

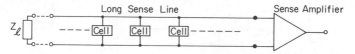

FIGURE 2.13-1 Long sense line with many storage cells.

The sense amplifier is connected to one end (Fig. 2.13-1), but what do we do with the other end of the line? Ultimately there must be a compromise between length of line, sense signal amplitude, and noise. We examine only some fundamental properties.

In the general case of a long sense line, a single cell read at any point sends out equal amplitude sense signals in both directions, one propagating toward the sense amplifier and one propagating toward the opposite end. The polarity of these two signals with respect to each other depends on whether the storage cell appears as a series or parallel voltage (or current) generator. Magnetic devices are series voltage generators as illustrated in Fig. 2.13-2. For long, ideal transmission lines, the two sections of the sense line each appear initially as a resistor of value Z_0, shown dashed. The total induced signal v_s is divided equally on the two ends, giving a positive voltage of $v_1 = v_s/2$ traveling toward the right (sense amplifier end) and a negative voltage $v_2 = -v_s/2$ traveling toward the left. If the load Z_l properly terminates the latter, a signal of amplitude $v_s/2$ is obtained (i.e., only half the total induced signal). If Z_l is made to be a short circuit, v_2 will be negatively reflected, giving a voltage $v_2' = +v_s/2$ traveling toward the sense amplifier. The latter signal will arrive at the sense amplifier at a time $2t_2$ later than v_1 as in Fig. 2.13-2b, where t_1 and t_2 are the electrical delays from the ends of the line to the cell in question. For very long sense lines, the second signal would be undesirable because it only increases the delay and does not add to the peak signal. If the line is made shorter, or if the peaking time of the signal becomes longer than $2t_2$, the signals begin to add as in Fig. 2.13-2c. This is the familiar "rabbit ears" signal with amplitude larger than $v_s/2$ but smaller than v_s. As the line delay becomes increasingly less than the signal peaking time, the two signals overlap more and more exactly. In the limit as t_2 becomes negligible, the two signals exactly overlap, giving the full sense signal of v_s.

Unfortunately, the desire for high capacity, high speed, and low cost pushes the design toward long sense lines with fast rising signals, hence less overlap in the two signal pulses. A compromise in the sense amplifier design versus shorter lines and more drivers becomes part of the overall design. An example of the sense problem for ferrite cores is given in Section 4.7.

If the cell provides a parallel voltage source that appears across the two sense conductors, the use of $Z_l = \infty$ (open circuit) will produce the rabbit

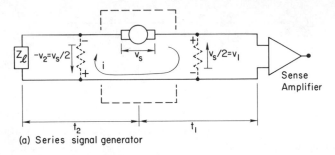

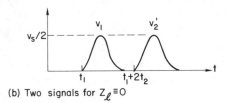

(a) Series signal generator

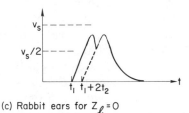

(b) Two signals for $Z_\ell \equiv 0$

(c) Rabbit ears for $Z_\ell = 0$

FIGURE 2.13-2 Signal propagation characteristics for series generator on a long line.

ears effect just described, with all the same problems. Integrated FET arrays use open circuited sense lines, but the lines are usually very short and appear more nearly as RC lines.

2.14 ULTIMATE LIMITS ON STORAGE DENSITY

Ultimate storage density and ultimate computational speed have interested researchers for years. These two fundamental matters are not totally independent, but we are concerned with storage density, approaching the subject from first principles, which neglect the practical problems.

Increasing storage density is a continuing goal of memory designers. In principle, passive devices such as that characterized by Fig. 2.3-1 could be composed of a single particle or element for storing information (e.g., magnetic spins or atomic nuclei), giving a very high storage density. However the probability of spontaneous switching of such elements due to thermal agitation is extremely large, making for storage times that are much too short for practical consideration. The spontaneous switching times can be greatly improved by using physical or logical redundancy. Both physical and logical redundancy require more particles or elements per bit, thereby reducing the density. Logical redundancy is acquired by coupling of particles through circuit connections; whereas physical redundancy achieves coupling through the physical forces of interaction within the storage medium. Since the latter is generally less complex to fabricate, we deal only with physical redundancy. Thus we now show that the probability of spontaneous switching of single elements is too large, then arguing heuristically that physical redundancy on the order of 100 coupled elements minimum is required for reliable storage. This represents approximately the ultimate limit. Using a storage element containing 10 times as many coupled elements as this minimum limit embodied in a ferrite spinel structure results in a very large storage density.

The spontaneous switching time for a single element storage cell can be derived as follows (Freiser and Marcus, 1969). Consider a memory composed of N identical and independent elements or bits. Let $P_N(t)$ be the probability that at least one stored bit has been lost (i.e., an error) within the N bits for some specified storage time t. Then the probability that no error has been made $Q_N(t)$ is given by $Q_N(t) = 1 - P_N(t)$. If $p(t)$ and $q(t)$ are the corresponding probabilities for the individual elements over the same storage time t, from elementary statistics we have

$$Q_N(t) = [q(t)]^N - [1 - p(t)]^N \qquad (2.14\text{-}1)$$

To obtain reliable storage over the specified time t, then $Q_N(t)$ must be nearly equal to 1, which requires $p(t)$ to be extremely small and also $Np(t) \ll 1$. Assuming these to be true for the moment, (2.14-1) simplifies to

$$Q_N(t)\Big|_{Np(t) \ll 1} = 1 - Np(t) + \frac{N(N-1)}{2!} p^2(t) - \cdots \qquad (2.14\text{-}2)$$

$$\approx e^{-Np(t)} \qquad (2.14\text{-}3)$$

Now if $1/\tau$ is the probability per unit of time that a single element will switch, the probability of a single element switching in the total storage time t is

$$p(t) = 1 - e^{-t/\tau} \qquad (2.14\text{-}4)$$

Since this must still be a small number, t/τ must be much less than unity, and (2.14-4) requires

$$p(t)\bigg|_{t/\tau \ll 1} = 1 - e^{-t/\tau} \approx \frac{t}{\tau} \tag{2.14-5}$$

Substituting (2.14-5) into (2.14-3) gives

$$Q_N(t) \approx e^{-Nt/\tau} \tag{2.14-6}$$

or

$$\tau = -Nt[\ln Q_N(T)]^{-1} \tag{2.14-7}$$

From these equations, we can derive the probability per unit time $1/\tau$ for a single element, and its reciprocal τ will represent the average lifetime over which spontaneous switching should *not* occur. To do this we must assume some values for the other parameter. For archival storage such as tape, a storage time of 30 years is considered adequate. If we use a tape with a capacity of $N = 10^8$ bits, $t = 30$ years $\approx 10^9$ sec, and assume $P_N(t) = 10^{-2}$ or $Q_N(t) = 0.99$, then (2.14-7) gives

$$\tau \approx \frac{-10^8 \times 10^9}{-10^{-2}} = 10^{19} \text{ sec} \tag{2.14-8}$$

$$\approx 3 \times 10^{11} \text{ years}$$

This rather long mean life expectancy would require the spontaneous switching probability for a single element to be $p(t) = t/\tau = 3 \times 10^{-10}$, an unrealistic value. The required τ for a main memory could be reduced substantially or $p(t)$ increased, since the size and storage time are both smaller for main compared to archival storage. If we assume a memory of only $N = 10^6$ bits and storage time of $t = 1$ day $\approx 9 \times 10^4$ sec, we have

$$\tau = \frac{10^6 \times 9 \times 10^4}{10^{-2}} = 9 \times 10^{12} \text{ sec}$$

$$\approx 3 \times 10^5 \text{ years}$$

and $p(t) = 9 \times 10^4/9 \times 10^{12} = 10^{-8}$.

These values are still unreasonable, and we must find some other way to reduce the switching probability. This can be done by physically coupling together many single elements into one larger cooperating unit, as occurs, for instance, in magnetic materials. Although a single electron spin has a large switching probability, the coupled unit has a smaller probability by orders of magnitude. Various arguments have been presented to explain this (Freiser and Marcus, 1969; Swanson, 1960), and Swanson has estimated that assuming thermal agitation to be the prime source of errors, a minimum of about 100 cooperating units (electron spins, dipoles) is needed at room temperature.

For some physical phenomena, 100 elements may not be sufficient to bring about the desired coupling. Let us assume that we need only 10 times this amount, or 1000 units for reliable storage, as well as space for isolating adjacent bits. We then want to determine the density that might be expected in, say, a ferrite spinel structure. The unit cell of a ferrite is about 8.4 Å on a side (Kittel, 1956). The cooperating units are the A and B sites for which there are 8 and 16 occupied, respectively, or a total of 24 metal ions or cooperating elements per unit cell. To accommodate 1000 elements would require 1000/24 = 42 unit cells, which would require a volume of approximately 25×10^3 Å^3/bit. Since we have already allowed space for separating bits within the factor of 10, the density would be the reciprocal of this, or about 4×10^{19} bits/cm^3. Though this value seems incredibly large, it should be noted that such densities are achieved in living organisms. For instance, typical bacterial DNA molecules can store on the order of 3×10^{19} bits/cm^3 (Freiser and Marcus, 1969). The major problem both in the biological systems and in any computer elements we might envision is the method of reading and writing, which has been purposely ignored. Biological systems accomplish this by reproducing an identical specimen at a given local environment according to the genetic code. The answer is hence at the same energy level as the storage and is physically inaccessible to other parts of the system. However in a computing system we would have to substantially raise the energy level of the stored information and make it accessible to other parts of the system: either the stored information would be located at some higher energy level (e.g., on paper and tapes) or it would be transcribed back to a low biological energy level within the brain of the individual who now acquires the information.

Practical limitations on storage have kept achievable densities many orders of magnitude smaller than any predictable ultimate limit (Keyes, 1969, 1972). Three major factors tend to limit both logic and memory sizes: first, losses in the form of power dissipation and the resulting difficulty in removing the heat as structures continue to diminish in size; second, losses in the form of increasing resistance, hence attentuation in the interconnecting lines as these get smaller; third, electromigration, which causes atoms to move in regions of high current densities and can lead to physical destruction of the material in such regions. Low temperature operation provides one means for reducing many of these limiting effects (Keyes et al., 1970).

3   Random Access Memory Devices and Cells

3.1 INTRODUCTION

This chapter replies on the fundamental phenomena described in Chapter 2 to devise various random access storage cells with two and three functional terminals.

The organization of a random access memory (Chapter 4) dictates the number of wires or terminals the basic storage cell must have. In 2D and $2\frac{1}{2}$D-2T organizations, two terminals or two wires are necessary as a minimum, whereas in $2\frac{1}{2}$D-3T and 3D organizations, a minimum of three wires or terminals is required. Additional wires are often desirable or even necessary to make a large array work well (e.g., noise isolation from bit/sense lines to amplifier), but they are fundamentally unnecessary. Thus any number of wires can be threaded through a magnetic core, which is used in all three types of organization. Likewise, magnetic films can have any number of wires, but because of the planar fabrication, they are more amenable to 2D and $2\frac{1}{2}$D-2T organization.

In principle, a transistor memory cell can be made with any number of terminals. However each terminal adds complexity and transistors to each individual bit, thus greatly increasing the cost and decreasing the on-chip density. We approach the cell structure in terms of the number of functional terminals available. The necessity and use of these terminals in any memory organization is discussed at length in Chapter 4.

Many phenomena and devices have been proposed for random access memory applications, but only a few have found practical applications. The major phenomena thus far studied or implemented for random access storage cells are magnetism, semiconductivity, superconductivitity, and ferroelectricity. Only the first two have found widespread usuage. Superconductivity still has potential, particularly in the form of Josephson tunneling cryotrons and investigative work continues. Ferroelectricity has an appeal because of its analogy to square loop magnetic structures, but with the advantage of planar fabrication. Much attention was devoted to this phenomenon in the 1950s and 1960s but its serious fundamental limitations were eventually revealed. This chapter covers devices employing each of these phenomena, with particular emphasis on magnetics, which dominated early and recent main memory technology, and semiconductors, which are the main new and near-future technology replacing magnetics. We spend considerable time on various transistor memory cells, to understand the fundamental tradeoffs in power, density, and speed. The infinite variety of random access cells is reduced to a few basic forms from which various perturbations can be more easily understood.

The older superconducting cryotrons, both in-line and cross-film devices, are discussed to show the similarity of the newer, faster Josephson device. A brief discussion of ferroelectric devices is included for historical interest, and to alert future inventors to potential problems in this field.

Random access read-only memories are a special case of a more general memory allowing the storage device to be much simpler. As a result, nearly every conceivable electrical device has been proposed, and many have been used, for such applications. A special section is devoted to some of the more notable read-only memory devices, past and present.

3.2 FERRITE CORE DEVICES

3.2.1 Principles of Operation and Evolution

Magnetic ferrite cores remained the dominant memory cells for about 20 years from the mid-1950s to mid-1970s. The cell itself consists of a small toroid made from pressed and subsequently fired ceramiclike magnetic ferrite material. Ideally, the material has a square BH loop as described in Section 2.6. A memory cell is made by passing two or more wires through the toroid as in Fig. 3.2-1. Let us examine such a device to see how it satisfies the fundamental requirements of Sections 2.3 and 2.4 for binary devices. Two stable states are provided by the points $+B_r$ and $-B_r$. Switching between these two is easily accomplished by controlling the polarity and amplitude of the applied current. A current of $i \geq i_c$ or $i \leq -i_c$ and subsequent removal

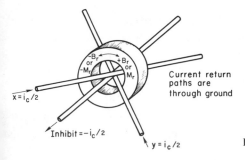

FIGURE 3.2-1 Magnetic core storage cell.

of current will switch the core into the $+B_r$ or $-B_r$, respectively. Coincident selection is accomplished by using two separate writing windings (e.g., wires x and y in Fig. 3.2-1), applying $i_c/2$ in each winding, and having only one core or one group of cores in the array residing at the intersection (coincidence) of the two windings. In 3D core memory organization, a third wire, the inhibit, is needed to cancel the x or y current for writing a "0" (see Section 4.7). Sensing is provided by the following property: upon switching from $+B_r$ (say, a stored "1") to $-B_r$ (stored "0"), the sense signal V_s is a negative pulse, whereas switching from $-B_r$ to $+B_r$ gives a positive pulse (Fig. 2.6-1). Thus sensing "0" and "1" is possible. The energy loss per unit volume is proportional to the area of the BH loop. Such a core has a well-defined threshold H_c, and this threshold makes it insensitive to disturb pulses on unselected cells. The two (2D) or three (3D) separate functional terminals are easily provided by separate windings along the toroid. Ease of having any number of separate terminals was a major advantage of core technology in its early history, since a single straight wire through the core opening serves as a single turn winding (Fig. 3.2-1). This represents the basic cell configuration used in all ferrite core memories. The various designs over the years have concentrated on reducing the size of the core for faster operation while simultaneously giving higher density, and reduction in the number of wires threaded through the core for cost reduction. The method of organizing this basic cell into a memory is considered in detail in Chapter 4. We concentrate on device and cell properties here.

3.2.2   Ferrite Core Media

Instead of ferrite, the original core memories used wound metal tape, such as 5 wraps of $\frac{1}{8}$ mil molybdenum/Permalloy 4/79%* on a ceramic bobbin (Rajchman, 1953). Such hand-made cores were much too expensive and were quickly replaced by ferrites (e.g., manganese-magnesium ferrite). This was a significant step toward reducing cost, and it allowed cores to be pressed in a mold. The evolution of ferrites from the earliest days consisted mainly of variations in the basic composition to achieve improved characteristics for ever-increasing tolerances and smaller size. To expedite fabrication, the early commercial cores were large, typically 0.080 to 0.050 in., requiring drive currents exceeding 1 A. Some manufacturers used even larger cores, in the range of 100 mils or more. A common size of second generation cores was 0.054/0.034 in. OD/ID by 0.016 in. height, strung with 32 double formex wire (0.009 in. OD) on 0.080 in. centers. Such a core required 1.1 A and 5×10^{-8} J for switching, and these rather large values were a serious problem in early memories. High speed arrays require fast rise times and the

* Permalloy = 80% nickel, 20% iron.

additional constraints of large current and power imposed severe requirements on the driving circuits. Thus the evolution of cores was toward smaller devices with lower current and power requirements, which also resulted in faster speed. The major cell parameters of importance in memory design are the drive currents, switching time, sense signal, and disturb tolerance. These are discussed in the following sections.

Ferrites are complex iron oxides with other metallic constituents. The general class of ferrites includes a wide variety of materials and crystal structures: hexagonal barium and related ferrites for high coercivity permanent magnets; orthoferrites (e.g., $GdFeO_3$) having a distorted perovskite structure; garnets, which are widely used as bubble and microwave materials; and spinels, which encompass nearly all memory core materials. The general formula for a spinel is MFe_2O_4 ($MO \cdot Fe_2O_4$), where M can be one or a combination of a wide variety of ions. For cores, the common ions are manganese, magnesium, zinc, copper, and lithium. The composition as well as the "firing" process determines all the important parameters, such as B_s, H_c, BH loop squareness, delta noise voltage (Section 4.7), temperature stability, magnetostriction, and disturb sensitivity. Typical saturation flux density ranges between roughly 1000 and 3000 G, with 2000 G being a good average value. These values are for the typical core after fabrication. The intrinsic flux density of the material is larger, but is diluted somewhat by the porosity and percentage of nonmagnetic second-phase material. Coercive force varies roughly from 1 to 10 Oe depending on the core size and switching speed desired.

3.2.3 Batch-Fabricated Core Devices

The fabrication problems associated with magnetic core devices led to the development of numerous alternatives for batch fabrication in the 1960s. The major problem is to simplify the stringing of wire through the cells and make smaller cores. Since ferrites can be molded easily into various shapes, and in principle the toroid need not be circular, a wide range of structures is possible. The design of ordinary transformers with U and I legs fitted together after the winding is in place serves as a starting point. One can easily conceive of a flat block of ferrite with posts representing the U legs of a square core. Wires can easily be placed in the channels and after all wiring is done, a top matching layer is used to complete the magnetic circuit. The waffle iron type memories (Bobeck et al., 1966) were very popular with inventors in the 1960s.

Other techniques attempted to coat wires directly with liquid ferrite much as is done in dipping ordinary candles. Very small diameter cores in the range of 0.005 in. have been produced by this technique (Brownlow and Grebe,

1967). An alternative technology with similar objectives was the plating of magnetic alloys on a metallic conductor (Higashi, 1966; Mathias and Fedde, 1969). All these alternatives did not significantly reduce the cost compared to the well-developed core plane techniques. Furthermore, the devices had numerous problems, such as poor switching characteristics in the waffle iron structures, due to the unsymmetrical magnetic circuit, applied fields, and air gaps, and none ever found significant commercial application.

3.3 FERRITE CORE SWITCHING CHARACTERISTICS

3.3.1 Switching Curves, Switching Time, and Relation to Coercive Force

The single most important parameter in the design of a ferrite memory is the core switching time. This parameter sets the core size, drive currents, final array delay, and ultimately the cost. The general "switching curve" of magnetic structures is described in Section 2.7, where it is shown that the speed of switching can be increased both by increasing the excess field and by operating in a faster mode region. This fundamental point, known *now* to be true for ferrites, was not understood in the early history of ferrite memories. This history is worthy of a brief discussion. In the early and mid-1950s it was thought that cores switched only by domain wall motion, which is a slow process. It was quickly recognized that this would greatly limit memory speed, and numerous other devices such as thin flat films and twistors were proposed as alternatives, since it was thought that they could be switched by the much faster rotational processes. There arose some speculation and controversy over the switching characteristics of cores, centering mainly around the question of whether the geometry of a toroid would permit rotational-type switching. The arguments against this were based on an assumed model of switching that would give large self-demagnetizing fields during switching, hence favoring domain wall motion. Experimental studies required generation and measurement of nanosecond pulses of high current and sensing of millivolt signals also in the nanosecond range. Such techniques became available in the late 1950s and the situation was clarified in 1958 when Shevel (1959) demonstrated the existence of three distinct modes of switching in various common ferrite cores. The measurements of the switching constant (inverse slope of switching curve—Section 2.7) versus applied field appear in Fig. 3.3-1. This spurred many subsequent studies of the switching characteristics such as the switching curves of Fig. 3.3-2. The three separate straight line portions follow the same form as the general switching curve of Fig. 2.7-1. In region III, a type of coherent switching does indeed take place, but in a rather complex fashion. To understand this, consider the toroid to

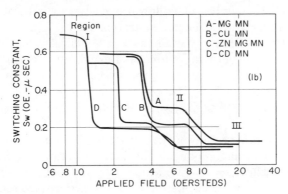

FIGURE 3.3-1 Switching constant versus applied field for four different ferrites. After Shevel, (1959).

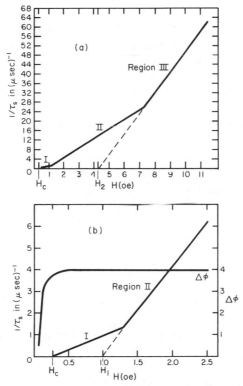

FIGURE 3.3-2 Switching curve for ferrite ($Mn_{0.57}Mg_{0.27}Zn_{0.24}Fe_{1.94}O_4$). (*a*) Entire curve. (*b*) Lower regions I and II magnified, with amount of flux reversal $\Delta\phi$ also shown. After Gyorgy, (1960).

be composed of a number of hollow, concentric cylindrical shells of infinitesimal wall thickness. The magnetization vectors can rotate coherently and independently within each of these shells. A helical pattern results within each shell, and the magnetization follows the pattern of a helix whose pitch begins at large negative values, then approaches zero as the midpoint in the reversal process is reached. The pitch then becomes positive, increasing in the opposite direction as the switching completes to the opposite state of magnetization.

The magnetization in a given shell has a small radial component M_r, in addition to the helical components. This radial component causes a radial demagnetizing field $H_r = -4\pi M_r$ within the given shell; but since M_r exerts no force on any other shell, there is no interaction between shells. This demagnetizing field causes rapid reversal as in the case of coherent rotation within a thin film. The result is a coherent rotation within each shell. However the direction and angular velocity of the magnetization vector may vary from one shell to another. A detailed treatment of switching is given by Gyorgy (1963).

The character of region III provides only an indirect indication that rotational switching might occur and, as such, it is not completely convincing. Direct observation of any rotational processes can be made by using a core in the form of a long cylinder. A sense loop along the cylinder axis will measure the usual circumferential flux change. A sense loop wrapped circumferentially around the cylinder will detect any axial or longitudinal flux change. If there are no coherent rotational processes, the longitudinal signal should always be zero. If part of the flux switches by rotation in unison, then a net signal will result. One such measurement on an MnCr ferrite with $H_c = 1$ Oe, $B_s = 2200$ G, using 10 Oe drive field showed that at least 30% of the flux reverses by a rotational processes (Elfant, 1963).

Switching Speed Versus Coercive Force

Based on previous relationships, it is easy to show that for faster switching of cores, a larger coercive force is needed. We already know from (2.7-1) that

$$\tau_s = \frac{S_w}{H_f - H_t} \tag{3.3-1}$$

where H_f is the full-select field for the full-select current and H_t is the threshold for that straight line portion of the switching curve of interest; that is, H_t is either H_c (i.e., H_w), H_1, or H_2 in Fig. 2.7-1. For proper design in a 3D organization, it is necessary to choose the half-select field $H_f/2$, applied to each of the x and y word lines, to be less than the disturb threshold field. This disturb threshold is approximately equal to but less than H_c (we discuss this more fully shortly). Thus we need

$$\frac{H_f}{2} \lesssim H_c \tag{3.3-2}$$

or

$$II_f \approx 2H_c \tag{3.3-3}$$

Substituting this into (3.3-1) and using $H_t = H_c$ gives

$$\tau_s \approx \frac{S_w}{2H_c - H_c} = \frac{S_w}{H_c} \tag{3.3-4}$$

where now the excess field becomes H_c. To speed up the switching, τ_s must be made as small as possible. If we have chosen a material with the smallest possible switching constant, we can speed up the switching only by increasing H_c. In actual memories, the speed is brought about by an increase in H_c plus a decrease in core size, which is necessary because just increasing H_c would only increase the drive current, and this is already a problem. The full-select drive current goes approximately as

$$i_f \approx lH_f = 2H_c l \tag{3.3-5}$$

where l is the mean core diameter. For a fixed value of i_f, H_c in (3.3-5) can be increased only by decreasing l by the same amount.

A relatively fast, semicoherent mode of switching is possible, but the required drive fields generally make this mode unworkable in a coincident selection memory array. The half-select disturb field, which would typically be one-half this large drive field, would cause significant switching and would eventually destroy the stored information. Thus cores are usually relegated to the slower, domain wall motion or incoherent regions. As such, cores then generally require 100 to 300 nsec to fully reverse states. To minimize this switching time, it is desirable to apply pulses with rise times shorter than the switching time; thus the driving field is essentially constant. If the pulse is terminated too soon, the core may not have completely switched states. Hence pulse width as well as pulse amplitude is important. This is illustrated in Figs. 3.3-3 and 3.3-4. If we apply a fast rise time step function of amplitude H_a, slightly larger than H_c, the core will be operating in region I. The core will switch by domain wall motion with a signal in a sense winding similar to that of Fig. 3.3-3a. If the drive field is suddenly terminated near τ_p, the core stops switching. If the step field is reapplied later, the core continues switching very nearly as if the drive field had never been interrupted (Fig. 3.3-3b). This is what one would expect with domain wall motion at a constant velocity

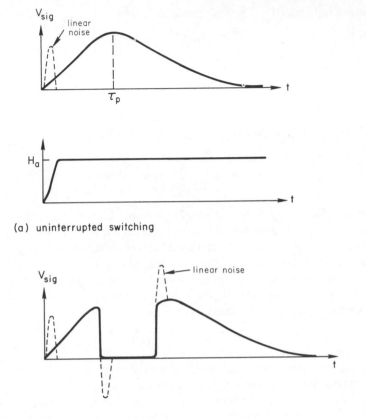

(a) uninterrupted switching

(b) interrupted switching

FIGURE 3.3-3 Sense signal obtained from ferrite core switching by domain wall motion in region I: $H_a \gtrsim H_c$.

proportional to the driving field. If the amplitude of the drive field is increased to be in region II, the situation is different. The uninterrupted switching occurs faster, as in Fig. 3.3-4a, which would be expected for incoherent rotation. However if the applied field is interrupted as in Fig. 3.3-4b, the initial portion remains as before. When the step function is reapplied, the core completes its switching by domain wall motion as evidenced by the long tail.

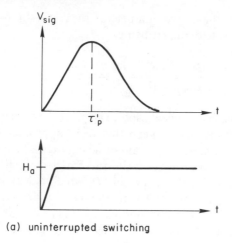

(a) uninterrupted switching

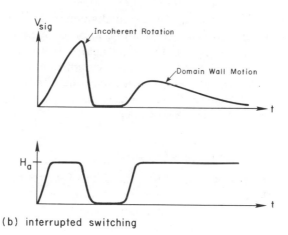

(b) interrupted switching

FIGURE 3.3-4 Sense signal obtained from ferrite core switching by incoherent rotation in region II: $H_a \gg H_c$.

3.3.2 Circumferential Drive Field of Toroid Versus Diameter

From (2.12-3) the circumferential field surrounding a circular wire is given by

$$H = \frac{0.16I}{D} \tag{3.3-6}$$

where D (in.) is the diameter of the circle at which the field is desired and is assumed to be larger than the wire diameter, and H and I are in oersteds and amperes, respectively. For large toroids of, say, 50/80 mils ID/OD, the field varies very little over these two diameters, the ratio of field at inside diameter to that at outside diameter being

$$\frac{H_{ID}}{H_{OD}} = \frac{OD}{ID} = \frac{80}{50} = 1.6 \qquad (3.3\text{-}7)$$

This is referred to as the geometrical aspect ratio. As the core is decreased in mean diameter, it is necessary to keep this ratio approximately constant to avoid disturb problems and to maintain sufficient excess field for switching. Thus a small core must have thinner walls and smaller signal. A 30 mil OD core then requires approximately a 19 mil ID, which is a typical core size. For a core size of, say, 12 mils OD with the same aspect ratio, an inner diameter of $12/1.6 = 7.5$ mils or a wall thickness of $(12 - 7.5)/2 = 2.25$ mils is required. This is about the thickness of a human hair, and such a core becomes difficult to fabricate and string into arrays. Such difficulties have limited cores to about the $13/19$ mil ID/OD range.

This variation in field over the toroid diameter places undesirable restrictions on the "excess field" that can be applied. We know from (3.3-3) that under ideal conditions, the full-select field is twice H_c and the excess field is H_c. However these conditions must be applied at the inner diameter, where the field is larger, to prevent a half-select field pulse from disturbing the inner region. Thus the excess field that switches the outer portions of the core is 1.6 times less than the ideal value.

3.3.3 Partial Switching and Disturb Characteristics

In all practical magnetic structures there exist microscopic domains of reverse magnetization in a supposedly "saturated" device. Half-select disturb pulses must be small enough not to cause these reverse domains to grow in size. Gyromagnetic effects are present with fast rise time pulses such as those encountered in memory. These gyromagnetic effects have been studied in detail for domain walls in thin films and have been found to be quite severe. Historically, such effects were uncovered in thin films some time after ferrites had long been employed in memory arrays. However the latter were then used at pulse rise times substantially greater than 100 nsec, where gyromagnetic effects are not very significant. As memory access times, hence pulse rise times, decreased, disturb characteristics became more important. The major question is, How important? Domain walls in ferrite cores are of the Bloch wall type (Fig. 3.5-4). In thin films, because of the geometry and polarity of applied fields, gyromagnetic effects are conducive to creeping, hence severe disturb characteristics. The inherent self-demagnetizing field is open flux thin films is a major factor in creeping. Coupled

and closed flux structures appear to be less susceptible, suggesting that toroidal structure is better, which is indeed the case. Furthermore, cores are used at
longer pulse rise times than open flux structures, producing less gyromagnetic
effects. Unfortunately, because of the geometry and lack of suitable techniques, domain wall structure and motion cannot be studied in cores in the
detail that is possible in thin films. As a result, the disturb characteristics of
ferrite cores represent empirical knowledge; we have little understanding of
the actual micromagnetic details. We consider some of the typical empirical
methods for measuring these disturb characteristics and some typical results.

The previous discussion (Figs. 3.3-3 and 3.3-4) demonstrated that pulse
width is quite important because it determines the total distance a domain
wall will move. Hence in characterizing the partial switching of cores, it is
imperative to make measurements over the range of pulse rise times and width
required for the intended memory design. Measurements at 5 nsec rise times
and 20 nsec pulse widths are of little value for a memory intended to have a
1 μsec access time, where both the rise time and width will exceed 100 nsec.

One common technique for presenting partial switching characteristics
is in the form of the so-called S curves, which can take several forms. The
writing characteristics as a function of pulse amplitude for a fixed rise time
and pulse width give a curve resembling that in Fig. 3.3-5. The core is reset
with a large pulse to negative saturation. A single pulse of given amplitude
and width will switch a varying amount of the core flux $\Delta\phi$ as the amplitude
is increased. A family of such curves for different pulse widths will specify the
field amplitude required to switch the core (typically the 90% point) within

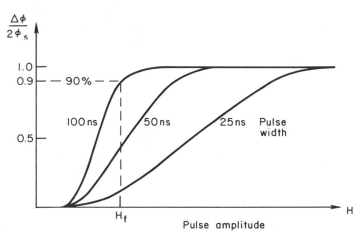

FIGURE 3.3-5 Writing characteristics of cores versus pulse amplitude and width for fixed
rise and fall times.

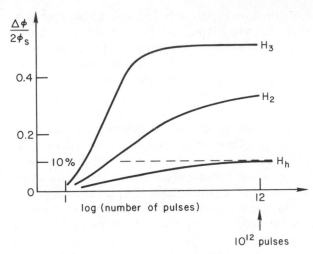

FIGURE 3.3-6 Disturb characteristics of cores illustrated by S curves for fixed pulse width (e.g., 100 nsec).

the pulse width. For instance, to achieve a required switching time of 100 nsec, a full-select field of H_f as shown would be required. It is next necessary to determine whether coincident selection will work for that core because of possible disturb switching. Any given word or core in an array must be capable of withstanding approximately 10^{12} disturb pulses. Thus we again can plot the percentage of flux switched as a function of the number of pulse disturbs between resetting of the core. A family of such curves for different pulse amplitudes but fixed rise time and the desired pulse width will give S curves like those in Fig. 3.3-6 (horizontal scale is logarithmic). The maximum half-select field H_h is usually chosen as that field for which the flux switched approaches the 10% point at large numbers of pulses, as shown. This half-select threshold as determined from the 10% disturb characteristics is roughly in the range of $0.8H_c$ but must vary with driving conditions. If these curves were measured for a pulse width of 100 nsec, then under ideal conditions, a coincident selection array would require H_h from the 10% disturb curve of Fig. 3.3-6 to be *equal* to or *less* than $0.5H_f$ from the 100 nsec switching curve of Fig. 3.3-5 to achieve 100 nsec writing time of the core, or

$$H_h \bigg|_{10\% \, \Delta\phi} \leq 0.5 H_f \bigg|_{90\% \, \Delta\phi} \qquad (3.3\text{-}8)$$

Failure to satisfy this condition indicates that we are attempting to achieve the required speed by using a large excess field that causes half-select disturbs.

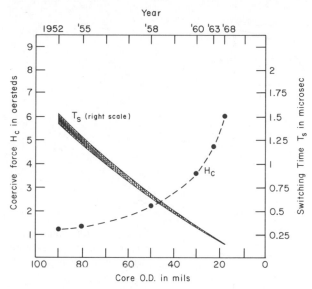

FIGURE 3.3-7 Evolutionary trend of ferrite core diameters and switching times.

We either must back off to a slower switching speed or choose a core with a larger coercive force. The larger coercive force will increase the disturb threshold H_h approximately proportionally, as well as increase the excess field. This may require the use of lithium ferrite cores instead of the more standard magnesium-manganese ferrites for higher H_c as well as smaller diameter cores, to achieve the drive fields. Serious problems have limited cores to switching times usually greater than 100 nsec. This has, in fact, been the evolutionary trend of ferrite cores, and in Fig. 3.3-7 the typical coercive force and switching time are plotted versus year, hence core diameter. The general trend over the years has been toward smaller cores, larger H_c, and faster core switching time. However the 100 nsec barrier presented some formidable restrictions on core fabrication and drive circuits that ultimately led to replacement by FET devices.

3.3.4 Sense Signal Amplitude

We wish to calculate the amplitude of sense signals in Figs. 3.3-3 and 3.3-4. The signal is given by

$$V_s = N \frac{d\phi}{dt} \times 10^{-8} \tag{3.3-9}$$

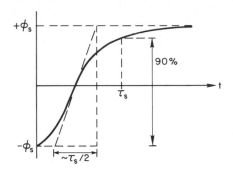

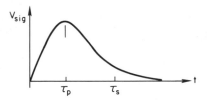

FIGURE 3.3-8 Approximate variation of flux and signal with time during domain wall switching of a ferrite core.

where V_s is in volts, ϕ in lines or maxwells, and t is in seconds. For a core wired into an array as in Fig. 3.2-1, $N = 1$ turn. A difficulty arises because the flux change with time is nonlinear, varies with driving field, and is not easily expressed analytically, as illustrated in Fig. 3.3-8. We are interested only in approximate peak values. If the switching time is taken as the 90% point of total flux change from negative to positive saturation, the peaking time τ_p is seen to occur at a point somewhat less than $\tau_s/2$. The peak signal will be given by the slope of ϕ versus t at τ_p. We can approximate this slope by using half the switching time; thus for domain wall motion

$$\left.\frac{d\phi}{dt}\right|_{\tau_p} \approx \frac{2\phi_s}{\tau_s/2} = \frac{4\phi_s}{\tau_s} \tag{3.3-10}$$

This only gives a ballpark number, depending on the actual circumstances. For faster switching modes in regions II or III of Fig. 3.3-1, the slope becomes more nearly

$$\left.\frac{d\phi}{dt}\right|_{\text{region II}} \approx \frac{2\phi_s}{\tau_s} \tag{3.3-11}$$

In most cases the actual value lies between these two approximations. Let us calculate these two values for some typical core parameters. If we are given the saturation flux density, diameters, and height of the core, the cross-sectional area is found to be

$$A = \left(\frac{OD - ID}{2}\right)H \tag{3.3-12}$$

where OD = outside diameter,
$\quad ID$ = inside diameter
$\quad H$ = height.

The change in flux is

$$2\phi_s = 2B_s A \tag{3.3-13}$$

We assume the switching time τ_s is given. Hence the induced signal from (3.3-10) is

$$V_s = \frac{4\phi_s}{\tau_s} \times 10^{-8} = \frac{4B_s A}{\tau_s} \times 10^{-8} \tag{3.3-14}$$

where V_s is in volts, B_s in gauss, A in square centimeters, and τ_s in seconds. For τ_s in nanoseconds and V in millivolts, (3.3-14) becomes

$$V_s = \frac{4B_s A}{\tau_s} \times 10^4 \tag{3.3-15}$$

with $B_s A$ in lines. Some typical values for an *assumed* B_s = 2000 G and τ_s = 200 nsec are given in Table 3.3-1. As the core size decreases, of course, the signal decreases, and this was the historical evolutionary path. At the same time, the array noise induced primarily from the rise and fall time of the applied drive fields (dashed lines in Fig. 3.3-3) becomes a more significant

TABLE 3.3-1 Approximate Sense Signals From Cores[a]

Core Dimensions[b] (mils)			$2\phi_s$ (lines)	$\dfrac{2\phi_s}{\tau_s/2} \times 10^4$ (mV)	$\dfrac{2\phi_s}{\tau_s} \times 10^4$ (mV)
OD	ID	Height			
50	30	12	3.1	310	155
31	19	9	1.4	140	70
21	13	6	0.62	62	31

[a] B_s = 2000 G, N = 1, $OD/ID \approx 1.6$, τ_s = 200 nsec.
[b] Actual core sizes vary among manufacturers.

problem. However the noise peaks generally do not coincide with the signal peak. By the use of a strobing circuit, the signal can be sensed within a narrow time window near the actual signal peak, thereby giving an improved signal to noise ratio.

3.4 OPEN FLUX PATH, THIN MAGNETIC FILM DEVICES

Thin magnetic films have found only very limited commercial applications, yet they received, perhaps, more detailed study than any previous technology. Despite these efforts, historically they proved to be an enigma, and there were many unforeseen problems. These difficulties have a direct bearing on cell and array design, fundamentally important aspects in all memory designs, which often are poorly understood. Because of this and the unique role films have played in the history of memory hardware (see Section 1.2), they are discussed here in some detail.

3.4.1 Principles of Operation

It was recognized early in the 1950s that significant cost reduction and density improvement could be obtained if a planar magnetic stucture could be achieved. The simplest planar structure would require a cell with an air gap to allow simple fabrication of the conductors. To understand this, suppose we start with a toriod having a very small effective air gap. To make the structure planar, we must unbend it to form a bar or rod for which the physical air gap has become quite large. We know from Section 2.6 and especially Fig. 2.6.2 that a large self-demagnetizing field H_D will shear the device BH loop. If H_D is a significant fraction of the coercive field H_c, a coincidently selected device will be difficult to operate. Thus it is necessary to reduce H_D to the smallest feasible value. If the length of our assumed rod in the direction of magnetization is made much larger than the radius, H_D gets smaller and smaller, approaching zero in the limit. Thus we can design a planar, open flux path structure with a nonsheared BH loop as is required. However the sense signal that is induced in a coil around the bar will be directly proportional to the area or square of the radius. For a fixed length bar, as H_D is reduced by reducing R, the penalty is a reduction in sense signal. An alternative is to hold R fixed and increase the length to reduce H_D. This approach is possible, but the density suffers from large cell size. Hence a compromise between cell size, magnetic characteristics, and sense signal is necessary.

In all flat, open flux path magnetic devices, this conflict between large sense signal and small self-demagnetizing field imposes some severe limitations on the density of such structures. Thus the first consideration in these devices is twofold: H_D and sense signal. Next we must deal with the switching and disturb characteristics. Ideally, the long thin bar postulated should be an ellipsoid of revolution, either a prolate or oblate ellipsoid. In such a case the self-demagnetizing field would be the same at all points within the device. For the small devices and fabrication techniques available, the structures are far from ellipsoids and in fact have more nearly square cross sections. As a result, there occur at the edges very large, local self-demagnetizing fields, which give rise to small edge domains of reverse magnetization. These effects and the resulting creeping phenomena are detailed later in Sections 3.5 and 3.6.

The practical consequences of an open flux structure typically result in a planar cell resembling that in Fig. 3.4-1. The films can be batch deposited onto a suitable substrate, after which the drive conductors can also be batch fabricated using photolithographic techniques. In fact, the early development of photolithography, now so important in semiconductor technology, was initially motivated by applications for thin films and cryotron cells. The magnetization vector **M** will always remain primarily in the plane of the film. If any $\mathbf{M}_z$ component normal to the film is encountered, it experiences a very large self-demagnetizing factor of $D_c = 1$ and a field

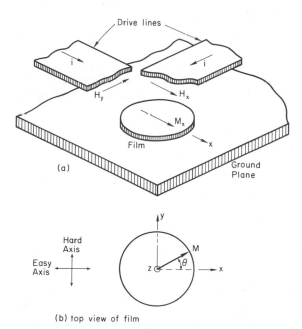

FIGURE 3.4-1   Open flux path, thin film cell structure.

given by H_D (Oe) $= M_z$ (G). This is orders of magnitude larger than the in-plane self-demagnetizing factor, hence we assume that the z component is always quite small.

The approximate self-demagnetizing field at the *center* of a thin circular film is given by (2.6-13). Assuming a Permalloy film of thickness $T = 1$ kÅ, residual flux density of $B = 10$ kG, and two different diameters of $d = \frac{1}{32}$ and $\frac{1}{16}$ in., the self-demagnetizing fields are 1.0 and 0.5 Oe, respectively. Typical coerciver forces are 2 to 4 Oe—which are not very much larger than H_D. This shows more explicitly the fundamental dilemma of thin films indicated earlier. For high speed and high density, we want a small coercive force and small diameter. A small diameter gives too large a self-demagnetizing field. This could be reduced by reducing the thickness, but then the coercive force increases and, more important, the sense signal deteriorates from an already marginal value (Section 3.5). Thus the density of such open flux path structures is limited by fundamental constraints, quite unlike that of such technologies as semiconductors, which are limited by photolithography and power dissipation.

A degree of freedom is available in this planar cell that was not possible in toroidal cores; namely, magnetic fields can be applied in orthogonal directions along the film plane. These directions are usually the easy and hard axes as indicated in Fig. 3.4-1b, with the corresponding in-plane magnetic fields H_x and H_y in Fig. 3.4-1a. Originally this was believed to be a major advantage, since orthogonal fields, combined with the necessity of in-plane magnetization only, are conductive to a rotational switching mode as discussed in Section 3.5. However partial switching and creeping effects precluded orthogonality from being a major advantage.

Fundamentally, a thin film works much like a core in that a half-select current in one conductor is insufficient to cause reversal. However a co-incidence of two half-select currents in the orthogonal lines is sufficient to cause reversal. One different and major disadvantage is that the "half-select" currents must differ quite significantly in amplitude. Because of "half-select" disturb problems along bit lines, the bit current that produces fields along the easy axis must be quite small; thus the word current must be larger, to achieve switching. This requirement has a profound influence on the overall memory organization as discussed in Section 4.8.

3.4.2 Thin Magnetic Film Media

One of the most difficult and enigmatic problems to plague the early history of thin film memories was the properties of the nickel-iron media. The alloys are so sensitive to the fabrication procedures that supposedly identical films prepared by different experimenters often had widely differing characteristics.

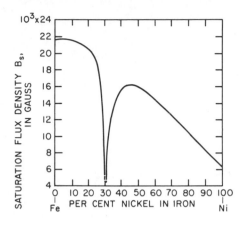

FIGURE 3.4-2 Saturation flux density of bulk nickel-iron alloy at 20°C. After Bozorth (1951, p. 109).

This is not surprising when one realizes that the films are so thin, typically 1000 Å, that the substrate surface, surface preparation, impurities, method of deposition, and so on, all impart some character to the film. As a result, many conflicting results are no doubt the artifact of some unknown fabrication difference.

To achieve the small self-demagnetizing factors already alluded to, it is necessary to use very thin films in the range of approximately 800 to 2000 Å. The required surface uniformity precludes the use of ferrites or any other particulate media. Rather, metallic alloys deposited by evaporation, electrodeposition, or sputtering are quite suitable and have been widely investigated and used. Nickel-iron alloys give quite useful parameters. Figure 3.4-2 shows the saturation flux density of bulk nickel-iron alloys as a function of the percentage of nickel, at room temperature. These values are quite representative of good quality thin films as well, since B_s is not very fabrication dependent. Film thickness beings to cause a decrease in the saturation magnetization only when the films become very thin, on the order of 100 Å (Pugh, 1963). Note that for pure iron and pure nickel, the saturation flux densities are

$$B_{\text{iron}} \approx 21,600 \text{ G} \qquad \text{and} \qquad B_{\text{nickel}} \approx 6200 \text{ G} \qquad (3.4\text{-}1)$$

The alloy flux density is not a linear combination of these two values because of the gradual crystal structure changes. Iron and nickel are body and face centered cubic, respectively.

Most of the other important parameters, such as coercive force H_c, anisotropy field H_k, and magnetostriction, are quite process sensitive. The coercivity of thin films depends on the thickness, composition, deposition parameters, and annealing. Wall motion coercive force in any real sample is

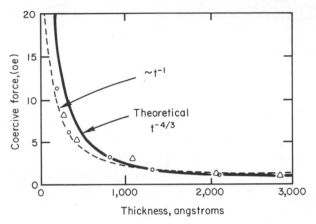

FIGURE 3.4-3   Wall motion coercive force (easy axis) versus thickness for 81% Ni-19% Fe films. After Tiller and Clark, (1958).

a very complex and poorly understood quantity. Experimental evidence suggests that it is mainly a function of film thickness (for $t < \approx 3000$ Å) and also a function of the *local* anisotropy. However the latter varies with local strains, impurities, composition, and any other effects that experimenters can invent to explain anomalies and inconsistencies. Neel (1956) derived the theoretical dependence of coercive force on film thickness to be the so-called $\frac{4}{3}$ law given by

$$H_c = \frac{C}{t^{4/3}} \qquad (3.4\text{-}2)$$

where C must be determined experimentally. More often the exponent is smaller than $\frac{4}{3}$, being more nearly $\frac{3}{4}$ or 1. In the experimental example appearing in Fig. 3.4-3, the 81% Ni–19% Fe films behave more nearly as t^{-1} compared to the theoretical $t^{-4/3}$ also shown. The latter has a proportionality constant of $C = 2.34 \times 10^4$ Oe-Å. A composition of 80% Ni–17% Fe–37% Co gives a roughly similar variation (Bradley, 1963). However the theoretical $\frac{4}{3}$ law was derived for Bloch walls, and it is known that as the thickness descreases well below roughly 1000 Å, cross-tie and eventually Neel walls are dominant. Theoretically H_c should be independent of thickness for Neel walls, but this quantity is very complex in between. This statement tends to be supported by the experimental results in Fig. 3.4-4, where the Bloch to cross-tie transition occurs near $t = 750$ Å. Above this value, the thickness variation of H_c is much as expected, but below this transition it is quite complex. Then we need to know how we can explain

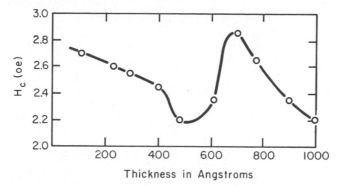

FIGURE 3.4-4 Wall motion coercive force (easy axis) versus thickness for permalloy films. After Middlehoek, (1961).

Fig. 3.4-3, which does not show similar anomalies. This question remains unanswered.

The anisotropy field H_k is quite sensitive to film stresses, either internal or induced by the substrate. Also the composition and impurities, especially stress-relieving additives, and annealing have a significant influence. Moreover, H_k is essentially independent of film thickness provided that thicker films do not induce stress. One typical example is given in Fig. 3.4-5 for compositions near zero magnetostriction. Typical values of H_k are between 2 and 10 Oe. The value of H_k can be increased by varying the angle of incidence of the evaporation vapor. The value shown is for normal (90°) incidence.

The magnetostriction constant is an extremely important parameter for practical film arrays. A large magnetostriction constant makes the film parameters quite sensitive to unavoidable stresses incurred during fabrication. The magnetostriction constant is near zero in the 80–83% nickel range, and Fig. 3.4-5 shows its variation versus composition for one set of film fabrication parameters. Also shown is the easy axis dispersion δ, which has a minimum of about 1° for compositions in the range of 80% Ni–20% Fe. More typical values are $\pm 3°$ for practical films. The exact values of all parameters vary somewhat for different fabrication procedures and variables such as substrate roughness, substrate cleaning process, substrate temperature (vapor deposition), angle of incidence, bath additives (electroplating), and many others. This is a source of much consternation, necessitating the careful measurement of parameters at all stages. Local composition gradients can and do give rise to significant variations capable of influencing switching behavior. As previously indicated, a commonly used alloy is Permalloy, which is 80% Ni–20% Fe. The major reason is the near-zero

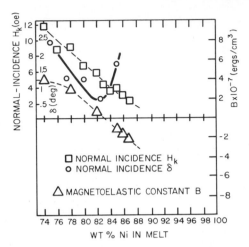

FIGURE 3.4-5 Evaporated film parameters for compositions near zero magnetostriction, substrate $T \approx 200°C$, $t \approx 1000$ Å. After Smith 1959, (1961); Smith et al., (1960).

magnetostriction constant. Other secondary advantages of this composition are that reasonable values of the other important parameters can be obtained, namely

$$\left.\begin{array}{l} B_s \approx 10{,}000 \text{ G} \\ H_c \approx 1 \text{ to } 5 \text{ Oe} \\ H_k \approx 2 \text{ to } 5 \text{ Oe} \\ \text{Easy axis dispersion } \delta \sim \pm 3° \end{array}\right\} \text{Permalloy}$$

3.5   THIN FILM SWITCHING CHARACTERISTICS

3.5.1   Quasi-Static Switching Processes in Thin Films

Ideal Case

In the early history of thin films, it was believed that because of the film geometry and capability of applying orthogonal fields, the devices could exhibit switching behavior similar to that of single domain particles. Under this assumption, very fast rotational switching would be expected, which could out perform ferrite cores by *at least* an order of magnitude. This improvement was found to be possible for certain conditions, but ultimately it was not feasible for random access cells. We consider the ideal quasi-static or low frequency switching behavior of films here, high frequency pulse switching afterward, and domain wall creeping and the influence of all these on cell design in Section 3.6.

The Stoner-Wohlfarth (1948) single domain theory is directly applicable. For a uniaxial thin films with easy axis in the x direction as in Fig. 3.4-1b, stable states exist for the orientation of the magnetization with any given applied field. However, switching of **M** to a different orientation can take place when a certain critical condition is reached. This critical condition can be shown to be

$$H_x^{2/3} + H_y^{2/3} = H_k^{2/3} \tag{3.5-1}$$

where $H_k = 2K/M_s$ is the anisotropy field. If there is shape anisotropy, it adds to H_k. The locus of points expressing this critical condition is known as the critical curve or switching asteroid (Fig. 3.5-1). The magnetization position for any applied fields is obtained by drawing tangents to the asteroid. For instance, if **M** is initially in the $+x$ direction and fields H_{x1} and H_{y1} are applied, the film magnetization will rotate to position M_1, which is tangent to the asteroid near the left side. If H_{y1} is held constant while H_x is increased to H_{x2}, then assuming that this combined field just barely exceeds the critical field H_k, M switches to the $-x$ direction and will be rotated in the position M_2 as long as the fields are applied. Removal of the fields will allow M_2 to relax to the $-x$ axis.

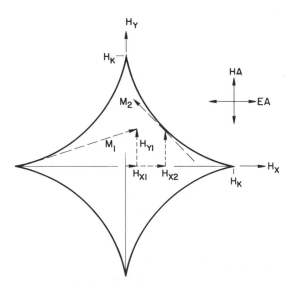

FIGURE 3.5-1 Critical switching curve for ideal, single domain, thin, film.

This idea model is based on the assumption of pure rotational switching. The easy direction *BH* loop is "square" with a coercive force of H_k, and the hard axis loop is a straight line with a saturation field of H_k.

Nonideal Characteristics

The idealized characteristics given above would be highly desirable for a random access cell. Unfortunately these characteristics do not exist in any real film. The easy axis *BH* loop has a coercive force considerably less than H_k, which presents serious cell design problems. The hard axis loop for a relatively good quality film and moderate drive field can approximate the ideal case, but with a rounding near saturation. However, the hard axis loops are usually open, as in Fig. 3.5-2. Another problem that arises for hard axis fields is the tendency for the film to split up into a multidomain structure when it is saturated in the hard direction and the field is removed. Both this problem as well as easy axis switching are compounded because a real film also has a distribution of easy axis. Rather than one well-defined easy axis, each local region of the film can have a slightly different easy axis orientation. In fact, it is this easy axis dispersion that gives rise to the open loop in the hard direction. This dispersion in good quality films is typically $\delta = \pm 3°$.

The easy axis switching and low value of H_c can be understood as follows. In all nonideal open flux structures, assumed initially to be saturated in the

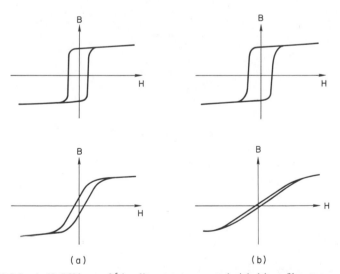

FIGURE 3.5-2   A 60 *BH* loop of $\frac{5}{8}$ in. diameter evaporated nickel-iron film: top = easy axis, bottom = hard axis. (*a*) 79% Ni-21% Fe, $t = 2760$ Å, $H_c = 1.5$ Oe, $H_k = 4.0$ Oe, $B_s = 10{,}270$ G, $M_s = 8.13 \times 10^5$ A/m. (*b*) 52% Ni-48% Fe, $t = 5160$ Å, $H_c = 1.98$ Oe, $H_k = 11.0$ Oe, $B_s = 14{,}830$ G, $M_s = 1.176 \times 10^6$ A/m.

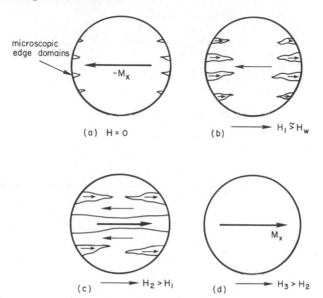

FIGURE 3.5-3 Approximate domain wall switching in thin films by slowly increasing easy axis field.

$-x$ direction, there exist edge domains of reverse magnetization as illustrated in Fig. 3.5-3a. If a slowing increasing $+H_x$ is applied at some field amplitude H_w, these edge domains start increasing in size from both edges (Fig. 3.5-3b). This field at which wall motion just starts is known as the wall motion threshold H_w and is less than the coercive field; that is $H_w < H_c$ (Methfessel et al., 1961a). Eventually some domains from opposite sides join in the center region (Fig. 3.5-3c). Thereafter, transverse motion of the domains walls in the $\pm y$ direction takes place to complete the switching (Fig. 3.5-3d). Such behavior is observed for films of all thicknesses and compositions of practical interest, although the value of H_w may vary. The same behavior, only more exaggerated, is observed with fast rising pulses as detailed in Section 3.6. Each successive magnetic state in Fig. 3.5-3 requires a small but nonzero increase in the applied field. This is partly due to the small but nonzero skew of the BH loop by the self-demagnetizing field (e.g., Fig. 2.6-2), partly to local stresses, inhomogeneities, and so on, which cause the domain walls to hang up, and partly to the presence of a small but finite energy stored within the domain wall. This wall separating the domains of reverse magnetization can be one of three types; a Bloch, cross-tie, or Neel wall (Fig. 3.5-4). The type and number of cross-ties per unit length vary with the film thickness.

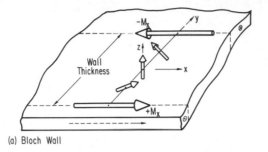

(a) Bloch Wall

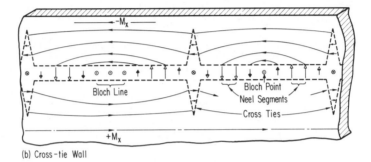

(b) Cross-tie Wall

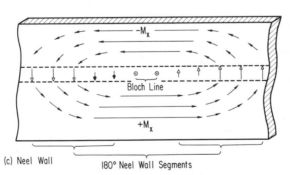

(c) Neel Wall   180° Neel Wall Segments

FIGURE 3.5-4   Schematic of three major wall types in thin films.

As a result of the switching behavior of reverse edge domains at low fields, the ideal, rotational critical curve of Fig. 3.5-1 must be modified for any real film. For the ideal critical curve, the film magnetization after removal of any external field can be in one of only two possible states; namely, the entire film is in either the $+x$ or the $-x$ direction. In other words, the critical curve separates two well-defined regions of irreversible, 180° switching. Since for the

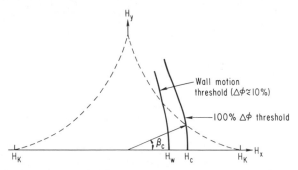

FIGURE 3.5-5 Quasi-static wall motion threshold curve with relationship to 100% $\Delta\phi$ and ideal critical curves.

real case there are essentially an infinite number of states of partial magnetization reversal (Methfessel et al., 1961b), any critical or threshold curve must specify the *final state* the film will have. *This is extremely important and is a source of endless confusion.* We always *start* with an *initially saturated film* for the *initial state*, but we consider threshold curves for various final states. If we modify the ideal low frequency critical curve to that of a real film, assuming that the final state will be 180° reversal of essentially 100% of M_s, the curve will be similar to that of Fig. 3.5-5 shown solid. Assuming a negligible self-demagnetization field, the complete reversal for fields along the easy axis will require an amplitude H_c as shown, where $H_c < H_k$. For a field at an angle to the easy axis, the real threshold crosses the ideal curve at some angle β_c. Typical values of critical angles β_c are 10° to 15° for the 100% $\Delta\phi$ threshold (dc) (Middlehoek, 1962). For fields at an angle $0 \leq \beta \leq \beta_c$, the film switches entirely by wall motion of the type represented in Fig. 3.5-4. For $\beta > \beta_c$, fields larger than H_k are required to reverse 100% of $\mathbf{M}$ to the opposite direction. As the applied field becomes more aligned in the hard direction, a point is reached where 100% of $\mathbf{M}$ can no longer be switched; rather, a multidomain state would result for a smaller easy axis component of the applied field. Hence the curve is asymptotic in the y direction as shown. This effect results from local easy axis and anisotropy dispersion within the film.

Unfortunately our new critical curve now takes on a new meaning. Whereas previously the ideal rotational curve allowed us to find the angle of rotation of $\mathbf{M}$ for any applied field by the use of tangents to the asteriod, *no such simple switching occurs in real films.* For fields applied at an angle greater than β_c, with amplitude corresponding to the ideal curve, 180° rotation of all the magnetization cannot occur. We can quickly deduce that some of the magnetization will reverse; hence a partially switched film must be the final state.

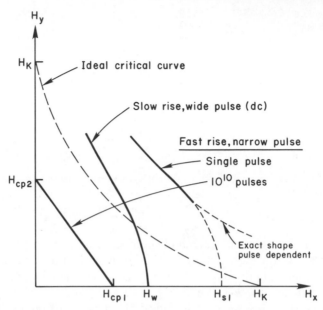

FIGURE 3.5-6   Effective switching threshold for onset of irreversible flux change ($\Delta\phi \gtrsim 10\%$) caused by fast rise time, narrow pulse fields.

This is indeed the case, but the domain configuration and switching behavior are complex. The net result is that if we slowly increase the applied field at some angle $\beta > \beta_c$, *partial reversal* will occur initially by rotation at H_k and finally the remaining reversal will occur by wall motion of the edge domains at a larger field. Unfortunately, fast rise time, narrow pulses produce additional effects that must be included. These effects can be interpreted and presented in several ways. One common approach is to essentially include the additional effects within the threshold, so that a new *effective threshold* is obtained. Several cases are illustrated in Fig. 3.5-6. If a fast rise time ($< \approx 100$ nsec), narrow pulse is applied to a saturated film, the rise time will attempt to decrease the effective threshold; but the pulse width may have insufficient time or energy to cause a measurable amount of wall movement. In such a case, the effective threshold may be larger than the previous quasi-static threshold. The latter is essentially the threshold for a slow rising, very wide pulse. If a large number of fast rising, narrow pulses are applied, their accumulated effects may cause substantial wall motion, hence the amplitude will have to be decreased to prevent creeping. The effective threshold is thus reduced as shown. Since the threshold amplitude depends on a summation of the individual effects of the rise time, fall time, and pulse width, these curves must be made at the pulse shape to be used in the memory design. This is always true.

Another way of characterizing the threshold fields is to assume that the quasi-static field remains fixed and include the separate external field due not only to pulse amplitude, but also to the gyromagnetic effects during rise time and fall time. A better understanding of wall motion and creeping results, although one must still resort to measurements with the intended pulse shape to obtain the necessary characteristics for cell design.

Insofar as memory cell design is concerned, we can conclude from the discussion that the ideal switching asteroid of Fig. 3.5-1 has very little utility. However it does serve as a point of departure for understanding real films. We saw some ways in which the ideal asteroid can be modified to be more useful in memory design. In the final analysis, the required pulse characteristics reduce to the S curves, such as those for ferrites in Fig. 3.3-6, obtained for the pulse shape of interest. The threshold curves of Fig. 3.5-6 can be obtained from these, if desired. Such S curves for films are considered in Section 3.6.

3.5.2 Dynamic Reversal and Switching Curves

As indicated previously, it was originally thought, or perhaps hoped, that thin films could be switched in a rotational mode, with a switching time of a few nanoseconds. This provided a very attractive alternative to the inherently slower ferrite cores. Rotational switching can be achieved in isolated devices, but large drive fields are required. In a memory cell, the rather severe disturb sensitivity of thin films precludes the use of large drive fields, and only moderate switching speed is feasible.

To understand dynamic reversal, we can use the quasi-static behavior of Fig. 3.5-6 as a guide. We saw that for a slowly rising dc field just slightly larger than H_k applied at some angle β, the magnetization first rotates, then forms a ripple pattern, and finally completes the switching by wall motion. If the slowing rising field is now replaced by a fast rise time pulse of amplitude just slightly larger than H_k, the quasi-static picture leads us to expect a similar process to take place, namely, fast rotation followed by slower wall motion. This is precisely what is experimentally observed, as shown in Fig. 3.5-7a.* Both the easy and hard axes sense signals show that for a drive field just slightly larger than H_k, the magnetization initially begins to rotate, as evidenced by the initial spike signals. Very quickly, however, the films degenerates into a wall motion mode as evidenced by the long, slow tail on the easy axis signal and essentially the disappearance of the hard axis signal.

---

* Historically, the pulse measurements were made first; the quasi-static model followed two years later.

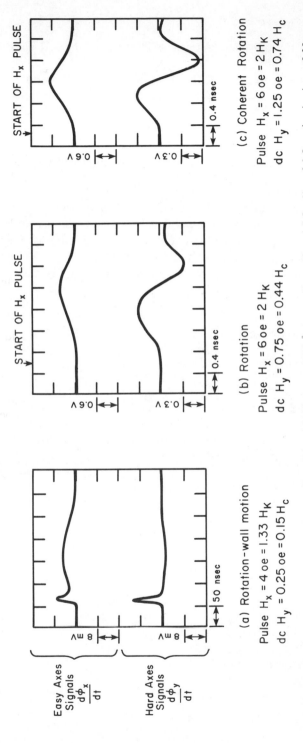

FIGURE 3.5-7 Pulse switching of thin magnetic film: 80% Ni-20% Fe, $t = 1500$ Å, 1 cm × 1 cm, $H_c = 1.7$ Oe, $H_k = 3.0$ Oe, pulse rise time ≈ 0.35 nsec. After Dietrich et al., (1960).

180

The total switching time is several hundred nanoseconds, as would be expected for wall motion.

When both the easy axis pulse and hard axis dc bias fields are increased, the switching process becomes faster and faster (Fig. 3.5-7b, c). It is speculated that the switching in Fig. 3.5-7b is a incoherent process because it is slower than the switching in Fig. 3.5-7c. However verification of this is difficult. Since the hard axis field is a dc bias, the initial and final states of **M** are at some angle to the easy axis. The pulse rise time was in the range of 0.35 nsec, and Fig. 3.5-7c indicates that the flux change occurs only slightly slower than this. The small but finite delay between the start of the pulse field to the start of the flux change is more pronounced in Fig. 3.5-7b. If we measure the reversal time as the total time from start of pulse to end of the sense signal, we find in Fig. 3.5-7c a value of less than 2 nsec, but this required a pulse field of $2H_k$ and a hard axis bias. The following conclusions can be drawn: the ideal rotational model is not valid; a drive field slightly larger than H_k produces slow, rotation-wall motion switching; fast rotational switching can be achieved but requires large driving fields on the order of $2H_k$ or more.

Switching Curves

Thin films can be characterized by switching curves of the type described in Section 2.7. Since orthogonal fields can be applied, however, there is now an additional degree of freedom. One common method for including this is to plot $1/\tau_s$ versus the easy axis drive field for various hard axis dc fields, as in Fig. 3.5-8. Three distinct regions are present, suggesting the three previous processes of domain wall motion, incoherent rotation, and coherent rotation. In the high field region at a hard axis field of $H_y = 0.333$ H_k and an excess field of approximately $(H - H_t) \approx 0.5$ $H_k \approx 1$ Oe., $1/\tau$ is 40×10^6 sec^{-1}. From (2.7-1), this gives an approximate switching constant of

$$S_w = \frac{1 \text{ Oe-sec}}{40 \times 10^6} \approx 0.025 \text{ Oe-}\mu\text{sec}$$

This is an order of magnitude smaller than ferrites; hence we expect the relatively fast switching at high fields as previously shown. At smaller drive fields, the speed is quickly lost.

Such curves are valuable for a fundamental understanding of film switching, but they are not very useful for cell design. In random access memory operation, the typical writing sequence is: apply hard axis field; apply easy axis field; remove hard axis field, remove easy axis field. The steps must be in that order, and the total cell writing time is the time to reach the final reversed state with **M** along the easy axis. The switching curves of Fig. 3.5-8 give only the first part of the write sequence and tell us nothing about how the film reaches the final state.

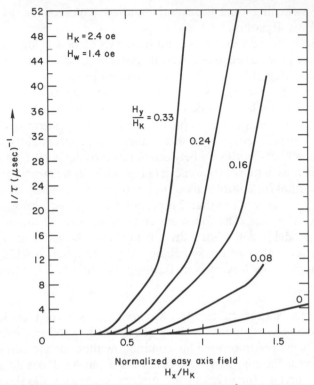

FIGURE 3.5-8   Switching curve for 80% Ni-20% Fe film, 1600 Å thick, for various normalized hard axis bias fields H_y/H_k. After Olson and Pohm, 1958).

3.5.3   Sense Signal

The sense signal can be calculated in a manner somewhat similar to that for ferrite cores (Section 3.3.4). There are two important differences, however. First, we can wind a sense coil to sense the easy axis, the hard axis, or any combination of flux change. Second, since films switch much faster in all modes, it is possible to have the time change in flux nearly follow the rising amplitude of the applied pulse, especially for rise times greater than roughly 5 nsec. However the tracking of the flux change with applied field is non-linear as the rise time varies. Both the point at which the peak $d\phi/dt$ occurs and its value are variable. Hence evaluation of the peak signal presents the same type of problem encountered with ferrites. As an approximation, we assume that the signal peaking time τ_p occurs at one half the field amplitude rise time (best case) and that the slope is

$$\left.\frac{d\phi}{dt}\right|_{\tau_p=\tau_R/2} = \frac{2\phi_s}{\tau_R} \tag{3.5-2}$$

TABLE 3.5-1   Ideal Sense Signal Amplitude
for Permalloy Thin Films[a]

Diameter		$2\phi_s$	V_s (peak)
cm	in.	(line)	(mV)
1	0.4	0.2	200
0.1	40×10^{-3}	0.02	20
0.01	4×10^{-3}	0.002	2

[a] $B_s = 10^4$ G, $t = 1000$ Å, assuming $2\tau_p = \tau_R = 10$ nsec.

or

$$V_s\bigg|_{\tau_p = \tau_R/2} = \frac{2B_s A}{\tau_R} \times 10^{-8} \tag{3.5-3}$$

where V_s is in volts, B_s in gauss, cross-sectional area A in square centimeters, and pulse rise time τ_R in seconds.

The sense signal using (3.5-3) is given in Table 3.5-1 for a Permalloy film 1000 Å thick, assuming $\tau_R = 2\tau_p = 10$ nsec, and various values of film diameter. It can be seen that a film of 0.004 in. diameter gives a very small (2 mV) signal. This film is large compared to common FET cell sizes, and the signal is relatively small. In fact, the linearly coupled noise is typically much larger, requiring balanced lines with careful fabrication control to achieve adequate signal to noise ratio.

The above analysis implicity assumes that the sense winding is perfect and links all the film flux. This is not always the case, especially as the films become small. The magnetic field external to circular thin films can be closely approximated by that of a uniformly magnetized oblate spheroid. Experimental verification and appropriate field equations are detailed in Matick (1964).

3.6   CREEPING AND ITS INFLUENCE ON THIN MAGNETIC FILM CELL DESIGN

In open flux, thin film structures, very small domains of reverse magnetization always exist on the edges of the otherwise saturated structure. An extremely small growth in the reverse domain is caused by applying a reverse pulse at an angle to the easy axis with amplitude *below* the normal dc wall motion threshold but above some other critical value. The application of millions of such pulses causes the reverse domains to gradually "creep," eventually leading to total demagnetization of the film. Creeping is thus defined as gradual demagnetization resulting from fields that are below the wall motion threshold. Creeping is most severe when a time-changing hard axis field of either polarity is applied in conjunction with a previously established easy axis field in the direction of the reverse magnetization (Hoper and Kayser, 1968; Olson and Torok, 1965).*

Creeping phenomena place limits on the maximum disturb fields that can be tolerated by unselected bits in a random access array. As a result, the full-select, or switching field of selected bits is greatly limited, giving rather slow, incoherent switching. This negates the inherent fast switching time possessed by thin films, since the speed is available only at rather large driving fields. In addition, creeping becomes worse as the bit size is reduced and as spacing to adjacent conductors is reduced. Both these characteristics have a great impact on density. In the final analysis, creeping prevented thin film arrays from achieving the orders of magnitude improvements in density and speed over ferrites that was originally envisioned. Creeping, combined with high fabrication costs, led to the gradual demise of thin films in the late 1960s.

Assuming a film to be saturated in the easy direction by a large field, the most severe creeping occurs when a time-changing field dH/dt of appropriate value is applied along the hard axis in the presence of a small, already established easy axis field that opposes the film magnetization, as in Fig. 3.6-1. If the hard axis field transition is reversed in direction (i.e., $-dH/dt$) while maintaining the same amplitude, rise time, and easy axis field, creeping will occur on its transitions also, as shown. The field parameters are assumed to be adjusted such that H_1/τ_R and H_2 are just above the creep threshold, ensuring that a large number of such pulses will eventually demagnetize the initial magnetization M_0. If the easy axis field is removed while the hard axis pulse remains, no creeping occurs (condition a in Fig. 3.6-2). However creeping can be induced by increasing the field amplitude of H_y to, say, $2H_1$. This increases dH_y/dt and induces creeping (conditions b). If the hard axis field is reduced back to H_1 and the easy axis pulse amplitude does *not* overlap with the hard axis rise and fall time, conditions c, no creeping occurs. If the easy axis pulse width is increased to overlap the hard axis transitions as in conditions d, creeping again occurs. The field parameters that characterize creeping depend on many variables that are not well understood. As a result, the designer must always measure these disturb characteristics for the given films with the given pulse rise and fall time because each film fabrication process endows the films with its own unique microcharacteristics. The S curves

---

* See Bourne et al. (1968) and Stein and Feldkeller (1967) for other creeping effects.

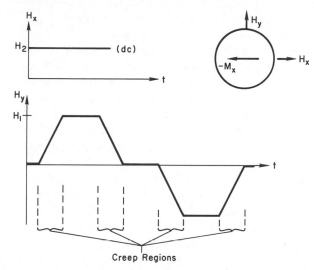

FIGURE 3.6-1 Fundamental condition for worst case creeping in thin films.

described Section 3.3.3 for ferrites are also very useful for thin films. Since two orthogonal fields are applied, and since the sequencing is most important, there are many possible ways of presenting these disturb characteristics. During a film memory "write" operation, the magnetization is first rotated into the hard direction by the word field. The easy axis bit field then determines the final state, either $+M_x$ or $-M_x$. If the hard axis word field is applied before the easy axis bit field, no dH_y/dt in the presence of an easy axis field is encountered. Once the film is rotated and the bit field is applied, however,

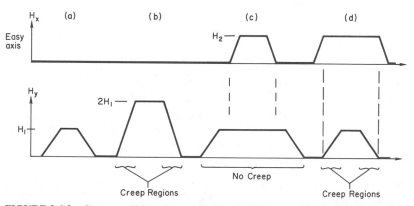

FIGURE 3.6-2 Creep conditions for pulses along both easy and hard axes of thin films.

the hard axis field must be removed before the easy axis field to obtain the final states. Thus at least one transition of dH_y/dt in the presence of an easy axis field must be encountered. Of course these writing fields do not disturb *that* bit, but they must be examined for possible disturb on other bits. In actual memory operation, the creeping occurs on half-selected films that receive an easy axis bit pulse on any given bit line but *no intentional* hard axis word pulse. However induced currents from various sources (see Section 4.8) produce undesired word currents in neighboring unselected word lines. Hence it is seldom possible to know a priori the exact disturb driving conditions.

If the memory is designed as described, so that the hard axis word field is applied before the bit field, *and if* the undesired word currents induced in neighboring lines follow the same pattern,* curves of the percentage of irreversibly switching flux $\Delta\phi/2\phi_s$ versus the logarithm of the number of pulse sequences for various pulse amplitudes are quite useful. The pulse sequence should be as close as possible to that expected in memory operation, including rise and fall times, timing, and so on. It should also be done for the correct size and shape of film element, since the self-demagnetizing field can have a significant effect as we have learned. For the case just given, the pulse sequence would resemble that of Fig. 3.6-3a. A family of curves for various easy axis bit fields and fixed hard axis field will yield S curves similar to those in Fig. 3.6-3b. Several such families for various hard axis amplitudes will provide the fundamental characteristics from which the allowable word and bit currents can be obtained in a memory array. The typical specification is to use bit and word currents that in a memory array produce only 10% irreversible flux change. Since the undesired induced word currents cannot be known until the memory array is designed, the final cell design cannot be specified without an array configuration.

The major effect of creep on the overall cell design in an array is to limit the bit current to smaller values than would normally be desired, which reduces the speed of writing. Also, because of the dependence of creep on the specific pulse parameters and sequencing, it is not feasible to present a generalized set of S curves for cell designs.† One must strike an engineering balance between the word and bit currents needed for the intended film switching speed versus the spacing of nearby conductors (density) that can be tolerated without excessive induced disturb currents. This balance becomes more significant and difficult as density and speed increase.

As a simple example, suppose we have specified the film size and required H_x and H_y at the film location to give a required speed. Then for disturb

---

* Not necessarily the case (e.g., current spreading in ground plane).

† For some specific examples of S curves see Dietrich (1962).

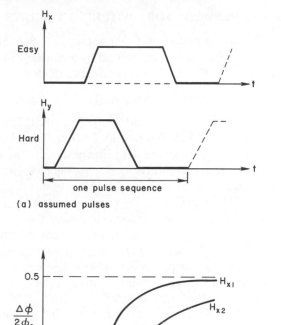

(a) assumed pulses

(b) family of S curves

FIGURE 3.6-3 S curves for representing magnetic film cell disturb characteristics.

consideration on half-selected cells, H_x will remain the same but H_y is not known. A family of curves like those in Fig. 3.6-3b with the given H_x corresponding to a 10% irreversible flux change will then specify the maximum permissible hard axis disturb field. The array conductors are then designed such that the amplitude of the required word field H_y will induce no more than the permissible disturb word field. In other words, H_y in Fig. 3.6-3b is some fraction of the actual driving word field, the fraction increasing as the density increases. Often, several iterations on the cell design, driving conditions, and array design are required. Current spreading in the ground plane (Section 4.8) and easy axis dispersion are also important considerations that can affect creep characteristics.

3.7 POWER–DELAY PRODUCT FOR SWITCHING CIRCUITS

For a given circuit configuration and technology, all switching circuits, including memory and logic, are characterized by a constant product of the power times delay over a substantial range of operation, or

$$\text{power} \times \text{delay} = K_1 \qquad (3.7\text{-}1)$$

where K_1 is in joules, power in watts, and delay in seconds. The value of K_1 varies with the technology and circuit configuration, but when these two are given, K_1 is fixed. Thus a fundamental principle results: we can increase the speed of a given switching circuit by increasing the power consumption; or inversely, we can reduce the power consumption, but only at the expense of more delay. It is desirable, of course, to keep K_1 as low as feasible. Typical approximate values for junction transistor cells are in the range of 300 pJ for early cells to tens of picojoules or less in more recent, advanced designs. FET cells are generally in the same range, but at a given design point for stable operation, they give lower power for larger delay, hence are attractive for random access main memory. Josephson junction switching circuits are capable of very low K_1, in the range of 0.005 pJ (Herrell, 1974). Advanced FET gates are capable of giving K_1 in the range of 0.1 pJ but are not yet economically feasible. The value of K_1 has continued to decrease with time for both memory and logic. Eventually some fundamental limits will be met, but when and how this will occur is difficult to determine (see Section 2.14).

In the mid-1970s two major computing systems appeared—the Amdahl 470, first delivered at year end 1975, and the Cray I machine. The former is a direct competitor of the IBM 370/168 and is faster in raw circuit speed. The Cray I is also faster in raw logic and memory speed. Both use levels of integration of the logic and memory that are commonplace. By what tricks can these systems achieve the improved speed at the same integration level and device sizes? The answer is that most of the speed is obtained simply by pumping in more power. More power obviously gives faster circuit speed, but it necessitates more cooling. This requirement affects the cost of making the system, especially the packaging and cooling, which in turn also affect the reliability of the system, maintenance, and so on. Thus the speed of an isolated circuit is not the only determining factor in a new design.

3.8 TRANSISTOR CELLS: GENERAL PRINCIPLES FOR TWO- AND THREE-TERMINAL CELLS

To be feasible in random access memory, any transistor cell must satisfy the four fundamental requirements in Section 2.3 and the additional three of Section 2.4. A transistor device by itself, either junction or field effect, satisfies a few of these but not all, particularly the more important ones. For instance, a transistor certainly dissipates energy, no doubt can be sensed externally, and can be energized an infinite number of times, but does not have two stable states (requirements d, c, b, and a of Section 2.3, respectively). A transistor by itself can have an infinite number of states, as determined by the externally applied voltages and currents (i.e., the boundary conditions). In a limited manner, a single device has two functional terminals (and one common terminal), since no current flows when only, say, the base or collector of a junction transistor or gate or drain of an FET is energized. However since the two stable states are not defined, the two terminal coincident writing capability cannot properly be judged (item c, Section 2.4). Unlike an FET, a junction transistor does not have a threshold, but again the two states being undefined, we cannot judge the adequacy of a threshold for writing (item a, Section 2.4). We see later that the FET threshold is fundamentally unnecessary but has some practical value in a memory cell. The conclusion clearly is that typical transistors of the type described in Sections 2.8 and 2.9 cannot provide storage by themselves. Additional components are required, in particular the devices must be used in some sort of circuit that satisfies the foregoing requirements. We consider these "circuits" or "cells" in the manner in which they historically evolved— namely, from the complex flip-flop to the more simple one-transistor cells.

Transistor Flip-Flop Cells

The requirement of two stable states can easily be provided by the classical Eccles-Jordan circuit of Appendix 1A. In fact, the original storage device in electronic computers (e.g., Eniac, Section 1.2) was the vacuum tube flip-flop circuit used in a register. However the large size and power requirements of each circuit plus the large number of bits needed for main storage precluded use of vacuum tubes, thus giving way to other technologies, primarily magnetics. Vacuum tube flip-flops nevertheless continued to be used in the CPU (e.g., IBM 650, 701, 704), since relatively few were required and the speed was quite high. Eventually the tube was replaced by the discrete transistor and still later integrated circuits in the CPU, giving even faster speeds, while memory continued to use magnetics, which were cheaper. The twin discrepancies in technology and speed of CPU versus main memory continued until the early 1970s, when the cost of integrated circuits became competitive with that of magnetics. The basic flip-flop circuit for memory applications appears in Fig. 3.8-1. The similarity to the original vacuum tube flip-flops is remarkable, the major differences being the lower power (no heaters, $B^+ \sim$ volts, few milliwatts or microwatts per bit), small size, all solid state (no vacuum), giving high reliability, and of course, lower cost, since thousands of transistors are fabricated simultaneously on one substrate.

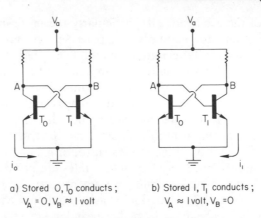

a) Stored O, T_0 conducts;
V_A = 0, V_B ≈ I volt

b) Stored I, T_I conducts;
V_A ≈ I volt, V_B = 0

FIGURE 3.8-1   Basic transistor flip-flop.

The circuit with its feedback or latching connections on the base allows the devices to operate in only *two* of the infinite number of possible states, as required. In addition, the states are stable, as we shall see shortly. This latching circuit of Fig. 3.8-1 satisfies the two stable state requirements of item *a* in Section 2.3. It does not require transistors with a threshold, nor even power gain; however gain is desirable in practical circuits to reduce power consumption. Unfortunately this circuit is still not a memory cell because it does not have two functional terminals or a means for coincident selection (item *a*, Section 2.4). This necessitates additional transistors, with a three-terminal cell being more complex than a two-terminal cell. Let us start with the basic flip-flop of Fig. 3.8-1 to understand its operation, then add necessary components to make it work as a simple two-terminal cell. Additional complexity can then be added to provide a three-terminal cell.

The operation of the basic flip-flop of Fig. 3.8-1 is as follows: the two transistors T_0 and T_1 form a normal flip-flop circuit as in Fig. 3.8-1a. When T_0 is turned on, current flows through T_0 to ground, putting node point A at ground. This in turn puts the base of T_1 at ground potential, thus holds T_1 off. If T_1 is off, node B must be at a voltage equal to the base-emitter voltage of T_0, which is typically 1 V, holding it on. Thus this would be a stable state with T_0 on and T_1 off, storing an arbitrarily labeled "0" (it could just as well be called "1"). To store the opposite state (i.e., a "1"), it is necessary to bring node B to 0 voltage and node A to some higher value. This can easily be done with two external voltage sources, one tied to point A and the other to B. This was essentially the way early flip-flop memory registers were operated, since there were few such storage bits. In a large, random access memory, however, we need some way to coincidentally select a specific location without selecting all locations. Of course this could be done by circuits used to select the external sources tied to points A and B, but this leads to very complex memory organization because then each cell would need its own two generators and separate writing from some external location. It is much simpler to bring these "external" sources into the cell itself and make them also do the coincident selection for the cell. Thus the fundamental principle for writing information is to bring node A to ground (with node B high or floating), hence T_0 conducting for a stored "0", or to bring node B to ground (with node A high or floating) and T_1 conducting for a stored "1." This is exactly what is done in several common flip-flop cells, and the manner in which it is accomplished leads to many different cell designs. To understand this, note that the flip-flop has only two access points, A and B, both of them functionally the same (i.e., to turn off one and turn on the other transistor). Although there are two physical terminals A and B, both must be simultaneously and inversely controlled externally at a given time; hence it is essentially a one-terminal device as far as memory organization is concerned. For useful memory implementation, the minimal requirement is that points A and B be coincidently selected, each by two additional terminals. This obviously requires at least one additional transistor for each node A and B as a minimum, and perhaps additional components, depending on the transistor characteristics and memory design specifications. This represents one major problem in transistor flip-flop cell design. The basic flip-flop circuit of Fig. 3.8-1 can be varied somewhat, but only to a very limited extent. Therefore most of the differences in flip-flop type cell design center around how points A and B are selected.

If terminals A and B are selected for writing by coincidence of pulses on two terminals as suggested earlier, a two-terminal device for 2D or $2\frac{1}{2}$D organization results. For 3D organizations, three terminals for selecting A or B must be provided, yielding additional cell complexity. To show how this selection and complexity can be added, we choose the MOS FET cell. Bipolar cell designs are considered later.

A basic MOS storage cell with two terminals to select either node A or B ($2\frac{1}{2}$D organization) is shown in Fig. 3.8-2. A coincidence of pulses on a word line (FET gates) and either of the two bit lines (tied to FET sources) results in a coincident writing into the cell. The operation of this cell is as follows. Recall that to write a "0" or "1," one node A or B must be brought to ground while the other node, B or A, must be floating or high. This is exactly what is done. The word line is normally at ground potential, whereas the bit lines "write 0" and "write 1" are both normally at $+V_b$, as shown. To write a "0" regardless of the initial state of the cell, a positive voltage is applied to the word line in coincidence with a pulse to bring bit line "write 0" to ground potential. The word pulse on the gate of T_2 turns it on and its source is at ground, bringing point A to ground potential. If the cell initially had been

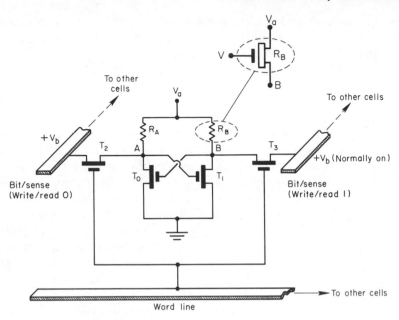

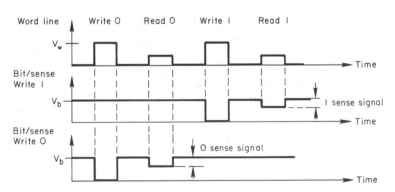

FIGURE 3.8-2 Two-terminal, six-MOS transistor flip-flop storage cell and pulse sequence (*n*-channel, enhancement FETs).

in the "0" state, point A already would have been at ground, and nothing would have happened. If the cell initially had been in the "1" state, point A initially would have been at $+V_a$ and T_1 conducting; but now A is brought to ground, causing T_1 to turn off and point B to increase to V_a, which causes T_0 to conduct; hence the cell switches to the "0" state. To write a "1," a word pulse is applied in coincidence with bringing bit line "write 1" to ground, and the same kind of behavior results. For reading, a word pulse is applied *without* a bit pulse. This word pulse causes both T_2 and T_3 to turn on. The node A or B that is at 0 V will cause a small current to flow out of an external voltage supply through an external load resistor, giving a small decrease in the normally "high" bit line voltage. The sensing is nondestructive because the word read pulse only strobes to see which state the cell is in. An important feature is that the current that flows through T_2 or T_3 during reading is supplied externally by the bit lines. This current does not flow through the cell load resistors but rather through the small "on" resistance of either T_0 or T_1. The power dissipation is minimized because the read current is supplied externally to node A or B.

Note that for reading, the bit lines become the "sense lines." Thus despite an inherent capability for coincident selection for writing such a cell, there is no coincident selection capability for reading; that is, all cells along a pulsed word line are read, hence this cell can be used only in 2D or $2\frac{1}{2}$D organization. This limitation in sensing results because in essence, this transistor cell is a two-input structure (i.e., word and bit/sense),* whereas magnetic cores, for instance, can have any number of inputs.

In the actual implementation of the MOS cells, the load resistors would, in fact, be biased MOS transistors as shown by the insert for R_B in Fig. 3.8-2. These are nothing more than resistors, but such resistors are easier to make from the same basic device rather than using a separate fabrication step. Since energy obviously is dissipated in the load resistors and transistors, we have essentially provided all the fundamental requirements of Section 2.3 and all but item *b* of Section 2.4, (i.e., insensitivity to disturb pulses on unselected cells). For an ideal circuit without tolerances, and so on, insensitivity to disturbs is provided by keeping the bit lines normally at a high voltage. When a word pulse is applied to turn on the node selection transistor, the "high" node remains high while the low node draws current through the load resistor of a bit driver. The external circuits act more as current sources, and the low node stays sufficiently below the "high" node to maintain the state. In actual circuits with tolerances, this disturb sensitivity requires additional consideration. Note that if both bit lines were normally "low," a disturb pulse that turned on the node selection transistors could leave the cell in an undetermined state, hence disturb sensitive.

The two-terminal cell of Fig. 3.8-2 can be enlarged to a three-terminal cell by the addition of another "functional" selection terminal that allows coincident selection of cells for reading in addition to writing. This can be easily accomplished by inserting another pair of transistors between the

---

* Although there are actually three inputs (word, write "0," and write "1"), the latter two serve only one function at a time, namely, bit writing or bit sensing.

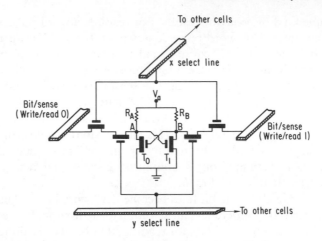

FIGURE 3.8-3   Three-terminal, eight-MOS transistor flip-flop storage cell.

node points A and B and their respective bit/sense lines (Fig. 3.8-3). We have, in essence, added another word line to the previous cell, now labeled x and y lines, and there must be a coincidence of pulses on x and y before either writing or sensing can take place through the bit/sense lines. Except for the small addition, the operation of the cell is basically the same as before. As previously mentioned, in actual implementation the resistors R_A and R_B are usually MOS transistors with their gates tied to the source or drain terminal, or a power supply. In addition, some changes in the voltage polarities are often used to simplify the external circuitry and achieve compatibility with bipolar transistor-transistor logic (TTL). However it should be remembered that the basic cell remains the same; only the practical details change, for various reasons.

The x and y lines in Fig. 3.8-3 can run orthogonal to each other, and we have a three-terminal cell that can be implemented in a 3D organization. The three terminals of the cell are (1) x select, (2) y select, and (3) bit/sense line pair.

In the 3D cell of Fig. 3.8-3, the digit (bit/sense) lines are isolated from nodes A and B by two transistors, and a direct connection is made only on a selected cell. Half-select disturbs on adjacent cells still leave the digit line isolated by at least one transistor; thus unlike the two-terminal cell, no disturb occurs, no matter what the voltage is on the digit lines. Hence in priniple, for three-terminal cells, the bit/sense line could be left floating, and we would have to apply only the proper voltages 0, V_a or V_a, 0 to A and B for storing "0" or "1," respectively. Thus, again in principle, the digit lines would not have to be

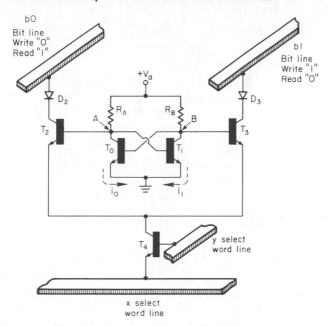

FIGURE 3.8-4 Early commercial integrated junction transistor memory cell with three functional terminals.

normally "on" in the three-terminal cell but they would in the two-terminal cell.

Actual implementation of MOS cells is very close to that described earlier. The early p-channel enhancement mode FET cells sold commercially used configurations very much like that in Figs. 3.8-2 and 3.8-3* except for rearrangement of the voltages. The IBM system 370 models 158 and 168 main memories make use of a two-functional-terminal, six device n-channel cell as in Fig. 3.8-2.

The same basic ideas concerning random access memory cell using MOS transistor flip-flops can be applied to bipolar transistor cells as well. In fact, the first commercial, mass-produced semiconductor memory cell used bipolar transistors in a 3D organization (three terminal cells), as shown in Fig. 3.8-4 (Farber and Schlig, 1972). There are some differences in detail, however, because of the need to keep the power dissipation per cell low (bipolar transistor cells tend to have high power dissipation) and the high speed that was desired in the design. Before discussing the operation of this cell, note the

---

* See for example, Texas Instruments Bulletin CW802 MOS Supplement, 1971, p. 67.

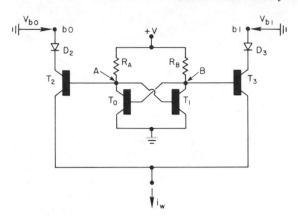

FIGURE 3.8-5 Simplified schematic of Fig. 3.8-4.

same basic flip-flop configuration with control of nodes A and B necessary for storing "0" or "1." The control of these nodes is accomplished by the coincidence of three functional terminals, x, y, and bit/sense pair just as before, hence a 3T, 3D cell.

The cell of Fig. 3.8-4 is simplified to that of Fig. 3.8-5 needing only a word pulse i_w and a bit pulse on either b_0 or b_1 for writing.* The bit lines are normally high (about 1.25 V) to maintain reverse bias on the collector-emitter junctions on T_2 and T_3. The cell of Fig. 3.8-5 contains two diodes that are essential to the cell operation. These diodes act as load resistors R_A and R_B in previous circuits, but now the load can vary, being made a large load in the leg that is being turned on and a small load in the leg that is being turned off. To see this, suppose that T_1 is initially conducting (stored "1"), which means that node B is near ground and node A is high (about 1 V); this will hold T_0 off (no base current), hence is a stable state. If we now wish to write a "0," it is necessary to get node A to ground and node B to $+1$ V (approximately). This is accomplished by first applying a negative bit pulse to the "0" bit/sense line to bring this normally "high" line to near ground potential. Bit line "1" remains high. Since node A is initially at $+1$ V and T_2 is off, the circuit formed through the base to collector (high resistance) of T_2 to the "0" bit line will back bias the diode D_2, giving a very large load resistor on T_2 (Fig. 3.8-6). This large load means that the transistor is easily saturated† and that a large base current, nearly equal to the emitter current,

---

* With a voltage $-V_x$, T_4 looks like a current source because of an additional load resistor in the emitter of T_4 in the actual array—see Fig. 4.9-5.
† For junction transistors, "saturation" means small collector current and small collector-emitter voltage (i.e., near the origin on the dc collector characteristics). This is just the opposite of the "saturation" region for an FET (large drain-source voltage).

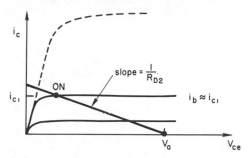

FIGURE 3.8-6 Transistor collector characteristics with large effective load resistor.

can flow. A word pulse current flowing in the direction shown will cause this to happen, and the base current, flowing out of node A through T_2 to ground is sufficient to bring node A near ground (within about 0.7 V, the base-emitter voltage) and switch T_0 on and T_1 off. Thus the high resistance of the back-biased diode D_2 is essential to allow sufficient base current to flow in T_2.

If the cell has already been in the "0" state, the action of diode D_3 (which looks like a small load resistor) would have been critical in preventing disturbance of the cell. For instance, in the "0" state T_0 is on, T_1 is off, and node B is at 1 V. Now when the word pulse current is again applied, a base current attempts to flow out of node B through T_1 toward ground. This word current must be supplied either by the base or collector of T_3.* If the load resistance presented to T_3 by diode D_3 had been large, the word current would have been supplied by the base of T_3 and the cell would have switched, hence would have been disturb sensitive. However bit line "1" is at a normally high potential; thus the word pulse current will forward bias diode D_3, giving a very small load. This means that T_3 cannot be saturated easily because of the small effective load line (Fig. 3.8-7). Therefore the word current is supplied by the collector and only a very small base current can flow (equal to about i_w/β, β = current gain of T_3), which is incapable of reducing the voltage at point B; hence no switching occurs, and the cell is insensitive to disturbs.

For reading, a word pulse is applied and a small sense current will flow either through T_2 or T_3, depending on whether node A or B is high. For a stored "0," B is high, and T_3 will conduct on application of a small word pulse. The current through T_3 (read stored "0") produces a negative voltage on bit line 1, and the use of a differential amplifier converts this to a negative signal. Similarly, a stored "1" will produce a current through T_2, a negative voltage on bit line "0," giving a positive sense signal out of the differential sense amplifier. The sensing is, of course, nondestructive with large sense

* Note that i_1 supplied by T_4 is really a current source.

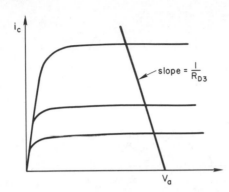

i_c

slope = $\dfrac{1}{R_{D3}}$

V_a

FIGURE 3.8-7 Transistor collector characteristics with small effective load resistor.

signals of 2 mA in 20 Ω load or 40 mV. For coincident selection of the cell, only one transistor T_4 is required, and the method of selection is obvious. The organization of the 3D cell on a chip is given in Section 4.9.

3.9 TRANSISTOR CELLS: EVOLUTION AND PRACTICAL CONSIDERATIONS

Integrated circuit memories came into existence by way of the rather complex six-device cell of Fig. 3.8-4. This technology was used for high speed caches (see Section 4.9) and proved to be quite feasible. Shortly thereafter, similar types of flip-flop cells having two instead of three functional terminals began to appear in main memory. These cells consumed large amounts of power and required many devices, two major factors in limiting density. Many other factors are also important, but the total number of bits per chip (including on-chip circuits) is a significant component of the ultimate cost. Hence we trace cell evolution from the point of view of increased density by way of lower power and fewer devices per cell. This is, in fact, the direction taken in transistor cell design.

For power dissipation, it is always necessary to consider both the static (standby) and dynamic (switching) power. In some cases one or the other dominates, whereas in other cells, both are important. The maximum total power dissipation for an air-cooled chip is in the range of 0.5 W or less.* Larger power dissipation requires special cooling such as forced air or liquid cooling, which is more expensive. Both the on-chip support circuits

---

* Compare, for example, the surface area of a silicon chip of 0.2 × 0.2 in. by two surfaces giving an area of 0.08 in.² versus that of a standard 0.5 W carbon resistor (0.375 × 0.15 in. diameter) with surface area of 0.176 in.². The silicon chip, although about a factor of 2 smaller, is typically mounted on a larger substrate. Thus 0.5 W is reasonable.

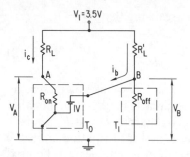

FIGURE 3.9-1 Static (standby) circuit of typical junction transistor flip-flop.

and memory cell dissipation must be included. If the total on-chip circuit power consumption P_c is known or can be approximated, the power dissipation per memory cell is related to the bits per chip by

$$\text{bits/chip (air cooled)} \approx \frac{0.5 - P_c}{p_m} \tag{3.9-1}$$

where P_c = total on-chip *circuit* dissipation (watts)
p_m = power dissipation per memory cell

Thus large-scale integration in terms of more bits per chip requires lower power cells, special cooling, or both.

The basic flip-flop circuit, either in junction transistors or FETs requires large silicon area and inherently dissipates excessive power. Most of the power is consumed during standby. To understand why power dissipation is large, assume in Fig. 3.8-1 that the left transistor of the flip-flop T_0 is "on" while T_1 is "off." The static circuit becomes essentially that of Fig. 3.9-1, where T_1 is characterized by a large "off" resistance R_{off}, T_0 is characterized by a fixed base-emitter voltage of about 1 V (a good value), and collector-emitter "on" resistance R_{on}, where R_{on} and R_{off} are functions of base current i_b and current gain β. Ideally we would like node A to have $V_A = 0$ and node B to have a voltage to maintain i_b of sufficient value to hold T_0 "on" such that V_A is as desired. The ratio of on to off resistance becomes important, and both values are determined by R_L for a given voltage. Also the power dissipation is determined by R_L as follows. Assuming $R_{\text{on}} = 0$ and $R_{\text{off}} = \infty$, we write

$$i_c = \frac{V_1}{R_L} \quad \text{and} \quad i_b = \frac{V_1 - 1}{R'_L} \tag{3.9-2}$$

The total standby power dissipation for this cell is

$$p_m = i_c^2 R_L + i_b^2 R'_L \tag{3.9-3}$$

Substituting the above current equations and realizing that $R_L = R'_L$ gives

$$p_m = \frac{V_1^2}{R_L} + \frac{(V_1 - 1)^2}{R_L} = \frac{[V_1^2 + (V_1 - 1)^2]}{R_L} \tag{3.9-4}$$

Of course we can make the power per cell as small as we like by increasing R_L. This requires a physically large resistor area (Fig. 2.8-4) in junction transistor technology, which limits the density. Alternatively, if R_L is made physically and hence electrically small, the large power dissipation limits the density, producing a dilemma. Various fabrication techniques can be used to give large R_L in a small area, but circuit operation limits the value of R_L to relatively small size. For instance, if R_L in Fig. 3.9-1 is made too large, then from (3.9-2) the base current begins to approach the emitter current. Transistor T_0 is then operating in saturation, which greatly slows the device switching speed. In addition, as these currents into nodes A and B become more equal, the state of the cell (i.e., "1" or "0") becomes more difficult to control by way of these nodes. We want smaller R_L for cell operation and large R_L for low dissipation. Obviously a compromise is necessary. Since we know that the bit lines are high during reading, when the bit transistors T_2 and T_3 are turned on by the word pulse, the read current is supplied externally, thereby minimizing read power dissipation. This is not the case in all cells (e.g., multiemitter cells, considered later).

In the above-described flip-flop, if we have $V_1 = 3.5$ V and $R_L = 6$ kΩ, the standby power from (3.9-3) is

$$p_m = \frac{3.5^2 + 2.5^2}{6 \times 10^3} = 3.1 \text{ mW/cell} \tag{3.9-5}$$

From (3.9-1) neglecting circuit power, the maximum number of bits per chip is

$$\text{bits/chip} < \frac{0.5}{3.1 \times 10^{-3}}$$

$$< 162 \text{ bits/chip}$$

Such a cell would be adequate for 64 or 128 bits/chip, air cooled. The cell power dissipation can be reduced by about a factor of 2, allowing 256 bits/chip. The difficulty is the large cell size.

3.9.1 Multiemitter Flip-Flop cell

The cell size just derived can be reduced by noting that the node voltages at points A and B need not be controlled by an external device alone but also can be varied by modifying the voltage on the emitters of T_0 and T_1 instead

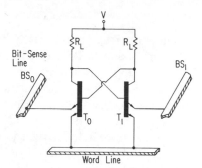

FIGURE 3.9-2 Two-terminal, multiemitter flip-flop cell.

of connecting them to ground. An early cell that achieved this with fewer devices is the multiemitter cell illustrated in Fig. 3.9-2. The bit/sense access points to the cell are coupled by way of a second emitter on the latch transistor. This eliminates the previous selection transistors T_2 and T_3 but also removes one functional terminal. Since the second functional terminal is a fundamental requirement, it is provided by way of the first emitters, serving as a common word line for all cells. This cell works much the same as the previous cell but with the bit/sense lines normally low. A transistor is turned off when both its emitters are high and turned on if one or both emitters are low. To write into the multiemitter cell, we must raise the potential of the bit lines, which raises the potential of the corresponding node. This procedure is just the opposite of that in the basic flip-flop. Hence if we continue to define a "1" as node B low with T_1 conducting, we must operate on node A to achieve this. For instance, if we wish to write a "1," T_0 is turned off by pulsing the word line and BS_0 simultaneously. The opposite is done to write a "0." At the quiescent state, no current flows in the bit/sense lines because they are at a slightly larger positive voltage than the "low" voltage on the word line. Emitter current at quiescence flows only into the word line. During reading, the word line is raised in voltage to a point sufficient to cause some of the emitter current in the "on" transistor to divert to the corresponding sense line, as shown. A differential sense amplifier is used as before. Note that the "1" signal appears on BS_1, although to write a "1," BS_0 had to be energized. The read current is supplied *internally* by the cell and flows through the load resistor. Since the peak of this read current, charging a capacitor, can be large at high speed, additional power dissipation can occur. This is one serious limitation of this cell. Nevertheless, it has found reasonably widespread commercial usage for low-scale integration in the range below 1K cells/chip. It has a definite density advantage over the basic six-device flip-flop.

3.9.2 Schottky Diode Flip-Flop Cell

The power and speed disadvantage of the multiemitter cell resulted essentially from the removal of an external supply at node points A and B. To maintain the *external* read current characteristics of the basic flip-flop without the large bit selection transistors T_3 and T_4, a modified configuration is required. These selection transistors are replaced by very small Schottky diodes, which can be fabricated directly on the collector contacts with a metal-n^+ junction. This provides the bit/sense line, hence one functional terminal. The word line is obtained from the emitters of T_0 and T_1 (Fig. 3.9-3). The cell structure and its operation are a combination of the basic flip-flop and the multi-emitter cells.

The R_L is very large, in the tens of kilohms, whereas R_c is a small (1 kΩ) resistor that is part of the inherent internal collector resistance in the n diffusion of Fig. 2.8-4. As we shall see, the read current does not come through R_L; thus R_L can be made large to give lower standby power without limiting the reading current, hence speed, or affecting cell operation.

The bit lines are normally biased at a small voltage V_{BS} and the word line is normally at a larger V_W. A voltage $V_W - V_{BS}$ back-biases the diodes,

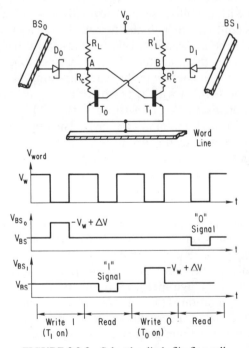

FIGURE 3.9-3 Schottky diode flip-flop cell.

isolating the bit/sense line from the cell. For writing, say, a "1" (i.e., T_1 on), the word line voltage is dropped to a low value while the "0" bit/sense line BS_0 is raised to some high value. If T_1 is initially off and T_0 is on, the diode D_0 will be forward biased, and a current will flow through T_0 to the grounded word line. A voltage will be developed across R_c which is sufficient to turn T_1 on. The current through T_1 must come through R'_L which, being large, lowers the voltage at node B sufficiently to turn T_0 off. Thus T_1 is latched on and T_0 remains off. For reading, the normally high word line is once again dropped to near ground potential and forward biases both diodes. Current will flow from one bit/sense line into whichever node, A or B, is low. If T_1 is on as previously, node B is low and current flows from BS_1 to the grounded word line, producing a small voltage drop on this line, as shown. Again, a differential amplifier is used to detect this signal. Note that in this cell, writing consists of *raising* the bit/sense line potential, as was done in the multiemitter cell. Thus writing a "1" requires energizing the "0" bit line as before, although the "1" signal is generated on the "1" sense line. In this diode cell, however, the sense current flows into the cell from the sense line, which means that the read current is external. This allows faster reading without large standby power as desired. This diode-coupled cell has become a popular type of junction transistor memory cell (mid-1970s).

All the foregoing cells are static in that the stored information remains indefinitely, as long as the power supplies are intact; they are also volatile, losing all information when the power supplies fail. Dynamic cells, those which require periodic refreshing, can be made much smaller at the expense of refreshing circuitry.

3.9.3 Four-Device Dynamic FET Cell

The six-device FET flip-flop cell of Fig. 3.8-2 requires large area and power, leaving much to be desired. There are many possible ways to improve this cell by removing various transistors, progressing first to four FETs, three, two, and finally one FET. Only the latter, the so-called one-device dynamic cell, has found wide acceptance, but we briefly consider several others along the evolutionary road.

The multiemitter cell of Fig. 3.9-2 has no direct analogy in FET technology. The diode-coupled cell of Fig. 3.9-3 can be implemented in FET devices with little change in the basic idea. It has the advantage of lower area and power, but it is still a static cell. The density gain is relatively small, however. More significant density improvements can be obtained by removing some of the devices. To see how this might be done, consider the FET flip-flop of Fig. 3.8-2. For a stored "1" in the quiescent state, T_1 is held "on" by charge on its gate, supplied by V_x through the load device into node A. This gate is really a simple capacitor in the quiescent state. Under *ideal* conditions, once

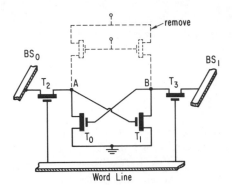

FIGURE 3.9-4 Four-device, dynamic FET cell with simple refresh (n channel).

this gate is charged, it should remain charged indefinitely. If this were the case, there would be no need to maintain the load devices and supply voltage V_x. In fact, if some other means could be provided to charge the gates of T_0 or T_1 as needed, the load devices could be eliminated altogether. This is precisely what is done in the four-FET device cell of Fig. 3.9-4. The load devices (shown dashed as they exist in the basic flip-flop) are now removed. The remainder of the cell and its operation stay intact, although some additional external circuits and operations are necessary. The various devices are far from ideal, and the charge on the gate of T_0 or T_1 eventually leaks off, requiring refreshing (i.e., the cell is dynamic). Fortunately refreshing is very simple. Both bit/sense lines are normally high, and the word line is low. The application of a word pulse automatically refreshes the correct stored information. For instance, if T_0 is off and T_1 is on (stored "1"), node B is at ground and node A is high. Suppose some of the charge has leaked off the gate of T_1, making the voltage at node A very slightly lower than the bit line voltage. When the word line turns on both T_2 and T_3, T_1 still shorts node B to ground while node A is charged back to the full bit line voltage. The current flowing into node B from line BS_1 generates a sense signal in a differential sense amplifier. Hence sensing and refreshing are identical operations. The cell is refreshed each time it is read.

The important idea in the cell just described was the storage of information in the form of charge on an FET gate. Stored "1"s and "0"s were represented by two different bundles of charge of the same polarity but stored on different gates. While two separate charge bundles give very good "1"–"0" discrimination, only one charge bundle is really necessary. We can discriminate "1s" and "0s" simply by the presence or absence of charge on a gate. Obviously this allows us to remove one of the storage FET devices in Fig. 3.9-4, say, T_0, leaving T_1, T_2, and T_3 as in Fig. 3.9-5. Recall that previously, writing and refreshing of a stored "1" was done through node A and sensing required

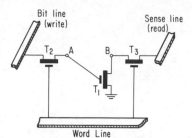

FIGURE 3.9-5 Three-device, dynamic FET cell (*n* channel).

node *B*. Hence both nodes and three devices are required in this cell, with separate bit and sense lines.

3.4.4 One-Transistor Cell

The concept of stored charge can be carried one step further. Rather than storing charge on the gate of an FET, we can use an ordinary two-terminal capacitor. The two physical terminals can be operated as two functional terminals in a diode matrix, for instance, as detailed in Section 4.11. This approach is not viable for storing charge, however, since all diodes must normally be back biased, charging all capacitors in the array. To use a linear capacitor for charge storage, it is necessary to isolate the capacitor from both the bit and word line. This requires a cell with at least *three* physical terminals, even though only *two* may be functional terminals. The way this is achieved can be deduced from the three-device cell of Fig. 3.9-5. Recall that previously when the word line voltage is raised, turning T_2 "on" with the bit line high, a very small refreshing charge flows into node *A* if the voltage at node *A* is high (stored "1"). If node *A* is low (no stored charge), a large charge (current) flows to charge the gate of T_1. This current through a resistor or FET device can be detected as a sense signal. Hence the bit line can also serve as the sense line, making the separate sense line as well as T_3 unnecessary. This leaves node *B* floating unconnected. Since this terminal is unnecessary, we can convert the device T_1 into a simple capacitor (Fig. 3.9-6). As Section 3.10 relates in detail, the capacitor can be obtained from a device that is part of an FET, having a gate and source but no drain. Hence the cell contains one FET device plus a storage capacitor of some sort. The common terminology "one-device cell" for this structure is somewhat misleading: it means only one *full* FET device. The same basic circuit—namely, a transistor and capacitor—can be implemented with a junction transistor as well as an FET as the next section demonstrates. The general principles of cell operation in terms of a discrete device and capacitor as depicted in Fig. 3.9-6 are described here. Actual cell structures and the resulting additional problems are discussed more fully in Section 3.10.

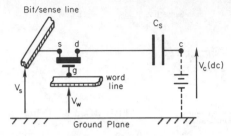

(a) general equivalent circuit

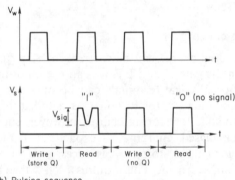

(b) Pulsing sequence

FIGURE 3.9-6   One-device, dynamic FET cell shown for positive dc voltage on capacitor.

In principle it does not matter which polarity of voltage is used on the capacitor electrode c—positive, negative, or ground. Nor does it matter which polarity of charge is stored on electrode c, either $+Q$ or $-Q$. The latter is determined by the voltage polarity used on the bit line in conjunction with that on electrode c. In FET cells these voltage polarities becomes important for practical reasons. Since a word pulse on terminal g connects s to d, externally it is necessary only to provide a voltage difference between s and c for storing charge on C_S. If c is at ground potential, s must be at some positive or negative voltage with respect to ground, and vice versa. To store no charge, there must be no potential difference between s and c when a word pulse is applied. Since the bit/sense line s and word line g provide the two required functional terminals, we do not have to provide any selection on terminal c. Hence we can simply fix it at any convenient potential and adjust the selection of the bit/sense line accordingly. Thus the complete cell read/write cycle can be done in many different ways, too numerous to list.

However some practical constraints introduced by actual FET cells make the following polarities attractive.

Polysilicon gate (self-aligned)	Positive V_c (dc)
	Positive V_s (bit line) during reading
	$V_s = 0$ for storing $-Q$ on electrode d $(+Q$ on $c)$
	Positive V_s for no stored Q
Standard process (diffused electrode d on C_S)	c at ground $(V_c = 0)$
	Positive V_s for reading
	Positive V_s for storing $-Q$ on electrode d
	$V_s = 0$ for no stored Q

Let us trace through the write/read cycles of the discrete cell in Fig. 3.9-6, using the voltage polarities for the polysilicon gate device just listed. As previously indicated, the FET gate is always turned on by the word line for any operation. With a positive voltage at electrode c, the storing (writing) of $-Q$ on electrode d would be accomplished by connecting the bit line to ground as in Fig. 3.9-7a. The dc voltage V_0 charges the capacitor with current flow as shown. Reading is accomplished by connecting the bit/sense line to a voltage V_0 through the sense amplifier impedance Z_r (Fig. 3.9-7b). The bit/sense line voltage cancels V_0 between electrode c and ground, leaving the potential stored on C_S connected across Z_r. A read current flows to discharge C_S, giving a small sense signal across Z_r as shown. Note that the polarity of the read current is opposite to that of the write current in Fig. 3.9-7a. The stored information is lost (destructively read), hence must be regenerated. An alternative scheme for reading appears in Fig. 3.9-7b: no voltage is used on the bit line; thus no sense current flows in this case. To store no charge (i.e., $Q = 0$), the bit line must be connected to a $+V_0$ as in Fig. 3.9-7c. If there had been some previous stored charge on C_S, it would be removed with a current flow (dashed in Fig. 3.9-7c). Note that this is the same as reading in Fig. 3.9-7b. Reading of this uncharged cell would be done as in Fig. 3.9-7d, which is identical to reading and writing in Figs. 3.9-7b and 3.9-7c, respectively, except now no read current flows. Since the stored information is obviously reinforced rather than destroyed, in principle, a regeneration cycle is unnecessary. However a given word in memory has both polarities of stored information, and we must always allow regeneration time in the cycle. The alternative scheme for sensing, proposed in Fig. 3.9-7b', would now *charge* the cell as in Fig. 3.9-7d', thus giving a sense signal across Z_r while destroying the information. A subsequent regeneration cycle would be required.

Ideally, the information stored on C_S should remain until the cell is destructively read. However in all real cells there are leakage paths that

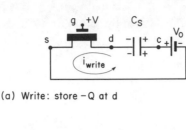

(a) Write: store −Q at d

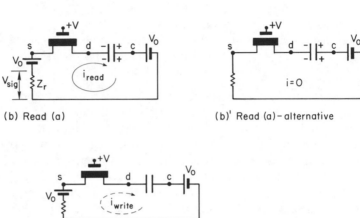

(b) Read (a)   (b)' Read (a)−alternative

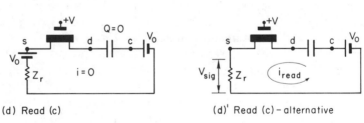

(c) Write : Store no charge

(d) Read (c)   (d)' Read (c)−alternative

FIGURE 3.9-7   Writing and reading steps of the FET one-device cell with positive dc voltage on storage capacitor.

create small but finite leakage current to gradually deteriorate the stored information. Thus the cell must be refreshed at a rate determined by the leakage time constant.

Regardless of the method of operation or sensing, the switching device must be capable of carrying current in both directions, one direction for charging and the opposite for discharging the capacitor. The following list summarizes some of the more important features of this cell.

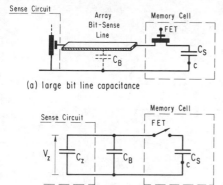

(a) large bit line capacitance

(b) simplified circuit

FIGURE 3.9-8 Sensing problem associated with the one FET device cell.

1. Two functional and three physical terminals.
2. Inherently destructively read.
3. Requires refreshing in practical cases.
4. Any polarity of voltages feasible, in principle.
5. Bidirectional current flow.

This cell is quite attractive for high density and large memories. However in such cases the stored charge is quite small and presents serious sensing problems. These arise as follows. In any FET array the bit/sense line essentially runs over a ground plane and is connected to the high impedance gate of an FET device (Fig. 3.9-8a). The bit line introduces a large capacitive load C_B. In such cases, a balanced sensing scheme with a differential FET flip-flop latch that precharges C_B can be used directly on the chip. Such a simple latch is workable when C_B is no more than roughly 10 times C_S. In large arrays, C_B can become much larger than $10C_S$. This greatly reduces the sense voltage obtainable from the cell and can even render the differential latch inoperable. A common method of overcoming this problem is the so-called charge transfer technique, which provides voltage gain (but not charge gain) out of the storage capacitor. There are also more complex sensing circuits, supplying charge gain as well as voltage gain. All these circuits require a balanced (differential) sensing scheme with a dummy sense line; not only do they offer better sensitivity, they are insensitive to variations in the threshold voltages of individual FET devices on the same chip (Heller et al., 1975).

MNOS

A truly "one-device" transistor cell is provided by the so-called metal nitride oxide silicon (MNOS) structure of Fig. 3.9-9. This is basically an FET with

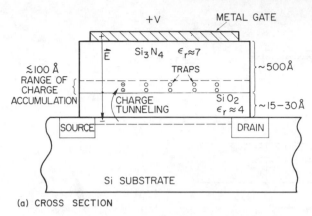

(a) CROSS SECTION

FIGURE 3.9-9   One-device cell using MNOS.

an additional gate insulation layer. Charge is stored in the interface states between the silicon and the silicon nitride. The cell coincident threshold, which is necessary for random access operation, is provided because the "turn on" threshold of this structure is now variable for the following reason. The application of a sufficiently large voltage across the gate insulator causes electrons to tunnel between the traps at (or near) the oxide–nitride interface and the silicon surface (the tunneling is into or out of the traps, depending on the polarity of the voltage). The charge condition in the traps alters the magnitude of the electric field impinging on the channel, hence changes the threshold of the device, just as oxide charge affects the threshold of a conventional MOS FET. Retention of charge in the traps is limited by leakage through the nitride layer, and appears to be in the range of 10^3 to 10^4 hr at present. It is evident that pulses of opposite polarity between the gate and channel are required to switch between the two states, the magnitude of this voltage currently being about 20 to 25 V, a rather large value. Such devices are sensitive to disturb pulses generally encountered on half-selected bit positions and require a memory design that avoids such disturbs.

3.10   INTEGRATED ONE–TRANSISTOR CELLS

The technology of the so-called one-device cell introduced in discrete form in Section 3.9 and shown schematically in Fig. 3.9-6 has become important for main memory. A workable cell can be made from a separate capacitor and transistor, as demonstrated previously. Since FET devices are required for the cell and the on-chip logic anyway, however, the capacitor might as well be made from a similar device if possible (Dennard, 1968). The gate of an

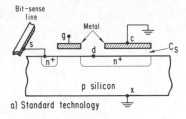

a) Standard technology

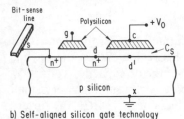

b) Self-aligned silicon gate technology

FIGURE 3.10-1 One FET device cell structure in two technologies.

FET is a capacitor and can be incorporated into the cell structure in several ways. Two common approaches for n-channel technology are illustrated in Fig. 3.10-1: the terminals corresponding to Fig. 3.9-6 are labeled appropriately. In Fig. 3.10-1a electrode d of the storage capacitor is provided by an n^+ diffusion, which also serves as the drain of the FET switch (i.e., internal connection). The capacitor electrode c and FET gate g are metal. Because of the n^+ diffusion under electrode c, the latter may be grounded for cell operation. The various write/read sequences are given in Section 3.9. This structure is made in a fashion following the standard process discussed in Section 2.9.1.

The self-aligned silicon gate process covered in Section 2.9.2 does not easily permit diffusion under a gate electrode. Hence the cell must take on the structure of Fig. 3.10-1b. The silicon region directly under the capacitor electrode c now behaves like an ordinary FET channel. Since we want this region to be a conductor, it is necessary to operate the cell with electrode c at some positive voltage V_0 that is larger than the channel threshold. This ensures that the capacitor electrode *within the silicon* will be inverted, hence conductive as required. The operation of this cell is exactly as detailed previously in conjunction with Fig. 3.9-7 for a discrete FET and capacitor. The leakage mechanism responsible for the need for refreshing is fundamentally important in this structure and occurs in the silicon region under the capacitor electrode c. A problem occurs whenever this region is unstable (i.e., not in electrical equilibrium). For the silicon gate device of Fig. 3.10-1b, this instability occurs whenever there is *no* charge stored on electrode d, corresponding to the excitation of Fig. 3.9-7c. This state was obtained by pulsing the bit

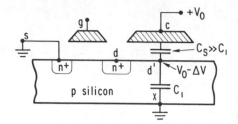

FIGURE 3.10-2 Unstable, zero stored charge state of the one FET device cell.

line to $+V_0$ with gate g on, so that the silicon surface d' under the capacitor is at V_0, pulling out all negative charge from this region. When the bit line excitation is removed as indicated in Fig. 3.10-2, the dc capacitor voltage V_0 appears between c and the substrate (assumed to be ground). A very small capacitance C_1 exists between d' and ground, but since $C_1 \ll C_S$, the surface at d' remains nearly at V_0 except for a small decrease of ΔV approximately equal to

$$\Delta V \bigg|_{C_1 \ll C_S} \approx \frac{C_1}{C_S} V_0 \tag{3.10-1}$$

Hence the surface is at a rather large positive potential. Within the p substrate, there are always holes and electrons that are thermally generated at some small but finite rate. The electrons are attracted to the positive surface, gradually accumulating until d' is indistinguishable from the "stored charge" state. The leakage current would eventually destroy all "zero charge" states, hence must be refreshed periodically. Fortunately the time for a significant amount of charge to accumulate is measured in milliseconds or longer. Such devices are capable of working with memory cycle times of 1 μsec or less, which means that a refresh on every tenth to hundredth cycle is sufficient.

Note that the leakage current attempts to take the cell into the "stored charge" or "1" state; hence a stored "1" is a stable state for the case shown. The unstable state always occurs when there is a potential difference, thus an electric field between the surface at d' and the substrate at x. It is the electric field that attracts charges into the surface region from within the substrate. Regardless of the potentials on electrode c or substrate x, such a condition always occurs at one time or another in the operation of this cell, making it impossible to avoid refreshing.

Integrated one-transistor cells can be fabricated in a variety of ways. An array using self-aligned polysilicon gates and recessed oxide isolation appears in Fig. 3.10-3. Since only one level of metal is commonly used, and since two orthogonal conductors are required, the bit line is a long diffusion and the word line is an aluminum line connected to the polysilicon FET gates. The capacitor electrode c is provided by the long polysilicon

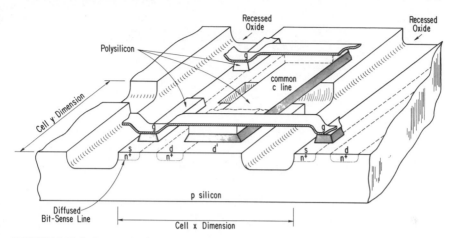

FIGURE 3.10-3 Isometric view of one FET device array using silicon gate and recessed oxide technology.

conductor, as shown. The entire region between the irregular silicon surface and various conductors would be filled with silicon dioxide (not shown) as described in Section 2.9. The metal word line must be insulated from this polysilicon capacitor electrode. The recessed oxide provides device isolation and also reduces the bit line to substrate depletion capacitance by reducing the perimeter of the bit line. This is very important in high density cells because the large bit line capacitance has a detrimental effect on sensing of the cell.

This one-transistor cell can be implemented with junction transistors rather than FET devices. If all the transistors of each cell are isolated from one another, the density is too low to be attractive. One method of improving this situation is to note that there are many common lines in the array of Fig. 3.10-3. Of the three physical terminals of any cell, one terminal will be common to all cells of the array, one terminal will be common to all bits of a word forming the word line, and finally, in the orthogonal direction, one terminal will be common to other cells to form the bit/sense line. Hence we can merge some of these connections internally within the diffusions. One possible approach is presented in Fig. 3.10-4. In principle, the single transistor of Fig. 2.8-4 is now made to have multiple n^+ contacts within one large p-base region. Since bidirectional currents must flow, the designation of emitter or collector is not important.* The common base becomes the word

---

* However because of the lack of symmetry in the collector-base-emitter structure, the current gain is poor in the normal reverse current direction. It is usually desirable to have higher gain in the direction of read current flow.

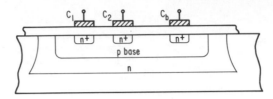

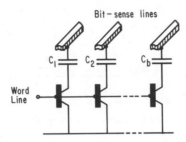

FIGURE 3.10-4 Integrated one-transistor cell using junction transistors (merged transistor cell).

line, and the number of n^+ regions diffused into the base is therefore equal to the number of bits per word. The storage capacitors are formed by a thin oxide and subsequent metal electrode, forming the bit/sense lines. These are connected between cells in an orthogonal direction as shown. Such a structure has potential for higher speed than an equivalent FET cell. One serious drawback is that this cell requires substantial on-chip logic for bit/sense selection (see Section 4.9) and regeneration. The typical junction transistor logic cells (e.g., Fig. 2.8-4) require larger area compared to FET logic; for an example, see Section 2.10. Hence the total bits per chip is typically less attractive.

3.11 SUPERCONDUCTING CELLS

3.11.1 Overview

Since the inception of the cryotron (Buck, 1956), superconducting devices have had strong appeal for potential storage applications. The original devices, both the wire-wound and in-line cryotrons, were projected to have very fast (subnanosecond) superconducting to normal switching times. However it was subsequently found that these devices are inherently slow, (see Section 1.2), in fact slower than ordinary semiconductors. Thus these early cryotrons were totally uncompetitive with devices of other tech-nologies. The subsequent introduction of the Josephson tunneling cryotron proved to be quite different and has resulted in a device that is one of the fastest known switching elements, with switching times measured in pico-seconds. In some memory cells (e.g., the current loop cell), either an ordinary or a Josephson cryotron can be used, whereas in others (e.g., the continuous film cell), only ordinary superconductors can be used. All memory cells that require ordinary superconducting to normal phase transition are totally noncompetitive with current integrated circuit memories. Thus we describe only briefly the cross-film and in-line cryotrons as well as the continuous film cell.

Section 2.11 relates the basic properties of superconductors from which various devices can be fabricated. Although many different devices have been proposed and implemented for both logic and memory, all such devices depend on one basic principle for operation—the transition from the super-conducting to normal resistance state on application of a sufficiently large magnetic field previously discussed. Though the normal resistance is typically small ($< 1 \, \Omega$), the superconducting resistance is identically zero, which means that the resistance ratio of normal to superconducting R_n/R_s is infinite. Thus the gate is nothing more than a switch that can be turned on or off, similar to a transistor. We have already seen in Section 2.3 that to implement *any* storage system at least 2 degrees of freedom in the form of two functional terminals are required, and for a random access superconducting storage cell, the two terminals can be provided by two conductors, each carrying a current, thus each supplying a portion of the critical field necessary to switch a superconductor to the normal state. The superconductor to be switched can be one of the current carrying lines, or it can be a separate, nearby superconductor. We also learned in Section 2.3 that the information must be in the form of stored energy. Superconductors typically accomplish this by means of a supercurrent that stores inductive energy $0.5 \, LI^2$ in a nonresistive loop. Single device cells are possible, but several gates are required as a rule. Numerous types have been implemented in working cells and arrays, and some are described shortly.

The superconducting gate provides the fundamental principles as well as the basic device from which memory cells are implemented. Hence we begin with the cross-film, in-line, and Josephson cryotron gates. Afterward, the various types of memory cell are easily understood.

3.11.2 Cross-Film and In-Line Cryotrons

The basic structures of the cross-film and in-line cryotrons are given in Fig. 3.11-1. The currents, hence the associated magnetic fields, are orthogonal for the cross-film structure and parallel or antiparallel for the in-line

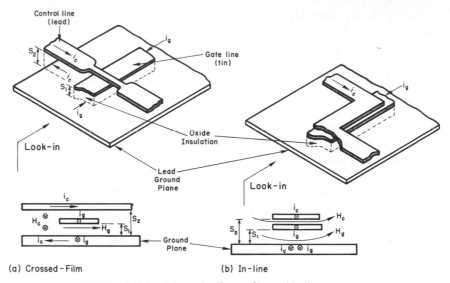

(a) Crossed-Film　　　　　　　　　　　　　(b) In-line

FIGURE 3.11-1　Schematic of cross-film and in-line cryotrons.

structure; the addition of the two individual currents in the separate conductors follows the rules established in Section 2.11. In both cases the under-conductor (closest to ground plane) is the gate whose resistance is controlled by a combination of current in the gate plus a magnetic field acting on this gate as produced by a current in the upper conductor, the control line. Thus the control line never has to go normal and can be made of a material such as lead, which has a high transition or critical temperature ($7°$K), whereas the gate, which must be switched, can be made from a low critical temperature metal such as tin ($3.7°$K). Thus these two structures really represent coincidently selected gates (switches) that can be fashioned into logic and memory devices, as we see later.

For logic devices, the incremental current gain is very important, since the gate current of one device must act as the control current of a subsequent logic gate. For the cross-film structure, this gain can be accomplished by the variation of the control conductor width where it passes over the gate as shown. Equations 2.11-20 or 2.11-21 can serve as idealized design equations. For the in-line structure, (2.11-16) and (2.11-19) are applicable. When the critical condition is exceeded, these devices switch by the rather slow phase boundary motion characterized by a velocity indicated in Fig. 2.11-4. In superconducting loop memory cells, the important parameters for speed are the switching speed of the device, the inductance L of the loop, and the "normal" resistance R_n of the switched superconductor. The L/R_n time constant determines the rate at which the supercurrents can decay, and the device switching speed determines how soon the decay can be *started*. Hence both are important. The device switching speed can be made reasonably fast for the cross-film structure, since the effective device area can be small. Also the inductance can be reasonably small. However the small device area also gives a rather small value of R_n, and L/R_n becomes too large. The value of R_n can be increased by increasing the length of the device as in the in-line geometry. However L also increases as does the device switching time, presenting a dilemma. The transition is complex, and there are other important details such as the rate of heat transfer to the environment (Brennemann et al., 1963). The net result is that for in-line structures of 0.006 in. gate (indium) and control (lead) width, 0.24 in. long and 7000 Å thick, the device delay time with 40% overdrive can still be 40 nsec or longer. For a somewhat smaller overdrive,* delay times of up to nearly 1 μsec may result. The problem is that the superconductor to normal phase transition has a latent heat requirement. If this uptake of heat at the moving boundary is supplied by the sample, it cools, thereby increasing the critical magnetic field and reducing the overdrive or excess field. The actual overdrive field varies critically with the thermal properties of the structure and could conceivably cause severe problems in a dense multilayered structure. The relatively slow switching speeds and numerous other problems have made memory cells with moving phase boundaries unattractive. The Josephson cryotron does not have such a transition or latent heat requirement and is the only superconducting device with any current potential to compete with integrated circuits.

3.11.3 Josephson Tunneling Cryotron

The Josephson junction of Section 2.11.8 provides the basic structure from which a two-terminal switching device can be made. A control line can be provided above the junction as in Fig. 3.11-2. This geometry is similar to the usual in-line cryotron, but there the similarity ends. The addition of the separate currents in control and gate line, though somewhat similar, requires special considerations for the Josephson junction. Since the switching of the junction requires no latent heat and no overdrive, the speed is orders of magnitude faster.

As explained in Section 2.11, switching from the zero voltage to nonzero voltage state occurs when the current density or magnetic field within the thin oxide exceeds the critical value. We *do not* want either the superconducting gate or control lines ever to go normal, and it is therefore

---

* Smaller than constant entropy critical field.

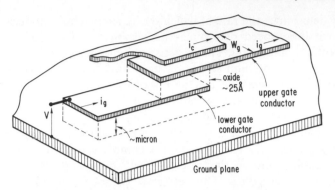

FIGURE 3.11-2   Single Josephson gate with control line.

important that the applied and induced currents and fields do not exceed the critical conditions of these lines.

The critical condition for the junction is derived in Section 2.11.7 but in terms of an external magnetic field. This field is now generated by a current in the control line with value given by (2.11-11) or

$$H_a = \frac{i_c}{W} \tag{3.11-1}$$

Substituting this for H_a in (2.11-27) for a long junction with $l > 2\lambda_J$ gives the approximate relationship for the maximum zero voltage gate current as

$$i_{max} = 2\lambda_J W J_1\left(1 - \frac{i_c}{WH_0}\right) \tag{3.11-2}$$

This is the equation of a straight line. For any given value of i_c, a value of i_g equal to or larger than i_{max} will cause the junction to switch to the nonzero voltage state. Thus two independent terminals are available for controlling the state of the device in a coincident mode. This is obviously useful for logic or memory, but we do not yet have a method for storing information. One circuit for achieving this is discussed later.

Since the speed of switching between the zero and nonzero voltage states is so fast, any memory cell speed will be determined solely by the inductance and normal resistance of the cell circuit and not by the device.

3.11.4   Current Steering in Superconductors

The classical, and still used method for controlling current flow with superconducting devices in memory and logic circuits is by means of current steering. To understand this, consider two identical superconducting gates

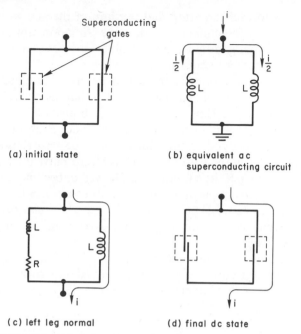

(a) initial state   (b) equivalent ac
                                         superconducting circuit

(c) left leg normal   (d) final dc state

FIGURE 3.11-3   Principles of current steering in superconducting circuits.

connected in parallel, as in Fig. 3.11-3. All lines are assumed to be of width W and a small distance S above a ground plane as in Figs. 3.11-1 and 3.11-2 with $W/S \gg 1$. The basic principle is applicable to any superconducting device that can be switched to a normal resistance. When both gates are superconducting, *if* terminal 2 is tied to ground, the equivalent circuit of each is an inductor (Fig. 3.11-3*b*). The inductance per unit length for a strip of width W, thickness T, separation to ground plane of S, and $W/S \gg 1$, is

$$L\Big|_{W/S \gg 1} = \mu_0 \frac{S}{W}\left(\mu_r + \frac{2\lambda}{S}\coth\frac{T}{\lambda}\right) \qquad (3.11\text{-}3)$$

For a thick conductor such that $T \gg \lambda$, this reduces to

$$L\Big|_{\substack{W/S \gg 1 \\ T/\lambda > 1}} = \mu_0 \frac{S}{W}\left(\mu_r + \frac{2\lambda}{S}\right) \quad \text{RMKS*} \qquad (3.11\text{-}4)$$

The effect of the superconductor on the total inductance of the line is to effectively add an additional insulator of relative permeability $\mu_r = 1$ and

* See Matick (1969), (6-67) and (6-69).

of a thickness λ to each side (top and bottom) of the actual insulator. In other words, the superconductor makes the situation appear as if the conductors were separated by an additional distance 2λ with an air (or free space) dielectric, a rather interesting result.

If a step function of current is applied to the input terminal, and if the inductances are identical, the current divides in half as determined by the equal ac impedances ωL. Thus $i/2$ flows in each branch. If one branch, say, the left side, is caused to go normal, a series resistance R_n is introduced (Fig. 3.11-3c). The final steady state supercurrent will see zero resistance on the right branch and R_n on the left branch. Thus all the current transfers to the right branch as shown. If the left branch is allowed to become superconducting once again, the current *does not* redistribute but continues flowing through the right branch as shown. Thus we have a method for controlling current flow. This technique is used not only in loop-type memory cells but also in cryotron tree decoders.

When both branches are superconducting, if terminal 2 is properly terminated in the appropriate characteristic impedance, each line looks like a transmission line with characteristic impedance (Matick, 1969 p. 319)

$$Z_0 \approx \frac{377S}{\sqrt{\varepsilon_r}\,W} \qquad \text{ohms} \qquad (3.11\text{-}5)$$

In most cases Z_0 is much larger than the normal gate resistance R_n. In such a case, the use of R_n for current switching is not feasible—the discussion of the cryotron tree decoder below gives one example where this is important.

3.11.5 Memory Cells Using Multiple Superconducting Gates

One of the oldest and still viable types of memory cell makes use of a superconducting current loop for storing information and the technique of current steering for writing and sensing. In Section 2.11.1 it was indicated that a current once established in a superconducting loop will remain indefinitely as long as the loop remains superconducting. We can thus logically represent a binary "1" or "0" by a supercurrent in the clockwise or counterclockwise direction of a current loop as in Fig. 3.11-4. To make such a device useful for random access memory, it must have at least two functional terminals

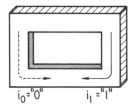

$i_0 = "0"$ $i_1 = "1"$

FIGURE 3.11-4 Two binary states of a simple superconducting current loop.

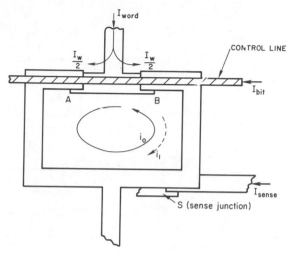

FIGURE 3.11-5 One-bit memory cell using three Josephson junctions (nondestructive read-out).

for reading and writing as well as a threshold for coincident writing (2 or $2\frac{1}{2}$D). The cryotron devices already described have the required thresholds as well as two separate function terminals, the gate and control line. However they do not provide the current loop needed for storage. Both functions can be provided by arranging cryotron junctions into the current loop in the manner that will allow writing of either polarity current and sensing of the stored information. All these can be accomplished by using three Josephson junction cryotrons in the loop, as in Fig. 3.11-5. Junctions A and B provide a means for coincident writing by means of current steering in the loop, and junction S provides nondestructive read-out of the cell. Suppose i_0 is initially stored in the loop and we wish to store i_1. If we apply a positive step function current I_w in the top terminal, it divides equally into the two branches as shown, assuming they have equal inductance. If a bit current I_b is applied in the control line with polarity as shown, it adds to the word current in junction A but subtracts in junction B (Fig. 3.11-6a). In addition to these two externally applied currents, the previously stored current i_0 adds or subtracts within each junction as shown. This stored current, as we see later, has magnitude $i_0 = I_w/2$. If the appropriate sums and differences of these three currents are greater than or less than the critical junction current I_{cr}, namely

$$A \qquad \frac{I_w}{2} + i_0 + I_b = I_w + I_b > I_{cr} \qquad (3.11\text{-}6)$$

$$B \qquad \frac{I_w}{2} - i_0 - I_b = |-I_b| < I_{cr}. \qquad (3.11\text{-}7)$$

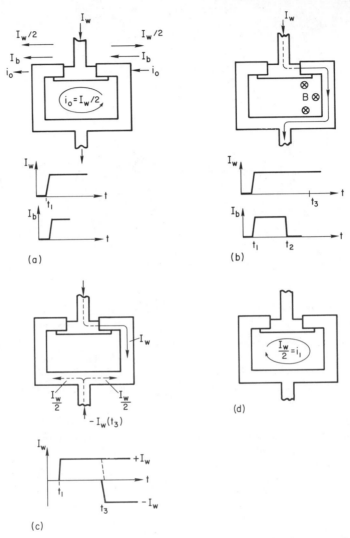

FIGURE 3.11-6 Sequential steps for writing into a superconducting storage loop.

junction A goes normal while B remains superconducting. By current steering principles, all the word current transfers to branch B as in Fig. 3.11-6b and the circulating current decays to zero. The bit current I_b can be removed, allowing junction A to become superconducting once again. The full word current must not switch junction B or

$$I_w < I_{cr} \tag{3.11-8}$$

To finally establish the circulating loop current, the word current must be turned off. To see how the circulating current comes about, we can approach the operation in two ways. The simplest conceptual view is to imagine that at time t_3, a negative step function of word current is applied (Fig. 3.11-6c). This is equivalent to turning off the previous word current. Since both branches of the loop are superconducting, this negative step current divides equally in the two halves, as previously, but in the opposite direction. The net current in the loop is obvious: $I_w/2$ flowing upward on the left side, $I_w - I_w/2 = I_w/2$ flowing downward on the right branch, and no net current into or out of the loop. Hence a circulating supercurrent of value $i_1 = I_w/2$ is left in the loop. Another way to explain the induced current is to note that in step b, with all the word current in the right branch, there is now a net magnetic flux linking the loop. Since the entire loop is now superconducting, any attempt to decrease this flux by turning off I_w will result in an opposing EMF and current to prevent this. Thus a circulating current is induced to produce the same total flux linking the loop. Since there will be flux contributions from current in both branches, the current need only be $I_w/2$ to produce the same total flux.

Note that if initially a current $i_1 = -i_0$ representing a stored "1" was present, the current conditions of (3.11-6) necessary for switching junction A would be

$$I_b > I_{cr} \tag{3.11-9}$$

But to perform the writing shown in Fig. 3.11-6, it was necessary to have $|I_b| < I_{cr}$, so junction B would not switch. We cannot now switch junction A, and the normal writing sequence will leave the cell unchanged. But this leaves a stored "1," which is what we are trying to write anyway; thus the cell is workable. When we wish to write a "0" starting from an initially stored "1," the bit current is reversed, causing junction B to go normal. All other operation are completely analogous to the previous case.

During the writing process, the energy stored initially in the loop by the circulating current i_0 was dissipated and subsequently an equal energy was stored but with an opposite current. There is no resistance and no dissipation during standby, only during switching. This stored energy dissipation represents the major power consumption of the cell and typically is roughly on the order of 10^{-11} J or less depending on cell size.

Sensing of the cell is quite simple. The right-hand branch of the current loop in Fig. 3.11-5 serves as the control line of the S junction. If a current i_1 is stored, a sense current with polarity shown adds to i_1 and together they cause S to go normal. This produces a sense signal of $2\Delta V$ on the order of 2 mV, or a 1 mV pulse traveling in each direction along the sense line (see Section 2.13). If initially i_0 was stored, this would subtract from the sense current and junction S would stay superconducting, giving no signal.

This cell has two functional terminals and hence can be used in 2D or $2\frac{1}{2}$D organizations. A three-terminal cell for 3D organization is conceivable — using two control lines, for instance. However because of decoding problems discussed later, $2\frac{1}{2}$D organizations that require only the simpler two-terminal cell are more practical.

In the above cell, the two binary states were represented by opposite polarity circulating supercurrents. It is possible to construct a simpler cell by using, say, a circulating current for a "1" and no current for a "0." This allows elimination of junction B and some changes in the writing sequence. One possible way is to redefine the bit control line in Fig. 3.11-5 as the word line and reset the entire word to all "0's" (no circulating current) with just a word pulse before coincidently writing "1's." Such a cell would be difficult to organize in a $2\frac{1}{2}$D one bit per chip scheme, hence may not be feasible in practical systems. Other undesirable features are that tolerances and signal to noise ratio become more critical.

3.11.6 Single Device Superconducting Cells Using Trapped Flux

All memory technologies strive to achieve a single device cell, and there are several such configurations possible with superconductors. One simple single device cell stores a circulating current in a superconducting ground plane at the intersection of a bit and word line. The basic principle for establishing the current can best be understood as follows.

In Section 2.11.3 we saw that it was possible to trap flux within the holes of a superconductor by applying a magnetic field to a superconductor above its critical temperature, then lowering the sample temperature. Supercurrents are induced when the field is turned off, giving a net flux trapped within the holes. The direction of the supercurrent flow can be reversed if the initial direction of the applied field is reversed. For a memory element, we can envision that this trapped flux and current can be used to represent stored binary information. However we do not wish to change the temperature of the sample, since this procedure is complex and slow. Rather, we want some means for trapping flux that can be accomplished with H fields or currents. This can be done by an external H field under proper conditions. To understand this, let us start with a superconducting sample with small holes, held at constant temperature at, say, liquid helium temperature ($\sim 4°K$) as in Fig. 3.11-7. If a small external field H_a is applied, supercurrents will be induced to exclude the field from the interior of the superconductor. If the holes are large enough, the H field will pass through as shown. Turning the field off is exactly the same as applying an equal and opposite H field. In such a case, the induced currents and field in the holes are exactly equal and opposite also; thus no flux is trapped. To trap flux, it is necessary for the applied field to exceed the critical field, permitting the superconductor to

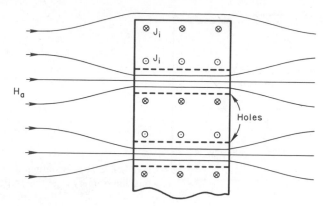

FIGURE 3.11-7   Cross section of superconductor with two holes and externally applied field.

become normal. Suppose this is done in Fig. 3.11-7; that is, H_a is increased to a point where $H_a > H_{cr}$. The supercurrents now see a resistance and are dissipated by I^2R losses so that the H field penetrates the entire sample, which is normal (Fig. 3.11-8). The H field within the sample holds it in the nonsuperconducting state. If we now slowly turn H_a off by applying, say, a slowly rising, equal, and opposite field $-H_a$, the field within the sample begins to decrease, eventually falling below H_{cr}. At this point, *if* the sample can switch back quickly to being a superconductor, the field, which is an infinitesimal amount below the threshold, must be excluded. This will induce supercurrents that because of the geometry, trap flux within the holes. Thus all external excitation is removed, but we have left some stored energy in the superconductor. This represents stored information that remains until intentionally removed. These *holes* are *not* essential for producing trapped supercurrents because they must be induced as described in either case. However the exact location of the external magnetic field generated by these trapped supercurrents is not well defined. In fact they can wander around through the sample, depending on inhomogenieties, and so on. Since we typically sense magnetic flux, it is desirable to confine the supercurrents

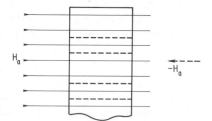

FIGURE 3.11-8   Field penetration when H_a exceeds the critical field.

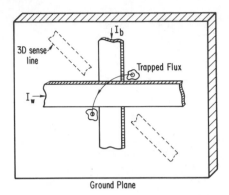

Ground Plane

FIGURE 3.11-9 Continuous superconducting film memory cell using trapped flux.

to positions that will produce the magnetic field as desired. Hence superconducting devices of this type typically have such pinning sites (holes) purposely introduced.

Note that in the foregoing case, the maximum amount of flux was trapped because we assumed that the normal to superconducting phase transition occurred much faster than the fall time of the applied field. If the opposite were true (i.e., if the field decreased very fast), we would be left with no trapped flux. In small practical devices with fast rise and fall time pulses, the applied field typically falls by some amount below H_{cr} before the sample can go normal. Thus some fraction of the maximum trapped flux is actually obtained.

This principle of trapped flux is used in numerous types of memory cells. One simple cell (Fig. 3.11-9) uses a continuous superconducting ground plane over which a word and a bit line are closely spaced. A coincidence of a word and bit current produce orthogonal fields or induced currents in the ground plane which add vectorally to give a maximum along the diagonal (dashed). The word and bit lines are made of materials to remain superconducting (but really do not have to be superconducting). The two currents are chosen so that one current alone cannot induce switching, whereas a coincidence will switch the diagonal region of the ground plane normal, trapping flux in a continuous loop along the diagonal. However the superconducting word and bit lines prevent these loops from forming directly under the cell, and the flux is ideally trapped at the diagonal edges as shown. In real devices, the trapped flux extends well along the edges of the drive lines. This trapped flux could represent a stored "1." A stored "0" could be either no trapped flux, or the opposite polarity flux obtained by no bit current or by reverse polarity, respectively. This provides a two functional terminal cell with coincident writing. For reading, the bit line can be used as a sense line. A large word current could be used to switch all bits along the word line with a sense signal induced by the changing trapped flux in appropriate cells. A three-terminal cell can be made, for instance, by including a separate sense line along the opposite diagonal as shown. This allows coincident reading as well as coincident writing as discussed in Sections 4.2 and 4.4. This cell has appeared in many forms, but all suffer from similar problems. The trapped flux or supercurrents are not very stable and can be moved about (Haering et al., 1963). In a real memory with fabrication and current tolerances, the cells tend to be disturb sensitive. Moreover, because of the orthogonal field addition, a full-select field is only $\sqrt{2}$ times larger than a half-select field, tending to aggravate the situation. The required cell uniformity over a large area made fabrication difficult and expensive, eventually leading to the demise of this cell in the early 1960s.

3.11.7 Cryotron Tree Decoder

Superconducting devices such as Josephson junctions are attractive for large, random access main memory because both the storage cell and logic decoding can be made from the same technology. In addition, superconducting transmission lines are nearly lossless at the pulse rise times of interest in the foreseeable future. However certain fundamental decoding problems inherent to all superconducting devices force the design toward a $2\frac{1}{2}$D, one bit per chip organization similar to transistor memory organizations. This prevents the full exploitation of superconductor properties for large, high speed random access memories but does not exclude their application. To understand this, let us first consider how decoding is done.

The most simple and desirable cryotron decoder consists of a simple current steering tree network (Fig. 3.11-10.) Each tree node consists essentially of a path equivalent to that of Fig. 3.11-3. The address register is connected to the control lines of the various branches of the tree as shown. A current in any control line switches that branch normal, thereby introducing a resistance, hence steering the applied current into the opposite branch. Every combination of an address selects one and only one of the eight drive conductors. For instance, for an address $A = 0$, $B = 0$, $C = 1$ with corresponding complements $\bar{A} = 1, \bar{B} = 1, \bar{C} = 0$, let us assume that all the "1" addresses supply a control current and switch that branch. Hence $\bar{A} = 1$ switches branch A_2 normal, steering current into A_1; $\bar{B} = 1$ switches branch B_2 normal, steering the current into branch B_1; $C = 1$ switches branch C_1 normal, steering the current into C_2. Hence array conductor number 1, binary 001, is selected as desired.

A serious limitation of such a decoder is that the series resistance introduced by the "normal" superconducting branch is quite small. For instance, if the devices in each branch consists of a Josephson device with the characteristics of Fig. 2.11-9, the normal resistance R_n on the straight line portion of the curve is on the order of 0.1 Ω, as shown. For the current steering to be effective,

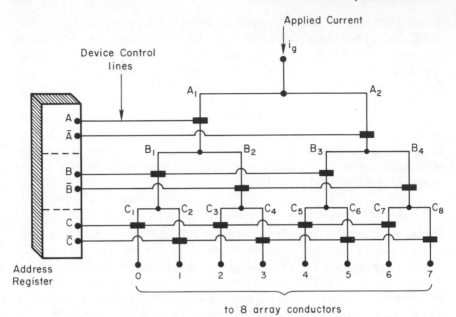

FIGURE 3.11-10   Three-bit cryotron tree decoder.

the resistance or impedance of the decoded array conductor must be less than this device resistance. If this is not the case, the equivalent resistance of an output node of the tree would be as in Fig. 3.11-11 for the previous address 001. The resistance introduced into branch C_1 is R_n, and the array line impedance is Z_0. When branch C_1 is switched, the current i_g at steady state divides into the two branches according to

$$i_1 = i_g \frac{Z_0}{2Z_0 + R_n} \tag{3.11-10}$$

$$i_2 = i_g\left(1 - \frac{Z_0}{2Z_0 + R_n}\right) \tag{3.11-11}$$

To make i_1 very small and i_2 nearly equal to i_g, we must have $R_n \gg Z_0$. Otherwise part of the current flows into each branch. A dilemma now arises. To make full use of the nearly lossless transmission line properties of superconductors, we want to make the array conductors very long, as is done in 3D organized ferrite core memories (Sections 4.4 and 4.7). This also reduces the number of decoders and drivers needed, both very desirable results. However a long line will be a transmission line with an effective impedance Z_0, which must be less than R_n. Let us calculate Z_0 for a possible long line. For a 0.001 in.

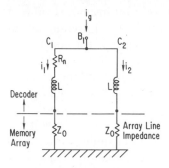

FIGURE 3.11-11 Equivalent circuit of output node of cryotron tree and corresponding array impedance.

(25 μ) wide array conductor above a ground plane, the dielectric insulation would have to be on the order of at least 1000 Å (0.1 μ) thick. Assuming silicon dioxide with a relative dielectric constant of $\varepsilon_r = 4$, the characteristic impedance from (3.11-5) is approximately

$$Z_0 = \frac{377}{\sqrt{\varepsilon_r}} \frac{S}{W} = \frac{377}{2} \left(\frac{0.1}{25} \right) \approx 0.75 \ \Omega \tag{3.11-12}$$

If the tree used Josephson devices with the previous value of $R_n = 0.1 \ \Omega$, then from (3.11-10) and (3.11-11), $i_1 = 0.47 i_q$, and $i_2 = 0.53 i_q$, obviously a poor design. Attempts to redesign the tree with larger R_n and smaller Z_0 are not very feasible. An alternative is to use array conductors that are much shorter than the pulse rise time and to short-circuit them on the opposite end (i.e., a very short transmission line with a short-circuited load impedance). Such an array conductor acts like a pure inductor. However such a constraint typically requires that the memory array be organized much like semiconductor chips (Section 4.9) with fully decoded chips and additional levels of off-chip decoding. This approach can provide a viable system, but it prevents full utilization of the advantages of superconducting transmission lines. However the latter might still be used to advantage for the chip and card interconnecting lines, provided suitable impedance matches can be supplied.

3.12 FERROELECTRIC MATERIALS AND DEVICES

Unlike magnetic phenomena, which data back to ancient times in the form of lodestone, ferroelectric materials are newcomers in science and technology. Since the first ferroelectric, Rochelle salt, was discovered in 1921, this field has experienced a great deal of basic research and has also seen many changes in practical applications, although no significant use in computer memory or logic has ever resulted.

During the 1940s, the need for high dielectric constant insulators spurred the interest in ferroelectrics, not only for capacitors used in radar, communciations, and other electronic applications, but as piezoelectric transducers for various applications (underwater sonic detection, etc.). The discovery of ferroelectricity in barium titanate (probably the second most famous ferroelectric) by von Hippel (1946) gave this field a significant boost. The desire to replace vacuum tubes with solid state devices also led to a great deal of interest in the so-called dielectric amplifier, which makes use of the voltage-controlled capacitance of such materials. These potential applications served to increase materials development, always one of the crucial problems. After World War II, the transducer and capacitor applications continued and expanded, and other interests were generated by this new, evolving technology. Although inherent materials problems as well as the development of the transistor led to the demise of the dielectric amplifier, part of the interests turned toward the nascent computer industry. In fact, ferroelectrics represent one of the oldest *potential* memory technologies, having been proposed as a memory storage element by Anderson (1952) only about a year after Forrester's (1951) publication using square loop ferrites for the same application. The 1950s witnessed a great deal of research on materials such as barium titanate and triglycine sulfate, as well as device development, but to no avail. The inherent materials problems, as well as the initial success of ferrite cores for memory, led to a gradual diminution of interest in ferroelectrics late in the decade. Individual investigators continued to study various aspects of this field and to publish papers, but the interest in ferroelectrics for memory has largely disappeared. As a result, the basic "square loop" ferroelectric device is only briefly described, along with some of its major limitations.*

Ferroelectric materials are characterized by a hysteresis loop of polarization (charge per unit area) P versus applied electric field E (Fig. 3.12-1). The polarization is defined as the number of electric dipole moments Ql per unit volume, completely analogous to magnetization M in Section 2.6.1. The electric field is the driving force, analogous to H in magnetic materials. The electric displacement D is analogous to magnetic flux density, and the three parameters are related by

$$D = \varepsilon_0 E + P \qquad \text{RMKS} \qquad (3.12\text{-}1)$$

where D = displacement (coulombs/cm^2)
   E = electric field (V/m)
   ε_0 — permittivity of free space ($=8.85 \times 10^{-12}$ F/m)
   P = polarization (dipole moment/vol, coulombs/m^2).

* See Dekker (1957), Jona and Shirane (1962), Kittel (1956), and Shirane et al. (1955) for additional information.

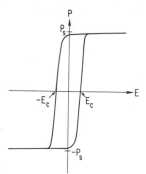

FIGURE 3.12-1   A 60 Hz hysteresis loop of polarization P versus electric field E of single crystal barium titanate at room temperature.

In all good ferroelectrics, P is very much greater than $\varepsilon_0 E$; thus

$$D \approx P \qquad (3.12\text{-}2)$$

For the most widely known ferroelectric, barium titanate ($BaTiO_3$), the hysteresis loop of Fig. 3.12-1 has approximate parameters (Anderson, 1952)

$$P_r \approx 15 \times 10^{-6} \qquad \text{coulombs/cm}^2 \qquad (3.12\text{-}3)$$

$$E_c \approx 2.5 \times 10^3 \text{ V/cm} \qquad (3.12\text{-}4)$$

This material is a relatively good dielectric, having a very large dc resistivity. To make a useful device utilizing the square loop characteristics, it is necessary to apply relatively large electric fields. This suggests a voltage on two metal plates that have the ferroelectric between them as the dielectric. This is nothing more than a capacitor, as in Fig. 3.12-2, and is, in fact the classical form of such devices. A positive voltage pulse applied to the metal electrodes will create an electric field as shown. If the separation S is much smaller than other dimensions, this field is very nearly

$$E = \frac{V}{S} \qquad (3.12\text{-}5)$$

If E is larger than the coercive field E_c or when V_a becomes greater than SE_c, the ferroelectric becomes polarized with $+Q$ on the top electrode, regardless of the previous state. Assume that the ferroelectric was initially in the opposite charge state with $-Q$ on the top electrode. When the positive pulse $+V_a$ is applied and exceeds SE_c, charge must flow, giving rise to a pulse of current as shown by the wave form for i. The charge on the top electrode reverses from $-Q$ to $+Q$ as shown, and the current reduces to zero. When the applied pulse falls to zero, the applied electric field does likewise, but some large charge remains on the plates, bound by the material polarization. This is completely equivalent to a permanently magnetized magnetic toroid with an air

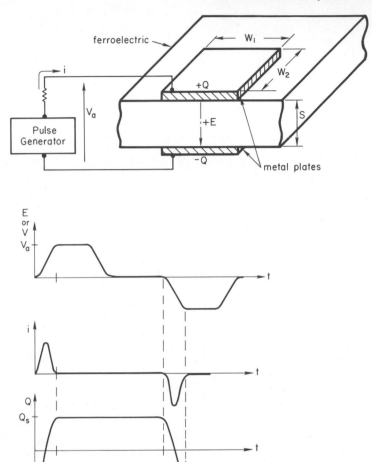

FIGURE 3.12-2   Typical ferroelectric capacitor device and charging wave form.

gap. The poles or charges remain after the external excitation is removed. These bound electric charges can be removed by reversing the polarity of the applied voltage and E field. If a negative pulse of $-V_a$ is now applied, the current flow will be in the opposite direction and the top electrode changes from $+Q$ to $-Q$ as shown, completely analogous to the previous case. Obviously there are two stable states, $+Q$ and $-Q$, which can be switched at will, hence have potential for binary storage. Unlike magnetic toroids that may have any number of wires, the ferroelectric device has only two electrodes

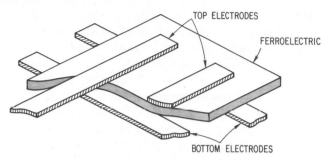

FIGURE 3.12-3   Array of ferroelectric capacitor devices for storage.

(i.e., has two physical and two functional terminals). Thus it can only be used in 2 or $2\frac{1}{2}$D organizations: 3D is not possible. Furthermore, it must be organized as outlined in Section 4.11. Despite these limitations, such devices are attractive because of their relatively simple structure. A storage array that lends itself readily to the organization in Section 4.11 can be fabricated with a set of orthogonal electrodes on top and bottom of a thin ferroelectric insulator (Fig. 3.12-3). This structure has potential for planar batch fabrication with high density, and interest in such applications motivated some of the original study. Unfortunately all suitable ferroelectric known to date have serious fundamental material difficulties.*

The fundamental requirements *a* and *b* in Section 2.3 specify that a binary device must have two stable states that can be cycled an infinite or at least very large number of times. Requirements *a* and *b* of Section 2.4 for a random access memory device specify a well-defined threshold and insensitivity to write disturb. Unfortunately ferroelectric materials do not satisfy these fundamental requirements.† To understand the first of these (i.e., unstable states), suppose in Fig. 3.12-2 that we continued to pulse the device with alternate plus and minus V_a pulses. Initially the switched charge Q would be as shown, with magnitude given by

$$Q = P_r(W_1 W_2) \tag{3.12-6}$$

where $W_1 W_2$ represents the area of the capacitor and P_r is the intrinsic residual polarization. After a short time, it would be noticed that the amount of charge switched was gradually decreasing, as though the vertical size of the PE loop were decreasing. Portions of the dielectric would appear to stop switching altogether, giving an effective decrease in area of the memory cell.

---

* An excellent, supplementary review of ferroelectric material limitations is given by Triebwasser (1962).
† They *do* satisfy *c* and *d* of Section 2.3 as well as *c* of Section 2.4.

This effect occurs in $BaTiO_3$ and potassium niobate ($KNbO_3$), but not in other materials such as triglycene sulfate (TGS) or Rochelle salt. In this example of decreasing switched charge, we can restore the original amplitude by increasing the amplitude of the applied pulses. In other words, the material does not have a well-defined threshold. The latter effect is more general, occurring in all known ferroelectrics and making these devices sensitive to half-select write disturbs. To understand this, we must consider the switching characteristics. The dynamic switching processes in ferroelectrics are similar in many respects to the domain wall switching processes in magnetic devices, especially thin, open flux path film devices. The switching characteristics can be represented by a switching curve of $1/\tau_s$ versus E such as that presented in Fig. 3.12-4 for three different ferroelectrics. Switching in ferroelectrics consists essentially of two processes: the nucleation of domains of reverse polarization, and the subsequent growth of these domains. The growth of these domains at relatively high field strengths is characterized by movement of the domain wall* with a nearly constant mobility. Hence the velocity is proportional to the applied field according to

$$\text{vel} \propto \mu E_a \qquad (3.12\text{-}7)$$

where μ is the mobility. Hence the reciprocal of switching time depends directly on the velocity divided by distance moved, suggesting a linear dependence of $1/\tau_s$ versus E at high fields. This is indeed the case. The high field straight line portions of these curves can be represented by a switching curve of the form

$$\frac{1}{\tau_s} = \frac{1}{S_f}(E - E_c) \qquad \text{[high field]} \qquad (3.12\text{-}8)$$

where τ_s is the required time to reverse the charge from $-Q$ to $+Q$ in Fig. 3.12-2, E is the externally applied electric field, and E_c is the extrapolation of that straight line portion of the curve to $1/\tau_s = 0$ (i.e., the threshold field for that region); S_f is the inverse slope of the ferroelectric switching curve, known as the switching constant analogous to (2.7-1) for magnetics. For the curves in Fig. 3.12-4a and b, the switching parameters for the high field straight line portions are approximately as given in Table 3.12-1. A small value of switching constant and large excess field $E - E_c$ are desirable for faster switching, just as in magnetics.

The low field switching process consists usually of nucleation of domains. As a result, the low field region of the switching curve deviates substantially

---

* Ferroelectric domain walls tend to be very thin, on the order of a few lattice spacings, in contrast to magnetic domain walls, which tend to be tens to hundreds of lattice spacings thick.

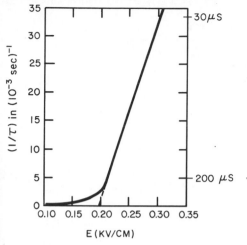

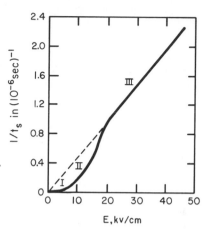

(a) Rochelle salt

(b) Tri-glycine sulfate in high field region

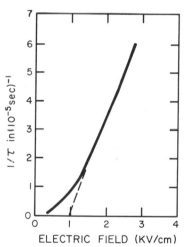

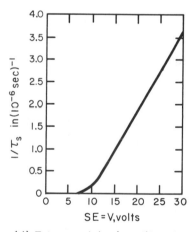

(c) Tri-glycine sulfate in low field region

(d) Tetragonal barium titanate

FIGURE 3.12-4 Reciprocal switching time versus electric field for three common ferro-electrics. (*a*) After Wieder (1958). (*b*) After Fatuzzo and Merz (1969). (*c*) Different sample from (*b*). After Pulvari and Kuebler (1958). (*d*) After Merz (1956); thickness specified only within 2.5 to 35 × 10^{-3} cm.

TABLE 3.12-1

	S_f (V-sec/cm)	E_c (V/cm)
Rochelle salt	0.003	0.2
Triglycine sulfate	0.02	0

from a straight line and can be expressed as

$$\frac{1}{\tau_s} = \frac{1}{\tau_0} e^{-E_0/E} \qquad \text{(low field)} \qquad (3.12\text{-}9)$$

where τ_0 and E_0 are material parameters, varying from one material to another. The "smaller field" at which the above exponential curve is valid varies considerably from material to material, as is evident from Fig. 3.12-4. Some typical values of the activation field E_0 are approximately

$$\text{barium titanate } E_0 \sim 10^4 \text{ V/cm}$$
$$\text{triglycine sulfate } E_0 \sim 3.8 \times 10^3 \text{ V/cm}$$

The intrinsic time constant τ_0 varies considerably not only from one material type to another but also between samples of the same material. Some typical values of τ_0 for barium titanate are 0.4 to 2.5×10^{-7} sec.

This switching curve is very much like the switching curve for magnetic materials but with some major differences. First, all the switching takes place by domain nucleation and growth as already described. *There are no known processes in ferroelectrics akin to rotational switching in magnetics.* The ultimate consequence of this is the tendency of ferroelectric devices to have very slow switching speeds. For instance, using (3.12-8) and the parameters of Table 3.12-1, triglycine sulfate operated at a full-select field of 20 kV/cm would switch in a time determined by

$$\tau_s = \left[\frac{1}{0.02} \times 20 \times 10^3 \right]^{-1} = 1 \times 10^{-6} \text{ sec} \qquad (3.12\text{-}10)$$

A 1 μsec device switching time is required even for a relatively large field, which is typical of ferroelectric devices.

Another and perhaps more significant difference between ferroelectrics and magnetics is that the value of E at which $1/\tau$ is zero (no switching) is zero or near zero field. In other words, there is no well-defined coercive field as shown in Fig. 3.12-4. This seems to be generally true for nearly all ferroelectrics, and it introduces severe half-select disturb problems. For an array operated as in Section 4.11, for a full-select field of some value E_1, the half-select write disturb field is typically $E_1/2$. For, say, triglycine sulfate (Fig.

3.12-4c, a half-select field of approximately 0.4 kV/cm would be needed to minimize half-select disturbs. The full-select field would then be 0.8 kV/cm: using the curve of Fig. 3.12-4c, the switching time for this field would be approximately

$$\tau_s = (0.3 \times 10^5)^{-1} \approx 30 \ \mu\text{sec} \tag{3.12-11}$$

Thus the device becomes quite unattractive for random access memory, assuming the distrub problem can actually be eliminated by the size of field. For Rochelle salt and barium titanate, the switching curves extend to very small values of E, making them less attractive.

One ferroelectric, $Bi_4Ti_3O_{12}$, appears to have a better defined lower threshold than the foregoing examples, with a value of 3 kV/cm (Cummins, 1965). However the threshold field is still time dependent and increases as the field, and hence as $1/\tau_s$ increases. This is a result of the apparent time dependence of the "internal bias" field, which is theorized to be the agent that stabilizes the low field switching characteristics.

The power dissipation of ferroelectrics during switching is moderate compared to other cells. Some typical parameters for a cell, assuming it could work, might be a full-select field of $E_a = 1$ kV/cm with $P_r = 25 \times 10^{-6}$ C/cm^2. The total energy dissipated in transversing the entire hysteresis loop is approximately

$$\text{energy/cycle} = 4P_r E_a \approx 0.1 \ \text{J/(cm}^3)(\text{cycle}) \tag{3.12-12}$$

If we assume that ferroelectric devices can be made with dimension comparable to semiconductor devices (a dubious assumption), typical dimensions might be $5 \times 5 \ \mu$ surface area $\times 1 \ \mu$ thick, giving a volume of 25×10^{-12} cm^3. The energy dissipated per cycle is then

$$0.1 \times 25 \times 10^{-12} = 2.5 \ \text{pJ/cycle}$$

If the device is cycled at a maximum rate of 10^6 Hz, the power dissipated per cell is

$$\text{power per cell} \approx 2.5 \ \mu\text{W/cell} \qquad (\text{at } 10^6 \ \text{Hz})$$

This value is rather small, but it is predicated on being able to achieve very thin ferroelectric layers, which is most unlikely. However, even if the power per cell increased by a factor of 100—to say, 0.25 mW per cell—this is still small. If single crystals are used, lapped to thicknesses measured in mils, the device volumes may become large enough to render dielectric heating a problem.

Finding a suitable ferroelectric material has continually been the major obstacle. One material difficulty is that the square loop properties needed for memory are obtained only in single crystals, which cannot be grown in thin film form or as a deposit onto another substrate. Hence the ease of planar fabrication available with silicon and other technologies (e.g., magnetic bubble materials) is not available with ferroelectrics. Many attempts have been made to produce suitable materials in thin film form (Masson and Minn, 1970), but the results have been discouraging. Likewise, attempts to *circumvent* the poor threshold characteristics have not been very successful. One attempt (Taylor, 1965) uses a very narrow writing pulse—much narrower than the full field switching time. Such a narrow pulse produces very little switching per disturb, but many of these pulses eventually deteriorate the stored information. Such operation only increases the tolerable number of disturbs but does not eliminate the threshold problem. The price paid for this increase is the need for accurate control of pulse width and amplitude, as well as timing of the two half-select pulses, which must add to produce full switching. Such schemes have not found practical applications.

If the material problems could be overcome—that is, if thin films with well-defined thresholds and stable residual polarization states could be obtained—ferroelectrics would still not be attractive compared to semiconductors. It is unlikely that the switching speeds could be improved by the orders of magnitude that would be necessary. Furthermore, the necessary on-chip circuits could not be made with ferroelectrics, hence would require a mixture of technologies. This is very undesirable and an unlikely development. One interesting possibility for such a mixture, however, is the use of a ferroelectric as the gate insulator of a field effect transistor. If a technology could be developed to yield a very thin, square loop ferroelectric film, a truly one-device FET cell could be imagined in which the stored polarization would hold an FET either on or off, depending on the state. Such a device might be useful in a slow write, fast read environment.

3.13   READ–ONLY MEMORY DEVICES

For random access memory applications, the writing process typically places more stringent requirements on the basic cell than does the reading process. Since a fixed or externally alterable read-only memory, by definition, is one that is only read, the cells do not have to provide random writing capabilities. The storage array (Section 4.13) reduces to a simple one-input OR array in which there either *is* coupling between word and sense line (input and output) OR there *is not* coupling. As a result, we would expect much simpler and less expensive cells to be feasible. This is indeed the case. In fact any two functional terminal device is a potential candidate for ROM, and almost every conceivable device has been attempted or proposed. A ROM cell must be capable of coupling a small quantity of energy from the word accessing mechanism, such as a word line, to a bit sensing means, such as a sense line. The devices need not be electrical but can be optical, acoustrical, and so on. It is clear that such a device can be linear or nonlinear. However, from the fundamental requirements of Section 2.3 and the organization of Sections 4.3 to 4.5, a linear cell cannot be used in 3D but is restricted to 2D or $2\frac{1}{2}$D organizations. A 3D memory requires coincidence for reading, which necessitates some threshold mechanism within the cell structure and three functional terminals. Such cells have been made, but they are more costly, hence most ROM cells essentially have two functional terminal.

It is impossible to cover all the devices that have been proposed for ROM. Thus we attempt to categorize similar ones under general, more basic cases, considering some of the more notable devices used in commercial systems. We deal almost exclusively with electrical cells and also those which are fixed or externally alterable. Slow write, fast read ROM is just a special case of ordinary random access memory.

Linear Cells

The three fundamental passive electrical components (linear resistors, capacitors, and inductors) are very attractive for coupling small quantities of energy from a word line to a sense line. Capacitors and inductors have the advantage that ideally, they dissipate no energy themselves, whereas resistors do. However all three components have been used. Resistors can be made in many ways (silk-screened resistor paste, diffused semiconductor lines, etc.*). A diode, semiconductor transistor, or FET makes a better resistor in many ways, and these are often used instead.

Linear capacitor cells are made in the classical sense of a capacitor, namely, two metal plates separated by a thin dielectric. Thin film technology is well suited to this scheme, as indicated in Fig. 3.13-1. At bit positions where large coupling (i.e., a " 1 ") is desired between word and sense line, the conductors are widened to give a larger capacitance. Conversely, at bit locations where a "0" or small coupling is desired, the conductors are not widened. Obvious there still exists some small but finite capacitance, not only between the word and sense line but also between the word line to ground, as well as sense line to ground (Fig. 3.13-1b). The signal to noise ratio as well as overall array performance depends on the relative values of these various capacitances. For high speed operation, the signal to noise ratio becomes very poor. One method for overcoming this is to use a balanced array (Fig. 3.13-2). A cell consists of two word lines and two sense lines above a ground plane. The word lines are driven by a balance voltage source with respect to ground, and the sense lines are read with differential amplifiers. To store a " 1," the

---

* See Dussine (1971, p. 84) for a commercial example.

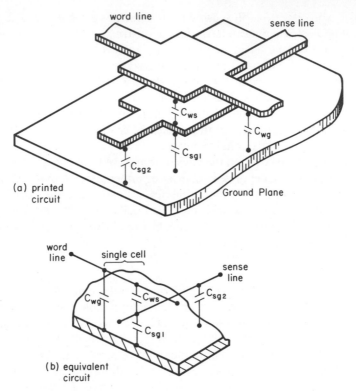

FIGURE 3.13-1   Fixed capacitor ROM cell (stored " 1 ").

capacitance between lines W_+ to S_+ and between W_- to S_- is increased by using the technique of Fig. 3.13-1. The large common node noise resulting from coupling between W_+ to S_- and W_- to S_+ is canceled by the differential amplifier while the differential signal is read. A "0" is just the opposite, giving a negative signal. This balanced capacitor scheme has been used extensively as a microprogrammed emulator in various computers (Abbas et al., 1968).

An externally alterable ROM can be made by inserting a simple conductive plate between the word and sense lines as in Fig. 3.13-3 at all locations where a "1" is to be stored. Such conductive plates can be small metallized regions on a Mylar or other dielectric substrate. The metallized regions can be removed externally (c.g., punched) at all predetermined "0" locations. Subsequently this information card can be inserted between the word and sense line. Such a scheme provides a simple, relatively quick way to change the stored information. However relatively uniform and consistent spacings must be maintained between the various conductors. Such a scheme, known as the card capacitor, has been used extensively for microprogrammed

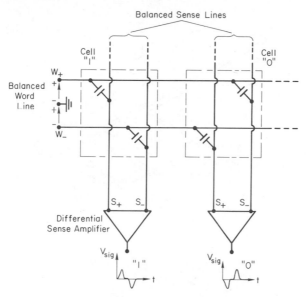

FIGURE 3.13-2 Balanced capacitor ROM cells and array.

emulators on the low end of commercial systems (Haskell, 1966). Similar but slightly modified forms of Fig. 3.13-1 have found other applications as well (EDN/EEE, 1971).

The basic idea of ROM using linear capacitor coupling as in Fig. 3.13-1 can also be achieved by the analogous linear inductor illustrated in Fig. 3.13-4. Inductive coupling to an underlying sense line is achieved by a small parallel segment of conductors to give a "1." If the two conductors run orthogonal to each other, no inductive coupling is present to give a stored "0." However there is still considerable stray capacitive coupling in both the "1" and "0"

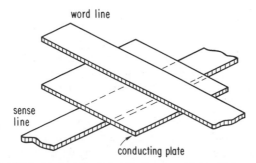

FIGURE 3.13-3 Externally alterable capacitor ROM cell (stored "1").

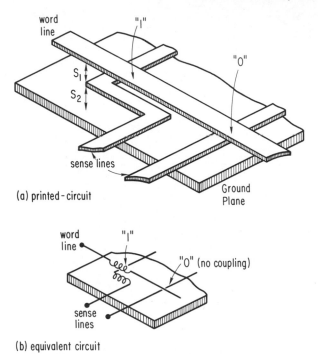

(a) printed-circuit

(b) equivalent circuit

FIGURE 3.13-4   Fixed inductor ROM cells showing "1" and "0."

states that gives rise to considerable noise. A balance scheme analogous to the balanced capacitor of Fig. 3.12-2 is possible. However linear inductor schemes tend to be more bulky and noisy than capacitor schemes, hence have not been as widely used.

Inductively coupled ROM becomes much more attractive when the coupling is increased by the use of a magnetic coupling element. As a result, a number of schemes have appeared. Two very similar versions that have found the most widespread application are transformed-type devices appearing in Fig. 3.12-5. The basic cell in both cases consists of a transformer, with the primary being the word line and secondary being the sense line. The difference between the two lies in the manner of interconnecting the cells in an array. If the primary windings of many cells are connected in series as word W_1 (Fig. 3.12-5a) a signal ("1") appears on each secondary sense winding for all transformers having a common W_1 primary winding. This can represent a word with each secondary sense winding designating the logical bit position in the word. Additional words are achieved by using multiple primary windings on all transformers where a "1" is desired at that bit position. If a "0"

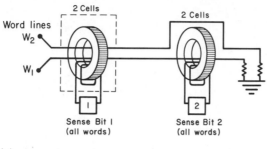

(a) one word per wire

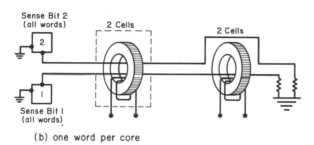

(b) one word per core

FIGURE 3.13-5 Inductive transformer ROM showing binary storage of $W_1 = 11$, $W_2 = 10$.

is desired, the primary winding of that word is made to bypass the proper bit position, as shown by word W_2, bit position 2 in Fig. 3.12-5a. The transformers in such an array have one sense winding and multiple word windings. The identical scheme but in a more elegant mechanical form (Taub and Kington, 1964) has been used extensively in the IBM 360/40 and various control units. Early versions of such schemes were used for code translation in crossbar telephone systems, the Bell Laboratories model 6 computer, the Atlas ground guidance computer, and the stabilization computer in the Polaris submarine.

The exact inverse of the foregoing scheme—namely, transformers with multiple sense windings and one word winding—is also possible (Fig. 3.12-5b). In essence, the sense amplifiers and word drivers have been interchanged. Excitation of one word winding induces signals on all sense lines passing through that transformer. Such a scheme, often referred to as a core "rope" ROM, has been used in space flights (Hopkins, 1964).

These inductive ROM devices were all essentially linear, since they did not depend on any nonlinear property for operation. An endless variety of linear devices appeared in the 1960s and these are described in review articles

(Dussine, 1971; Taub, 1963; Lewin, 1965). Nonlinear inductively coupled ROM devices are not only possible but have some advantages. One fundamental technique makes use of magnetic material with a very well-defined saturation characteristic to allow simple external alteration of the stored information as follows. Suppose in Fig. 3.12-5a that each bit position in the array has a separate transformer so that word lines do not share a common cell. For the example shown of 2 words × 2 bits, there would be four transformers or cells, with the word line storing a "1" at each cell location. A "0" can be stored by placing a small permanent magnet over the transformer of the desired cell. The magnet saturates the transformer, hence reduces the coupling to essentially zero. The advantage of such a scheme is that the fields of permanent magnets can be made to extend over large dimensions; thus the magnets can be external to the physical structure of array. Two schemes that use this basic idea but with rather different internal transformers cells are the twistor (Bobeck, 1957; DeBuske et al., 1959; Looney, 1959) and the thick magnetic film (Matick, 1966) ROM schemes.

Most of the foregoing ideas were developed and used in the 1960s. The advent of high density integrated electronics in the late 1960s was destined to change this situation. A single diode, junction transistor, or FET device makes an excellent ROM cell, with the information stored by the presence or absence of a device at each bit location. Such arrays are easily achieved with high density, using planar semiconductor technology, and many such arrays are commercially available. Two major disadvantages are as follows: a new mask set must be constructed each time the information is changed, and once the array is fabricated, the information content is not changeable. The first condition makes prefabricated information schemes very expensive. This has been circumvented by fabricating a cell at each bit location and including within each cell a means for externally programming the array. Each cell contains a fusible link such as nichrome, which melts at a given current, thus opening that cell connection within the array. This "write 0" current is much larger than that normally used in ROM operation but not large enough to harm the cells. Thus all arrays can be fabricated identically and programmed at any time.

The second disadvantage of preprogrammed arrays just mentioned can be a serious shortcoming—for example, during the development of a processor, where mistakes as well as changes are bound to occur. In such cases, it is desirable to have ROM arrays that can be changed externally, even if this writing time requires minutes or hours. Many slow write, fast read transistor cells can be envisioned, but most suffer from the low density incurred in such designs. A popular scheme that allows high density is the floating gate, avalanche-injection metal oxide semiconductor FET known as a FAMOS devices (EEE, 1971). The FAMOS is essentially a silicon gate FET with no electrical connection to the gate. The gate region serves only as a means to store or not store charge, which inverts the channel or holds it off, respectively. To store charge in a p-channel device, a large negative voltage (about 30 to 50 V in 0.2 mil technology devices) is used at the source (or drain) to ground. An avalanche of electrons charges the gate, which produces positive charges at the surface of the n silicon, inverting it and allowing conduction between source and drain. This stores a " 1 " at each avalanched bit location. Essentially, the charge remains indefinitely in well-made devices. The charge can be removed by flooding the array with ultraviolet light. This stores all "0's." Selective avalanching is used to store "1's" where desired. Undoubtedly numerous other ROM devices will appear as integrated circuit technology becomes more advanced. The major concerns for ROM cells are density and cost per bit. These factors are interrelated, and both depend on cell complexity. To be attractive, ROM cells must be less complex and substantially cheaper than random access cells.

4 Random Access Memory Principles and Organization

4.1 INTRODUCTION

The term "random access" is usually associated with the main memory tied to a central processing unit of a computer. This is by far the most common and largest use of random access memory systems, yet other types of memory, technically speaking, can also be randomly accessed. Thus although most of this chapter is devoted to the main memory type of random access system, there are separate sections on read-only and associative memories, which are certainly accessed randomly.

In Chapter 1 we saw that in the early history of computers, main memory was essentially on a par with the CPU; in fact, the CPU clock cycle was often dictated by the main memory cycle time. However as technologies advanced, the speed of CPU circuits increased dramatically while the speed of main memory tended to saturate (Fig. 1.1-3). This created a gap between processing speed and memory speed, and numerous computer architectures have been devised to bridge it. We also saw in a very general way in Chapters 1 and 2 (particularly in Sections 1.3 and 2.2) that random access memory is more expensive than nonrandom access storage systems, and at the same time, the latter necessarily are slower than random access memory. These conditions are a consequence of the basic construction of either having dedicated wiring and transducers, which are costly but fast, or sharing many transducers, which is inexpensive but slow. The concept of sharing transducers to reduce cost is not limited to nonrandom access systems but is one major distinction between the various types of organizational structure of random access memories (3D, 2D, etc.). We study the various types of organization in this chapter to see the tradeoffs in relative cost versus speed. We examine the basic organizational methods in their pure form without regard to the actual cell or technology, but simply in terms of the number of functional terminals used on each cell. All practical memories are organized in these forms, although some small variations in the exact layout of the cell or array are used for practical reasons. For instance, in a $2\frac{1}{2}$D organization, a cell with three functional terminals can be achieved with just two wires through a core: one wire

246

with two ends serves as one functional terminal, whereas each end of the second wire serves as a separate terminal, one for bit drivers and the other for sense amplifiers on a common bit/sense line. Other cells use three separate wires for three functional terminals and a slightly modified $2\frac{1}{2}$D array organization. In any case, the basic organization remains the same. A relative comparison of the cost and speed of the various organizations indicates the advantages and disadvantages of each.

Various implementations of these organizational techniques in actual memory design are considered in some detail. We concentrate mainly on ferrite cores, thin films, and integrated transistor circuits but also touch on others. Numerous devices have only two physical terminals, and these special cases are considered separately. This organization, which takes the form of a matrix, has much more general applicability and is used as the organizational structure of selection matrices. Reducing circuit count, hence cost, is desirable not only for the memory array itself, but also for the devices that are used as the address decoder to select and drive the physical wires of the array. Selection matrices are often used as such decoder-drivers, and many forms have been devised—some to provide large currents from low current transistors such as the load sharing matrix switch, and others for speed or low cost. Certain types of selection matrices are identical in principle to the memory array operation using devices with two physical terminals. This is quite reasonable because the physical wire of a memory array (e.g., a word or bit line) is nothing more than a "device" with two physical terminals, hence is selected much like a two-terminal cell.

The incompatibility of the memory array fabrication with that of the peripheral circuits used to be a serious problem with most memory systems. Magnetic memories either strung on wires such as cores or evaporated and electroplated on metallic conductors (thin films, plated wires, etc.), were fabricated quite differently from the transistor circuits required to decode, drive, and sense these arrays. As devices become smaller and smaller, one is forced to seek compatible fabrication methods for the array and circuits. Such compatibility problems are difficult to treat in any fundamental way, hence are not considered. Nevertheless it should be recognized that this important driving force in main memory technology has resulted in the appearance of transistorized memory systems in the early 1970s and will continue to be a principal factor in all future memories.

In typical computer operations, a word in main memory is read more often than it is written with the ratio of read to write varying roughly from $\frac{3}{1}$ to $\frac{10}{1}$ or more. Occasionally this can be used to advantage both in the design of elements or cells and in the overall architecture. However we do not consider such special cases, except for the limiting case of read-only memory.

4.2   GENERAL CONSIDERATIONS FOR MEMORY ORGANIZATION

The following sections cover each organizational structure and its variations in considerable detail and perform some engineering analysis on the circuit cost and array delay of each type. Before becoming involved in these details, some general discussions and summary of the advantages and disadvantages of each is very helpful to put the details into proper perspective. There are three broad classes of organization: the two, three, and two and a half dimensional organizations. The 2D and 3D types require a basic storage cell with two and three terminals, respectively, whereas $2\frac{1}{2}$D can use either type of cell. In their pure forms there are variations within these three types: there are basically two types of 3D, the series and parallel connections on the selection lines. Two basic types of $2\frac{1}{2}$D are distinguished primarily by the use of a two- or three-terminal cell. One could argue that the $2\frac{1}{2}$D organization using a three-terminal cell is just a segmented 3D memory, which is true. However additional decoding is required, very much like that in the 2D-2T cell organization, such decoding being unnecessary in a pure 3D structure. Hence the common usage of the term "$2\frac{1}{2}$D." The 2D organization has no fundamental variations but only practical variations in the geometrical layout of the arrays or planes.

In the discussion of the details of memory organization, it is important to understand the meaning of a memory word, since it is commonly used. To avoid confusion, it is necessary to define physical word and logical word. In 3D and 2D organization, the two are identical, but in $2\frac{1}{2}$D (which is becoming more common), physical and logical words can be quite different. A logical word is the total number of bits that are retrieved and delivered to the output buffer register (OBR) or to the CPU in one memory cycle or fetch. A physical word in $2\frac{1}{2}$D is several logical words that are energized simultaneously, though only one is delivered to the OBR. A physical word is simply the number of bits strung along the word selection lines, where the latter are the lines other than the data bit lines. The seemingly subtle distinction is important, since not all bits along any given line need be selected during reading or writing. The manner of selection represents the fundamental distinction between the various organizations. Thus

physical word = total number of bits strung along word selection lines

logical word = total number of bits sensed and gated into OBR on one read cycle

Obviously, if one knows the size of the OBR, the maximum size of the logical word is known.

In addition to the word addressing mechanism, there must be a bit selection mechanism for storing "1" and "0" in the proper positions of the chosen logical word. This will become clear shortly.

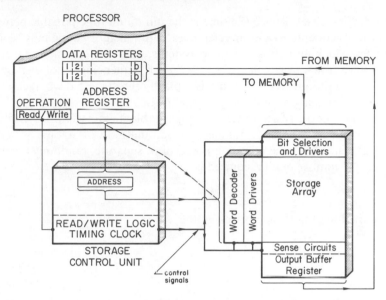

FIGURE 4.2-1 Schematic of general random access memory system showing interface to processor.

To build a useful memory, a number of essential functions must be provided (Fig. 4.2-1). The CPU generates two pieces of information required by the memory system: an address specified by n binary bits located in an address register, and the required operation, read or write. In addition, the CPU must supply the data for a write operation, or the destination for a read operation. As with all memory or storage systems, a storage control unit is necessary to assist in carrying out all the gating, timing, and logical functions corresponding to the CPU request. A given operation of either read or write requires a series of well-defined sequential events to take place. The address must be gated out of the address register into the decoder; for a write operation, the data must be gated into the selected bit lines. Once the word and bit pulses are provided, the information goes into or comes out of the array after a variable time delay. For a read operation, it may be necessary to strobe the sense amplifiers or output buffer latches at the proper time for signal detection. The data must then be gated to the proper CPU register. If the cells are destructively read, the regeneration must be initiated after the data are latched in the output buffer register. All the sequential events are paced by clock pulses generated in the storage control unit. Since any sequence of words can be accessed at any random time, the cycle time must allow time for the worst case (e.g., the shortest reference followed by the longest reference or other worst case). Thus cycle time is the minimum time possible between initiation of sequential, random references. A full memory cycle may require only a few clocking pulses in simple systems, or many complex sequences such as in the one-device cell of Fig. 3.9-7. Such sequencing is not seen by the user; rather, random access memory is typically run such that worst case and best case referencing have the same cycle time.

The total number of separately distinguishable memory entities available is equal to the total possible number of combinations of n bits, which is simply 2^n. Thus for a memory composed of N separate, randomly accessed entities, the number of bits required is

$$N = 2^n \qquad\qquad (4.2\text{-}1)$$

Taking the log of both sides gives

$$\log N = \log 2^n = n \log 2 \qquad \text{or} \qquad n = \frac{\log N}{\log 2} = 3.321 \log N = \log_2 N$$

$$(4.2\text{-}2)$$

In such a system, n must always be an integer (even or odd), since we can either have an address bit or not—there are no fractional bits in a binary system. Thus 2^n or N must be an even number. Sometimes $N = W$, the number of total words in a memory, and in other cases, $N = \sqrt{W}$ or other sectional part. In any case, these parts, which are really physical conductors of some sort, must be grouped in "even" numbers, indeed, in groups of 2^n, to make efficient use of the address bits. The required number of address bits n is independent of the organization of the memory, and N is thus equal to W_l, the total number of logical words that can ever appear in the output buffer register. This is a fundamental relationship: various memory organizations are, in one sense, just different ways of making use of the n bits available. In some cases n is divided into two equal groups of $n/2$ for 3D organization, into (usually, not always) unequal groups for $2\frac{1}{2}$D, or not divided at all for a 2D organization. Thus in Fig. 4.2-1, the decoders and word driver array shown as a unit may consist of two or more separate arrays for $2\frac{1}{2}$ or 3D organization.

The major advantages and disadvantages of the various organizations are as follows:

3D, *Series Connection.* Requires very low drive circuit count with low circuit loading, hence low power requirement and low circuit delay; however the array delay is quite long because of the long lines in series.

3D, *Parallel Connection.* Because lines are in parallel, both array delay and circuit count are low; however since circuit loading is high, both circuit power and circuit delay are large.

Note that with 3D series and parallel, the properties are reversed: series has large array delay but low circuit delay and power, parallel has low array delay but large circuit delay and power.

$2\frac{1}{2}$D, *Three Terminal Cell.* A compromise between 3D series and parallel, giving medium array delay, circuit count, circuit power, and circuit delay; requires coincident selection during reading as well as writing; can use destructive read-out cell similar to that in 3D.

$2\frac{1}{2}$D, *Two Terminal cell.* A further compromise on $2\frac{1}{2}$D-3T cell requiring a less complex cell.

2D. Gives small array delay, low circuit power, and low delay; but considerable selection required on word lines which gives a high circuit count; a nondestructive read-out cell is desirable but not fundamentally necessary.

In the design of a memory system, the choice of organization is made strictly in terms of the tradeoff between total cost and speed. Of course, for a given device technology with a fixed number of functional terminals on the basic cell, one may be limited in this choice; that is, a two-terminal cell cannot be used in a 3D array. Internal array connections for two- and three-terminal cells are shown in Fig. 4.2-2. The latter cell requires more conductors within the array, which decreases the cell density but requires few decoding circuits. The manner in which the ends of these conductors are logically connected to the peripheral circuits at the array edges distinguishes between the various organizations as we see later.

The selection of a memory organization for specific design is intimately bound to the overall memory design and is nearly always an iterative process of trial and error. Generally, the overall computer architecture specifies only the memory size in both total number of logical words and bits per logical word, the read access time, read/write cycle time, and maximum total cost, without concern for the technology or organization. The memory designer must then choose the technology and organization that will give the desired size and speed at the lowest possible cost. The total cost and speed or delay of the memory are determined at least by all the components of the storage and control unit of Fig. 4.2-1. It can be seen that both the cost and delay have contributions from many parts—the address decoders, word and bit line drivers, array delay, and sense amplifiers with OBR latches. The drivers typically require high power, high speed circuits, whereas the sense amplifiers and latches are very low level, low power circuits, with high stability and low noise. The address decoders can take on many forms, ranging from magnetic matrix selection switches and diode selection matrices, to integrated circuit logic trees.

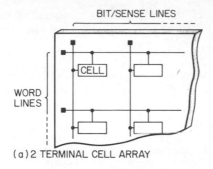

(a) 2 TERMINAL CELL ARRAY

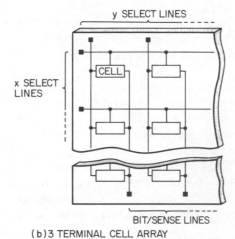

(b) 3 TERMINAL CELL ARRAY

FIGURE 4.2-2 General forms of basic memory arrays or planes.

As we see later, the speed can be increased by going from a 3D series organization to 3D parallel to $2\frac{1}{2}$D to 2D, in that direction; however the circuit count and complexity usually increase in the same direction, but not in a simple manner. Since, moreover, such other factors as the array technology and cell structure change for different organizations, no general principles can be established. In designing a ferrite core memory, the first consideration is core switching time, which is a major factor in determining cycle time, module size, and cost. The core switching time dictates the speed, amplitude, pulse width, and power of the driving circuits. For a chosen core and switching time, the driving and sensing circuits must be designed and the cost determined. Although switching time is a very important part of the cycle time, it can be changed substantially by the choice of organization, which is reflected back into the circuit as well as array cost. On the other hand, for a semiconductor integrated circuit memory, the first considerations are the technology (e.g., bipolar or FET), the cell structure (e.g., a flip-flop two- or three-terminal cell or single device cell), and bits per chip. If a two-terminal cell is chosen, $2\frac{1}{2}$D organization is a natural consequence. Thus the choice of organization is not nearly as straightforward as would be desired. In fact other practical considerations having nothing to do with speed or cost may bear very substantially on the choice of organization. This is especially true in semiconductor memories in which the bit density is large and the size of the silicon chips or array containing the bits is very small, making many pin connections to such chips impossible. This condition has a strong influence on the organization. We now consider each of the organizations in their pure form, then examine the practical implementations in specific technologies.

4.3 TWO-DIMENSIONAL ORGANIZATION

The simplest method organizationally, but the most expensive approach for achieving word and bit addressing, is the so-called 2D or "word"-organized geometry (Fig. 4.3-1). This scheme has a number of advantages and disadvantages. The word selection mechanism uses linear decoding; if there are W words (physical = logical word) the decoding must select 1 out of W words. For large arrays, this becomes complex and expensive. To build, say, a

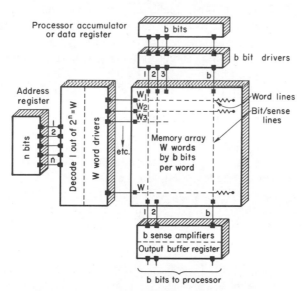

FIGURE 4.3-1 Schematic of 2D organized memory.

memory or 1M words, the address decoder must select one out of 10^6, requiring more than 10^6 selection devices plus necessary word drivers, which can number up to 10^6, a rather sizable amount of circuitry.

The reason for the term "two-dimensional" organization is obvious from Fig. 4.3-1 since the array has only length and breadth, W and b. However in some technologies (e.g., thin film magnetics, cryogenics, transistors) it is not possible, or not desirable from a volumetric standpoint, to put the entire array on one substrate. The one substrate in Fig. 4.3-1 would be divided into several along the bit/sense lines, and interconnections would be made between the substrates. This might be done in a thin film memory; for instance, if the word lines and bit/sense lines are on 0.010 in. centers, and the substrates, with all deposited layers, are 4×1 in., a maximum of 400 words $\times$ 100 bits/word could be accommodated on a substrate—actually less, since allowance for end connections must be included. Thus something on the order of 300 words $\times$ 64 bits/word would be reasonable. A 4096 word memory would require more than 13 such substrates with appropriate interconnections. The substrates do not have to be laid out in one plane, but can be folded one under the other if desired. Other possible physical structures include fabricating the arrays orthogonal to that shown, permitting the word lines to run perpendicular to the substrates. The wiring for the word lines becomes complex and expensive to achieve, however discouraging this type of organization.

In 2D, no decoding is required on the bit lines because the CPU data register in Fig. 4.2-1 contains one bit for each bit of the memory word (i.e., one-to-one correspondence between the data bits and bit drivers). The data bits from the CPU accumulator either turn on or hold off the corresponding bit drivers. Likewise, no decoding is required on the sense lines, since there is one sense amplifier for each bit in a word.

The number of bits in the address register is then simply given by

$$n = 3.32 \log W = \log_2 W \qquad (4.3\text{-}1)$$

The number of transducers* or circuits that must be connected to a 2D array is easily deduced. Each word line must have one driver and each driver must be connected to one logic gate on the last stage of the decoder of Fig. 4.2-1. Thus minima of W drivers and W gates in the last stage of the decoder are required. More than W gates are required in the entire decoder, whether it be a selection matrix or a logic tree, but we include only the output stage, which constitutes the largest part. One driver is needed for each bit line and

---

* A transducer is taken to indicate any circuit or set of circuits or devices that must convert one type of energy, such as the dc power supply, into another type, such as a word or bit pulse of proper rise time, duration, and amplitude, or small signals into logic level voltages, and so on.

one sense amplifier for each sense line, thus b bit drivers and b sense amplifiers are necessary. These transducer requirements are summarized in Table 4.5-2.

In Fig. 4.3-1 it is apparent that if the memory consisted of a very large number of words (e.g., 65K) and relatively few bits per word (e.g., 64), the physical structure would be very long but narrow—that is, very long in the direction of bit/sense lines but short in the direction of the word lines. This arrangement, though most simple conceptionally, is not only cumbersome in structure but extremely costly in terms of the number of circuits required for its operation. Table 4.5-2 calls for W drivers and W decode gates (last stage), and these requirements can be the dominating factor in a large memory (e.g., a 500K word memory would require more than 500K drivers and 500K decode gates). This circuit count is larger than that of most large size computers. However, it is also to be noted that at least for small memory sizes, where the array is more nearly square, 2D organization gives the minimum wiring delay. Thus this type of organization is most suitable for small memories where speed is important. This can be understood by examining the relative cost per bit and delay.

For a given total number of bits N, the total storage array cost, exclusive of circuits, varies only by small factors as the organization changes. However total circuit cost and array delay can vary significantly. Since cost variations due to organizational changes are difficult to characterize in a general way, we consider only circuit cost and array delay in all subsequent analysis. An absolute cost and delay can be obtained only for a specific technology implementation. To understand the tradeoffs, we will use nonnumerical multiplying factors for circuit cost and delay per bit.

4.3.1 Two-Dimensional Circuit Cost Per Bit

Let us assume the total circuit cost of decoder and word line driver for each word line is some known value C_{w2}, and likewise the total cost of both bit driving and sensing together is C_{b2} for each bit line.* Since there are W word lines and b bit/sense lines, we have

$$\text{total circuit cost} = C_{w2}W + C_{b2}b \qquad (4.3\text{-}2)$$

The circuit cost per bit is obtained by dividing by the total number of bits N, to get

$$C_{T2} = \frac{C_{w2}W + C_{b2}b}{N} \qquad ¢/\text{bit} \qquad (4.3\text{-}3)$$

---

* We could separate the costs for word decoding and driving, bit driving, and sensing, but no additional insights are obtained. The subscripts $w2$ and $b2$ indicate word lines 2D and bit lines 2D organizations, respectively.

Obviously C_{T2} is a function of the two variables W and b. Assuming W and b to be totally independent, for a fixed value of b, C_{T2} must decrease monotonically as W increases (i.e., no minimum). Likewise, for a fixed value W, C_{T2} must decrease monotonically with increasing b. In any array design, however, W and b are related by

$$N = Wb \qquad \text{or} \qquad b = \frac{N}{W} \qquad\qquad (4.3\text{-}4)$$

As a result, along a contour of constant N, the value of C_{T2} will have a minimum, hence an optimum value of W and b. These are the relationships of interest to us. To determine this optimum condition for a fixed value of N, it is necessary to express (4.3-3) in terms of only N and W or only N and b. Choosing the former, we can substitute (4.3-4) for b into (4.3-3) to get

$$C_{T2} = \frac{C_{w2}\,W}{N} + \frac{C_{b2}}{W} \qquad \text{¢/bit} \qquad\qquad (4.3\text{-}5)$$

For a given memory size N, we can now find the best value for W to give minimum circuit cost per bit by taking the derivative of (4.3-5) with respect to W, holding N, C_{w2}, and C_{b2} constant, setting it equal to 0, and solving for W. Doing this

$$\frac{dC_{T2}}{dW} = \frac{C_{w2}}{N} - \frac{C_{b2}}{W^2} \equiv 0 \qquad\qquad (4.3\text{-}6)$$

Solving (4.3-6) gives

$$\text{optimum } W = \left(N\,\frac{C_{b2}}{C_{w2}} \right)^{1/2} \qquad\qquad (4.3\text{-}7)$$

If the circuit costs are equal ($C_{w2} = C_{b2}$), we would expect the minimum cost per bit to occur for a minimum periphery, devicewise, along the array (i.e., a square array). Assuming cost equality to be the case, then (4.3-7) and (4.3-4) give

$$W = N^{1/2} \qquad \text{and} \qquad b = \frac{N}{W} = N^{1/2} \qquad \text{for} \qquad C_{w2} = C_{b2} \qquad (4.3\text{-}8)$$

Thus for this case W equals b for minimum circuit cost. Unfortunately, as indicated previously, in practical main memories the number of words greatly exceeds the bits per word, which leads to a nonoptimum cost layout.

In the devices of many of the older technologies such as thin film, the word drivers were required to deliver more current and larger power than bit drivers necessitating more expensive transistors. This cost, added to those of the required decoders on word lines, made the word line cost larger than the bit line cost. Assuming this to be the case, namely, $C_{w2} > C_{b2}$, then for a given fixed total number of bits N, (4.3-7) indicates that the number of words should be decreased and (4.3-4) indicates that the number of bits per word b should be increased. However b is fixed by the CPU architecture and a larger memory forces the designer along the path of high cost. Hence the organization is more applicable to smaller arrays, such as in scratch-pad memories.

If we design for the optimum value of W as given by (4.3-7), the optimum cost per bit obtained by substituting (4.3-7) in (4.3-5) is

$$\text{optimum } C_{T2}\bigg|_{\text{opt } W} = 2\left(\frac{C_{w2}\,C_{b2}}{N}\right)^{1/2} \qquad \text{¢/bit} \qquad (4.3\text{-}9)$$

where C_{w2} = total word line circuit cost per word

C_{b2} = total bit/sense line circuit cost per line

N = total number of bits in memory

4.3.2 Two-Dimensional Delay

The total delay of any organization is a sum of the appropriate array and circuit delays. The maximum array delay occurs during reading and occurs at the bit located farthest from the word drivers and simultaneously farthest from the sense amplifiers. This is the worst case, since a read pulse must propagate down the full length of the word line to interrogate the bit, then the signal must travel the full length of the sense line. During writing, the word and bit pulses can travel simultaneously; thus the writing delay is the maximum of either the word or bit line delay. If we assume the delays *per bit* along word and sense lines are d_{w2} and d_{s2}, respectively, the total array delay is the sum of b delays along the word and W delays along the sense line or

$$D_{A2} = d_{w2}b + d_{s2}W \qquad (4.3\text{-}10)$$

In memory design, we are interested in optimizing the total delay, since we already know the delay per bit, whereas previously the cost *per bit* was important. To optimize the total array delay along the constraint of fixed N, we can substitute (4.3-4) for b to get

$$D_{A2} = d_{w2}\frac{N}{W} + d_{s2}W \qquad (4.3\text{-}11)$$

Proceeding as before, the optimum number of words for minimum delay is obtained by taking the derivative of (4.3-11) with respect to W, equating to 0 and solving for W to get

$$\frac{dD_{A2}}{dW} = d_{s2} - \frac{Nd_{w2}}{W^2} \equiv 0 \qquad (4.3\text{-}12)$$

or

$$\text{optimum } W\bigg|_{\substack{\text{min} \\ \text{delay}}} = \left(N\frac{d_{w2}}{d_{s2}}\right)^{1/2} \qquad (4.3\text{-}13)$$

and

$$\text{optimum } b\bigg|_{\substack{\text{min} \\ \text{delay}}} = \left(N\frac{d_{s2}}{d_{w2}}\right)^{1/2} \qquad (4.3\text{-}14)$$

The optimum delay is obtained by substituting (4.3-13) into (4.3-11) to get

$$\text{optimum } D_{A2} = 2(Nd_{w2}d_{s2})^{1/2} \qquad (4.3\text{-}15)$$

All these equations are summarized in Table 4.5-1.

Note from (4.3-13) and (4.3-14) that for equal delays per bit along the word and sense lines, the optimum array delay for a fixed value of N is achieved with a square of $N^{1/2}$ on each side, just as for the cost condition of (4.3-8). As before, this merely indicates that a square geometry has maximum area within a minimum periphery. When the word and sense line delays are unequal, the optimum array geometry will shift as before.

4.4   THREE-DIMENSIONAL ORGANIZATION

There are two basic types of 3D storage: the series and parallel connections for the selection lines. The series 3D organization has long been used in ferrite core arrays and is very economical in terms of transducer count, but it is also the slowest in terms of array delay. Because it is so common, this type is usually thought of as being the only 3D organization. However the parallel version is also used, particularly in semiconductor memories. We consider both fundamental types.

In the classical 3D series organization, the x and y selection lines are connected in series between planes as in Fig. 4.4-1a, and the bit/sense lines are connected in series *on* a plane as in Fig. 4.4-1b. A general three-terminal cell is depicted, and only one x and one y line. The bit/sense line could be one line as in a three-wire core memory, or two separate wires, one for the

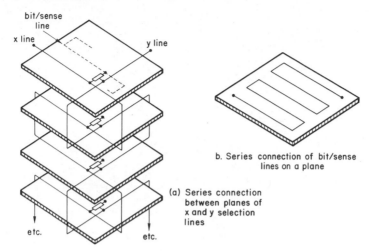

FIGURE 4.4-1   Schematic of 3D series organization in 3D geometry.

inhibit function, and one for sensing as in a four-wire core memory. A more specific embodiment of the 3D series organization is shown in Fig. 4.7-1. The bit line is more commonly referred to as the inhibit line in ferrite core arrays, for reasons that will become obvious; in other 3D devices (e.g., semiconductor flip-flop cells) it is called a bit or digit line because it does not "inhibit" a cell as it does in a core array. The 3D series array need not be laid out in a 3D geometry but also can be arranged in a planar geometry as in Fig. 4.4-2; since the peripheral circuits are contained in small modular

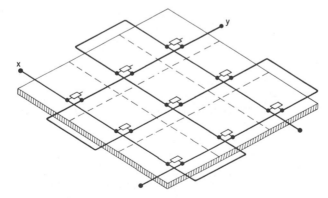

FIGURE 4.4-2   Schematic of 3D series organization in planar geometry.

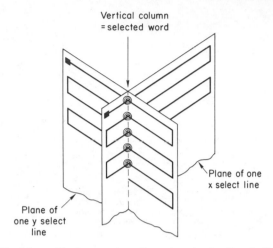

FIGURE 4.4-3 Word formed by intersection of x and y selection lines in 3D core array (bit/sense line not shown).

packets, however, additional wiring delays and interconnections from the distant bit planes to the circuits make this planar layout impractical in many cases.

The basic selection principle requires the use of an x-select, a y-select, and a bit (or inhibit) line for writing and an x-select, a y-select, and a sense line for writing. The planes of each x- and y-select line intersect in one vertical column (Fig. 4.4-3) to select an entire physical word. Thus there are as many bits per logical word as there are bit planes. Energizing an x and y line would store all "1's" in the word; a "0" is stored on any given plane by applying an inhibit current to cancel out the y-select field as described in Section 3.9. If the cells were not cores but rather transistor flip-flops as in Fig. 3.8-3, a coincidence of the x, y, and "1" bit lines or the x, y and "0" bit lines will store appropriate "1's" and "0's." For reading, energizing the x and y lines serves to read all bits of the word with proper "1" and "0" signals appearing on the sense lines for each bit.

Thus for 3D organization, the logical words are themselves coincidently selected, not just the physical word lines and bits. The array is typically broken into a square of $W^{1/2} \times W^{1/2}$ logical words by b bits/word. The number of address bits required for decoding is still $n = \log_2 W$. This is easily seen as follows: each side of the $W^{1/2} \times W^{1/2}$ array requires selection of one out of $W^{1/2}$ physical lines or a number of address bits of

$$n_1 = \log_2 W^{1/2} = \tfrac{1}{2}\log_2 W \quad \text{per side} \tag{4.4-1}$$

But there are two sides. Thus the total number of address bits required is

$$n = 2n_1 = 2 \times \log_2 W^{1/2} = \log_2 W \qquad (4.4\text{-}2)$$

There is no saving in address bits, but there is considerable economy in total circuit count in the decoding circuitry. For instance, on the last stage of the decoder for a selection of one out of $1\text{K}' = 1024$ physical words, $W = 1\text{K}'$ gates are needed for a straightforward 2D array. For 3D, however, the total number of gates in the last stage of the decoder is $2W^{1/2} = 2(1\text{K}')^{1/2} = 2 \times 32 = 64$. This is quite a substantial saving, since now a considerable amount of the decoding is done within the memory device. Putting additional stringent requirements on the device is costly, but usually a substantial net savings results nevertheless. The circuits required for various functions on a typical array are summarized in Table 4.5-2. The total array delay and circuit cost per bit for the 3D series connection can be obtained in a general way as was done in Section 4.3 for the 2D organization. Let us assume the array consists of $W^{1/2} \times W^{1/2}$ words and b bits per word for each module. If this module is not sufficient to contain as many words as are needed, identical modules with the same cost per bit and delay will be added in parallel.

4.4.1 Three-Dimensional Circuit Cost Per Bit

The total number of bits is N per module. Let the cost of the x and y drivers be identical and equal to C_{w3} ¢ for each line, where the subscript $w3$ indicates 3D, series connection, word lines; let the inhibit and sense line circuits, added together, cost C_{z3} ¢/line. Since the module is $W^{1/2} \times W^{1/2} \times b$ bits, the total circuit cost per bit is

$$C_{T3} = \frac{1}{N}(2C_{w3}(W)^{1/2} + C_{z3}b) \quad ¢/\text{bit} \qquad (4.4\text{-}3)$$

As previously in the 2D analysis, we wish to find the optimum cost for a fixed value of N and the corresponding number of words W and bits b. Thus we wish to express (4.4-3) in terms of W and N only, making it possible to take the derivative with respect to W with the constraint that $N = $ constant. This allows both W and b to vary to their optimum values under the constraint that $Wb = N$. In practice, we normally would be given a fixed value of b, hence could not allow b to vary. For now, we wish to investigate the case of allowing b to be optimized as well as W, which will give the unrestrained optimum as a function of N. Afterward we will hold b fixed to see the consequence. This unrestrained optimum is obtained by making use of

$$W^{1/2} \times W^{1/2} \times b = N \qquad \text{or} \qquad b = \frac{N}{W} \qquad (4.4\text{-}4)$$

Substituting (4.4-4) into (4.4-3) gives

$$C_{T3} = \frac{2C_{w3}}{N} W^{1/2} + \frac{C_{z3}}{W} \quad ¢/\text{bit} \tag{4.4-5}$$

For a given size module of fixed bits N, we can now find the optimum array dimensions for minimum cost. This can be done by taking the derivative of (4.4-5) with respect to W and set equal to 0 or

$$\frac{dC_{T3}}{dW} = \frac{1}{2}\left(\frac{2C_{w3}}{N}\right)W^{-1/2} - C_{z3}W^{-2} \equiv 0 \tag{4.4-6}$$

Solving for the optimum value of W gives

$$\left.\text{optimum } W\right|_{\substack{\text{min}\\\text{cost}}} = \left(\frac{C_{z3}}{C_{w3}} N\right)^{2/3} \tag{4.4-7}$$

and for the optimum number of bits/word

$$\left.\text{optimum } b\right|_{\substack{\text{min}\\\text{cost}}} = \frac{N}{W_{\text{opt}}} = \left(\frac{C_{w3}}{C_{z3}}\right)^{2/3} N^{1/3} \tag{4.4-8}$$

When the costs of the word and of the inhibit/sense circuits are identical, we would expect a cubic module to give minimum cost per bit. Substituting $C_{w3} = C_{z3}$ into (4.4-7) and (4.4-8) gives

$$W^{1/2} = b = N^{1/3} \tag{4.4-9}$$

which is a cube as expected. In our analysis we allowed both b and W to vary, to give the array configuration with minimum circuit cost. In practice, the value of b is usually fixed, and we wish to pick an array size to meet the speed requirement and give as low a cost as possible. If we fix b, the array with minimum circuit cost, under the foregoing assumptions, is that with a number of words given by (4.4-7). If we let the costs of the word and sense/inhibit circuitry be identical, the module with fixed b and optimum circuit cost is the cube given by (4.4-9). Hence when b is fixed, the optimum module size N is fixed. If we allow W or N to increase or decrease beyond this value while b is fixed, the circuit cost per bit will increase. Before we can decide on the final module size, we must consider other factors such as the array fabrication cost per bit as a function of W and the array delay. We investigate the delay for 3D organization below, and a comparison of cost and delay for $2\frac{1}{2}$D versus 3D in Section 4.6. For now, it is interesting to note that for core arrays, some typical module sizes are $W = 4096$ words and $b = 64$ bits/word, which is a perfect cube of $64 \times 64 \times 64$.

The optimum cost per bit is now easily obtained by substituting the optimum W into (4.4-5) to get

$$\text{optimum } C_{T3}\bigg|_{\text{opt } W} = 3\left(\frac{C_{w3}{}^2 C_{z3}}{N^2}\right)^{1/3} \text{¢/bit} \qquad (4.4\text{-}10)$$

where C_{T3} = optimum circuit cost per bit (total) for 3D, series word line connection

C_{w3} = circuit cost/line of each x and each y word line

C_{z3} = circuit cost/line of inhibit/sense line together

4.4.2 Three-Dimensional Delay

The maximum array delay, neglecting the width of applied pulses, occurs during reading and depends slightly on the actual location of the sense amplifiers with respect to the drivers. For the worst case, we will have to wait for a full x or y line delay plus a full sense line delay. In ferrite core 3D series organization, factors other than the maximum word and sense line delay significantly influence cycle time. The major factor arises from timing problems on the inhibit pulse during writing. When a "0" is stored, an inhibit line must be energized in advance, to ensure cancellation of either the x or y line pulse. This inhibit pulse must remain on until either the x or y line pulse is removed from the cell in question. If the inhibit pulse is turned on too late or removed prematurely, the bit will be switched partially or fully, giving erroneous storage. In some worse case bit positions, a part of the inhibit delay plus time for overlapping must be added to the y or x line delay and can increase the cycle time. In $3T - 2\frac{1}{2}D$, no such time sequences are required. This problem is specific to ferrite cores and does not occur in 3D transistor flip-flop as long as the x, y, and bit pulses overlap long enough to switch the cell. We do not include these timing problems in our delay calculations, but they can be significant. Timing problems are discussed in the sections on specific memory types. Assuming that the x and y lines are of equal length, the delays per bit d_{w3} also are equal, and the sense line delay per bit is d_{s3}, the worst case delay is

$$D_{A3} = \text{word line delay} + \text{sense line delay}$$
$$= d_{w3} W^{1/2} b + d_{z3} W \quad \text{nsec} \qquad (4.4\text{-}11)$$

where d_{w3} and d_{s3} are in nanoseconds per bit. Since $b = N/W$, (4.4-1), can be simplified to

$$D_{A3} = d_{w3} N(W)^{-1/2} + d_{s3} W \qquad (4.4\text{-}12)$$

We see later that the delay is rather large, and in many cases it can be reduced by the 3D parallel or $2\frac{1}{2}D$ organization. Even though we seldom have a choice for W and b in actual design, the optimum values for minimum delay can be found by setting the first derivative to zero for a constant total bit size N or

$$\frac{dD_{A3}}{dW} = -\frac{1}{2}d_{w3}N(W)^{-3/2} + d_{s3} \equiv 0 \qquad (4.4\text{-}13)$$

Solving for W gives the optimum value for minimum delay at a fixed value of N. This is the minimum, since the second derivative is positive. Hence

$$\text{optimum } W\bigg|_{\substack{\text{min} \\ \text{delay}}} = \left(\frac{1}{2}\frac{d_{w3}}{d_{s3}}N\right)^{2/3} \qquad (4.4\text{-}14a)$$

and

$$\text{optimum } b\bigg|_{\substack{\text{min} \\ \text{delay}}} = \frac{N}{W} = \left(\frac{2d_{s3}}{d_{w3}}\right)^{2/3}N^{1/3} \qquad (4.4\text{-}14b)$$

If the delays per bit on word and sense line are equal (i.e., $d_{w3} = d_{s3}$), for fixed N, the optimum array delay from (4.4-14a) and (4.4-14b) is obtained with

$$W = \left(\frac{N}{2}\right)^{2/3} \quad \text{and} \quad b = \frac{N}{W} = (4N)^{1/3} \qquad (4.4\text{-}15)$$

The dimension (i.e., number of wires), along the x and y directions of the array, for minimum delay under the above assumption, is

$$x = y = W^{1/2}\bigg|_{d_{s3}=d_{w3}} = \left(\frac{N}{2}\right)^{1/3} \qquad (4.4\text{-}16)$$

Thus the ratio of the vertical z to x or y dimension would be

$$\frac{z}{x} = \frac{b}{W^{1/2}}\bigg|_{\substack{\text{min delay} \\ d_{w3}=d_{s3}}} = \frac{4N^{1/3}}{(N/2)^{1/3}} = 8^{1/3} = 2 \qquad (4.4\text{-}17)$$

Thus b should be twice the x or y dimension to achieve minimum delay under these assumptions. Substitution of the optimum number of words from (4.4-14a) in (4.4-12) gives for the optimum delay, when N is fixed,

$$\text{optimum } D_{A3} = 1.5(2d_{w3}d_{s3}{}^2N^2)^{1/3} \qquad (4.4\text{-}18)$$

This relation is valid only for W and b optimized according to (4.4-14a) and (4.4-14b). Unfortunately in 3D organization b is fixed by the computer architecture and W is then chosen as large as possible to stay within a prescribed delay constraint. This does not follow the path of minimum delay except under special conditions. The foregoing equations are summarized in Table 4.5-1.

4.4.3 Three-Dimensional Parallel Organization

There is no fundamental reason for not replacing the series connection of the x lines or y lines in Fig. 4.4-1 by a parallel connection (Fig. 4.4-4). Under certain conditions the latter will reduce the array delay, but the penalty is the increased drive current requirement. In ferrite core arrays, where the delay results strictly from transmission line propagation time, the delay is decrease by the same factor that the current is increased. But the drive currents for core arrays are quite large at the outset, necessitating the series connection. Since transistor flip-flop cells have much lower current requirements, a certain amount of paralleling is possible and has been used. The bit and sense lines remain the same for both cases.

The cost per bit of the parallel 3D scheme is identical in form to that for the series 3D except the cost of the x and y word drivers is larger for identical cells and modules. Thus the circuit cost per bit for the parallel 3D organization is

$$C_{T3p} = \frac{2C_{w3p}}{N} W^{1/2} + \frac{C_{z3p}}{W} \quad \text{¢/bit} \qquad (4.4\text{-}19)$$

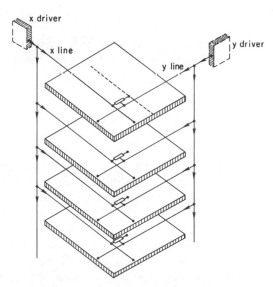

FIGURE 4.4-4 Schematic of 3D parallel organization showing x and y selection lines.

where C_{w3p} and C_{z3p} represent the costs per circuit on the word line and the bit/sense line, respectively, with p referring to parallel connection. The optimum word and bit sizes as well as optimum cost per bit are analogous to the series connection with appropriate values of the circuit costs as already discussed.

The parallel connection does not always reduce the array delay. In some cases, such as highly integrated FET arrays in which the delay results from RC time constants, the delay can be independent of the connection. In general, the delay can be reduced by a parallel connection only when the pulses are limited by the propagation velocity $v = [LC]^{-1/2}$ type of behavior. *Assuming this to be the case*, the previous series array delay will be reduced by the parallel connection; the worst case delay will again occur during reading and will be the sum of the total delay on an x or y line (assumed equal) plus the delay on the sense line or

$$D_{3p} = d_{w3p}W^{1/2} + d_{s3p}W \qquad (4.4\text{-}20)$$

But for the same cell and selection method at the cell level, the delays per bit must be the same for series or parallel; thus the total delays for the series and parallel connections become

$$\text{series } D_{3s} = d_{w3}W^{1/2}b + d_{s3}W \qquad (4.4\text{-}21)$$

$$\text{parallel } D_{w3} = d_{w3}W^{1/2} + d_{s3}W \qquad (4.4\text{-}22)$$

Obviously the word line delays represented by the first term in (4.4-21) and in (4.4-22) are quite different, the series term being b times larger than the parallel term. Since b can be as large as 64 to 100 bits/word, the reduction in delay by the parallel connection can be quite large, particularly if $W^{1/2}$ is on the order of b, which typically is the case (e.g., 4K' word $\times$ 64 bits/word, giving $W^{1/2} = b = 64$).

4.5   2.5-DIMENSIONAL ORGANIZATION

For a 2D memory we need a device with two functional terminals; likewise for 3D we need three functional terminals. The two fundamental forms of $2\frac{1}{2}$D use a device with either two or three terminals. We denote these as 2T-$2\frac{1}{2}$D and 3T-$2\frac{1}{2}$D, respectively. These two types have the same organizational form and in fact are identical in the writing process. The major difference appears during reading, where the 3T cells are coincidently selected and the 2T cells are not. This distinction is important in $2\frac{1}{2}$D organizations, which uses cells that are read destructively. Since the $2\frac{1}{2}$D organization is between 2D and 3D, it is possible to start with either of the latter and evolve to the $2\frac{1}{2}$D form. Since nearly all main memories today are $2\frac{1}{2}$D, we do it both ways, to obtain a very clear understanding of the problems and advantages. We start with the 2D array and evolve the $2\frac{1}{2}$D organization using two terminal cells, since this is more easily visualized, then we show the advantage of a three-terminal cell in the same configuration. Afterward we evolve the $2\frac{1}{2}$D organization for both the two- and three-terminal cells from the 3D organization.

Let us now evolve $2\frac{1}{2}$D from 2D organization. A fundamental difficulty with the 2D array of Fig. 4.3-1 is that there are many word lines equal to the total number of logical words, and these word lines are short, each containing only the bits of that word. In all main memory systems, the number of logical words greatly exceeds the number of bits per word, the former being in the thousands or millions and the latter usually varying from 16 to 72 bits/ word. This produces a very long, narrow array with long delay in the bit/sense line direction and a large number of physical words to decode. To reduce both this delay and the large number of physical words, we can organize the array to ensure that a physical word contains more than one logical word, in particular, let

$$W_p = \frac{W_l}{s} \tag{4.5-1}$$

where W_p = number of physical words
W_l = number of logical words
s = segmentation: $s > 1$ for $2\frac{1}{2}$D; $s = 1$ for 2D

The number of logical words is that always specified for a memory (e.g., 32K′). Two simple ways to accomplish this segmentation are presented in Fig. 4.5-1, where each logical word is shown to have 4 bits. In principle, the two arrays are identical and differ only in the way we have labeled bits belonging to a given logical word. In practice, the two labelings differ only by virtue of the practical problems encountered in making physical connections to the arrays and connections of the sense lines, as we see shortly. Further evolution of the organization depends on whether we have a two-terminal or a three-terminal cell. The former is simpler, so first assume a 2T cell. For such a cell, we would have a bit/sense line just as in the 2D cell, and writing must always be done coincidently. Thus a selection of the proper physical word line and four of the corresponding bit lines with correct pulses on each, for "1" or "0," would write the information into the desired logical word. Note that the number of address bits required for writing is n_1 bits for decoding one out of W_l/s physical word lines and n_2 bits for decoding one out of s segments in each group or

$$n = n_1 + n_2 = \log_2 \frac{W_l}{s} + \log_2 s = \log_2 W_l \tag{4.5-2}$$

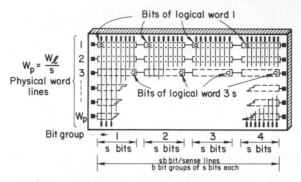

a) Bit-organized groups of bit/sense lines

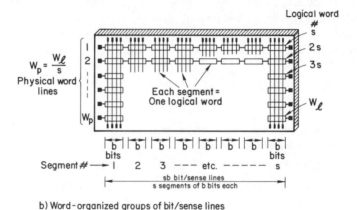

b) Word-organized groups of bit/sense lines

FIGURE 4.5-1 Schematic of $2\frac{1}{2}$D organization using two terminal cells: $b = 4$, $s = 8$, $W_l = 48$.

This is exactly as we expect, since 2 raised to the power of n must always equal the total number of words available in a memory. The bit line segment can be selected in various ways. Selection matrices are often used in core memories; semiconductor memories use decoding gates.

There can be no coincidence for reading, since the bit line is now the sense line. Hence the entire physical word must be read, which requires only n_1 address bits for decoding and gives us sb sense signals. Obviously additional decoding of the sb signals to just b signals must be done by the remaining n_2 address bits. In Fig. 4.5-1a the decoding must select one out of s lines in each bit group, whereas in Fig. 4.5-1b a selection of one out of s groups is necessary; these are essentially the same, requiring selection of four sense lines out of $4s$ total sense lines in both cases. This decoding must be done outside the device cell, on the sensing end of the bit/sense line, in fact, it can be done completely

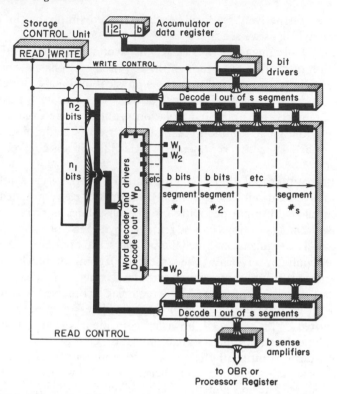

FIGURE 4.5-2 Schematic of $2\frac{1}{2}$D organization using two terminal cells and word-organized segments of bit/sense lines.

analogous to the bit line decoding during reading. One such approach is shown schematically in Fig. 4.5-2, which is just a more complete system of Fig. 4.5-1b.

Note that in the $2\frac{1}{2}$D-2T organization when a physical word is read, all logical words along that physical word are "read" in that they all receive a read pulse. If the cells are destructively read, the entire physical word must be sensed and regenerated, which is a complex and expensive operation. Nevertheless, this is sometimes done. For instance, the one-device, FET memory array of Section 3.10 organized as in Fig. 4.9-8, is a two-terminal, destructively read cell that requires complete regeneration of a physical word, even though only one bit of that word may be sensed. Other advantages, such as higher bit density, offset the less desirable destructively read cells. The $2\frac{1}{2}$D-2T organization is more ideally suited for nondestructive read-out (NDRO) cells, which are more expensive and usually less dense. Hence an engineering tradeoff is required. The extensive sensing and regeneration needed for a destructively read cell can be removed simply by the use of a three-terminal cell, as we see shortly.

The 2T-$2\frac{1}{2}$D organization of Fig. 4.5-1b is often used in NDRO thin magnetic film memories, even though the cell itself often has a separate bit line and sense line, giving a cell with three physical terminals. Functionally, the cell is operated as a two-terminal device, the separate bit and sense lines being required for noise and isolation problems. The organization of Fig. 4.5-1a is the most commonly used for 2T transistor flip-flop memory cells, where each segment s represents a single chip. This is covered in more detail later.

Two shortcomings of the 2T configuration of $2\frac{1}{2}$D are as follows: a non-destructive-read-out device is highly desirable for any practical implementation, and additional decoding on the sense lines is required during reading. Both the restrictions can be removed by the use of a three-terminal cell, still in $2\frac{1}{2}$D organization. Since the bit and sense lines are now separate either functionally or physically, the sense lines of common bits for all words can be arranged in numerous configurations. Using a 3T cell, the writing remains the same as before for a 2T cell, requiring a coincidence of word and bit pulses on appropriate lines, with the sense lines remaining idle while data are stored. With a 3T cell, however, coincident selection is also used during reading, which produces signals only at the cells of the desired logical word, not from the entire physical word as before with a 2T cell. In other words, only b signals are generated rather than sb, and we are free to arrange the sense lines so that no segment selection is required during reading. This can be accomplished with a slight modification of the sense line arrangements in Fig. 4.5-1. More specifically, we can connect appropriate groupings of sense lines either in series or in parallel, giving b groups of sense lines, with only one signal ever appearing within any one group. Hence this is the logical word desired. The series connections for the corresponding bit and word organized arrangements of Fig. 4.5-1a and b appear in Fig. 4.5-3a and b, respectively. Only the sense lines are shown for simplicity—the bit lines would be identical to those for 2T cells. The parallel connections for the corresponding cases are given in Fig. 4.5-4a and b. Of course it is conceivable that it may not always be possible to connect the sense lines in series or parallel, in which case decoding will be required as with the 2T cell. However, this condition is usually avoided whenever possible. For various reasons to be discussed later, $2\frac{1}{2}$D organizations usually employ the series connection for ferrite cores and parallel connection for semiconductors.

Continuing with the 3T-$2\frac{1}{2}$D organization, coincident selection during reading results in only the desired logical word receiving the full read pulse: all other cells along the selected x and bit lines receive half-select pulses just as during writing. Thus if destructively read cells are used, only one

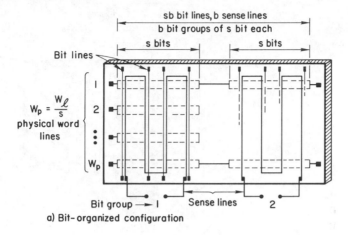

a) Bit-organized configuration

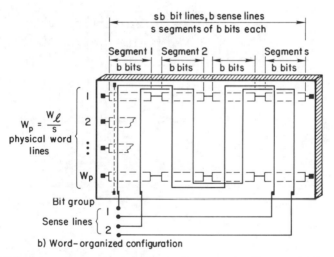

b) Word-organized configuration

FIGURE 4.5-3   Schematic of series sense line configurations for $2\frac{1}{2}$D organization using three terminal cells: $b = 2$, $s = 4$, $W_l = 16$.

logical word must be sensed and regenerated. This represents one major advantage of the 3T cell over 2T cell for $2\frac{1}{2}$D organization, namely, destructively read cells can easily be incorporated in the former, whereas they involve the expense of much additional circuitry in the latter. Since ferrite cores are read destructively, they are used in a 3T version when implemented in $2\frac{1}{2}$D.

Even though the 3T cell can eliminate segment selection on the sense lines during reading, we still must select the "bit" lines in addition to word

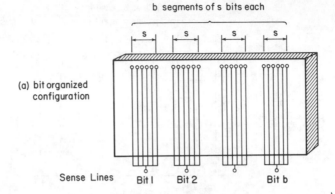

b segments of s bits each

(a) bit organized configuration

Sense Lines   Bit 1   Bit 2   Bit b

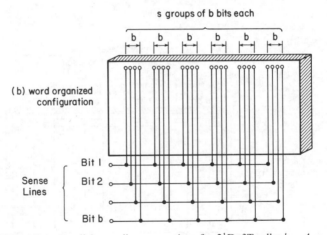

s groups of b bits each

(b) word organized configuration

Sense Lines   Bit 1   Bit 2   Bit b

FIGURE 4.5-4   Parallel sense line connections for $2\frac{1}{2}$D, 3T cells: $b = 4$, $s = 6$.

lines. This requires more external decoding during *reading*, which is not needed in the 2T case. However these decoders and bit drivers are needed during writing, hence are already available, and no additional circuitry is needed. Compare the schematic of the memory organization for such a case in Fig. 4.5-5 with Fig. 4.5-2.

Thus the important factors to be decided on in choosing between a 2T and a 3T cell used in $2\frac{1}{2}$D organizations are the relative advantage of non-destructive read-out versus destructive read-out cells traded against the resulting sense line selection and information regeneration required for 2T cells. The word and bit lines are essentially the same in both types, hence

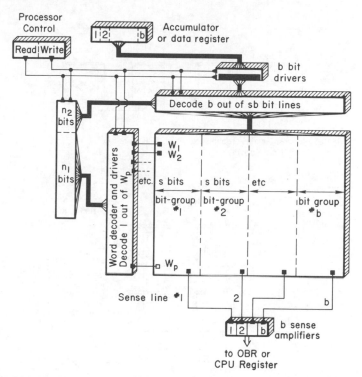

FIGURE 4.5-5   Schematic of $2\frac{1}{2}$D organization using three terminal cells and bit-organized groups of sense lines.

writing is also identical; the reading mechanisms, given the implications just mentioned, are the prime differences. In ferrite arrays, another practical advantage of the 3T cell in $2\frac{1}{2}$D is that there are fewer cells switching along any x or y line, which produces a smaller word line "back voltage" for the same drive current, thus reducing the breakdown voltage requirement on the drive transistors. The circuits required for various functions around the array are summarized in Table 4.5-2 for the 2T and 3T cells.

We now consider evolution of $2\frac{1}{2}$D from 3D organization with serial sense lines, deriving circuit cost and array delay expressions for comparison with the other organizations. This requires at the start a 3T cell (e.g., a core). In a 3D series organization, there are two significant contributions to the array delay, namely, the x or y word line delay and the sense line delay. We are again neglecting the pulse width and inhibit overlap problem. We can more easily visualize these delay contributions by schematically laying out the 3D module in two dimensions as in Fig. 4.5-6a. The sense line is only shown on the last bit plane and in an oversimplified form for a core memory;

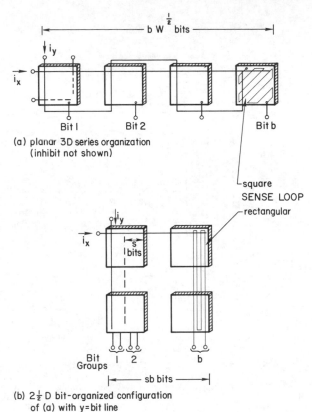

(a) planar 3D series organization
(inhibit not shown)

(b) $2\frac{1}{2}$D bit-organized configuration
of (a) with y=bit line

FIGURE 4.5-6   Evolution of $2\frac{1}{2}$D from a 3D series organization for a general case.

inhibit lines are not shown.* The x or y line delay can easily be cut in half by rearranging the four bit planes into the square pattern of Fig. 4.5-6b with a $2\frac{1}{2}$D organization. There are now twice as many physical x and y lines to be selected, but smaller delay. If the sense lines within each bit group are connected in series as in Fig. 4.5-3a and the wires run parallel to the y lines rather than on the diagonal, the sense line must still thread the same number of bits; thus the delay is reduced only by approximately $\sqrt{2}$ as a result of the geometry change. A larger decrease in sense delay could be obtained with the parallel connection of Fig. 4.5-4a, but this is not always possible, especially in large core modules. Approximately the same delay as the parallel connection could be obtained by leaving all sense lines separated and performing

* A more exact 3D wiring diagram is that of Fig. 4.7-1.

decoding and switching on the sense lines during reading, similar to that necessary in the 2T case of Fig. 4.5-2.* However this requires additional circuits and negates one of the advantages of the 3T cell in $2\frac{1}{2}$D. Nevertheless, this tradeoff in speed versus cost must always be made in memory design, and can only be done for specific implementations. It is thus seen that a $2\frac{1}{2}$D organization using 3T cells is just a segmented 3D array.

4.5.1 2.5-Dimensional Circuit Cost per Bit

In the circuit cost analysis of $2\frac{1}{2}$D, we have available many ways to vary the sensing circuit cost per line with a 3T cell by the method of connection of the physical sense lines, which in turn affects the delay. The 2T cell does not have quite that much freedom, but many different selection schemes are still possible on the bit lines and sense lines. Thus we assume that each word, bit, and sense line separately has some given cost per physical wire in the array: the sense circuit cost per line can be lowered by series or parallel connections of bit groups, and the exact cost per line will vary considerably with the specific embodiment. We simply assume this cost to be given and analyze $2\frac{1}{2}$D analogous to 2D, except now we include the circuit cost of bit and sense line separately. Let $C_{w2.5}$, $C_{b2.5}$, and $C_{s2.5}$ be the circuit costs per physical line for the word (x), bit (y), and sense lines of the array, where the bit and sense line circuits include any additional cost for segmentation. Then the cost analysis closely follows that of 2D. The total circuit cost per bit is just the cost per line times the number of physical lines in each direction. For the general case using either a 2T or 3T cell and any sense line configuration, the $2\frac{1}{2}$D array dimensions are W_l/s physical word lines by sb bits per physical word line, where, as before, W_l is the specified number of logical words and the total bits size of the memory is

$$N = W_p sb = W_l b \quad \text{or} \quad b = \frac{N}{W_l} \tag{4.5-3}$$

Thus the circuit cost per bit is

$$C_{T2.5} = \frac{1}{N}\left[C_{w2.5}\left(\frac{W_l}{s}\right) + sb(C_{b2.5} + C_{s2.5}) \right] \tag{4.5-4}$$

To optimize the circuit cost under the constraint of a fixed N, we can eliminate b in (4.5-4) as was done in the previous 2D and 3D analysis. Substituting (4.5-3) gives

$$C_{T2.5} = \frac{W_l}{N}\frac{C_{w2.5}}{s} + \frac{s}{W_l}(C_{b2.5} + C_{s2.5}) \tag{4.5-5}$$

* This is segmented as in Fig. 4.5-3b rather than bit-grouped as in Fig. 4.5-3a.

In the previous cases with 2D and 3D, we found that the optimum circuit cost per bit forced a specific relationship between W and b. Hence for a given value of b, the optimum W and the array size for minimum circuit cost are fixed. In $2\frac{1}{2}$D, we are now free to change the array dimensions simply by the selection of the value of segmentation s. This is one major difference between $2\frac{1}{2}$ and 3D. Hence s is a design parameter that can optimize the circuit cost, if we know the optimum value of s. This value can be found by taking the derivative of (4.5-5) with respect to s and equating it to zero or

$$\frac{dC_{T2.5}}{ds} = \frac{-W_l}{N} C_{w2.5} s^{-2} + \frac{C_{b2.5} + C_{s2.5}}{W_l} \equiv 0 \qquad (4.5\text{-}6)$$

Solving for s gives

$$\text{optimum } s\bigg|_{\substack{\text{min} \\ \text{cost}}} = W_l \left[\frac{C_{w2.5}}{(C_{b2.5} + C_{s2.5})N}\right]^{1/2} = \frac{N}{b}\left[\frac{C_{w2.5}}{(C_{b2.5} + C_{s2.5})N}\right]^{1/2}$$

$$(4.5\text{-}7)$$

Obviously s can be a noninteger value in general. The best integer value must be chosen. The optimum number of physical words for minimum circuit cost is the number of required logical words divided by the optimum s given by (4.5-7) or

$$\text{optimum } W_p\bigg|_{\substack{\text{min} \\ \text{cost}}} = \frac{W_l}{\text{opt } s} = \left[\frac{(C_{b2.5} + C_{s2.5})N}{C_{w2.5}}\right]^{1/2} \qquad (4.5\text{-}8)$$

If the circuit cost per wire on the word line equals the sum of bit plus sense line, a simple value for the optimum s results, namely

$$\text{optimum } s\bigg|_{C_{w2.5}=C_{b2.5}+C_{s2.5}} = \frac{W_l}{N^{1/2}} = \frac{N^{1/2}}{b} \qquad (4.5\text{-}9)$$

As indicated in Fig. 4.5-1, the width of a $2\frac{1}{2}$D array *along* the word line direction is sb, and length along the bit line direction is W_l/s. The optimum values for these dimensions of the array in terms of number of bits or physical wires can be obtained by using (4.5-7) for the optimum value of s and (4.5-8) for the optimum value of W_p. Using the above assumption for circuit costs, namely,

$$C_{w2.5} = C_{b2.5} + C_{s2.5}$$

the optimum number of physical words is obtained by substituting this into (4.5-8) to get

$$\text{optimum } W_p = N^{1/2} = (W_l b)^{1/2} \qquad (4.5\text{-}10\text{A})$$

The optimum value of sb for the same cost assumption is obtained directly from (4.5-9) as

$$\text{optimum } sb = N^{1/2} = (W_l b)^{1/2} \qquad (4.5\text{-}10\text{B})$$

As would be expected, for equal circuit cost along the length and width, the optimum array is a square. The advantage of $2\frac{1}{2}$D is that we can choose s to ensure that this is the case, at least approximately, except for the small deviation resulting from nonintegral values of s.* Thus W_l can be varied independently of b while still allowing the optimum array configuration for minimum circuit cost. We did not have this freedom in 3D, since the value of b fixes the value of W for minimum circuit cost.

The optimum cost per bit can be obtained by substituting the expression for s from (4.5-7) into (4.5-5) to get

$$\text{optimum } C_{T2.5}\bigg|_{\text{opt } s} = 2\left[\frac{(C_{b2.5} + C_{s2.5})}{N} C_{w2.5}\right]^{1/2} \qquad (4.5\text{-}11)\dagger$$

Note that this is identical in form to (4.3-9) for 2D except for the separation of the bit and sense line circuit costs for $2\frac{1}{2}$D.

4.5.2 2.5-Dimensional Delay

The maximum delay in a $2\frac{1}{2}$D organization depends strongly on the sense line configuration. There are three possibilities: the sense lines in a given bit group can be in series, in parallel, or unconnected but selected separately. We assume the series case and take the delay as the sum of word line plus sense line delays. For series connection, the sense line always has W_l bits in series.‡ Thus the total delay is

$$D_{2.5} = d_{w2.5} sb + d_{s2.5} W_l \qquad (4.5\text{-}12)$$

where $d_{w2.5}$ and $d_{s2.5}$ are the word and bit line delays per bit for $2\frac{1}{2}$D organization. We can optimize this either with respect to W_p, W_l, or s. Choosing the former, we know that

$$sb = \frac{N}{W_p} \quad \text{and} \quad W_l = sW_p \qquad (4.5\text{-}13)$$

---

* This occurs when $W^{1/2}$ and $b^{1/2}$ are not perfect squares. However typical values are $W = 4096$ words and $b = 64$ bits/word: $W^{1/2} = 64$, $b^{1/2} = 8$.

† The same expression could be obtained as was done for 2D and 3D, namely, by taking the derivative of C_T with respect to W_p or W_l, equating to 0, finding optimum W, and substituting that into (4.5-5). Obviously the optimum must be the same either way.

‡ A parallel sense line connection would reduce the sense line delay only if it were of the propagation velocity type. Otherwise it most likely would be the same as the series case.

TABLE 4.5-1   Generalized Circuit Cost and Delay per Bit for Various Random Access Memory Organizations[a]

	2D	$2\tfrac{1}{2}D$ (series sense line)	3D (series word line)
Total circuit cost/bit	$\dfrac{C_w W + C_b b}{N}$	$\dfrac{C_w W_p + (C_b + C_s)sb}{N}$	$\dfrac{2C_w W^{1/2} + C_z b}{N}$
Optimum circuit cost/bit	$2\left(\dfrac{C_w C_b}{N}\right)^{1/2}$	$2\left[\dfrac{C_w(C_b + C_s)}{N}\right]^{1/2}$	$3\left(\dfrac{C_w^{2} C_z}{N^2}\right)^{1/3}$
Optimum array configuration for minimum cost	$W = \left(N\dfrac{C_b}{C_w}\right)^{1/2}$	$W_p = \left[\dfrac{N(C_b + C_s)}{C_w}\right]^{1/2}$	$W = \left(N\dfrac{C_z}{C_w}\right)^{2/3}$
	$b = \left(N\dfrac{C_w}{C_b}\right)^{1/2}$	$s = \dfrac{N}{b}\left[\dfrac{C_w}{N(C_b + C_s)}\right]^{1/2}$	$b = \left(\dfrac{C_w}{C_z}\right)^{2/3} N^{1/3}$
Total array delay	$d_w b + d_s W$	$d_w sb + d_s W_l$	$d_w W^{1/2}b + d_s W$
Optimum array delay	$2(N d_w d_s)^{1/2}$	$2(s N d_w d_s)^{1/2}$	$1.5(2 d_s d_w^{2} N^2)^{1/3}$
Optimum array configuration for minimum delay	$W = \left(N\dfrac{d_w}{d_s}\right)^{1/2}$	$W_p = \left(\dfrac{N d_w}{s d_s}\right)^{1/2}$	$W = \left(\dfrac{N d_w}{2 d_s}\right)^{2/3}$
		$s = \dfrac{N}{W_p^{2}}\dfrac{d_w}{d_s}$	
	$b = \left(N\dfrac{d_s}{d_w}\right)^{1/2}$	$sW_p = \dfrac{N}{b} = $ fixed	$b = \left(\dfrac{2 d_s}{d_w}\right)^{2/3} N^{1/3}$

[a] Parameter definitions

C_w = circuit cost per physical word line (all)

C_b, C_z = circuit cost per unit line, combined for bit/sense line for 2D and 3D, respectively

C_b in $2\tfrac{1}{2}D$ = circuit cost per bit line including segmentation

C_s in $2\tfrac{1}{2}D$ = circuit cost per sense line including segmentation

d_w = delay per bit along word line

d_s = delay per bit along sense line

N = total number of bits

W, W_l = total number of words (logical)

W_p = number of physical words ($2\tfrac{1}{2}D$)

b = bits per word

Note.   Appropriate values of parameters must be used for each organization (e.g., C_w will be different for 2D and 3D).

Substituting these into (4.5-12) gives

$$D_{2.5} = d_{w2.5} \frac{N}{W_p} + d_{s2.5} s W_p \qquad (4.5\text{-}14)$$

Taking the derivative and equating to zero gives

$$\frac{dD_{2.5}}{dW_p} = -d_{w2.5} N W_p^{-2} + s d_{s2.5} \equiv 0 \qquad (4.5\text{-}15)$$

Solving this gives

$$\text{optimum } W_p = \left(\frac{N d_{w2.5}}{s d_{s2.5}} \right)^{1/2} \qquad (4.5\text{-}16)$$

Substitution of (4.5-16) into (4.5-14) gives the optimum total delay as

$$D_{2.5} \Big|_{\text{opt } W_p} = 2(s N d_{w2.5} d_{s2.5})^{1/2} \qquad (4.5\text{-}17)$$

Equation 4.5-16 can be solved for the optimum value of s in terms of N and W_p to get

$$\text{optimum } s \Big|_{\substack{\text{min} \\ \text{delay}}} = \frac{N d_{w2.5}}{d_{s2.5} W_p^{2}} \qquad (4.5\text{-}18)$$

For a fixed N and fixed b as we assume here, the number of logical words is fixed, since $W_l = N/b$. But since $W_l = s W_p = $ fixed, W_p and s cannot be optimized separately but only together, as related by (4.5-16) and (4.5-18).

A summary of the optimum cost and delay relationships for the three cases discussed, with appropriate assumptions, is given in Table 4.5-1. The minimum circuit or transducer requirements at various points of any array are listed in Table 4.5-2 for several organizations.

4.6 RELATIVE COMPARISON OF CIRCUIT COSTS AND ARRAY DELAYS FOR 2.5-DIMENSIONAL VERSUS THREE-DIMENSIONAL ORGANIZATION

It is impossible to make an absolute cost and delay analysis without specific implementations and actual designs. Each memory technology has its own peculiarities that impose restrictions or ground rules (e.g., core arrays have delta noise, which does not exist in semiconductor arrays, whereas the latter are fabricated only in small arrays called chips). As a result, we discuss only a few aspects of the relative merits of $2\frac{1}{2}$D versus 3D arrays based on the circuit

TABLE 4.5-2   Circuits Required for Various Random Access Memory Organizations[a]

Function	2D	$2\frac{1}{2}$D, 2T Cell	$2\frac{1}{2}$D, 3T Cell	3D Series
Decoding gates				
Word lines (last level)	W	$W_l/s = W_p$	$x = W^{1/2}$	$2W^{1/2}$
Bit lines	0	design dependent	$y = bW^{1/2}$	
Read/write drivers				
Word lines	W	$W_l/s = W_p$	$x = W^{1/2}$	$2W^{1/2}$
Bit lines	b	$b(+sb$ switches$)$	$y = bW^{1/2}$	b
Sense amplifiers	b	$b(+sb$ switches$)$	b	b
Address bits				
Word lines	$\log_2 W$	$n_1 = \log_2 W_p$	$2 \log_2 W^{1/2}$ $= \log_2 W$	$2 \log_2 W^{1/2}$ $= \log_2 W$
Bit lines	—	$n_2 = \log_2 S$	—	—

[a] W_l = total number of logical words, W_p = total number of physical words, b = bits per logical word, s = segmentation $(2\frac{1}{2}$D$) = W_l/W_p$.

cost and array delay analysis of Sections 4.4 and 4.5. In essence, this analysis is confined to certain specific consequences of the physical geometry and external circuit connections of the two organizations. These comparisons are fundamental and are valid for any technology, within the limitations of the assumptions made. For actual memory arrays, additional constraints would have to be superimposed on these, as is done in Section 4.7 for $2\frac{1}{2}$D versus 3D ferrite cores. We wish to compare the array delays and circuit costs of 3D versus $2\frac{1}{2}$D organizations, using the relationships derived in Table 4.5-1. We assume that the bits per logical word is fixed by the CPU architecture at $b = 64$ bits, and we determine array delay and circuit cost as the number of logical words varies. From this, certain conclusions will be obvious—namely, that 3D gives lower circuit cost and $2\frac{1}{2}$D gives smaller array delay.

We know from Section 4.4 that when b is fixed, we *cannot* optimize the 3D geometry for either optimum circuit cost or delay. Hence for 3D organization, we must use the expressions for total array delay and total circuit cost per bit from Table 4.5-1. On the other hand, for $2\frac{1}{2}$D organization, even with a fixed value of b, we can pick the segmentation s to optimize either delay or circuit cost, or somewhere in between if we wish. We arbitrarily pick s to optimize the $2\frac{1}{2}$D circuit cost per bit. For expediency, we assume that for the circuit costs in Table 4.5-1,

$$C_w = C_z \equiv C_3 \quad \text{in} \quad 3D \tag{4.6-1}$$

$$C_w = (C_b + C_s) \equiv C_{2.5} \quad \text{in} \quad 2\tfrac{1}{2}D \tag{4.6-2}$$

and for the delay values

$$d_w = d_s \equiv d_3 \quad \text{for} \quad 3D \tag{4.6-3}$$

$$\equiv d_{2.5} \quad \text{for} \quad 2\tfrac{1}{2}D \tag{4.6-4}$$

The delay assumption is reasonable in some technologies such as cores and magnetic films but may or may not be acceptable in integrated circuit arrays, depending on the technology and design. Likewise, the circuit costs may be reasonable in certain cases but not in others.

Since we choose to optimize the circuit cost per bit in $2\tfrac{1}{2}D$, the expressions for the two organizations, using (4.6-1), (4.6-2), and Table 4.5-1, give

$$\text{total circuit cost/bit (3D)} = C_{T3} = C_3\left[\frac{2}{b(W)^{1/2}} + \frac{1}{W}\right] \tag{4.6-5}$$

$$\text{optimum circuit cost/bit } (2\tfrac{1}{2}D) = C_{T2.5} = \frac{2C_{2.5}}{N^{1/2}} \tag{4.6-6}$$

But since $N = Wb$, substituting this into (4.6-6) gives

$$\text{optimum } C_{T2.5} = \frac{2C_{2.5}}{(Wb)^{1/2}} \tag{4.6-7}$$

where W is the number of logical words. Numerical values for (4.6-5) and (4.6-7) are given in Table 4.6-1 for $b = 64$ bits and various values of W. Note that as the number of words increases, the circuit cost per bit of 3D becomes increasingly better than $2\tfrac{1}{2}D$ for a fixed value of $C_{2.5}/C_3$, as shown by the $2\tfrac{1}{2}D/3D$ column in Table 4.6-1. At a module size of 4K′ words, the circuit cost ratio is $5.3C_{2.5}/C_3$. This specifies that if we wish to have equal circuit cost per bit at this size, the individual circuits of $2\tfrac{1}{2}D$ must be 5.3 times cheaper than those of 3D, which is not very likely.

Since we optimized the $2\tfrac{1}{2}D$ organization for minimum circuit cost, we cannot simultaneously optimize the array delay. Hence we must use the expressions for total array delay for both $2\tfrac{1}{2}D$ and 3D in Table 4.5-1 or, substituting (4.6-3) and (4.6-4),

$$\text{total delay 3D} = D_3 = d_3(bW^{1/2} + W) \tag{4.6-8}$$

$$\text{total delay } 2\tfrac{1}{2}D = D_{2.5} = d_{2.5}(sb + W) \tag{4.6-9}$$

TABLE 4.6-1 Comparison of $2\frac{1}{2}$D and 3D Arrays for $b = 64$ bits and various W

Total Words W	Circuit Cost per Bit			Array Delay		
	3D	$2\frac{1}{2}$D (opt)	$2\frac{1}{2}$D/3D	3D	$2\frac{1}{2}$D	$2\frac{1}{2}$D/3D
1 K'	$19.5 \times 10^{-4}\, C_3$	$78 \times 10^{-3}\, C_{2.5}$	$4\, C_{2.5}/C_3$	$3.07 \times 10^3\, d_3$	$1.28 \times 10^3\, d_{2.5}$	0.42
4 K'	$7.3 \times 10^{-4}\, C_3$	$39 \times 10^{-4}\, C_{2.5}$	$5.3\, C_{2.5}/C_3$	$8.2 \times 10^3\, d_3$	$4.6 \times 10^3\, d_{2.5}$	0.56
8 K'	$4.6 \times 10^{-4}\, C_3$	$27.6 \times 10^{-4}\, C_{2.5}$	$6\, C_{2.5}/C_3$	$14 \times 10^3\, d_3$	$8.9 \times 10^3\, d_{2.5}$	0.64
16 K'	$3.05 \times 10^{-4}\, C_3$	$1.95 \times 10^{-4}\, C_{2.5}$	$6.4\, C_{2.5}/C_3$	$24.6 \times 10^3\, d_3$	$17.4 \times 10^3\, d_{2.5}$	0.71

Since we optimized s for minimum circuit cost, from (4.5-9) or Table 4.5-1 we write

$$s_{\text{opt cost}} = \frac{N^{1/2}}{b} = \frac{(W_l b)^{1/2}}{b} \tag{4.6-10}$$

Substituting this into (4.6-9) gives

$$D_{2.5 \, \text{opt cost}} = d_{2.5}[(Wb)^{1/2} + W] \tag{4.6-11}$$

where W is the number of logical words.

The ratio of 3D delay to the $2\frac{1}{2}$D delay, obtained as the ratio of (4.6-8) to (4.6-11), gives

$$\frac{D_{2.5}}{D_3} = \frac{d_{2.5}}{d_3}\left[\frac{(bW)^{1/2} + W}{b(W)^{1/2} + W}\right] \tag{4.6-12}$$

Note that the term in brackets in (4.6-12) must always be less than 1. Also, in many cases, the unit delay is independent of organization: for such cases $d_3/d_{2.5} = 1$, hence the $2\frac{1}{2}$D delay will be less than the 3D delay. Numerical values for these two equations and the ratio are given in Table 4.6-1. Note that as W increases, the delay advantage of $2\frac{1}{2}$D over 3D appears to diminish, as evidenced by the ratio approaching unity. This results because we optimized the $2\frac{1}{2}$D array for minimum circuit cost, not for the best delay. Hence as the array gets larger, we would probably want to consider a different value for the segmentations s.

It is clear from this analysis that based on the geometry and circuit connections to the array, 3D gives a more efficient use of the individual circuit, whereas $2\frac{1}{2}$D allows us to more efficiently arrange the wiring for less array delay. In core array design, the decision to use a $2\frac{1}{2}$D or a 3D organization is not quite so simple. In practice we are given a certain speed objective, bits per word, and often the technology as well (e.g., core size). The goal is to design a module of maximum size and minimum cost within these objectives. For a given delay, it is obvious that for the above assumptions, a larger value of W is possible in $2\frac{1}{2}$D than in 3D. For purposes of illustration, suppose that the required speed limits a 3D array to 4K' words and a $2\frac{1}{2}$D to 16K' words. If the cost ratio remained the same as in Table 4.6-1, the cost ratio for the two organizations is now only $19.5C_{2.5}/7.3C_3 = 2.7C_{2.5}/C_3$. If the per unit circuit cost can be lowered for $2\frac{1}{2}$D, it may be competitive. Phase reversal (see Section 4.7) can reduce the number of bit line circuits in half, giving approximately a $\sqrt{2}$ improvement. Other factors not considered can become important, and the final choice depends on specific details.

The foregoing analysis is particularly applicable to core arrays. In integrated circuit memories with a low or moderate number of bits per chip, (e.g., 4K or smaller), the on-chip circuits occupy only a small portion of the area. In addition, they are fabricated using the same technology as the array, which means that their cost is usually small relative to the total array cost. Hence lower total cost per bit is achieved by increasing the number of bits per chip. This requires the simplest possible cell structure—typically a two-terminal cell—and this excludes 3D organization. The design then centers around the best type of $2\frac{1}{2}$D structure. The factors of power dissipation and error correction for chip failure become important and are considered in Section 4.9.

As the density and bits per chip increases, the necessary on-chip circuits begin to occupy an increasing percentage of the chip area in many cases so their cost becomes very significant. No simple, general design principles are applicable for all cases. As higher levels of integration are achieved, the tradeoffs between cell structure, circuits, and organization grow in complexity.

4.7   FERRITE CORE MEMORY ORGANIZATION

The classical 3D, four-wire series core memory module (Fig. 4.7-1) is a specific embodiment of the fundamental 3D series sense line configuration of Fig. 4.4-1 and operates exactly as previously described. Writing is accomplished by the coincidence of an x and a y pulse for "1" or x, y, and z for a "0." Reading is destructive, and each word must be regenerated (write cycle) after a read cycle. All other cores along energized x, y, and inhibit lines will receive half-select disturb pulses during writing and those along x and y lines during reading. All cores must then be capable of sustaining a large number of disturbs. This organizational scheme has been used extensively and has been a significant factor in the power and growth of computers. This organization gives a low peripheral circuit count compared to other organizations as shown in Tables 4.5-1 and 4.5-2. In the early days of ferrites, these circuits constituted a very significant portion of the total memory cost.

Fundamentally, there is no reason not to use the parallel word line connection of Fig. 4.4-4 if adequate current drivers are available. However the already large current requirements on the series drivers would be increased by the factor b, since b lines would now be in parallel rather than in series, requiring b times as much current. Since b is typically 32 to 72 bits/word and the half-select current can be from 0.5 to 1 A, a selected x line in the parallel connection would require from 16 to 72 A with a fast rise time and megahertz repetition rates. This is an extremely difficult and expensive way to drive; therefore all 3D core arrays use the series connection. In fact, even

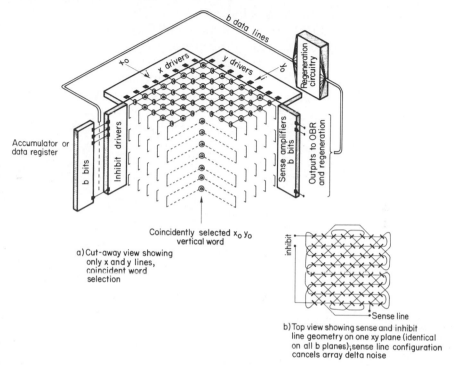

FIGURE 4.7-1   Schematic of 3D, four wire core array.

the series connection places severe requirements on the transistor drivers, so load sharing matrix switches were invented in the early history of cores as a means to achieve high power, economical drivers. This represented one of the first major evolutionary changes in core memories, and many such ingenious array driving schemes were developed (see Section 4.10).

The classical 3D four-wire array has a number of inherent problems that resulted in the gradual evolution of the 3D three-wire array and the $2\frac{1}{2}$D three-wire array. The choice between a 3D or $2\frac{1}{2}$D three-wire scheme intimately involves the economics of each manufacturer's product. Thus both have been used by different manufacturers as successors to the 3D four-wire scheme. It is also possible to devise a $2\frac{1}{2}$D two-wire core array as well as a 2D scheme. In considering the evolution of these arrays, we first discuss fundamental problems encountered in core array design and afterward point out some of the practical problems and motivating forces responsible for core array evolution.

In any core array design, either $2\frac{1}{2}$D or 3D, the word and bit lines must be arranged through the cores in the proper direction to allow writing and reading at all bit locations. This is not difficult to do by itself, but another problem inherent in cores—namely, "delta noise"—must be solved simultaneously. Delta noise can be reduced by proper arrangement of the sense wires but places a limit on the maximum number of half-selected cores that can be strung on any one sense line. This, in conjunction with the need for proper arrangement of word and bit lines, leads to complex sense line patterns and limits on core plane sizes. We now consider in detail the delta noise problem for both $2\frac{1}{2}$D and 3D organizations and evolve the complex sense line configuration of Fig. 4.7-1*b* from a more elementary scheme.

4.7.1   Delta Noise

Delta noise occurs in core arrays because the *BH* loops of cores are not ideal and variations (deltas) occur not only between supposedly identical cores, but also between different segments of the *BH* loop of a given core. To understand the source of delta noise and how it might be reduced, consider two cores strung on a single drive wire with two sense wires *S* (sum) and *D* (difference) as in Fig. 4.7-2*a*. For the moment, the cores are assumed to have identical hysteresis loops, and the loops are assumed to be semiideal as in Fig. 4.7-2*b*. The reason for using flux ϕ instead of flux density *B* becomes obvious shortly. The ϕH loops are thus assumed to have equal slopes for small positive or negative fields, in both the positive or negative saturation state; in other words, it is assumed that

$$\Delta\phi_0 = \Delta\phi_1 = \Delta\phi_0' = \Delta\phi_1' \qquad (4.7\text{-}1)$$

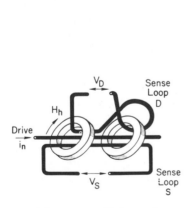

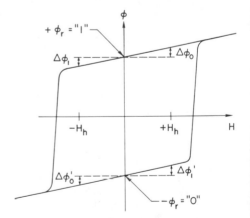

(a) two cores with Sum and   (b) semi-ideal ϕH loop with assumed
    Difference sense loops   equal slopes in both residual states

FIGURE 4.7-2   Fundamentals of delta noise in core arrays.

Thus a given half-select drive of i_h or H_h will cause equal amounts of flux change, no matter which direction the field is applied in or which residual state the cores happen to be in at the moment. In Fig. 4.7-2a, since sense loop S passes through both cores in the same direction as the drive current, the individual flux changes for the two cores always add to give a total flux change of $2\Delta\phi_0$. A voltage directly proportional to the time rate of change of the total flux is obtained, or

$$V_S = \frac{d\phi}{dt} \propto 2\Delta\phi_0 \qquad (4.7\text{-}2)$$

If there were many such cores rather than 2, they would all add and could give a large noise signal.

Sense loop D on the other hand has one core polarity reversed, since it passes through one core in a direction opposite to the drive current. Hence a half-select drive field always causes the individual core noise signals to cancel. Under the ideal conditions, V_D is always identically zero, no matter what residual state, "1" or "0," the two cores happen to be in. If there were three cores instead of two, only two could cancel and a noise signal proportional to one $\Delta\phi_0$ would be obtained. Likewise for any *even* number of cores, the noise can be eliminated by threading the sense wire in opposite directions through "paired" cores. For this hypothetical case of identical cores and symmetrical ϕH loops, the delta noise is always zero. Delta noise arises because the ϕH loops tend to be unsymmetrical for positive and negative excitation for a given core; furthermore, the loops of supposedly identical cores have small differences. In other words, in Fig. 4.7-2b the values of $\Delta\phi$ may not be equal. In one given core, we typically have

$$\Delta\phi_0 = \Delta\phi_0' \qquad \text{and} \qquad \Delta\phi_1 = \Delta\phi_1' \qquad (4.7\text{-}3)$$

but

$$\Delta\phi_1 > \Delta\phi_0 \qquad \text{and} \qquad \Delta\phi_1' > \Delta\phi_0' \qquad (4.7\text{-}4)$$

The inequality results because the inherent magnetization or flux density follows such an unsymmetrical loop for most magnetic materials (see Figs. 5.2-2 through 5.2-4 for examples). If both cores in Fig. 4.7-2a had these characteristics, and if one core were initially in the opposite residual state from the other core, one core would switch by an amount $\Delta\phi_0$ and the other by $\Delta\phi_1$. The two components would still subtract, there would be a net difference between them of

$$\Delta\phi_\delta = \Delta\phi_1 - \Delta\phi_0 \qquad (4.7\text{-}5)$$

Hence a *delta* noise would be generated for this pair of cores, of value

$$\delta V = \frac{d}{dt} \Delta\phi_\delta \quad \text{V/pair} \tag{4.7-6}$$

This particular component of the delta noise resulted strictly from the inequalities of (4.7-4). Suppose both the above-mentioned cases were initially in the same residual state (i.e., both storing "0" or both storing "1"; then a half-select drive would produce equal flux changes in the two cores, assuming they were identical. Thus in this initial state, the delta noise is still zero. However the $\Delta\phi_1$ or $\Delta\phi_0$ for two cores can be different because the material volume density, hence magnetization, can vary, as well as the cross-sectional area. Since $\phi = BA$, any variation in B or A will be reflected as differences in, say, $\Delta\phi_1$ of two otherwise identical cores. In other words, manufacturing tolerances become important. For a string of many cores on a wire with the sense line reversed on paired cores, the delta noise will vary with the stored information and variations in core materials. The worst case occurs when alternate "1's" and "0's" are stored in paired cores, and when the stored "1" cores have minimum B and A while the stored "0" cores have maximum B and A. In actual arrays with large numbers of cores, we would not expect this "worst possible" case to occur, but rather some average or statistical distribution. Thus the average delta noise flux for the general case can be expressed as in (4.7-5), where the flux change are now some typical average values over many cores or

$$\text{average } \Delta\phi_\delta = \langle\Delta\phi_1\rangle - \langle\Delta\phi_0\rangle \tag{4.7-7}$$

Clearly the delta noise is reduced by threading the sense line through cores on common drive lines such that the sense line passes through as nearly equal numbers of cores as possible in the same and opposite directions as the half-select current. This is commonly referred to as pairing of cores, but of course any two cores in one plane having their sense lines in opposite directions can be considered paired, provided the sense line delay is not important. In such cases the difference between, say, $\Delta\phi_1$ for different cores should average out to zero, leaving only the difference between $\Delta\phi_1$ and $\Delta\phi_0$, or $\Delta\phi_1'$ and $\Delta\phi_0'$, as the source of delta noise. In large arrays the time coincidence of the individual noise signals from paired core may become important, and this would require them to be in close proximity. The latter usually happens without deliberate design. However in such cases the probable difference between comparable flux changes, such as $\Delta\phi_1$, of adjacent cores becomes more significant and can now contribute to the delta noise.

It is clear that the delta flux for a given set of cores will be very small. However in large arrays the delta noise is additive and can become quite severe. For example, in an array of 64×64 words per plane in 3D, the number of half-selected cores in that plane would be $2(64) - 1 = 127$ cores. There are thus 63 paired cores and one that is unpaired. If each pair of cores gives a delta flux of 2% of the residual flux ϕ_r, the total delta noise flux is

$$\text{total } \Delta\phi_\delta = 63(0.02\phi_r)$$
$$= 1.26\phi_r \qquad (4.7\text{-}8)$$

The total "1" sense signal is proportional to $2\phi_s$; thus the signal to delta noise ratio in such a case would be

$$\text{signal/delta noise} = \frac{2\phi_r}{1.26\phi_r} = 1.6 \qquad (4.7\text{-}9)$$

This is not particularly good, since other noise sources will add to the delta noise. Hence delta noise places restrictions on the ϕH loop and is an important limiting factor on the number of cores that can be strung on any one sense loop.

The necessity of a "paired" sense winding configuration for delta noise reduction has a very profound effect on the overall wiring configuration. The primary problem in establishing a wiring pattern is the need to wire the x, y, and inhibit windings to write a "1" or "0" in the selected core, and the sense line must be superimposed on top of this to achieve delta noise reduction. This leads to the complex geometrical arrangement not only in the 3D, four-wire configuration but in others as well, as we see below.

4.7.2 Evolution of Core Array Organizations

It should be understood that the primary factor responsible for the evolution of all memory systems is the desire for lower cost and higher speed. Since there are many contributing parameters, all interrelated, there is no one single view of this evolutionary process. Thus we present some of the important problems, not necessarily in order of importance, to see how they enter into the array structure.

In the fabrication of any core array, some of the cores always crack during the stringing (wiring) operation, requiring very costly hand repair work. The number of cracked cores decreases as the number of wires through the core decreases. For example, the number of cores cracked during nonautomated (hand) stringing varies with the number of wires through the core approximately as follows (Harding, 1971):

$$\begin{array}{lll}
4 \text{ wires} & 20 \text{ cracked in } 100K & \\
3 \text{ wires} & 10 \text{ cracked in } 100K & (4.7\text{-}1) \\
2 \text{ wires} & 1 \text{ cracked in } 100K &
\end{array}$$

Thus it is desirable to eliminate some of the wires through the core to reduce the array fabrication cost. This requires some additional circuitry, which increases the circuit costs and may, or may not offset the reduced array cost. However another factor favors a reduction in the number of wires, namely, core switching speed. As we saw in Section 3.3, the reciprocal of the switching time is directly related to the applied excess field over and above the coercive force, and the switching speed can be increased by making the core smaller or using larger drive currents. Since circuits for generating larger currents at higher speeds were not feasible, smaller cores were necessary (Fig. 3.3-7). Fewer wires through the core allows smaller cores to be used, which allows faster switching. Smaller cores also introduce lower inductance, hence smaller back voltage on the word and bit lines, and possibly smaller propagation delay, all very desirable. Thus there is significant motivation to reduce the numbers of wires, irrespective of whether the organization is changed to $2\frac{1}{2}$D or remains at 3D.

These considerations are valid for any implementation or organization. Some problems specifically related to the 3D, four-wire array of Fig. 4.7-1 are as follows. First, the cores must be arranged in the "box" fashion, which provides minimum core density per unit area, and longer lines; a significant improvement in packing density and wire length can be achieved by a parallel arrangement of cores. Another problem associated with the 3D four-wire scheme is that during the writing of a "0," the inhibit pulse must be wide enough to cancel the x or y pulse for the worst case delay. In a core that is fathest from the x or y drive circuit, the inhibit pulse must remain on, even after the x driver has been turned off, for a time equal to the propagation delay of the x line (i.e., until the word current is removed from the farthest bit cell). Then the inhibit driver can be turned off. This need for overlapping inhibit pulse increases the cycle time and can be eliminated only with a $2\frac{1}{2}$D organization, which doesn't require an inhibit pulse.

One advantage of the 3D, four-wire scheme is the dc isolation of the inhibit and sense lines. However the inhibit and sense windings thread through the same cores, and thus are redundant to a certain extent. The major advantage is the low circuit count. The first evolutionary change in array design was the use of three wires instead of four.

4.7.3   Three-Dimensional, Three-Wire Core Array

The 3D, three-wire scheme reduces array cost and allows the use of smaller cores with faster switching times, which increases the speed. In this system the x and y lines remain as before, but the third line must serve both the inhibit function during writing and the sense function during reading. The standard sense wire of Fig. 4.7-1*b* for a 3D, four-wire system gives the required delta noise cancellation but does not allow a current in the sense wire to inhibit all cores of a plane. The inhibit function requires the inhibit wires to run parallel to the x or y wires, whereas for delta noise cancellation the sense line must reverse direction through half the cores on each x and y wire. This can be implemented in two ways. In both approaches the sense/inhibit wires run parallel to the y (or x) line: the delta noise cancellation is obtained by using the "box" core arrangement of Fig. 4.7-1b to pair cores, while the other literally reverses the sense direction over half the cores to form a "bow tie" pattern. These two cases are illustrated in Fig. 4.7-3a and b,

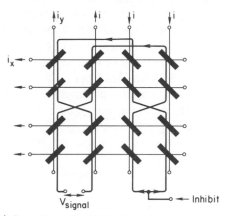

(b) Bow-tie sense-inhibit line with parallel cores

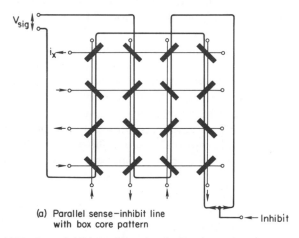

(a) Parallel sense-inhibit line
   with box core pattern

FIGURE 4.7-3   Sense/inhibit configuration for 3D, three wire core memory planes.

respectively. Note that the box core configuration will have a lower core density by about a factor of 2 than the parallel column (bow tie) arrangement, hence longer delay.* However the box configuration allows the sense wires to run directly through all cores of a column and is thereby amenable to semiautomated core stringing.† The bow tie sense configuration requires a crossover in the midplane, hence necessitates hand stringing.

In both these cases, the inhibit function is supplied at the midpoint of the sense loop with equal currents of the same polarity flowing in both legs. The reason for this is quite fundamental. The inhibit function requires large currents and voltages, whereas the sense signals are very small compared to inhibit pulses. Thus the amplifiers must work at low level with high amplification. Any large pulses on these sense amplifiers could cause damage if special precautions are not provided or as a minimum, will saturate them and require long recovery times. Thus the major problem in 3D, three-wire design is the inhibit/sense line configuration and circuits. To protect the sense amplifier, it would be desirable to drive the inhibit function from one end of the line with the sense amplifier at the other end; during writing, if the sense amplifier end of the line could be at ground potential, the sense amplifier would not be affected. During reading, the sense amplifier must respond to a signal across the two ends of the sense line. This type of operation can be achieved only with a balanced system in which the inhibit functions are the common mode but the sense function is the differential mode. This is exactly what is done, and there are several schemes, each with advantages and disadvantages. One possible way to achieve this is represented in Fig. 4.7-4a, which is an "unfolded" schematic of the sense/inhibit line of Fig. 4.7-3b. The inhibit/sense line is connected at three points—at the two ends and at the midpoint. One drawback is that the inhibit driver must now supply twice the normal inhibit current, since the current splits in two equal halves. Under ideal connections, only the two ends of the line, points p and q, need be connected to a differential sense amplifier with a high common mode rejection and points p and q each tied to ground through Z_0, the line characteristic impedance. Three problems arise in practice. First, the characteristic impedances of the two halves of the line cannot be maintained equal, this means that the common mode impedances, and hence voltage from point p to ground and point q to ground, are not equal, which can give a large differential signal $V_p - V_q$ into the sense amplifier. Since the inhibit current is large, this differential noise could swamp the sense amplifier, causing a recovery problem. Second, the unequal impedances can produce unequal

---

* About twice as many parallel cores can be strung along one y line compared to the orthogonal box configuration.
† This is the wiring scheme used in the IBM 360 core arrays of the mid-1960s.

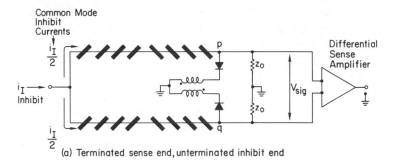

(a) Terminated sense end, unterminated inhibit end

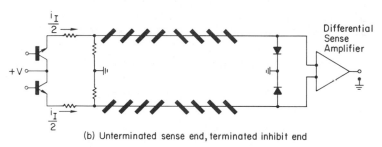

(b) Unterminated sense end, terminated inhibit end

FIGURE 4.7-4 Unfolded sense/inhibit wiring of 3D, three-wire core plane of Fig. 4.7-3b showing common mode inhibit drive and differential sensing.

inhibit currents in the two halves, which is most undesirable from the standpoint of tolerances. Third, the common mode voltages V_p and V_q to ground can be very large, perhaps 100 times the sense signal or larger, and this would require a sense amplifier with a common mode rejection of better than 100 to 1, which is quite difficult to achieve. All these difficulties can be alleviated by using the transformer and diodes connected as shown.* The transformer connection maintains an equal division of current, since any increase in current in one winding will cause an increase in current or decrease in impedance of the other side. This also equalizes the common mode voltages V_p and V_q to ground. Furthermore, the transformer lowers the common mode impedance of points p and q to ground for common mode voltages only, and looks like an open circuit (large inductance) to the differential sense signal, as desired. Thus this arrangement has all the requirements for

---

* This transformer is often referred to as a balun, but it is not a balun in the strict sense. This transformer is, in principle, an ordinary transformer with a center taped winding, the center tape being connected to ground. Its operation is quite different from that of the classical balun; see Matick (1968).

performing sense/inhibit on one wire. One serious problem, however, is that for large modules that require long sense lines (e.g., 4096 cores/section), the sense signal amplitude is reduced in half and the effective pulse width can be doubled. This results because the sense signal propagating in the two directions away from a switched core (Section 2.13) can arrive at very different time delays at the sense amplifier. Suppose, for instance, that the core nearest point p in Fig. 4.7-4a is switched for reading; since the core acts as a series generator, one-half the signal propagates toward the right and one-half toward the left. Obviously the signal toward the right arrives immediately at the sense amplifier. If that toward the left has a sufficiently long delay, the familiar "rabbit ears" signal appears (Fig. 2.13-2); with half the signal amplitude and twice the pulse width. There are a number of possible solutions; for example, the signal propagating toward the left could be terminated by appropriate resistors equal to the line characteristic impedance on the left-hand end of the line, just as on the right. This unfortunately yields a half-amplitude signal that may be intolerable in some cases. Alternatively, the signal amplitude at the sense amplifier could be doubled back to the original value by removing the terminating characteristic resistances Z_0 on the sense amplifier end as in Fig. 4.7-4b. This gives a positive voltage reflection coefficient and doubles the voltage pulse with the original signal pulse width. However this reflected signal must travel toward the left, and we must wait for it to be absorbed in the left-hand terminating resistors. For the worst case, which is that of a core switching at the far left-hand end, the total signal propagation is one electrical length to the sense amplifier and another for the reflected wave to get back. Timewise, this is essentially no better than the previous circuit; however, we now have approximately the full original signal amplitude, which improves the signal to noise ratio and can be quite significant in large arrays. The common mode during writing experiences multiple reflections or ringing and cannot be ignored. The common mode impedance is reasonably large, but usually smaller than the sense line impedance; on the sense amplifier end, we would like the common mode voltages to be shorted to ground, to ease amplifier common mode rejection; but a perfect match is desirable at the far left-hand side. This is nearly achieved by the circuit of Fig. 4.7-4b, with the far end terminating resistors providing large damping to the common mode. Irrespective of the method of termination, unfortunately, the unequal propagation time delay for certain core positions is a major factor in limiting the array size for a given system speed.

4.7.4   2.5D, Three-Wire Core Arrays

Although 3D, 3-wire configurations lower the array cost considerably and allow smaller cores to be used for faster switching time, the array delays are only slightly reduced by the change in the sense line configuration.

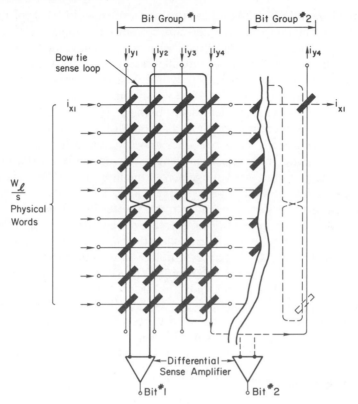

FIGURE 4.7-5   Schematic of $2\frac{1}{2}$D, three-wire core array showing phase reversal on y lines and bow tie sense loop for delta noise cancellation.

Further reduction in the array delay requires a new organization. The three terminal, three-wire core lends itself readily to $2\frac{1}{2}$D-3T organization, and it has been used in some commercial cores systems (Gilligan, 1966). The typical configuration uses the series sense winding and scheme similar to that of Fig. 4.5-3a. One such example for a core array appears in Fig. 4.7-5. In $2\frac{1}{2}$D there is no inhibit function required; thus all the cores can be parallel and all x and y current polarities are the same for the same stored information. However the "bow tie" sense loop configuration must be employed to cancel delta noise, as shown. Each "bit group" constitutes a bit plane or part of a bit plane with a series sense line. Note that for such a case, when either reading or writing, only one bit (y) line within any given bit group is excited at any one time. Hence the bit line and the sense line are coupled over only a very small electrical length, namely W_p/s bit cell spacings, rather than over the entire length W, as are the inhibit (bit) and sense lines in 3D. Typical values might be coupling over $W_p/s = 256$ core spacings in $2\frac{1}{2}$D versus 4096 in 3D. This greatly reduces the linearly coupled noise voltage appearing at the sense amplifier during writing and alleviates the recovery time problem, allowing further reduction in the cycle time. This represents a major advantage of $2\frac{1}{2}$D core memories over 3D. In addition, the word and bit lines are shorter, giving shorter electrical delay both for terminated pulses and for multiply reflected common mode signals on all lines. With the method of balanced driving used, the driver lines appear essentially a short-circuited transmission lines. If the electrical length can be made shorter than the applied pulse rise time, the voltage across the input to the line can be substantially smaller than that of a long line. Thus a lower voltage transistor is needed to drive the same current into the shorter line. This condition can be satisfied in $2\frac{1}{2}$D core memories. Another advantage is the elimination of the overlap timing delay of the inhibit with x and y word pulses that was necessary in 3D. In $2\frac{1}{2}$D core arrays, moreover, the number of y line drivers can be cut in half by the use of "phasing" of the y lines on adjacent bit groups. For instance, the y_4 line of bit group 1 in Fig. 4.7-5 can be connected in series with y_4 of bit group 2: since the y current direction reverses with respect to the x current on adjacent lines, no disturb problem is encountered. This technique is used to lower the typically larger circuit count of $2\frac{1}{2}$D arrays.

As we discussed in Section 4.6, the sense line takes the overall geometrical form of a rectangular array rather than the "square" form in the 3D array of Fig. 4.7-3. As more segments are added to optimize the overall $2\frac{1}{2}$D array, the sense array becomes more rectangular (i.e., longer and thinner), which increases delta noise in the sense loop. This is one disadvantage of $2\frac{1}{2}$D, but the cores can be placed closer together to give a smaller delay because of reduction of the electrical length.

4.7.5   2.5D, Two-Wire Core Arrays

In the $2\frac{1}{2}$D, three-wire organization, a sense line can thread through all cores of a bit group and the bit lines can be separated as in Fig. 4.7-5. When a $2\frac{1}{2}$D two-wire organization is attempted, the bit and sense line(s) are the same physical line, necessitating some changes. With only two wires, a $2\frac{1}{2}$D, 2T cell and array configuration such as that of Figs. 4.5-1 and 4.5-2 is relatively simple but requires excessive circuitry and has all the previously discussed problems of a destructively read 2T cell. This can be improved by using a 3T cell array such as that of Fig. 4.5-3. However this approach requires coincident selection during reading, which means that one wire must provide two functions simultaneously. This can be done by proper arrangement of the array and circuitry. The signal versus noise problems

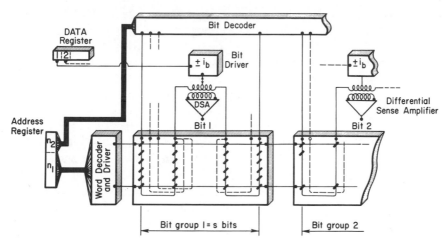

FIGURE 4.7-6   Schematic of $2\frac{1}{2}$D, two-wire core array using three terminal cells, bit-organized array configuration, and phase reversal. After Harding (1971).

are very similar to the situation encountered in going from four to three wires in 3D—namely, the large bit voltages during both reading and writing must be isolated from the sense amplifier and still allow the small signal to be sensed. The techniques for achieving this are identical in principle to those of 3D, three-wire arrangements. In one basic scheme (Fig. 4.7-6) "phasing" on the bit lines is used to reduce the number of bit drivers (i.e., to double the value of s for the same number of bit drivers). In principle, this array is the same as the fundamental form of Fig. 4.5-3a, with the sense winding serving also as the bit winding. The bit decoder matrix selects only one line from any bit group, both for reading and writing. The polarity of the bit current, in combination with the word current i_x, ensures that only one core ever switches in each bit group during both reading and writing. A string of b such bit groups along the physical word line gives the required b bits per logical word.

4.7.6   Two-Dimensional Core Arrays

It was pointed out in Section 4.3 that 2D organization is not practical for large memories with normal word lengths. This is particularly true for core arrays used in large main memories. However one problem accompanying $2\frac{1}{2}$D core arrays makes the 2D scheme more attractive. As previously indicated, core switching time has become an important factor in the overall memory speed. However the core switching constant appears to have been reduced as much as possible (Section 3.3), and the only way to decrease switching time is to use the concept of partial switching. This technique requires a 2D organized array because the cores are quite disturb sensitive in the partially switched state and could not tolerate the half-select pulses present in the $2\frac{1}{2}$ and 3D organizations. The 2D scheme would tend to further increase the speed except for one offsetting factor: because of the poorer signal to noise ratio in the partially switched state, two cores per bit are needed. (Rhodes, et al., 1961; Amemiya et al., 1966). This makes the array lines longer and increases the cost, tending to make the 2D scheme unattractive. Experimental arrays were built as early as 1961, but the increased speed has not been sufficient to justify the greater complexity and attendant cost; hence 2D core arrays have not appeared in commercial systems. Examples of various ferrite core memory organizations are given in Gilligan (1966), Harding (1971), and Russel et al. (1968). A rather complete description of a very early core memory used in the ORDVAC computer can be found in C. V. Smith (1959).

4.7.8   Sense Delay of Core Arrays

In ferrite core arrays, any switching of the cores, either partial or full adds to the line inductance, increasing the delay per unit length given by $T_0 = (LC)^{1/2}$. Most core arrays use series windings that contain many cores (e.g., 4096), but only one gives a full signal during a read cycle. The signal current then flows in the sense line in both directions and is too small to cause any significant switching of the cores along the sense line. Hence the sense line impedance and delay is essentially that of a line in air. Linear capacitive and inductive coupling effects to nearby conductors are important, but the cores themselves have only a second-order effect on the sense signal propagation characteristics.

4.8   MAGNETIC FILM MEMORY ORGANIZATION

Magnetic film memories can be organized in much the same way as ferrite cores. In fact, since the size of the magnetic core is reduced while the total number of bits in the array is increased, many of the same problems exist in both technologies. This is particularly true of the linear noise coupling between conductors of the array and often leads to balanced sense lines similar to those of Figs. 4.7-3 through 4.7-5.

Flat, open flux path, anisotropic magnetic films are not attractive for use in a 3D organization for various reasons. First, they are intended for higher speed operation than are cores (e.g., $<0.5\ \mu sec$ cycle time), and 3D organization is not particularly well suited for high speed. Second, and more important the switching characteristics of such flat films do not lend themselves readily to 3D organization. As Section 3.4 indicated, anisotropic films work best with orthogonal and parallel applied fields. Hence the physical conductors must lie parallel or perpendicular to one another as in Fig. 3.4-1. The switching characteristics are very dependent on the orientation of the applied fields relative to the easy axis because the anisotropy is built into the crystalline structure. There is a very large shape anisotropy in the circumferential direction in ferrite cores which makes them insensitive to all but circumferential fields. Hence cores may have the conductors at 45° angles to the plane of the core without changing the switching characteristics. In other words, cores are insensitive to the angle of orientation, whereas films are quite sensitive. If we attempt to organize a 3D, four-wire array similar to the core array of Fig. 4.7-1, using films with switching characteristics given by Fig. 4.8-1 and assuming that a rotational mode is needed for speed, the following problems result. For rotational switching, we typically apply a perpendicular word field and a plus or minus bit field for storing a "1" or "0." The latter is employed in lieu of the inhibit line. The word field could be supplied by the coincidence of x and y word lines, but with the conductors parallel to each other at each film location as in Fig. 4.8-2. For writing a given bit such as film 11, a field of H_0 is supplied by x_1 and likewise H_0 from y_1 to give a total field of $2H_0$ at point f in Fig. 4.8-1. A bit field of $+H_b$ or $-H_b$ will exceed the critical field and write a "0" or "1" as desired. However all other bits in that plane that lie along conductors x_1 and y_1 will receive a half-select disturb pulse of value H_0 added vectorially to H_b indicated as point d in Fig. 4.8-1. As discussed in Section 3.5, the critical margins and open flux structure make such a film very disturb sensitive. A "0" bit could be totally erased by many such half-select disturbs in the "1" direction, and vice versa. The applied half-select disturb fields can be reduced by using a 2D or $2\frac{1}{2}$D two-terminal cell type configurations such as those of Figs. 4.3-1, or 4.5-1 and 4.5-2. In such cases, since there is only one word line,

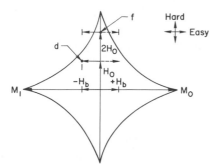

FIGURE 4.8-1 Switching asteroid and applied fields for thin films in 3D organization.

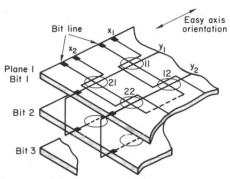

FIGURE 4.8-2 One possible 3D configuration of a thin film array.

unselected bits of a given plane receive only a disturb field of value H_b and no hard axis field in Fig. 4.8-1. This greatly improves the disturb characteristics and permits moderate sized arrays to be built. However for large arrays working at high speed, the tolerances on individual film cells over a large substrate are very difficult to control, resulting in disturb characteristics similar to those for 3D organization. An alternate is to use many small, interconnected arrays. However this is expensive and undesirable. It was ultimately a combination of such tolerance problems coupled with the resulting cost/performance tradeoff that led to the demise of flat film memories. Examples of specific designs are given in Jones and Bittman (1967), Pohm and Zingg (1968), and Raffel et al. (1961).

Many attempts were made to circumvent these tolerance and disturb problems by the use of coupled film structures (Bobeck et al., 1966; Chang, 1967). The basic idea was to make the film structure look more like a core, but one having small air gaps. Coupled film structures can reduce the self-demagnetizing fields of single films, giving better disturb characteristics. If the coupled film is used in the form of a continuous sheet or keeper over the array, other advantages can be obtained within the array operation. A magnetic keeper close to the word lines serves to confine the magnetic field to a smaller region around a driven word line. This reduces coupling to adjacent unselected word lines and reduces the disturb problem discussed previously. The net results of coupled structures are improved disturb characteristics, allowing more tolerance on drive and film parameters, reduced drive requirements, and higher densities. Unfortunately the additional complexity made the arrays expensive, and the density was still greatly limited because of the large local self-demagnetizing fields inherent in all open flux structures (see Section 2.6). Magnetic bubbles offer a method to circumvent this, and interest in magnetics switched from flat films to bubbles in the early 1970s.

Flat film magnetic arrays have other difficulties in addition to the disturb tolerance. One very serious problem is the noise induced on sense lines by the word and bit lines, during both writing and reading. The applied word and bit fields must be quite uniform over the area of the film. This requires either a flat or slitted strip line configuration. However a minimum of two orthogonal conductors and often two parallel (bit and sense) and one orthogonal (word) line are required. The linearly coupled noise into the sense line becomes quite severe and requires special geometries and differential sensing to achieve a reasonable signal to noise ratio.

Influence of Creep on Thin Film Memory Organization

The foregoing discussion has shown that the desire for high speed switching of thin films essentially eliminates the use of a 3D organization, leaving only 2 or $2\frac{1}{2}$D. We now consider the effect of creep or disturb characteristics (Section 3.6) on the latter two organizations and see that it places severe constraints on $2\frac{1}{2}$D. In the $2\frac{1}{2}$D thin film array in Fig. 4.8-3a, which is word organized analogous to Fig. 4.5-3b, we have four physical and eight logical words; thus $s = 2$. For writing, a relatively large word current i_w is applied in combination with a smaller plus or minus bit current as discussed previously. The word current creates a large hard axis field as in Fig. 4.8-1, and the small easy axis bit field determines the state. The hard axis word field can be applied before the easy axis bit field, which is the better condition

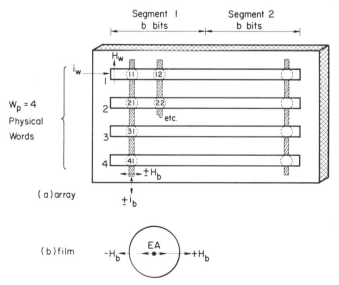

FIGURE 4.8-3 $2\frac{1}{2}$D word-organized thin film memory: $W_p = 4$, $W_l = 8$, $s = 2$.

for reducing creeping. To ensure proper writing, the hard axis word field must be removed first, which is the worst case for creep to occur (Section 3.6). But since we are *writing* into the film, why worry about creep? The answer is that creep affects other films in the array. First, a given word current in a selected physical word line will induce small but nonzero currents in adjacent unselected word lines, giving a small hard axis field on unselected neighboring films. A group of b bit lines corresponding to the selected logical word of segment 1 or 2 will all receive pulses. Since these bit lines run over all four physical words, the unselected neighboring films receive the same bit field in combination with a smaller hard axis disturb field. This is the worst case for disturb to occur and is a source of many constraints. This particular disturb problem does not affect the memory organization but rather requires the word lines to have larger separation than would be desired, severely compromising array density. The memory organization is influenced by another disturb problem, namely, that created by the word pulse on the selected line. If, say, segment 1 in Fig. 4.8-3 is selected for writing, all films in segment 2 receive the same hard axis field. Even though no easy axis field is applied to these films in segment 2, the hard axis field must be large and typically can be larger than the disturb thresholds for this condition. Whenever writing is performed, therefore, either the entire physical word must be written or regeneration must be performed after writing. Either case requires sb sense amplifiers and sb drivers, which negates part of the advantage of $2\frac{1}{2}$D. In other words, the array operates more nearly as a 2D array. The easy axis skew and dispersion problems further compound this restriction, since a "nominally" hard axis field will have a component along the easy axis of some skewed films or some dispersed parts of each film.

We may consider trying to change the disturb thresholds and write fields to a point where $2\frac{1}{2}$D becomes feasible without the limitations noted. This is possible in principle, but it would require more stringent control of the film parameters, which would be more costly. The result would be a shifting of cost from one part of the system to another. This approach is generally unworkable in large arrays because of the tolerances.

Another serious problem encountered in thin film arrays is current spreading in the ground plane (Liniger and Schmidt, 1966). Any unidirectional pulse sequence has low frequency and dc components. When pulses at a high repetition rate are applied to the word lines in Fig. 4.8-3, the low frequency components spread over the ground plane and create a significant hard axis bias field on the films. This bias field amplitude varies with position in the plane and can also vary slowly with time, depending on the word line sequencing pattern. Clearly this affects both the writing of a given film and the disturb characteristics of adjacent films. Since the direction of the hard axis field is unimportant during writing, we could conceivably use some method of alternate polarity sequencing on successive word lines. However this would require bipolar drivers with additional logic, complicating the system and increasing the cost. The bit pulses are bipolar on average, and thus do not have a dc component. Also they are of smaller amplitude, which means that any local unipolar pulsing for, say, a series of write "1's" generates less bias field than the unipolar word pulses.

Another serious problem is the linearly coupled noise, which becomes more serious at high frequencies. Usable signal to noise ratios usually require a balanced drive or sensing scheme that further complicates the array. A fundamental problem in thin film structures is the need to create a magnetic field to produce the desired effect on the films. However at high frequencies, an electric and magnetic field occur simultaneously. The electric field, undesired because it generates large noise, cannot be avoided, but only circumvented by adequate design. Semiconductors do not inherently have this problem within the device itself, although similar noise problems occur in adjacent array conductors.

4.9 TRANSISTOR MEMORY ORGANIZATION

Transistor memories have a distinct advantage over nearly all other technologies in that the peripheral circuits can be made from the same fabrication processes and in many cases, the decoding, driving, and sensing can be done with the identical device with simple changes in the fabrication masking. Decoding circuits can easily be fabricated on the same chip as the storage devices themselves, thus greatly simplifying the interface problem between the CPU and memory. There are several differences between transistors and core arrays, however, which give rise to slightly different array configuration for transistor memories. Some of the important differences are as follows:

1. The number of storage cells (bits) per chip that can be successfully fabricated is considerably less than the total basic storage module (BSM) size, even considerably less than the number of total words desired.
2. The chip that can be successfully fabricated is very small, typically 0.2 in. on a side or smaller; thus the number of required external pin connections becomes critical.
3. The basic two-terminal MOS FET cell of Fig. 3.8-2 allows coincident selection (word and bit line) for writing, but no coincident selection for reading, as discussed previously; a 3D cell can be made, but at the expense of having a more complex cell, lower density, and higher cost.

These affect the organization of arrays in different, but interrelated ways. The basic question is, Given a specific number of cells per chip, how do we organize the chip into words of memory?

In 3D core arrays, we had to put the x lines (and y line) all in series from one plane to another because of the large current requirement (cores are current-sensitive elements). In theory, we could parallel all x lines along a given vertical plane, and likewise all y lines, to achieve a much faster array; but the practical problems posed by a high speed, high current driver force us into series operation and long delays. Large currents are not required in transistor memories; in fact, quite small currents suffice in many circuits, permitting the use of a 3D parallel conductor selection scheme, as found in actual memory systems (Alying and Moore, 1969). The same paralleling of selection conductors can be used in $2\frac{1}{2}$D organization, and since $2\frac{1}{2}$D requires a simpler (hence cheaper) cell, this is often the design that is used in commercial systems.

4.9.1 Transistor Memory Organization When Number of Logical Words Equals Bits per Chip

To understand transistor memory organization, let us take a $2\frac{1}{2}$D, two terminal cell and consider the possible ways of organizing a memory system. First consider building a 256 word $\times$ 4 bit/word memory from chips containing 256 bits each. The chip is an array of 16 word lines $\times$ 16 bit/sense line pairs. Thus four chips are needed. How do we connect these chips together to form a 256 word $\times$ 4 bit/word random access memory? If we use the simple, straightforward $2\frac{1}{2}$D organization of Fig. 4.5-2, the organizations of Fig. 4.9-1 results. In Fig. 4.9-1a, four segments are used, requiring $W_p = W_l/s = 256/4 = 64$ physical words. These 64 words are decoded by an off-chip decoder, as are the four segments; for simplicity, only one decoder is shown for the segments, whereas in general, one for the bit lines and one for sense segment decoding would be needed. In Fig. 4.9-1b, the 16 word lines are tied in series from chip to chip, and 16 segments are used. Since the word decoder must decode only one out of 16 words, this decoder could be put on chip to simplify fabrication. The 16 bit/sense line pairs of each chip are now segmented into four groups of 4 bits/group, or 16 total groups for the four chips. In Fig. 4.9-1c a square organization is used: 32 physical words, 8 segments, and a one out of 32 word decoder. All these organizations are feasible in principle, but there are certain drawbacks and difficulties. First, the word line is rather long in Fig. 4.9-1b and sense line is long in Fig. 4.9-1a, not only giving a long delay (if delay is important) but possibly serious pulse deterioration, as well (this cannot be decided without a specific embodiment and known parameters). Next, two types of chips are required in Fig. 4.9-1b, one with decoders and one without decoders. This is very expensive and, even more important, the chips without decoders in Fig. 4.9-1a, b, and c require many interconnections and pins (16 pins for the word lines on two sides in b, 16 for sense lines in a, and on all four sides in c. This is a

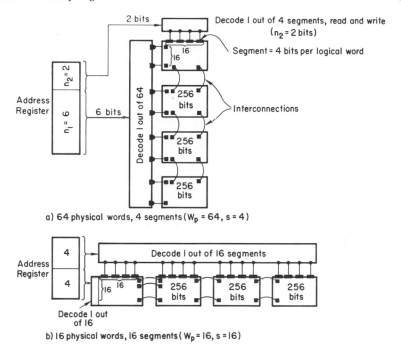

a) 64 physical words, 4 segments ($W_p = 64$, s = 4)

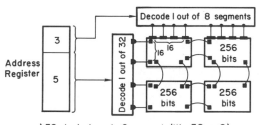

b) 16 physical words, 16 segments ($W_p = 16$, s = 16)

c) 32 physical words, 8 segments ($W_p = 32$, s = 8)

FIGURE 4.9-1 Possible $2\frac{1}{2}$D organization for 256 words by 4 bits/word transistor memory using chips of 16 × 16 bits.

difficult condition to achieve, and becomes even more difficult and un-reliable as the density increases. It is desirable to remove pin connections as much as possible. The decoded chip only requires four pin connections for the address lines, suggesting that each chip be decoded with on-chip decoders. Another important consideration, especially if one wishes to buy or supply "off the shelf" components, is the word length variation. Suppose we wish to increase the word length to six bits instead of four. This would be an extremely complex task with the above organizations.

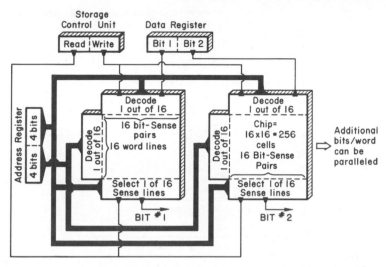

FIGURE 4.9-2   Typical bit-organization integrated circuit memory of 256 words $\times$ 2 bits/ word using fully decoded chips; number of words = cells/per chip, 1 bit/chip $2\frac{1}{2}$D.

All the above-mentioned objections can be removed by the organization of Fig. 4.9-2 (only two bits are shown). This example is organized as one bit per chip, which is quite commonly used. Additional bits can be added to the system for any specified number of bits per word with very little change— word lines and various data paths are paralleled as shown.

The input lines into the bit decoder and sense decoder specifying read or write are single digit (one bit on or off) lines that activate or do not activate the ENABLE input of the decoder. This ENABLE is a very important function, since it serves in later example as a "chip selector," which allows easy expansion of a standard chip of small size into a large memory array (to be considered next). The ENABLE provides another level of decoding capability that can be done off-chip but selects the desired chip when necessary.

A fundamental problem with fully decoded chips is that when all the input address are normally off (at, say "0") this still represents a real address, hence selects one of the word or bit lines. Therefore the *word driver or bit driver must be normally off and can be turned on only after the decoding is completed.* This introduces additional delay but cannot be avoided.

4.9.2   Transistor Memory Organization When Number of Logical Words Exceeds Bits per Chip

When the memory requirement in total number of bits exceeds that of a single chip, it is necessary to interconnect a large number of chips in two directions to achieve the required words and number of bits per word. In the previous case, essentially, we had only to expand in one direction to achieve the bits per word. Now the major concern is the accomplishment of this interconnection.

Since chips are mounted in modules or carriers, modules mounted into cards, and cards plugged into a board for the final system (to supply power and connections to other parts of the computer, etc., as in Fig. 4.9-6, e.g.), there results a hierarchy of organization that can take on many different forms. Form in turn depends on the total number of words and bits per logical word required by the system versus the number of cells per card that can be implemented easily; thus the best organization is not always obvious. The primary factors influencing card structure are power dissipation and required speed. Since the cells always dissipate energy, both standby and during switching, high density means large power dissipation on a chip. If the memory is to be run at high speed (high repetition rate) and if the switching speed is a significant factor, chips with more than one bit per chip can have a larger power dissipation at small local spots, making possible eventual failure. Under such circumstances, it is desirable to distribute the switching power over a larger area, and in $2\frac{1}{2}$D organization this would mean organizing as one bit per chip. Unfortunately the power dissipation problem cannot be easily addressed without a particular embodiment—the power dissipated per cell varies greatly from one cell design to another, and the local heating depends on the density, line widths, substrates, and other factors and must be considered in any detailed design. For our purpose, we sidestep the power problem and investigate some possible ways to interconnect a large memory from small chips.

Suppose we wish to build a 1024 word $\times$ 8 bit/word memory using the chips already described of 256 bits each (16 $\times$ 16 array). Since the cells are two-terminal structures, the organization must still be $2\frac{1}{2}$D. As with the previous case of 256 words, we can conceive of many organizations similar to those in Fig. 4.9-1 that will implement a larger array. However they will suffer from the same shortcomings as before: long lines, many pin connections, difficulty of expansion, and so on. The previous organization of one bit per chip can circumvent many of these difficulties, except that now there will be 10 address register bits, requiring additional decoding. Thus we must determine where and how this additional decoding is to be done. If we wish to maintain a uniformity of the chip layout (organization) and also minimize pin connections to each chip, it is desirable to use chips as before— namely, a decoder to select one out of 16 word lines, and a decoder to select one out of 16 (pair) bit/sense lines. This, again, will require only eight address bits; obviously, therefore, two bits must be decoded elsewhere. We can use the ENABLE function previously described to select a given chip. One possible way to do this is illustrated in Fig. 4.9-3. Since the 4 bit word address will

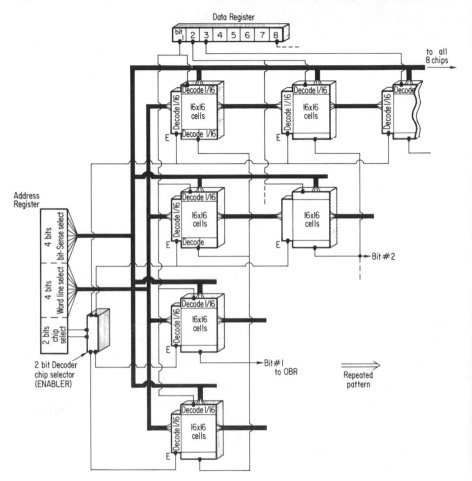

FIGURE 4.9-3 Integrated circuit memory organization with number of words larger than cells per chip; 1024 words × 8 bits/word, $2\frac{1}{2}$D one bit/chip (sense line selection and read/write control lines not shown).

attempt to decode all four groups of chips simultaneously, an additional selection capability is required, namely, the ENABLE function on the decoder of each chip (and one more pin connection). The enable function requires special considerations and implementation. In some technologies, it is not easily or conveniently placed directly on the decoder. In such a case, the ENABLE can be combined with the "turning on" of the drivers after the decoding has taken place. The "chip select" pulse can be used to trigger the drivers, but it must be delayed long enough to ensure that the decoding is completed; otherwise the wrong word may be selected. Such a combined ENABLE and driver delay scheme is used on the IBM FET main memories in the system 370 models 158 and 168.

It could be argued that when designing a full memory system for a given CPU architecture, when expansion of the word size is not a problem, a one bit per chip organization is not necessary, and the organization in terms of one character or one word per chip has considerable merit. However certain practical problems must be considered, the most important one being chip failure. With high density integrated circuits, a simple failure, such as one external pin connection opening, can render the entire chip inoperative. With many such chips mounted and interconnected on a carrier, the failure cannot possibly be found and corrected immediately. In large systems the resulting down time could be quite expensive. Hence some means is desired to prevent a simple failure from crippling the entire system. If the memory is organized as one bit per chip, the use of a parity bit and single bit error correction logic can circumvent the problem of single chip failures, since this now represents only one bit of the word. If two chips of the same word should both fail, we are faced with the previous problem. However the probability of this occurring becomes progressively smaller, and the use of double bit error correction is not usually warranted.

In the design of semiconductor memory systems the choice of organization is often influenced by many practical concerns other than those given thus far. For example, Section 4.5 indicated that a two-terminal cell in $2\frac{1}{2}$D organization *almost* requires a nondestructive read-out cell to be practical. Whereas NDRO is very desirable, it is not fundamentally necessary, but rather requires one sense amplifier on each sense line and a means for regenerating all the bits along the physical word line after reading. In high density integrated circuits memories, this design is feasible in some cases, particularly if the basic cell is very simple and provides high density at low power, since a few additional sense amplifier circuits on a chip may be trivial in terms of the silicon real estate required. The savings in real estate provided by a small, low power dissipation cell can usually offset the additional sense amplifier area by a large factor. This is the case for random access memory designed from the one-device cell of Fig. 3.10-1. The device is functionally a two-terminal cell that is destructively read out. The cell, for large memories, is thus limited to $2\frac{1}{2}$D organization. One may segment such a scheme as one bit per chip, one byte per chip, one word per chip, or various combinations. In any case, assuming that the physical words are always larger than logical words, some segment selection is required for any organization. Conceptually as well as in terms of layout of the system, the segmentation schemes of Figs. 4.5-1 and 4.5-2 are often more desirable than one bit per chip scheme

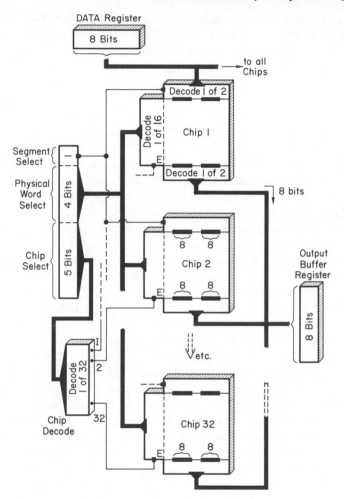

FIGURE 4.9-4   Alternate $2\frac{1}{2}$D transistor memory organization of 1024 words using 8 bits/chip.

of Figs. 4.9-2 or 4.9-3. However the very practical problem of chip failure quite often *forces* the designer to use a one bit per chip organization. Nevertheless, semiconductor memories can be designed to provide multiple bits per chip. Figure 4.9-4 presents an example of a typical organization providing 8 bits/chip and using the previous 256 bit chips. Each chip contains two bit/sense segments, hence 32 logical words. Thirty-two such chips yields 1024 words at 8 bits/chip. Note that in this case, the off-chip decoder must be larger; also all eight data bits go to each chip and come out to the OBR, thus requiring more pin connections than previously. To see this, let us count the signal pin connections required for each case.

Chip Pin Connections

Fig. 4.9-3	Fig. 4.9-4
4 word address	4 word address
4 bit/sense address	1 bit/sense address
1 data in	8 data in
1 signal out	8 signal out
1 chip select	1 chip select
1 word write select	1 word write select
1 bit write select	1 bit write select
1 sense read select	1 sense read select
14 pins/chip	25 pins/chip

The data in, signal out pins could be shared, changing these totals to 13 and 17, excluding power and ground. Thus the one bit per chip organization has a pin advantage in addition to other benefits.

4.9.3 Three-Dimensional Transistor Memory Organization

The problems encountered in attempting to organize a memory from three-terminal transistor cells are much the same as those accompanying two-terminal cells. The number of physical words and the number of logical words placed on one chip or module depend on power dissipation, pin limitations, and so on. In addition, as Chapter 3 demonstrates, three-terminal cells are more complex, dissipate more power, and require more silicon real estate. As a result, 3D semiconductor organizations are seldom used except for special applications where they have a particular advantage. Such a case is the first example given below.

4.9.4 Examples of Commercial Transistor Memory Organizations

The first mass-produced semiconductor memory used bipolar transistors in the cell configuration of Fig. 3.8-4, introduced by IBM in 1968 and used in models 25, 85, and 195. Because of this rather unique position in memory evolution, the overall characteristics of this configuration are described in some detail.

The smallest storage unit consists of 64 cells on a 112 × 112 mil silicon chip. The transistors are *npn* double diffused, with p^+ junction isolation made

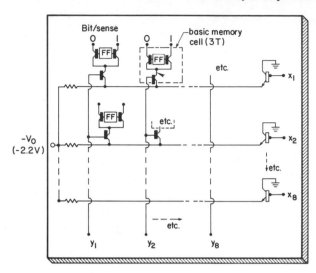

FIGURE 4.9-5   Cell and chip organization of IBM 64 bit/chip monolithic memory.

using 0.2 mil photolithography. Each chip in the system contains only 64 cells plus 8 x-word line select transistors, as in Fig. 4.9-5; no other circuitry is contained on the chip. The cells are three-terminal structures, each has an x, a y, and a bit/sense pair, 3D coincidently selected on the chip. However, the remainder of the memory is organized as a $2\frac{1}{2}$D, similar to that of Fig. 4.9-3, or as a one bit per chip system, although with additional groupings and decoding of chips to achieve a large size. Only one bit out of the 64 on any given chip is used for any given word, (i.e., one bit per chip), the logical words being formed from groups of chips, requiring 72 chips for a full 72 bit word. This memory is organized on pluggable cards containing 512 words × 18 bits/word. Two chips are mounted on a $\frac{1}{2}$ in. ceramic module, 72 modules/ card (7 × 9 in. multilayered pluggable card: Ayling and Moore, 1969; Agusta, 1969). All other circuitry, including drivers, decoders, and sense amplifiers, is on separate chips that are mounted on the same card, as shown schematically in Fig. 4.9-6.

The performance of this system is as follows: "1" signal = 2 mA (into 10 Ω); card access time (read) ≈ 25 nsec; full system access time ≈ 40 nsec; cycle time ≈ 60 nsec.

Figure 4.9-7 is a photograph of the actual 64 bit chip of Fig. 4.9-5, overlayed on a core memory plane of the same vintage. It can be seen that the chip requires the same area as about six cores or a factor of at least 10 improvement in areal density. Higher levels of integration currently in use have made this

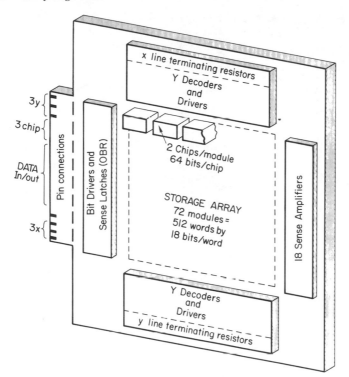

FIGURE 4.9-6 Schematic of high speed buffer card organization representing the first mass-produced, commercial monolithic memory: chip shown in Figs. 4.9-5 and 4.9-7.

ratio even more dramatic, and it will continue to improve. Mass-produced bipolar transistor memories have been and are being used in other configurations also (Ayling and Moore, 1971; Gater et al., 1971). However field effect transistors reduce both processing cost as well as power dissipation and have overtaken the main memory market.

4.9.5 Memory Organization Using the Two-Terminal, One-Device Cell

The so-called one-device memory cell of Fig. 3.9-6 is becoming more popular for main memory because of its small size and low power dissipation. The device has two independent functional terminals plus a common ground (or voltage source) terminal, making it suitable only in 2 or $2\frac{1}{2}$D organizations. In addition, the cell is destructively read out (DRO) and requires periodic refreshing, since the stored charge leaks away slowly. The DRO character of the cell does not present a serious problem because the method for sensing

FIGURE 4.9-7 First mass-produced commercial semiconductor memory chips containing 64 bits, 664 components on 0.11 in. silicon chip, overlayed on ferrite core array.

low levels of charge already includes much of the regeneration circuitry. The need for periodic refreshing of the stored charge means that there must be additional circuitry and also causes a slight increase in the average cycle time over long periods, since typically one cycle in 100 to 1000 must be reversed for refreshing. If such devices are organized as one bit per chip, the overall organization would be identical in principle to that in Fig. 4.9-3. Each chip then would have to contain separate decoders for the word lines and for the bit/sense lines. One requirement not shown in Fig. 4.9-3 is as follows: since all cells along a given word line are destructively read, a separate sense amplifier and data latch must be present on every sense line of each chip. For instance, for a square chip consisting of $w^{1/2}$ words × $w^{1/2}$ bits/word (i.e., w bits/chip), the chip would resemble that in Fig. 4.9-8. The on-chip decoder must select one of $w^{1/2}$ word lines. This could be done with FET NOR gates in one level of decoding. One level of decoding would require a fan-in of $\log_2 w^{1/2}$ or $0.5 \log_2 w$. For $w = 1024$ bits/chip, the one-level decoder gates must have a fan-in of 5, which is reasonable for FET gates. Since the common bit/sense line for such devices is a diffused line of high resistance, the bit and sense circuitry could be placed in the center of the chip rather than on the edges, to reduce the RC time constant by half. The bit/sense line decoders, bit drivers, sense amplifiers, and output buffer register latches are lumped in the areas designated BS, and so on. The logical

(a) Chip schematic

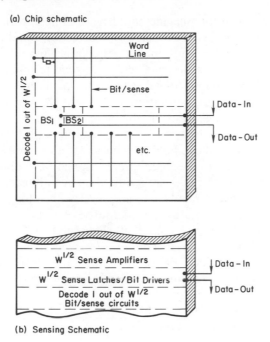

(b) Sensing Schematic

FIGURE 4.9-8 One bit per chip organization for the one-device, two-terminal MOS FET cell.

operation of such an array is as follows (assuming that this chip has been selected by the chip-select circuit). During reading, the word decoder selects one word line. A pulse applied to this word generates sense signals on all sense lines that the pulse crosses. These signals must be sensed on each line, a sense latch (chip output buffer register) must be set for each, and the desired sense signal is then decoded from among the multiple signals as in Fig. 4.9-8b. Since the cells along the selected word are destructively read, it is essential that the signal pulse be latched into an appropriate "1" or "0" for each sense line. Following the read cycle, with the same word selected, a write cycle is automatically initiated by the memory control unit. The sense latches are connected to all bit drivers, and pulsing of the word line writes (regenerates) the data back into that word. The word line is then turned off, followed by discharging of the bit lines and resetting of all sense latches to appropriate levels.

During writing, it is first necessary to read all the bits along the selected word line and latch all the sense latches. Then one of these latches—namely, the selected bit—is changed to the proper state, if incorrect, whereupon all the bits of that word are written back into that word with a maximum of one different bit. Of course this scheme could be organized with multiple bits per chip such as in Fig. 4.9-4, but then error correction could not be used to compensate for a bad chip. Thus one bit per chip is often used.

It can be seen that this destructively read, two-terminal cell requires a read operation followed immediately by a write operation for either reading or writing data. This requires additional time, but the saving in density is typically significant enough to justify the increase.

Refreshing of the stored information is done automatically by the storage control unit. A typical cell can hold the charge for a few milliseconds. If the cells require refreshing, say, every millisecond, then for a chip of 1024 bits organized as 32 words, 32 cycles are required every millisecond. If we interleave these cycles between regular memory cycles, then for a memory with a 1.024 μsec cycle time operating continuously, one out of every 32 cycles must be a refresh cycle for each chip. If all chips can be refreshed in parallel, only a very small increase in average cycle time is incurred in this case. Much greater chip densities are possible than that just described; 8 to 16K' bits on a fully decoded chip are becoming commonplace.

4.10 MATRIX SELECTION ARRAYS

In typical random access memory operation, one conductor (e.g., a word line or a sense line) must be selected from among many similar lines. This selection can be done with a standard logic tree decoder where the straightforward decoding of n bits into one out of 2^n locations requires a minimum of 2^n logic gates and often considerably more. For large memories, the number of required logic gates can become unreasonable, as shown in Section 1.9. Since the logic gates themselves contain several devices (transistors, resistors, diodes), the actual device count can become quite large. In addition, the connecting wire pattern may be very complex, and at times impossible, in integrated circuits that are restrained to one, or at most, two wiring levels of metal. An alternative, and older technique is to use a matrix selection array to decrease the device count, as well as to simplify the interconnection pattern. Numerous such selection arrays have been invented and used over the years. The magnetic matrix switch was one of the older techniques used for selecting word and inhibit conductors in the original 3D core arrays. The large currents required for early cores led to the improved load-sharing matrix switch but was still rather expensive and cumbersome. Improvements in semiconductors led to the replacement of magnetic selection arrays by diode selection arrays. Since cores require bipolar currents (i.e., in both directions at different times), and since noise can be reduced by using a balanced drive scheme, the selection matrix becomes a balanced drive, double diode array. To under-

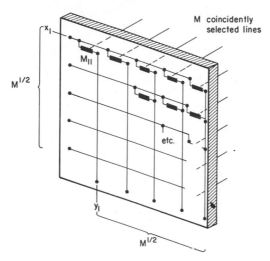

FIGURE 4.10-1 Fundamental principles of matrix selection arrays.

stand how the latter works, it is expedient to first consider a simple diode selection matrix for unipolar currents, then a balanced drive diode matrix for unipolar currents, and finally the double diode array for balanced drive and bipolar currents. These three diode selection matrices are very valuable in the next section. Thus the selection arrays to be considered are (a) magnetic matrix switch, (b) load sharing matrix switch, (c) diode matrix for unipolar currents, (d) balanced drive, diode matrix for unipolar currents, and (e) balanced drive, double diode matrix for bipolar currents.

First we discuss some general aspects of selection matrices. The selection principle used in all matrix selection arrays depends on the same coincidence principle employed in selecting bits in a memory array. This requires some kind of threshold (i.e., nonlinear) device at each coincident point. The basic scheme appears in Fig. 4.10-1. Suppose we wish to select one of M lines of a memory array. A selection array of $M^{1/2} \times M^{1/2}$ threshold devices with suitable characteristics can be wired for coincident selection with an array of $M^{1/2}$ horizontal and $M^{1/2}$ vertical wires as shown.* To select one of the M lines, say, M_{11}, it is necessary to apply pulses simultaneously to the matrix wire x_1 and to y_1. Only the device at the intersection must switch, and it must be capable of supplying the necessary drive current or voltage into the M_{11} line. All other devices along x_1 and y_1 will receive a disturb pulse, but because of the simplified function provided by this matrix, the devices can be operated so that the disturb is usually of no consequence. Assuming that

---

* The array need not be square.

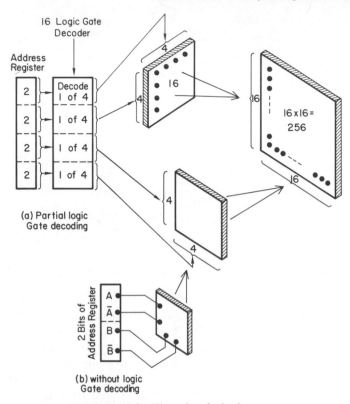

FIGURE 4.10-2   Hierarchy of selection arrays.

the selection array can be made to work, we have reduced the problem
of selecting one out of M to that of selecting one out of $M^{1/2}$, but on two edges,
for a total of 2 out of $2M^{1/2}$. Each of the edges of this array can likewise be
selected by another array, giving a hierarchy of selection arrays as shown in
Fig. 4.10-2a. For the example given, only 16 logic gates are needed instead of a
minimum of 256 if no selection arrays were used. This was very important
in early core memories, since the logic gates were bulky, expensive, power-
consuming vacuum tubes, whereas the selection arrays could be simple
ferrite cores similar to those in the memory. In principle, logic decoders are
not needed; rather, the selection array hierarchy can be extended down to
the address register, as in Fig. 4.10-2b. Since one element of every array must
be turned on for every selection, the complements $\bar{A}$ and $\bar{B}$ of the address
bits then serve to implement an array that can select one out of four.
One difficulty is that the address registers seldom have sufficient power to
drive the matrix; then additional drivers are needed. Furthermore, a hierarchy

with multiple levels becomes cumbersome to interconnect. Two levels have been used, but only one selection array is sufficient as a rule, since the required number of logic gates is already decreased dramatically.

4.10.1 Magnetic Matrix Switch

One of the oldest types of selection switch simply placed magnetic toroids at each intersection of the array wires in Fig. 4.10-1. To provide ease of operation, an additional winding was inserted through all cores, as in Fig. 4.10-3. A direct current supplied to this winding biases all cores to some point p_1 as in Fig. 4.10-3b. The current supplied in the x line just cancels this bias field and causes no switching. A coincidence of an x and a y field switches the core to point p_2, inducing a pulse in the selected M line. When either or both x and y fields are removed, the dc bias field resets the core. All other cores along the selected x and y lines receive disturb pulses, but obviously this condition is of no consequence because all cores are maintained at a quiescent bias field. In such a scheme, the BH loop threshold or squareness is not critical. The induced drive current is proportional to the saturation flux level and number of turns. Many other coincident selection schemes are possible, but the dc bias scheme was one of the more common techniques in early core memories.

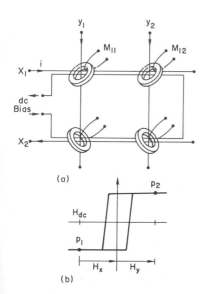

(a)

(b)

FIGURE 4.10-3 A dc biased, magnetic matrix selection array.

4.10.2 Load Sharing Matrix Switches

In early core memories, the high currents and fast run time pulses often required that several independent driving sources be tied in parallel to produce one high power driver. If such drivers were duplicated for each x and y line of the above selection arrays, either the cost would be prohibitive or the memory size would be drastically limited. In these selection arrays, only one x and one y line need be energized at one time. As a result, many schemes were invented to allow the high power driver to be shared by switching it to the needed line. This requires additional logic, as explained below. The fundamental principle used in magnetic load sharing matrix switches is shown in Fig. 4.10-4. There are two pairs of drivers, A, $\bar{A}$, B, and $\bar{B}$. The complements are needed because of the requirement for bipolar pulses. One driver of each pair is always used to select one of the two cores; hence two drivers always share in supplying the energy to each core. The only difference between the cores is the direction by which each individual wire passes through. The windings are arranged such that any two combinations will select one of the cores to give either a positive or negative current pulse. For instance, with the winding direction given, turning on drivers A and B produces a positive current in core 1, whereas $\bar{A}$ and $\bar{B}$ give a negative current (polarity arbitrary). The currents through core 2 cancel when core 1 is selected, and vice versa. Obviously additional logic is required to turn on the appropriate low power drivers.

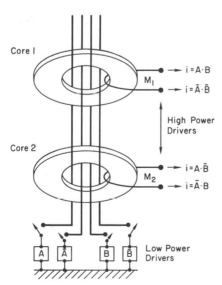

FIGURE 4.10-4 Load sharing magnetic matrix switch.

It should be noted that these cores do *not* provide a selection matrix like that in Figs. 4.10-1 or 4.10-3. Rather, these "matrix switch" cores would be connected to the selection array x lines in Fig. 4.10-1 and another identical matrix switch connected to the y lines. In this manner, the drivers A and B have to supply only half the current required by the selection array. The matrix switch can be expanded to 16 cores using 16 pairs of low current drivers (Constantine, 1958), with each supplying only $\frac{1}{16}$ of the total load. For example, two such switches could be used on the x and y lines of the 16×16 selection array of Fig. 4.10-2a. It can easily be seen that such switches do not reduce the circuit count but rather increase the number of components. However such switches did permit low power, high speed transistors (the only ones available) to supply high power at high speed, and in various forms they were used in early core arrays. The structures were rather cumbersome but effective. When the evolution of ferrite memories to smaller cores and improvements in semiconductors led to simplification and lower cost, magnetic matrix switches and selection arrays were replaced by diode selection arrays. Additional information on magnetic selection arrays and matrix switches can be found in Christopherson (1961), Forrester (1951), Merwin (1956), Morgan (1959), and Rajchman (1952 and 1953).

4.10.3 Diode Selection Matrix for Unipolar Currents

The basic form for a diode selection matrix is represented in Fig. 4.10-5. The diodes provide the threshold element for coincidently selecting one of the linear loads M. The selection of any given load, say, M_{11}, is as follows.

Initially all x lines are at 0 V and all y lines are at $+V_y$, reverse biasing all diodes in the array. Selection of M_{11} requires that line y_1 be disconnected from V_y and connected to ground. Simultaneously, line x_1 must be ungrounded and raised to same voltage V_x. Now diode D_{11} becomes forward biased and will conduct with very low resistance if V_x has the proper value. Any load in series with D_{11}, such as M_{11}, will experience a voltage pulse of essentially V_x to ground, minus the small forward drop through the diode. All other diodes in the array remain reverse biased.

The above switching sequence can be achieved with transistors connected to the x and y lines as shown. The bases of the transistors must be tied to additional logic circuits in the storage control unit for proper sequencing. Initially transistors T_3, T_4, T_7, and T_8 are conducting while all the others are off; thus all x lines are grounded and all y lines are at V_y as required. To select M_{11}, T_3 and T_7 are turned off while T_1 and T_5 are turned on, thereby grounding y_1 and raising x_1 to V_x. Thus D_{11} is forward biased and current can pass through the load M_{11}.

Such diode arrays provide a substantial reduction in device count compared to using logic gates. As an example, suppose we wish to select one out

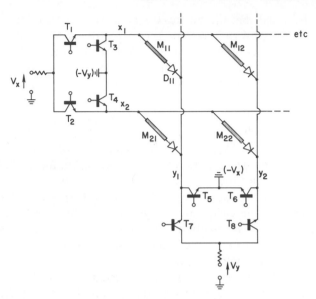

FIGURE 4.10-5   Schematic of diode selection matrix providing unipolar pulses.

of 256 resistors from $n = 8$ address bits. The resistors might be word or bit lines in a memory array. A straightforward logic decoder would require more than 256 logic blocks, hence many devices (transistors, diodes). A simple diode array of 16×16 would require only 256 diodes plus logic gates to select one out of 16 x lines and one out of 16 y lines, a substantial reduction in total device count. The logic gates would trigger the necessary gating functions by pulsing the base of the appropriate transistor to turn it on or off.

In the operation of the array just described, the diodes must be either highly reversed biased by V_y or highly forward biased by V_x. Thus the threshold characteristics of the diodes need *not* be very sharp, which is desirable. Also, making V_x slightly less than V_y causes all other diodes along the selected x_1 line that experience a reverse bias voltage of amplitude $V_y - V_x$, to remain reverse biased. Thus half-select disturbs are inconsequential.

4.10.4   Balanced drive, Diode Selection Matrix

In the previous diode array, when a load M_{11} is selected, one of its terminals is connected to ground through line y_1. If the M loads are word or bit lines of a memory array, such a "single ended" drive scheme, in which one terminal is grounded, often results in extremely large electrical coupling to adjacent sense lines. Reduction of this noise can be accomplished by using a balanced drive where one end of the load is raised to $+V_0$ and the other end to $-V_0$, so that the sense line at the center is essentially at 0 V, midway between these two voltages. This can easily be achieved by making few small changes in the array of Fig. 4.10-5. The ground contact between transistors T_3 and T_4 is now tied to $-V_y$, and the ground between T_5 and T_6 is tied to $-V_x$ as indicated in parentheses. In the quiescent state, the x lines are all at $-V_y$ and the y lines at $+V_y$, which means that the loads are essentially at 0 voltage. As before, the selection of M_{11} first requires T_3 and T_7 to be turned off. When T_1 and T_5 are turned on, however, line x_1 is at $+V_x$ and line y_1 is at $-V_x$, giving the desired balanced drive.

4.10.5 Balanced Drive, Double Diode Selection Matrix for Bipolar Currents

In the operation of most memory arrays, it is necessary to be able to supply either positive or negative current pulses upon command (for reading or writing, store "1" or "0," etc.). The previously described diode matrices can supply only unipolar currents, hence are not suitable in most applications. The situation can be improved very simply by using two diodes and an additional y line for each load in Fig. 4.10-5. The essential idea is as follows. In Fig. 4.10-5, the diode allows current to flow through the load in only one direction. Suppose that now we build an identical matrix but simply reverse the direction of the diode and reverse the sequencing of the transistors: the array will work as before, but with an opposite current polarity. Now we can superimpose these two arrays, connecting all common points and eliminating any duplicate wires. The result (simplified) appears in Fig. 4.10-6 in terms of one element of the matrix. A positive current through load M_{11} by way of diode D_{11} is obtained exactly as before: line x_1 is connected to $+V_x$, line y_1 to $-V_x$ and line y_1' to $-V_x$. Diode D_{11} then conducts, giving a balanced drive, while D_{11}' is reversed biased. To reverse the current polarity by way of diode D_{11}', line x_1 is connected to $-V_y$, line y_1 to $+V_y$, and line y_1' to $+V_y$. Now D_{11}' conducts while D_{11} is reversed biased. The quiescent point, hence voltages on all unselected lines, can be obtained with unselected x lines at $+V$, unselected y lines at $+V$, and unselected y' lines at $-V$. Under these conditions, all unselected diodes experience either 0 V or a negative (reverse bias) voltage as required.

This type of double diode selection with transistor switches was one of the more common selection schemes used on core memories in the late 1960s and early 1970s. One example of the use of such arrays in a small, 3D, three-wire core memory module is given in Lake, 1972. Other versions of the same basic double diode selection principle are shown in Gilligan (1966) and Russel et al., (1968).

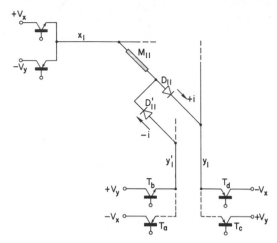

FIGURE 4.10-6 Balanced drive, double diode selection matrix for bipolar currents showing only one element of the array.

4.11 MEMORY ORGANIZATION FOR DEVICES WITH TWO PHYSICAL TERMINALS

We have already seen that for random access memory applications, a device or cell must have at least two independent, isolated functional terminals to allow reading and selective writing to be performed. This permits organization in a 2 or $2\frac{1}{2}$D array. For a 3D array, at least three independent isolated functional terminals are required, the functional aspect meaning that the terminals must perform totally different functions. In the basic transistor flip-flop cell in Fig. 4.11-1a, there is only one isolated, functional terminal, either node A or B; both nodes perform the same function—for example, writing ("1" or "0") or reading—since only one terminal can be used at a time. The ground connection to each cell serves as the necessary return electrical connection, but because it is common to all cells, it cannot be used as a functional array connection terminal. Hence we must tie additional components (transistors) to nodes A and B to be able to provide additional terminals at the cell level, making the cell more complex and expensive. This is unavoidable, however, if we are to be able to arrange such devices in an array.

A number of devices (e.g., ferroelectric, switchable resistors) are inherently two physical terminal devices and unlike ferrite cores or thin films, cannot have any additional terminals, not even a common ground. One device of this type is illustrated in Fig. 4.11-1b. If an array of such devices is fabricated

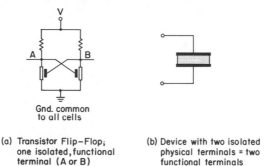

(a) Transistor Flip–Flop;   (b) Device with two isolated
    one isolated, functional   physical terminals = two
    terminal (A or B)   functional terminals

FIGURE 4.11-1   Memory cells with two physical terminals.

on one substrate such that all share a common connection, (e.g., ground plane), they fall into the category of one-terminal devices as with the transistor flip-flop cell. Under the circumstances, it would be necessary to add components to the device to achieve a workable cell for random access memory. If the devices can be fabricated with both terminals isolated from all other devices, however, the device can be the basic cell and can be organized into an array with no additional components in some cases (e.g., ferroelectrics) or with the addition of a series diode for sneak path elimination in other cases (e.g., switchable resistors).

To build a random access memory, the device or cell must have some threshold for coincident selection writing. Since these devices have two-terminals they can be used in 2D or $2\frac{1}{2}$D organization only; hence coincident reading (3D organization) is not possible. These devices must be put into some sort of array—the most obvious and simple one being a 2D array like that in Fig. 4.11-2. The selection process is very similar to that used in the diode selection array of Fig. 4.10-5, except here we must provide at least three separate functions: write "1," write "0," and read. All these operations must, of course, be done with just two wires connected to the device. Coincident selection is obtained by applying the appropriate sources or sinks $(+V, +i, -V, -i,$ or ground) to the desired x and y lines (e.g., x_1 and y_1 to select device F_{11}). The coincidence thus consists of a proper voltage on x_1 and a proper voltage on y_1; this device will receive the sum of the amplitudes of the potentials or currents applied to the selected x and y line, which will exceed its built-in threshold, causing it to switch, whereas all other devices will see just an x or y potential, not both (i.e., half-select disturb). Thus this coincidence potential must be capable of being varied to write a "1," write a "0," or read, without disturbing other unselected locations. To be more specific, it is necessary to choose a particular device and implement it in an array. We do this next for the case of the classical ferroelectric device.

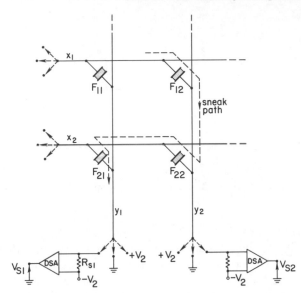

FIGURE 4.11-2 One possible array organization for two physical terminal, ferroelectric devices.

4.11.1 Ferroelectric Array

The square loop ferroelectric device of Section 3.12 is the electrical analog of the ferrite core with one exception: cores can have any number of physical terminals, whereas a ferroelectric capacitor has only two. Hence it must be used in an array such as that in Fig. 4.11-2. To ensure performance of all the desired functions, each x and y line must be capable of being separately connected to a positive voltage, a negative voltage, or ground. In addition, one of these lines must link to the sense amplifier for reading, one possibility being as shown.

Let us now trace the process of "write 1" followed by "read," then "write 0" followed by "read," into the element F_{11}: the polarities are arbitrary. To write a "1," line x_1 is switched to $-V_1$ and line y_1 is switched to $+V_2$. All other x and all other y lines are at ground. Under these conditions element F_{11} will experience a voltage $V_x + V_y$, whereas other devices on line x_1 will experience a voltage $-V_1$ to ground and those on line y_1 will experience a voltage $+V_2$ to ground. The necessary condition is that $V_x + V_y$ must exceed the device voltage threshold V_T (proportional to E_c) in Fig. 3.12-1, whereas the half-select disturb voltages V_1 or V_2 alone must not disturb the stored information in nonselected cells. To read the same cell, x_1 is connected to $+V_1$, and y_1 is connected to $-V_2$ through the small sensing resistor as shown. The voltage across F_{11} is now in the opposite direction, causing it to reset to "0." The switching will cause a small displacement current to flow through F_{11} which must pass through R_{s1}, producing a small voltage pulse. This is sensed by the differential sense amplifier (DSA) as a "1" signal. This last resetting step is identical to writing a "0" into F_{11}. If we now attempt to read F_{11}, the applied voltage will be of the same polarity. No switching can occur; thus no current and no voltage appear on R_{s1}.

If such a memory is organized as one bit per array, only one sense amplifier is required, and it can be switched to the appropriate y line during reading. If a multiple bit per array organization is used, multiple sense amplifiers must be used.

4.11.2 Sneak Path Problem

In arrays such as these, sneak paths are always present and may cause noise problems. To understand this, consider the step of reading a "0" stored in F_{11}. Negligible current flows through F_{11}, hence no signal results. However the other devices in the array can produce difficulties. Suppose that any small voltage across any device will cause some shuttling of the electric flux (which, though very small, is nonzero*). This can give some unwanted signals on line y_1 and can appear as a "1" signal instead of "0" in the sense amplifier. For instance, when a voltage is applied to line x_1, device F_{12}, which is half-selected, can allow a very small current to flow into line y_2. This signal can then flow through F_{22} into line x_2, and through F_{21} into line y_1. For a large array of devices, many such sneak paths exist. Each may contribute only a very small noise signal, but many of these, if they add linearly, can produce a noise signal equal to or larger than a "1" signal. If this occurred, incorrect information would be registered by the sense amplifier. Any devices in such arrays have potential sneak paths with the severity depending on the exact device characteristics. In some cases, diodes in series with the devices can reduce the amount of sneak signal per element, thereby allowing a larger array to be implemented. For instance, diodes such as in Fig. 4.10-5 placed in series with an array like that of Fig. 4.11-2 might help. For the sneak path shown, the diode in series with F_{22} would be in the direction opposite to the current flow, hence would present a large resistance, greatly attenuating the sneak signal. The value of such a scheme depends, of course, on the exact device characteristics relative to those of the diodes.

Other two-terminal devices such as switchable resistors can be wired into an array very similar to that of Fig. 4.11-2 (Matick, 1972). The selection process uses the basic principles described in this section and Section 4.10.

---

* These changes may be reversible (e.g., back and forth on the saturated slope of the hysteresis loop).

4.12   ASSOCIATIVE OR CONTENT ADDRESSABLE MEMORY

In all random access memories discussed thus far, the address of the word desired had to be sepcified before the address could be decoded and the proper word selected. In many computer applications, a different set of circumstances exists; one may not know the address of the word desired, but instead would like to determine all addresses of words that have particular pieces of information stored within a specified portion of the word length. For example, if the memory contains information about all employees of a given company, we may wish to know the names of all employees in a given department. Of course this information could be found by a sequential search of each word over the known bits (which contain the department number); but we would have to search for a match on each word in memory, which would require many machine cycles. An associative memory would allow the entire search to be completed in one memory cycle, a considerable saving for large files.

For the general case, an associative memory must be capable of operating both in the associative mode and in the typical random access read/write mode. For the latter mode, the usual address register, word and bit drivers, and sense amplifiers are used. During an associative interrogation the normal address register is not used; rather, all words are excited simultaneously, as well as the bits of each word over which the search is desired. The latter bits are prespecified and are known as the search field or mask. The compare functions performed over the search field can be *equal to*, *greater than*, *less than*, combinations of these, or other logic. In any case, ultimately the required compare must be done over the entire search field. We can think of an associative array as performing this function at two levels. Referring to Fig. 4.12-1, first some logic according to a prescribed truth table is done at each local bit level, to produce a bit "flag" F_{mn} indicating the results. Then the individual bit flags of the search field of each word are logically combined in the *search field comparator* to give the final yes/no compare result for each word. Finally a normal random access is made to the words that satisfied the search requirement. Thus the associative interrogation consists basically of three parts:

1. Interrogate each bit of search field for match and produce a bit flag.
2. Compare bit flags of each word for match and produce a word flag.
3. Interrogate matching words.*

To associatively address the memory, it is necessary to specify the exact bit locations over which the search is to be carried out. It is not possible in

---

* Step 3 may not always be done, but the system must be capable of doing this as desired. For example, we may wish to know only the number of words that provided a match.

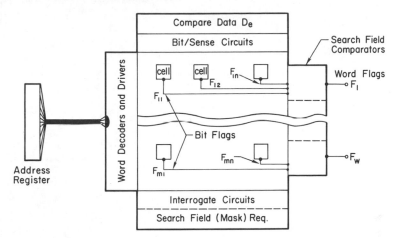

FIGURE 4.12-1 Schematic of general associative memory organization showing individual bit and word flags.

this case to specify a match of, say, 10 bits, anywhere in words of, say, 64 bits length. This type of search could be done by sequentially moving the search field along the words, but it would require additional memory cycles. Thus, the search field location must be known before we can address the memory, and this is a serious limitation in many types of file searching.

The complexity of the basic associative cell as well as the search field comparator depends on both the logical compare operation that must be performed and on circuit characteristics of the cell devices. To understand this, we first deduce the minimum number of terminals required on an associative cell for any logical compare operation and the constraints required to achieve this. After the general considerations, specific examples for "compare equal" and "compare unequal" logic cells and array organization are presented.

Let us now look at general associative cells in an array to deduce the minimum cell requirements. Figure 4.12-2 gives more details of the array organization of Fig. 4.12-1 using an undefined cell with any logic function. The cell is shown with essentially five terminals—a normal read/write word line, a bit line, a sense line, an interrogate line I, and a flag bit line F_{mn}. For normal random access, the interrogate and flag lines are not used. For associative operation, we must be able to interrogate any prespecified search field bit positions of all words; hence a separate interrogate line is needed for each bit position, and it must logically connect the same bits of a word as the bit line, as shown. The bit flag lines must logically connect all bits of a word, hence must run in the same direction as the word line. Since

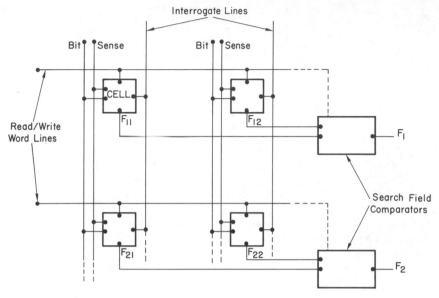

FIGURE 4.12-2 General associative array configuration.

we already know the bit and sense line for 2 or $2\frac{1}{2}$D organization can be the same line, it is clear that the five terminals named can be reduced immediately to four. Now the question is, Can we further reduce this number by allowing one terminal to serve several functions? Note that during normal read/write operations the interrogate line is unnecessary. During an associative interrogate, the external data for comparison can be supplied to the bit lines, the interrogate lines can be used to excite only the correct search field bits of all words, and the word line is unused. Since the word line and bit flag lines logically connect the same bits, the word line can serve as the bit flag line, provided the word lines can be connected in parallel to all bits of a word. If this is possible, the basic associative cell must contain a minimum of three functional terminals. If the word line cannot be used as the bit flag line, an additional terminal is required, and this is undesirable. Whether the word line can be used this way depends on the cell devices and the polarity of the bit flag signal. If this is not possible, either the individual cell flag lines must share a spare, common flag line, or all must be individually connected to the search field comparator, as shown schematically in Fig. 4.12-2. A very complex array wiring scheme is required in the latter case. If the bit flags cannot use the word line, it is at least highly desirable that all bit flags of a word be capable of sharing the same physical line. Cells can be designed to share the use of the word line for the bit flag line as well, as we shall see.

Some conclusions resulting from the above discussion can now be summarized:

a. A minimum of three functional terminals is required for a basic associative cell.

b. To achieve the minimum of three terminals, the normal read/write word line must serve as the bit flag line in the associative mode. This requires the bit flag signal logic to be compatible with the word line physical connection to all cells of that word.

c. If compatibility is not possible, an additional cell terminal is required. If these flag terminals are not capable of parallel connections among bits of a word, additional array complexity results.

d. An associative cell requires considerably more complexity than a comparable random access cell, hence is expected to be larger and slower.

4.12.1 Associative Cell for "Compare Equal"

To understand the general discussion, let us start with the basic two-terminal MOS flip-flop storage cell of Fig. 3.8-2 and add sufficient logic to convert it into a three-terminal associative cell for performing a "compare equal" function (we consider inequalities afterward). Each memory cell must have the local capability of comparing its previously stored contents S_{mn} with an externally supplied data bit D_e, producing a local bit flag F_{mn}. For the "compare equal" function assumed here, the flag must produce an indication that S_{mn} AND D_e are both "1," OR S_{mn} AND D_e are both "0." This function can be expressed more formally in standard logic terminology as $S_{mn} \cdot D_e + \bar{S}_{mn} \cdot \bar{D}_e$. When a match occurs, this logic function, which must be performed within the cell, can produce either a "1" flag signal F_{mn} or a "0" flag signal $\bar{F}_{mn}$ (i.e., no signal). Thus at the cell level the logic performed can be either

$$F_{mn} = S_{mn} \cdot D_e + \bar{S}_{mn} \cdot \bar{D}_e \qquad (4.12\text{-}1)$$

or

$$\bar{F}_{mn} = S_{mn} \cdot D_e + \bar{S}_{mn} \cdot \bar{D}_e \qquad (4.12\text{-}2)$$

Associative memory cells can be designed with either logic function. Although the difference between these two flags may seem conceptually trivial, the choice can have significant practical consequences on the implementation of the search field comparators in Figs. 4.12-1 and 4.12-2. In certain integrated circuit type cells, the use of the logic function of (4.12-2) allows the comparator

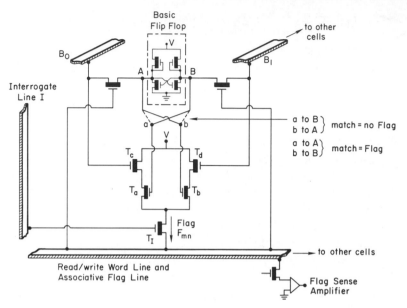

FIGURE 4.12-3 Associative memory cell for "compare equal," derived from basic MOS two-terminal flip-flop.

function to be automatically obtained in a very simple manner, whereas the use of (4.12-1) would require additional complexity.

Continuing with the basic storage cell of Fig. 3.8-2 the nodes A and B are again the important access points. The associative interrogation logic must compare the previously stored voltages at nodes A and B with an external data bit D_e represented either by a voltage pulse on B_0 with B_1 at ac ground ($D_e = 0$) or a voltage pulse on B_1 with B_0 at ac ground ($D_e = 1$). Also, it is desirable that the logic of the cell allow us to use the word line as an associative flag line. The interrogate line I must just allow the flag to go into the word line or not. This can be accomplished with a single FET, represented in Fig. 4.12-3 by T_I. The cell flag logic circuit, contained within the dashed box, must have four inputs, one each from B_0, B_1, node A, and node B. Four FETs can be used as shown, but now we must determine how points a and b are to be connected to nodes A and B. The connections indicated with solid lines (i.e., a to B and b to A) give the function of (4.12-2)—no flag signal current when a match occurs. The connections shown in dashed lines give the other logic flag: namely, a signal on a match. The former connection requires the search field comparator to be an OR function, and the latter requires an AND comparator. If the flag signals of all cells along the word line are tied in parallel to the word line, an OR logic function results. Hence the

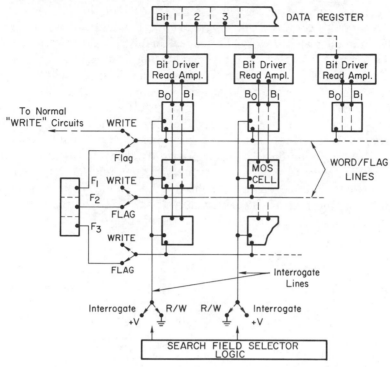

FIGURE 4.12-4   Schematic of associative array using three-terminal MOS cell of Fig. 4.12-3.

first connection (solid lines in Fig. 4.12-3) is necessary. Any word with a perfect match on all bits of the search field will produce no flag current. Any one or more mismatches will produce a flag; hence the desired words are those without flag signals. The method by which such an array could be achieved is shown in Fig. 4.12-4. During normal read/write operation, the bit/sense lines and word lines are connected and operated as in Sections 3.8 and 4.9. For an associative interrogation, the word lines are connected to low impedance sense amplifiers. The desired interrogate lines, corresponding to the bits of the search field, are switched by the search field logic to a voltage pulse to activate only the interrogated bit positions of all words. The bit/sense lines bring in the desired external search data bits as they would ordinary data. All words that have one or more mismatches in the search field produce a signal in the flag register. Indeed, since the register can be made to set or reset on this signal, the register itself can have either "0" or "1" represent a match. Assuming the flag bits retain their logical polarity, the register will contain all "1's" except for the word or words producing a match over the entire search field. Additional logic circuitry is now needed to convert the flag register into a true address for a subsequent read-out of the matched word. This is reasonably straightforward.

Note in the foregoing example that during an interrogation cycle, an associative flag line (word line) can contain a signal current of value as small as the signal of one cell to as large a signal as that from all bits, or b times a single signal. The latter would occur when all bits along a word gave a mismatch. Since b can be 64 or larger, the sense amplifier must be capable of limiting the input signal to prevent saturation and subsequent long recovery times. In addition, the flag signal acts as a word pulse would in normal writing of the cells. Since the interrogate data can be the opposite of those stored on some cells, a large voltage on the flag line would attempt to "write" the data into the interrogated cells, a most undesirable situation. This disturb sensitivity problem requires special design of such cells and limits on the maximum flag voltage.

4.12.2   Associative Cell for "Compare Unequal"

In many applications (e.g., associative replacement algorithms) it is desirable to identify words whose search field value is greater than or less than a given value. In the previous case of simple equality, all bit positions of the search field must be equal simultaneously, and there are only two possible states: all equal or not all equal. In an inequality comparison, a fundamental problem arises. A local bit flag can be either on or off, indicating two possible states (e.g., equal or not equal). In an inequality comparison of two bits S_i and D_i, we can have

$$S_i = D_i, \qquad S_i > D_i, \qquad \text{or} \qquad S_i < D_i \qquad (4.12\text{-}3)$$

a total of three conditions. When we wish to compare the binary value of a string of several bits, a bit-by-bit comparison is no longer valid. It is necessary to compare the various bit positions of the string relative to one another under certain circumstances. For instance, suppose we wish to compare the binary value of two bits $S = S_2 S_1$ with that of $D = D_2 D_1$ to find all words with $S > D$. If we compare the higher order bit S_2 with D_2, then if S_2 is less than D_2, or if S_2 is greater than D_2, the final result is determined, irrespective of the relative value of S_1 to D_1. However if $S_2 = D_2$, the final compare is determined by S_1 relative to D_1. It should be apparent that to accomplish this, the three local states of the bit cell, given by (4.12-3), must be provided, and this requires two separate flags at the cell level. In addition, the flags must be combined in a more complex manner than previously; hence the search field comparator has to be more complex. For instance, suppose we wish to provide a word flag for all words that have

$$S > D \qquad (4.12\text{-}4)$$

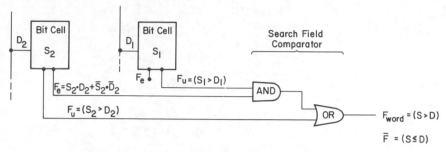

FIGURE 4.12-5   Schematic of a 2-bit inequality associative compare.

where S and D are two bits, as previously. The basic associative cells are assumed to give the two flags for equal F_e and unequal, F_u as

$$F_e = S_i \cdot D_i + \bar{S}_i \cdot \bar{D}_i \qquad (4.12\text{-}5)$$

$$F_u = (S_i > D_i) \qquad (4.12\text{-}6)$$

One way to do this is shown in Fig. 4.12-5. If the higher order bits position satisfies (4.12-6)—in other words, if $S_2 > D_2$—the lower order bit is irrelevant. Hence this flag directly provides the word inequality flag through the OR circuit. If the high order bits S_2 and D_2 are equal, satisfying (4.12-5), the low order bits S_1 and D_1 determine the inequality. If S_1 is greater than D_1 AND if $S_2 = D_2$, the search field satisfies (4.12-4) and the word flag is turned on. Since the "equal" flag on the low order bit is not used, if $S_1 = D_1$, no bit flag is provided at the AND gate and no flag results. If both S_2 and S_1 are less than D_2 and D_1, no bit flags are turned on, and no word flag can result. Notice that the word flag is "1" for $S > D$ and "0" for $S \leq D$; that is, the word flag follows the inequality set at the bit flag level. To get a word flag to indicate $S \geq D$, we could reverse the bit flag to indicate $F_u = (S_2 < D_2)$, which would change the word flag to indicate $F = (S < D)$, and $\bar{F} = (S \geq D)$. A simple inverter could be used to give a "1" for the latter. In any case, the equality part of the word flag inequality (i.e., "greater than or equal to") follows the bit flag, as shown in Table 4.12-1. Obviously as the complexity of the logic increases, so does the complexity of the associative cell and search field comparator.

A nontechnical summary of the literature on associative memories for 1956 to 1966 is given in Hanlon (1966). Some novel uses of associative memory in virtual memory hierarchies are considered in Section 9.13. In addition, an example of an associativelike directory without the use of fully associative bit cells is given in Sections 9.10 and 9.11.

TABLE 4.12-1

Bit Flag (unequal)	Word Flag
$F_u = (S_i > D_i)$	$F = (S > D)$
	$\bar{F} = (S \leq D)$
$F_u = (S_i < D_i)$	$F = (S < D)$
	$\bar{F} = (S \geq D)$

4.13   READ–ONLY MEMORY

If one adheres strictly to the definition of read-only memory (Section 1.3), it is difficult to determine the first technology for such usage. The mud tablets of early man and electrical resistance cards for early twentieth century firing tables (Section 1.2) were examples of simple ROM. Automatic telephone switching systems of the early 1900s made use of translators that were ancestors of modern read-only memories.* In the early 1960s, card changeable twistor ROMs (Barrett et al., 1961) were installed in central exchanges of the Bell System. As used on computers, the function table on the Eniac was perhaps the first such example of a ROM (externally changeable), although it was limited mainly to storing input data and mathematical tables. The concept of microprogramming by way of an externally alterable ROM was first developed by Wilkes on Edsac II, a follow-on to Edsac (Wilkes and Stringer, 1953; Wilkes et al., 1958). The intent was to use ROM as a decoder between the instruction of the user (actually ROM word addresses) and machine language (content of the ROM words). Thus the user could design his own machine language or in essence, redesign the internal machine data flow just by changing the contents of the ROM. The concept became quite popular in the early 1960s, but few such user-designable machines have been built. Rather, ROM found its first major use as an inexpensive way to do "emulation" in the IBM system 360, as well as for microcode translation in such special purpose computers as the controllers for disk and tape drives. All these applications can be classified as microprogram control, and ROM has been used extensively for this purpose in large computers (Tucker, 1967; Schwartz and Klein, 1968) as well as small desk and hand-held calculators. Such applications are beyond our scope, but a few fundamental points that reflect on ROM are considered. The reader should understand the fundamentals of the CPU cycle time discussed in Section 1.4. To carry out a machine cycle, many combinatorial logic nets in Fig. 1.4-1 require "control" inputs,

---

* For a review of ROM history see Dussine (1971), Lewin (1965), and Taub (1963a).

and any given net likewise may require several control inputs. A collection of all the control inputs necessary to carry out a given machine cycle is called a microinstruction and can be stored as one word of a ROM. The individual controls on each combinatorial net are referred to as "microorders."* Thus a word or microinstruction of the ROM consists of a collection of microorders. Each word read out of the ROM performs a new machine instruction. To be effective, a *ROM for microcoding must operate at a cycle time equal to that of the processor.* Fortunately for such application, the size of the ROM need be only several thousand words of less than 100 bits/word for large computers, and considerably smaller for calculators. Small size coupled with relative simplicity allows ROM to be faster than random access memory.

As indicated in Section 1.3, there are many varieties of read-only memory (postable, slow write, fast read; externally alterable, etc.). The pure form is that which is fixed during the manufacturing process and cannot be changed (written) except by changes in the physical hardware. It should be clear that lower cost is obtained by removing all or most of the writing functions of a random access memory. Hence the devices must be nondestructively read, and this is one fundamental requirement. However the cell can be essentially fixed in one state, hence read-disturb problems are then of no concern, which further lowers the cell cost.

Random access ROMs can be organized very much as ordinary random access memories in 3D, $2\frac{1}{2}$D, or 2D. However cells for use in 3D require threshold characteristics, hence are more difficult to fabricate and are almost never used. Most early cells were linear devices and were used in the $2\frac{1}{2}$D, 2T cell configuration of Fig. 4.5-1. Since the required word length is in the range of 100 bits or less, while the number of words is in the thousands, $2\frac{1}{2}$D with segment selection on the sense lines is more economical than a 2D organization. In a pure ROM with no electrical writing capability, the bit line is unnecessary, leaving only a word line and a sense line. A linear cell, such as a resistor, capacitor, or inductor, is connected between the word and sense line at all desired locations where "1's" are required and is left out for "0's." In such an array, a read pulse on one selected physical word line will generate a "1" signal from every stored "1" bit location. The proper logical word must be decoded from the physical word, but no regeneration is required because the reading is nondestructive. The simplicity of both the cells and array typically allow read-only memory to be cheaper and faster than a similar random access memory.

Linear bit cells used in a ROM array will have two physical terminals and typically are organized in an array similar as that shown in Fig. 4.11-2. As

* See Tucker (1967) for excellent review and example of microprogramming using ROM, and Mallach (1972) for excellent review of emulation.

a result, sneak path currents can become very significant in large arrays and must be taken into consideration in the array design (Taub, 1963b).

The diode selection array of Fig. 4.10-5 is essentially a ROM. The loads M, rather than being word lines, can be fusible links that are either removed to remove a diode in the array, or allowed to remain. Thus the diodes can be programmed into the OR array as desired and a very simple ROM results. One slight change is that all bits along a given x line are read simultaneously, which simplifies the y line selection scheme (i.e., there is no coincident selection).

The fusible link MOS cell (Section 3.13) is essentially an improved version of this concept. An MOS device is simpler and more economical to make than a diode, and these properties have led to the appearance of various commercial forms of programmable MOS arrays.

In a similar manner, the magnetic selection matrix of Fig. 4.10-3 can be fashioned into a coincidently selected ROM. The array can be programmed by inserting or deleting the magnetic cores. This is essentially a 3D ROM; but it requires a three-terminal cell that is more complex than the 2 and $2\frac{1}{2}$D, 2T cells. A three-terminal semiconductor cell could also be devised, but since this is uneconomical, as pointed out previously, most ROMs use a two-terminal cell, hence 2 or $2\frac{1}{2}$D organization.

As mentioned in Section 3.13, there is an almost limitless variety of ROM cells, each with certain advantages and disadvantages. Whatever the cell, the basic array organization takes on one of the two or three fundamental forms decribed in this chapter.

Early computer versions of externally alterable ROM such as twistors (Barrett et al., 1961) card capacitors (EDN, 1971; Haskell, 1966), and Balanced Capacitors (Abbas et al., 1968; Taub, 1963b) had relatively low density by modern standards. Maximum bit densities were in the range of 500 bits/in.^{2}, and typically much less. A 16K' bit planar module fabricated with array bits on both sides would require about 32 in.^{2} of each side of the module for 8K' bits. The supporting electronics, including drivers, decoders, and sense amplifiers with latches, could be placed on a thin module of 100 in.^{2}* In contrast to this, an integrated circuit ROM of early–mid-1970 vintage can store 2K' bits fully decoded on a chip of approximately $0.2 \times 0.2 = 0.04$ in.^{2}. Eight such chips would give 16K' on a module slightly larger than $8 \times 0.04 = 0.32$ in.^{2}. The module density improvement is about a factor of 300. This factor results from comparing maximum densities of the mid-1960s technology with semiconductors of early to mid-1970s. Integrated circuit densities are becoming available of 8 times or more the foregoing value, giving a density improvement measured in the thousands. This

* Based on actual prototype design using thick film ROM at 256 bits/in.^{2} (Matick et al., 1966).

density, coupled with low cost and better compatibility of semiconductor arrays with the CPU technology, has resulted in semiconductor ROM finding extensive use in all controlling functions.

Programmed Logic Array Application of ROM

In the early 1970s, the advent of large-scale integrated circuit ROM arrays made the known concepts of programmed logic arrays (PLA) quite attractive, and they began to appear in use. Although we do not dwell on PLAs, a few fundamental points should be understood. The storage medium array of a ROM is just a large OR array. If we pulse any given word, an output signal is obtained if bit 1, OR bit 2, OR bit 3, and so on, has a stored "1." This by itself is not sufficient to perform complex logic; rather, an AND array is also necessary. The latter can be obtained from the decoding logic on the word lines, since any decoder is fundamentally just AND logic. Section 4.10 shows some implementations in arrays. However these decoders only select "one out of 2^n words" for any given address n. More powerful logic can be obtained by customizing the AND decoder to select several different numbers of words for any given address. In this way, each minterm of a logic truth table can be implemented term by term, and complex logic, both sequential and combinatorial, can be performed (see Carr and Mize, 1972; Hemel, 1970; Kvamme, 1970).

Additional, simple logic can be added to the input of the AND array for even further advantages. The major point is that the arrays are in essence simple read-only memory arrays, and both the common ROM storage array that performs OR logic and the word decoders that perform AND logic, must work together as a unit to perform complex logic functions.

4.14 BASIC STORAGE MODULE INTERLEAVING ARCHITECTURE

In early computers of the mid-1950s and early 1960s the main memory requirements were in the range of 10^5 to 10^6 bits and cycle times of 12 to 2 μsec (see Table 1.1-1). For such sizes and speed, it was possible to build the entire main memory as one unit, using ferrite core arrays. The CPU logical address was used to decode one word out of one box, the main memory box. However the advent of the so-called third-generation computers in the mid-1960s required increases in speed and size of main memory, and this was no longer possible. In such cases the designer produced a module of maximum size compatible with the speed and cost requirements. The largest size module that can be fabricated while achieving the required speed, tolerances, and other specifications is known as the basic storage module (BSM). To achieve larger total main memory capacity without sacrificing

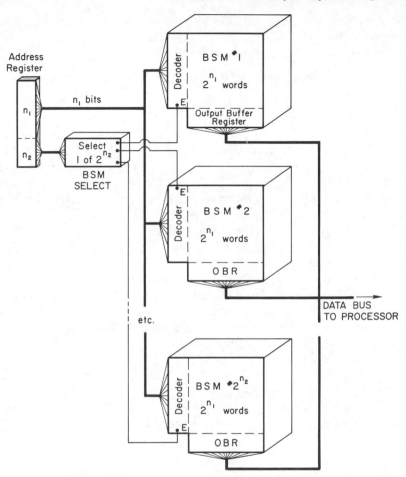

FIGURE 4.14-1 Extending memory capacity using basic storage modules (BSM); data-in and power bus not shown.

speed, additional architectural design is required. In the simple case, all the BSM's necessary decoders or selection matrices, drivers, sensing circuits, and so on, are contained within the module. Enlarging the memory capacity simply calls for paralleling the signal paths and segmenting the CPU address register to include additional capacity (Fig. 4.14-1). Additional decoding is required because each BSM contains only enough decoding to handle its own capacity, and all BSMs are identical. This additional decoding is completely analogous to that used in conjunction with transistor memory chips in Figs. 4.9-3 and 4.9-4. The fully decoded chips are in essence a more elementary BSM.

When a large number of words are required, the paralleling of BSMs sometimes introduces additional problems. The parallel connections increase the loading effects on circuits and may necessitate additional drivers, hence additional delay. These effects are typically small but not negligible. The parallel connection of many BSMs usually introduces a more serious problem, namely, the cable delay of the interconnecting transmission lines. Main memory is packaged as a separate box with several BSMs per box. As more boxes are added, the physical spacing requires longer cable lengths, which sets a limit on the maximum size of memory that can be parallel without degrading the cycle time. Some typical sizes of BSMs are 4K' words × 64 bits/word for core arrays at the higher speeds. The maximum BSM size of core arrays is about 16K' words. Early semiconductor BSMs were generally in the same range; and they continue to grow as the level of cell integration increases. If we wish to implement a 4M' word memory with, say, 4K' BSMs, we must obviously connect 1K' memory modules in parallel. This becomes unwieldy; thus larger BSM sizes are desirable at a given speed.

In Fig. 4.14-1 if the address register, BSM selector decoder, and other control functions of the control unit are fast enough, any BSM can be accessed at any time relative to all other BSMs. One module cannot be run at a rate faster than its cycle time, but this is the only restriction. Because of this independence of each BSM, it is possible to obtain an "apparent" increase in main memory speed by interleaving the BSM accesses. This feature requires additional hardware in the control unit and also places constraints on the memory reference sequences, but often it can be used to great advantage in large, high speed computers. Interleaving permits the CPU to reference memory at the CPU clock rate as long as a sufficient number of sequential references are made to different modules. The latter condition is not always possible but it is nearly so with respect to memory references made by the CPU versus the I/O processor in Section 9.1. The I/O processor is likely to be transferring a page into one memory module while the CPU is referencing another. If so, no cycle stealing is necessary. Another important use of interleaving is in the storing of a page or block of cache in alternate main memory BSMs. As discussed more fully in Section 9.3, when a miss occurs to the cache, it is necessary to transfer the page from main memory as fast as possible. Storing words of a given page in different BSMs permits the transfer to be done essentially at the cache speed except for the first access. This interleaving concept has been used on many commercial computers. Of course additional delays are encountered because of the bus delay paths between various BSMs as well as the added logic delay. However the former are usually more significant and are present whether the BSMs are just paralleled or interleaved.

5 Magnetic Recording Fundamentals

5.1 INTRODUCTION

This chapter is concerned primarily with the fundamentals of magnetic recording systems that are applicable to all saturated magnetic recording systems using a magnetic head (transducers) for reading and writing, in conjunction with a medium that moves relative to the transducer. The concepts discussed here are applicable to disks, tapes, strips, drums, and other related magnetic systems. Subsequent chapters deal with the systems and operational aspects of disks and tapes separately.

Chapters 2 and 3 indicated that random access memory is fast and expensive because of the large number of dedicated transducers used for operation. Chapter 2 further discussed how a lower cost, but slower storage system could be devised by sharing transducers and by not having a "wired-in" storage medium. Chapter 1 made the large storage needs for many applications apparent, and larger storage with faster access time is becoming increasingly important. Hence the goal of storage systems remains to provide the largest possible storage capacity with high speed operation and at low cost.

These requirements are somewhat contradictory in that high speed tends toward small capacity and high cost (per bit), whereas large capacity and low cost tend towards slow speed. Magnetic recording represents a compromise between these conflicting demands, providing large storage capacity at low cost and slow access times, although data rates can be large. Low cost is achieved through the sharing of transducers, and through using a movable and in some cases, a removable (changeable) medium, for greater flexibility. Many of the implications of this philosophy in the overall operation are systems problems and are discussed later with reference to specific systems (tape, removable disk, etc.).

The basic requirements for magnetic recording, which are the same for all storage systems as given in Section 2.2, are as follows:

1. Storage medium.
2. Writing mechanism.

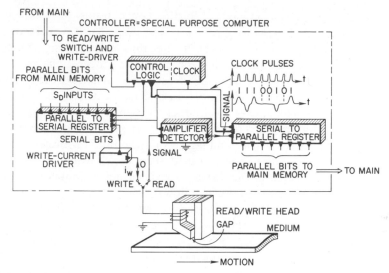

FIGURE 5.1-1   Essential features of a simplified complete magnetic recording system.

3. Sensing and reading mechanism.

4. Addressing mechanism.

The various types of memory systems differ in the way each of these is implemented. This chapter covers the ways these functions are accomplished in
magnetic recording, starting with the medium, then writing, reading, and
addressing techniques. These four essential parts for a simplified but nevertheless complete magnetic system (Fig. 5.1-1) consist of a controller (a
sometimes large computer) to perform the addressing and other functions as
well as write current generation and signal detection; serial/parallel conversion registers; a read/write head with an air gap to provide the magnetic field
for writing and to sense the stored flux during reading; and finally the medium.
The wired-in cells, array, and transducers of random access memory have
been replaced by one read/write transducer that is shared among all stored
bits, and a controller, also shared. Coincidence for reading and writing
is obtained by mechanical motion of the medium relative to the head.
Chapters 5 through 7 are organized in terms of these four basic requirements,
with additional sections and concepts as needed. This chapter concentrates
on concepts and principles that are applicable to all digital magnetic
recording; Chapters 6 and 7 relate the specifics of sequential and direct access
systems, respectively. Before discussing in detail each of the four basic
requirements, let us summarize the problems and approaches pertinent to
magnetic recording, to put the following sections into perspective.

In essence, the field of magnetic recording concentrates on achieving at reasonable cost the following goals: (*a*) *increasing density* by recording stored bits closer together in the medium while (*b*) simultaneously providing adequate *signal to noise ratio* during the readback process. The means of effecting these goals can vary greatly, but in each case, all parts of the system— from the medium, to the read/write transducers, electronic circuits, and organizational characteristics—affect either the density, the signal to noise ratio, or both. Thus implementation of the four system requirements introduces constraints on density and signal to noise ratio. We refer to these two goals again and again in subsequent sections, showing how various design parameters can effect the density, signal, or noise. Some of the more important points to be learned are as follows.

To achieve higher density, it is necessary to write a binary bit in the smallest possible space, and to place other bits as close to the first bit as possible. In the more common codes (NRZ or NRZI) a stored "1" bit is represented by a signal transition of magnetization within the medium from $+M_r$ to $-M_r$, or vice versa. In practice, the space occupied by many sequentially recorded information bits, hence density, is dictated largely by the properties of the recording medium and the read head (i.e., readback coupling). Contrary to what one might offhand suspect, the write head is not the major factor in determining the recorded density. In fact, it is possible to write bits at a much higher density than they can be read and converted to digital signals. This insensitivity to the write head results because the writing is done by the trailing edge of the write head fringe field and can give very sharp, closely spaced transitions compared to the reading process, where the entire fringe field of the stored bit pattern couples to the read head to give a broad sense signal.

After being written, the information must not only be capable of being sensed by giving a large signal to noise voltage out of the read head, but also this signal must be converted into digital form. The sensing and subsequent conversion to digital form via strobing or clocking are two separate and equally important problems in the total reading process, the first (signal amplitude and signal to noise ratio) being determined mainly by the medium and head parameters, and the latter being determined by the bit coding scheme, clocking technique, linearity of the electronic circuits, and tolerances in all parts of the system.

The minimum size of one stored bit (i.e., one transition) is determined by the minimum transition length required within the medium to change from $+M_r$ to $-M_r$, or vice versa. In nearly all magnetic recording systems the minimum spacing at which adjacent bits can be placed with respect to a given bit is not governed by an increase in self-demagnetization; rather, the bit spacing is determined by the distortion of the sense signal when adjacent bits are too close (bit crowding).* This results from the overlapping of the fringe field from adjacent bits when they are too close, and this total, overlapped magnetic field is picked up in the read head, giving an induced signal different from that produced by a single transition. This is just another way of saying that the fringe field of a bit has a significant, nonnegligible value for rather large distances—in fact, larger than the spacing at which the adjacent bits can be placed by the write head.

Ideally, the signals coming out of the read head would be a series of sharp pulses separated by a fixed distance, hence easy to convert to binary digits. Because of the nature of the readback process and the finite air gap, however, the signal more nearly represents an analog signal in which the amplitude, shape, and time position (phase) of the bits in the signal vary from one position to another. This makes the clocking of the read signal for conversion without errors much more difficult, particularly as the density increases. Assuming the clocking and conversion to digital form can be done without error (a poor assumption), one obtains in essence a series of discrete bits "1" and "0" without any individual identity. The only way to recognize particular pieces of stored information is through the sequence of pulse patterns. This then leads to the use of special sequences of pulse patterns such as gaps, address markers, and numerous other coded patterns that can be recognized by the logic hardware built into the storage control unit. In all cases this is a special purpose computer attached to the storage unit to provide numerous logic capabilities for storing and retrieving information. These special patterns, along with other aids, are referred to as the *stored addressing information* and constitute at least part of the "addressing mechanism." The total addressing mechanism takes on different forms depending on the system and can vary from very simple (e.g., start–stop gaps on tape or simple gaps on disks) to disks with very complex formated stored addressing information with considerable rotational position information. The total addressing mechanism is always provided by the storage control unit in combination with this stored addressing information. This chapter discusses only the general form of the latter; the manner in which the storage control unit uses this stored information is covered more fully for specific systems in Chapters 6 and 7.

In summary, the most important practical factors limiting density are in the readback process. Writing in terms of flux changes per unit length can be done at a very high density. The difficulty arises in the signal to noise ratio

---

* Although self-demagnetization increases and becomes important at very high densities, it usually is not significant at lower densities where bit crowding is the major factor. Even at higher densities, bit crowding still dominates, since H_c can be made large enough to resist the self-demagnetization forces.

when one attempts to read this recorded information and to specify which are the "1" and the "0" bits. Readback ability is determined by many factors, starting from the medium, through the read head, and back into the clocking and sensing circuits; it is a function of such factors as noise caused by a nonuniform magnetic medium, surface roughness, head to medium separation, read head air gap and head design, clocking accuracy, and linearity of circuits. This chapter attempts to show why these factors are important and how they are interrelated. Many additional and important engineering design aspects of magnetic recording are considered elsewhere (IBM 1974).

5.2 MAGNETIC RECORDING MEDIA

Although numerous media are used for magnetic recording, two common types have dominated since the early days of computers: these are flexible media (primarily tapes) and thin magnetic coatings on hard surfaces such as disks and drums.

The most common, and by far the largest storage medium in use has been and continues to be 0.5 mil thick iron oxide, γFe_2O_3, on a flexible carrier such as Mylar, which is 0.5 in. wide, 1 mil thick, and generally rolled on reels 2400 ft long. A typical reel of tape has the following dimensions: 10.5 in. diameter and $\frac{23}{32}$ in. thick at the mounting hub. Tapes are usually enclosed in a plastic case of $11\frac{5}{8}$ in. diameter and $1\frac{3}{16}$ in. height. A typical reel recorded at 800 bpi (see Section 1.7) can store more than 10^8 bits in a physical structure that is smaller than most books and easily transported. The details of magnetic tape and its manufacture are presented in Chapter 6.

Disk and drum recording substrates are rigid surfaces such as polished aluminum rather than flexible substrates like tapes. Magnetic drums, since earliest times, have used electroplated nickel-cobalt as the magnetic medium. Such materials could also be used for disks, but the latter have been mainly fabricated from γFe_2O_3 as used for tape. Details specifically related to disks are given in Chapter 7.

The remainder of this section dwells on the medium parameters that affect the density and signal to noise ratio of the medium itself. Particular emphasis is placed on the fundamental magnetic properties desired versus those obtainable from various magnetic materials. Because of its widespread and common usage, γFe_2O_3 is treated more specifically, although other materials are included.

All common magnetic recording media consist of a magnetic part (the magnetic material) and a nonmagnetic part. Both parts affect the density and signal to noise capability of the medium. Thus the overall requirements of the medium must be obtained by varying two sets of parameters, namely, the magnetic and nonmagnetic variables. These two sets are interdependent and together determine the overall medium parameters. The overall medium parameters that affect density and signal to noise ratio are as follows:

a. Particle size in oxide and grain size in metallic media.

b. Coercive force H_c.

c. Residual flux density B_r.

d. Thickness.

e. Surface roughness.

f. Uniformity of characteristics over large area.

Items *a* through *e* determine the density and signal to noise ratio over a small, localized area. Item *f* determines the repeatability of the characteristics over the entire medium.

The magnetic and nonmagnetic variables at our disposal for varying these six parameters are as follows:

Magnetic Material Parameters

1. Intrinsic coercive force H_c.

2. Saturation magnetization I_s (or M_s).

3. Particle (or grain) shape and size.

4. Particle (grain) orientation.

5. Intrinsic anisotropy.

These magnetic parameters are determined by the material composition and method of fabrication.

Some of the variable nonmagnetic material parameters are as follows.

1. Carrier substrate smoothness and uniformity.

2. Carrier dimensional stability.

3. Solvent-binder wettability.

4. Adhesive properties of binder and carrier.

When the medium is fabricated from acicular particles of γFe_2O_3, the magnetic particles are suspended in a solvent to provide a fluid matrix for orientation, along with a nonmagnetic binder (glue) to hold them to the carrier substrate. The variables at our disposal interact in a complex way to yield the final medium. Let us now consider each of the overall medium parameters to see how each is affected by the various magnetic and nonmagnetic material parameters.

Particle or Grain Size   In the ultimate limit, the dimensions of a stored (recorded) bit cell will be equal to the dimensions of the magnetic particles or grains (smallest possible magnetic domain) composing the medium. Thus the ultimate goal of medium design is to achieve atomic sized particles with the required parameters and to disperse these uniformly over a large area.* To understand this, some discussion of particle magnetics is necessary. All magnetic materials require some ordering of the atoms that make up the material, to provide a net magnetic moment. The ordering can occur over a large macroscopic array of atoms, which would be a single crystal capable of being handled and measured, or it can occur over a very small microscopic dimension, referred to as a particle or grain. Atomic exchange energy, which gives rise to local magnetic ordering in an ensemble of atoms, occurs over very small distances of a few atoms; thus magnetic ordering in very small particles is possible if the ordering is not destroyed by other forces such as magnetoelastic coupling, anisotropy, and self-demagnetization (magnetostatic energy). These forces can be either an aid or a hindrance, depending on their magnitude, their direction (sign or direction of orientation), and how they are used. Magnetoelastic coupling and anisotropy are intimately related, and together they determine the coercive force of the material or particle. The self-demagnetizing force, as we saw in Section 2.6, simply reveals the amount of self-destructive force present for a given amount of magnetization B_r or M_r.

The ultimate particle is one that can stay magnetized when saturated in a given direction: because of the large self-demagnetizing forces inherent on the edges and in corner regions of all structures except ellipsoids of revolution (Section 2.6) the ultimate particle is a prolate spheroid (cigarlike), having a circular cross section and an aspect ratio a/c of about 10:1 up to 100:1; for γFe_2O_3 the actual dimensions should be in the range of

$$a = 1 \text{ k\AA} = 0.1 \mu$$
$$c = 50 \text{ to } 100 \text{ \AA}$$

Coercive Force. As we know from Section 2.6, the coercive force is that parameter which resists the self-demagnetizing field H_D of the material. To provide a reasonable residual flux density B_r, the coercive force must be at least comparable to, preferable larger than, the self-demagnetizing field. As the recording density increases, H_D increases; hence we must expect to go to larger values of H_c for higher density. The coercive force is determined primarily by the magnetoelastic and anisotropy parameters of the material used. Any switching of M is always accompanied by a change in the dimensions of the magnetic material (i.e., magnetostriction), and the

---

* Current particle sizes are quite sufficient for high density; other practical factors more important in limiting density are surface roughness, head to medium separation, and servoing (disks).

relationship is determined by the magnetoelastic constant. The latter can be greatly altered by the addition of various other atoms or by stress built into the material (e.g., stress from the carrier substrate). The larger the stress, the larger or smaller the coercive force, depending on the direction of applied stress, the polarity of magnetostriction, and the direction of measurement of H_c relative to the above-mentioned variables.

Anisotropy measures the ability of M to remain oriented in a preferred direction of magnetization. Crystalline anisotropy can be built into the particles to provide a larger H_c in one direction; that is, a larger applied field is necessary to change the magnetization perpendicular to the anisotropy axis. Also, shape anisotropy can ge used to achieve the same effect—a long thin bar is more easily magnetized along its long axis than along its short axis.

Under ideal conditions, the anisotropy can be used to determine the coercive force. For an array of ideal, *spherical* single domain particles, there is no shape anisotropy. If only crystalline anisotropy is present, the particles must switch by rotation against this built-in restraining force. The coercive force must then be equal to the anisotropy field given adjacent to (3.5-1) or

$$H_c = H_K = \frac{2K}{I_s} \tag{5.2-1}$$

On the other hand, for an array of single domain particles with only shape anisotropy and all aligned in one direction, the coercive force for an external field applied along the long or a axis of a prolate spheroid is given by Stoner and Wohlfarth (1948) for pure rotational switching as

$$H_c = (D_b - D_a)B_s \tag{5.2-2a}$$

with H_c in oersteds and B_s in gauss* or

$$H_c = (N_b - N_a)I_s \tag{5.2-2b}$$

with H_c in oersteds and I_s in emu per cubic centimeters. The maximum possible value of H_c will be obtained for very long, thin, prolate spheroidal particles with D_a approaching 0, so that $D_b - D_a \approx D_b$. From (2.6-10) we know that

$$D_a + D_b + D_c = 1 \tag{5.2-3}$$

But for our case, $D_b = D_c$ and $D_a \approx 0$, thus substituting into (5.2-3) gives

$$D_b = \tfrac{1}{2} \tag{5.2-4}$$

* For ideal single domain particles, $B_r = B_s$.

Thus from (5.2-2a), shape anisotropy gives

$$\max H_c \bigg|_{D_a \sim 0} = 0.5B_s \qquad (5.2\text{-}5)$$

with H_c in oersteds and B_s in gauss. For cases in which both crystalline and shape anisotropy exist, the two effects must be added to get

$$H_c = \frac{2K}{I_s} + (N_b - N_a)I_s \qquad \text{cgs units} \qquad (5.2\text{-}6)$$

For the above general ideal case, the coercive force has two terms, one that increases with increasing I_s and one that decreases with increasing I_s. In many cases, one or the other dominates. It can be seen that large coercive forces could be obtained for single domain particles using only shape anisotropy with the correct values for I_s, N_b, and N_a. This is not possible to achieve in practice because of the difficulty in producing such small single domain particles of uniform shape. Thus the coercive field is determined by a noncoherent rotational model that does not lend itself to easy expression.

Residual Flux Density B_r. The magnitude of the playback signal is directly proportional to the magnitude of B_r. Thus for maximum signal, maximum B_r is desired. As we know, however, large B_r gives a large self-demagnetizing field, which decreases the density, necessitating a compromise. As for the media, the flux density is determined entirely by the moment of the constituent materials and the amount of dilution. Intrinsic values (material with no air gaps) of B_s for several materials are given in Table 5.2-1. When an oxide consisting of particles, such as a powder, is mixed with binders and solvents, ideally the net B decreases linearly with the amount of dilution. If the coating consists of 20% particles and 80% nonmagnetic binders (by volume) all uniformly dispersed, the flux density is 20% of its value for a single particle. Unfortunately the particles are not always uniformly dispersed but rather cluster in groups. These groups can have a certain amount of closed flux paths within their structure, which reduces the externally sensed B, hence can reduce the effective flux density by more than the dilution factor. This reduction of B from clustering is not usually significant in γFe_2O_3 because quite adequate value of B_r can be obtained.

Thickness. The medium thickness is an important parameter because of its effect on density. A thick medium causes the change in magnetization to be spread over a distance larger than that caused by a thin medium, producing bit crowding in the readback process as shown in Section 5.4. Hence a very thin medium is desired for high density. However a large signal requires large flux or large thickness, and again a compromise is necessary. For oxide coatings, the thickness is governed mainly by the particle size, the ability to

TABLE 5.2-1 Intrinsic Properties of Magnetic Recording Materials

Material	σ (emu/gr)	Density^a ρ (gr/cc)	$I_s = \sigma\rho$ (emu/cc)	$B_s = 4\pi I_s$ (G)	H_c (Oe)	$S = I_r/I_s$ Oriented	Particle Shape (a/b)	Particle Size, Long Axis (μ)	K (ergs/cc)
Oxide Particles									
γFe_2O_3	74	$\sim$5.07–4.6	375	$\sim$4,700	$\sim$100	0.46	Equiaxed	0.05–0.3	-4.64×10^4
			340	4,300	250–380	0.75–0.8	Acicular	0.2–0.7	
$\gamma Co_xFe_{2-x}O_3$									
$x = 0.04$	50	4.67	233	2,930	400	0.7	Cubic	0.05–0.08	10^6
$x = 0.6$	44		205	2,575	600	0.7	Cubic	0.05–0.08	10^6
Fe_3O_4	92–84	4.9–5.2	$\sim$450	$\sim$5,650	$\sim$300	0.52	Equiaxed	$\sim$1	-1.1×10^5
					300–335	0.7	Acicular	0.2–0.7	
					350–400	0.7	Platelets		
$Co_xFe_{3-x}O_4$									
$x = 0.04$	80	5.185	415	5,215	600–800	0.1	Cubic	$\sim$0.2	3×10^5
$x = 1$	70	5.32	372	4,680	750–980	0.65	Cubic	0.004–0.016	6×10^5
					1200			0.04–0.05	
CrO_2	90–100	4.8	430–480	$\sim$6,000	60–400	0.5	Cubic	wide range 0.2–10 long 0.03–1 wide	2×10^5
Metal particles									
Iron	159		$\sim$1714	$\sim$21,500	645	0.57	Acicular	0.025	4.8×10^5
Iron-cobalt (73–27)	107				1000	0.9			
Cobalt	150		$\sim$1422	$\sim$18,000	900	0.83			4.3×10^6
Metal films									
Iron	218		1700	$\sim$21,500	$\geqslant$800	0.95			4.8×10^5
Co-Ni-P	$\sim$120		$\sim$1100	$\sim$14,000	1300	0.8			

^{a} Particle density usually less than bulk because of packing factor.

wet the particles to prevent clustering, the roughness of the substrate, and the mechanical limitations in laying out a small surface of uniform thickness.

Surface Roughness and Uniformity. These are determined mainly by the amount of clustering of magnetic particles, the uniformity of magnetic and nonmagnetic particle sizes, the surface characteristics of the substrate, and the mechanical tolerances in the coating process.

Another important uniformity problem is posed by variations over time. The addressing of recorded bits is not wired in but rather requires physical coincidence of the bits with the read/write heads. The tolerances on this physical coincidence become more severe as density increases. Hence the mechanical and thermal stability of the carrier substrate becomes very important, as we would expect, and special attention must be given to these problems, although we do not treat them here.

Thus the final material requires consideration of all the foregoing magnetic and nonmagnetic factors and the possible ranges of parameters that can be achieved. We now discuss the ranges of parameters for the more common magnetic materials used or considered for recording.

5.2.1 γFe_2O_3

The most commonly used magnetic material for disk and tapes has been gamma iron oxide (γFe_2O_3).* The basic magnetic material in crystalline form has a spinel structure (cubic symmetry) that is closely related to magnetite ($Fe_3O_4 = FeO \cdot Fe_2O_3$), the latter being the basic material used, with substitutions, in magnetic cores. The Curie temperature is difficult to measure because it transforms to the nonmagnetic rhombohedral structure, αFe_2O_3, above 350°C. Values reported for Curie temperature range between 680°C (Bozorth, 1951, p. 470) and 590°C (Bate and Alstad, 1969, p. 824). In any case, it is substantially above room temperature. The saturation flux density B_s is 5000 G and the maximum coercive force for oriented materials is about 380 Oe. For magnetic recording, fine particles of γFe_2O_3 are made and suspended in an organic binder. These particles usually consist of multiple crystallites (small crystals) with a needle shape (acicular); length is between approximately 0.2 μ and less than 1 μ, and widths (diameters) are typically between 0.03 and 0.1 μ, giving about a 7:1 aspect ratio. The particles are irregularly shaped and can vary widely (Fig. 5.2-1a).

---

* The gamma (γ) is a metallurgical designation applied to any compound. It indicates the low temperature metastable phase as contrasted to the α phase, which is a high temperature stable phase. As applied to Fe_2O_3, the γ phase has a cubic spinel structure that is ferrimagnetic with a net moment. The α phase is rhombohedral and also ferrimagnetic, but the oppositely directed moments nearly cancel, giving a very small net magnetization.

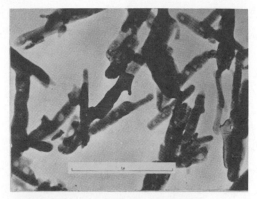

(a) Electron micrograph

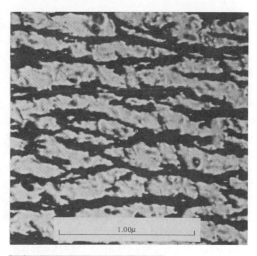

(b) Photomicrograph

FIGURE 5.2-1   Micrographs of γFe_2O_3 particles. Courtesy of G. Bate. (*a*) Unoriented particles showing irregular shapes with dendrites and cavities. (*b*) Partially oriented acicular particles.

Suppose a batch of this iron oxide powder is compressed into a convenient shape while still maintaining a random distribution of the particle axes orientations with respect to each other. If now a magnetic field is applied in one given direction, the individual particles, because of their acicular shape and random physical orientation with respect to this applied field, will exhibit different coercive forces as well as varying amounts of remanent flux

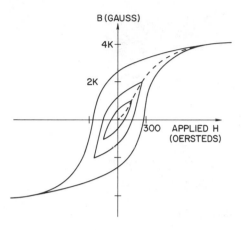

FIGURE 5.2-2 *BH* loops (major and minor) for unoriented bulk powder sample of γFe_2O_3 (approximate).

density in this direction. A collection of noninteracting, randomly oriented, uniaxial, single domain particles will have a remanance of $0.5B_s$. The long acicular particles under consideration, though not single domain, will show a similar effect with a somewhat larger remanent magnetization. Hence the composite *BH* loop in this direction will have a poorly defined coercive force and low residual flux density (i.e., poor squareness ratio). A typical example such as that in Fig. 5.2-2 has these characteristics, with a squareness ratio of $2500 \div 4250 = 0.59$ as expected. In this form the material is unattractive for recording. To improve the magnetic characteristics, the particles are oriented in one direction (Fig. 5.2-1*b*) and held in place on the carrier substrate by a binder. To accomplish this, the particles are suspended in a wet mixture of solvent and organic binder at a loading factor (amount of magnetic material) of about 30 to 40%, depending on the application. This reduces the saturation magnetization or flux density to 30% or 40% of the intrinsic value or to B_s of roughly 1000 to 2000 G. If the particles are now oriented in a large magnetic field and the binder is allowed to dry, a considerable improvement in magnetic properties results (Fig. 5.2-3). Along the direction of orientation, a well-defined coercive force and improved squareness ratio are obtained. The *BH* loop perpendicular to the orientation, (i.e., Fig. 5.2-3*b*) shows the behavior expected for a partially aligned, nonuniform ensemble of particles. The residual flux density is considerably reduced, which is desirable because the material is now less susceptible to off-axis magnetic fields. A considerable amount of information about the particle switching behavior can be deduced from these *BH* loops. If the particles were perfectly symmetrical (e.g., spheres), the magnetic alignment or anisotropy would be due to only crystalline anisotropy (Section 3.5). From

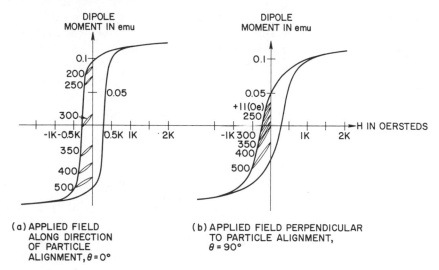

FIGURE 5.2-3 Hysteresis loops of typical γFe_2O_3 tapes on Mylar substrate; magnetic coating thickness, 9.9 μ, particle loading, 40% by volume. Courtesy of G. Bate and R. Thornley, IBM.

(5.2-1) the switching or coercive field for single domain particles or for pure rotational switching would then be equal to the anisotropy field or

$$H_c = H_K = \frac{2K}{I_s}$$

For γFe_2O_3, $K = -4.64 \times 10^4$ ergs/cc (Speliotis, 1967; Takei and Chiba, 1966) and I_s is about 390 emu/cc, giving $H_c = 240$ Oe. If, on the other hand, the particles were perfect prolate spheroids with, say, an axial ratio of 10:1, then from (5.2-5) the coercive field for single domain particles or pure rotational switching would be

$$H_c\bigg|_{D_a/D_b \ll 1} = D_b B_r = 0.5 B_r \tag{5.2-10}$$

For single domain particles of γFe_2O_3, B_r is approximately 5000 G, giving $H_c \approx 2500$ Oe. The measured value is about 300 Oe. Thus the first value calculated from crystalline anisotropy is slightly too small, and the second value calculated from perfect shape anisotropy is much too large. The particles in Fig. 5.2-1 clearly show some elongated shape of irregular sizes, whereas in Fig. 5.2-3 there is improvement with alignment. Thus we can conclude that the particles are not single domain and that the switching must occur by some incoherent switching mechanism.

High density recording requires very thin media with small particle size, large coercive fields, and reasonably large B_r. With γFe_2O_3, the thickness can be controlled to some extent by using a thinner coating, although surface roughness and uniformity become significant problems. The magnetization is generally large enough for higher density. However improvements in particle size and coercive field require new materials. Therefore a number of other materials have been studied for many years as potential high density media. Some of these are discussed below.

5.2.2   Other Oxides

$Co_xFe_{2-x}O_3$

If some of the iron in γFe_2O_3 is replaced with cobalt, smaller particle sizes can be obtained, as well as an increased intrinsic coercive force, mainly due to the increased crystalline anisotropy, as given in Table 5.2-1. Coercive fields as large as 600 Oe have been obtained with good squareness ratios. Unfortunately the saturation magnetization is considerably smaller, although this need not be a drawback for high density. The major disadvantages are the rather large temperature dependence of the coercive field and its stability at elevated temperatures as a function of time.

Magnetite, Fe_3O_4, and cobalt-substituted magnetite have interesting properties for recording. Coercive fields considerably larger than those possible with γFe_2O_3 have been obtained. In addition, a somewhat larger magnetization is also obtained which can provide a large sense signal. Possible problems involve long-term stability of the magnetic properties and susceptibility of the remanent magnetization to rather small stray fields.

CrO_2

Chromium dioxide has been used for some time in video and audio recording but only to a minor extent in digital recording. Table 5.2-1 indicates that it has reasonable properties. This material is ferromagnetic, hence has a larger magnetization than the oxides discussed earlier. When small particles are suspended in a binder and solvent with typical loading factors, the resulting BH loops are quite attractive. Figure 5.2-4 shows one example of typical commercial tape with H_c of about 460 Oe and squareness ratio of about 0.8. The Curie temperature of about 120°C is rather low, making thermal stability a consideration. The material is more expensive to produce than γFe_2O_3.

5.2.3   Metallic Magnetic Films

Many of the problems associated with particulate coatings can be eliminated by using metallic particles or metallic films. The single most important parameter limiting high density recording is film thickness. For oxide

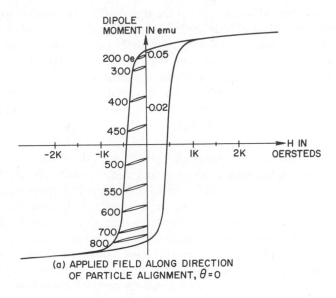

(a) APPLIED FIELD ALONG DIRECTION
OF PARTICLE ALIGNMENT, $\theta = 0$

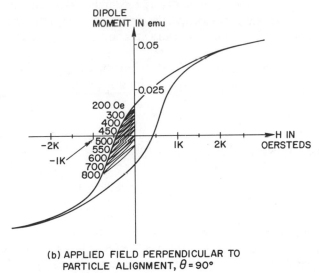

(b) APPLIED FIELD PERPENDICULAR TO
PARTICLE ALIGNMENT, $\theta = 90°$

FIGURE 5.2-4 Hysteresis loops of CrO_2 tapes; magnetic coating thickness, 3.8 μ; particle loading approximately 40% by volume. Courtesy of G. Bate and R. Thornley, IBM.

particles, a smaller thickness reduces the flux that can be coupled to the read head, causing signal amplitude to deteriorate. The dilution or loading factor of particulate in binder is mainly responsible, since it substantially reduces the effective magnetization and cannot be eliminated. Metallic films can be deposited on carrier substrates without any dilution; hence the full strength of the magnetization is available for the readback process. In addition, metallic films are generally ferromagnetic, hence have inherently larger magnetizations than those of the ferrimagnetic iron oxides. Metallic particles require dilution in a binder just as do the oxide particles, but the larger magnetization compensates for the loading factor. Metal particles as well as various alloys can be made from iron, nickel, and cobalt, displaying a very wide range of parameters. Alloys can be deposited by electroplating, by chemical or electroless deposition, or by vacuum deposition. All these techniques are well known and some have been used commercially. Early magnetic drums were electroplated nickel and nickel-cobalt, and the first commercial tape (Univac) consisted of a nonmagnetic metal base plated with a magnetic layer (Eckert et al., 1952, p. 16). Metallic alloys can be deposited in very thin layers with very smooth surfaces, both highly desirable for high density. The major difficulty is the higher cost and difficulty in maintaining uniform magnetic properties over very large areas. An excellent review of magnetic recording materials, methods of preparation and properties is given by Bate and Alstad (1969).

The relatively high coercive force and stabilizing curing process make data recorded on magnetic media relatively insensitive to external fields and environmental extremes (Geller, 1976).

5.3 WRITING FUNDAMENTALS AND CODING

In principle, the writing transducer in all magnetic recording is simply the toroidal structure of Fig. 2.6-1 or 3.2-1 with an air gap. In magnetic recording, the fringe field does the writing and the air gap must be designed to have maximum fringe field as shown in Fig. 5.3-1. A significant amount of the gap field extends into the region below the head. A recording medium, either tape or disk, would be located some distance h below the head as shown. Since the stored bits are written along the length of the medium, the x component of the fringe field determines the writing of information.* This fringe field is maximum directly over the gap at $x = 0$ and falls off on either side as x increases or decreases; a typical curve for some arbitrary head to medium

---

* The easy axis of the medium is "oriented" in this direction, thus is less sensitive to the vertical component B_z—see previous section.

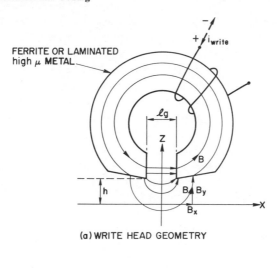

(a) WRITE HEAD GEOMETRY

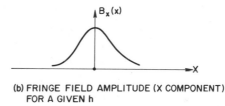

(b) FRINGE FIELD AMPLITUDE (X COMPONENT)
FOR A GIVEN h

FIGURE 5.3-1 Schematic of write head geometry and corresponding fringe field.

separation h appears in Figure 5.3-1b. This function B_x versus x determines the shape of the sensitivity function, which is all-important in both writing and reading and is considered in detail in what follows.

It should be pointed out that for writing, the actual fringe field $B_x(x)$ is important because it determines the strength of the field being applied to the medium, whereas for reading, the sensitivity function denoted by S_x, which is proportional to $B_x(x)$, is important in determining both the amplitude and shape of the read signal as detailed in Section 5.6.

The fringe field B_x verus x is a characteristic of a given magnetic head design and varies from one head to another. However the general shape is much the same for all well-designed heads. This function obviously changes for various values of h, getting smaller and also spreading out over larger values of x as h increases.

To understand both the writing process and the rationale for the various codes used in magnetic recording, we start with the writing of one bit in a stationary medium. The resulting magnetization in the medium can be obtained from the medium BH loop, together with the fringe field B_x versus x of the head. We can then allow the medium to move, to obtain various magnetization patterns that will represent the actual dynamic writing process. Dynamic writing, which is done by the trailing edge of the head, allows us to place single magnetization transitions at various positions along the medium. The minimum spacing between these transitions represents the fundamental maximum flux changes per unit length or maximum ideal density. To interpret these transitions, variations in spacing must be used to represent data; also clocking information interleaved within the data is required for high density. Various coding schemes are possible for relating the positions of such magnetic transitions to the stored data and any clocking information, if used. We will evolve the various coding schemes from very simple to the very complex.

5.3.1 Static Writing

Let us assume that the medium is initially saturated in the negative M_s direction (arbitrary direction) and we wish to store one bit of $+M_s$ in a static medium. To determine the magnetization pattern in the bit, it is necessary to know the MH (or BH) loop of the bit. However this loop will be greatly influenced by the self-demagnetization of the bit, and this cannot be known until the magnetization pattern of the bit is identified. Since this complicates matters greatly, we simply assume some general shape to the MH loop to see how the bit pattern is derived. Later, this difficulty partly disappears because the actual bit patterns are long regions of magnetization with small transitions between. It is the transition regions that contribute the demagnetization (poles) and determine the density. For now, let us assume that the bit geometry and medium possesses an MH loop with self-demagnetizing field as in Figure 5.3-2a; a magnetic head at some distance h above this medium is further assumed to produce a magnetizing field shown as H_x versus x in Fig. 5.3-2b. This $H_x(x)$ curve, to a first approximation, is the same as the $B_x(x)$ curve, being related by $H_x(x) = B_x(x)/\mu_0$. This relationship is valid when the medium is in positive or negative saturation because we assumed the MH loop to have a flat top, hence permeability of μ_0 in these regions. The relationship breaks down when switching occurs, since the permeability becomes nonlinear. However we are mainly interested in the end points and general patterns, and for now we assume the relationship to be generally valid. The actual switching process has not been amenable to calculation; this is treated more fully in Section 5.8. The medium and the head are stationary relative to each other, which implies either that they are physically stationary, or that the write current is applied and removed very quickly compared to any physical motion. Using these two pieces of data, we can construct the magnetization within the medium as follows.

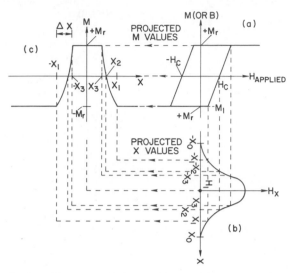

FIGURE 5.3-2 Static writing of one bit in a medium initially in the $-M_r$ state. (*a*) Assumed *BH* loop for bit. (*b*) Assumed fringe field for write head. (*c*) Resultant *M* versus *x* in medium.

The function $H_x(x)$ specifies the magnetizing force created on the medium by a given head geometry and write current; the *MH* loop specifies what happens to the medium magnetization *M* for an applied field *H*. Proper superposition of these two curves should give us the magnetization in the medium as a function of *x*. This can most easily be obtained by a graphical construction, point by point. The amplitude of the $H_x(x)$ function must project along the *H* axis of the *MH* loop; then for chosen values of x_1 along the *x* axis of $H_x(x)$, the driving field H_1 is obtained and is projected up to the loop to give the value of magnetization M_1 (equals M_r in this case), expected for that value of x_1 as shown. Thus both M_1 and x_1 are known and can be graphically projected onto a new curve of *M* versus *x* for the medium (Fig. 5.3-2*c*). This can be done for various points x_2, x_3, and so on, as shown, to give the final curve of *M* versus *x* in the medium. Several things should be noted from this example; first, the total distance Δx required in the medium from x_1 to x_3 (or $-x_1$ to $-x_3$) for the magnetization to reverse direction depends on the slope of the *MH* loop (i.e., the self-demagnetizing field) and also on the shape of $H_x(x)$ (i.e., sensitivity function). As the self-demagnetizing field is reduced, the vertical sides on the *MH* loop become steeper; therefore the spread from x_1 to x_3 decreases, approaching zero for an infinitely steep side, which is, of course impossible.* Also, as the sensitivity

* The self-demagnetizing effects are treated more fully in Sections 2.6 and 5.8.

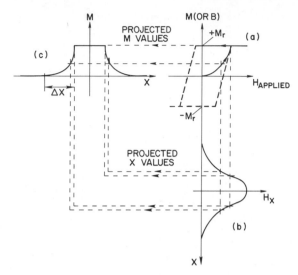

FIGURE 5.3-3 Static writing of one bit in an initially demagnetized medium, $M_r = 0$. (*a*) Assumed *BH* loop for bit. (*b*) Assumed fringe field for write head. (*c*) Resultant *M* versus *x* in medium.

function becomes sharper with steeper sides, this transition region grows more narrow. Also note that the width of the region from x_3 to $-x_3$ over which the medium is in the $+M_r$ state is directly related to the width of $H_x(x)$. However we see shortly that the latter spacing is relatively unimportant and that the transition region Δx really represents the stored information in most practical recording, hence is the region of interest.

Let us continue for now with the finite bit patterns. If the medium were initially demagnetized, the *MH* loop would resemble that in Fig. 5.3-3*a*. Since very small fields will cause some switching, the new *M* versus *x* in the medium will be more spread out (Fig. 5.3-3*c*). The actual bit patterns in the medium for these two cases would be similar to those in Fig. 5.3-4; case *a* obviously gives a sharper transition region, thus a smaller Δx. These transition regions Δx were derived for very ideal cases with simplifying assumptions about the self-demagnetization effects. A more detailed discussion is given in Section 5.8.

5.3.2 Dynamic Writing

The above example of static writing can be thought of as being accomplished with a steady current applied in the write head when the medium is stationary, or alternately with a moving medium and a very fast, narrow pulse or write

TRANSITION REGIONS

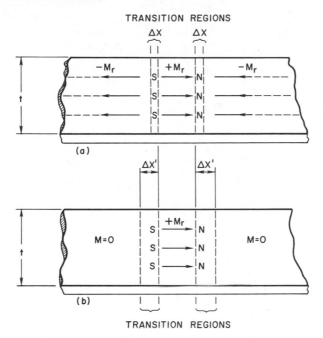

(a)

(b)

TRANSITION REGIONS

FIGURE 5.3-4 Medium magnetization transitions for static writing of one bit. (a) Medium initially at $-M_r$. (b) Medium initially demagnetized ($M_r = 0$).

current. The latter method is reasonable for writing as long as the electrical time constants are fast enough to ensure that the medium motion does not smear out the magnetization pattern beyond the required spacings to achieve a given density. In actual recording, the medium is always moving. However the write current can consist of very narrow pulses, or it can be a steady current that changes only when necessary. The current waveform depends on the code used (Section 5.3-3). For now we briefly consider the magnetization patterns that result in the medium for a pulsed and a switched, steady current.

Assume that the medium is initially demagnetized and write current pulses can produce an $H_x(x)$ sufficiently fast to give a magnetization pattern like that in Fig. 5.3-4b. This situation is shown schematically in Fig. 5.3-5a at time $t = 0$. A very narrow current pulse produces a region of $+M_r$, with the length of the so-called bit cell x_b being a fixed value determined by the length of the air gap, the head to medium spacing, and other fixed parameters. The medium is allowed to move for a time t_1, hence distance vt_1, which is greater than x_b. A negative current pulse is then applied, producing a second

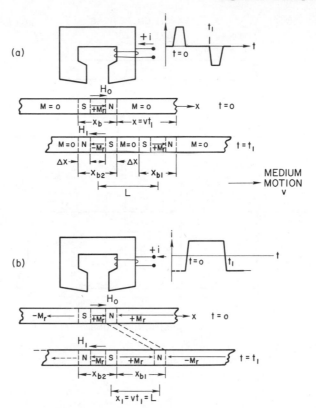

FIGURE 5.3-5 Principles of dynamic writing process. (*a*) Pulse writing (equivalent to RZ). (*b*) Switched current writing (equivalent to writing "1's" in NRZI).

bit cell of length x_b but with $-M_r$ polarity, as shown in the lower medium position at time t_1. As the medium moves along, various magnetization regions of length x_b can be placed as desired. A restriction is the above limit on the time spacing of pulses, namely

$$t_1 > \frac{x_b}{v} \tag{5.3-1}$$

Otherwise the bit cells would overlap and interfere. Note that the length of the bit cells x_b is fixed, whereas the spacing between cells $x = vt_1$ can be varied by varying the pulse repetition rate t_1.

In the above case let us allow the current to reverse direction in violation of the restriction of (5.3-1) and determine the resulting magnetization pattern. Assume, as in Fig. 5.3-5*b*, that a negative current has been applied for some time while the medium has been moving to the right, producing a long region of $-M_r$. At time $t = 0$ the current is switched positive, which instantaneously produces a bit cell of $+M_r$ and length x_b just as before. However the current remains positive while the medium moves to the right. The north poles also move to the right, but since the field is still on, the south poles remain stationary with respect to the write head. In other words, the bit cell length x_{b1} increases as long as the current is maintained. If at some time $t_1 = x_1/v$ the current is again switched negative, another bit cell of $-M_r$ and length x_{b2} will be created, as shown. If the negative current is maintained, the north poles under the left-hand leg of the head will remain stationary with respect to the head or will be effectively shifted toward the left in the medium, while the south poles under the right-hand leg will remain stationary in the medium as the medium moves. Thus we are essentially left with two transitions Δx, of south and north poles separated by a distance L, which equals x_1 in this case. Note there had to be a slight change in definition of the bit cell length x_{b1} because the second transition of south poles is no longer part of the first bit cell but rather belongs to the second. In some codes more than one transition can exist per bit cell. The distance L is determined only by the timing of current switching t_1 and medium velocity. The width Δx of the transitions is fixed by physical parameters, but their spacing is variable. In effect, the transitions have been written by the trailing edge of the write head and can be placed very close together. This type of writing using switched currents, hence the trailing edge of the head, is very commonly used in most systems. The previous scheme of pulsed currents is feasible and has been used (RZ code), but it is less practical. The concept of writing by the trailing edge of the head is very important in that it essentially removes the writing process as a factor determining the achievable densities on practical systems. The writing process as discussed with respect to Figs. 5.3-2 through 5.3-4 can produce very sharp transition regions Δx because the writing process within the medium is highly nonlinear. These transitions can be placed very close together by trailing edge writing, to permit the achievement of high density. The reading process is essentially linear and places the most severe limits on practical density.

Thus far in the discussions of recorded transitions, the thickness has been neglected for simplicity. In actual recording, the thickness is a very important parameter in determining the density. The ideal writing situation produces very narrow transitions Δx, which are uniform with respect to medium depth, and it can place these at any desired spot on the medium. The minimum spacing of even such ideal transitions is determined by the readback problems such as bit crowding. The adverse effects of medium thickness only smear out the transitions and further increase the minimum spacing between successive transitions (i.e., reduce density). The effects of thickness

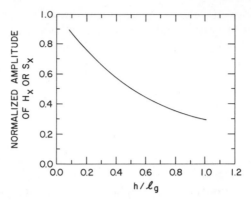

FIGURE 5.3-6 Amplitude of normalized horizontal component of magnetizing field or sensitivity function of a Karlquist head as a function of the normalized head to medium spacing.

can be seen in a simple-minded way by considering only that the writing field $H_x(x)$ is larger (for all x) at the top surface than it is at the bottom surface of the medium. For instance, the peak amplitude of S_x, which is directly proportional to the peak of H_x, varies with z (Fig. 5.3-6). In typical cases the top surface might be at $h/l_g = 1$ and the bottom might be at 5. Thus the medium experiences a significant variation in magnetizing force as a function of thickness. If we view the writing process as static and make the same, rather oversimplified assumption of the self-demagnetization of the transition as in Figs. 5.3-2 and 5.3-3, we can construct the expected magnetic transition on the top and bottom surfaces as in Fig. 5.3-7, where the lower H_x at z_2 tends

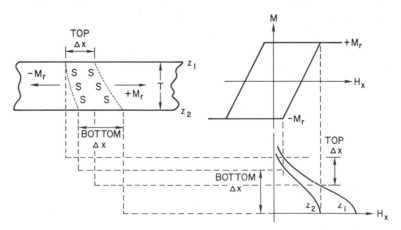

FIGURE 5.3-7 Thickness dependence of static writing for an assumed constant self-demagnetizing field of the recorded bit.

to both increase Δx and shift it to one side. Since the self-demagnetizing effects are all-important in determining the actual shape of the transition region (Section 5.8), this simplified picture cannot be taken as strictly true. A detailed treatment of the magnetization as a function of depth is not available.

Thus far we have neglected the vertical z component of the writing field and any possible vertical components of magnetization. This is a reasonable first approximation because the horizontal component of magnetization is dominant, and vertical components usually produce small perturbations on the magnetization and subsequent readback voltage (Section 5.4). The vertical component of the write field can be relatively large. For an idealized head, for example, Figs. 5.3-12 and 5.3-13 show the peak of the vertical field to be at least half that of the horizontal field. However the medium is *purposely* made to be *less sensitive* to the *vertical* field. In fact, the particle alignment and crystal anisotropy (Section 5.2) are purposely introduced to reduce the z component of magnetization as much as possible. However it cannot be reduced to zero, and its effects distort the sense signal as Section 5.4 reveals. Determination of the vertical magnetization within the medium is extremely difficult and has never been done by direct methods. Typically one can guess from the amount of distortion of the sense signal what approximate value of z magnetization is present. All subsequent calculations and analyses neglect the vertical magnetization as a first approximation, adding it later as a correction factor, if necessary.

5.3.3 Codes

The pulsed writing scheme of Fig. 5.3-5a records a full bit cell at one time. As the medium moves and various bit cells are written, the resulting pattern would look very similar, magnetically, to bits stored in a thin, flat film memory medium. If the medium is initially demagnetized and "0" bits are stored as $-M_r$, with "1" bits as $+M_r$, the bit pattern would resemble that in Fig. 5.3-8a; associated with each bit is a discrete magnetized region, and this method of recording is known as return to zero (RZ), since the magnetization returns to the demagnetized state between each bit. Note that in this and all subsequent cases, the writing current wave form as a function of time is identical in form to the magnetization as a function of distance. These demagnetized regions between bits require considerable real estate on the medium and reduce the bit density. As a result, numerous methods have been devised for storing information, and these are referred to as *codes*. The selection of a code for a given application depends on many factors but ultimately reduces to the density obtainable versus complexity of the readback process, hence total cost; that is, the readback process is the major density-limiting factor. Coding is one of the many parameters that affect the readback capability of a system. The parts of the readback process

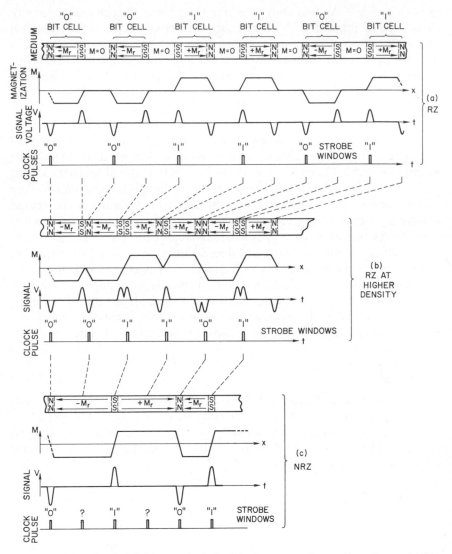

FIGURE 5.3-8 Bit cell definitions and relationships between various coding schemes. (*a*) RZ. (*b*) RZ at higher density. (*c*) NRZ. (*d*) NRZI. (*e*) DF or FM. (*f*) PE. (*g*) RB.

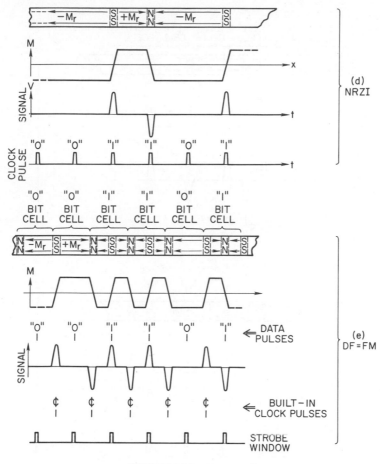

FIGURE 3.5-8 (*continued*)

that are heavily dependent on coding are mainly the code clocking requirements and the sense signal polarities generated by the code. The signal
polarities are important for two reasons: they affect the clocking capability,
and they determine whether a recorded "0" will appear different from a
"dropout" on the medium. The latter is very important in minimizing data
errors. The clocking problem is described in more detail in Section 5.4,
but a few important points should be understood here. The major clocking
consideration of a code is whether a self-generated clock pulse is inherent
or an external clock is required during readback. The problem is that during
writing, an external clock must be used to space recorded bits at the desired

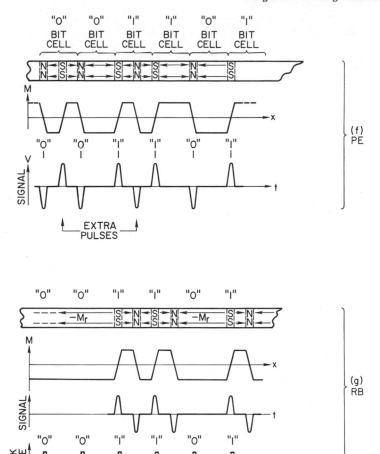

FIGURE 5.3-8 (*continued*)

intervals. At high density, however, the drift in the clocking circuits could be very substantial, making it impossible to strobe the information accurately during readback. This becomes more critical as density increases; thus it is desirable to have a code that inherently provides, on every bit cell, some means to synchronize or trigger the strobing of the readback signal. This can be done by including a separate clocking signal within the bit cell, but the recorded density is affected, although this is not significant. Another technique is peak detection. For codes that give a distinct signal for every "1" and every "0," the signal itself can be used with a peak detector for sensing without an external clock trigger. Thus the following discussion of codes concentrates on signal polarities, clocking capability, and the distinction between "0" and dropouts.

For the RZ code described earlier (Fig. 5.3-8a), it is obvious that two signals are obtained for every stored bit and the "0" and "1" are distinctly different. Using the arbitrary polarities for bits and induced signals shown, a "0" is a negative pulse followed by a positive pulse; a "1" is just the opposite—a negative followed by a positive pulse. The extra pulse per bit cell could be used as a trigger for strobing the signal, or since a "1" is different from a "0," peak detection could be used. Thus this code is inherently self-clocking. Also, the signal characteristics of a "0" are clearly different from those of a medium dropout, which is no signal. However before writing, the medium must be preerased to neutral magnetization, usually with a high frequency current. This procedure is advantageous in that it reduces spurious noise, which is often a serious problem, but it requires a more complex procedure and hardware compared to self-erasing codes. The major drawback with this code, however, is the relatively low density resulting from the two transitions per bit cell and the region of neutral magnetization between bits.

To see how the various codes are related, let us start by increasing the density of the RZ code. Referring to Fig. 5.3-8a, if we push these bits closer together, a pattern similar to that in Fig. 5.3-8b will result at some small separation, and further reduction in the bit separation will eventually give the pattern of Fig. 5.3-8c. The latter coding scheme is workable; it is known as nonreturn to zero (NRZ) and gives a higher bit density than RZ. Note that in this case there is a change (reversal) in magnetization only between changes in the stored bit pattern from "1" to "0," or vice versa. Also, a transition from "1" to "0" gives a negative pulse, and a transition from "0" to "1" gives a positive pulse. The difficulty with this method of coding is that a sense signal is generated in the read head *only* when a change in M takes place, or only when the stored bit pattern changes between a "0" and "1." If the bit pattern consists of a "0" followed by ten "1's," then all "0's" again, only two sense signals are generated, one at the beginning and one at the end of the group of ten "1's." In digital computers, all circuits represent each "1" as a pulse and each "0" as no pulse (or negative pulse). If we wish to transfer this group of ten stored "1's" to a logic register, additional circuitry would be needed to generate these ten pulses. We could use an external clock pulse as shown, in combination with the signal. A clock pulse and no signal generates a bit with polarity equal to that of the last pulse; a clock with a signal pulse generates a "0" if the signal is negative, and a "1" if the signal is positive. Besides the usual problem with externally generated clocks, this code presents a serious error problem. A spurious error in reading a given signal pulse will cause all subsequent bits to be in error until the next signal pulse is encountered and correctly read. For instance, in Fig. 5.3-8c if the first "0" was incorrectly read as a "1," the second bit, which should also be "0," will be read as "1." The third bit, stored as "1," if correctly read, will terminate propagation of the errors. If the second "0" were actually a long string of "0's," many uncorrected bit errors would result. A further problem is that a medium dropout is indistinguishable from a stored bit with no transition.

The lack of self-clocking and the error propagation in NRZ can be rectified by a slight change in the coding scheme. The difficulty with NRZ coding is that a string of "0's" and a string of "1's" are indistinguishable, both giving no signal. So let us now generate a pulse for all stored "1's" and no pulse for all stored "0's." This coding scheme and bit pattern (Fig. 5.3-8d) is known as nonreturn to zero, inverted (NRZI) and is by far the most commonly used in tape recording. The term "inverted" is appended to NRZ for the NRZI code because the resulting magnetization wave form, which equals the writing current wave form, is identical to the inverted and shifted wave form for NRZ. Thus the frequency spectrum of these two must be identical. This code uses a magnetization change from either $-M$ to $+M$, or vice versa, each time a "1" appears in the bit pattern. Because of this, both positive and negative signals appear for alternate "1's" in a series, making for a clear distinction between "1's" and "0's" in the code. Thus the error propagation of NRZ is eliminated. An error in reading any given bit in NRZI will be an error in *that* bit only; subsequent bit detection is independent of previous bit polarity, which is desirable. Single bit errors are easily corrected in multitrack systems such as tapes by the use of parity.

The clocking advantage of NRZI over NRZ is less obvious and can be realized only for special cases. For clocking, we would like to have at least one signal pulse available for each bit cell. Neither of these two codes has this property built into the cell code. However NRZI provides a pulse for each stored "1." On multitrack/character systems such as tapes, the use of odd parity across a character ensures at least one signal pulse for every character (see Section 6.3). Since NRZ does not have a distinct signal for "1's" or "0's," the use of parity cannot ensure a clock pulse for every character. Thus NRZI has a distinct advantage in such cases. Unfortunately, like NRZ, NRZI cannot distinguish a "0" from a dropout, and both codes present certain system problems. In any code it is necessary to recognize the beginning of a data record. This may be done, for instance, by a string of "0's." However since a dropout in the medium would be sensed as a string of "0's," a more complex method is necessary if dropouts are to be tolerated. Also, a dropout in the middle is equivalent to recorded "0's," leaving some ambiguity in reading stored records. Both codes give higher density than RZ but both have inherent limitations. If we wish to go to even higher density, the clocking problem in NRZI becomes a serious limitation. It is clear that for a single track per character system such as disk,* parity across a character cannot be used for clocking; hence a different code is necessary. One common code used widely on disks, known as double frequency (DF), simply stores an additional clock pulse in each bit cell. This code is described below. Continuing with NRZI and higher density, Section 6.4 demonstrates that even on multitrack/character systems the use of parity for clocking has serious limitations resulting from skew of the tracks. As density increases, it is necessary to provide some means for self-clocking within each bit cell of every track. Tape systems generally use phase encoding, which is described after double frequency.

Double Frequency (DF) or Frequency Modulation (FM)

If we wish to use an NRZI-type code on a single track/character system, some clocking information must be added to each bit cell. A very simple way to do this is to add a " 1 " signal at the beginning of a bit cell of each NRZI bit. In other words, interleave a string of "1's" into the NRZI code, shown by the "built-in clock pulses" in Fig. 5.3-8e. These clock pulses then trigger the signal strobing circuits to provide a "strobe window" at the data positions as shown. Since there is a trigger for every bit, no accumulated timing errors can result. Obviously each bit cell must now be capable of two magnetic transitions rather than one, hence the name "double frequency." This requires all circuits and transducers to operate at higher frequencies, which is a problem. However the bandwidth is typically smaller than that of NRZI, and this somewhat offsets the high frequency disadvantage. A dropout on the medium looks like a "0" just as in NRZI, but now the clock pulse is lost as well. Hence dropouts are serious and must be accommodated.

In *phase encoding* (PE), also known as phase modulation (PM), a signal is generated for every bit: a "1" is a positive pulse, and a "0" is a negative pulse (Fig. 5.3-8f). This provides a means for self-clocking by the use of peak detection. Note that a string of "1's" or of "0's" produces extra transitions within the bit cell and an extra signal pulse. Thus the bit cell must be capable of two transitions per bit, requiring higher frequency response but a narrower bandwidth than NRZI, similar to DF. The extra signal pulse obtained on only some bits requires the detector logic to deal with these appropriately.

The workhorse of commercial systems has been NRZI for tapes and low density, phase encoding at higher density, and double frequency for disks. Nevertheless other codes have been used at various times and deserve a brief description.

---

* That is, characters and records are stored serially along a single track, hence only one read/write head per surface.

Return to Bias (RB)

Magnetic transitions are stored only for " 1 " data bits with no transitions for
"0's," just as in NRZI. However a " 1 " bit has two magnetic transition per bit
cells, like RZ. In between " 1's," the magnetization returns to negative saturation, which also represents stored "0's" (Fig. 5.3-8g). Since a string of "0's"
gives no signal, a separate means for clocking is required. Since the polarity
and pulse character are distinct for " 1's" and "0's" a separate parity track
can provide this clock in multitrack/character systems. The required bandwidth of the reading channel must be higher than NRZI; thus the density
is about half that of NRZI, other things being equal. Dropouts are still
indistinguishable from a stream of "0's."

Modified Return to Bias (MRB)

If RB is modified so that the magnetization for "0's" and between two
"1's" returns to the demagnetized state, we have modified return to bias
(MRB). In essence, this is equivalent to RZ in Fig. 5.3-8g, with the write
current pulses (i.e., magnetization change) removed for all "0" bit cells.
It has the same disadvantages as RB.

   Under worst case conditions (i.e., a succession of all "1" signals), phase
modulation (PM) and DF requires twice as many magnetic transitions as
NRZI for the same recorded information. If the spacing between transitions
necessitates the same minimum length x_0 on the medium, NRZI theoretically gives twice the density of PM or DF. However, density is limited more
by clocking accuracy than by transition length; therefore PM and DF give
higher density in practice. Nevertheless, though providing the necessary
clocking information, these codes have essentially cut in half the number of
information bits per cycle of bandwidth of the system as compared to
NRZI. Therefore alternative techniques, which provide clocking information
without seriously reducing the information per bandwidth cycle, are desirable.

   In systems whose recorded density is limited by intersymbol interference
or bit crowding, the center to center spacing of transitions must have some
minimum length x_0. As a result, it is desirable to have alternate codes
that supply adequate clocking information but allow more data bits to be
stored while still maintaining the minimum transition spacing x_0 (i.e., more
information per bandwidth cycle). Fundamentally, this can be done by
providing clock transitions only where they are needed and omitting them
where they are unnecessary. In DF coding, for instance, the clock transitions
included for bit cells containing "1's" are unnecessary, but they are very
desirable for bit cells that contain successive "0's." To see what advantage
this might have, let us start with the DF magnetization pattern of Fig.

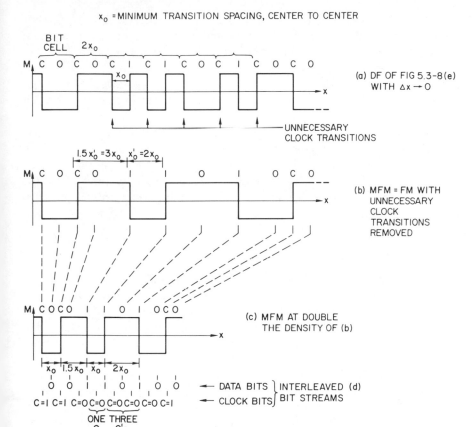

FIGURE 5.3-9   Evolution of MFM from the DF code.

5.3-8e, redrawn in Fig. 5.3-9a but with the transition regions Δx very small, approaching zero width. The minimum transition spacing is assumed to be some fixed value x_0. Let us now provide clocking transitions only between successive "0's," thereby allowing us to remove all those pointed to at the bottom of Fig. 5.3-9a. If these transitions are removed, the magnetization versus x becomes that represented in Fig. 5.3-9b. Note that the data information is identical but the minimum spacing between transitions x_0' is now double that previously, or $2x_0$. Obviously we can now pack the same bits in half the medium length (Fig. 5.3-9c) and still maintain the minimum transition spacing of x_0. In effect we have doubled the linear density along the medium. This coding (Fig. 5.3-9b, c) is known as modified frequency modulation (MFM). However we cannot conclude that the overall recording density is doubled just by renaming transitions. The allowable peak shift of the signals becomes more critical when a peak detection scheme is used, because transition spacings can be noninteger multiples of x_0—in fact, can be $1.5x_0$ as shown. Since this spacing of $1.5x_0$ may contain a "0" and a "1," the allowable peak shift in the signal is reduced. This lowers the overall density gain to somewhat less than a factor of 2, but a significant increase can often still be obtained (e.g., 1.5 times improvement).

The fact that the spacings between transitions do not have to be integer multiples of x_0 is a significant departure from all previous codes, which required integer multiples for the maximum density configuration. If this notion is generalized to allow transition spacings of any multiple of x_0, the general form of run-length limited (RLL) coding is obtained. In practical cases, the multiple varies from 1 (i.e., minimum of x_0) to some upper limit. The fundamental concept is as follows.

Run-Length Limited (RLL) Code

The evolution from DF in Fig. 5.3-9*a* to MFM in Fig. 5.3-9*b* and *c* was obtained by removing the clock transitions at unnecesary points and keeping them only between successive "0's." Another way of looking at this, and more to the point for RLL, is to consider that the clock information stream in DF is set to "0" at all points except between successive "0's," where it is deliberately made "1." These interleaved clock bits and the data bits appear in Fig. 5.3-9*d* for the double density case. It can be seen that if we now consider the clock and data bits to be our storing code, there is a maximum of three "0's" and a minimum of one "0" between two successive "1's." This is the essence of RLL. The distinction between data and clock transitions no longer exists, and there is a specified maximum k and minimum d number of "0's" between two successive "1's," denoted as

$$d \leq z \leq k \tag{5.3-2}$$

For MFM, obviously $d = 1$ and $k = 3$. Although the minimum transition spacing is still x_0, the strobing for data must be done at intervals of $0.5x_0$. Thus the price for higher density is more stringent tolerances on the location of transitions within the medium. In the ordinary codes described earlier, each bit of a given data stream was stored directly as a bit of information on the medium, totally independently of other bits in the data except for the insertion of clocking transitions. In RLL codes, this independence no longer exists. The incoming data stream is broken into groups of m bits per group (Fig. 5.3-10). The m bits are then transformed by the RLL code into a new sequence of n bits, which represent the information stored on the medium. The new sequence of bits n must satisfy the condition of (5.3-2); namely, there is a maximum and minimum number of "0's" between successive

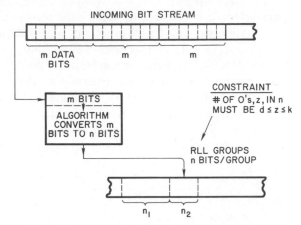

FIGURE 5.3-10   Basic principles of Run Length Limited codes.

"1's" of the stored bits. The minimum number ensures a minimum transition spacing of x_0, and the maximum number ensures pulses frequent enough to maintain adequate clock synchronization. The recipe by which this transformation is carried out is stored as an algorithm within the logical portion of the system and must be used in the inverse mode during readback.

If the coded information is to be stored at a timing spacing r cm/bit, and if the minimum physical spacing between bits x_0 is larger than r, the value of d must be

$$r \text{ cm/data bit} \times d \text{ data bits/transition} = x_0 \text{ cm/transition} \quad (5.3\text{-}3)$$

where x_0 is usually specified by the overall system technology, hence is a given constant, thus fixing the product of r and d; r and d are then design parameters. If d is large, r is small, which means higher density. But larger d requires a more complex RLL coding scheme and less peak shift in the signal. If d is reduced to produce a simpler code, the density decreases. We also would like k to be as large as possible for higher density, but since its value determines the overall clock synchronization capability, this becomes more critical as d increases.

The feasibility of RLL codes depends on the ability of the code to transform the m bits of each information character $I_1, I_2, \ldots, I_m$ into a corresponding code word of n bits, $c_1, c_2, \ldots, c_n$, each of which satisfies (5.3-2). In general cases, this mapping between information and code word is not fixed but may vary with the information sequence. In other words there are multiple modes of operation, and the particular mode depends on the previous code word and the next information character. Multiple mode operation permits high efficiency with short code word length n, which is very desirable. For a given set of parameters, it is possible to specify the theoretical increase in total stored information per unit length over, say, an NRZI with clocks interleaved at every $(k + 1)/(d + 1)$ bit. Increases of 80 and 140 % are possible in certain cases.* In practical systems, the achievable density is limited by various physical parameters and would generally be closer to a 25 % increase. Coding schemes and techniques for determining simple realizations of various codes have been described extensively in the literature (Franaszek, 1970; Gabor, 1967; Tang, 1969).

The characteristics of the more common codes are summarized below.

Return to Zero (RZ)

a. Two signal pulses for every stored bit.

b. Stored "0" $= -V$ followed by $+V$.†

c. Stored "1" $= +V$ followed by $-V$.†

d. Self-clocking via extra pulse plus polarity distinction between "1" and "0."

e. A "0" signal is clearly different from a dropout.

f. Large bit cell gives low density.

Nonreturn to Zero (NRZ)

a. Signal only for change from "1" to "0" or "0" to "1."

b. "1" following a "0" = positive signal pulse, thereafter all "1's" give no pulse.

c. Ambiguity in signal requires some recorded means for signaling the beginning of a record.

d. Not self-clocking; clocking is critical—if one bit is in error, all succeeding bits are in error until next signal pulse is encountered.

e. No simple means for parity error detection and correction in multitrack (tape) systems.

f. Medium dropout is indistinguishable from a stored bit with no signal.

Nonreturn to Zero, Inverted (NRZI)

a. Signal pulse only for stored "1's."

b. Stored 1 = positive or negative pulse; stored "0" = no pulse.

c. Ambiguity in signal requires some means for signaling the beginning of a record.

---

* For example, $d = 1, k = 5, m = 3, n = 5$, and $d = 2, k = 5, m = 2, n = 5$, respectively.
† Alternate definitions for either "0" or "1" could be as follows: positive or negative pulse preceded by negative or positive pulse, respectively.

d. Non-self-clocking; clocking is critical—accumulated clock time error can result in lost bits.

e. Inherent means for clock synchronization using parity storage in multi-track (tape) systems.

f. An error in reading a bit is only an error in that bit, *not* in succeeding bits, as in NRZ.

g. Medium dropout is indistinguishable from stored bit with no signal.

Double Frequency (DF) (Frequency Modulation, FM)

a. Signal generation is identical to NRZI.

b. Interleaved clock pulse on each bit cell removes clocking sensitivity, therefore can be used on single track records.

c. Dropouts are still indistinguishable from no signal, but the clock synchronization pulse also is usually lost; hence dropouts require special consideration.

Phase Encoding (PE)

a. Signal generated for every stored bit.

b. Stored "1" = positive signal pulse.

c. Stored "0" = negative signal pulse.

d. Self-clocking by virtue of property *a.*

e. Additional logic required to remove extra signal pulses.

f. Theoretically has lower density than NRZI because of two transitions per bit cell, but in practice, self-clocking gives PM higher density.

In NRZI recording the current in the write head is either in the plus or minus maximum current position and the trailing edge of the head does the writing. To get maximum density, the rise time of the head must be much smaller than the time it takes for the medium to move across a distance of one bit. This distance is easily calculated for tapes and disks as follows.

The common fast tapes move at 200 in./sec and store 800 bpi or 1.25×10^{-3} in./bit; the time for the medium to move across one bit is

$$\frac{\text{sec}}{200 \text{ in.}} \times \frac{1.25 \times 10^{-3} \text{ in.}}{\text{bit}} = 6.25 \ \mu\text{sec/bit} \qquad (5.3\text{-}4)$$

The fastest tapes move at 250 in./sec and store 6400 bpi, giving

$$\frac{\text{sec}}{250 \text{ in.}} \times \frac{0.156 \times 10^{-3} \text{ in.}}{\text{bit}} = 0.625 \ \mu\text{sec/bit} \qquad (5.3\text{-}5)$$

Typical tape head time constants are generally well below 1 μsec as required.

For disks, a better time constant is needed. Typical disk speeds are 2400
3600 rpm for a 14 in. diameter disk, giving linear velocities at the outer edge
of the circumference of

$$\frac{2400 \text{ rev}}{60 \text{ sec}} \times \frac{44 \text{ in.}}{\text{rev}} = 1760 \text{ in./sec} \tag{5.3-6}$$

and

$$\frac{3600 \text{ rev}}{60 \text{ sec}} \times \frac{44 \text{ in.}}{\text{rev}} = 2640 \text{ in./sec} \tag{5.3-7}$$

For the higher speed system, a typical bit density is 4040 bpi,* which means
that time required to pass over one bit is

$$\frac{\text{sec}}{2640 \text{ in.}} \times \frac{\text{inch}}{4040 \text{ bits}} = \frac{10^6}{11.75} = 85 \text{ nsec/bit} \tag{5.3-8}$$

Thus the disk head must have a time constant well below 85 nsec, which is
quite small, requiring small, well-designed structures.

In writing, a clock pulse is used to gate the bit pattern out of a data register
into a drive circuit, which generates the correct pulse polarity (also on
command from the clock pulse) as shown schematically in Fig. 5.1-1. The
data to be stored usually come from main memory and comprise a parallel
sequence of b bits. For the case shown, these bits are stored serially in the
recording medium, necessitating some conversion, which is supplied by the
buffer register. The parallel bits set the buffer register directly by way of the
set-direct inputs, all in one clock cycle. The data are clocked out serially
into the necessary logic and drive circuitry to store the information.†

5.3.4 Idealized Writing Head

The field produced by actual recording heads is very difficult to calculate
without a number of simplifying assumptions. As a result, a number of
approaches have been used. One of the oldest and most popular characteriza-
tions is that of an ideal head according to Karlquist (1954). The head is
assumed to have infinite pole tip lengths and infinite permeability (Fig.
5.3-11a). The scalar magnetic potential is assumed to be a linear function
across the air gap. This is just another way of saying the field is assumed
constant and uniform for all points within the gap between the pole pieces,

---

* The IBM 3330 disk system.
† In tape systems, typically characters are stored in parallel by the use of seven or nine heads in
parallel.

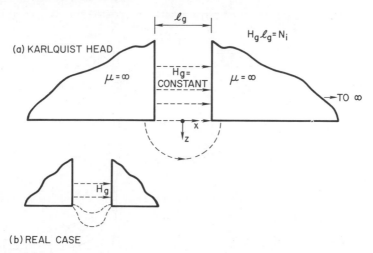

FIGURE 5.3-11 Idealized head analyzed by Karlquist showing gap field deviation from real case (note origin differs from that of Fig. 5.3-1 and all other coordinate systems used in this chapter).

as shown, including the position $z = 0$.* The last assumption represents the major departure from the real case, even assuming infinite permeability. The fringe field should be distorted outward at $z = 0$ as in Fig. 5.3-11b. However such a case does not allow simple closed form analytical expressions, whereas the assumption of uniform field at $z = 0$ does. Hence for a current i in a winding of N turns on the head as in Fig. 5.3-1, the field at $z = 0$ is the same as that inside the gap and is a constant of value

$$H_g - \frac{Ni}{l_g} \tag{5.3-9}$$

Under these assumptions, the field pattern below the gap is given by

$$H_x(x, z) = \frac{H_g}{\pi} \left(\tan^{-1} \frac{l_g/2 + x}{z} + \tan^{-1} \frac{l_g/2 - x}{z} \right) \tag{5.3-10}$$

$$H_z(x, z) = \frac{H_g}{2\pi} \ln \left[\frac{z^2 + (l_g/2 + x)^2}{z^2 + (l_g/2 - x)^2} \right] \tag{5.3-11}$$

This required assumption of uniform H_g at $z = 0$ is a good approximation for distances that are about $l_g/3$ or greater. Since this is usually the case, the Karlquist head serves as a good analytical description of the head field.

* The coordinate system origin is displaced from that of Fig. 5.3-1.

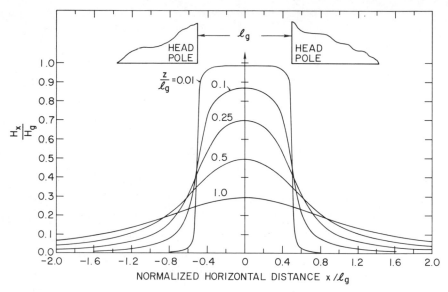

FIGURE 5.3-12   Normalized horizontal field component for idealized (Karlquist) head.

These fields scale directly with air gap length, making it convenient to normalize all dimensions and field amplitudes by dividing by l_g and expressing the field relative to H_g. Doing this gives

$$\frac{H_x(x_n, z_n)}{H_g} = \frac{1}{\pi}\left(\tan^{-1}\frac{1 + 2x_n}{2z_n} + \tan^{-1}\frac{1 - 2x_n}{2z_n}\right) \qquad (5.3\text{-}12)$$

$$\frac{H_z(x_n, z_n)}{H_g} = \frac{1}{2\pi}\ln\left[\frac{z_n^2 + (0.5 + x_n)^2}{z_n^2 + (0.5 - x_n)^2}\right] \qquad (5.3\text{-}13)$$

where $x_n = x/l_g$, and $z_n = z_0/l_g = h/l_g$

$H_g \approx Ni/l_g$ (RMKS) = field intensity (only x component) at point $x_n = 0$, $z_n = 0$ (i.e., $h = 0$)

These two field components are plotted in Figs. 5.3-12 and 5.3-13 for typical normalized dimensions.

A simplified expression for the peak value of H_x as a function of z at $x = 0$ is given by

$$\left.\frac{H_x}{H_g}\right|_{x=0} = \frac{2}{\pi}\tan^{-1}\frac{1}{2z_n} = \frac{2}{\pi}\tan^{-1}\frac{l_g}{2z} \qquad (5.3\text{-}14)$$

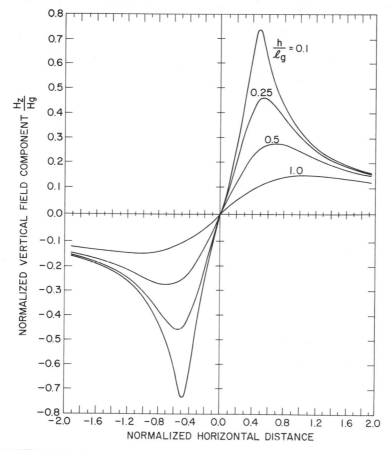

FIGURE 5.3-13 Normalized vertical field component for idealized (Karlquist) head.

At a distance far below the gap, where $z \gg l_g$, $\tan^{-1} \alpha \approx \alpha$, and the expression simplifies even further to

$$\left.\frac{H_x}{H_g}\right|_{x=0} \approx \frac{1}{\pi}\frac{l_g}{z} \qquad \text{or} \qquad H_x \approx \frac{Ni}{\pi z}\text{(RMKS)} \qquad \text{for} \quad z \gg l_g, x = 0$$

Such large distances are avoided whenever possible however: this expression serves only as a limit check.

The variation of the peak amplitude of H_x over a distance equivalent to a standard tape 0.4 mil thick, for typical dimensions and a gap field of 5000 Oe appears in Fig. 5.3-14. Clearly a very wide variation in writing field can exist. The presence of the medium during the actual writing process should tend

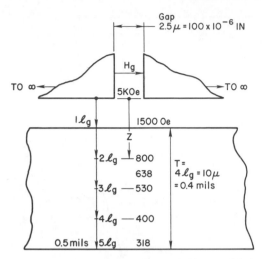

FIGURE 5.3-14 Peak horizontal component of write field created by a Karlquist head at various points for typical tape dimensions.

to even out this variation somewhat, but whether it does, and to what extent, remains an unsolved problem in magnetic recording (Section 6.3 gives examples of depth of recording vs. transition length and density).

The assumptions required for the idealized head produce an H_x versus x function (Fig. 5.3-12) that is more narrow in the x direction than can be achieved. Magnetic materials may have permeabilities in the tens of thousands, but the value is far from infinite. Furthermore, the large permeability μ is obtained for relatively small fields and falls off for larger fields. Small fields are obtained during reading, whereas large currents and drive fields are necessary during writing. Hence the assumption is more applicable to reading. A smaller μ will give a larger field value at large values of x (i.e., the field spreads out more). In addition, eddy currents in both the head and the medium during writing will broaden this field. It would thus be desirable to directly measure the field intensity of any given head. However the very small dimensions of modern heads, with gaps of l_g in the range of 50 to 100 μin., make measurement very difficult. Since any conceivable probe would be larger than the gap, the probe would measure an average field H over some large area. One way to overcome this problem is to scale up the head to larger dimensions, measure the field, and normalize the results. Very little work along these lines has been done. Chapman (1962) has measured the vertical component for a moderately scaled up head. (The dimensions of probe and head did not permit accurate measurement of the x component

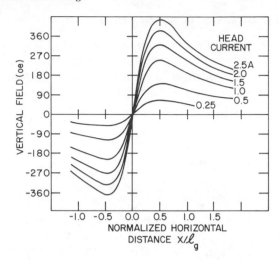

FIGURE 5.3-15 Measured vertical field component at $x = 0$, produced by a head with $l_g = 7$ mils at a distance $h = l_g$ for various currents in head winding. After Chapman (1962).

at any close distance to the head.) The measurements were obtained with a Hall probe on a mu-metal write head with a gap of $l_g = 0.007$ in. The field H_z for one value of head to medium plane spacing of $h/l_g = 1$ is given in Fig. 5.3-15. The value of H_g, the field in the gap, can be estimated by using (5.3-11) as an approximation. From Fig. 5.3-15, at $x_n = 0.5$, the field at 2.5 A is about 450 Oe; thus $H_z = 450$, $x_n = 0.5$, $z_n = 1$. Substituting these in (5.3-13) gives

$$H_g = \frac{2\pi}{\ln 2} H_z = \frac{2\pi}{0.69} (450) \qquad (5.3\text{-}16)$$

$$\approx 4000 \text{ Oe}$$

From Figs. 5.3-12 and 5.3-13 at $z_n = 1$, we see that the peak vertical component is about half the peak horizontal component. For writing in γFe_2O_3 at $z_n = 1$,[*] we would need a horizontal field of about 450 Oe or a vertical component half the above value. Hence the gap field would have to be in the range of 2000 Oe (G) or more, and it is clear that a large gap field is required for writing. In fact, the value is larger, since the medium extends to a distance larger than $z_n = 1$: the effective medium thickness is typically a few tenths of a mil, (e.g., 0.25 mil).

---

[*] Typical allowable maximum head to medium separation.

5.3.5   Equivalent Current Sheet for Karlquist Head

One of the most important observations concerning the above described fields, which becomes extremely important in Section 5.6, is that the fields of (5.3-10) and (5.3-11) are *identical* to those of an infinitely long current sheet of Section 2.12 of total width $l = 2d$. The fields for any point in space, using $d = l/2$ and z for y_p in (2.12-10) and (2.12-11) are

$$H_x(x, z) = \frac{J}{2\pi} \left(\tan^{-1} \frac{l/2 + x}{z} + \tan^{-1} \frac{l/2 - x}{z} \right) \tag{5.3-17}$$

$$H_z(x, z) = \frac{J}{2\pi} \ln\left(\frac{(l/2 + x)^2 + z^2}{(l/2 - x)^2 + z^2} \right) \qquad \text{RMKS} \tag{5.3-18}$$

where the vertical distance is z, with a negative coordinate system, and $J = i/l$ or the total current divided by total sheet width. The foregoing relations are equal to (5.3-10) and (5.3-11) if we let $H_g = J/2$. Note also that as the air gap length l_g becomes very small approaching zero, the equivalent current sheet width l also approaches zero or a point current source. For all dimensions larger than l, the field of the sheet becomes the field of a single wire of small diameter. Thus the field of the Karlquist head for small l_g and/or distances much larger than l_g must be identical to (2.12-12) and (2.12-13) except for a constant; therefore it can be deduced to be

$$H_x = \frac{H_g}{\pi} \frac{z}{x^2 + z^2} \qquad \text{and} \qquad H_y = \frac{H_g}{\pi} \frac{x}{x^2 + z^2} \tag{5.3-19}$$

where a negative coordinate system is used with origin at the center of the gap as in Fig. 5.3-11. The equivalence between heads and current loops is very important in understanding induced signals (Section 5.4) and reciprocity (Section 5.6).

5.4   SENSING AND READING FUNDAMENTALS

In practical magnetic recording systems, the recording density is limited for the most part by the ability of the system to reliably and accurately read the stored information. For a system with fixed dimensions in terms of gap spacing, head to medium spacing, and so on, it is usually possible to record (with appropriate electronic equipment) at a higher density than it is possible to read. This results from several factors: the writing is done by the trailing edge of the head, thus can be quite sharp, whereas the read signal is determined by the sensitivity function, which depends on the read gap spacing, among other things. Other important problems in reading are strobing (clocking) and variations in head to medium spacing. Of all these problems, that of strobing (i.e., extracting the desired signal from noise with timing jitter superimposed) is perhaps one of the most difficult obstacles in the achievement of higher densities. We consider all these problems.

Determining the stored information is a more involved process in magnetic recording than in random access memory. In the latter, assuming that a reasonable signal to noise ratio exists, each sense and read cycle that produces only one logical word is triggered by a clock pulse, and all subsequent words are likewise triggered from a fixed or at least known reference point. In addition, the location of the information is physically fixed; therefore the worst case delays are known ahead of time and are accounted for in the cycle and access times. In magnetic recording, information that is written by one head is sensed either by a separate head or by the same head at a subsequent time. Unlike random access memory, the exact location of the stored information is not known, and in addition, many bits are read out serially as in Fig. 5.4-1. If the system is clocked (strobed) externally, the clock intervals during sensing and reading must be identical, within certain tolerances, to the clock intervals used during writing. If they are not reasonably identical, the read cycle will be strobed at time intervals different from those used for writing, and there will be ambiguity or error in the readback. As we shall see, the transducer used for sensing the stored bits can be very simple, but the total

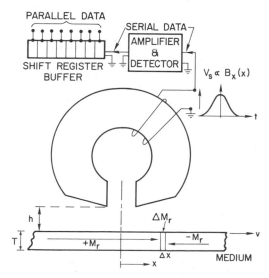

FIGURE 5.4-1   Schematic representation of the readback process.

problem of strobing and reading the information is more involved. We consider first the sense transducer and then the total reading problem.

Sensing is done in a manner completely analogous to that of writing. The sensing could be done by the write head, which is the case with disks; but for most tape systems, separate heads are provided to allow reading of information immediately after writing (for checking purposes), while writing of new information continues.

The most important basic principle needed to understand the reading process is that of reciprocity of the read signal with the sensitivity function (Section 5.6). If the medium is very thin and the magnetic transition Δx is very small, approximating a step function, the reciprocity theorem states that for a linear readback system, the signal as a function of time is identical in shape to B_x or S_x as a function of x. More specifically, we have from (5.6-12)

$$V_s(t) = v W_2 T 2 M_r S_x(x) \qquad (5.4\text{-}1)$$

The sensitivity function S_x is essentially the mutual inductance of the read head to the medium per unit of cross-sectional area of the medium, and it varies with x. The conversion from spatial dependence to time dependence comes about from the velocity in (5.4-1). Since the velocity is a constant when the medium is in motion, $v = dx/dt = x/t$ or $x = vt$. Thus time and distance are linearly related and can be interchanged as long as v is a constant.

To understand how the readback signal is obtained, we can make use of the simplified form of the reciprocity theorem for a very narrow gap head, considering only the x component of magnetization. These simplifying assumptions permit the read head to be replaced by an infinitely thin vertical coil (Fig. 5.4-2). A single transition of north poles is assumed to exist near the coil as shown (the south poles are assumed to be far removed on both sides of this transition). It is clear that for position p_1 of the coil with respect to the transition, the flux through the coil is in the negative x direction; at position p_2 the net flux is zero, and in position p_3 the flux is in the $+ x$ direction (Fig. 5.4-2b). If the transition were thus moved from left to right, the induced signal would have a wave form similar to that in Fig. 5.4-2c. The signal can be positive or negative, depending on the sense coil connection. Thus a single transition Δx produces a single voltage pulse in the read head, with the peak occurring, ideally, when the head is directly over the transition. In actual systems, the peak can be shifted from its ideal position because of interference from other transitions (bit crowding), vertical component of medium magnetization, thickness-dependent effects such as that in Fig. 5.3-7, and other conditions. We consider the effects of bit crowding and vertical magnetization later.

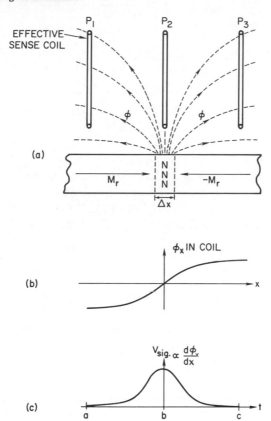

(a)

(b)

(c)

FIGURE 5.4-2   Readback flux and signal induced in a sense coil equivalent of a simple, narrow gap head.

EXAMPLE

Let us calculate the peak sense signal for the following parameters:

velocity $v = 200$ in./sec $= 5.1$ m/sec
thickness $T = 50$ μin. $= 1.27 \times 10^{-6}$ m
track width $W_2 = 0.050$ in. $= 1.26 \times 10^{-3}$ m
residual $M_r = 1 \times 10^5$ A-turns/m (1257 G)
read head $=$ write head with peak field B_x $(x = 0)$ of 10^4 G or 1 Wb/m^2
for 1 A in 100 turns at given head to medium separation.

We can calculate the peak $S_x(x = 0)$ from (5.6-1) as

$$S_x(x = 0) = \frac{B_x(x = 0)}{i} = \frac{1 \text{ Wb/m}^2}{1 \text{ A}} = \frac{1 \text{ H}}{\text{m}^2} \tag{5.4-2}$$

From (5.4-1) we have

$$V_s(\text{peak}) = vW_2\,T2M_r S_x(x = 0)$$
$$= 5.1 \times 1.26 \times 10^{-3} \times 1.27 \times 10^{-6} \times 2(1 \times 10^5) \times 1$$
$$= 1.7 \times 10^{-3} = 1.7\,\text{mV}$$

This signal is small but feasible. The parameters we assumed are approximately those for a high performance tape system. Signals of 1 mV or less are common, although the older, lower density systems give larger signals. In disk systems, the track width is considerably smaller to permit higher arcal density, but the velocity is considerably larger. If we wish to use the same parameters and sense signal for a tape and disk system, we can estimate the allowable reduction in track width. In (5.4-1), assume that all parameters for these two cases are identical except v and W_2; hence

$$\frac{V_d}{V_t} = \frac{v_d W_d}{v_t W_t} \equiv 1 \qquad \text{or} \qquad \frac{W_t}{W_d} = \frac{v_d}{v_t} \tag{5.4-3}$$

where subscripts t and d represent tape and disk. Typical velocities are 200 in./sec for tape and 2400 rpm for disks; the latter converts to 1600 in./sec at the edge of a 14 in. disk. Using these values, we can tolerate approximately

$$\frac{W_t}{W_d} = \frac{1600}{200} = 8 \tag{5.4-4}$$

Typical values in commercial systems are W_t about 45 mils and W_d about 5 mils, with a ratio very nearly equal to 8.

The use of the foregoing principles concerning sensitivity function for analyzing magnetic recording can best be understood by considering Figs. 5.3-1 and 5.4-1. If the medium is in motion and saturated at, say, $-M_r$, and an instantaneous reversal of write current is applied, the instantaneous field pattern of the write head for some value of h will be as in Fig. 5.3-1. The trailing edge of this field will induce a sharp, nearly step function change in magnetization as previously discussed (Fig. 5.4-1). If the write current were removed and the transition moved under the head at constant velocity, the induced sense signal would have a shape identical to $B_x(x)$ in Fig. 5.3-1, with x replaced by vt: the identical shape would be contingent on having the change in magnetization occur over a very small Δx compared to the gap width, and on having the thickness of the medium very small compared to the head to medium spacing (i.e., $T \ll z_0$). This represents the ideal case, which is never achieved. When these constraints are not true, as in a practical system, the sense signal spreads out in time, reduces in amplitude, and lowers the density. We can make use of the principle of induced signal from a step function change in M_r for the ideal case to understand practical situations.

A major problem in magnetic recording is obtaining an adequate sense signal from which the stored data bits can be extracted. Many factors affect not only the sense signal itself, but also the data extraction or binary conversion process. We first consider the circumstances under which the signal's amplitude and wave form are affected. These include bit crowding with resultant amplitude reduction, peak shift, or dc level shift; the effect of finite spread in ΔM_r rather than step function change; and the effects of finite medium thickness and of vertical components of magnetization in the medium. The discrimination process, which is most seriously effected by clocking, is covered afterward.

5.4.1 Bit Crowding

A recorded "1" in NRZI is ideally represented by a step change in magnetization from $-M_r$ to M_r, or vice versa. This ΔM_r would give an ideal sense signal as illustrated in Fig. 5.4-1. For high density, the next stored "1" should be as close to this one as possible. Since the second ΔM_r will be in the opposite direction, the sense signal will be negative (Fig. 5.3-8d). If the two bits (i.e., two ΔM_r's) are far apart, the sense signal will have the shape of two sensitivity functions $S_x(x)$, one positive and one negative, separated by the length L, which separates the ΔM_r's as in Fig. 5.4-3. Now as the distance L is decreased, the two sensitivity functions $S_1(x)$ and $S_2(x)$ begin to overlap and subtract

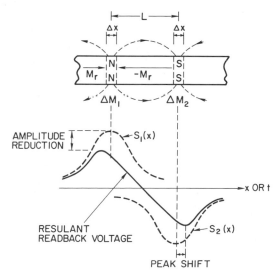

FIGURE 5.4-3   Readback wave form distortion caused by bit crowding of two ideal, adjacent step transitions showing resultant amplitude reduction and peak shift.

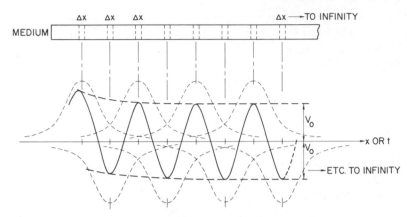

FIGURE 5.4-4   Readback wave form distortion from bit crowding of a sudden, long string of ideal step transitions (approximate).

from each other as shown, giving both a reduction in signal amplitude and a shift in the position, hence time, where the peaks occur (peak shift). As L further decreases, the amplitude reduction and peak shift increases until at $L \gtrsim 0$ the two signals nearly overlap and cancel each other. For higher density, a very narrow $S(x)$ is clearly desirable, to permit L to be smaller, with less distortion of the resultant signal.

The above case considered only two successive step function changes in ΔM_r. Of course in actual recording we may encounter a very long string of successive changes in ΔM_r (i.e., a string of "1's" in NRZI). If there is a long series of step changes, additional distortion in the signal can arise. For instance, in Fig. 5.4-4 there is a shift in the apparent dc level of the signal, or a droop. There will be only a small peak shift on the end signals (first and last) and none on the center peaks because of symmetry. Furthermore, the initial part of the signal will have a droop as before, but the droop will eventually level out, leaving only a reduced amplitude signal in the middle region with no dc level shift. This is obvious because in the middle of a long string of ΔM's. the signal must be symmetrical about the zero line as shown. Some normalized curves for the peak amplitude reduction and peak shift for two successive ΔM's and various head to medium spacings h are given in Figs. 5.4-5 and 5.4-6 for the idealized sensitivity functions of Fig. 5.3-12.

5.4.2   Signal Reduction for Head to Medium Separation

Of course if the medium is far away from the read head, no sense signal can be induced. In typical recording systems, the bits are quite small and the external field is the physical entity that is sensed by coupling it to the read

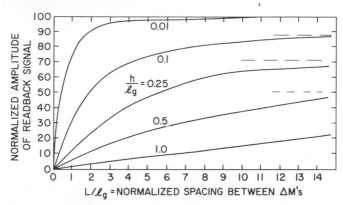

FIGURE 5.4-5 Normalized curves of peak readback signal versus bit spacing for two step ΔM's and various head to medium spacings, using sensitivity function of ideal head (Fig. 5.3-12).

head as it passes by the gap. The amplitude of the external fringe field falls off very rapidly with distance, and very close head to medium spacings must be maintained for reliable data readback and writing. The reduction in signal amplitude as a function of head to medium separation can be obtained from the sensitivity function amplitude versus z, as given in Fig. 5.3-6 for normalized dimensions: the signal falls off rapidly for close spacings but less rapidly for large spacings, as would be expected.

5.4.3 Signal Distortion

Distortion Due to Nonstep Magnetization Change

In all magnetic recording, the change in magnetization from $\pm M_r$ to $\mp M_r$ takes place over a finite distance as explained in Section 5.3. When the distance Δx is finite and comparable to the gap length l_a, the sense signal is

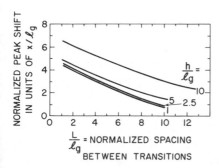

FIGURE 5.4-6 Normalized curves of peak shift versus bit spacing for two step ΔM's and various head to medium spacings (peak shift normalized to l_g units of space) using idealized sensitivity function (Fig. 5.3-12).

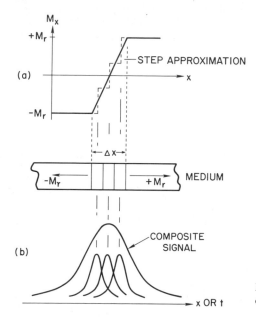

FIGURE 5.4-7 Readback wave form distortion for nonstep change in ΔM.

reduced in amplitude and spread out in time. This effect can be seen by again using superposition of the ideal cases. We can break the actual magnetization change into increments of small steps in ΔM (Fig. 5.4-7a). The sensitivity function for each step then has an amplitude equal to a fraction of the total magnetization change it represents. Also the position of each fractional sensitivity function is displaced by the appropriate amount (Fig. 5.4-7b). The composite signal will be lower in amplitude and broader than that which would be obtained for a step change of ΔM_r. If the value of Δx is known, the so-determined composite sensitivity function can be used to reevaluate the bit crowding signal distortion. Since this bit crowding becomes worse as Δx increases, a narrow transition is very desirable.

Distortion Due to Finite Medium Thickness

In all the cases thus far we have implicitly assumed either that the medium was very thin or that its thickness T was much smaller than the medium to head separation. These conditions are seldom if ever obtained, and the medium thickness is one of the more important parameters affecting recording density. The manner by which the readback signal is affected can be determined similar to that done previously for a nonstep change in ΔM. In this case, the medium is divided into thin, horizontal strips as in Fig. 5.4-8 and the fractional sensitivity function is assumed constant for each strip. Since all these strips are located at different separations from the head, a different

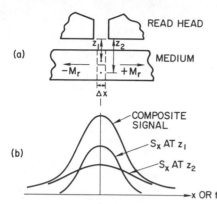

FIGURE 5.4-8 Readback wave form distortion for finite thickness medium.

sensitivity function must be used for each (Fig. 5.4-8b). As the strip progresses further away from the head into the medium, the fractional sensitivity function becomes broader in space or time and lower in amplitude. The composite effect on the readback signal is very similar to that caused by a nonstep change in ΔM. Thin media are evidently desirable for high density, to reduce bit crowding distortion of the wave form.

Distortion Due to Vertical Components of Magnetization

If the amount of vertical magnetization present within the medium is known, the resulting induced signal can be determined much as previously. In this case we must make use of the z component of the sensitivity function, which will have the form of the vertical field produced by the read head. For an idealized head, this sensitivity function will have the form given by (5.3-13) and Fig. 5.3-13, with the appropriate conversion from H_z and S_z as discussed in Section 5.6. This function will be distorted for a read head, but the form will be the same. For now, we assume that the medium has a vertical and horizontal component of magnetization such as that in Fig. 5.4-9b. The transition regions Δx are assumed to be small enough to be considered step functions. The corresponding horizontal and vertical components of the sensitivity function S_x and S_z are assumed to be those of Fig. 5.4-9c. Since the readback process is linear, the two components of induced voltage resulting from these two sensitivity functions can be added. Since the transitions are assumed to be step functions, the total signal is proportional to

$$V_{\text{sig}} \propto M_x S_x + M_z S_z \qquad (5.4\text{-}5)$$

Note that for the medium motion assumed (i.e., toward the right), the trailing edge write field, which is on the right side as in Fig. 5.4-9a, produces M_x and M_z components of the same polarity. Hence the sensitivity functions of

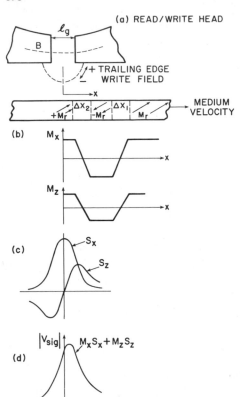

FIGURE 5.4-9 Readback wave form distortion resulting from vertical component of magnetization. (*a*) Head and write field orientation. (*b*) Medium magnetization and components. (*c*) Components of sensitivity function. (*d*) Resultant readback wave form showing shift in direction of motion.

Fig. 5.4-9*c*, with appropriate scaling factors, can be added with the polarity shown for transition Δx, and with only a negative sign for Δx_2. The resulting signal, (Fig. 5.4-9*d*) is no longer symmetrical about the vertical axis; thus a vertical magnetization introduces an undesirable peak shift. This peak is shifted in the direction of the medium motion as shown for all transitions. Thus it is clear why the medium is made to be less sensitive to the vertical writing field. Note that the asymmetrical signal distortion due to vertical magnetization is very similar to that caused by bit crowding; namely, the peak shifts to one side and the signal becomes more spread out over time on one side but narrower on the other. Vertical magnetization always shifts the peak of the signal in the direction of the medium motion regardless of the direction of motion, as long as reading and writing are performed in the same direction. This is because the writing is done by the trailing edge field as shown. Bit crowding shifts the peaks of two interacting bits further apart. In some case this may compensate for the peak shift due to M_z, whereas it sometimes adds to the peak shift.

For the more general case, distortions due to nonstep magnetization changes, finite medium thickness, and so on, can be handled exactly as previously with only the appropriate value of S_z included. The problems introduced by peak shift are related to clocking and are discussed next.

5.4.4 Clocking

The sensing tranducer reads the entire magnetization pattern on the medium, which is a continuously varying voltage as a function of time. This signal for various coding schemes (Fig. 5.3-8) is basically an analog signal coming from the transducer. The fundamental problem in the readback process is to accurately and reliably convert this read signal, which can have a very peculiar wave form, into its binary equivalent. The processing of stored information is done by the CPU, which can understand only binary information in which "1's" are usually represented as positive pulses and "0's" by either a negative pulse or no pulse in combination with a clock pulse. Since many common systems use codes that indicate "0's" by the absence of a pulse (e.g., NRZI), the clock pulse at the proper instant of time is essential because the absence of a pulse is the same as no information; all digital systems are strobed or energized by a clock pulse that reads the information as "0" when no pulse is present.

To understand the clocking problem in magnetic recording, we start with a simple hypothetical case and proceed to more complex cases. Let us assume that the recorded information generates a single positive pulse for stored "1's" and a single negative pulse for stored "0's" as in Fig. 5.4-10.* This signal is essentially binary already, but it must be converted from a serial bit stream into parallel bytes, for instance. To accomplish this, we might feed the serial bit stream into a serial input shift register that reads, say, a byte or multiple bytes, then transfers the information in parallel to main memory. This resets the register and allows it to continue to read the serial data coming in. To properly operate the shift register, the serial data signal would have to be dissected into several parts. In principle, the dissection could be done as follows. The shift register requires three inputs, a clock pulse for activation the reading and shifting, a "1" input for "1" bits, and a "0" input for "0" bits.† The register must shift every data pulse ("1" or "0"); thus the clock pulse could be generated by a simple full wave rectifier as in Fig. 5.4-10b. The data pulses for the "1" and "0" input of the shift register could be obtained from positive half-wave rectification and negative half-wave rectification, respectively, (Fig. 5.4-10c, d). Both logically and with

---

* This bit stream is what one would get for a stream of alternate "1's" and "0's" (i.e., $101010\cdots$) in phase modulation. However any series of "1's," series of "0's," or combinations will generate more complex patterns in PE, as discussed in Section 5.3.

† For example, a standard RS shift register built from master-slave flip-flops.

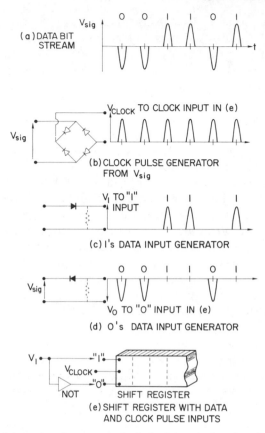

FIGURE 5.4-10   Schematic of one method of obtaining clock pulses from a simple self-clocking code.

regard to hardware we do not need V_0 from Fig. 5.4-10d, since it could be obtained from V_1 in Fig. 5.4-10c by using a NOT gate as in Fig. 5.4-10e (i.e., the absence of a signal when a clock pulse is applied is logically a "0"). The latter point is very important because in some coding schemes the "0's" are not provided as signals (i.e., no pulse for "0") and the clocking then becomes all-important, especially when a string of "0's" is obtained, as we consider shortly. The advantage of this self-clocking scheme is that no matter what the internal clock pulse cycle was during writing, a discrete, identifiable signal can easily be recorded in the shift register (provided the data were, in fact, stored.) It would not matter in the readback process if the writing clock cycle varied, since the shift register records and shifts according to the clock pulses generated by the data, which could have widely varying periods between pulses with no effect on what is finally read as data.

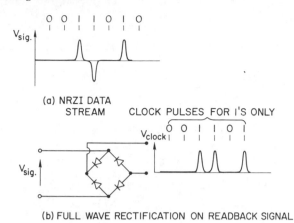

FIGURE 5.4-11   Schematic showing inadequacy of full wave rectification for obtaining clocking pulses for NRZI code.

This simplified case is an example of self-clocking for data readback, that is, a unique pulse is obtained for all data both "1" and "0." To increase linear bit density, it is desirable to push adjacent regions of magnetization as close together as possible, as in Fig. 5.3-8b through d. This results in numerous coding schemes, the most common one being NRZI. In this scheme a stored "1" is represented by a flux or magnetization change and a "0" as no change. Furthermore, "1's" can be either positive or negative pulses, as shown in Fig. 5.3-8d and reproduced in Fig. 5.4-11. Now the basic question is, How do we generate the clock pulse? Obviously we have no problem for "1's"; a simple full wave rectifier as before will suffice, giving the results of Fig. 5.4-11b. For "0's," however, there is no clock pulse available, and it must be generated internally by the same clock used for writing, for instance. This represents one fundamental problem in magnetic recording. The clock pulse period can vary, and if the period during reading is significantly different from that during writing, the clock pulses will misalign with the data pulses and incorrect data may be shifted into the buffer shift register. This is especially likely to happen if a single clock generator is used and we are attempting to read a long string of "0's" followed by a string of "1's" in NRZI, as in Fig. 5.4-12. Suppose the clock period during writing is constant (Fig. 5.4-12a). A string of 0000110 would be recorded (Fig. 5.4-12b), with bit cells of equal length. If now during the readback process the clock period has increased and begins drifting (Fig. 5.4-12c), it is quite possible for the drift to accumulate, and after a period of time the clock pulse may coincide with the wrong data pulse, such as the fourth clock pulse during reading in Fig. 5.4-12c; the data readback will now be 000100 instead of the original

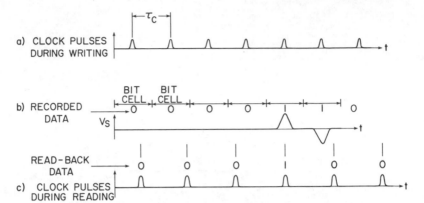

FIGURE 5.4-12   Effect of clock period drift on readback data in NRZI using one clock.

0000110. Of course, numerous cases could occur, and the prevention of error would require very accurate control of the clock period for essentially the life of the system. For very low densities, this control is not difficult; as the densities increase, however, the bit cell dimension as well as the sense signal amplitude decreases and the noise increases. This requires that the clock pulses during reading and writing coincide more and more closely, to obtain a reasonable signal to noise discrimination (i.e., to distinguish a "1" from a "0" and from noise). Clock period drift cannot easily be controlled to the tolerances required for high density; for example, on tape moving at 250 in./sec recording 6400 bpi, the bit cell time period τ_b is

$$\tau_b = \frac{1}{6400 \text{ bits}} \frac{1 \text{ sec}}{250 \text{ in.}} = 0.624 \times 10^{-6} \text{ sec/bit} \qquad (5.4\text{-}6)$$

If we were to specify an arbitrary constraint for the clock drift of no more than a total of 20 % τ_b drift over a total time of 100 bit cells, the constraint of the clock drift $\Delta\tau_c$ would be

$$100\Delta\tau_c \leq 0.20\tau_b = 0.2(0.624 \ \mu\text{sec}) = 0.125 \ \mu\text{sec}$$

or

$$\Delta\tau_c \leq 0.125 \times 10^{-2} \ \mu\text{sec} = 1.25 \text{ nsec}$$

The clock period would then have to be controlled to an accuracy of about ± 1 nsec for long periods (e.g., months or years). This would be quite a difficult task; hence another clocking method is needed or a different code must be chosen that is self-clocking on readback. Both schemes are used in practice; for very high density, phase modulation is used in tape systems,

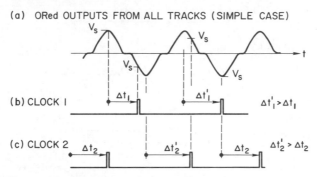

FIGURE 5.4-13 Double clocking principles in multitrack NRZI code with clock period drift during reading (no drift during writing).

whereas the double frequency code is commonly used on disks. For lower density using NRZI, a double clock can circumvent the clock drift problem. The double clocking is especially useful for NRZI on tape that uses multiple tracks in parallel (i.e., read and write a byte or character). By using odd parity across the byte (see Fig. 6.3-5), we ensure that there will always be at least one signal pulse present for every character or byte. All track signals, for clocking purposes, can logically be tied into an OR gate and peak detector. The OR guarantees at least one signal for every character to be read, and the peak of this signal triggers the clock that provided the time interval to the next pulse strobing point of all the tracks individually as in Fig. 5.4-13a. This strobe pulse may occur at the peak or off-peak of the next pulse as in Fig. 5.4-13b; but in either case a second clock period is triggered by the peak of this second signal, irrespective of where the strobe pulse may happen to have landed (Fig. 5.4-13c). Figure 5.4-13 represents the case when, for instance, the clock intervals during writing were fixed, giving evenly and accurately spaced bit cells, but the clocks varied during reading. The opposite case could also happen, that is, the clock intervals varied during writing but were constant during reading, or a combination when the clocks varied during both writing and reading. The latter is the worst case, as in Fig. 5.4-14 in which during writing $\Delta t'_2$ or its equivalent was smaller than Δt_2 but during reading (Fig. 5.4-14c) the opposite is true: $\Delta t'_2$ is greater than Δt_2. The sense signal at this strobe point can be very small as shown if the clock pulse variations are not well confined. Figure 5.4-14b illustrates the same situation for $\Delta t'_1$. The major advantage of double clocking is that even though the time periods Δt_1 and Δt_2 of each clock may vary, there never can be an accumulated drift, as for a single track and one clock. Nevertheless, even for the double clock system, as the density increases, the timing problem for the exact instant of trigger of each clock and the clock

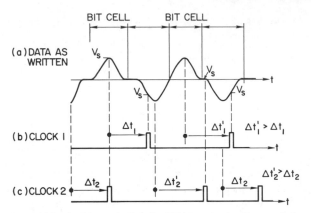

FIGURE 5.4-14   Double clocking principle in NRZI code showing variations both during writing and reading.

timing intervals Δt_1 and Δt_2 become more critical. A self-clocking system is desirable, and this is what is used in high density tapes and in medium to high density disks. Additional magnetic transitions must be placed within each bit cell, which theoretically lowers the density compared to NRZI because the latter requires fewer transitions per bit cell, allowing close packing of data bits for a given bit crowding. However the clocking problem is the limiting factor in practical cases; hence self-clocking schemes are necessary.

Although inductive magnetic heads have been used extensively for the readback process, magnetoresistive sensors have received considerable attention (Bahr 1972; Hunt 1961; Thompson 1975). A uniaxially anisotropic strip of Permalloy (see Section 3.3) will experience a few percent change in electrical resistance when subjected to a suitable dc magnetic field. This resistance change can be sensed by a small current flowing through the element. The magnetorestrictive sensing scheme has several advantages: the signal amplitude is independent of the medium velocity, the element can be quite small, and it is quite sensitive for such applications. Since magnetoresistive elements do not generate suitable external magnetic fields, they are not used for writing.

As the transducers become increasingly small, both the inductive and magnetoresistive heads begin to encounter readback problems because of the so-called Barkhausen noise, which is generated in the read head as it is magnetized by a bit cell. This phenomenon is characteristic of all magnetic structures that switch by domain wall motion, and the read/write heads fit into this category. The domain walls, hence magnetization of the read head, switch by small jumps rather than in continuous fashion as the applied field is increased. Normally this effect is averaged and swamped out by large sense signals; however when the tracks are very small, the heads are very small and the jumps in magnetization begin to be significant. These can cause such detrimental effects as spurious noise or loss of magnetic permeability (Bajorek and Thompson, 1975).

5.5 ADDRESSING MECHANISM FUNDAMENTALS

In random access memory, the addressing mechanism is wired into the memory system and a full logical word (b bits in parallel) is retrieved on each memory cycle (Fig. 4.3-1). The desired information is uniquely and totally specified by the address bits that are initially entered into the address register—the decoder selects one logical word within a very small time (usually two or three logic level delays), and read or write pulses go directly to the logical (physical) word. In magnetic recording, one could obtain b bits in parallel for each read cycle, once the information is found, by paralleling "b" write and read heads; but there is no "wired-in" addressing mechanism to permit one to go directly to the desired physical location. Since the medium moves with respect to the transducers, the basic addressing problem in magnetic recording is to find the desired information. This important problem requires additional mechanisms to achieve the addressing. Tapes, disks, drums, strips, and so on each have specific addressing techniques as well as internal variations (e.g., several different disk addressing techniques), which are considered separately in Chapters 6 and 7. For now, we concentrate on the general principles and problems in addressing for both reading and writing.

To better understand the addressing mechanisms in all magnetic recording, let us start with a very simple system and attempt to write one simple data record that must be subsequently located and read. This will indicate that certain basic capabilities must be present. Then we will progress to a more complex case of closely packed multiple records, still in the simple system, finding additional requirements are necessary. As we move on to an even more complex case, we discover the basic addressing problem in magnetic recording, namely, the need for "stored addressing information" (SAI). Although in actual practice the clocking information is part of the SAI, we do not consider it here because theoretically we could design perfect clocks, hence clocking would not be a part of the SAI. However we would need some SAI to write and locate the data even in a perfect system. Therefore clocking is not a fundamental part of the SAI but rather is a practical part. Clocking problems are discussed in Section 5.4. We assume there that we have a perfect clock; thus there is *no* ambiguity in the data bit location for any and all codes.

For our simple system we assume a large magnetic medium that can be moved relative to one stationary magnetic head; the same head is used for reading and writing. We can move the medium either continuously in a circle (disklike) or back and forth (tapelike) with perfect mechanical alignment on the given track. The medium is very large, and we wish to store one data record of say, R_1, bits and subsequently find and read it.

For this simple case, the writing is easy. At any given time, with medium in motion, we turn on the writing pulse currents with polarity determined by the data to be stored and the coding scheme used, and with pulse intervals geared to some internal clocking pulse. The recording will stop when no more data pulses are left. Now we wish to locate and read back the data. This is a little more difficult. If there is no other information stored in the medium, we can move it until some pulses are generated in the read head and transfer the bits into a flip-flop type of shift register. Reading starts when signals are received and stops when the signals are no longer available. This scheme would be workable and quite simple if the stored data generated, say, positive pulses for stored "1's" and negative pulses for stored "0's" as in Fig. 5.4-10a. This signal would tell us where and exactly how long the data are with no ambiguity; it would be an ideal pulse pattern.

Now we wish to record additional data records on the same medium, tightly packed for efficient utilization of the storage space. For a back and forth tapelike system, we stopped reading immediately after the last data pulse was obtained. To write a new record, we can just simply start the medium moving once again and begin writing whenever it is up to the correct speed (reading and writing can be done only when the system is at the correct speed). Thus a blank space between records is needed for starting and stopping; this is the interrecord gap (IRG). Writing and medium motion stop when all the data have been sent to the system, and this can be determined with logic circuits. If we now wish to read, say, only the second record R_2, we can move the medium back to the first Gap IRG_1, stop then start forward, read until IRG_2 is sensed, and then stop. We do not really have to sense the IRG_2 to know when to stop if we know the length of the data record R_2; just read for a prespecified data length. Thus for the sequential medium under the assumed constraints, all we need is an IRG between each record. The same is true if many records are stored. Suppose, however, we store (write), 100 records as R_1 through R_{10}, each of varying but known data length and starting at the beginning of the medium. If we wish then to read R_{10}, we would reset to the beginning, start reading forward, counting IRGs as we pass them, and when we reach the tenth IRG, start reading data for a certain specified (known) length of record and stop. This should place us within IRG_1. Thus we could find any record, provided we knew something about where it is located. When we wish to search and compare on stored data, the procedure becomes more complex, requiring a small program. Nevertheless it can be done with the SAI being nothing more than the IRG's as before.

If, however, our medium is continuously rotating (disklike) and we wish to write, locate, and read records in addition to the one previously stored, the process becomes more involved. The writing in one track can be sequential, very much like tape, except that there is no start and stop time, hence no need for an IRG in this simple case. Unfortunately, there are several problems; first we can add more records until we get back to the original record. If there is not enough room for the last record, it must be removed and placed elsewhere. This maneuver requires some logic control, but it can be done. If we planned ahead so that all the records just fit, we have a circular track completely filled with data bits. Now let us locate record R_{10}. There is no beginning nor end of the track and no IRGs; thus there is no way either to initiate counting or to continue to count records as in the tape. Let us put an index marker at the beginning of the first track to denote our beginning reference point for recording. The mark can be sensed electronically and used to trigger some logic circuits. But even with this capability, there is no simple way to find the desired record. If we know the complete format of all tracks (i.e., number of bits), we can initiate a counter at the index point, count a prespecified number of bits to reach R_{10}, and start reading. This is possible but difficult. Sometimes R_{10} is the last record on the track, and we may have to count 40K to 80K or more bits.* This is difficult and costly to do with logic hardware, thus suggesting the inclusion of some additional SAI. We might argue that we could search the records by content for equality; but since we lack an IRG to designate the beginning of each record, we would have to compare all possible bit patterns over a prespecified mask or bit size. This again would be quite difficult and subject to ambiguity resulting from possible matches obtained from overlapping portions of two records. Let us put in some gaps to separate records: now we intend to search some prespecified portion of each record until a match is found and read the remaining portion of the record. This could work if the search field were the first part of the data, ensuring that reading after a match would give the entire record. However if the search field happened to be somewhere in the middle, we would have to count bits as before to obtain a full revolution minus backspacing, to be able to read the full records. This becomes quite complex and requires expensive logic hardware. Thus both ways of locating the records would benefit greatly from additional SAI.

Therefore let us put gaps between records to assist in searching on the data

---

* For example, outer diameter of a typical medium density 14 in. disk storing 2K bpi gives 80K bits total.

itself, and let us ease the bit counting problem by placing many markers, called sector markers, around the circumference, using one counter to count the sectors and another to count bits within a sector. This essentially provides a two-level addressing scheme, which is much easier to handle in hardware. If we had 100 sectors, for instance, the sector counter need only count to 100 and the bit counter to 80K/100 or 800, both much more reasonable. A few of the logic hardware requirements for these are as follows. A binary counter of 17 places (17 toggle flip-flops) would be needed to count to 80K (can count to $2^{17} = 128K'$), and probably we would choose a synchronous counter design to avoid propagation delays through all 17 places.* The latter is quite a complex logic circuit. The counter for 800 bits would require a 10-place binary toggle shift register ($2^{10} = 1K'$), and the 100 bit counter would require seven places—both still quite complex. We do not wish to discuss yet the design of the controller, which is a computer attached to the drive unit to do all the logical functions, but we need to understand the problems. In the foregoing example, we could consider using only 16 sectors (requiring a four place binary counter) and not counting bits. This simplifies the hardware but complicates the record retrieval. If data can be written only starting at a sector mark, we can specify that data must also be read starting at a sector mark. Then in general, a large group of records must be read into main memory, and finer addressing must be done by a program through the CPU. This is actually how many systems work. Such an organization requires a great deal of prior knowledge about the format and composition of the records by the programmer; and when a program is written to accomplish this finer addressing, it will contain a large amount of SAI. Thus the SAI has been removed from the hardware or data records and transferred to the program, which resides in main memory during execution. Hence the SAI is stored in main memory, but usually in a very compact, non-redundant form.

Such a system is more amenable to fixed length, well-organized records. If variable length records with a great variety of formats and organization are to be handled, additional SAI would be very helpful. This is duscussed more fully in Section 6.5.

Thus we have seen that for systems using shared transducers, the absence of wired-in addressing capability requires some additional information or special features for data location and retrieval. This is a fundamental feature of all storage—not only computers but also books, pencil and paper files, and probably even the human brain about whose retrieval mechanisms little is known.

---

* "Synchronous" means that the output is available after one or very few logic level delays, thus avoiding the propagation delay through serially connected flip-flops.

5.6 RECIPROCITY THEOREM AND SENSITIVITY FUNCTION

The reciprocity theorem described in this section is a consequence of certain fundamental laws of electric and magnetic fields and provides relationships that are true in general. Its value in magnetic recording is that the consequence of this theorem often reduces to a very simple form that allows us to determine the shape of the sense signal from a single magnetic transition Δx in a very simple way. Even in the more general cases, it provides a powerful analytical technique for determining the readback signal. Without this method, the calculation of the signal is extremely complex. The idea of using reciprocity of mutual inductance to express sense signals for magnetic recording was first suggested by the famous physicist L. Brillouin and was derived by Hoagland (1963).

We first define the horizontal and vertical components of the sensitivity function to be

$$S_x(x, z) = \frac{B_x(x, z)}{i} = \frac{\mu_0 H_x(x, z)}{i} \quad \text{H/m}^2 \tag{5.6-1}$$

$$S_z(x, z) = \frac{B_z(x, z)}{i} = \mu_0 \frac{H_z(x, z)}{i} \quad \text{H/m}^2 \tag{5.6-2}$$

$$\mathbf{S}(x, z) = \mathbf{S}_x(x, z) + \mathbf{S}_z(x, z) \tag{5.6-3}$$

where i is the write current flowing in N_R turns on the head and produces the total magnetizing field $H_x(x)$ or $H_z(x)$, which for an idealized head, would have the form shown in Figs. 5.3-12 and 5.3-13. Thus the sensitivity function has the same functional form as the field created by the head in question. The consequences of the reciprocity theorem are as follows. The laws of mutual inductance show that the sense signal as a function of time must be related to the sensitivity function $S(x)$ as a function of x. In general, if we *happen* to know ahead of time what the x and z components of magnetization are as a function of x in the medium, the signal is proportional to the integral of the product of the magnetization times the derivative of $\mathbf{S}$, or conversely, is proportional to the integral of the product of $\mathbf{S}$ times the derivative of $\mathbf{M}$. More specifically, referring to Fig. 5.6-1, for any given magnetization distribution in the medium, we can determine the total flux linking the sense loop as a function of $x_p - x_m$, the position of the magnetization with respect to the loop. Note that the coordinate system origin is taken at some arbitrary position within the medium as shown. Allowing the medium to move at constant velocity or $x_p \propto vt$ and determining the resulting time

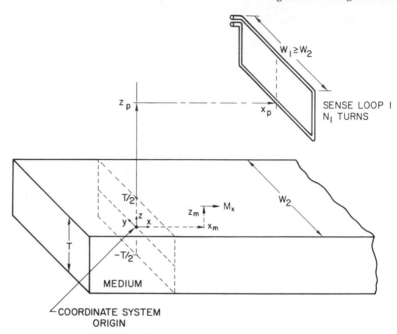

FIGURE 5.6-1   Coordinate system for reciprocity.

change of flux in the sense loop, the result is found to be

$$
|V_x(t)| = \frac{\partial}{\partial x_p}\left\{ vW_2 \int_{-T/2}^{T/2} dz_m \int_{-\infty}^{\infty} M_x(x_m, z_m) S_x(x_p - x_m, z_p - z_m) dx_m \right\}
$$

(5.6-4)

The term under the right-hand integral expresses the product of S_x and M_x for a given value of x_p and x_m (i.e., fixed separation $x_p - x_m$ between the magnetization and sense loop). The integral sums this product over all values of x_m for a fixed x_p, and the derivative $\partial/\partial x_p$ outside the integral sums these over all time. We must be careful in applying the latter derivative. As the medium moves relative to the sense loop, x_p obviously changes, yet within the integral we can allow either x_m or $x_p - x_m$ to be a time variable, but not both simultaneously. If we allow $x_p - x_m$ to be the dependent variable so that x_m is independent of x_p, (5.6-4) reduces to

$$
|V_x(t)| = vW_2 \int_{-T/2}^{T/2} dz_m \int_{-\infty}^{\infty} M_x(x_m, z_m) \frac{\partial}{\partial x_p} S_x(x_p - x_m, z_p - z_m) dx_m
$$

(5.6-5)

If we allow $x_p - x_m$ to remain constant while x_p varies, x_m varies with x_p (i.e., x_m is the dependent variable). In such a case, the derivative in front of the integral in (5.6-4) would have to operate on M_x. Note in this case that dx_p must equal dx_m; thus $\partial M_x/\partial x_p = \partial M_x/\partial x_m$. This permits the reciprocity equation to be expressed in its more common and perhaps more useful form, namely,

$$|V_x(t)| = vW_2 \int_{-T/2}^{T/2} dz_m \int_{-\infty}^{\infty} \frac{\partial M_x}{\partial x_m}(x_m, z_m)S_x(x_p - x_m, z_p - z_m)dx_m \quad (5.6\text{-}6)$$

in RMKS units. Only the amplitude is expressed here, since the polarity depends on the sense coil connection relative to the medium motion.

When vertical components of magnetization are present in the medium, the following similar expression for its induced signal can be obtained:

$$|V_z(t)| = vW_2 \int_{-T/2}^{T/2} dz_m \int_{-\infty}^{\infty} \frac{\partial M_z}{dx_m}(x_m, z_m)S_z(x_p - x_m, z_p - z_m)dx_m \quad (5.6\text{-}7)$$

in RMKS units. The x component is usually much larger, but the peak of the total signal is slightly shifted in the direction of motion by the vertical component. Reversal of the medium motion reverses the polarity of both components.

Note an extremely important point: the magnetization does not have to be produced by S for this analysis to be valid; rather, M can be induced by any means. Only the trailing edge of S usually produces small transitions as described in Section 5.3. It can be seen that if M varies in a complex manner over x and z, the evaluation of the sense signal will be difficult. Fortunately the foregoing expressions often reduce to simple form for typical recordings. We saw in Section 5.3 that the written information consists of very narrow transitions Δx, with very nearly uniform M_x everywhere else. Let us approximate the magnetization change at one of these transitions as in Fig. 5.6-2.

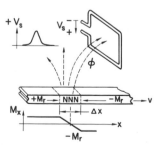

FIGURE 5.6-2 Coordinate system and readback signal polarity for linear reversal of magnetization from $+M_x$ to $-M_x$.

Assume that M_x is at $+M_r$ for negative values of x and changes linearly to $-M_r$ over the distance Δx. The subsequent, more general example shows that such a transition used in the reciprocity expression of (5.6-6) results in

$$|V_s(t)| = vW_2 \int_{-T/2}^{T/2} \int_0^{\Delta x} kS_x \, dz \, dx_m \qquad (5.6\text{-}8)$$

where $k = 2M_r/\Delta x$.

If we further assume Δx is very small such that S_x is essentially a constant over Δx, the integral with respect to dx is that of a constant or

$$|V_s(t)| = vW_2 \int_{-T/2}^{T/2} (kS_x \Delta x) dz \qquad (5.6\text{-}9)$$

But

$$k\Delta x = \frac{2M_r}{\Delta x} \Delta x = 2M_r \qquad (5.6\text{-}10)$$

Substitution of (5.6-10) in (5.6-9) simplifies the latter to

$$|V_s(t)| = vW_2 \int_{-T/2}^{T/2} 2M_r(x_p, z)S_x \, dz \qquad (5.6\text{-}11)$$

This is a more specific form of reciprocity. The final and most useful form can be obtained by assuming that the thickness of the medium is very small such that S_x does not vary substantially over T (we assumed that M_x does not vary with z). If this is true, the above integral over dz becomes an integral of a constant or

$$|V_s(t)| = vW_2 T2M_r S_x \quad \text{volts} \qquad (5.6\text{-}12)$$

where $v =$ velocity (m/sec)

$\quad W_2 =$ width of magnetized region (m) (track width)

$\quad\ \, T =$ thickness of medium (m)

$\quad M_r =$ residual magnetization (A/m)

$\quad\ S_x = x$ component of sensitivity function (H/m^2; includes the turns N_R on the read head*)

The signal polarity is determined as shown in Fig. 5.6-2.

For the simplified form to be valid, recall that it is necessary for both Δx and T to be small enough to prevent S_x from varying substantially over these dimensions. If this is not true, we can break the various dimensions into smaller regions for which it is true, then integrate over each region separately.

---

* If S_x is given per turn, multiply by N_R.

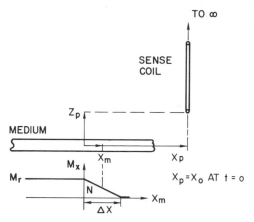

FIGURE 5.6-3 Coordinate system and magnetization variation for a linear transition from $+M_x$ to 0.

Since the separate integrals are all constants that are linearly added, we are permitted to use superposition as in Section 5.4 to construct the total signal. If we have a step function change in M_x, clearly Δx is vanishingly small and one part of the requirement is valid.

EXAMPLE

Let us use the reciprocity theorem to calculate the signal produced by one magnetic transition of any length Δx, with only horizontal magnetization in a very thin medium, using the sensitivity function of an infinitely thin sense coil. The medium is assumed to have magnetization as in Fig. 5.6-3. It is fully magnetized at M_r for negative x_m and decreases to zero over a transition region of length Δx and is zero thereafter.* At time $t = 0$, the origin of the medium is separated from the sense coil by a distance $x_p = x_0$ as shown. The medium moves toward the right, which means that x_p changes as $x_p = x_0 - vt$. The medium magnetization is

$$M_x = M_r\left(1 - \frac{x_m}{\Delta x}\right) \tag{5.6-13}$$

The derivative of M_x with respect to x is obviously zero except in the transition region, where it is equal to $-k'$, where

$$k' = \frac{M_r}{\Delta x} \tag{5.6-14}$$

* The required south poles would be at some distance to the far left.

Substituting this into (5.6-6) and changing the limits on x from 0 to Δx, we get

$$|V_x(t)| = vW_2 \int_{-T/2}^{T/2} dz_p \int_0^{\Delta x} k' S_x(x_p - x_m, z_p) dx_m \qquad (5.6\text{-}15)$$

where k' is half the value of k in (5.6-10) because of the different magnetization state. This of course changes the amplitude but not the analytical form of the signal. Since the medium is assumed to be very thin, the integral over dz_p is a constant equal to T, and (5.6-15) reduces to

$$|V_x(t)| = vW_2 Tk' \int_0^{\Delta x} S_x(x_p - x_m, z_p) dx_m \qquad (5.6\text{-}16)$$

To obtain an analytical expression for the signal, we need a sensitivity function. If we assume a very thin sense coil of N_R turns, the sensitivity function is obtained by substituting (2.12-12) or (5.3-19) into (5.6-1) with appropriate coordinate variables, giving

$$S_x = \frac{\mu N_R}{2\pi} \frac{z_p}{z_p^2 + (x_p - x_m)^2} \qquad (5.6\text{-}17)$$

Substituting this into (5.6-16) gives

$$|V_x(t)| = \frac{vW_2 Tk'}{2\pi} \mu N_R z_p \int_0^{\Delta x} \frac{dx_m}{z_p^2 + (x_p - x_m)^2} \qquad (5.6\text{-}18)$$

Integration of this equation and substitution of (5.6-14) for k' gives the final signal as

$$|V_x(t)| = \frac{\mu v W_2 T}{2\pi} N_R \frac{M_r}{\Delta x} \left(\tan^{-1} \frac{x_p - \Delta x}{z_p} - \tan^{-1} \frac{x_p}{z_p} \right) \qquad (5.6\text{-}19)$$

This normalized voltage, as expressed by the arctangent terms in parentheses, is plotted in Fig. 5.6-4 versus normalized distance x_p/z_p for one case of $\Delta x = z_p$. The peak occurs at the point $x_p/z_p = 0.5$, since the middle of the transition Δx occurs at this point for this case.

The same voltage expression can be obtained by expressing the linear transition of width Δx by a constant pole charge density of ρ_v poles per unit volume over the same distance Δx. However the analysis is much more complicated compared to that using the reciprocity theorem. Hence the latter is more desirable.

In general, the reciprocity theorem is valid for any linear head whose sensitivity function or external field can be constructed from equivalent

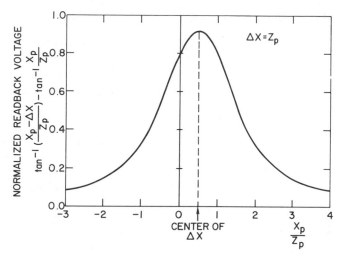

FIGURE 5.6-4 Normalized readback voltage for linear transition of width $\Delta x = z_p$ in a very thin medium read by a narrow gap head.

current loops or sheets. For the general case when both the sensitivity function and medium magnetization are complex functions of x and z, the determination of the signal can become somewhat complex. Fortunately the simple expression of (5.6-12) for a step function magnetization transition is often a reasonable first approximation. The nonlinear character of the medium produces very narrow transitions Δx. If S_x varies significantly over Δx, the transition can be represented as a superposition of smaller transitions as previously discussed. A more serious problem is the linearity of the readback process. Because of the air gap in the read head, the current is linearly related to the flux through the head. However during readback a small transition is moving past a complex magnetic head structure, and the actual flux pickup by the head is difficult to calculate in any general way. If the head structure is idealized, the entire readback becomes linear and simplified.

Reciprocity is important because S_x or B_x for a given read head configuration can be calculated or measured, and the result gives the response for the step function transition. Of course we could start with a step function and just measure the sense signal as a function of time, eliminating all this messy detail with sensitivity functions. However such a case becomes more difficult to simulate accurately as density increases and all dimensions get smaller. We can calculate approximate $B_x(x, z)$ more readily, hence the best possible response can be found from a given head design. Other practical factors make it worse but the limit is at least known.

5.7 DENSITY–LIMITING FACTORS

Two fundamental limits to the theoretical maximum recording density are the signal to noise ratio of the readback process and the particle size limits of the medium. An analysis of the channel signal to noise for reasonable ultimate parameters gives linear densities in the range of 5×10^5 bpi and areal densities greater than 10^{10} bits/in.^{2}

The ultimate possible bit density that can be tolerated by the medium itself is determined by the size of the magnetic particles. This assumes that the read/write heads and other engineering design goals can be achieved to reach the limits, which may or may not be true. The particle must remain magnetized against the destructive forces of self-demagnetization as well as thermal energy. Using either acicular particles for their shape anisotropy, or materials with large crystalline anisotropy, known materials could conceivably give densities of 10^{10} to 10^{11} particles/in.^{2} with a thermal relaxation time (to spontaneously reverse) of 30 years. Assuming that the remainder of the system could store one bit per particle, this becomes the areal density. Thus both the channel noise and particle size limitations appear to be capable of more than 10^{10} bits/in.^{2} as an ultimate limit. The most advanced magnetic recording system, projected for the 1980s, is in the range of (roughly) 50K bpi $\times$ 2000 tpi, giving a density of about 10^8 bits/in.^{2}. This is clearly a long way from the theoretical limit cited.

5.7.1 Practical Density

As in all engineering design that attempts to achieve the ultimate in sophistication, a compromise between conflicting demands is necessary. So it is in magnetic recording that the practical factors tending to give high density in one respect tend to reduce the density in another way. We have seen that writing is not the problem as far as density is concerned; rather, the difficulty lies in the readback process. Since the read signals are already quite small, it is desirable to increase the sense signal, or at least keep it constant. Large sense signal implies a large medium thickness (i.e., large amplitude of S_x or inductance), large B_r, and a very narrow sensitivity function, to avoid bit crowding and peak shift. In addition to large sense signal amplitude, for the read-back process it is desirable to have a self-clocking coding scheme to ensure good discrimination for conversion of the code to binary.

If we write the data at high density, the separation between the ideal transition simply gets smaller, which produces a larger self-demagnetizing field and requires a larger coercive force to support this self-demagnetization if we wish to keep B_r fixed. To prevent degradation of the sense signal as the density increases, it is necessary to reduce the medium thickness to avoid speading of the signal as in Fig. 5.4-8 from an effective change in the head to medium spacing.

To prevent further signal degradation from bit crowding and peak shift, it is necessary to have a narrow sensitivity function, which means a small air gap in the read head. A small gap reduces the external flux or $H_x(x)$, and since we have already indicated that a large H_c is necessary to support the larger self-demagnetizing field, we must use a larger write current or more turns on the write head, and both alternatives are undesirable. More turns means larger inductance, with a larger head time constant; to switch the write current in a larger inductance and achieve the desired density, we may have to slow down the medium motion, thus compromising the access time.

5.7.2 Media

The practical limit on the transition region length Δx, hence the practical density the medium can support in typical medium coatings, arises primarily from the limits of self-demagnetization. If the transition region is too small, the self-demagnetization field will exceed the coercive force; therefore some demagnetization or spreading of the transition region will occur until Δx is large enough to just be balanced by the coercive force (see Section 5.8). Under the assumption of magnetization only in the x direction (plane of the medium) and assuming one arctangent transition within the medium, as discussed in Section 5.8, the self-demagnetizing field can be calculated everywhere within the medium. The condition for minimum transition length is that the maximum self-demagnetizing field be equal to or less than H_c. Using this with the assumption that the transition length (yet to be determined) is much greater than the medium thickness, the minimum length is given by (5.8-29) or

$$\Delta x_{min} = \pi a_{min} = \frac{\pi T}{4}\left(\csc\frac{H_c}{8I_r} - 1\right) \qquad \text{for } H_c < 4\pi I_r = B_r, \quad (5.7\text{-}1)$$

$$\Delta x_{min} = 0 \qquad \text{for} \quad H_c > 4\pi I_r = B_r \qquad\qquad (5.7\text{-}2)$$

Thus we realize the importance of H_c in determining density; in particular, as H_c becomes equal to or larger than the maximum possible self-demagnetizing field for any geometry, (5.7-2) shows that the transition length Δx approaches zero, as would be expected, and is in agreement with that derived previously by other considerations.

Equation 5.7-1 can be further simplified by assuming the medium thickness to be much smaller than a, giving

$$\Delta x_{min} = 2\pi T \frac{I_r}{H_c} \qquad \text{for} \quad T \ll a \qquad\qquad (5.7\text{-}3)$$

where I_r is in emu per cubic centimeters and H_c in oersteds.

It is interesting to note that the quantity $T(I_r/H_c)$ is often used as a figure of merit for recording surfaces, which is quite reasonable because it expresses very roughly the density capability of the medium *and* the recording system. For small Δx, hence high density, we wish to make $T(I_r/H_c)$ very small. To get large signals, however, the quantity TI_r should be large, and to enable the electronics to provide the necessary write currents and head fields with fast rise time pulses, H_c should be as small as possible.* Thus the recording system (reading, writing, and electronics) requires this quantity to be very large (i.e., TI_r large, H_c small), and it is not surprising that it represents a type of overall balance of the system.

5.8   THEORETICAL ANALYSIS OF RECORDED TRANSITIONS AND READBACK WAVE FORMS

This chapter has emphasized that linear density in terms of transitions per unit length is limited not by the writing process but by the readback process. As the density increases, however, the specific characteristics of the transitions, and their mutual interactions, can influence the readback process in subtle but important ways. Thus a complete understanding calls for knowledge of both the magnetization pattern induced during writing and the voltage wave form generated by this pattern during reading. Ideally, we would like to be able to determine the exact magnetization pattern, which includes the transition regions, as a function of position, then to use this pattern to determine the exact readback signal. These variables should be obtained in terms of the physical and magnetic properties of the recording system such as the medium thickness, coercive force H_c, residual magnetization M_r, nonlinear permeability (BH loop), head to medium spacing, and write and read head air gap length. Unfortunately the real problem is much too complex to allow this.

In Sections 5.3, particularly Figs. 5.3-2 and 5.3-3, we graphically derived **M** versus x for a very idealized case, and assuming that the self-demagnetization field is known. This is not the case; rather, the self-demagnetization field H_D must be calculated from the magnetization pattern. The self-demagnetizing force is a function of the geometrical position of the magnetic poles and cannot be determined until **M** versus space is known. But since **M** experiences a reverse field from the self-demagnetization, H_D and **M** are interrelated and require a self-consistent calculation to be exact. The problem is complicated further because the magnetization in the medium has a small reversible component (minor loops) that reduces M_r slightly when the head

---

* For example, from (2.6-1) the write field is portional to the ampere-turns on the head, and large H_c requires large write currents. Large current with fast rise times require special circuits, whereas small currents can be supplied with small integrated circuits.

is removed far from the medium, but increases M_r when the head is brought near once again. To make the problem manageable, various simplifying assumptions are used in practice. We now investigate several approaches to see how they approximate or relate to the actual problem. We deal separately with calculation of the magnetization pattern in terms of the transition length, and the calculation or determination of the readback signal from this transition.

5.8.1 Transition Length

There are two typical methods of calculating the magnetic transition length, and both make use of simplifying assumptions. In both approaches the medium magnetization is assumed not to vary with distance into the medium (i.e., no variation of **M** with thickness). This is probably a reasonable assumption for thin media, but not for thick media. Such a variation across the thickness theoretically could be obtained with a computer solution, but it is extremely complex and would require excessive computation time. Thus no accurate knowledge of the magnetization variation through the thickness is available. It should be pointed out that such variations through the thickness are sometimes given but are basically incorrect. For instance Pear (1967) gives such a pattern based on the write head field pattern and an assumed BH loop for the bit in which the latter implicitly assumes a value for the self-demagnetizing field of the bit. But this self-demagnetizing field cannot be calculated until **M** as a function of position is known, and vice versa, and this requires a "self-consistent" calculation. Hence the magnetization pattern derived in such a fashion is fundamentally incorrect; it may turn out that the final self-consistent calculation does not (or does) change the pattern drastically, but this must be shown, not assumed. All the theoretical analyses that follow are based on the assumption of no variation in the magnetization pattern with thickness.

In the first and most common approach for analyzing the transition pattern, the functional form of M_x as a function of distance x is assumed; then the length of the transition region Δx is calculated. This approach permits analytical relationships to be derived between the quantities of interest, since simple analytical functions of M as a function of position are reasonable.

In the second approach, the functional variation of **M** with distance is not assumed; instead the value of **M** is determined by a self-consistent calculation based on iteration of points within a grid. A value of **M** is assumed at each point of the grid, the total H field at each point is evaluated to see whether it satisfies the necessary conditions on **M** as a function of H (intrinsic BH loop), adjustments to **M** are made where necessary (iterations), and the problem is recalculated until the solution converges.

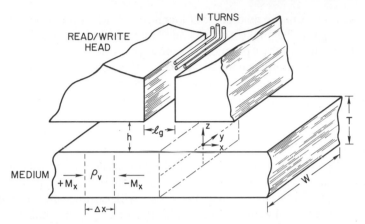

FIGURE 5.8-1   Geometry and coordinate system used for theoretical analysis.

In the first analysis, we determine the maximum self-demagnetizing field as a function of transition width Δx for two different assumed functions of **M** versus x. This maximum self-demagnetizing field is set equal to the coercive force and the value of Δx that satisfies this requirement can be easily determined. In these calculations with assumed M_x as a function of x, it is implicitly assumed that during writing, the recording head effectively shunts part of the external field of a transition to reduce the self-demagnetization to a value such that the written transition is smaller than the final value. When the head is removed, the ensuing self-demagnetizing field causes the transition to increase in size until the maximum value of self-demagnetizing field equals H_c, with the magnetization versus x following the assumed functional form.

Referring to Figs. 5.8-1 and 5.8-2, the magnetization is assumed to lie entirely along the x direction (no y or z components) and to be a constant value of $+M_r$ or $-M_r$ at all points except within the transition regions Δx. There must always be at least two transition regions with $+\rho_v$ and $-\rho_v$ and usually more. We are interested in calculating the length Δx of one transition region, which requires calculation of the total internal H field (self-demagnetizing field) within the region Δx; this field within one Δx region will change if other opposite-poled adjacent regions are too close, giving a larger self-demagnetizing field. For the moment, we assume that the spacing between transitions is large, and only the volume pole density of one region need be considered. We allow closer spacing later to demonstrate the effect. We use two functional forms for $M(x)$, namely, a linear and an arctangent function.

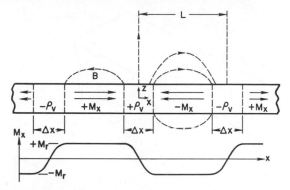

Figure 5.8-2   Medium with transitions and only x components of magnetization.

Linear M_x Versus x

Here we have

$$M_x = \frac{2M_r x}{\Delta x} \tag{5.8-1}$$

This requires a volume pole distribution given by

$$\nabla \cdot M = -\rho_v \tag{5.8-2}$$

but

$$\nabla \cdot M = \frac{dM_x}{dx} = \frac{2M_r}{\Delta x}$$

hence

$$\rho_v = \frac{-2M_r}{\Delta x} \tag{5.8-3}$$

or a constant charge density thoroughout the region Δx.

We assume a very wide recorded bit in the y direction so that $W \gg T$, $W \gg \Delta x$ and calculate the field for any position x, z inside and outside the transition region. The constant charge density within a transition region can be broken into a large number of elemental sections, and one is shown in Fig. 5.8-3. Each element has a length W and cross-sectional area $dx\,dz$. We wish to calculate the magnetizing field produced by this element at any given point in space, and to integrate over all such constant charge elements of the transition region Δx. We are only interested in the maximum value of

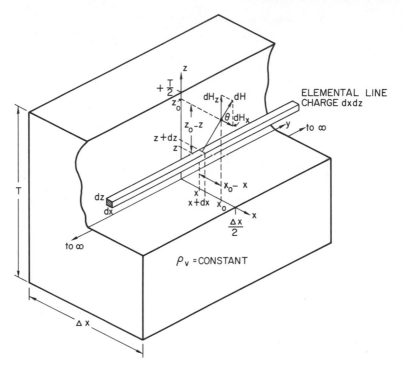

Figure 5.8-3 Transition region Δx with constant ρ_v broken into elemental line charges of cross-sectional area $dx\, dz$.

this field within the transition, which occurs along the middle plane formed by the xz axes. Since the width W of the transition is assumed to be much larger than either the transition length Δx or medium thickness T, the field of each elemental section can be considered to be that of an infinite line charge with a charge per unit length of $\rho_v\, dx\, dz$. The field at the center of an infinite line pole charge is

$$dH = \frac{4\pi\rho_v}{2\pi r}\, dx\, dz \qquad (5.8\text{-}4)$$

Substituting (5.8-3) for ρ_v gives

$$dH = \frac{4 I_r}{\Delta x r}\, dx\, dz \qquad (5.8\text{-}5)$$

Where H is in oersteds and M or I in emu per cubic centimeter.

The field components within the xz plane at any general point P with coordinates x_0 and z_0 are given by

$$dH_x(x_0, z_0) = dH \cos \theta = \frac{4I_r}{\Delta x} \frac{x_0 - x}{(x_0 - x)^2 + (z_0 - z)^2} \, dx \, dz \quad (5.8\text{-}6)$$

$$dH_y(x_0, z_0) = 0 \quad (5.8\text{-}7)$$

$$dH_z(x_0, z_0) = dH \sin \theta = \frac{4I_r}{\Delta x} \frac{z_0 - z}{(x_0 - x)^2 + (z_0 - z)^2} \, dx \, dz \quad (5.8\text{-}8)$$

Integration gives

$$
\begin{aligned}
H_x(x_0, z_0) &= \int_{-\Delta x/2}^{\Delta x/2} \int_{-T/2}^{T/2} \frac{4I_r}{\Delta x} \frac{x_0 - x}{(x_0 - x)^2 + (z_0 - z)^2} \, dx \, dz \quad (5.8\text{-}9) \\
&= \frac{2I_r}{\Delta x} \left[A \ln \frac{C^2 + A^2}{D^2 + A^2} + B \ln \frac{D^2 + B^2}{C^2 + B^2} \right. \\
&\quad \left. + 2C \left(\tan^{-1} \frac{A}{C} - \tan^{-1} \frac{B}{C} \right) + 2D \left(\tan^{-1} \frac{B}{D} - \tan^{-1} \frac{A}{D} \right) \right]
\end{aligned}
$$

$$(5.8\text{-}10)$$

$$
\begin{aligned}
H_z(x_0, z_0) &= \frac{2I_r}{\Delta x} \left[C \ln \frac{C^2 + A^2}{B^2 + C^2} + D \ln \frac{D^2 + B^2}{A^2 + D^2} \right. \\
&\quad \left. + 2A \left(\tan^{-1} \frac{C}{A} - \tan^{-1} \frac{D}{A} \right) + 2B \left(\tan^{-1} \frac{D}{B} - \tan^{-1} \frac{C}{B} \right) \right]
\end{aligned}
$$

$$(5.8\text{-}11)$$

where

$$A = z_0 - \frac{T}{2}, \qquad C = x_0 - \frac{\Delta x}{2} \quad (5.8\text{-}12)$$

$$B = z_0 + \frac{T}{2}, \qquad D = x_0 + \frac{\Delta x}{2} \quad (5.8\text{-}13)$$

These fields are the self-demagnetizing fields at any point x_0, z_0. We wish now to determine the point at which the H_x field is maximum, to be able to specify that this maximum self-demagnetization must just equal the coercive force, then calculate from (5.8-10) the value of Δx that will satisfy the condition.* This point of maximum self-demagnetization occurs at $z_0 = 0$ and $x_0 = \Delta x/2$, which is at the edge of the transition and in the center plane

---

* Note that H_z is nonzero except at $x = 0$, hence tends to align the magnetization with a vertical component M_z; but we have assumed this away in the analysis.

formed by the xy axis. This can more easily be seen by first letting $z_0 = 0$ to get

$$H_x(x_0)\Big|_{z_0 = 0} = \frac{2I_r}{\Delta x}\left[T \ln\frac{D^2 + T^2/4}{C^2 + T^2/4} + 4\left(D \tan^{-1}\frac{T}{2D} - C \tan^{-1}\frac{T}{2C}\right)\right]$$

(5.8-14)

We know from first principles that since the net magnetization I is zero at $x_0 = 0$, the self-demagnetizing field must be zero, and this is found to be the case if substituted into the equation. The maximum value of H_x occurs at $x_0 = \Delta x/2$ or $D = \Delta x$, $C = 0$, and equating that to H_c gives

$$H_x\Big|_{\substack{x_0 = \Delta x/2 \\ z_0 = 0}} = H_c = 2I_r\left[\frac{T}{\Delta x}\ln\left(1 + \frac{4\Delta x^2}{T^2}\right) + 4\tan^{-1}\frac{T}{2\Delta x}\right]$$ (5.8-15)

We can perform a simple limit check on the foregoing analysis as follows: if the transition length goes to 0, the demagnetizing field becomes that of an infinitely thin, infinitely wide plane. Therefore letting $\Delta x = 0$ in (5.8-15), the ln term is zero, $\tan^{-1}(T/2\Delta x) = \pi/2$, and

$$H_D = 2\frac{I_r}{\Delta x}\left(4\Delta x\frac{\pi}{2}\right) = 4\pi I_r$$

as it should be.

The transition length Δx from (5.8-15) involves a transcendental equation. Some simplified expressions can be obtained for certain limiting cases. For instance, if $4\Delta x^2/T^2 \ll 1$, then

$$\ln\left(1 + \frac{4\Delta x^2}{T^2}\right) \approx \frac{4\Delta x^2}{T^2}$$ (5.8-16)

and (5.8-15) simplifies to

$$H_c = 2I_r\left(\frac{4\Delta x}{T} + 4\tan^{-1}\frac{T}{2\Delta x}\right)$$ (5.8-17)

But since $\Delta x/T \ll 1$ and $\tan^{-1}(T/2\Delta)$ is on the order of unity to $\pi/2$ radians, the first term is negligible and

$$H_c\Big|_{(4\Delta x^2/T^2) \ll 1} \approx 8I_r\tan^{-1}\frac{T}{2\Delta x}$$ (5.8-18)

or

$$\Delta x = \frac{1}{2}\frac{T}{\tan(H_c/8I_r)} = \frac{T}{2}\cot\frac{H_c}{8I_r}$$ (5.8-19)

Once again, as a check, when $H_c = 4\pi I$, the transition length should reduce to zero. If this value is substituted for H_c in (5.8-19), $\cot(H_c/8I_r) = \cot(\pi/2) = 0$, and Δx reduces to zero as it should. Equation 5.8-19 is an approximation often seen, but it contains many unrealistic implicit assumptions. It obviously is good only for cases when the transition length is much smaller than the medium thickness and also only when the vertical component of magnetization is negligible. These two conditions are contradictory: a large Δx transition in a thin medium (i.e., $\Delta x/T \gg 1$) will have the magnetization mainly in the x direction, but a small Δx transition in a thick medium as assumed in (5.8-18) will have a z component of I. In addition, (5.8-19) is not satisfied for any useful recording materials. For instance, for (5.8-19) to be valid we must have $\Delta x/T = \frac{1}{2} \cot(H_c/8I_r) \ll 1$ or $H_c/8I_r \ll \pi/4$. If we choose an upper limit of $H_c/8I_r = \pi/4$ this requires

$$H_c \gtrsim \frac{\pi}{4} 8I_r = 2\pi I_r \qquad (5.8\text{-}20)$$

Even for γFe_2O_3, I_r is in the range of 100 emu/cc, requiring $H_c \gtrsim 628$ Oe which is not obtained with this material. For other suitable materials (e.g., metals), H_c is higher, but I_r is considerably larger, too (e.g., $H_c \approx 800$ Oe but $I_r \approx 800$ emu/cm^3). Thus (5.8-19) is not very practical and (5.8-15) must be used. Nevertheless, some conclusions are possible from (5.8-19). To make the transition small, it is necessary to have a large ratio H_c/I_r and/or small T. Thus the dependence on medium parameters is evident—for a given magnetization I_r, higher density as determined only by self-demagnetization requires thinner media and larger H_c, as could be determined from first principles without such lengthy analysis.

Arctangent I_x Versus x

It is assumed that the magnetization follows the function

$$I_x = \frac{2}{\pi} I_r \tan^{-1} \frac{x}{a} \qquad (5.8\text{-}21)$$

as in Fig. 5.8-4. The transition length is usually taken arbitrarily as the intercept on the x/a axis of the tangent to the curve at $x = 0$ as shown. This intercept occurs at a value of $x_0/a = \pi/2$ for which $I/I_r = 2/\pi$. Since the transition extends symmetrically on both sides of the origin, the transition length must be twice the x_0/a intercept or

$$\frac{\Delta x}{a} = \frac{2x_0}{a} = \pi \qquad (5.8\text{-}22)$$

or

$$\Delta x = \pi a \qquad (5.8\text{-}23)$$

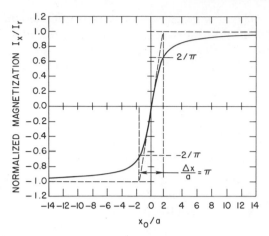

FIGURE 5.8-4 Assumed arctangent magnetization function $I_x/I_r = (2/\pi)\tan^{-1}(x/a)$, transition length $\Delta x = \pi a$.

To find Δx it is necessary to determine a. Again the magnetization is assumed to be only in the x direction (i.e., no z or y component). We can now proceed exactly as previously in the linear case except

$$-\rho_v = \nabla \cdot I = \frac{dI_x}{dx} = \frac{2I_r}{\pi} \frac{a}{x^2 + a^2} \tag{5.8-24}$$

Solution of this equation gives the x and z components everywhere (Potter, 1970), both inside and outside the medium, as

$$H_x(x_0, z_0) = 4I_r \left[\tan^{-1} \frac{(T/2 + z_0)x_0}{x_0^2 + z^2 + a(|T/2 + z_0|)} \right.$$

$$\left. + \tan^{-1} \frac{(T/2 - z_0)x_0}{x_0^2 + a^2 + a(|T/2 - z_0|)} \right] \tag{5.8-25}$$

$$H_z(x_0, z_0) = 2I_r \ln \frac{x_0^2 + (|T/2 + z_0| + a)^2}{x_0^2 + (|T/2 - z_0| + a)^2} \tag{5.8-26}$$

where I_r is in emu per cubic centimeter (and in x direction only) and H is in oersteds.

The maximum total self-demagnetizing field (sum of x and z components) occurs at the medium surface $z = T/2$ and near the edge of the transition (note there is no sharp boundary for ρ_v as in the linear case, since a small ρ_v exists for a very long x distance). This results because there is a significant z component H_z, which is larger than H_x over this portion of the transition

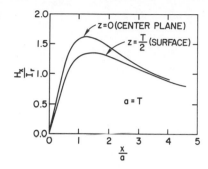

FIGURE 5.8-5 The x component of the self-demagnetizing field versus x for two values of z, assuming an arctangent magnetization transition with $a = T$.

for thick media. However since we assumed that there was no z component of magnetization, we implicitly assume that other mechanisms make the vertical self-demagnetizing field unimportant. This is nearly true—particle shape anisotropy (Section 5.2) and alignment keep the vertical component, which we assumed to be zero, relatively small. Thus since we need be concerned only with the x component, H_x is maximum along the center plane $z = 0$ at a distance of about $x/a = 1.3$. This is shown in Fig. 5.8-5, where H_x versus x is plotted for both the surface and center plane ($z = T/2$ and 0). If we set $H_x(\text{max})$ at $z = 0$ equal to H_c, the result is

$$H_x(\text{max})\bigg|_{z=0} = H_c = 8I_r \tan^{-1}\left[\frac{T}{4a}\left(1 + \frac{T}{2a}\right)^{1/2}\right] \qquad (5.8\text{-}27)$$

To find the minimum transition lengths, we must solve (5.8-27) for the minimum a or, upon inverting,

$$a_{\min} = \frac{T}{4}\left(\csc\frac{H_c}{8I_r} - 1\right) \qquad (5.8\text{-}28)$$

Since by definition we arbitrarily specify $\Delta x = \pi a$, we have

$$\Delta x(\text{min}) = \frac{\pi T}{4}\left(\csc\frac{H_c}{8I_r} - 1\right) \qquad (5.8\text{-}29)$$

for any value of $\Delta x/T$, provided $H_c \leq 4\pi I_r$.

As a check, we know from first principles that when $H_c = 4\pi I_r$, the transition length should reduce to zero. If we substitute this value for H_c in (5.8-29), $\csc H_c/8I_r = \csc \pi/2 = 1$ and Δx goes to zero.

Although the functional form of (5.8-29) is different from that derived previously for a linear M versus x assumption (5.8-19), the major conclusions remain the same; namely, Δx varies directly with T, and decreasing Δx requires an increase in H_c/I_r. Figure 5.8-6 plots (5.8-15) (linear transition) and (5.8-29) (arctangent transition) in normalized form to show the variation of

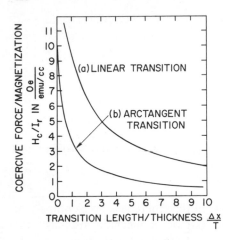

Figure 5.8-6 Coercive force versus ratio of transition length to thickness for assumed linear and arctangent transitions.

transition length versus H_c. For γFe_2O_3 on tape, I_r is about 100 emu/cc and H_c about 300 Oe, giving $H_c/I_r = 3$. From Fig. 5.8-6, this would require $\Delta x/T$ of 6 and 1.4 for the linear and arctangent transitions, respectively. We can easily understand why the linear transition function gives a larger $\Delta x/T$ than the arctangent by plotting the self-demagnetizing field as a function of x for the two cases (Fig. 5.8-7). The x component of field at the edge of the transition is more than twice as large for the linear case, hence would be

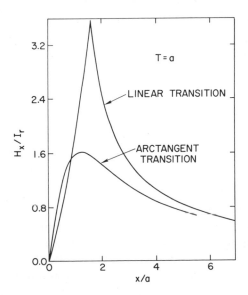

FIGURE 5.8-7 Comparison of demagnetizing fields for linear and arctangent transitions of equal length along the center line $z = 0$, $y = 0$. After Potter (1970).

expected to give a much larger Δx.* The arctangent function appears to be a more reasonable approximation than the linear function. We compare these with the self-consistent calculations later in this section.

When the medium is very thin such that $T \ll a$, a simple expression can be obtained for the transition length. If we let $T/a \ll 1$ and recognize that $\tan^{-1} \theta \approx \theta$ for very small arguments, (5.8-27) becomes

$$H_c \bigg|_{T/a \ll 1} = 8I_r \frac{T}{4a} \tag{5.8-30}$$

or

$$a = 2T\frac{I_r}{H_c} \tag{5.8-31}$$

Hence the transition length becomes

$$\Delta x \bigg|_{T/a \ll 1} = \pi a = 2\pi T \frac{I_r}{H_c} \tag{5.8-32}$$

This is a well-known expression derived in Bonyhard et al. (1966) specifically for thin media. It is seen to be a limiting case of the thick media, as it should be. However a word of caution is necessary about the use of the general equation in the foregoing analysis, particularly (5.8-29) for transition length. It was assumed that the z component of magnetization is zero, which is more nearly true in thin media with $T/a \ll 1$. For thick media into which narrow transitions are written, a vertical magnetization component will appear, violating the assumptions on which the analysis was based.

For the more general case we should include a vertical component of magnetization M_z, as in Fig. 5.4-9. Since the medium parameters are chosen to minimize this component, we might expect it to be small: M_z is typically estimated to be less than 20% of the horizontal component. Hence it is reasonable to calculate Δx assuming only an M_x; if we know the value of M_z, this can be included, assuming it also follows an arctangent function given by

$$\mathbf{M} = \frac{2}{\pi}(iM_x - jM_z)\arctan\frac{x}{a} \tag{5.8-33}$$

As before, there is no variation with z, only with x.

In Section 5.4 (e.g., Fig. 5.4-9) we graphically constructed the total readback signal expected when a vertical magnetization component is present, using the reciprocity theorem. Under the assumption that both components

---

* For the arctangent function H_z is larger than H_x over considerable portions; thus the $\int H \cdot dl$ is preserved for both linear and arctangent cases.

follow the arctangent function of x, that there is no z variation, and that the magnitudes of M_x and M_z are known, the readback voltage as a function of time can be specified exactly. One further unknown is the sensitivity function for the read head. Assuming the idealized Karlquist head, (5.3-12) and (5.3-13) give us the necessary form for $H = H_x + H_z$. Using all the foregoing assumptions, the readback voltage for horizontal and vertical arctangent magnetization functions is obtained* by combining (5.6-6) and (5.6-7) into the generalized form

$$V_{sig}(\bar{x}) = 4\pi v N_R W \times 10^{-8} \int_{-\infty}^{\infty} \int_{h}^{h+T} \frac{\partial M(x - \bar{x}, z)}{\partial \bar{x}} \cdot H(x, z) dx \, dz \quad (5.8\text{-}34)$$

$$= 4\pi v N_R W \times 10^{-8} M_x [f(\bar{x}) + f(-\bar{x})] + M_z [q(\bar{x}) - q(-\bar{x})] \quad (5.8\text{-}35)$$

where

$$f(\bar{x}) \equiv \frac{a}{\pi l_g} \int_{-\infty}^{\infty} dx \int_{h}^{h+T} \frac{\tan^{-1}[(l_g/2 + x)/z]}{(x - \bar{x})^2 + a^2} dz$$

$$= \frac{h + a + T}{l_g} \tan^{-1}\left(\frac{l_g/2 + \bar{x}}{h + a + T}\right) - \frac{h + a}{l_g}$$

$$\times \tan^{-1}\left(\frac{l_g/2 + \bar{x}}{h + a}\right) + \frac{1}{2l_g}(l_g/2 + \bar{x})$$

$$\times \ln \frac{(l_g/2 + \bar{x})^2 + (h + a + T)^2}{(l_g/2 + \bar{x})^2 + (h + a)^2}, \quad (5.8\text{-}36)$$

$$q(\bar{x}) \equiv \frac{a}{2\pi l_g} \int_{-\infty}^{\infty} dx \int_{h}^{h+T} \frac{\ln[(l_g/2 + x)^2 + z^2]}{(x - \bar{x})^2 + z^2} dz$$

$$= \frac{h + a + T}{2l_g} \ln[(l_g/2 + \bar{x})^2 + (h + a + T)^2]$$

$$- \frac{h + a}{2l_g} \ln[(l_g/2 + \bar{x})^2 + (h + a)^2]$$

$$= \frac{1}{l_g}(l_g/2 + \bar{x})\left[\tan^{-1}\frac{l_g/2 + \bar{x}}{h + a + T} - \tan^{-1}\frac{l_g/2 + \bar{x}}{h + a}\right]. \quad (5.8\text{-}37)$$

* The signal polarity in (5.8-35) can be positive or negative depend'.g on winding direction, connection to oscilloscope, and so on; it is important only to be consistent and to maintain the same polarity throughout.

where N_R = number of turns on read head

$\quad\quad v$ = velocity (cm/sec)

$\quad\quad \bar{x}$ = vt ($=x_p$ in Section 5.6)

$\quad\quad W$ = track width (cm)

$\quad M_x, M_z$ = horizontal and vertical magnetization (emu/cc: same as I_x/I_r)

$\quad\quad h$ = head to medium spacing (cm)

$\quad\quad l_g$ = head air gap (cm)

$\quad\quad T$ = medium thickness (cm)

$\quad\quad a$ = arctangent transition parameter = $\Delta x/\pi$

$\quad \Delta x$ = horizontal spacing between points where M_x/M_r crosses the $\pm(2/\pi)$ amplitude values

$\quad V_{\text{sig}}$ = total readback signal (V)

Note that a and h always appear additive together, hence their separate effects on the signal are not separable. These expressions reduce to simpler forms under certain simplifying conditions. For instance, if the air gap becomes much smaller than the other dimensions, we have

$$|V_{\text{sig}}|\Big|_{l_g \to 0} = 8N_R vW \times 10^{-8}\left\{\frac{M_x}{2} \ln \frac{\bar{x}^2 + (h + a + T)^2}{\bar{x}^2 + (h + a)^2}\right.$$

$$\left. - M_z\left[\tan^{-1}\frac{\bar{x}}{h + a + T} - \tan^{-1}\frac{\bar{x}}{h + a}\right]\right\} \quad (5.8\text{-}38)$$

This equation shows clearly that making the air gap arbitrarily small compared to a, h, and T does *not* make the signal pulse width arbitrarily small.

If the medium thickness is made very small compared to the other dimensions, the general equation reduces to

$$V_{\text{sig}}\Big|_{T \to 0} = 8N_R vW \times 10^{-8}\frac{T}{l_g}\left[M_x \tan^{-1}\frac{l_g/2 + \bar{x}}{h + a}\right.$$

$$\left. + M_x \tan^{-1}\frac{l_g/2 - \bar{x}}{h + a} + \frac{M_z}{2} \ln \frac{(l_g/2 + \bar{x})^2 + (h + a)^2}{(l_g/2 - \bar{x})^2 + (h + a)^2}\right] \quad (5.8\text{-}39)$$

A further reduction is often possible; as T becomes much smaller than l_g, h, and Δx, the vertical magnetization becomes negligible and we could set $M_z = 0$ in most cases. Note that this is true only when T is much smaller than the other parameters. When they are all of comparable size, M_z is not necessarily negligible.

If we let just the transition parameter a become small, the expression for the voltage does not simplify greatly. However if we let both the transition length

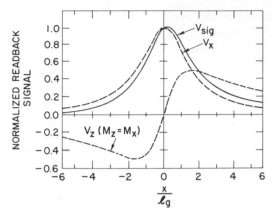

Figure 5.8-8 Readback wave form distortion resulting from vertical magnetization and an assumed arctangent transition:

$$M_z = 0.2M_x, \ T/l_g = 1.25, \ (h + a)/l_g = 1.0.$$

and medium thickness get small, the limiting expression is

$$V_{\text{sig}}\Big|_{\substack{a \to 0 \\ T \to 0}} = 8N_R vW \times 10^{-8} \frac{T}{l_g} \left[M_x \tan^{-1} \frac{l_g/2 + \bar{x}}{h} \right.$$

$$\left. + M_x \tan^{-1} \frac{l_g/2 - \bar{x}}{h} + \frac{M_z}{2} \ln \frac{(l_g/2 + \bar{x})^2 + h^2}{(l_g/2 - \bar{x})^2 + h^2} \right] \quad (5.8\text{-}40)$$

Note that in all three limiting cases, no one dimension alone can control the signal pulse width, hence density. It is clear that all four parameters, a, h, l_g, and T must be reduce roughly by proportional amounts to reduce the signal pulse width and allow higher density. This was pointed out in Section 5.7 in a general way. These relationships show the behavior more specifically.

The actual signal distortion introduced by a vertical components of magnetization can best be seen by an example. Since this tends to be a second-order effect, a large value of M_z is necessary to give significant distortion. It is possible for M_z to be 0.2 M_x in some cases, although in very thin media a smaller value is more probable. Assuming this value for M_z, the resulting signal wave form is as shown in Fig. 5.8-8: the dashed curves represent the signal components that would be obtained for only M_x, and only M_z with amplitude equal to M_x.* It can be seen that the peak is shifted slightly in the direction of medium motion as derived in Section 5.4.

---

* Recall that the total signal is obtained by adding to V_x the amount of V_z proportional to M_z (0.2V_z in this case).

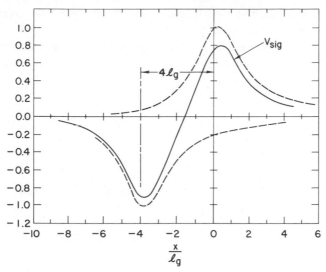

Figure 5.8-9 Readback wave form distortion resulting from both vertical magnetization and bit crowding, using two isolated arctangent transitions of Fig. 5.8-8 spaced a distance $L = 4l_g$ apart.

When bit crowding is present in addition to vertical magnetization, the single curve of Fig. 5.8-8 can be used to construct the total signal by using superposition as in Section 5.4. Figure 5.8-9 presents such a case for two arctangent-type bits with $M_z = 0.2\ M_x$ and a physical center spacing of $L = 4l_g$ (i.e., the spacing between the two isolated V_x functions of Fig. 5.8-8 is $4l_g$). As a numerical example, if $l_g = 100$ and $h = a = 50\ \mu\text{in.}$ then $T = 125$, $\Delta x = \pi a = 157$, and $L = 4l_g = 400\ \mu\text{in.}$ The spacing between bits would be $400 - 157 = 243$, which is comparable to Δx. The additional peak shift from bit crowding adds to the peak shift because of M_z on the positive pulse but subtracts from that of the negative pulse. The amplitudes of the two pulses are also different as would be expected.

5.8.2   Self-Consistent Calculation

Rather than assuming a functional form for the magnetization as a function of x, it would be desirable to calculate it from first principles while including the intrinsic magnetic BH loop characteristic of the media. This can be done to a certain limited extent by means of a self-consistent calculation. The practical complexity of the problem has still required assumption of only horizontal x components of fields, hence only for cases of the media thickness being much less than the effective length. The details of the various self-consistent calculations are much too lengthy and involved to present here.

Instead some of the more pertinent results from the rather complete and detailed calculations are summarized.

A number of rather extensive and detailed self-consistent calculations have been done under the following conditions (Potter and Schmulian, 1971):

1. Thin media of $T/l_g = 0.1$, hence only horizontal magnetization (i.e., $M_z \equiv 0$).
2. Medium characterized by typical BH loop with major and minor loops and squareness ratio $S = M_r/M_s$ (S can vary but will be 0.9 for most of the results presented here).
3. Normalized head to medium spacing $h/l_g = 0.5$.
4. Writing is performed with a write current of finite switching time, while medium moves.
5. Writing current linearly reverses polarity (e.g., $+I_0$ to $-I_0$) over a distance corresponding to a normalized medium movement of $x/l_g = 0.25$.
6. Medium magnetization is 800 emu/cc and $H_c = 300$ Oe.
7. Write and read head geometries are assumed identical for any given set of calculations.

The calculations were done for two head geometries, one with infinite pole pieces assuming Karlquist fringe fields, and another with finite pole pieces of length $l_p/l_g = 1.25$ (the actual, numerical calculations used $l_g = 1 \ \mu$).

The normalized magnetization as a function of normalized position for a single isolated transition is given in Fig. 5.8-10 for the just listed conditions. The reversal of writing current begins at the point when midpoint of the air gap is at $x = 0$. The transition length is taken to be the same as for the

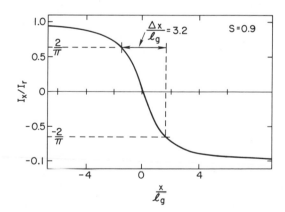

Figure 5.8-10 Normalized magnetization as a function of position, obtained from self-consistent calculation: see text for other parameters. After Potter and Schmulian (1971).

arctangent transition, namely, the distance between the plus and minus $2/\pi$ magnetization points (note that I_x/I_r approaches ± 1 asymptotically). For this case, the normalized transition is $\Delta x/l_g = 3.2$: for an air gap of $l_g = 1\ \mu$, the transition width would be $3.2\ \mu$. The linearly switching write current reverses in a normalized distance of 0.25, which is more than an order of magnitude smaller than the calculated transition length. Hence it does not contribute significantly to Δx.

These self-consistent calculations show a number of important, subtle points that *cannot* be obtained from the previous two analytical approaches. For instance, assuming $M_z = 0$, two ΔM_x transitions that are sequentially "written" and subsequently "read" (i.e., written and ready by means of self-consistent computer calculations) produce an asymmetrical readback voltage. The pulses for the two bits not only have significantly different amounts of peak shift but also significantly different amplitudes (Fig. 5.8-11c).

The significance of this analytical technique and its results can best be understood by calculating the readback signal of two transitions in a very simple way and progressively becoming more exact. Let us assume that two step function transitions (i.e., Δx approaching zero) are somehow written into the medium, separated by a normalized distance $x/l_g = 2.5$. For a Karlquist read head at a separation of $h/l_g = 0.5$ and assuming a very thin medium, the readback signal is as shown in Fig. 5.8-11a: the individual pulses for the isolated transitions are the dashed curves, and the resultant is obtained from superposition of these two, just as in Fig. 5.4-3. The two pulses must have the same amplitude and peak shift (the peak shift is insignificant with this spacing and scale). The pulses are normalized to unity at the peak. Now using the same head, the same normalized dimensions, and the same bit spacing, the self-consistent transition of Fig. 5.8-10 gives a wider transition length for z single, isolated transition. Two such readback pulses for *isolated* transitions are shown dashed in Fig. 5.8-11b, separated by the same spacing $x/l_g = 2.5$. The medium is essentially moving toward the left; therefore the first transition is centered at $x = 0$ and the second at $x/l_g = 2.5$. Each isolated pulse is slightly asymmetrical, being shifted toward the left in the direction of motion. The pulse width of these self-consistent transitions is more than double that of the step transitions in Fig. 5.8-11a. If these two pulses are superimposed, the resultant is as shown (solid). There is a significant amount of peak shift and a very slight difference in the amplitude (positive amplitude is smaller) because of the asymmetry in the isolated pulses.

Instead of superimposing the two isolated pulses of Fig. 5.8-11b, let us analytically write two transitions sequentially using self-consistent theory. The conditions under which the first and second transition are written will be substantially different; hence we might expect even greater asymmetry. The

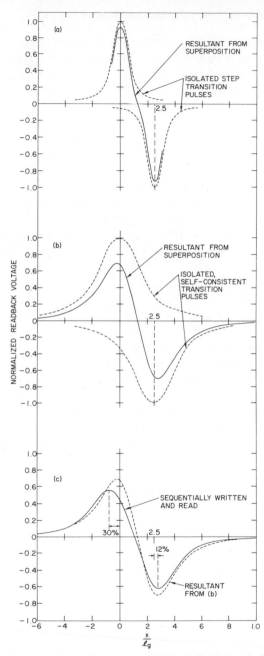

Figure 5.8-11 Comparison of calculated bit crowding readback signals for progressive refinement in the analyses, assuming only horizontal medium magnetization, a Karlquist head for writing and reading, with $h/l_g = 0.5$, $T/l_g = 0.1$, and bit spacing of $x/l_g = 2.5$.
(*a*) Superposition of two-step ΔM_x transitions.
(*b*) Superposition of two separately computed transitions using self-consistent theory.
(*c*) Self-consistent calculation of two sequentially written and read transitions: dashed curve shows resultant wave form from *b*. Curves *b* and *c* after Potter and Schmulian (1971).

calculated signal for two such sequentially written and subsequently read transitions appears in Fig. 5.8-11c. For comparison, the wave form of Fig. 5.8-11b obtained by superposition of isolated pulses is shown dashed. It can be seen that substantially more peak shift as well as amplitude difference is obtained. This comes entirely from the asymmetry in the written transitions and has two fundamental origins: (1) the writing of the second transition causes partial erasure of the first transition, (2) the total demagnetizing field acting on the first transition is larger than that on the second transition because of the assumed initial condition that the medium is everywhere at $+M_r$. These results cannot be obtained by any other analytic technique.

It should be noted that the waveform distortion obtained here for bit crowding using self-consistent theory with no vertical magnetization is similar to that obtained in Fig. 5.8-8 for an assumed arctangent magnetization with a vertical magnetization component instead of bit crowding. Another result that can only be obtained with self-consistent calculations is the effect of the BH loop squareness ratio S on the readback wave form. The effect is relatively small for modest changes in S; nevertheless decreasing S will increase the pulse width and amount of asymmetry. For instance, reducing the squareness ratio from 0.9 to 0.8 increases the readback pulse width (at the 50% level) by 4%. This would be difficult to measure accurately in a practical system, but it does show that loop squareness can be a small contributing factor to signal degradation.

5.8.3 Finite Pole Tip Head and Density

Finite pole tip heads comprise another important area in which self-consistent calculations are necessary. In the quest for even higher density and low cost, the engineer is led to consider batch fabricate heads to achieve the small dimensions required (Chynoweth et al., 1973; Chynoweth and Kayser, 1975; Romankiw and Simon, 1975). Vertical head structures have a pole tip length that is usually comparable to the gap length (Fig. 5.8-12). For such a head, the horizontal field reverses sign near the outside edges as shown. This field pattern has a very important effect on recorded transitions. Figure 5.8-13 shows the normalized readback signal for two sequentially written and subsequently read transitions with the same spacing as in Fig. 5.8-11 and with $l_p/l_g = 1.25$. The signal from the Karlquist head of Fig. 5.8-11c is given for comparison (dashed curve). Each signal is normalized to the voltage peak of its own isolate transition for that particular geometry. It can be seen in this case that the finite pole tip head produces a readback signal that is narrower and more symmetrical than the infinite (Karlquist) pole tip length head. Most of this improvement occurs during the readback process. These initial results indicate that such heads may be not only feasible but necessary for higher density.

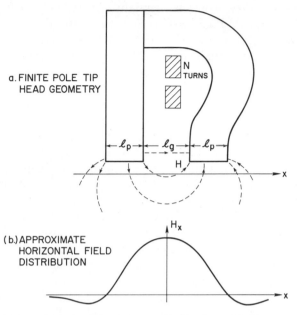

a. FINITE POLE TIP
HEAD GEOMETRY

N TURNS

ℓ_p ℓ_g ℓ_p

H

x

(b.) APPROXIMATE
HORIZONTAL FIELD
DISTRIBUTION

H_x

x

Figure 5.8-12   Finite pole tip head showing reversal of horizontal field component near outer edges of tip.

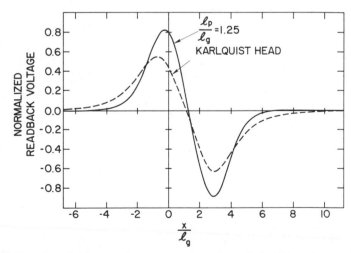

$\dfrac{\ell_p}{\ell_g}=1.25$

KARLQUIST HEAD

NORMALIZED READBACK VOLTAGE

$\dfrac{x}{\ell_g}$

Figure 5.8-13   Effect of finite pole tip head on readback wave form of two sequentially written and read transitions on $x/l_g = 2.5$ center spacing, using self-consistent calculations and $l_p/l_g = 1.25$. All other parameters and dashed curve are same as Fig. 5.8-11. Each signal is normalized to the voltage peak of its own isolated transition for that particular geometry (after Potter and Schmulian, 1971); $x = 0$ at peak of self-consistent, isolated pulse as in Fig. 5.8-11.

5.8.4 Ratio of $\Delta x/T$ From Self-Consistent Calculations

If we use the normalized transition length of Fig. 5.8-10, $\Delta x/l_g = 3.2$. This value was obtained numerically (Potter et al., 1971) for the following specific parameters.

$$T = 0.1 \ \mu$$
$$l_g = 1 \ \mu$$
$$h = 0.5 \ \mu$$
$$H_c = 300 \ \text{Oe}$$
$$I_r = 800 \ \text{emu/cm}^3$$

Thus,

$$\left.\frac{\Delta x}{T}\right|_{I\ =800\,\text{emu/cm}^3} = \frac{3.2}{0.1} = 32 \tag{5.8-41}$$

If we translate this to γFe_2O_3 assuming $I_r = 100$ emu/cc, the product $I_r T$ must be a constant of value

$$I_r T = 800 \ \text{emu/cm}^3 \times 0.1 \ \mu = 80 \ \text{emu-}\mu/\text{cm}^3$$

The thickness for the new case must then be

$$T = \frac{80 \ \text{emu-}\mu/\text{cm}^3}{100 \ \text{emu/cm}^3} = 0.8 \ \mu = 0.032 \ \text{mils}$$

This thickness is still very small and satisfies the basic assumption on which the self-consistent calculations are based. Thus for this case, under the above assumption and definition of Λx, we have

$$\left.\frac{\Delta x}{T}\right|_{I_r = 100\,\text{emu/cm}^3} = \frac{3.2}{0.8} = 4 \tag{5.8-42}$$

5.8.5 Comparison of $\Delta x/T$ for Various Theoretical Analyses

Our theoretical analyses give different ratios of $\Delta x/T$ for any given medium, namely,

$$\frac{\Delta x}{T} = \frac{1}{2} \cot \frac{H_c}{8I_r} \qquad \text{linear } M_x \text{ vs. } x \tag{5.8-43}$$

$$\frac{\Delta x}{T} = \frac{\pi}{4} \left(\csc \frac{H_c}{8I_r} - 1 \right) \qquad \text{arctan } M_x \text{ vs. } x \tag{5.8-44}$$

The self-consistent calculation requires numerical solution for a specific case such as the one previously noted. For γFe_2O_3 with $H_c = 300$ Oe and $I_r = 100$ emu/cc, the ratios for these three cases are as follows:

$$\frac{\Delta x}{T} = 6 \qquad \text{linear } M_x \text{ vs. } x \tag{5.8-45}$$

$$\frac{\Delta x}{T} = 1.4 \qquad \text{arctan } M_x \text{ vs. } x \tag{5.8-46}$$

$$\frac{\Delta x}{T} = 4 \qquad \text{self-consistent calculation} \tag{5.8-47}$$

The linear analysis gives a large ratio, the arctangent a small ratio, and the self-consistent a value between the two. We would expect the self-consistent to be more accurate, but this has never been proved.

5.8.6 Relationship Between Thickness and Flux Changes per Inch

The number of magnetization changes per unit length equals the number of Δx transitions per unit length. This is generally referred to in the art as the flux changes per inch (fci). Thus fci = number of Δx per inch. The relationship between fci and bpi depends on the code used. In NRZI code, each Δx represents one "1," which means that the maximum value of fci equals the maximum number of bits per inch. In phase encoding and double frequency codes, two transitions maxima are required per bit, hence

$$\text{max fci} = \text{bpi} \qquad \text{for} \quad \text{NRZI} \tag{5.8-48}$$

$$\text{max fci} = 2\,\text{bpi} \qquad \text{for} \quad \text{PE and DF} \tag{5.8-49}$$

Since the ratio of $\Delta x/T$ is supposedly fixed for any given medium, we can express the recorded transition thickness in terms of the fci. In medium to high density recording, the separation between transitions approximately equals the transition length; thus the number of transitions per unit length is

$$\text{fci} = \frac{1}{2\Delta x} \tag{5.8-50}$$

with Δx in inches. But

$$\frac{\Delta x}{T} = \text{constant} \qquad \text{or} \qquad \Delta x = TK \tag{5.8-51}$$

Substituting this into (5.8-50) gives

$$T = \frac{1}{2K(\text{fci})} \tag{5.8-52}$$

where K is either 6, 1.4, or 4 for the linear, arctangent, and self-consistent calculations, respectively. If we assume that the latter is most accurate, $K = 4$, and from (5.8-52) we have

$$T\Big|_{\Delta x/T = 4} = \frac{1}{8(\text{fci})} \tag{5.8-53}$$

$$-\frac{1}{8(\text{bpi})} \quad \text{for} \quad \text{NRZI} \tag{5.8-54}$$

$$=\frac{1}{16(\text{bpi})} \quad \text{for} \quad \text{PE and DF} \tag{5.8-55}$$

This is an approximation that can be used to estimate the recorded thickness. Some examples are given in Section 6.3.

A serious limitation for all these theoretical results is the lack of specific correlation with experimental results. Although many of these subtle effects, such as asymmetry, are seen in practice, experimental relationships to actual causes are very difficult to establish because many factors can contribute to signal distortions. We saw, for instance, that the self-consistent calculations for a thin medium assuming *no* vertical calculations gave read-back wave form distortion very similar to that obtained for a thick medium with vertical magnetization but an assumed arctangent function of x. Other effects such as nonlinearities in the sensing system, eddy currents in the reading and writing head, and eddy currents and penetration effects in the medium, can also distort the signal by small amounts and are hard to separate from each other. On top of these are other experimental difficulties, such as unwanted unavoidable medium noise and thickness variations, and variations in the important physical dimensions. Extremely well-controlled experiments are necessary to establish the fundamental relationships with theory. Such measurements are more urgently needed as density increases. Self-consistent calculations can serve as a guide in such work, and more complete analysis including the vertical magnetization would be helpful.

6 Sequential Access Storage Systems

6.1 INTRODUCTION

Electronic shift register memory and storage systems are basically sequentially accessed; however we consider only tape and tapelike systems.

This chapter deals primarily with the fundamental characteristics of the more common tape systems and formats (Frost, 1970; Greenblatt, 1972; Sebestyen 1973). A wide variety of tape systems of other types attempt to exploit certain characteristics to advantage in particular applications (Murphy, 1971), but these are not included here.

The term "sequential access" refers to the manner in which the stored information is read from the medium; hence it also implies the manner in which it was originally written. Since the most common sequential media have a beginning and an end (i.e., tape and tapelike structures), the information is written (and read) in a sequential manner, starting at the beginning of the medium, and each new piece of information is started where the last one left off. Unfortunately this description in itself does not adequately describe a sequential system, since a single track on a magnetic disk is also sequentially written and read. In fact, the more simple track formats for disks (Fig. 7.6-1b) are the same, in principle, as tape formats. The major difference is that the tracks on disks are very short, whereas tapes are long; in addition, disk tracks are continuous, the end joins the beginning, whereas tapes are discontinuous; disks are in constant motion, but tapes start and stop; disks usually have movable heads, which give direct access to one of many tracks (then a sequential search of that track), whereas tapes have seven or nine fixed heads and tracks. Other distinctions become evident later; the point is that "sequential access storage" (SAS) identifies a system with respect to degree and is not a rigid distinction (i.e., common tapes are completely sequential and disks are partially sequential). In principle, a tape could be made in the form of a loop and accessed much the same as a disk with a combination of direct and sequential accessing. Thus we apply "sequential" to systems that are entirely sequential.

The major advantage to sequential systems is their low cost, and because of this factor, magnetic tape has been used as the medium for mass storage since its introduction in the 1950s (see Section 1.2). By far the most common tape (measured in number of reels in use) is $\frac{1}{2}$ in. wide tapes of γFe_2O_3 (see Section 6.2) on a Mylar substrate, and this chapter concentrates primarily on such tapes.

As in the previous and following chapter, SAS systems are discussed in terms of the four fundamental requirements for all storage systems: (1) medium, (2) writing mechanism, (3) reading mechanism, (4) addressing mechanism. We also cover sequential processing with an example, and density limiting factors.

6.2 TAPE MEDIA CHARACTERISTICS, MANUFACTURING PROCESS, AND CRITICAL PARAMETERS

The most common tape medium continues to be a coating approximately 0.5 mil thick of γFe_2O_3 on a 1 mil Mylar substrate. The thickness of both coating and substrate has continually decreased over the years and even varies among manufacturers at a given time, but 0.5 and 1 mil are reasonably nominal figures.*

Tape is commonly manufactured in five steps, each step being a continuous process in itself. These steps are as follows:

1. Coating. Oxide applied to substrate, oriented, and dried.
2. Curing. Chemical bonding of oxide.
3. Ironing or surface smoothing.
4. Slitting and cutting to length.
5. Testing.

The coating process starts with a continuous roll of Mylar substrate about 7500 ft long (3 times final tape length) and of varying widths of from 24 to 48 in. The Mylar substrate is initially (as received in raw form) about 1.5 mils thick and is etched (by a corona discharge) to provide good adhesion of the oxide coating; the final Mylar thickness is about 1 mil. A relatively thick oxide coating is applied to the Mylar substrate by various means such as a gravure coating roller (Fig. 6.2-1), after which the coating is smoothed down to a uniform thickness (about 0.5 mil) by means of smoothing rollers. Next the magnetic particles are oriented (see Section 5.2) along the long (axial) direction of the tape, by passing the tape between orientation magnets. Since this orients the entire tape along its axis, the self-demagnetizing field is essentially zero; thus the particles remain oriented and the orienting field need be applied for only a short time, even though the coating is not yet dry.

---

* IBM tape for type 2400 systems has a nominal oxide thickness of 0.4 mil and a total thickness of between 1.6 and 2.2 mil.

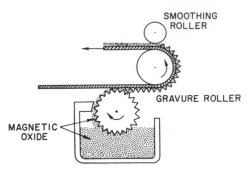

FIGURE 6.2-1 Schematic of gravure coater.

The next step in the continuous process is to dry the coating. This ensures that the particles remain oriented, the surface becomes hard, and the tape can be rewound into spools, completing the coating step.

The rolls are next placed in an oven at about 140°F for 2 days to allow the coating to cure. The chemical reaction ensures binding of the oxide magnetic particles with nonmagnetic carriers and to the substrate.

After the curing step, the surface is ironed by rollers to reduce the surface roughness from as large as 6 μin. (0.25 mils) to the 2–4 μin. range. This surface smoothing reduces head to tape separation, which can be a serious problem in loss of signal as we saw in Chapter 5.

These wide, long rolls must now be cut into standard size tapes of $\frac{1}{2}$ in. by 2500 ft (approximately). This is done by means of a high precision slitter, giving tapes of 0.4975 $\pm$ 0.001 in. wide and about 2400 ft long, including leaders. The actual usable length varies somewhat among manufacturers but is close to 2400 ft between markers (usable length). These tapes are wound on typical reels of $10\frac{1}{2}$ in. diameter and $\frac{23}{32}$ in. high at the mounting hub. The reels are enclosed in a plastic case.

The final testing step is done to ensure uniform quality. The actual tests performed vary among manufacturers and range from an exhaustive actual recording test of the entire tape, to ensure zero permanent defects at the rated density, to a listing of the maximum number of defects. Permanent defects are often caused by excessive bumps (hills) within the coating. These spots are easily detected in testing, and when found they are immediately removed by stopping the tape and automatically using a precision knife edge to remove the bump. If the bump resulted from excessive material (hill), its removal with the knife edge should restore the tape to the proper thickness and recording characteristics. If the bump was due to buckling of the surface (e.g., a nonmagnetic layer underneath), removal of the bump leaves a spot with little or no magnetic material, hence a permanent defect. This can easily be checked by recording once again over the spot. If a permanent defect is present, the tape can be cut and the nondefective parts used as smaller tape lengths (desirable in some applications). The quality of the tape is an important factor, particularly as density increases.

The magnetic medium itself (γFe_2O_3) has changed very little in composition since earliest times. The major changes have been an ever-decreasing particle size, smoother surface finishes, and fewer defects or holes (dropouts) in the oxide after deposition on the carrier substrate. All these advances have been necessary to achieve higher and higher density. The principle advance in the carrier (substrate) has been a change from acetate to Mylar, primarily for smoother surface and dimensional stability. The magnetic properties are detailed in Section 5.2. Magnetic loading factors for tape are typically in the range of 40%, with resulting BH loops as in Fig. 5.2-3.

An approximate estimate of the coercive force required for typical tapes can be obtained by assuming a worst case bit pattern, calculating the maximum self-demagnetizing field to be expected, and recognizing that H_c must be equal to or greater than this. One serious difficulty is that actual magnetization patterns as a function of depth into the surface, and also as a function of distance along the surface, are not well known. Hence we assume a sinusoidally recording flux pattern along the tape surface with no variation with thickness, and an infinitely wide strip. The latter assumption is quite reasonable because the width to length ratio of tape bits is typically greater than 10:1 (see Fig. 6.3-7). Assuming sinusoidal flux changes of 1 mil per bit cell or wavelength $\lambda = 2$ mils (i.e., 100 fci), an effective recording thickness of $t = 0.25$ mil and $B_m = 1$ k G, (2.6-14) gives for the magnitude of the maximum self-demagnetizing field

$$H_D(\max) = 10^3(1 - e^{-\pi t/\lambda}) = (1 - e^{-0.393})10^3$$
$$= 324 \text{ Oe}$$

This is reasonably close to the values of coercive forces typically used in tapes or disks (about 300 Oe).

It is easily seen that as the bit density is increased, the self-demagnetization, hence H_c for the assumed sinusoidal pattern, will increase unless the thickness is reduced such that t/λ remains constant. For instance, if λ decreases to 0.2 mil while the thickness remains constant at 0.25 mil, we have

$$\pi \frac{t}{\lambda} = \pi \frac{0.25}{0.2} = 3.93$$

$$H_D = 10^3(1 - e^{-3.93}) = 980 \text{ Oe}$$

Obviously reducing the thickness by the same factor will bring H_c back to 324 Oe. This is effectively what is done in practice for two reasons. First,

TABLE 6.2-1   Parameters of Typical Recording Tapes [Berkowitz et al. 1968; Bate and Alstad, 1969][a]

	Commercial γFe_2O_3 (Fig. 5.2-3)		Experimental Cobalt- γFe_2O_3		Commercial CrO_2 (Fig. 5.2-4)	
Coating thickness (μ)	9.9		3.8		3.8	
Surface roughness (arbitrary, relative units)	1		0.54		0.55	
Loading factor	40%				approx. 40%	
Saturation magnetization						
I_s (emu/cc)	103		152		170	
B_s (G)	1290		1900		2140	
Angle between applied field and average particle orientation	0°	90°	0°	90°	0°	90°
Coercivity H_c (Oe)	286	262	586	512	460	450
Squareness ratio I_r/I_s	0.74	0.41	0.8	0.7	0.8	0.3

[a] All oriented materials are at room temperature.

materials with such large H_c are more difficult to produce. Second, large H_c would require exceedingly large writing field, which are very difficult to produce with fast response time. Massive writing heads with slow response time would tend to compromise the density; therefore reduction of the recording thickness is essential for high density. Table 6.2-1 summarizes important parameters for various tapes.

As discussed in Section 5.2, very well dispersed magnetic particles in a nonmagnetic matrix are necessary to achieve both a well-oriented coating and a uniform medium. This requires the particles to be essentially isolated from one another as much as possible. Thus the binder and solvent must "wet" the particles to completely coat them and to prevent clusters from forming. Clusters of particles not only form bumps on the surface, which can result in loss of signal due to separation of the tape from the read/write transducer, but are also easily torn away from the substrate by mechanical contact with the heads (tapes are operated in contact with the read/write heads). Thus mechanical properties as well as magnetic characteristics of the medium are very important. Since the magnetic particles must spread uniformly over the substrate with a thickness typically of 0.5 mil (12 μ) or less, the solvent is used primarily to allow thin uniform coatings to be applied and also to furnish a temporarily fluix matrix for aligning the particles in a magnetic field. The binder serves mainly to hold the particles to the substrate and to isolate the particles from one another. There are no perfect solvents and binders, thus particles typically cluster in groups of a few particles per cluster in good coating to hundreds in poor coatings. Particle isolation and perfect alignment cannot be obtained simply by applying a larger field during orientation. Such fields are ineffective on clusters of particles that form closed magnetic field structures.

The phenomenon of dropout occurs in all magnetic tape and results in an unusable portion of tape. "Dropout" simply means a portion of the tape cannot be adequately recorded or read, and data have been or will be lost at these points. Dropouts occur either when the magnetic coating is not uniform, thus presenting a hill on the surface, when particles cluster and present a bump (sharp hill) that eventually will be worn away, or when sections of the coatings are devoid of magnetic particles. Thus defects of any kind that can make the medium ineffective lead to dropouts or defects. Since dropouts can vary in size and effect, a defect that is fatal at one density (high) may be totally unnoticeable at a lower density. Hence such defects must be tested for at the rated density for which the tape is intended. These defects are a major contributor to the random noise induced in the read head during sensing, becoming more significant as the density increases and sense signal decreases.

Contrary to popular notions, tape media are relatively insensitive to hostile fields and environmental extremes, provided reasonable care is taken (Geller, 1976).

6.3 WRITING MECHANISM

The information stored in the magnetic tape media is very similar in principle to that which would be stored in, say, a thin, flat film random access memory (i.e., small magnetized spots in the plane of the film*). One would expect the media cost for sequential and random access systems to be roughly similar for equal volumes and equal automation of the production.† Thus the way to bring about large cost reduction is to eliminate all the array wiring and share as many transducers as possible. This is precisely what is done in tapes (and disks).

Tapes are organized and recorded by tracks, and each track has one write head and (usually) one read head. The heads are grouped into units of seven

---

* See Section 5.3 for details of coding schemes and resulting bit patterns.
† This is a slight exaggeration: thin films require more critical control on the individual spots, hence higher cost.

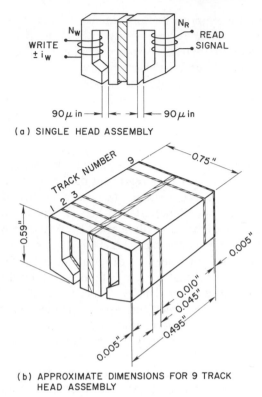

(a) SINGLE HEAD ASSEMBLY

(b) APPROXIMATE DIMENSIONS FOR 9 TRACK
HEAD ASSEMBLY

FIGURE 6.3-1   Typical read/write head geometries for magnetic tape recording.

or nine read/write heads (total of 14 or 18 gaps) for seven- and nine-track systems, respectively (Fig. 6.3-1). The details of the actual recording process are given in Chapter 5. We are concerned only with track formats and writing problems specific to tapes.

The two most common recording codes used for tapes are nonreturn to zero, inverted (NRZI) and phase encoding (PE). In NRZI, during writing there is always a current in the write head of positive or negative polarity; hence the writing process is destructive or self-erasing, since all old information is destroyed. A similar situation exists for PE coding; that is, it is self-erasing, although the current polarities are more complex, as indicated in Fig. 5.3-8*f*. Unlike analog recording, therefore, saturation digital recording ideally requires no preerase mechanism; but since numerous practical problems can leave partial magnetization (e.g., between tracks), an erase mechanism is usually included.

In a typical drive mechanism (Fig. 6.3-2) the file reel is mounted on the left and the take-up reel on the right. The tape passes at constant velocity

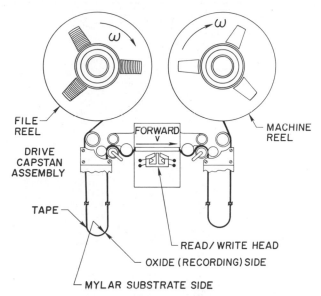

FIGURE 6.3-2 Typical tape drive mechanism: reference track 1 is nearest the front (observer) end.

from left to right in the forward direction over the read/write head assembly as shown, with the oxide surface facing downward, in contact with the heads. The characters thus normally run from right to left along the tape surface in this position. Early tape systems ran at relatively slow velocities of 18.75 and 37.5 in./sec. More typical tape units run from 100 to 250 in./sec (see Table 6.4-1).

The information on tapes is recorded parallel by character; that is, each alphanumeric character is stored in a column (e.g., as in Fig. 6.3-3). There are numerous codes used for representing information in computers, and three of the more common ones appear in Table 6.3-1.

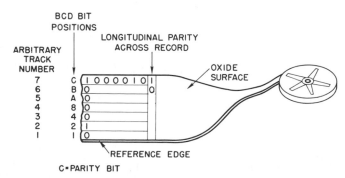

FIGURE 6.3-3 Tape track and record format for six-bit BCD code.

TABLE 6.3-1

								Bit Configuration	
								EBCDIC	
			Symbols					ASCII[a]	
			BCDIC				Punched	BCDIC	
Decimal	Hexadecimal	Report	Program	ASCII	EBCDIC		Card Code	BA8421	0123 4567[b]
0	00			NUL	NUL		12-0-1-8-9		0000 0000
1	01			SOH	SOH		12-1-9		0000 0001
2	02			STX	STX		12-2-9		0000 0010
3	03			ETX	ETX		12-3-9		0000 0011
4	04			EOT	PF		12-4-9		0000 0100
5	05			ENQ	HT		12-5-9		0000 0101
6	06			ACK	LC		12-6-9		0000 0110
7	07			BEL	DEL		12-7-9		0000 0111
8	08			BS			12-8-9		0000 1000
9	09			HT			12-1-8-9		0000 1001
10	0A			LF	SMM		12-2-8-9		0000 1010
11	0B			VT	VT		12-3-8-9		0000 1011
12	0C			FF	FF		12-4-8-9		0000 1100
13	0D			CR	CR		12-5-8-9		0000 1101
14	0E			SO	SO		12-6-8-9		0000 1110
15	0F			SI	SI		12-7-8-9		0000 1111
16	10			DLE	DLE		12-11-1-8-9		0001 0000
17	11			DC1	DC1		11-1-9		0001 0001
18	12			DC2	DC2		11-2-9		0001 0010
19	13			DC3	TM		11-3-9		0001 0011
20	14			DC4	RES		11-4-9		0001 0100
21	15			NAK	NL		11-5-9		0001 0101
22	16			SYN	BS		11-6-9		0001 0110
23	17			ETB	IL		11-7-9		0001 0111
24	18			CAN	CAN		11-8-9		0001 1000
25	19			EM	EM		11-1-8-9		0001 1001
26	1A			SUB	CC		11-2-8-9		0001 1010
27	1B			ESC	CU1		11-3-8-9		0001 1011
28	1C			FS	IFS		11-4-8-9		0001 1100
29	1D			GS	IGS		11-5-8-9		0001 1101
30	1E			RS	IRS		11-6-8-9		0001 1110
31	1F			ITB(US)	IUS		11-7-8-9		0001 1111
32	20			SP	DS		11-0-1-8-9		0010 0000
33	21			!	SOS		0-1-9		0010 0001
34	22			"	FS		0-2-9		0010 0010
35	23			#			0-3-9		0010 0011
36	24			$	BYP		0-4-9		0010 0100
37	25			%	LF		0-5-9		0010 0101
38	26			&	ETB		0-6-9		0010 0110
39	27			'	ESC		0-7-9		0010 0111
40	28			(			0-8-9		0010 1000
41	29			)			0-1-8-9		0010 1001
42	2A			*	SM		0-2-8-9		0010 1010
43	2B			+	CU2		0-3-8-9		0010 1011
44	2C			,			0-4-8-9		0010 1100
45	2D			−	ENQ		0-5-8-9		0010 1101
46	2E			.	ACK		0-6-8-9		0010 1110
47	2F			/	BEL		0-7-8-9		0010 1111
48	30			0			12-11-0-1-8-9		0011 0000
49	31			1			1-9		0011 0001
50	32			2	SYN		2-9		0011 0010
51	33			3			3-9		0011 0011
52	34			4	PN		4-9		0011 0100
53	35			5	RS		5-9		0011 0101
54	36			6	UC		6-9		0011 0110
55	37			7	E0T		7-9		0011 0111
56	38			8			8-9		0011 1000
57	39			9			1-8-9		0011 1001
58	3A			:			2-8-9		0011 1010
59	3B			;	CU3		3-8-9		0011 1011
60	3C			<	DC4		4-8-9		0011 1100
61	3D			=	NAK		5-8-9		0011 1101
62	3E			>			6-8-9		0011 1110
63	3F			?	SUB		7-8-9		0011 1111

[a] For 8 bit ASCII-8, add higher order bit = 0, and use ASCII symbol (i.e., use EBCDIC bit configuration for decimal values 0–127).

Relationship Between BCD, ASCII, and EBCDIC Codes for Symbol Representation

		Symbols					Bit Configuration	
		BCDIC						EBCDIC
						Punched	BCDIC	ASCII[a]
Decimal	Hexadecimal	Report	Program	ASCII	EBCDIC	Card Code	BA8421	0123 4567[b]
64	40			@	SP	no punches		0100 0000
65	41			A		12-0-1-9		0100 0001
66	42			B		12-0-2-9		0100 0010
67	43			C		12-0-3-9		0100 0011
68	44			D		12-0-4-9		0100 0100
69	45			E		12-0-5-9		0100 0101
70	46			F		12-0-6-9		0100 0110
71	47			G		12-0-7-9		0100 0111
72	48			H		12-0-8-9		0100 1000
73	49			I		12-1-8		0100 1001
74	4A			J	¢	12-2-8		0100 1010
75	4B	.		K	.	12-3-8	BA8 21	0100 1011
76	4C	□	)	L	<	12-4-8	BA84	0100 1100
77	4D	[		M	(	12-5-8	BA84 1	0100 1101
78	4E	<		N	+	12-6-8	BA842	0100 1110
79	4F	‡		O	|	12-7-8	BA8421	0100 1111
80	50	&	+	P	&	12	BA	0101 0000
81	51			Q		12-11-1-9		0101 0001
82	52			R		12-11-2-9		0101 0010
83	53			S		12-11-3-9		0101 0011
84	54			T		12-11-4-9		0101 0100
85	55			U		12-11-5-9		0101 0101
86	56			V		12-11-6-9		0101 0110
87	57			W		12-11-7-9		0101 0111
88	58			X		12-11-8-9		0101 1000
89	59			Y		11-1-8		0101 1001
90	5A			Z	!	11-2-8		0101 1010
91	5B	$		[	$	11-3-8	B 8 21	0101 1011
92	5C	*		\	*	11-4-8	B 84	0101 1100
93	5D	]		]	)	11-5-8	B 84 1	0101 1101
94	5E	;		⌐	;	11-6-8	B 842	0101 1110
95	5F	△		_	⌐	11-7-8	B 8421	0101 1111
96	60	-		\	-	11	B	0110 0000
97	61	/		a	/	0-1	A 1	0110 0001
98	62			b		11-0-2-9		0110 0010
99	63			c		11-0-3-9		0110 0011
100	64			d		11-0-4-9		0110 0100
101	65			e		11-0-5-9		0110 0101
102	66			f		11 0 6-9		0110 0110
103	67			g		11-0-7-9		0110 0111
104	68			h		11-0-8-9		0110 1000
105	69			i		0-1-8		0110 1001
106	6A			j	¦	12-11		0110 1010
107	6B	,		k	,	0-3-8	A8 21	0110 1011
108	6C	%	(	l	%	0-4-8	A84	0110 1100
109	6D	⋎		m	_	0-5-8	A84 1	0110 1101
110	6E	\		n	>	0-6-8	A842	0110 1110
111	6F	—		o	?	0-7-8	A8421	0110 1111
112	70			p		12-11-0		0111 0000
113	71			q		12-11-0-1-9		0111 0001
114	72			r		12-11-0-2-9		0111 0010
115	73			s		12-11-0-3-9		0111 0011
116	74			t		12-11-0-4-9		0111 0100
117	75			u		12-11-0-5-9		0111 0101
118	76			v		12-11-0-6-9		0111 0110
119	77			w		12-11-0-7-9		0111 0111
120	78			x		12-11-0-8-9		0111 1000
121	79			y		1-8		0111 1001
122	7A	ƀ		z	:	2-8	A	0111 1010
123	7B	#	=	{	#	3-8	8 21	0111 1011
124	7C	@	'	|	@	4-8	84	0111 1100
125	7D	:		}	'	5-8	84 1	0111 1101
126	7E	>		~	=	6-8	842	0111 1110
127	7F	√		DEL	"	7-8	8421	0111 1111

[b] Numbers 0–7 indicate EBCDIC bit positions (arbitrary): 0–3 = higher order and 4–7 = lower order binary bit positions.

TABLE 6.3-1 (*Continued*)

Decimal	Hexadecimal	Symbols BCDIC	Symbols EBCDIC	Punched Card Code	Bit Configuration BCDIC BA8421	Bit Configuration EBCDIC 0123 4567[b]
128	80			12-0-1-8		1000 0000
129	81		a	12-0-1		1000 0001
130	82		b	12-0-2		1000 0010
131	83		c	12-0-3		1000 0011
132	84		d	12-0-4		1000 0100
133	85		e	12-0-5		1000 0101
134	86		f	12-0-6		1000 0110
135	87		g	12-0-7		1000 0111
136	88		h	12-0-8		1000 1000
137	89		i	12-0-9		1000 1001
138	8A			12-0-2-8		1000 1010
139	8B			12-0-3-8		1000 1011
140	8C			12-0-4-8		1000 1100
141	8D			12-0-5-8		1000 1101
142	8E			12-0-6-8		1000 1110
143	8F			12-0-7-8		1000 1111
144	90			12-11-1-8		1001 0000
145	91		j	12-11-1		1001 0001
146	92		k	12-11-2		1001 0010
147	93		l	12-11-3		1001 0011
148	94		m	12-11-4		1001 0100
149	95		n	12-11-5		1001 0101
150	96		o	12-11-6		1001 0110
151	97		p	12-11-7		1001 0111
152	98		q	12-11-8		1001 1000
153	99		r	12-11-9		1001 1001
154	9A			12-11-2-8		1001 1010
155	9B			12-11-3-8		1001 1011
156	9C			12-11-4-8		1001 1100
157	9D			12-11-5-8		1001 1101
158	9E			12-11-6-8		1001 1110
159	9F			12-11-7-8		1001 1111
160	A0			11-0-1-8		1010 0000
161	A1		~	11-0-1		1010 0001
162	A2		s	11-0-2		1010 0010
163	A3		t	11-0-3		1010 0011
164	A4		u	11-0-4		1010 0100
165	A5		v	11-0-5		1010 0101
166	A6		w	11-0-6		1010 0110
167	A7		x	11-0-7		1010 0111
168	A8		y	11-0-8		1010 1000
169	A9		z	11-0-9		1010 1001
170	AA			11-0-2-8		1010 1010
171	AB			11-0-3-8		1010 1011
172	AC			11-0-4-8		1010 1100
173	AD			11-0-5-8		1010 1101
174	AE			11-0-6-8		1010 1110
175	AF			11-0-7-8		1010 1111
176	B0			12-11-0-1-8		1011 0000
177	B1			12-11-0-1		1011 0001
178	B2			12-11-0-2		1011 0010
179	B3			12-11-0-3		1011 0011
180	B4			12-11-0-4		1011 0100
181	B5			12-11-0-5		1011 0101
182	B6			12-11-0-6		1011 0110
183	B7			12-11-0-7		1011 0111
184	B8			12-11-0-8		1011 1000
185	B9			12-11-0-9		1011 1001
186	BA			12-11-0-2-8		1011 1010
187	BB			12-11-0-3-8		1011 1011
188	BC			12-11-0-4-8		1011 1100
189	BD			12-11-0-5-8		1011 1101
190	BE			12-11-0-6-8		1011 1110
191	BF			12-11-0-7-8		1011 1111

[a] For 8 bit ASCII-8, and higher order bit = 0, and use ASCII symbol (i.e., use EBCDIC bit configuration for decimal values 0–127).

| | | Symbols | | | Bit Configuration | |
| | | | | | BCDIC | EBCDIC |
Decimal	Hexadecimal	BCDIC	EBCDIC	Punched Card Code	BA8421	0123 4567[b]
192	C0	?	{	12-0	BA8 2	1100 0000
193	C1	A	A	12-1	BA 1	1100 0001
194	C2	B	B	12-2	BA 2	1100 0010
195	C3	C	C	12-3	BA 21	1100 0011
196	C4	D	D	12-4	BA 4	1100 0100
197	C5	E	E	12-5	BA 4 1	1100 0101
198	C6	F	F	12-6	BA 42	1100 0110
199	C7	G	G	12-7	BA 421	1100 0111
200	C8	H	H	12-8	BA8	1100 1000
201	C9	I	I	12-9	BA8 1	1100 1001
202	CA			12-0-2-8-9		1100 1010
203	CB			12-0-3-8-9		1100 1011
204	CC		⌐	12-0-4-8-9		1100 1100
205	CD			12-0-5-8-9		1100 1101
206	CE		⊦	12-0-6-8-9		1100 1110
207	CF			12-0-7-8-9		1100 1111
208	D0	!	}	11-0	B 8 2	1101 0000
209	D1	J	J	11-1	B 1	1101 0001
210	D2	K	K	11-2	B 2	1101 0010
211	D3	L	L	11-3	B 21	1101 0011
212	D4	M	M	11-4	B 4	1101 0100
213	D5	N	N	11-5	B 4 1	1101 0101
214	D6	O	O	11-6	B 42	1101 0110
215	D7	P	P	11-7	B 421	1101 0111
216	D8	Q	Q	11-8	B 8	1101 1000
217	D9	R	R	11-9	B 8 1	1101 1001
218	DA			12-11-2-8-9		1101 1010
219	DB	.		12-11-3-8-9		1101 1011
220	DC			12-11-4-8-9		1101 1100
221	DD			12-11-5-8-9		1101 1101
222	DE			12-11-6-8-9		1101 1110
223	DF			12-11-7-8-9		1101 1111
224	E0	≠	\	0-2-8	A8 2	1110 0000
225	E1			11-0-1-9		1110 0001
226	E2	S	S	0-2	A 2	1110 0010
227	E3	T	T	0-3	A 21	1110 0011
228	E4	U	U	0-4	A 4	1110 0100
229	E5	V	V	0-5	A 4 1	1110 0101
230	E6	W	W	0-6	A 42	1110 0110
231	E7	X	X	0-7	A 421	1110 0111
232	E8	Y	Y	0-8	A8	1110 1000
233	E9	Z	Z	0-9	A8 1	1110 1001
234	EA			11-0-2-8-9		1110 1010
235	EB			11-0-3-8-9		1110 1011
236	EC		⊣	11-0-4-8-9		1110 1100
237	ED			11-0-5-8-9		1110 1101
238	EE			11-0-6-8-9		1110 1110
239	EF			11-0-7-8-9		1110 1111
240	F0	0	0	0	8 2	1111 0000
241	F1	1	1	1	1	1111 0001
242	F2	2	2	2	2	1111 0010
243	F3	3	3	3	21	1111 0011
244	F4	4	4	4	4	1111 0100
245	F5	5	5	5	4 1	1111 0101
246	F6	6	6	6	42	1111 0110
247	F7	7	7	7	421	1111 0111
248	F8	8	8	8	8	1111 1000
249	F9	9	9	9	8 1	1111 1001
250	FA				12-11-0-2-8-9		1111 1010
251	FB			12-11-0-3-8-9		1111 1011
252	FC			12-11-0-4-8-9		1111 1100
253	FD			12-11-0-5-8-9		1111 1101
254	FE			12-11-0-6-8-9		1111 1110
255	FF		EO	12-11-0-7-8-9		1111 1111

[b] Numbers 0–7 indicate EBCDIC bit positions (arbitrary): 0–3 = higher order and 4–7 = lower order binary bit positions.

The older and at one time very common binary coded decimal interchange code (BCDIC) uses six binary bits, hence can accommodate only 64 alphanumeric characters. This proved to be too few for general computing needs involving both data processing and mathematical or scientific calculations. Thus the seven-bit American National Standard Code for Information Interchange (ASCII), which allows 128 characters, and the eight-bit extended binary coded decimal interchange code (EBCDIC), which allows 256 characters, were devised. At present, many bit configurations in the latter code do not have an assigned meaning, to permit future expansion. IBM systems 360 and 370 make extensive use of EBCDIC: since these systems are eight-bit byte oriented, the use of ASCII in such systems requires special definition. An expansion of this code to the so-called ASCII-8 system merely requires an addition of a higher order "0" bit and the use of ASCII symbols. As such the ASCII-8 bit configuration becomes identical to EBCDIC for decimal equivalent 0 through 127. Since ASCII is a seven-bit code, it has no entries for decimals 128 through 255 in Table 6.3-1.* There are numerous other codes, as well as optional features to those mentioned, especially in the area of data communications. However BCDIC, ASCII, and EBCDIC are the more common codes in computer application.

These codes, represent only the logical relationship between alphanumeric data and the equivalent binary representation. When information expressed by any of these codes is recorded on tape, a parity bit is always stored with each character, to reduce recording and readback errors. Thus the six- and eight-bit codes require seven- and nine-track tapes, respectively. Since this parity is independent of the standard code, one may use even or odd parity.

The information that is written on the tape often comes from the standard card (72 columns × 12 rows) of Fig. 6.3-4 with appropriate punch positions as in Table 6.3-1. Since the cards are punched according to one standard and the code on tape is one of several standards, a one-to-one correspondence does not exist and some conversion is necessary. Conversion is done by the CPU via main memory—the cards are read into main memory, and the data are processed and converted to the desired tape code, which is then written on tape. The programs for conversion differ for each code, but these are usually supplied by the manufacturer. Not all information written on tapes comes from cards; any data stored in the main memory can be written on a tape in large, modern computing systems. There are also available key-to-tape input systems.

A group of read/write heads, equal in number to the number of tracks, is

---

* In many applications, such as terminals and printers using ASCII, the first 33 (decimal 0 to 32) and last (decimal 127) characters are omitted for obvious reasons, leaving only 94 symbols.

PUNCH
ROW

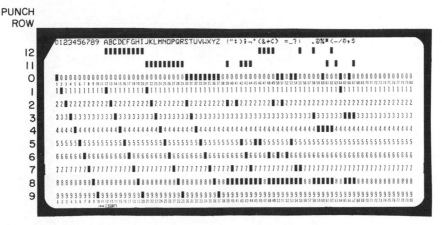

FIGURE 6.3-4 Card punch positions for some IBM system 360/370 characters.

used for parallel writing and reading. In all systems, one of the read/write heads is always a parity track to provide a parity bit across the character (e.g., Figs. 6.3-3, 6.3-5, and 6.3-6). On nine-track systems, the parity track and other most frequently used tracks in EBCDIC are placed in the center region of the tape, away from the edges, to ensure that in case the tape edges (hence the outer tracks) get damaged, the parity and information bits will not be lost. The seven-track BCD code does not have a set of "least used" tracks. In addition to parity for each character, a parity bit (usually of polarity opposite to that of the character parity bit) is written at the end of a record (Figs. 6.3-3 and 6.3-5). These parity bits assist in locating and correcting errors that may inadvertently enter. In addition, odd parity across the character in NRZI recording ensures at least one "1," therefore one signal pulse for

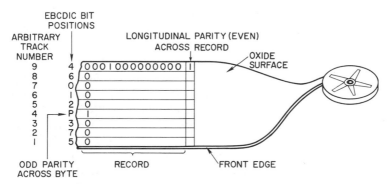

FIGURE 6.3-5 Tape track and record format for eight-bit EBCDIC code.

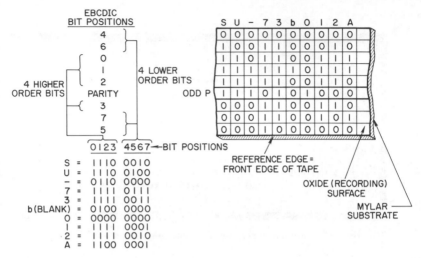

FIGURE 6.3-6 Example of data recorded on tape in EBCDIC code. (Tape shown upside down from recording position of Fig. 6.3-2, hence characters are reversed left to right.)

every character, which greatly aids the clocking on readback. Since tapes are operated in contact with the heads, both are subject to wear (the oxide coating is a very abrasive surface). Dirt may also enter, interfering with the writing or reading process.

The layouts of tracks on tape for seven-track and six-track IBM systems appear in Figs. 6.3-3 and 6.3-5. The physical track numbers start at the reference edge, which is the front edge of the tape nearest the observer when the tape is mounted. An example of a portion of a record (without longitudinal parity check) for one typical system is given in Fig. 6.3-6. The tape is shown with oxide face up.

To further limit possible errors, the information written on tape is often read immediately afterward by a separate read head mounted as close as is reasonably possible to the write head (Fig. 6.3-1a). With this technique, one can be assured that the intended information is recorded except for peculiar and most unlikely cases in which an intermittent reading error might exactly cancel an intermittent writing error.

Typical track dimensions range as follows: seven-track tape, 0.050 in. track width and 0.020 in. separation between tracks (0.070 in. center to center); nine-track tape, 0.045 in. width and 0.010 in. separation (0.055 in. center), and 0.005 in. on each edge. These dimensions can vary slightly among manufacturers and for different tape systems. The magnetic transitions Δx produced by a NRZI code for an arbitrary bit pattern are shown in Fig. 6.3-7.

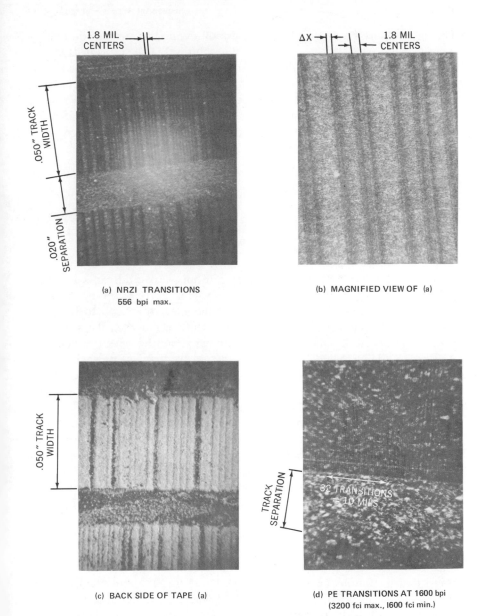

(a) NRZI TRANSITIONS
556 bpi max.

(b) MAGNIFIED VIEW OF (a)

(c) BACK SIDE OF TAPE (a)

(d) PE TRANSITIONS AT 1600 bpi
(3200 fci max., 1600 fci min.)

FIGURE 6.3-7 Magnetization transitions recorded on 0.4 mil thick γFe_2O_3 tape as seen via Bitter patterns under a microscope. (*a*)–(*c*) Arbitrary bit pattern for NZRI at 556 bpi maximum. (*c*) "Print through" fringe field. (*d*) Alternate pattern of "1's" and "0's" (3200 fci) with six unipolar bits (1600 fci) near upper right corner.

The patterns are made visible by the use of a colloidal suspension of very fine magnetic particles in a liquid (Bitter solution). The solution is spread on the tape and allowed to dry; observation through a microscope clearly shows the separate transitions for which Δx is approximately 0.001 in. long.

It is well known that a given tape (e.g., 0.4 mil γFe_2O_3), can be recorded over a wide range of bit densities. If the self-consistent relationship of Section 5.8 is valid, we would expect the effective recorded thickness to decrease as the density increases, as given by (5.8-54) and (5.8-55) or

$$T\Big|_{NRZI} \approx \frac{1}{8}\left(\frac{1}{bpi}\right)$$

$$T\Big|_{\substack{PE \\ DF}} \approx \frac{1}{16}\left(\frac{1}{bpi}\right)$$

with $\Delta x = 4T$. For NRZI recording at 556 bpi, we would expect T to be about 0.225×10^{-3} in. At a higher density such as 1600 bpi using phase encoding (i.e., 3200 fci), we would expect the effect thickness to be about 39 μin. The actual variation of recording depth versus density in a thick medium is not well known, but it is known that the effective thickness decreases with increasing density. The actual mechanism of such surface flux reversal is not understood. It is known, however, that the unswitched underlayer of the thick medium does not improve the recording process. Rather, higher densities are easier to achieve with thinner media.

Figure 6.3-7 gives an example of these two different densities recorded on the same type of 0.4 mil thick tape. At 556 bpi recorded in NRZI, we would expect the recorded transition to be on $1/556 = 1.8$ mil centers, with the transition length of about half this, or 0.9 to 1 mil, as in Fig. 6.3-7a and b. If our thickness calculation is reasonable, we would expect the transition to be saturated only through a little over half the tape thickness. Whatever the effective thickness, it is clear from Fig. 6.3-7c that the transition fringe field has a finite value on the back side of the tape which is at least 1 mil away. At 1600 bpi recorded in phase encoding, which requires 3200 transitions/in. maximum, we would expect 3.2 transitions/mil (0.313 mil centers) or 32 transitions in 10 mils. The transition length required is about half the center spacing or about 0.16 mils, as in Fig. 6.3-7d, where the required 32 transitions are within 10 mils. If the previous thickness calculation of 0.039 mil, based on the self-consistent analysis of self-demagnetization is correct, these transitions should be saturated only in a surface layer of about one-tenth the tape thickness. The actual thickness of recording is not known, but clearly it must be less than the total thickness.

One could easily conclude that a thinner medium is not really necessary but rather, it should be possible to use a thick medium and just record on a surface layer. As a rule, however, this can be done only under laboratory conditions with well-controlled parameters. In actual operating systems, variation in the critical parameters can cause serious problems. For instance, an increase in the writing current can cause the transition to spread through a larger thickness and a larger Δx, which is most undesirable. Also variation in the head to medium spacing, coercive force, and other parameters can cause serious problems in overall reliability. Thus a thinner medium is a practical necessity for higher density.

Even though tape systems are operated nominally in contact with the head, variations in the tape surface roughness, momentary buckling during start/ stop, and other practical problems can cause the tape to separate from the head. The design must take this worst case into consideration and allow for a certain amount of head to medium separation h, during both writing and reading. The normalized sensitivity functions as a function of x for various values of h are given in Figs. 5.3-12 and 5.12-13, and the peak of the former is plotted as a function of h in Fig. 5.3-6. Some typical tape system parameters are $l_g = 100$ μin., approximately, with a maximum head to medium separation of about half this, or $h = 50$ μin., giving $h/l_g = 0.5$. From Fig. 5.3-6, this would reduce the signal to about 50% of its theoretical maximum value. From Fig. 5.3-12, it is also seen that considerable additional spreading of the transition, hence the signal, is encountered. This is another factor that degrades bit density.

6.4 SENSING AND READING MECHANISM

The general reading mechanism for tapes is that outlined in Section 5.4. The tape is moved across the read/write heads at constant velocity and generates a signal of amplitude given in (5.4-1). Typical sense signals of about 1 mV were previous calculated for some typical parameters and velocity of 200 in./sec. As the velocity decreases, the number of turns is often increased to maintain the signal within the millivolt range.

Skew

During the writing processes, the tape is moved past the write head and is guide only by the mechanical alignment of the tape edge against a grooved channel. It is desirable to have the tape edges perfectly parallel to each other, moving parallel to the gap length. This may actually be the case, for example, during writing, but reading may occur much later, and because of the mechanical nature of the guiding mechanism, the tape may then traverse under the read head at some small angle with respect to the alignment during writing.

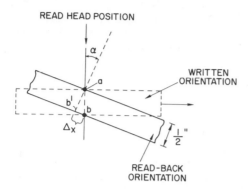

READ HEAD POSITION

WRITTEN ORIENTATION

READ-BACK ORIENTATION

FIGURE 6.4-1 Schematic of tape skew resulting from different orientation during reading and writing.

This condition (Fig. 6.4-1) is referred to as skew. The skew angle α can be quite small but can produce a significant misalignment in terms of linear displacement between the original bits and subsequent reading positions. For example, suppose the data were written in the orientation indicated by the dashed lines in Fig. 6.4-1 and subsequently read in the orientation shown by the solid lines. The stored bit at point a would be properly aligned, but that at point b would be skewed to point b'. For 0.5 in. tape with a skew of only 0.1°, point b' would be $0.5 \sin 0.1 = 0.5 \times 0.00175 = 8.8 \times 10^{-4}$ in. away from point b. In a system storing, say, 1600 bpi, this distance would correspond to $1600 \times 8.8 \times 10^{-4} = 1.4$ bits, that is, a skew of 1.4 bit cell positions, which is intolerable. The tape skew must be controlled more accurately than this for the system to function properly. The maximum skew is often specified in terms of the total time variation permitted between the inside and outside track of the tape for a given linear density and tape velocity. For instance, a typical specification is less than 2 μsec variation (inside to outside track) for 800 bpi moving at 112.5 in./sec. This would then allow a maximum variation of

$$112.5 \text{ in./sec} \times 2 \times 10^{-6} \text{ sec} \times 800 \text{ bpi} = 0.18 \text{ bit}$$

or a skew of less than 20% of a bit cell dimension; for 0.5 in. tape, this translates into a skew of less than 0.03°, a rather small variation. No skew correction would be required for the system. As the linear density and velocity increase, however, the skew time variation would become more significant for the same skew angle, and some provision must be included to compensate for this.

Fortunately the skew does not vary rapidly as the tape is being read: for example, if the tape is skewed a small amount, it will remain the same while several inches of tape is moved past the read head. This permits each record, before being read, to be deskewed by means of "deskewing buffers." There

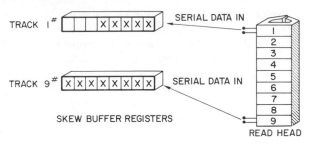

FIGURE 6.4-2 Schematic of deskewing buffers.

are many ways to accomplish this, with one simple possibility as follows. During the writing process, a known bit pattern is stored in front of a block of records. During readback, this pattern is read into a deskewing register and is recognized by the logic built into the controller. Only the two end tracks need be read, and the prerecorded pattern might enter as shown in Fig. 6.4-2. As soon as one buffer is filled with the correct bit pattern (tested by the controller), the number of empty spaces remaining in the other is counted or easily sensed; this information is then used for shifting the bits, which are sensed by each of the nine tracks to properly align the correct bits for each character (byte). This deskewing is all accomplished by the logic built into the controller and is not usually "seen" by the user. At high bit density, the mechanical alignment that would be required to avoid skewing is nearly impossible to achieve. As the linear density continually increases, built-in deskewing becomes increasingly important, and more sophisticated techniques will be required.

Three very important parameters in the operation of tape systems are data rate, tape speed, and rewind time. The data rate is an important parameter indicating the speed with which data can be transferred to and from main memory. It can easily be found from the linear velocity and bit density

$$\text{bps} = v \times D_b$$

where v is in inches per second and the bit density D_b is in bits per inch. This neglects any gaps that may be present to separate records or blocks. For instance, a tape running at $v = 250$ in./sec and a density of $D_b = 3200$ bpi would give

$$\text{bps} = 3200 \times 250 = 800,000 \text{ bits/sec}$$

If eight tracks are read in parallel, the data rate would be 800K bytes/sec. If gaps are present, the effective data rate will be lowered. This is actually a rather high speed tape unit; slower speed units operate at 800 bpi and 100 in./sec giving a data rate of 80K bytes/sec. Even on the high performance systems,

TABLE 6.4-1   Typical Parameters of Common Tape Systems

Tape Speed (in./sec)	Data Rate (K bytes/sec)	Density (linear) (bpi)	Rewind Time (sec)	Recording Code
18.75	15	800	minutes	NRZI
37.5	30	800	minutes	NRZI
75	120/60/41.5/15	1600/800/556/200	45–100	PE/NRZI
100	160/80	1600/800	72	PE/NRZI
112.5	180/90	1600/800	55–97	PE/NRZI
125	200/100	1600/800	55	PE/NRZI
200	320/160/111.2	1600/800/556	45–60	PE/NRZI/NRZI
250	800	3200	45	PE
200	1250	6250	45	

these data rates, coupled with the slow sequential nature of tapes, are not sufficient to keep many medium to high speed computers busy. For instance, if we assume a CPU of 1 MIPS and $I/B = 2$ (see Chapter 1), this CPU needs data at the average rate of

$$10^6 \text{ IPS} \times \tfrac{1}{2} \text{ byte/inst.} = 0.5 \times 10^6 \text{ byte/sec}$$

Although the high performance tapes may be able to supply the data almost fast enough, this will be true only for short periods. Once a full block is used up and an IRG is encountered, the CPU becomes idle until the next block begins transfer.

All modern tape units use the NRZI code on lower density systems and phase encoding at higher densities (usual at 1600 bpi and above). A summary of some typical tape parameters is given in Table 6.4-1.

6.5   ADDRESSING MECHANISM AND STORED ADDRESSING INFORMATION

Tape systems have no way to externally define a physical location on the medium; that is, there are no accurate means for counting the number of bit locations traversed—no synchronizing tracks or any other special aids. Thus the addressing mechanism must be contained within the stored information (see Section 5.5). On a typical tape (Fig. 6.5-1) the recorded information consists of two parts, the stored addressing information (SAI) and the actual desired data. The SAI is always used in locating a record and the data sometimes serve as additional addressing information (e.g., comparison of a field in data for coincidence). Each data record has an SAI area associated

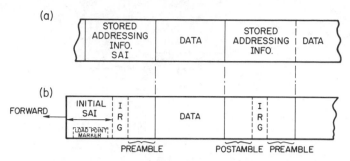

FIGURE 6.5-1   General format for data and SAI on tape.

with it such that the tape consists of alternate sections of SAI and the data areas. The SAI is thus a space between the data records, and it contains a certain amount of information but is nonprogrammable by the user; its two main functions are to indicate to the system the beginning and end of data records, and to provide an interval for the tape to be accelerated and decelerated for stopping, starting, moving backward, forward, and so on. The latter gap is called the interrecord gap (IRG). As we saw in Chapter 5, the reading and writing process in magnetic recording requires the medium to be moving at constant velocity. Since the mass of the tape and its drive motor are finite, a certain amount of time is required to accelerate and decelerate the tape to a constant velocity (IRG). In addition, some character information must be contained with the SAI interval for signaling the beginning and end of a record, as well as deskewing information. These characters are automatically placed in the interval during writing and are not seen by the user.

The relationship between the actual data areas, the stored addressing information interval, and the inter record gap is presented in Fig. 6.5-2. The IRG, shown as a gap of length $2x_0$, contains no stored information and is only the interval required to stop and start the tape. The SAI data gaps x_1 and $x_4 - x_3$, which precede and follow the IRG, contain varying lengths and different kinds of information, depending on the particular system. In most cases, however, they are not programmable by the user; the data are automatically inserted by the controller. The portions of the SAI gaps on either side of the IRG (more specifically; those preceding and following data), contain different kinds and amounts of information depending on the coding scheme and can also differ among manufacturers. In PE, both the preamble and postamble (Fig. 6.5-1b) typically consist of a string of "1's" followed by "0's," or vice versa. The preamble synchronizes detection circuits for distinguishing "1's" from "0's." The postamble serves two

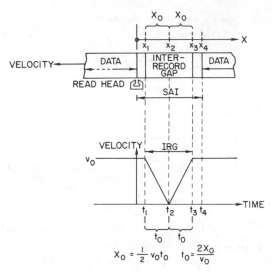

FIGURE 6.5-2 Approximation of the acceleration and deceleration of tape within the IRG interval.

purposes; to signal the end of data in a block or record, and to allow reading backward (in which case the functions of postamble and preamble are reversed). A preamble is not necessary in NRZI, since "1's" and "0's" are unique. The postamble consists typically of some empty spaces followed by the longitudinal parity bits shown in Fig. 6.3-3 for seven-track systems. For NRZI in nine-track systems, the postamble typically contains cyclic redundancy bits in addition to the longitudinal parity (Fig. 6.3-5). The standard IRGs for several tape types are given in Table 6.5-1.

An estimate of the actual acceleration and deceleration times can easily be obtained for any tape system from a knowledge of the IRG. As we approach and then enter a typical IRG, the velocity is seen to be constant outside the gap, suddenly decreasing to zero after some small distance within the gap, as in Fig. 6.5-2. If we approximate the velocity by a straight line (i.e., constant deceleration a_0), the distance traversed is related to time by

$$v = a_0 t \qquad \text{or} \qquad \frac{dx}{dt} = a_0 t$$

Simple integration then yields the result that the distance to decelerate or accelerate (assumed equal) is given by

$$x_0 = \tfrac{1}{2} v_0 t_0 \qquad \text{or} \qquad t_0 = 2 \frac{x_0}{v_0}$$

TABLE 6.5-1 Tape Inter-
record Gaps (IRG)

Density (bpi)	IRG[a] (in.)
7 tracks	
200	
556	0.75
800	
9 tracks	
800	
1600	0.6
6250	0.3

[a] Standard accepted by most of the industry.

where v_0 = normal tape velocity. From Fig. 6.5-2

$$x_0 = x_2 - x_1$$

But since x_0 is half the total IRG size, the time to accelerate or decelerate the tape is given by

$$t_0 = \frac{2(\text{IRG}/2)}{v_0} = \frac{\text{IRG}}{v_0}$$

As an example, a typical system has $v_0 = 200$ in./sec, IRG = 0.6 in.; thus we get

$$t_0(\text{max}) = \frac{\text{IRG}}{v_0} = \frac{0.6}{200} = 3 \text{ msec}$$

This is quite a small time in which to start or stop the capstan motor and tape, so special mechanical and electrical design is required.

Clearly the time allotted to the IRG is quite small, and reducing it by any substantial amounts presents some formidable problems. As the speed v_0 continues to increase (as it has in past systems), the acceleration time t_0 will have to be decreased to keep the IRG constant. This gap already occupies a significant amount of space and can consume a considerable portion of the recorded surface when the record length is short. Suppose, for instance, we are recording records 1K bytes long on tape with a density of 1600 bpi for each track, with nine tracks in parallel (8 bits + parity), a 1K byte record occupies only

$$\frac{1\text{K byte}}{1600 \text{ bpi}} = 0.63 \text{ in.}$$

A tape fully recorded with such records would consist of alternate areas of 0.6 in. IRG, 0.63 data, 0.6 in. IRG, and so on, as in Fig. 6.5-3. Thus the efficiency of tape utilization is $0.63 \div (0.63 + 0.6) = 0.51$ or 51%.* In addition, the access time to a random record is greatly increased because many gaps must be traversed. If efficiency and random access are important, larger data areas, hence fewer IRGs, are necessary. This is accomplished by grouping records together in blocks with no IRGs between records; rather, the IRGs are inserted between the blocks.† Now the blocks look like single records in the previous case of no blocking. The records within a given block can have additional markers to separate one record from another, if desired; however this is accomplished in the programming, not by the hardware. Related blocks of records are usually organized into a file, designated on tape by an "end of file" marker as shown. The "end of file" gap is a special sequence of bits. The gap format varies with code used and among manufacturers but commonly consist of a blank tape for 3.75 to 3.9 in. followed by some special bit codes varying in length from about 4 to 40 linear bit spaces (again depending on the specific system). A tape mark such as hexidecimal 7F is often used. Since this mark is provided by the controller, the user need not be concerned with its details. The distinction between records, blocks, and files is best understood by an example. If we are attempting to store the file "student" in Fig. 8.4-3, there are several possibilities; we could store the "CURRENT STUDENTS" as one block with each student entry as a record (25K records total), the "COURSES 72" could be stored as another block, with each line entry as a record; likewise for "AVG 72" or other data. Since these blocks are all related in some way, we could organize them all as one file, if desired. However these blocks also may be related to other dissimilar blocks; hence we may wish to store each block as a file or various combinations (even with duplicated storage). More information about the total file is needed before the final organization is achieved. In any case, it should be clear that since there are no IRGs within a given block, the entire block must be read; it is not possible to stop in the middle of a block and start again.

Since tape is a discontinuous medium with a beginning and an end, a means is needed to indicate this to the system, namely, the "load point" and "end of reel" markers in Fig. 6.5-3. These markers are shiny reflectors

---

* This neglects nonusable space for the preamble and postamble, but these require very little length (e.g., 40 bits each).
† This process is referred to as blocking of records.

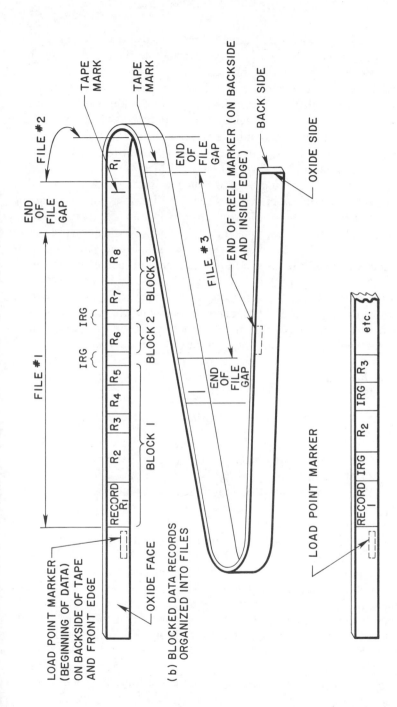

FIGURE 6.5-3 Data record format on tape.

465

created by thin, vapor-deposited aluminum on transparent adhesive tape. About $1 \times \frac{3}{16}$ in. in size, they are fastened manually to the tapes during final testing and are sensed by separate photocell detectors in the tape drive unit.

As discussed earlier, position location on the tape is done by way of the SAI. Because of the high bit densities involved and the limits of mechanical tolerances, it is not feasible to mechanically count and thereby locate the physical position of a tape within a bit spacing. In principle, it is conceivable that a separate clock and position track could be recorded on the tape to provide position information, easing the record location problem. In addition, a programmable SAI could be used, much as is done in disks, to further aid in retrieval. We would still need a fixed IRG for stopping and starting distances however, so all these aids would be in addition to the existing ones.

To what extent do these additional aids help, and how much do they cost? The aids are of little value for purely sequential processing, since we know exactly where we are and what to do for each step and each record or block of records. For purely random processing, the tape still must be moved back and forth (stopped and started), regardless of whether we know how far and which direction to go. The distance to go and the direction can be determined for the most part from the structure of the data and simple algorithms included in the processing program. The access time for starting, stopping, and moving become the critical factors because of the long, sequential string of the data, and our additional aids are of very limited value.

6.6 SEQUENTIAL PROCESSING: EXAMPLE

Tape requires sequential storing of records, since there are no other ways to address the data. Records or blocks (groups of records) can be of varying length, but all blocks are separated by fixed length gaps. Thus there is no way to directly update a tape file; only indirectly updating, by use of additional tapes for temporary storage followed by rerecording, is possible. All this additional activity is required because addressing on tape cannot get down to the "fine" level of bytes nor even parts of the records (i.e., fields) but must deal with the blocks as one unit. The usual solution is to transfer a block into main memory, where the finer addressing mechanism can be used to avoid all the sorting activity, and so on. However one reel of 2400 ft tape may contain more than 10^8 bits of information, and the records requiring sorting may be scattered over the entire length or a significant fraction of it. This would, of course, require a large main memory of 10^8 bits for the worst case just to store the data. Even if only $\frac{1}{100}$ of the tape is needed, this requires 10^6 bits of main memory, which is larger than the amount allotted to many systems, or even if available, requires too much storage for such a simple operation.

For the problems requiring sorting over the entire tape, the "sort" procedure itself can become very complex, necessitating sophisticated sorting algorithms as well as several passes into and out of the main memory; the tape would be broken into segments, each segment sorted separately, and finally all would be merged together to produce the sorted tape. Thus although much of the information needed in tapes for addressing can be stored within the records (name, ID number, etc.), the mechanism for actually addressing is all external, by way of a program. This is very unlike a random access memory, where the "fine structure" addressing is available. Since the large storage required is seldom available in main memory, however, one has little choice.

Thus sequential processing of records on tape can be quite involved, comprising several steps for simple types of operation. As an example, suppose an "accounts receivable" system is organized such that as customer payments are received, they are recorded on tape sequentially, in order of receipt. Suppose there are 20 accounts, all on one tape, and the records are partitioned into two blocks of 10 records each. Suppose that in one case, the payments were received in the order shown in Figure 6.6-1 starting with block 1 and continuing through block 2. After all 20 have been received, it is desirable to reorder them in numerical order on one tape for other processing in the future. How do we do this? It *is* possible to simply search the tape first for record number 1, write it on a second tape, search (sequentially) for record 2, write it as the second tape, then 3, 4, and so on. However since each record must be interrogated to see what number it is, and this

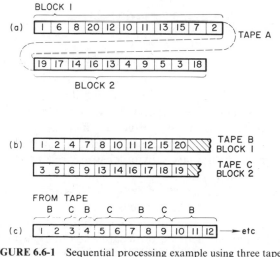

FIGURE 6.6-1 Sequential processing example using three tapes.

must be done sequentially, we would have to search, in the example given, from one end of the file (record 1) to the middle (*R*2) to the end (*R*3), backwards to (*R*4), forward to (*R*5), and so on. Since the file might occupy a significant portion of the tape, which is 2400 ft long, the searching could take several minutes to traverse from end to end of the file, and such a sequential processing could take nearly an hour of back and forth tape movement, not to mention the excessive and unnecessary wear on the tape. Thus this method is avoided whenever possible.

A better technique is as follows. Complete blocks of records can be transferred into main memory and sorted as a unit. Assuming the blocks are actually reasonable size (e.g., 10K bytes) and the main memory of our processor is sufficiently large, each block will be sorted and stored on a separate tape, block 1 on tape B and block 2 on tape C as in Fig. 6.6-1*b*. Now these tapes can each be searched sequentially for the numerical order, since each block is ordered within itself. The tapes would have to move only from one record to another sequentially, the programming then taking the correct record number, reading that record and placing it sequentially on tape D as in Fig. 6.6-1*c*. The two tapes B and C are thus interwoven with the correct numerical ordering. Since each block is only scanned once in Fig. 6.6-1*c*, a very substantial saving in processing time is obtained.

It should be pointed out that commercial data processing accounts for (very approximately) 80% of all computer processing. Most uses of tape processing involve quite simple functions, often merely computerized automation of clerical operations such as payroll, accounts receivable, inventory, statements (banks, insurance, stocks), and many related functions.

6.7   DENSITY–LIMITING FACTORS

Although theoretically and even in practice the writing of data is not the major problem for linear density, nevertheless practical limits on certain parameters can result in errors in the recorded data. The two most serious practical problems giving rise to inaccurate data are tape surface roughness and dropouts. Surface roughness can greatly increase the head-to-medium spacing during writing as well as during reading, as discussed in Section 5.4, causing a magnetic field that is insufficient to record the desired data. Reducing surface roughness is a prerequisite for higher density both in writing and in reading. Likewise, reducing the size and number of dropouts or defects is a prerequisite for higher density. A defect such as a clustering of magnetic particles (with closed flux paths internally) or absence of magnetic material may be too small to be noticeable at one density but may be a serious dropout at a higher density when the bit size approaches the size of the defect. These dropouts and other defects not only result in poorly recorded data but also increase the random noise induced in the sense head during reading. As density increases, it is obvious from Section 6.4 that the skew must be controlled more accurately with better tape guiding, or more sophisticated skew buffers must be included. As the bits become smaller and thinner, the signal amplitude grows smaller. A larger velocity would improve the signal but also would increase the noise amplitude generated by the medium nonuniformities. A certain minimum signal to noise ratio must be maintained, which necessitates improvements in the medium uniformity.

Next to surface roughness and defects, perhaps the most important parameter affecting density is the medium thickness. Obtaining a thin tape medium that is uniform over large areas, contains no dropouts at a specified density, and is relatively inexpensive to manufacture, presents an interesting challenge.

Thus far we have addressed only one aspect of the problem, namely, the linear density. The areal density is perhaps even more important, and it is limited more severely by the track density rather than by the linear bit density. Track density is very low because of the practical difficulties encountered in spacing the tracks closer together. As a result this problem has received considerable attention. One practical solution that is gaining popularity is the use of a "rotary head." The basic idea is represented in Fig. 6.7-1. A read/write head is recessed into a polished cylinder that rotates at a high velocity ω. The tape is wound in a helical fashion around the cylinder such that the edge of the tape makes an angle θ with the cylinder axis. The tape is moved in this helical direction at a velocity v, which is much less than the angular velocity of the head. Hence the tape is nearly stationary as the head moves across the track of length L (Fig. 6.7-1b). After recording this track of length $L = W/(\sin \theta)$, the head must rotate around the cylinder. During this time, the tape moves some small distance such that when the head appears at the tape edge the second time, a new track position is ready for recording. Obviously the spacing between tracks is determined by the diameter of the rotating cylinder, its angular velocity ω, and the tape velocity v. Very close track spacings, in the range of hundreds of tracks per inch, can be obtained this way. Rotary heads that use this basic principle are employed in the Ampex Terabit Recording System (Damron et al., 1968; Damron and Kietz, 1968) and the IBM 3850 mass storage system (*Computer Decisions*, 1974)*. Note that in this arrangement, the tracks can be made addressable by accurate control of the linear positions of the tape around the cylinder. Thus such systems can have the track addressing advantage of disks while maintaining the flexible medium

---

* The 3850 stores about 10K transitions/in., equivalent to about 7K run length coded data bits/in.: tracks are 15 mil wide and 67 tpi.

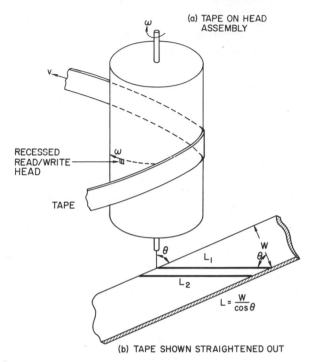

(a) TAPE ON HEAD ASSEMBLY

RECESSED READ/WRITE HEAD

TAPE

(b) TAPE SHOWN STRAIGHTENED OUT

FIGURE 6.7-1   Rotary head recording on a flexible medium.

and contact recording advantages of tape. Such systems may eventually replace ordinary tape.

Although substantial room for improvements remains with respect to track widths, some practical limits must be reckoned with. The problem of defects or nonuniformity in the medium gives rise to noise in the read head. For a given defect size and density within the medium, as the track width is reduced, these defects generate more noise. This occurs simply because a point is reached at which the defects become a significant part of the magnetic bit cell being sensed. Further reduction in defect size and density will reduce the unwanted noise. Even assuming a perfect medium, however, other practical factors limit the track size (e.g., the so-called Barkhausen noise discussed in Section 5.4).

6.8 TAPE STORAGE CONTROL UNITS

The most common type of storage controller system is that appearing in Fig. 9.2-1. Section 9.2 explains the necessity of this unit apart from the CPU.

We lump together all the I/O processor logical functions required for tape operation under the heading of "controller," irrespective of where it physically resides. For IBM-like systems, this includes the channel and control unit, whereas for CDC-like systems the peripheral processor unit (PPU) and so-called "controller" are included. The practical implementation of these functions in terms of system configurations such as in Figs. 9.2-2 and 9.2-3 becomes intimately involved with computer resource management, throughput, and efficiency for the intended application, all subjects beyond our scope.

All controllers are special purpose, dedicated or semidedicated computers with a logical structure tailored to the particular application. A controller can typically control a number of tape drive units (e.g., 8 or 16). The control is carried out by means of a stored program, written by a user or a systems programmer. Thus a controller must be able to address one of several tape units, decoding and executing control instructions, and these instructions must operate on the data register, either writing its contents on tape or reading data from tape into the register. The data path width between the CPU, the controller, and the tape unit is typically one character wide, which is equivalent to seven or nine tracks. The control instructions are often referred to as commands and have a format somewhat different from that of CPU instructions. However they are completely analogous, having an address

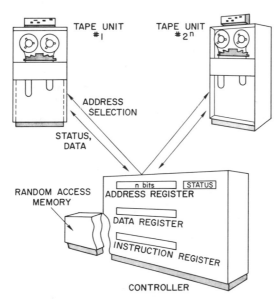

FIGURE 6.8-1 Block diagram of multiple tape drives connected to a tape control unit.

and operation part as minimum components. The address selects one of the several tape units by way of an ADDRESS register, and the operation is decoded in the COMMAND register as in Fig. 6.8-1. This is completely analogous to the central processor addressing of a word of main memory. One difference is that in the latter, the time to write or fetch the information from main memory is fixed and all subsequent operations are clocked accordingly. In tape operations, the time to read or write is highly variable; it is possible in complex systems to have a request for a second tape unit before the first one has been successfully processed. Hence some logical means must be provided to indicate the status of a given tape unit currently residing in the address register. The status information and its subsequent use may be very simple, such as a lockout until the first tape unit is completely processed, or very complex, involving priorities, type of command being processed, and so on.

In principle all the commands must be contained in the final object program, which resides in a random access memory. The location of this memory varies with system architecture; it can be a selected portion of main memory to which the controller has access, as in IBM systems, or portions of it can reside within the controller (i.e., PPU) as in CDC systems (Fig. 9.2-3).* In any case the commands must be stored and accessible. In typical user programs, a tape instruction need not contain all the underlying commands; rather, the instruction essentially calls a subroutine that contains the necessary commands and is provided by the systems program. However these operations or commands must be supplied somewhere in random access memory, and the exact details can vary significantly.

Some of the commands available to the systems programmer that are fundamental to tape operation are as follows:

READ	(READ BACKWARD)
WRITE	(WRITE BACKWARD)
REWIND	Back to load point marker
ERASE GAP	Write end of file gap (tape does not stop)
WRITE TAPE MARK	
FORWARD BLOCK	Advance to next IRG
FORWARD FILE	Advance to first IRG after tape mark
BACKSPACE BLOCK or FILE	Analogous to FORWARD

Some systems do not have all these functions, whereas others have additional features (testing status, bad track indication, etc.). Each command is decoded and executed by the controller in conjunction with the tape unit, and if

---

* For this reason, Fig. 6.8-1 shows the memory separately.

appropriate, the CPU. Many operations, such as parity generation and checking, exact form of the tape mark, writing or reading stored addressing information preceding the following data (Fig. 6.5-1), and encoding the incoming data to the recording code, are provided within the controller logic circuits and are done in many different ways. The details are available in manufacturers' manuals.

7 Direct Access Storage Systems

7.1 INTRODUCTION: DEFINITION OF DIRECT ACCESS

This chapter deals primarily with the fundamental characteristics of the more common disk systems. The widely used programmable recording format (IBM) is contrasted with a nonprogrammable format (CDC) to show the fundamental differences, and the advantages and disadvantages of each. Systems of the former type are available from a wide variety of manufacturers. In addition, numerous other disk systems are available (see Modern Data series 1968–1976, *EDN/EEE*, 1972; Frost, 1970; Greenblatt, 1972). The fundamentals and concepts presented here are applicable in general.

It should be clearly understood that a "direct access storage" (DAS) system is not a randomly addressable store in the sense of random access main memory; nor is it purely sequential like tape—rather, it is in between. Direct access storage systems in use today require basically two logical operations to access the desired information; one part is direct in that it is possible to go directly to one area (track or head) of the total storage, but from then on, a sequential-type operation over a smaller portion of the storage area (track length) is necessary. The "direct" part of the operation is done either mechanically (in movable head systems) or electronically (in fixed head systems). Since the total storage of such systems can be very large and it is possible to go directly to a rather small, local portion (one track) of the entire store, the name "direct access storage" has become common.

In essence, one can think of DAS as consisting of short pieces of tape, each piece formed into a continuous loop, and the loops continuously rotated past a read/write transducer. Many such tape pieces can be placed together on a flat circular surface such as a disk, or on a cylindrical surface such as a drum. Clearly, access to any information within, say, one track or one byte of a given tape piece, will be fundamentally the same as accessing the long, uncut tape originally. As added advantage, however, the tape is short, it is in continuous motion, and it is in a continuous loop, making each piece of stored information accessible once for each revolution. Thus a DAS system can greatly reduce the amount of sequential accessing compared to long tapes, but only at a price.

Chapter 4 revealed that in random access memory the address of any desired word is *exactly* specified in the address register with no further user intervention or concern. The decoder interprets the address and goes directly to the physical word for read-out. The address uniquely specifies the desired information both logically and physically. In sequential (tape) systems, just the opposite is true—there is no unique address, hence no way to go directly to the desired information either logically or physically. One must know a great deal about the stored information (which block it is in, the format for comparing a known piece with the desired input information, etc.). Likewise, with a DAS system, one must have a significant amount of knowledge about the file before the desired information can be found; otherwise a sequential search is necessary, and this can be quite time-consuming.

Many addressing problems associated with tape result from its purely sequential mechanical nature and cannot be circumvented even with additional aids such as separate addressing tracks as postulated in Section 6.5. However these aids can be quite useful in DAS systems if one wishes to implement them for additional cost and additional complexity. This chapter demonstrates that the major differences between various DAS systems center around the type and complexity of these aids (e.g., stored addressing information (SAI), stored clocking tracks), and they must be understood fundamentally to appreciate the advantages and differences between various DAS system organizations and formats. We devote considerable discussion to this subject and consider in detail several commercial systems.

Our principal concern in this chapter is with the physical attributes of the DAS systems, to show what built-in mechanisms are available for storing and retrieving the desired information. In other words, except where noted, we assume that there is no operating system and no systems programming aids on the system, and that the mechanisms available to us are those the systems programmer must use to implement a more sophisticated "user" system. The hardware functions and organization are often dictated or strongly influenced by how files are organized and used, but we do not discuss these here. Chapter 8 covers the details of building files of various kinds, including both the physical properties of DAS systems and the inherent properties of the file.

There are two major types of DAS device in use: the disk and the drum. We give particular emphasis to disks, however, because they are more generally and widely used than drums.

As in the previous two chapters, we discuss DAS systems in terms of the four fundamental requirements for storage (medium, writing mechanism, reading mechanism, and addressing mechanism). We start with the general characteristics of fixed and movable head systems, proceed to the four requirements listed, undertake a comparison of the fundamental differences between various commercial systems (i.e., different SAIs), and examine the density limiting factors for disks and the methods for addressing disks, with examples.

7.2 GENERAL CHARACTERISTICS AND PARAMETERS: MOVABLE HEAD AND FIXED HEAD SYSTEMS

To reduce cost compared to random access memory, it is necessary to share transducers as much as possible, and this leads to a shift register type system that lacks "wired-in" cells. If we accept the fact that mechanical shifting of data is cheaper than electronic shifting, we must move the read/write transducers relative to the storage medium. To circumvent the effects of the slow access time of tape, we must eliminate the long narrow medium, as well as the start/stop requirement. Hence we are naturally led to cutting the tapes into pieces, stacking them side by side, making a loop, and spinning it in a circular motion in the form of a cylinder (drum) or disk. Of course, we could spin the transducers, leaving the medium stationary, but since electrical connections must be made to the transducers, not to the medium, it is easier mechanically and electrically to hold the transducers stationary. Other factors (mass of the heads, flying height control, etc.) also favor moving the medium. We thus arrive at a configuration resembling that in Fig. 7.2-1. Since we can store data in tracks of very narrow width, thus can have many tracks on our disk or drum, we need to know how many transducers and tracks there must be. To keep the cost per bit of the medium itself as low as possible, we wish to store as many tracks as possible in the medium. Then we must decide whether to use one transducer per track or just one transducer, sharing this component even further by moving it from one track to another (i.e., a movable or fixed head system). To decide this question, considerably more information is necessary. Both fixed head/track and movable head systems are used in disks, whereas drums are exlusively fixed, one head per track because drums can be made mechanically very strong and stable, hence can be rotated at very high speeds (e.g., 13,000 rpm). This feature allows the possibility of fast access time on a relatively cheap medium. The use of one transducer moved from track to track would greatly degrade the access time; therefore one head per track is the logical choice. This increases the cost, but fast access time is the key feature of drum storage. Unfortunately the achievable storage density is also reduced, and because of this disadvantage, coupled to the lack of easy removability, removable disk packs are more widely used.

Continuing with the disk, a fixed head system similar to the drum is reasonable but cannot be rotated nearly as fast. If we choose to use one transducer and move it, the moving mechanism will be quite expensive. High cost

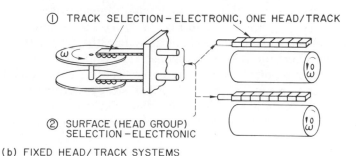

FIGURE 7.2-1 Schematic of direct access systems.

may suggest stacking several disks in parallel, each with one transducer per recording surface, and moving the transducers in parallel as in Fig. 7.2-1. This is precisely what is done in practice, primarily to achieve lower cost. The most common type by far has been the movable head system, although fixed head/track systems are available. Fixed head/track obviously has a substantially better average access time but at a higher price. The important parameters from a user's standpoint are the access time and data rate.

7.2.1 Access Time

Movable head systems require "seek time" or time for the arm to move the magnetic head to the proper track, plus rotation time (rotational delay), which is the time for the correct record on the track to spin around to the head or

$$t_{access} = t_{seek} + t_{rot}. \tag{7.2-1}$$

For fixed head systems, the seek requires electronic switching only and can be neglected compared to the rotation time. The actual rotational delay obviously depends on chance (where the disk position happens to be when an operation is requested) and can vary from zero to a full rotational delay. Over a large number of requests, the rotational delay will have an even distribution over all possible values, giving an average delay of half the rotation time. Since disks and drum speeds are rated in revolutions per minute, this gives

$$\text{average rotational delay} = 0.5t_{\text{rot}}$$

$$= 0.5 \times \frac{60 \ (\text{sec/min})}{\text{speed (rpm)}} \quad \text{sec/rev} \quad (7.2\text{-}2)$$

The seek time for arm movement depends on the distance (i.e., number of tracks over which the head must be moved). This delay increases rapidly for small numbers of track movements but levels off and increases less rapidly for large numbers of tracks (e.g., as in Fig. 7.2-2). This is because the activator is usually an underdamped mechanical system that has a transient and steady state (constant velocity) response. The underdamped (oscillatory) transient response, often referred to as the "settling time," dominates for small arm movement (i.e., barely reaches steady state and must stop), whereas for large distances, the steady state (constant velocity) delay time dominates, giving nearly a linear relation between delay and number of

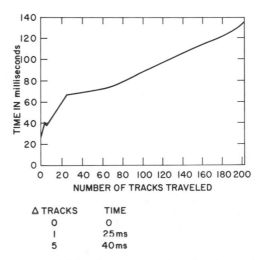

Δ TRACKS	TIME
0	0
1	25 ms
5	40 ms

FIGURE 7.2-2   Arm movement delay time versus number of tracks traveled for typical DAS drive.

tracks in this region of the curve. The ratio of seek time for 200 tracks compared to one track movement can be 5:1, which is quite substantial, with the larger movement requiring 130 msec. Since average rotational delays are typically in the range of 16 to 30 msec, it is important in organizing a file to try to limit arm movement as much as possible, by storing data on successive surfaces (i.e., within a cylinder). When arm motion is necessary, the data should be organized in adjacent or nearby tracks. Obviously the organization of the stored records can have a significant effect on the access time.

7.2.2 Data Rate

Once a data area is found, the information is read (or written) serially for each head. In some systems, all data bytes or characters are stored serially by one head, whereas in other cases several heads are used in parallel, such that a byte is stored within one clock pulse but physically it is recorded on several different surfaces. A larger data rate can be obtained with the parallel system, but additional data buses and circuits must be incorporated at higher cost.

The bits stored on a track are synchronized to a fixed clock, ensuring that the bits per track remains constant.* Hence the bit density is lower on the outer tracks and increases for the inner tracks. The density in bits per inch is thus either an average value or maximum value and is not always clearly identified by the manufacturer. Most often the highest density at the innermost track is used. If this radius r_0 is known, the data rate can be calculated from

$$\text{data rate (bits/sec)} = \text{density (bpi)} \times \text{rpm} \times \text{min/60 sec} \times 2\pi r_0 (\text{in./rev})$$

$$(7.2\text{-}3)$$

Alternately, if the data rate, density, and rotation speed are known, the radius for the density can be calculated easily. For instance, for a system specified as having 4040 bpi, 6448×10^3 bits/sec, and spinning at 3600 rpm, the density is rated at a radius (from 7.2-3) of

$$r_0 = \frac{\text{data rate} \times 60/\text{min}}{2\pi \times \text{density} \times \text{rpm}} = 4.25 \text{ in.} \qquad (7.2\text{-}4)$$

Such a system uses a 7 in. radius disk, recording a 2 in. wide band, hence the density is rated at the inner track. For systems operating several heads in a parallel mode, the data rate is multiplied by the number of parallel paths.

---

* Some systems use two or more clocks over two or more regions to take advantage of higher total bit count possible on the outer track.

7.3 DAS MEDIA*

The first mass-produced commercial computer, the IBM 650, used a drum as the main memory. The drum consisted of electrodeposited nickel-cobalt on a 4 in. cylinder, 14 in. long. An earlier drum on the Manchester computer (not commercially produced; see Section 1.2) used electroplated nickel. The process of electrodeposition can provide a very smooth, uniform surface, particularly on a drum geometry that lends itself to a uniform current density at the surface during plating. Various elements or combinations can be electroplated, but iron has too low a coercive force, and because it oxidizes readily, it deteriorates. Nickel does not deteriorate and can be made with a much higher coercive force, in the range of 100 Oe. Although the latter value was sufficient for densities on the earliest system (in the range of 136 bpi or about 7.5 mils/bit), it is inadequate for higher densities.† Nickel-cobalt can increase the coercive force up to about 800 Oe if desired; the coercive force can be controlled to some extent. Thus nickel-cobalt with a B_s of about 14,000 G is very attractive for high density. However maintaining uniformity during electrodeposition is very difficult because of numerous factors that are more easily controlled on cylinders than on flat disks; thus this process has not been used extensively for disk media. For disks up to densities of at least 6400 bpi, γFe_2O_3 particles suspended on a binder and coated on polished aluminum disks are quite suitable. The coating may consist of 20% magnetic particles and 80% epoxy, plus many other ingredients to give the desired adhesion, thickness, and other properties. One technique for doing this is as follows. A mixture of iron oxide particles in a suitable solvent and binder is placed in the center region of the disk to be coated and the disk is spun at high speed (e.g., 3600 rpm). The centrifugal forces on the mixture cause it to spread out in a somewhat spiral fashion. Since the linear velocity is greater at the outer edges, the mixture normally tends to be thinner at the outer edges, getting progressively thicker as one proceeds inward toward the center. This is a serious problem and limits the band of recording that one can use for this spinning technique between certain radii, which are a function of the recording parameters.‡ Of course the outermost edge would be selected for maximum storage capacity. To be able to use a larger portion of the disk, some manufacturers employ a different method of coating, more like tape, in which the oxide and binder are mechanically placed and spread over the disk surface. Since the coatings

---

* Material parameters and other important characteristics are detailed in Section 5.2.

† For example, a circular spot 7 mils in diameter, 1 μ (25.4 kÅ) thick made of nickel with $B_s = 8$ kG would have a self-demagnetizing field of about 100 Oe.

‡ The IBM/360 DAS 2311, 2316 uses a 14 in. disk with a 2 in. wide outer band. Thickness varies from about 30 μin. at the inner band edge to 50 μ at roughly 0.7 in. from the edge.

are quite thin, typically 50 μin., and getting thinner, spreading becomes increasingly difficult to control. A spraying technique is often used to obtain thin coatings. The spinning technique allows very thin coatings to be applied with uniform thickness in a circumferential direction, but varying in the radial direction. An ideal binder would overcome this variation by means of a special mixture in which the viscosity over a certain region varied inversely with the force applied to deform it.

Disks, unlike tapes, are not in contact with the read/write head; hence the material thickness is more critical for high density recording.

Estimate of Medium Thickness for Disks

If we wish to record at a linear density of, say, 2200 bpi, using DF coding requires 4400 transitions/in. The center spacing of these transitions must be the reciprocal of the latter value. The actual transition should be no more than about half the center spacing, giving

$$\Delta x \Big|_{2200 \, bpi} < \frac{1}{2}\left(\frac{1}{4400}\right) = 144 \, \mu\text{in.}$$

From Section 5.8, and as in Section 6.2, if we again use $\Delta x/T \le 4$, the medium thickness should be

$$T \approx \frac{144}{4} \approx 30 \, \mu\text{in.}$$

This is typically the value of T used for such disk recording. The gap length is typically 100 μin., thus Δx approximately equals l_g. At double the density of 4400 bpi we would expect to require l_g about 50 μin., $\Delta x = 57 \, \mu$in., and a recorded thickness of 15 μin. The actual medium depth might be larger, but only the top portion would be saturated.

7.4   WRITING MECHANISM

The writing process and associated design parameters are detailed in Chapter 5. We consider here only some additional points that are pertinent to disks. Since DAS disk and drum media are in constant motion, it is necessary to keep the heads and medium separated a finite, but small distance; otherwise excessive wear would occur in a very short time. The linear density depends on the separation and its tolerances, high density obviously requiring a close spacing. To achieve a well-controlled spacing, the head is generally "flown" aerodynamically on an "air bearing." This is simply a cushion of air that is dragged along by any rotating surface; though very small, it is nevertheless finite. The effect of this cushion on the head to medium separation can be adjusted by the aerodynamic design of the head assembly, the amount of pressure (forcing head toward medium), and the rotation speed.

In disk technology, the read/write head is very expensive because the miniature, critical structure does not readily lend itself to automation. The cost of the heads alone approaches 50% of the total disk drive cost in some cases, depending on the total number of heads and the extent of other built-in hardware capability. In any case it is clear that low cost means movable heads until practical batch-fabricated heads become feasible. Thus it is typical to use only one head and one gap per surface on a movable head system. The same structure (i.e., same gap and winding) is used for reading and writing. Hence it is not possible to read immediately after writing, as is commonly done in magnetic tape; if one wishes to check the writing process, a full revolution of the disk must be tolerated.

To keep the cost low, it is desirable to avoid track following servo systems. For the same reason, however, it is also desirable to keep the track density as large as possible. How does one design a system to achieve a reasonable balance? For the typical interchangeable disk pack type systems, one proceeds as follows. The absence of track servoing requires special consideration of the track width and signal strength. For a 50 μin. read gap and nominal head to medium spacing, a 5 mil track is needed. Mechanical tolerances on track alignment and following for interchangeable disk packs can be maintained to typically between ± 0.0005 and 0.0015 in. (approximately). If the width of the read/write head is 5 mils, a variation due to mechanical tolerances can cause a loss of 20 to 25% in signal, which is not tolerable. It would be desirable to have the read head about 2 to 3 mils wider than the actual written track width; then variations in the head position relative to the track would not change the signal. This could be done with two separate gaps, one for reading and one for writing, as for tapes. However the edges of a written track are never as strongly magnetized as the center region because of reduction of the write field from the geometrical fringing effects. We have neglected geometrical fringing in all previous analysis, since it is difficult to include this effect accurately. For large tracks widths such as those in tapes, the edge effects are not important. For very narrow tracks such as those used in disks, however, they can be quite significant. Rather than using two separate gaps for reading and writing, a better signal to noise ratio is obtained with the tunnel erase technique provided by heads such as those in Fig. 7.4-1. During the writing process, a wide track of about 8 mils is recorded. At the same time, the tunnel erase gaps are energized with constant negative polarity to erase any transitions in the two narrow edge regions. This leaves a 5 mil recorded track with strong magnetization and signal, while also providing low noise, demagnetized bands between the tracks. The overhang of the read/write gap during reading, plus mechanical tolerances, dictate that

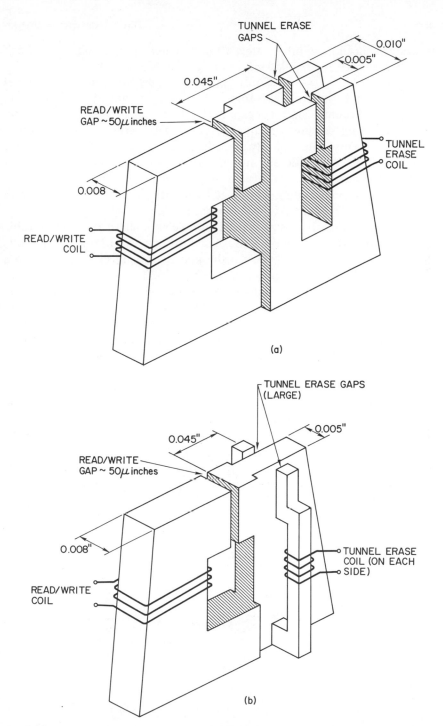

FIGURE 7.4-1 Approximate read/write head geometries for typical disks. (*a*) In-line tunnel erase gaps used in IODISC-1000, IBM 2311. (*b*) Quadature tunnel erase gaps used in IBM 2314.

tracks be spaced on approximately 10 mils centers, giving 100 tpi. As track density increases, track following servo systems become a necessity.

The heads of Fig. 7.4-1 are only approximate, nominal cases. The actual dimensions and geometries vary somewhat among manufacturers and among the systems. Accurate control of gaps in the 50 μin. range is a difficult requirement and manufacturing techniques as well as geometries have been evolved to achieve it. Heads are typically made from ferrite, laminated soft magnetic alloys, or both. As the density further increases (both track and linear bit density), the use of batch-fabricated, thin film heads such as those in Fig. 5.8-12 will become more common (Chynoweth et al., 1973; Chynoweth and Kayser, 1975; Romankiw and Simon, 1975).

The aerodynamically designed head module, module carrier, and movable arm assembly are shown in Fig. 7.4-2. A slightly convex surface of the module provides the aerodynamic lift when the unit is brought close (50 μin.) to a spinning disk. The carrier provides a flexible bed to allow the module to follow variations in the disk surface position (wobble). Pressure is exerted on the carrier, forcing the module toward the disk while the aerodynamic lift of the module forces it away. The balance of these two forces gives a well-controlled flying height that can follow the surface position variation with considerable accuracy.

Since the medium must not be in contact with the heads, the normal and maximum head to medium separation is larger than that in tape systems. Again, the writing density can be higher than the limits imposed by readback, but large head to medium separations can introduce significant broadening of the written transitions width Δx, which is most undesirable. From Fig. 5.3-12 we know that for a given head gap l_g, the sensitivity function becomes broader as the head-to-medium separation h increases. But since a large h is necessary, the only alternative to keep the transitions narrow is to

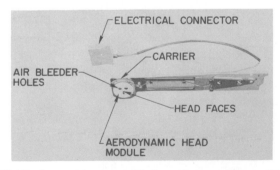

FIGURE 7.4-2   Arm and head assembly for typical movable arm disk systems.

decrease the head air gap length. A 50 μin. gap is adequate at densities of 2200 bpi. Typical write currents are generally less than 100 mA peak, with sense signals of a few millivolts peak.

For a rotating disk, the linear velocity of the disk surface as it passes the head will increase with the radius of the track from the center. If a fixed *time* is used between recorded transitions, the linear bit density will be greater at smaller radii, and vice versa. The maximum density is fixed by the various design factors, hence must be set at some given track radius, usually an inner track. If recording is done over a large variation in disk radius, the outer tracks will have a very low density, hence wasted space. In such cases several zones can be used with different *real time* between recorded transitions in each zone.* This requires additional electronics as well as medium thickness control over a larger portion of the disk. An alternative is to use only the outer portion of the disk and a fixed time between transitions, and to just tolerate the small variation in linear bit density.†

The maximum data rate for writing and reading with one head can easily be obtained from (7.2-3) in terms the disk rotation speed, linear bit density, and the disk radius at which the density is specified. The latter is not usually given, rather, the data rate, linear bit density, and rotation speed are specified in operating manuals. The relationships between these is given by (7.2-4), where r_0 is the radius at which the density is specified; since this is typically the innermost radius of the band, it represents the maximum density. Average data rates are typically in the range of 1 to 12×10^6 bits/sec per head. Higher rates can be obtained by parallel connections of heads. Typical bit densities are 2200 to 4400 bpi.

7.5 SENSING AND READING MECHANISM

The fundamentals of the readback process and design parameters are covered in Chapter 5. Section 5.4 showed that the reduced signal due to smaller track width is compensated by a larger linear velocity compared to tapes.

Since the same gap is usually used for both reading and writing, much of the discussion of Section 7.4 deals with the sensing mechanism as well. A major consideration in disks is the track following capability of the head during reading. At 100 tpi, there usually is no special track following capabilities. The mechanical tolerances on alignment can be maintained to an

---

* CDC disk systems described later (Bryant Corp.) are organized in this manner, using 39 in. diameter, nonremovable disks.
† All IBM systems to date use a 2 in. band (approximately 9 to 13 in. diameter) on 14 in. disks.

accuracy that permits this, as described in Section 7.4. But at higher track densities, the mechanical tolerances become critical and some additional means for servoing is usually required. Some systems, such as those described in Section 7.6, have a separate disk that contains clocking and tracking information. An entire group of heads on a disk drive, for instance, are fixed mechanically relative to one another, but the entire group follows a track prerecorded on the separate disk. This provides a limited but sufficient amount of track following capability.

For removable disk pack systems, continued improvements in density will require special implementations such as the integrated heads within the disk pack* or new techniques and technologies.

7.6 ADDRESSING MECHANISMS: FUNDAMENTAL REQUIREMENTS FOR RECORD ADDRESSING AND FORMATING IN DAS

Several basic requirements must be incorporated into the design of disk systems, and the way these requirements are implemented determines the variations among commercial systems. There are no absolute standards for implementation; rather, each design is undertaken with a clear view of the intended application. We discuss these fundamental requirements and see how they are implemented in several commercial systems.

In rotating disks or drum DAS, the information is recorded in continuous tracks either with a single movable head for all tracks on a surface or with a fixed head for each track, and with possibly several surfaces (Fig. 7.2-1). We are interested only in the absolute minimum requirements for locating and subsequent reading or writing a data area on a single surface. Once we can do this for one surface, we can organize the data on multiple surfaces in any number of ways, such as a record on only one surface (serial by bit), all bytes of a character in parallel on parallel disks, or any combinations. Since each surface has the same basic requirements, and since surface selection is accomplished by a simple electronic switch as in Fig. 7.2-1, we specify the basic requirements for only one, therefore for each surface. For either a movable or a fixed head system, we must be able to accomplish the following.

R1. Select a given track on a specific surface, either by moving the heads and therefore arms (movable head system) or by electronically selecting one head on a specific track (fixed head system).

R2. Verify the position (track and surface); in a movable head system, the mechanical positioning and servoing can be in error, requiring verification. In a fixed head system, mechanical tolerances and other problems

---

* For example, the IBM 3340 records at 5600 bpi and 300 tpi.

can result in misalignment or excessive head to media spacing between a head and its associated tracks. A check of the electronic head selection for possible errors is also desirable. Hence verification is always the first line of business.*

R3. Have a well-defined reference point for counting, clocking, and position reference.

R4. Record (write) data positions along a track.

R5. Locate a previously stored record.

R6. Know when to start reading the located record and when to stop the data transfer to main memory.

All these functions should be done efficiently, with as little wasted storage as possible. This is not a fundamental requirement but a practical one.

Numerous other requirements (error detection and correction, identification of unusable tracks and alternates, etc.) are important but are due to practical problems and, in principle, could be eliminated with more expensive systems and special precautions. The six requirements above are basic and cannot be eliminated even in principle, since they are an intimate part of the storage and retrieval problem. The manner in which these requirements are implemented varies substantially from one manufacturer to another, as well as between different systems of a given manufacturer.

With respect to R1 (track selection), it has already been pointed out that both movable and fixed heads are used. The major differences between systems lie in the total number of tracks, hence heads, on a fixed head system; on a movable head system, the difference resides in the choice of actuator (hydraulic or electromechanical) for moving the arms.

With the exception of R1, all the other requirements must have some form of SAI. The SAI can take either of two forms: (a) being very close to the data it is associated with, to be called "adjacent SAI" (e.g., on same track in adjacent regions), or (b) being far away, on another track, surface or in some other form, to be called "remote SAI" (e.g., index markers, clock and sector marks recorded on separate surface). It should be clear that all serve the same function, namely, to help write and locate data.

With respect to R2, position verification is handled in different ways, but it is always "adjacent SAI," since we may wish to read or write immediately after verification, hence should verify as close to the data as possible.

To write records with a known point of origin as well as to have a point

---

* In principle the user does not *have* to verify position each time but can take his chances; should an error occur, it is a fundamental requirement that position verification be possible, to permit the error to be found. In addition, we see in Section 7.10 that the position verification can be used in some cases as an address for stored records.

for future and continuing reference (R3), all systems have some form of index marker to signify the start of the track. This arbitrary reference point, placed anywhere initially, can be a physical mark (but electronically sensed) or stored bits on a separate surface. This is less critical than position verification and can be done with "remote SAI."

Writing and locating records at various positions along a track (R4 and R5) can be accomplished with either adjacent or remote SAI, and both methods are used in practice.

For R6, knowing when to start and stop reading requires some adjacent SAI. The exact method for implementing all this dictatcs, in a very general way, the format of the records stored on DAS. The format selected determines the storage utilization efficiency of the system, which in turn depends, on the particular application, being good for some and less efficient for others.

All formats for stored records require the use of some "adjacent" SAI, (Fig. 7.6-1a). Some form of information must precede the data to separate the various pieces of data from one another and as an aid in addressing specific records. In the simplest formats (Fig. 7.6-1b), the SAI is a gap, usually but not always of fixed length, with some coded information that is interpreted by the controller hardware (similar to tape gaps). This gap is not (usually) accessible to the programmer. The advantages of this system are that few bits are required for the SAI, and the overall electronics can be relatively simple. The main disadvantage is that the system is more suitable to well-organized data such as those found in scientific or engineering calculations.

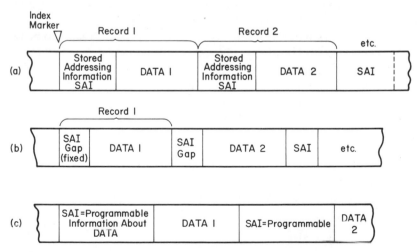

FIGURE 7.6-1 Fundamental track formats for DAS systems. (*a*) General case. (*b*) Simple format using gaps for SAI. (*c*) Complex format using programmable SAI.

With slight modifications, this is essentially the format in use on CDC 6639 and 7638 disk systems (see Section 7.7). It is not intended for use in a general environment, where highly variable data lengths are continually encountered.

When a highly variable and general type of data is to be recorded, a more complex format such as that in Fig. 7.6-1c is desirable. Here the adjacent SAI contains gaps resembling those in Fig. 7.6-1b, but more important, it has areas that are programmed information about the data and are invaluable aids in locating records. In essence this is the format used in IBM system 360/370 disk systems, but with substantially more detail. The disadvantages are the large amount of storage space consumed by the SAI in many cases, and the additional complexity of the electronics and programming when the full capabilities are used.

The amount and complexity of the "remote SAI" also determines the flexibility of the system and the cost. The addition of a separate disk for indexing, clocking, and sector addressing can greatly aid in implementing R3, R4, and R5 but necessitates considerably more hardware and logic capability in the system.

With this foundation, we can discuss the details of several actual systems of the simple and complex types for disks. Although we contrast specific embodiments of the programmable and nonprogrammable systems in terms of IBM and CDC systems, the concepts are applicable to many other manufacturers and in fact can be generalized.

7.7 CHARACTERISTICS OF NONPROGRAMMABLE TRACK FORMAT SYSTEMS (CDC–LIKE DAS)

7.7.1 Movable Head Systems

The fundamental components of two movable head disk systems are illustrated in Fig. 7.7-1 and 7.8-1. Disks in a stacked series are mounted on a common shaft and rotated at reasonably high speeds (1800 to 3600 rpm) in unison. The read/write heads are mounted on arms that extend between the disks, one head for each surface (top and bottom), and can be moved in and out of the stack. All arms, therefore all heads, are linked together and are moved in unison by one actuator, either hydraulic or electromechanical. In a multiple disk system as shown, the user has the ability to move the arms in and out to select a particular location on the disk surface, as well as the capability to select one of the given read/write heads. The former is mechanical, therefore slow, requiring milliseconds, whereas the latter is electronic and essentially instantaneous as far as using the system is concerned.

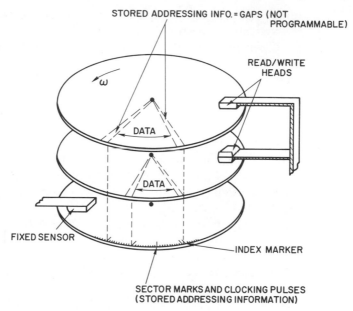

STORED ADDRESSING INFO.= GAPS (NOT PROGRAMMABLE)

READ/WRITE HEADS

DATA

DATA

FIXED SENSOR

INDEX MARKER

SECTOR MARKS AND CLOCKING PULSES (STORED ADDRESSING INFORMATION)

FIGURE 7.7-1   Fundamental addressing features of CDC 6639 and 7638 disk systems.

These two systems differ primarily in the complexity and method of implementing the SAI. The system of Fig. 7.7-1 uses, basically, the data format of Fig. 7.6-1*b*, which is nonprogrammable gaps for data record separation, representing a very simple type of "adjacent SAI." The remote SAI in this case is relatively complex and is contained on a separate disk. For the IBM 360 system, the adjacent SAI is, in essence, the format of Fig. 7.6-1*c*, which is programmable. The remote SAI in this case is quite simple, being mainly an index marker. There is another IBM system, chiefly for use of S370, which makes use of both a complex adjacent SAI (format same as S360) and a complex remote SAI (separate disk with sector addressing, etc.). Let us now consider the details of the first system. No attempt is made to cover all facets of organization and use; rather, the fundamental components are presented, and these can serve as a solid foundation for learning the various details.

7.7.2   Fundamentals of CDC 6639 and 7638 Disk Systems

Very little SAI is contained within the data record itself, the SAI on track being primarily fixed gaps determined by the hardware. The records consist of data sections preceded by a "preamble" and followed by a "postamble"

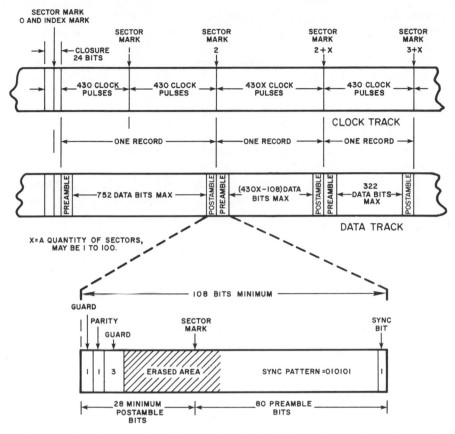

FIGURE 7.7-2 Schematic of track formats for clock and data tracks of Fig. 7.7-1 for CDC 6639.

as in Fig. 7.7-2. To facilitate both placement and searching of records, the remote SAI is contained on a separate disk that provides the *index mark*, a series of sector marks, and clock pulses as in Fig. 7.7-1. The index mark again signifies the beginning of the track and acts as a reference point. The surface is divided into sectors of equal length with numbers that are addressable. Records can only start (start recording preamble) at a sector mark. Since the sector marks can be addressed, this technique provides additional addressing capability and represents remote SAI which is supplementary to the limited amount on the recorded track. As in Fig. 7.7-1, each stack of disks has one sector-clock track that is sensed by a fixed head and is not accessible to the user. The actual data can extend beyond one sector length as shown and can end in the middle of a sector; however the latter wastes storage space, since the next record must start at the next sector mark. Thus records are usually "blocked" to fit the available space as nearly as possible.

Let us now look at this system to see how the fundamental requirements of Section 7.6 are satisfied.

R1. Track selection on a surface has already been mentioned: all arms are moved in parallel.

R2. Position verification of the track and head is provided by the first four bytes or first 48 bits* of the data field of each sector, thus satisfying R2 of Section 7.6. Since read and verify position can be done immediately before reading data, no time is lost, whereas verify position and write data costs one sector because of switching times from read to write; read verify must be done on the previous sector.

R3. The reference mark requirement is implemented by a magnetically stored bit pattern (index) signifying the beginning of all tracks and enabling the first record to be easily marked as well as initiating the clock for counting (specifying) sectors to follow.

R4. Recording at various positions and locating records is provided primarily by the sector marks.

R5. Locating records is done by a combination of sector addressing and gaps on the tracks.

R6. Information to start and stop reading data is provided by the preamble and postamble gaps.

Efficient storage utilization is highly dependent on the size and type of data records, and their inherent ability to be organized into blocks of length comparable to the sector size.

Thus all these systems have the basic requirements. Figure 7.7-2 shows that the CDC 6639A disk can record a maximum of 43,000 bits/track, including preamble and postamble. The preamble is 80 bits, and the postamble is a minimum of 28 bits and 100 sectors maximum. In the 7638 system, the density is increased to 86,930 bits/track, but only 40 sectors are now available. The preamble and postamble are larger, being approximately 165 and 66 bits, respectively, although they can vary. Both systems use 39 in. diameter disks rotating at 1800 rpm. The total system, which consists of many disks on several spindles (disk drives), can be organized in many different ways. These CDC systems read 16 tracks in parallel.

* CDC systems use 12 bits/byte; systems are word oriented, 60 bits (5 bytes) per word.

7.8 CHARACTERISTICS OF PROGRAMMABLE TRACK FORMAT SYSTEM (IBM S360/370)

In the IBM 360/370 systems, the basic track formats are the same for all DAS systems, hence for all disk systems, being of the variety shown in Fig. 7.6-1c. However some of the physical hardware does vary among systems. Here we are concerned with both the simplest 2311 and 2314 type disk systems used on S360 and the more complex 3330, which is used on S370.

The basic hardware components of the 2311 and 2314 type disk and drive appear in Fig. 7.8-1. In addition to the hardware components to select a track (cylinder) and a surface (head), a separate nonrecording metal shield is included on the bottom of the disk packs, which contain only an index marker. This marker, which is a physical slot in the shield, is sensed by a photocell and represents the only rotational position information about the disk. All other information must be stored on the track. The record format of the track is basic to the 360 and 370 systems and provides the flexibility of the systems to handle records of varying size, organizational structure, and searching parameters. Before discussing the track format, it is necessary to understand the "cylinder" concept of disk file organization.

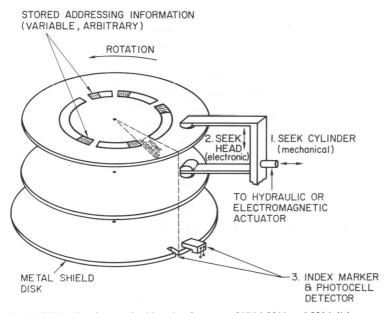

FIGURE 7.8-1 Fundamental addressing features of IBM 2311 and 2314 disk systems.

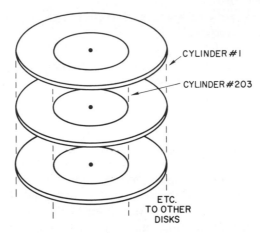

FIGURE 7.8-2   Cylinder concept for storing data files.

7.8.1   Disk Cylinders

Since all the movable arms move in unison and are positioned at one point (track) at a time, and since this is a slow process compared to electronically selecting a head, data for a specified file are usually written and read on "cylinders" to keep the access and searching time as low as possible. A cylinder is thus represented as a column of one specific track on all successive disks as shown in Fig. 7.8-2. If there are a total of 203 tracks per disk surface (IBM 2311), there are 203 maximum possible cylinders (200 + 3 spares). Thus if a user stores a file on one cylinder—requiring, for example, all tracks (disks) within that cylinder—and he wishes to search the file for a record of unknown position in the file, only one movement, maximum, is required of the head assemblies. Each disk can be read separately but usually only sequentially, that is, one surface within a given cylinder for each disk revolution. Thus a search of all disks within a given cylinder made up of 20 disk surfaces will require 20 revolutions but only one arm movement.

7.8.2   S360/370 Disk Track Format

The basic structure of the track format is illustrated in Fig. 7.8-3, where the index marker and "home address" are located as indicated in Fig. 7.8-1. All tracks have identical formats, hence all have a "home address."

The parts of the track format in Fig. 7.8-3 are as follows:

Index Marker. Physical beginning of all tracks; as previously indicated, denoted by a slot on separate plate and sensed by photocell for 2311 and 2314 systems.

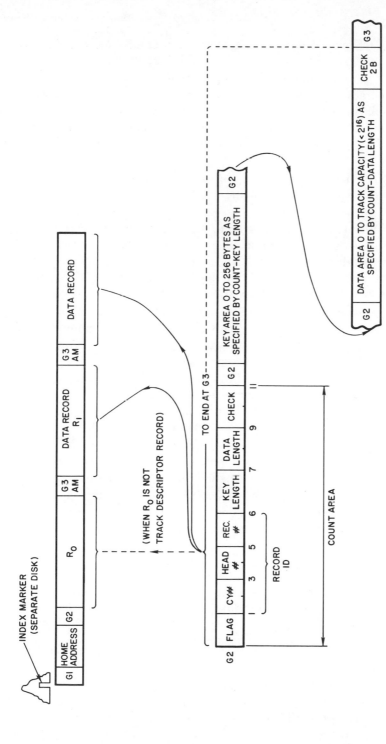

FIGURE 7.8-3 Fundamental feature of track format for IBM S360/370 disk systems.

495

*Gap G*1. Separates index marker from home address; fixed length for given system but can range from 36 to 72 bytes among systems.

Home Address. Immediately after index marker (slot on bottom plate); one per track, home address provides a reference point for programmer to begin a file or start a search as well as indicate (flag) if track is operable and its address (cylinder and head number in binary notation); it is not (normally) changed by programmer, thus is always fixed. Flag tells whether track is operable.

*G*2. Fixed length, separates home address from count area of data record (can be from 18 to 36 bytes in different systems).

R_0. Can be either the first data record of the file or a track descriptor record. When used as a data record, it is like any other record such as R_1. Since various parts of a surface often become inoperable because of head crashes or other malfunctions, R_0 is often used as a programming aid, to enable the entire contents of that track (primary track) to be moved to another (secondary) track if a portion of the primary track is inoperable.

Data Records. Consist generally of three basic parts (the COUNT, KEY, and DATA areas), separated by gaps of the *G*2 variety as shown.

Count Area. Flag, cylinder, and head number are similar to that in home address. This redundancy allows the user to check the actual number of heads and cylinders without having to wait for the address marker and home address; also it can be used as a physical address as we show later. The remaining information serves to describe the subsequent record to the system and programmer. Record number (1 byte in binary notation) specifies the sequential number of the record on the track, maximum of 256 (2^8).

Key Length. One byte binary, specifies to the system the actual number of bytes in the key area; zero key length indicates that no keys are used.

Data Length. Two bytes binary, similar to key length in function, to specify actual number of bytes in data area. Zero indicates no data. Within the count area, the cylinder, head, and record numbers are called the record ID and can be addressed as a unit (see Section 7.10).

Check. Two bytes used for error detection and checking.

It should be obvious that since each record has its own count area, variable record lengths as well as formats (keys or no keys) are easily handled.

*G*2 *Gap.* (As before.) Separates count and key areas.

Key Area. Contains actual keys associated with data (see Section 8.4), length specified by count–key length and can vary from 0 to 256 (2^8) bytes.

*G*2 *Gap.* (As before.) Separtes key and data area.

Data Area. Contains the actual stored information and can vary from 0 to 64K' bytes (2^{16}) as specified by the two binary bytes in the count–data length.

Check. Two bytes for checking and error detection.

*G*3. Special gap containing an "address marker" to indicate to the control unit that a count area follows.

It can be seen from both the above systems that "adjacent SAI" with its own gaps is very important to the hardware (e.g., controller) for locating specific records or parts of the records on a given track. Gaps contain a string of bytes that are written as well as recognized by the controller, hence contain no data. In essence, they are part of the programmable SAI, although they are not under the control of the user but are completely handled by the controller. They occupy a nonnegligible portion of the recorded bits and must be taken into account when juding the storage efficiency of any file system.

Let us now examine this system to see how the six basic requirements of Section 7.6 are implemented.

R1. Track (and head) selection is provided by the hardware as previously.

R2. Position verification is contained in the "adjacent SAI" stored with each record in count area or home address.

R3. Reference point is provided by the index marker, which in combination with home address is essentially the only "remote SAI."

R4. Write at various positions along a track is provided by the address marker gaps *G*3.

R5. Locate records is done in various ways by use of the adjacent SAI stored as count, ID, or key, or by use of these in conjunction with the data, as will be seen.

R6. Start and stop reading is provided by the data length specificd in the count area, in conjunction with gaps *G*2.

Thus all the fundamental requirements are accounted for.

The somewhat complex track format of Fig. 7.8-3 is more than just an attempt to circumvent the lack of random addressing in DAS. There are certain problems fundamental to file organization and the way people use them, as detailed in Chapter 8. This complex format attempts to provide flexibility and versatility to the user in organizing a file. One could argue that this is not fundamentally necessary. For instance, a search for any given piece of data could be done by searching on the stored data, thus requiring no additional stored addressing information except fixed gaps as in tape. This could be done by comparing certain bits in the record with known bits (i.e., a person's name or number), but there are several problems. First, it would be necessary to ensure that the bits used for compare are unique to that record; otherwise, of course, there would be errors. In addition, this procedure is slow because it is sequential, and in many search cases the bits used for compare come after the desired stored information, requiring another full rotation. Even more important, some additional logical functions (hardware, software, or both) would be needed to specify the *exact* location of that record for subsequent reading. Such logic is already built into the formatted track. The key and or count area can be used for unique identification of the record and the data can be read out of the data area immediately after a match condition has been obtained. If the search is done explicitly on data stored within the record (i.e., associative compare), of course this formatted track has no fundamental advantage. The search would be done, if at all possible, on a prior data record, and when a match occurred, the data area after the next address marker would be read. This would eliminate the need for an additional full rotation but would require knowledge of the previous record, which is essentially SAI stored in the user's head or in the program.

Figure 7.8-3 indicates that the "adjacent SAI," which includes rather long gaps, can occupy a significant amount of storage. Thus it is desirable, for an efficient system, to have data records that are proportionally long. The technique of blocking (Fig. 6.5-3) is therefore often used as with all systems (tapes and disks), but blocking is a programming option or feature and is not fundamental to the hardware operations per se; that is, the hardware has no knowledge of the logical structure of the data. Physically, information is stored as data records that can be single physical records, multiple physical records (blocks), scientific data, mathematical tables, numbers, constants, or whatever one chooses. The data record represents the smallest piece of information that can be written or fetched (i.e., equivalent to a word or byte in main memory). Fetching a data record is still rather coarse; the record may contain many fields, and only one of these may be desired. Any "finer" addressing requires transfer of the entire data record into main memory for resolution of the separate records and separate bytes.

The two previous sections revealed that the CDC system has sector addressing (rotational position via sector/clock track) but a nonprogrammable SAI on track. The IBM system discussed does not have sector addressing but has a programmable SAI on track. Each system has its own advantages and disadvantages. As one might suspect, it is possible to combine the sector addressing capability with a programmed SAI for greater versatility and improved performance. This is precisely what is done in the IBM 3330 disk file system.

7.8.3   IBM 3330: Basic Characteristics

The IBM 3330 has a separate disk, similar in principle to that of Fig. 7.7-1, but it contains 128 sector marks, allowing the rotational position to be known to within 360/128 or about 2.8°. These sectors can be addressed separately with sector commands (e.g., read sector, set sector); thus the entire system provides a "finer" (more detailed) addressing capability than either of the other two.

No attempt is made to describe the complete system, since operating manuals are easily obtained. Nevertheless, a number of points of special interest deserve mention. The density is quite high, being 4040 bpi maximum, $\times$ 192 tpi on model 1, for an areal density of

$$4040 \text{ bpi} \times 192 \text{ tpi} = 775,680 \text{ bits/in.}^2$$

which is approaching 10^6 bits/in.^{2}. One surface of a disk can store about 5.25M bytes or 42M bits/surface. A complete system consists of eight disk drives storing 100M bytes/drive (per disk pack, which is removable) or 800M bytes for the system, or a capacity approaching 10^{10} bits of storage. Model 2 achieves double density by storing twice as many tracks per inch at the same linear bit density, giving approximately 200M bytes/disk pack. The rotation speed of both is 3600 rpm, which means that the time for one rotation is 16.7 msec or an average rotational delay of $16.7/2 = 8.4$ msec. Nominal data rates are 806,000 bytes/sec or about 6.4M bits/sec. The head flying heights and the storage medium are both 50 μin. The actuator arm seek time is comparable to earlier systems: 10 msec cylinder to cylinder, and 55 msec maximum.

The major hardware improvements have been in the areal density with the added capability for rotational position sensing (RPS) and sector queueing. Although the density and speed have been improved over earlier systems, the rotational position feature has been particularly important. This feature allows other important parts of the overall computing system, namely, the channel and control unit, to be freed from the disk drive for most of a record search time; hence they can be performing other operations such as controlling other disk drives. For instance, suppose we request a record that is in sector 1 and on interrogation, we find that we are just entering sector 2; the channel and control unit can be released for nearly $16.4 \times (127 \div 128) = 16.2$ msec, which is a long time, during which many other CPU input/output instructions can be performed. On other disk systems without rotational position sensing (e.g., one index mark and no sectors), the control unit must remain connected to the drive, since there is no way to know when the index mark might suddenly appear. For systems with sector marks, releasing of the connection could be done if the logic were provided in the controller. All these additional features require considerable logic hardware, and a system with high density and large storage capacity is desirable to keep the cost per bit down. Most of the additional features of the 3330 are built into the control unit. Many of these relate to the system 360/370 architecture and aim at improving the overall system efficiency.

7.9 VARIATIONS IN DISK SYSTEMS

The foregoing examples demonstrate widely different ways to achieve the basic addressing requirements of Section 7.6. It should be apparent that there are numerous other possibilities, and in fact such variations do exist. Some disk systems that use physical holes for sector marks include more than one sector, allowing addressing to be done at the beginning of each sector, thus providing additional SAI.

IOMEC Corp. IODISC 1000 (removable disk cartridge, i.e., one removable disk + one fixed disk) uses 8 or 12 sector marks (two models) and one index mark, all placed on a small vertical hub rather than on a horizontal disk. A similar technique is used in the HP 7900A disk system, except 24 sector slots and one index slot are placed on the hub. The IBM 2314 disk drive uses 20 sectors plus one index as in Fig. 7.8-1. The methods are all similar in principle, but this type of sectoring is considerably less expensive *and* less flexible compared to sectors stored on a separate disk. No attempt is made to discuss all the available commercial systems (see *Modern Data* series 1968–1976; *EDN/EEE*, 1972; Frost, 1970; Greenblatt, 1972); the systems mentioned were chosen at random.

In addition to the physical attributes of the hardware, there are differences among various systems with respect to the method of organization. These differences are not fundamental to DAS but arise because of the overall architecture of the computer with which it is interacting. For instance, the number of surfaces read in parallel, the number of disks stacked on one drive mechanism, the number of drive mechanisms paralleled as one system, and the number of bits used to represent one byte (character), are variables that differ greatly. Since this book is concerned mainly with fundamentals, these parameter variations are not discussed.* Future systems will incorporate higher densities and speeds, with perhaps additional aids to simplify the addressing difficulties. However the same principles will apply; only the method of implementation will be different.

7.10 DAS ADDRESSING TECHNIQUES AND EXAMPLES

The next subject of interest is the use of the hardware and formats of disk systems for data processing. In most cases the "user" has available a high level language such as Fortran, Cobol, or PL/I, and a complex operating system; thus the details of the disk or other I/O are completely hidden. However since *someone* must provide all the details to perform the necessary

---

* Manuals on any given system are easily obtained from the manufacturer.

operations, let us consider how a user, without the aid of a high level language or operating system, actually stores and retrieves data records in symbolic machine code.

In all disk systems, there are three fundamental operations available to the user as follows:

a. Position operations. Used only to move the arms (heads) to the appropriate cylinder, to electronically select a particular disk surface of the cylinder, or to do both; also some method of recovering from a positioning error is required to reset the arm and head to some initial position. As far as the user is concerned, no data are transferred between the DAS and CPU.

b. Read operations. Used to read the data from disk into main memory once the desired record is found.

c. Write operations. Used to write data from main memory into a specified location on a head and cylinder (i.e., a specified track and position on a disk surface).

In addition, a fourth function must always be provided within the controller hardware, although fundamentally it need not be available as a programming operation.

d. Read and Compare—search Selected Areas of Disk. This function is necessary to indicate the cylinder and/or head position, and more important, the circumferential distance along the disk track at any time. Fundamentally, the latter must be provided in some form to the user. In one form it may allow the user to identify fixed positions on the disk, to be able to initiate read or write operations (e.g., sectors). In other forms it may allow the user to identify variable, but previously specified positions on the disk track (e.g., count, key areas). In addition, this function provides for the *practical requirement* of position verification, which is standard practice before reading or writing any data area but is not a fundamental requirement. No data transfer to CPU occurs for this operation.

The commands available for any given system must be assembled together to form a program that will store and retrieve information of a given nature, such as the files in Sections 8.3 and 8.4. Since random addressing is not possible and large blocks of data are stored as units, the exact location of a desired piece of data is often not known, nor can the location be calculated. It may be necessary to search the entire file to find the desired data, and the program for various types of searching can become quite complex. Thus manufacturers often supply programming systems or "operating systems" that take advantage of macroinstructions to greatly simplify the programming. One macroinstruction may generate many machine commands for, say, searching an entire file on many disk surfaces and keeping track of the start and stop of search, data location when found, and numerous details. These programming systems nevertheless make use of the built-in hardware commands, and our concern is with the latter rather than the former, that is, we want to investigate the commands available to the programmer, who must write the programming system for users. The numerous file organization techniques are discussed in Chapter 8.

Within any given commercial system, there are typically subsets of the four basic operations just listed. In the CDC 7678 disk system, the subsets are relatively simple:

a. *Position Operation.* Performed by margin select, position select, head select. The first two mechanically select the correct cylinder and the last electronically selects a group of 16 heads. This system has a data path of 16 bits between disk and controller and organizes the disk and heads into various groupings.

b. *Read operation.* Performed by read select.

c. *Write operation.* Performed by write select.

d. *Read and Compare.* This function is automatically done by the controller during a read or write select operation. The user must specify the sector in which the operation is to start; the controller reads and compares (i.e., searches) the sector positions and automatically initiates the operation on a compare equal.

In a system using programmable SAI, the subsets are somewhat more extensive. We now consider some of the more useful fundamental programming operations corresponding to the IBM format of Fig. 7.8-3.

7.10.1   Position Operations

Seek Cylinder. Mechanical motion of arm to correct cylinder.
Seek Head. Electronic selection of head, therefore surface.

The "seek time," which is the amount of time required to move only the arms, is usually comparable to the rotational delay. However the seek time varies considerably with the distance the arm must travel. Figure 7.2-2 shows the arm movement delay versus the number of cylinders (tracks) over which the arm must move for one system. For a small number of cylinders (e.g., < 5), the seek time nearly equals the total rotational delay (25 msec in this case).* If the arm must move over the entire disk surface, the seek delay can reach 135 msec. This has important implications in

---

* The rotational delay must be added to the seek time.

designing a file; all data should be stored on adjacent cylinders as much as possible, to keep the arm movement, hence seek time, as small as possible.

7.10.2 Read Operations

Read Data. Usually chained from a search command, permitting search and read to occur on same revolution. If not chained, the DATA following the next address marker is read.

Though the reading of the desired data is the ultimate goal, it is necessary to be able to read other portions of a track to arrive at the correct location. As a result, other commands also allow reading of the home address, count, key data, count-key-data, and track descriptor record. Fundamentally, these are read and compare (i.e., search) operations.

7.10.3 Write Operations

Before data can be written, a track or record must be initialized; this is done with commands that write home address, track descriptor record, or count-key-data. The actual data are written by write data, which must be chained from search ID or search key equal. Write key and data must be chained from search ID equal.

It is standard practice to verify after writing. This should be done by performing a read such that no data are transferred to the CPU, although data are transferred to the controller. The DAS instruction or command formats allow such operations. Note that since such disk systems have only one head, which is used for reading and writing, an additional revolution is necessary for verification.

7.10.4 Read and Compare: Search Operation

As might be suspected, the simplest, fastest search requires the user to have the most prior information about the desired information and organization of the file, whereas the most complex and slowest search takes place with the least amount of prior information. Before any search can begin, the head and cylinder must have been set to the desired position (with its delay time). Once this is done, the search can begin, and the desired record can be directly under the head, so there is no rotational delay; or the head may have just passed the desired record, giving the maximum delay of one complete revolution time. On the average, over many searches, the delay is half the rotational time, usually specified as the average rotational delay. Of course this must be added to the seek time delay. There are many combinations and variations of searching possible, but the basic techniques available are as below.

Search ID (C, H, R#). When the specific address (cylinder, head and record number) are known, one can go directly to the desired information with small delay. The head and cylinder must be set with a "seek" command, and the count area of each record on the given track is to be compared with the desired count area for equality (or high or low). As soon as the desired match is located, the data record (or key) of that record can be read out with a read command without any additional delay (i.e., another rotation of disk is not required). This command represents "direct addressing" but requires considerable prior information, which may not be available.

Search Key. Searches key areas of all records on the head and cylinder previously set by a "seek" command. This command is useful when the C, H, and R numbers are not known but the key is known. This method requires, or course, that the file be organized by "keys" (see Section 8.4). The search can be started at a previously set cylinder and head (e.g., beginning of the file) and can sequentially search through the keys of records on all heads and cylinders by the addition of appropriate control bits or programming by the user. As with search ID, the data can be read immediately, once the desired match (high, low, equal) of key areas with the chosen key is obtained. This technique is as close to *random* processing or random addressing as one can get in a disk system.

Search Key and Data. Similar to the previous case except that it searches key areas and specified bits of the "data record" for match (high, low, equal). When a match is obtained, however, the remaining portion of that data record cannot be read, but the next (sequential) record (after the address marker gap) can be read without a full revolution. Thus this technique is useful to obtain a record based on data and key stored in the *immediately preceding* record.

Search Home Address Equal. This is self-explanatory.

The 3330 has, of course, a read sector capability that provides the angular position of the disk as a further aid in addressing.

DISK ADDRESSING EXAMPLE

To better understand the technique of disk addressing, let us consider a simple example making use of the ID portion of the track format. Suppose we are given a file consisting of the year-to-date tax withholding for each employee of a company. The file is stored on disk, organized by identifiers (ID) as follows. The withholdings are stored as the data of reach record; all records are 258 bytes long, including the identifier and any other SAI; total track capacity is 5160 bytes and is the same for all tracks; each record has a unique identifier; the file is written entirely on cylinder #10, with the first entry beginning at head #0 (i.e., first surface). The problem is to find the withholding tax for John Doe, who is entry 226 in the file. This can easily be done as follows.

Since each record is 258 bytes long and the total track capacity is 5160 bytes, the track capacity is 5160/258 = 20 records/track. Thus the first 20 entries in the file are on the first surface or head #0, the second 20 entries are on the second surface or head #1, and so on. Hence entry 226 is located as follows

$$\frac{226}{20} = 11 + \frac{6}{20}$$

Thus it must be on the eleventh surface or head 10, and the sixth record on that surface. The symbolic program for finding this would be

> Seek cylinder #0
> Seek head #10
> Search ID = 226
> Read data

From Fig. 7.8-3, the record ID area contains the cylinder, head, and record number, and the "search ID = 226" instruction verifies the cylinder and head selection before reading the data. If written in machine code, the symbolic program would have to be converted to the correct binary operation codes for the instructions (commands) and the correct binary addresses for the cylinder, head, and ID numbers.

In this example, we might have initially stored the file on one surface rather than on one cylinder. However this could have resulted in many arm movements and excessive delay if many different entries were accessed. Organization by cylinder is generally faster, although exceptions may arise. The programmer must make this decision based on the properties of the disk system and those of the file and likely access patterns.

7.11   DIRECT ACCESS STORAGE CONTROL UNITS

The reader should be familiar with Section 9.2 to understand the rationale for having a special purpose, dedicated computer in addition to the CPU. As was done with tape systems (Section 6.8) we lump together all the disk I/O processor logical functions under the heading of disk controller. For CDC systems, this includes a PPU (Section 9.2) and a disk "controller"; for IBM systems, this includes the channel and DAS control unit. This controller is completely analogous to the tape controllers, typically serving several disk units and having address, data, command, and status functions as in Fig. 6.8-1. Some of the major differences are that the data formats as well as coding are quite different, more operations are available on disks for accessing records, and most often the data are purely serial.

CDC 6639 and 7738 systems operate on 12 and 16 surfaces in parallel, representing 12 and 16 bit bytes, respectively. This is analogous to a tape that operates on a full character as a time. The majority of other systems operate on serial data, storing characters and records along one track in a manner similar to that in Fig. 5.1-1. This figure gives only a few of the more simple functions provided by the controller. Many of the additional functions, particularly those affecting the user, have been covered in Sections 7.6 through 7.10. All instructions must be decoded and logically carried out by the controller with proper timing, encoding, decoding, current wave form generation, and so on. The circuit design details are not any different from those required in the CPU.

The many additional yet necessary functions that are hidden from the user include speed control, air filtration and pressurization, and servicing facilities.

Since controllers perform only a small set of well-defined functions, they provide an excellent opportunity for the use of read-only memory to control the various functions. Extensive use has been made of read-only memories for such microprogramming. A given instruction provides the address of a word. This word or microinstruction has several times more bits than the original instruction (address), and hence supplies logical information for controlling various gates as well as the address for the next microinstruction. For additional information on architectural and design considerations, see Ahearn et al. (1972) and Brown et al. (1972).

7.12   DENSITY–LIMITING FACTORS

Sections 5.7 and 6.7 discussed numerous factors that influence density. Most of these factors are also important in disks. One notable difference between disk and tapes is the requirement for a well-controlled flying height h in the former. The density is strongly dependent on h and it represents one of the major practical limiting factors. Flying heights of 50 μin. are quite common in the systems described previously. Improving this by a factor of 10 to, say, 5 μin. represents a formidable challenge. However such advances will be necessary to achieve higher densities.

It is difficult to present the practical limits in any fundamental way because they are a function of how much one is willing to pay. However it is interesting to note the following: to a first crude approximation the spacing L between transitions on commercial disks is equal to the sum of the head air gap, head to medium spacing, and medium thickness, or

$$L \approx l_g + h + T \tag{7.12-1}$$

In commercial systems, these three lengths are very nearly equal, or

$$l_g \approx h \approx T \tag{7.12-2}$$

This characteristic cannot be proved to be a requirement, but it probably reflects a balance in the amount of investment versus return in each of the three key components of the system.

One fundamental that can be employed in conjunction with the foregoing is that to maintain an air cushion or bearing (i.e., pressure) between the head and medium, h must be larger than the mean free path λ of the air molecules, or

$$h \geq \lambda \tag{7.12-3}$$

The value of λ at standard temperature and pressure is about 2.5 μin. and is known as the Knudsen number. If we take λ to be the minimum value for h, this value in conjunction with (7.12-1) and (7.12-2) gives a maximum practical transition spacing center to center of

$$L \gtrsim 3\lambda = 7.5 \times 10^{-6} \text{ in./transition}$$

or a maximum linear density

$$\frac{1}{L} = 133K \text{ transitions/in.}$$

One could conceive of various methods to circumvent this limit (e.g., using higher pressure or a different gas to lower the value of λ). These measures would increase the cost and complexity, but they may be ultimately necessary. Currently, recorded densities are far below this limit, and considerable room for improvement exists by just reducing the parameters in (7.12-1).

8

File Organization
and Data Structure

8.1 INTRODUCTION*

In Chapters 6 and 7 we learned that inexpensive sequential and direct access systems could be obtained only by sharing transducers and having no wired-in selection capability. This, unfortunately, requires a substantial amount of stored addressing information, both "adjacent" and "remote" in disks. The need for SAI resulted strictly from the hardware and its limited built-in facilities for finding any given record. In structuring files, we find that with few trivial exceptions, we must store even more *information* with the data to help locate that which we seek; this new and additional stored addressing information is called *file addressing information* (FAI). We must incorporate FAI because of the way humans organize and use data, which results from the fact that the way data naturally occurs is not the only way it can or will be used. This leads to multiple interconnections between various pieces of data. Superimposed on this is the need for an efficient system in terms of storage. The FAI is used to provide the logical interconnections with reasonable storage requirements for its own storage.

This chapter reveals that in many types of data processing, the structure of the file is dictated as much by the characteristics of the information (data) being stored as by the characteristics of the storage system used. Thus using the same storage system, one type of data might give a very efficient (in terms of storage utilization), easily searched file, and another type might give just the opposite. We consider several examples to illustrate the importance of the data in determining the overall file characteristics.

As with sequential and direct access type systems (Chapters 6 and 7), it is important when studying file organization to separate the basic facilities that are available to the systems programmer from the facilities provided by the operating systems. The latter are programs prewritten by the manufacturer and are usually available to the user to ease the programming burden. We do not consider the prewritten programs because there are many

---

* For additional information see Buchholz (1963), Codd (1970), Elson (1975), Knuth (1973), Leftkovitz (1968), and Lum et al. (1971).

508

variations; rather, we examine only the basic functions, which can be put together in any number of ways.

The primary considerations in organizing a file include the intended use of the file and the types of searching and updating that are likely to be needed. In general, the more versatile the organization becomes, the more complex it will be, and also, the less efficient in terms of the amount of additional FAI. Two of the primary tradeoffs are the access time to find a given piece of information versus the file organization technique, and the amount of FAI versus the organization technique. In certain cases the file can be organized by its inherent characteristics to give a very fast, efficient file, but this does not generally happen; instead, the inherent characteristics tend toward an inefficient file. We cover some of these examples to understand the basic characteristics and tradeoffs.

8.2 FUNDAMENTAL CONSIDERATIONS IN FILE DESIGN AND ACCESS METHODS

Life itself is a process of continuing change and renewal, and attempts to remain fixed or static result in a backward motion relative to the rest of the world. Thus one might expect that the things man does must also be subject to change, including placing data in files. With very few exceptions, no data of any kind remain fixed or constant but are continually subjected to updating, corrections, deletions, and additions. This is evidently true of commercial data files (customer accounts, income and expense statements, employee files, etc.), but it also holds for such "fixed" data as scientific measurements and tables of properties of matter. Over time, the latter are subjected to refinement of measurements or calculations, discovery of errors, addition of new properties, and so on. Thus files must be designed with change in mind. This fundamental need to be able to make insertions, deletions, and corrections represents one of the most difficult parts of file design and leads to many techniques for accomplishing "changeability."

In addition to changeability, there is a fundamental need for cross-referencing, or data searching various pieces of information (e.g. "all employees in Department X" or "all blue cars" or "all blue cars with V-8 engines"). When designing a file, one may know some of the types of searches and cross-references desired, but one seldom knows or even can guess at all the types of searches to be made. Thus the designer must anticipate these to a certain extent and make provisions whenever possible. Regardless of how well a file is designed, it will never be perfect and can never satisfy all possible demands.

The many variations and combinations of techniques used for file structuring and searching not withstanding, there are three fundamental ways to organize and/or access data records in a file, independent of the type of memory used.

1. *Sequential*. Records are organized sequentially as data become available, with no spaces between records and no separate means for identification; accessing is accomplished by searching the entire file, starting at one point and continuing one record after another until the desired one is found based on some self-contained identifying information (e.g. name, ID). Even if a random access memory is used, the address is unknown, requiring sequential searching.

2. *Direct*. Records are stored according to some physical hardware address that can be specified in a number of ways, thus leading to numerous variations; accessing is accomplished by first determining the physical address (this may have to be calculated or looked up in a table, etc.), then going directly to that address as fast as the hardware will permit (e.g., unique keys).

3. *Indirect*. Records are organized in a manner that is between or a combination of sequential and direct. There are several variations, but in each the specific address of the desired record is not known and must be found or determined by preliminary sequential steps that eventually lead to the desired address, hence the term "indirect" (e.g., lists, nonunique keys).

We discuss each of these in more detail, and specific examples are given in subsequent sections.

Sequential organization and searching in its pure form applies mainly to files stored on tape and tapelike media for which there is no physical mechanism enabling one to determine a specific location on the tape (i.e., no physical address). Hence searching must rely entirely on information stored in the records. Furthermore, since tape can only move forward or backward in a sequential manner, retrieval of a specific piece of information stored on tape usually requires searching a large number of records. Therefore this type of organization and medium is used whenever possible for files that lend themselves to sequential processing, such as a payroll, where every record requires processing, sequentially, one after another, rather than one out of a large number.

Direct access lends itself to implementation to both random access memory and DASD (direct access storage devices—disks, drums). Since files are almost never stored in main memory, however, we limit ourselves to DASD in terms of file organization.

8.3 FILE STRUCTURE OF SIMPLE DATA RECORDS WITH SELF–CONTAINED UNIQUE IDENTIFIERS: EXAMPLES

Let us consider a simple but instructive example in which it is desirable to store a table of sin θ to five places (5 decimal numbers = 5 bytes each) for $1°$ intervals of θ (i.e., θ from 0 to 359). Since the record can be sequential and numerically ordered (0 to 359), the simplest method would be a programmable track format such as that in Fig. 7.8-3 but without keys. If the file started at the beginning of the track, the track records would be as in Fig. 8.3-1 using only count area and no keys. The ratio of stored data to stored addressing information will be less than 5:11, indicating very inefficient use of the disk. A more efficient file would store groups of say, 20 angles per data record, which would increase the ratio to about (5 × 20):11 or about 9. However, the sine of any given angle will then require some additional processing, although the result may be found faster.

In the simple case of Fig. 8.3-1, keys are not needed because we know that the sine of any angle (integer values of angle) is stored in record number equal to that angle (i.e., sin 60 is stored in record 60). Now the question is, Where is record 60? Suppose there are only 40 such data records per track (not realistic, since there are more likely to be 2000 to 3000 bytes/track, depending on record format); then the entire file will require nine tracks (i.e., 360 records ÷ by 40 records/track = 9 tracks). We can determine the exact location from the data record ID. Assuming data are stored only on one surface, the record number can go only to 40 on any given track and then the cylinder number is incremented to second cylinder (same surface, next track), and the record number repeats again from 0 to 39. The location of sin 60 or record number 60 is obtained simply by dividing 60 by the number of records per track or, since we are storing on one surface, the number of records per cylinder: thus

$$\frac{60 \text{ records}}{40 \text{ records/cylinder}} = 1 \text{ cylinder and remainder of } 20$$

Thus record 60 is on cylinder 1, record 20 on that track (note that the first cylinder was number 0).

Keys are not needed in this case because the record number is the sine of the desired angle and provides a unique identifier. Thus we could find sin 60 by

Seek cylinder 1
Search ID equal 60 (meaning cylinder 1, head 0, record 20)
Read data

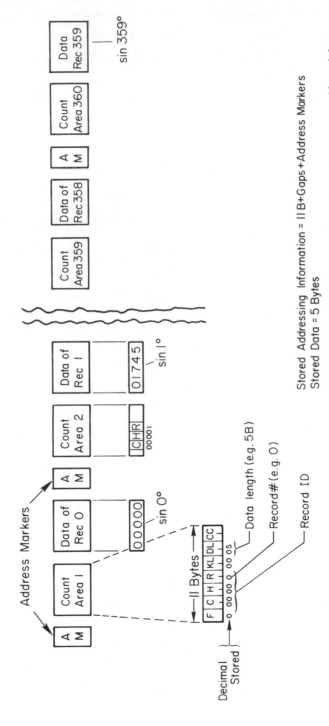

FIGURE 8.3-1 Simple data record storing sin θ to five places in 1° intervals with self-contained, unique identifiers using programmable track format.

512

Thus this file is directly organized without keys, since the ID is unique and unchanging. This example is a very simple one not often encountered in practice. Not only is the file inefficiently organized, but such mathematical functions are computed by simple subroutines rather than being stored in tables. Furthermore, the files are usually more complex and less obvious to organize except for scientific data, for which the file is usually very well-organized and easily structured.

8.4 FILE STRUCTURE OF COMPLEX DATA RECORDS AND TRADEOFF IN SIZE VERSUS SEARCHING CAPABILITIES: EXAMPLES

As an example of a complex file system, let us consider storing all necessary administrative information about students in a large university. We wish to store the following information: student name, identification number, college address, permanent home address, all courses taken and grade in each, and semester point average. The university consists of 20,000 students maximum at any one time and 2000 courses. The most simple-minded (and most inefficient) method of constructing such a file appears in Fig. 8.4-1a. The formatting is quite arbitrary, allowing 20 characters maximum for the address and 4 characters for each of the 2000 total courses offered by the university.

Each line of the file shown is all the information in that file about a given student, and represents a logical record. Each logical record as shown would consist of

$$5 + 12 + 6 + 20 + 8000 + 56 = 8099 \text{ char/record}$$

If each logical record were stored, for instance as a disk track, in the format shown, the logical record and physical record would be one and the same thing. We later break the record into pieces and store each piece in a separate file so that the logical record is no longer the physical record—this requires additional pieces of stored information and additional programming, but it produces a more efficient and useful file in some cases.

For the case in Fig. 8.4-1, since there are a maximum of 20,000 logical records (students), the total storage required for such a file would be

$$\text{total size} = 2 \times 10^4 \times 8.099 \times 10^3$$
$$= 16.198 \times 10^7 \text{ char.}$$

If one character equals one byte or 8 bits, the file requires about $8 \times 16 \times 10^7 = 128 \times 10^7$ bits, or more than a billion bits. This is an enormous mass storage requirement for such a simple file, and obviously another way must be found to organize it. To simplify the file, first note that all the 2000

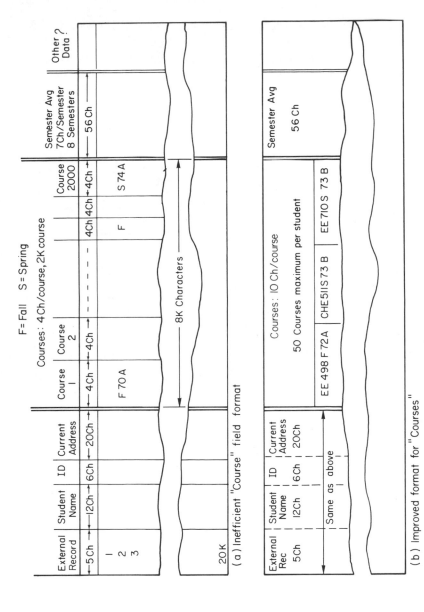

FIGURE 8.4-1 Complex data record storing student file and organized by fields, for two formats.

listed courses, only a fraction will be taken over a period of four or even eight years (graduate students) by any given student. Thus we could reduce the "course" area to 50 fields and allow 10 characters per field, to include each course number, when taken, and grade, as in Fig. 8.4-1b. However this only reduces the storage needed to

$$5 + 12 + 6 + 20 + 500 + 56 = 599 \text{ char./record}$$

or

$$\text{total size} = 2 \times 10^4 \times 5.99 \times 10^2 = 11.98 \times 10^6 \text{ char.}$$

or about $8 \times 12 \times 10^6 \approx 10^8$ bits.

The file is still rather large, however, and it contains many blanks (e.g., freshman have few courses, sophomores somewhat more). Thus there may be ways to achieve further reduction in total size. First, however, we must deal with other problems that have been totally neglected thus far. A few of these are as follows. Shall the file be a continuous one, allowing year after year additions of students? We must allow for drops and additions during a given year, but how do we number the students and subsequently search the file? Will searching be done on different fields at different times (i.e., in name one time, ID, courses, or other fields at a subsequent time)? Will the processing be random or sequential? Many such questions are quite important and need thorough consideration before beginning to design a file system. Since the final design depends on the specific uses and circumstances, we make the following assumptions and proceed to investigate the various ways in which the file could be organized.

1. We will keep only current students in the file; all others will be relegated to other files.
2. We will have a maximum of 25,000 logical records in the file; that is, a five-digit number for record number (20K students plus 5K for additions, since the enrollment cannot be controlled that accurately).
3. We need random processing (addressing) of single, individual logical records.
4. We wish to search the entire file, for example, for all students who have taken course "EE 498".

Random processing (assumption 3) requires some way to uniquely identify each student record. To do this, we would like a series of sequential numbers ranging from 0 to 25,000 just as was available in the case of storing $\sin \theta$ in Section 8.3. We could use the numerical record number in Fig. 8.4-1,*

---

* The numerical record number would be used in this case as the actual record number in the file in physical, sequential order, to permit the file to be addressed by record number.

but we face a dilemma. Suppose student 1 leaves school; we wish to remove his name from this file, place it in another, noncurrent file, and fill #1 with a new name. Thus #1 is not unique, since we can have more than one student with that number. In fact, on various printouts, the old student will appear as #1, and if a new student is substituted afterward, subsequent printouts will have a new name for #1, leading to confusion and errors if there is an attempt to identify the record by "#1." Thus a better numbering scheme is needed. Names are, of course, unique, but they do not easily translate to sequential numerical values.

For an unchanging file as the sin θ example of Section 8.3, the file entries never change, and unique identifiers can be assigned or easily determined for such well-organized data. For any given file as it stands at any point in time, we ideally always desire unique identifiers, but only one for each record and in numerical sequence. This would give a very efficient file, with no "overflow." However the requirement for additions and deletions to the file causes the major problem. Thus to allow for additions (and deletions); the identifier must be as large or larger than the total number of students we would ever expect to place into the file.

Student ID numbers present one possibility for unique identifiers. No two students will ever have the same ID within any reasonable period of time. For example, ID numbers have digits (assumed in this case) of 0 to 999,999 or maximum of 10^6 students. If 25×10^3 students maximum are expected per year (20K plus 5K for additions and deletions), the six-digit ID can accommodate

$$10^6 \text{ students} \div 25\text{K students/year} = 40 \text{ years}$$

Forty years is probably longer than the file in its present form will last; therefore student ID numbers provide a distinct possibility. One difficulty is that ideally the requirement is for the identifiers to be as numerically sequential as possible, and to vary from minimum to maximum by 25K. If the IDs are assigned sequentially, this ideal will be very nearly true, deviation being caused only by small deletions and additions over the year and large changes at the end and beginning of each year. Under these circumstances, we could use the ID and convert it with minimum effort, into a specific, unique address. Suppose, for instance, that the IDs for the current year range from 125,000 to 150,000 (125,000 to 145,000 + 5000 spillover). It is apparent that if we drop the highest order digit (i.e., 1) and use 25,000 as our zero reference point, we have a unique identifier set ranging from 0 to 25K.

We still do not have a unique disk address for each identifier, but we can easily develop one as follows. We need to convert each ID into a track number and an internal record number along the track (the latter should not be confused with the external record number assigned arbitrarily in

Fig. 8.4-1). Typically on movable head disk systems, records are stored sequentially within one cylinder, to eliminate excessive movement, which wastes time. On fixed head disks, this is not a consideration, and since there are hundreds of tracks per surface but usually only 10 to 20 surfaces, it may be simpler to store the records sequentially on one surface. For the moment we will not worry about whether the "tracks" are numbered along one surface of one disk or are incremented from one disk surface to the next. We can arbitrarily number the tracks any way we please and delay specifying the correct disk position until an actual system is implemented.

To get the IDs into track and internal record number, we can use the hashing method in the following program, which would be part of our systems I/0 program.

1. Delete the highest order bit and divide remaining ID number by prime number* close to 25K; discard the quotient but keep the remainder.
2. Divide the remainder in 1 by the number of records per track (a known value when the file is finally designed) to get a second quotient Q_T and remainder R.
3. Relative disk address is given by

$$\text{track } \# = Q_T + T_0$$

where T_0 is some reference point (i.e., the beginning track number of our file). The internal record number along this track is $R + 1$, starting with first record as $\#1$ or R starting with first records as $\#0$, where R is obtained as in step 2.

For example, suppose we found when done that we could store 15 records/ track on our disk system. We could then assign all records to tracks and internal record numbers by using steps 1 to 3. Then we could find the location of ID $\#125031$ as follows:

1. $25,031/25,000 = 1 + 31$.
2. Discard quotient 1.

$$31/15 \rightarrow Q_T = 2, R = 1$$

3. Address is thus

$$\text{track } \# = Q_T + T_0 = T_0 + 2$$

Internal record number along this track is 1 or 2, depending on whether numbering starts from 0 or 1. If $T_0 = 0$, address is second track, second record.

---

* A prime number is not divisible without a remainder by any number except itself and unity.

This system would be "direct" organization, since every ID converts to a specific track and internal record number, thus requiring at most, one movement of the access arm to the proper track (directly to the track) and a small sequential search or count to find the current record on that track.

If the student IDs had not converted nicely to specific identifiers, we could have taken one of several alternatives.

If the IDs were not in order, we could still use the hashing technique, but we would encounter the overflow problem, which might result in the need to move the access arm more than once—first to the home track, then to the next track referenced by the home track, then to a subsequent track if necessary, as referenced by each track, until the desired identifier (key) is found. It is advantageous on movable head disks to have the subsequently referenced overflow tracks on a different surface of the same cylinder; thus the access arm (slow mechanical) does not have to be moved and only switching between heads on different surfaces (fast electronic) is needed. However this cannot always be assured because overflow sometimes must go to a different cylinder. In either case, the file is referred to as "indirectly organized," since it is not possible to go directly to the overflow records.*

Another "direct organization" of the case of IDs that are not well organized would be an indexed system. This concept is extremely simple in principle, merely being a table in which each ID is mapped into a specific address, as for example, in Fig. 8.4-2. The IDs in this case could take on any values, including nonnumeric values. The disadvantage, of course, is that the table requires considerable storage space itself. It is usually stored in main memory, since otherwise it would require additional file organization and access time to read it into main memory and determine the corresponding address for a given ID.† A further disadvantage is that to locate a particular address corresponding to a given ID requires a search of the index table, such as a binary search (Section 8.7). This necessitates several CPU cycles, although the approach is still considerably faster than access time on the disk. Thus once the correct address has been found by the CPU in the index table, only one "seek" is required by the disk access arm. Hence this technique is usually called "direct organization," which refers only to the disk operation. In essence, it is really an indirect organization scheme if one includes the entire system, not just the disk arm movement; but the total time to find the record is determined, in the worst case, by the long seek time of the access arm because it is the dominating factor. Since the dominating factor is "directly" accessed by one seek time, it is arbitrarily called direct organization.

---

* It is still, of course, direct access to the nonoverflow or "home track" records. Keeping overflow to a minimum is a major requirement, with 20 % overflow being an acceptable value in many cases; see Buchholz (1963)].

† This form of organization is possible, however.

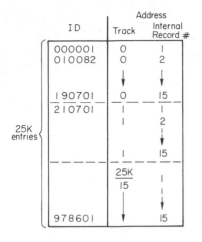

FIGURE 8.4-2 Direct organization of the student file using an index table to map IDs into addresses.

We assume that the first method of IDs giving unique addresses works for this file and go on to consider the "courses" field as in Fig. 8.4-1.

Assumption 4 about the file requires that we be able to retrieve information based on nonidentifier fields in the record (i.e., we want "all students who have taken EE498" or "EE498 and CS221" or other combinations, and we do not know the IDs or external record numbers). Unfortunately there is no simple way to do this "information retrieval." It would be necessary to transfer each logical record sequentially into main memory and write a program to search the various fields for appropriate matches, and store the IDs of all matches in a separate table, for example. The program and details for doing this would depend on how the "course" fields were organized. In any case, this represents an unsolved problem in information retrieval and is not considered further. Rather, we neglect the retrieval problem and treat methods for organizing the course fields to reduce the total size of storage required for this file.

The "course" field organization of Fig. 8.4-1b remains quite inefficient. Considerable conservation of empty slots could be achieved by using a "list" type of organization in which, say, only a student's name, ID, and address are included in the physical record. However at the end of each record, two separate spaces are provided: one to point to "courses" and one to point to "semester averages" as in Fig. 8.4-3. These pointers literally point to a new file with names "COURSES 72" and "AVG 72," for example, and the track, head, and internal record numbers. The names are symbolic in this example and in practice would locate the disk drive or disk pack (or both) that contained the required information. If these new files happened to be on the same disk, only the track, head, and record numbers would be

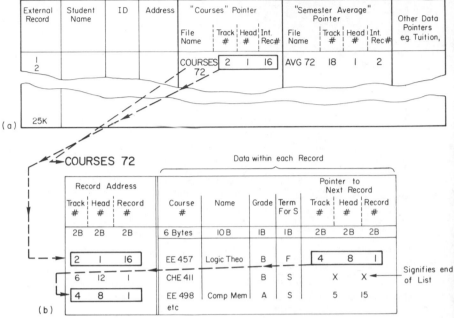

FIGURE 8.4-3 A simple list organization. (*a*) "Current students" file. (*b*) "Courses 72" file.

needed. In either case, the pointers indicate the location of the first "course" or "semester average" for that student.

The new file (e.g., "Course") would contain records and each itself would have pointers to point to subsequent records within that file for that student, as in Fig. 8.4-3*b*. Note that the first pointer in "Current students" pointed to a new file, whereas the subsequent pointers in "Courses 72" point to records within that file.

This list organization has many advantages as well as disadvantages. The list can be stored in sequential order on a track, for instance, and no empty slots are required for subsequent data. Later entries are easily added by merely inserting a pointer into the last entry, the physical record being stored at any convenient location. In fact, it is not necessary for the new records to be placed on the same physical disk, rather new records can be located on separate disk packs and separate disk drives. Thus list organization allows for easy expansion without completely rewriting the entire file, as would be required in a purely sequential file.

Quite often, various types of searches are made which do not require the entire logical record of a given student but may request just the address, or semester average, or tuition payment status of a given student. Thus if we wish to know the tuition status of the individual represented by a given ID number, it would be necessary to read the entire record of Fig. 8.4-1a or b into main memory and select the proper field for the answer. This would require transferring and storing into main memory large amounts of information, most of which is irrelevant. When the logical record is not exceptionally large, however, this is actually faster than searching the list, although a great deal of storage space is wasted with this organization of Fig. 8.4-1. A list greatly compacts the data. Furthermore, many data sets consist of very large logical records. By using a "list" file, a very large logical record can be constructed—for example, by putting additional pointers at the end of the records in Fig. 8.4-3a. If an organization as in Fig. 8.4-1 were used, not only would it be inefficient, but transfer time into main memory and the space in main to hold it could be excessive (assuming the entire record were transferred, which is not always the case—it is possible to "mask" the data coming off a disk). But if the entire record of, say, 1K bytes (= 8K bits) is transferred at a rate of 200K bits/sec, the record requires a transfer time of

$$\frac{8K \text{ bits}}{200K \text{ bits/sec}} = 0.040 = 40 \text{ msec}$$

In Fig. 8.4-3b note that if each entry is a data record on a disk file, the ratio between data record/SAI can be quite small, giving an inefficient file (e.g., 18 bytes of useful data vs. 11 bytes count and six for pointers); with gaps and address markers, this gives almost a ratio of 1:1 or worse. A somewhat more efficient, but less versatile system would be to group courses in sets of, say, four courses per record as in Fig. 8.4-4, since few students ever take less than for courses at any one time. This would improve the storage utilization somewhat but requires more knowledge about the organization of each field, which field is desired, and so on.

If all the logical information about each student were not linked together somehow, it would be necessary to have separate "identifiers" stored with each piece of the logical information. This itself would consume significant storage space and cause confusion. That is, we could not use the ID number again for a new "course" file in Fig. 8.4-3b because that number has already been used and has been given a unique address for each number. Rather than invent new numbers, which would not be known to those using the file anyway, it is expedient to use pointers that never have to be made known to the user (other than the systems programmer). Thus pointers are used, since the unique identifiers have already been used up and inventing new ones would not be meaningful to the persons actually using the file (administrative clerks, etc.).

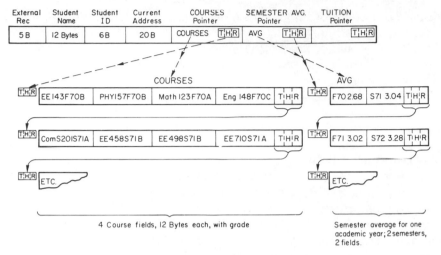

FIGURE 8.4-4 Variation of list organization for student file using four course fields per record.

8.5 MEMORY–TYPE REQUIREMENTS FOR FILE STRUCTURING

In the example of the student file it was pointed out that searching on "courses" was not possible because the file was organized around the student ID number as a unique identifier. If we wish to search for all students who have taken course EE499, it is necessary to transfer each record (or part of record) into main memory and dissect the "courses" fields in a sequential manner. This time-consuming process is very inefficient, but we have no alternative in this example, which represents an unsolved problem in information retrieval. Then we must ask whether we could or should use main memory or perhaps even content addressable (associative) memory for such information retrieval applications. The advantage of main memory storage is that we can randomly address much smaller pieces of stored data (individual bytes characters, words, etc.) and need not allow for SAI, as is required on a disk. The question to be answered is whether this provides unique capabilities or whether some problems are inherent in the data file structure and use.

Let us consider the "student" file and examine first the problem of addressing a record, and second the information retrieval problem on "courses." Unfortunately, even with this file in main memory, we still face the difficulty of specifying a unique, meaningful address for each record. We can store records initially in alphabetical order corresponding to numerical memory addresses, say words 1 through total actual records (25K). After a number of additions and deletions have been made, however, the numerical addresses no longer will correspond to the alphabetical order of names. Thus we must either keep a separate, external index of memory addresses for each record, or resort to the previous technique of developing a unique memory address from the stored data. This problem exists, irrespective of the memory addressing scheme (excluding associative memory); it is an inherent result of the structure of the stored data and the need for additions and deletions.

Now let us examine the question of information retrieval on the fields "courses." If the student file as organized in Fig. 8.4-1a were stored completely in main memory, would it be easier to organize the file as well as search it for information to find all students who have taken EE499? Before answering this, we must set some guidelines. Namely, we do not have infinite memory at zero cost; rather, we must constantly strive to produce a file structure that is as compact as possible, just as in the previous case of the file on disk. Thus if we store Fig. 8.4-1a in main memory, we will once again have many empty slots with an inefficient file. However we would be able to do the searching mentioned before, since all the fields are well organized. Moreover we know, for instance, that the course EE499 would be in say, the second course field, and we could search sequentially on that field very easily while it is in main memory. Of course, we could do the same with the file on disk, but this would require transferring each record sequentially into main memory first. The only advantage of main memory for storing the contents of the file would be the elimination of the transfer times.

As before the organization of Fig. 8.4-1a is much too inefficient to merit consideration as a possibility, suggesting an organization such as Fig. 8.4-1b. We assume that the hardware of the computer allows us to address each field, several fields, or each entire record as a unit. In Fig. 8.4-1b the course fields are not labeled; thus we do not know where EE499 may be stored for any given record. In fact, any specific course will be located somewhat randomly within the course fields. Therefore unless we know the field address of each course for each student, we are no better off than we were with the disk storage. To know each field address would require a hard copy (paper) of the entire field, and the search could be performed on the paper rather than via the computer. This, of course, defeats the purpose of the computerized file. We want the computer to be able to find the required information without our knowing precisely where it is stored.

In the organization of Fig. 8.4-1a an associative memory would be useful because a given field could be addressed for *all* matches on one memory cycle, that is, we know the search mask or search field for interrogating the memory (see Fig. 4.12-1). However for the organization of Fig. 8.4-1b we do know which field to search on; thus we would have to search each field separately, but we can do all words simultaneously. For a total of 50 fields, we would have to do 50 searches, or 50 complete cycles to locate all records that might contain EE499. Nevertheless, this is a considerable saving over $25,000 \times 50$ searches, which otherwise would be required. Therefore associative memory is helpful for a file organization of Fig. 8.4-1b, whereas using main memory rather than disk only saves the transfer time required for the latter.

Once again, as with disk, the organization of Fig. 8.4-1b is rather inefficient, requiring a memory of about 10^8 bits. Thus we would use another organization, the list organization of Section 8.6 being one possibility. For the nonindexed organization with random addressing (i.e., unique identifier) and more than one course per record as in Fig. 8.4-4, an associative memory would be used in a manner similar to that described for searching the file of Fig. 8.4-1b—we would have to search on all fields for a match of a given course, for instance. However, if there were only four course fields per record, only four associative memory cycles would be required, yielding a substantial saving, provided we knew the structure of the records (e.g., courses), to be able to mask the proper bit (byte) positions for comparison. Unfortunately since we still would lack a way to link the "courses" record with the appropriate student, it would be necessary to track backward. Thus associative memory is not very helpful without a reorganization of the file.

An associative memory could be useful in the index type of random organization of Fig. 8.4-2. For such a large index relating nonunique identifiers to a unique disk address, the search times can become quite long. For a binary search (Section 8.7) through 25K items, the maximum number of tries is $\log_2 (25K) = 14.6$, or 15 search cycles maximum, and about 8 on average for random distribution. The use of an associative memory to store such an index would greatly speed up the searching. In fact, associative registers are sometimes used for a different, but very similar problem, namely, that of searching indices in a cache–main memory hierarchy system (see Chapter 9).

Thus for searching files on actual data, associative memory is not particularly useful unless each record contains all the information associated with it (physical record = logical record) and the field structure of each record is well known, permitting proper masking for searching on desired fields. This requirement generally results in a structure similar to that of Fig. 8.4-1a, which is much too redundant, hence large. When a list-type file is structured to circumvent these problems, associative memory is not particularly useful without additional FAI for backward tracing.

We have thus seen that associative memories can be quite useful in certain limited types of file searching. The natural question is then, Why are associative memories not more widely used in computing systems? The answer is, Because of cost and usage. Associative memories cost considerably more than main memory, thus must find very wide, general usage to be economically justified. Yet it is hard to justify associative memory because it does not have very broad applicability in computing problems. As technology, particularly that of large-scale integrated circuits, progresses, associative memory will eventually be economical and may become more commonplace in many applications.

8.6 SIZE VERSUS SEARCHING CAPABILITY FOR LIST ORGANIZATIONS

In the example of the student file, we started with the simple arrangement of a matrix consisting of long records for each student (e.g., Fig. 8.4-1). This resulted in a very long file that wasted considerable storage space, although the organization was very simple. The need for much more efficient storage utilization led to a list organization as one possible solution. This is a very typical situation, matrix organization usually being large and inefficient in storage utilization. We did not consider the tradeoff in that example of the size and organization versus searching capabilities because no specific objectives were set. Tradeoffs cannot be ignored in the design of complex files, since the searching capabilities required by the user determine the possible organizations, which in turn, often produce a conflict between size and searching requirements. That is, small size generally means more difficult searching, whereas easy searching often leads to large file sizes. Hence a compromise is necessary.

As an example, let us consider organizing a file for a parts inventory situation. Let us suppose that we are asked to design a file for use on disk to keep track of 20 models of cars, and each car is made of varying numbers of subassemblies (SAs). Each car has at least 10 SAs but no more than 30, and there are 30 maximum possible SAs. Each SA is composed of from 1 to 100 parts; there are a total of 1000 parts, and all are used. The problem is to design a file that records the SAs needed for each car, the parts list for each SA, a way to find all cars that use a given SA, and all SAs that use a given part. In addition, each model, SA, and part has a 5 byte sequential numerical identifier that is unique. All characters and digits are counted as 1 byte each.

As usual, the requirements will be to provide a file organization that has a minimum amount of storage and requires a minimum amount of searching (access time). These turn out to be conflicting requirements because the data are structured in opposition to the method selected for search. For instance, the data structure requires that we maintain a listing of all SAs for each (therefore every) car, and all parts for each SA. However the searching requires us to be able to find all cars for each and any SA and all SAs for each

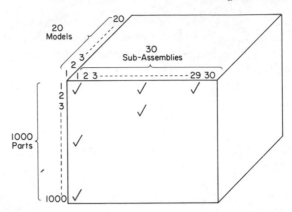

FIGURE 8.6-1   Parts inventory file using a 2D matrix for each model entry.

and any part; clearly this is just the opposite of the listing. This suggests (but does not prove) that there are two general ways to organize the file, one for minimum storage and another for minimum searching. We next demonstrate that this is the case.

Let us organize the file by means of a list structure. It can easily be shown that any simple matrix structure that lists all parts, all SAs, and all cars is much too wasteful in storage. For instance, if we were to use a matrix as in Fig. 8.6-1 consisting of a 2D record of parts by SA for each car model, putting a check mark in the appropriate box (as in the student file of Fig. 8.4-1a), we could accomplish all the requirements for searching. However there would be considerable redundancy and numerous blanks in the matrix. Redundancy results because any given SA uses the same parts for all models; thus any two models using the same SA would have duplicate check marks for the parts listing of that SA. Even more significant, each model can have from 10 to 30 SAs and each SA of from 1 to 100 parts. If we take a simple arithmetic average and say the average is 20 SAs per car with 50 parts per SA, the storage used is 20 × 50 = 1000 slots per model × 20 models = 20K slots filled in the matrix, while there are 1K × 30 × 20 = 0.6M slots available, obviously a very inefficient organization.

Improvements in the matrix, such as that used in Fig. 8.4-1b for the "student" file will help, but a list organization can greatly improve the storage problem. Therefore we drop the matrix and proceed to a list structure. Here we are immediately faced with the question of searching efficiency versus storage efficiency. The way files are naturally used often leads to conflicting demands on the file organization. In the manufacturing process, we need to know which SAs are required to produce each model so that the

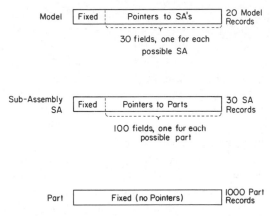

FIGURE 8.6-2 List organization for minimizing storage of parts inventory file.

model can readily be assembled. Likewise, we also need to know which parts are required to produce each subassembly. This is the natural data hierarchy, and one way to organize it would be to have each model record contain an identification (pointer) of all SAs it requires, with each SA containing an identification (pointer) of each part it requires. A general outline of this structure appears in Fig. 8.6-2. If we wish to assemble a given model, of course, we know or can easily find the SAs required and can order them as necessary; likewise for a given SA, we can easily determine the parts needed for its completion. It should be noted that since the identifiers used as pointers in Fig. 8.6-2 are unique (e.g., the five digit identifier given in the problem), this organization tends to minimize the storage requirement for the problem. This is because the longer number of fields required for the data association is on the SA records (100 fields needed, one for each possible part), which are few records in number (i.e., 30 SA records). At the same time, the part records, of which there must be 1000, are very short with no pointers. Thus the large record count occurs on a short record length, whereas the short record count (both SA and car in this case) occurs on the long record length.

   If the only searching we ever had to do was to determine the SAs for a given car, or parts for a given SA, the problem would be essentially done, except for the details of the actual file records. However files are seldom used in only one searching mode. In fact, it is safe to say that for any file containing useful collections of data, sooner or later every possible searching combination will be requested by users (given sufficient time of usage). In addition, changes will need to be made, since progress always initiates changes.

   For our problem at hand, both these situations will likely arise. Suppose one SA has been found to be defective and it is necessary to recall for changes all models using that SA. We would then like to be able to easily find all such models; this could be done with the organization depicted in Fig. 8.6-2, but every model record would have to be searched to see whether the SA appeared in that record. For the case given here, the numbers are small enough to allow this to be done, but a large file with thousands of records equivalent to the "model" in this example, would call for a very long search time. Extremely lengthy search times may be acceptable on occasions; but this is not always the case, especially for on-line or time-shared systems.

Another problem associated with the use of this system is the need to make changes. Suppose a new, cheaper material is found for making a certain part and now we wish to find which SA will be affected by this development. The same comments apply here as in the case of finding all models for a given SA. The searching can be done but it is difficult, becoming harder as the size of the file increases. If we wish to organize for easy searching, the easiest way to find all SAs that use a given part is to somehow maintain within each part record an identification of all the SAs it is used in. Likewise, for finding all cars that use a given SA, we would want to maintain an identification within each SA of all the cars in which it is employed. This could be done by using pointers in each parts record to both identify and point to the appropriate SA, and likewise, using pointers in each SA record to identify and point to the appropriate model. One possible way is that shown in Fig. 8.6-3. The difficulty with this organization is that now the longest record is associated with "parts," which requires the largest record count (i.e., 1000). Thus this organization, though making the searching easier, leads to a larger storage requirement than previously. There are possible organizations that permit a better compromise between these two extremes, but in

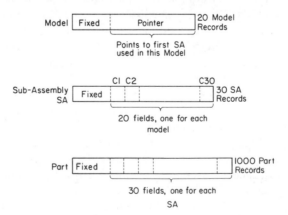

FIGURE 8.6-3   List organization for easy searching of parts inventory file.

any case, before attempting to work further, the designer must decide or know from the user, the basic criteria for the file. These points are very essential parts of file design, namely, to specify all the basic requirements for searching and organization, as well as the constraints on search time versus storage requirements.

8.7 BINARY SEARCH TECHNIQUE

In many types of data retrieval problems it is necessary to search an indexed file or table to find the desired information. The index can be based on keys and the desired information can be the data record or actual address of a record related to that key. The keys in this case do not convert to unique addresses, or the file may be located on a piece of hardware that does not use key searching (e.g., tapes). Suppose, for example, that a file of N records is organized by keys but stored on tape in a random sequence (i.e., not in key sequence). If a specific record is desired from this file, the entire file (N records) must be transferred to main memory and searched for the desired record. A sequential search could be used, starting at the first record, comparing its key with the desired key, on to the next, and so on, until the key match is obtained. However this would require looking at $(N + 1)/2$ records on the average, which is slow. There are numerous ways to speed up the search, including the binary search technique.

If the keys are numerical, they can be ordered in numerical sequence. Note that the keys do not have to be simple, sequential numbers separated by one decimal digit; after sorting, for example, they might be ordered as shown in Fig. 8.7-1. To perform a search, the middle key $\#N/2$ is addressed (Search 1 in Fig. 8.7-2) and compared to the desired value; if the desired key value is higher numerically, the lower half of the key area is divided in half again and another comparison is made. If the desired key is still larger

Record or Key #	Key Value K_N	Data
1	5100	Adams J.---
2	5210	Brams R.---
3	5300	etc.
4	6329	
.		
.		
.		
.		
N	8432	----------

FIGURE 8.7-1 Arrangement of N records in memory after sorting on key values.

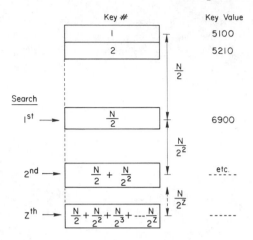

FIGURE 8.7-2   Binary search technique by successive division on key number and comparison on key value.

numerically than the desired key, the remaining half-area is again divided in half, and so on. In this way, the direction of the search is always known, and substantial saving in the number of search operations can be obtained. The maximum number of searches required to find any key is easily derived as follows. The first search is to key number $N/2$. If N is an even number, this leaves $N/2$ key entries in the upper half-field between the key numbers $N/2$ and N. The upper half-field between 0 and $N/2$ will have one fewer entry that has not been tested. Hence the worst case occurs when the desired key falls in the lower half-field.* This lower field is likewise divided in half, and the second search is performed on key number $N/2 + (N/2)\frac{1}{2}$, as Fig. 8.7-2. For the worst case, no match occurs and the search must continue to the lower half of the second field. The search continues in like manner until one of several events occurs, depending on the value of N. If N is a power of 2, then when

$$\frac{N}{2^z} = 1 \tag{8.7-1}$$

the number of the key searched at the zth position in Fig. 8.7-2 must be an odd number, since $N/2 + N/2^2 + N/2^3 + \cdots$, excluding $N/2^z$, must be even. Hence we can be, at most, one key number away from the last number N. Assuming we test this final key to be certain it is the desired value, the

---

* This could have been reversed by choosing $N/2 + 1$.

maximum number of searches is

$$S_{max} = z + 1 \tag{8.7-2}$$

The value of z can be obtained from (8.7-1), namely,

$$N = 2^z \quad \text{or} \quad z = \log_2 N \tag{8.7-3}$$

Therefore the maximum number of searches, when N is a power of 2, is

$$S_{max} \leq 1 + \log_2 N \tag{8.7-4}$$

When N is *not* a power of 2, the value of z in (8.7-3) is not an integer and (8.7-4) is ambiguous. However for N values between two successive powers of 2, the maximum number of searches does not change. For instance, suppose

$$2^{z_1} \leq N < 2^{z_2} \tag{8.7-5}$$

$$z_2 = z_1 + 1 \tag{8.7-6}$$

Then the maximum number of searches is constant at

$$S'_{max} = 1 + z_1$$

for N within these limits. When $N = 2^{z_2}$, then S'_{max} increases by 1 and remains constant at this value until N equals the subsequent power of 2.

As an example, consider a file consisting of, say, from 1024 to 2047 records in main memory, organized as previously: N can range from

$$2^{10} \leq N < 2^{11}$$

where $z_1 = 10$ and $z_2 = 11$. A binary search for any record would require, at most, $1 + z_1 = 11$ accesses to main memory, which is quite a substantial improvement over a sequential search. Of course the CPU and a small program are also required, but this overhead is generally quite small.

9 Memory Hierarchies and Virtual Memory Systems

9.1 INTRODUCTION

This chapter deals primarily with the more advanced type of memory heirarchies, the virtual and cache memory systems. First we present the evolution of memory hierarchies as well as virtual memory systems. Section 9.2 analyzes the simple type of storage hierarchy to point out the need for multiprogramming and additional I/O processing hardware. The remainder of the chapter is devoted to the fundamental requirements, design, and several commercial implementations of virtual hierarchies, including both the cache and the usual virtual memory systems.

9.1.1 Evolution of Storage Hierarchies

Hierarchies appear to be a fundamental necessity whenever large discrepancies arise in the speed or capacity of functional parts of any computing system. The human brain itself is composed of at least a three-level hierarchy (Fig. 1.10-2). Large gaps exist in both speed and capacity of the three levels, although much remains to be learned about this complex hierarchy.

Early calculators did not have large functional discrepancies, hence did not use storage hierarchies. For instance, the early Hollerith-type calculators and IBM-Harvard Mark I (Section 1.2) were electromechanical. The speed of the arithmetic unit was governed by the speed of electromechanical relays and was measured in fractions of a second. Memory and storage in the form of cards and paper tape could be read and written at comparable speeds, hence could adequately match the speed of the arithmetic unit. The shift to electronic switches for the arithmetical operations created a gap between the storage and calculating speed.

The first electronic calculator, Eniac, had a hierarchy consisting of 20 temporary storage registers and 312 words (40 bits/word) of externally alterable read-only memory, all backed up with punched cards for storing intermediate results. The read-only memory was known as the function table and was altered by means of switches on the front panel. Arithmetic operations required a few milliseconds each. Since the small capacity of electronic main storage was inadequate for most problems, the speed of the system was determined by the rate of punching and reading the secondary storage cards. This rate, about 0.3 sec/card, was much too slow for the types of problem being solved and those envisioned by physicists and engineers. Hence the second major electronic computer and the first stored program computer, Edsac, used an electroacoustic memory that more nearly matched the CPU speed and was backed with a drum. In these and subsequent early computers, the major decision was the choice of memory technology, and the CPU was built around this essential component.

The two laws postulated in Section 1.1—(1) the law of expanding CPU power and (2) the law of expanding storage—were set into motion at this time, although they were not recognized as laws. These two laws created significant gaps between various functional parts of the computer that evolved ultimately to the various storage hierarchies currently in use. The two laws promoted important advances in CPU and storage technology, and as a result, the first type of simple hierarchy used in Edsac grew primarily in size. Tapes were added early in computer history to provide larger backing and archival storage (i.e., law 2). The first tape was added to the National Bureau of Standard's SEAC* in the early 1950s to back up the 512 words of mercury delay line and 512 words of Williams tube memory. The first commercial tape was introduced by Univac in 1951 (Table 1.1-1). The introduction of core storage in 1955 was a significant step to improve CPU power (i.e., law 1), and disks were added in 1956 to help bridge the gap between tapes and core storage. This essentially completed the generic types of storage systems from which innumerable hierarchies have evolved.

The second type of memory hierarchy evolved from the first law. The continued improvement in CPU speed created a speed gap between the main memory and CPU (Section 1.1). This gap became significant in the late 1950s and was quickly recognized as one potential limitation on the computational power of computers. Attempts to bridge this evolving gap first took the form of the so-called scratch pad or slave memory (Wilkes, 1965). This, in essence, is a small, fast, random access memory that stores the recently used words addressed out of main memory. Since many subsequent memory references require the same words, the reference goes directly to the scratch pad and gives an increase in the effective overall memory cycle time. This idea has been implemented in many machines such as the Ferranti Titan (Atlas 2) and the Univac 1110.

The scratch pad served as a precursor to the cache type of paged hierarchy. The difficulty with the scratch pad is that the hit ratio (Section 9.4) is not very large, typically being a maximum of 70 to 90% for instructions alone and generally less than 80% for operands (alphanumeric data) (see,

---

* Standard Eastern Automatic Computer, see Greenwald, et al. (1953).

e.g., Tucker, 1966). Only words previously referenced by the program are stored in the scratch pad. A high probability exists that a different, but physically very close word will be needed next. Hence the concept evolved of paging into the scratch pad not only the referenced word but many nearby words. A number of years and considerable work was required to accumulate sufficient statistics to determine the potential improvement and design parameters of such paged systems. Further evolution resulted in the cache–main memory hierarchy described in Section 9.12. The first was introduced in the IBM model 85 and subsequently appeared on other systems. Thus the second type of hierarchy bridges the speed gap between main memory and the CPU and evolved out of the first type of hierarchy under the influence of the law of expanding CPU power.

As an alternative to the scratch pad concept for bridging the CPU–main memory gap, the concept of "interleaving" memory modules was introduced in the 1960s. Since main memory normally consists of a number of independently working basic systems modules (Section 4.14), sequential words are stored in these separate modules. The modules are clocked with the same overall clock period, but the memory modules are initiated at different times separated by a fraction of the total period. Thus if subsequently referenced words reside in different modules, an effective increase in cycle time can be achieved. In general cases, this technique can provide only a limited improvement, since one does not know which word will be next referenced. If all words were referenced in an orderly, sequential fashion, interleaving would solve the cycle time problem. Such operation is not usually the case. Another drawback is that considerable additional storage control for storing words is required. This interleaving technique is nevertheless used. It is particularly useful on cache–main memory systems where rapid transfer of a page into the cache is necessary. In such cases, the pages are of known size and the entire page can be transferred in an orderly, sequential fashion when needed. Hence efficient interleaving can be built into the system. We do not distinguish this interleaving scheme as a separate hierarchy.

The third type of hierarchy also evolved from the original type but under the influence of the law of expanding storage. The early hierarchies were generally of the most simple kind, such as the first example in Section 9.2. Main memory was loaded from, say, a tape, and the CPU worked on this until all processing was completed. Thereupon a new segment of information was loaded into main memory, and so on. It was the job of the programmer to divide a large problem into independent segments such that no two segments were required at any one time. Thus for large, complex programs, the burden was placed on the user to ensure efficient operation of the system. As shown in Section 9.2, this I/O problem led to the introduction of multiprogramming to provide a more balanced system utilization, but this did

FIGURE 9.1-1   Evolution of storage hierarchies from the original, simple type.

not solve the user's problem. Rather, multiprogramming addresses primarily the system utilization, and the programmer has an ever-larger burden of problem segmentation and storage allocation. As systems grew both in size and complexity, this burden became too great and the memory hierarchy evolved to the third type, the so-called virtual memory. The evolution of these forms is shown schematically in Fig. 9.1-1. Thus the term "memory hierarchy" is ambiguous and can mean any of many possible configurations. Two very common types of hierarchy in use today are the main memory–disk virtual store and the cache–main memory hierarchies.* Although the former is referred to as "virtual storage," the latter makes use of the identical principles and concepts, hence is a virtual store in a fundamental sense. The essential difference is that the cache–main memory hierarchy is aimed only at bridging the speed gap between main memory and the CPU, whereas the main memory–disk hierarchy attempts to bridge the capacity gap between main memory and secondary storage. The use of the term "virtual storage" for the latter is thus more descriptive but tends to mask the similarity to the cache concept. Because of this, in discussing virtual memory systems we refer to the small, fast memory as *primary storage* and the slower, larger, less expensive memory as *secondary storage*. In a cache–main memory system, the cache is obviously the primary storage and main memory is the secondary storage. In the disk–main memory virtual system, the latter is primary storage and the disk is secondary storage. Section 9.3 outlines the general fundamental requirements of virtual storage, which are applicable both to the cache–main memory and the main memory–disk hierarchies. The differences lie mainly in the implementation of the required functions, with cache systems having more hardware for high speed, whereas "virtual" systems are implemented more in software by way of complex operating systems, mainly for low cost and greater flexibility. Each of these types— namely, the disk or drum paged into main memory, and the main memory paged into cache—represents a two-level virtual hierarchy. It is possible to have both types present simultaneously, giving a three-level virtual hierarchy

* Another type is that of a small, fast, array working out of a larger, slower random access array such as that described in Section 9.12.

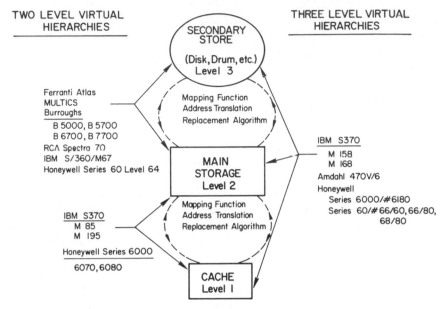

TWO LEVEL VIRTUAL HIERARCHIES

THREE LEVEL VIRTUAL HIERARCHIES

SECONDARY STORE

(Disk, Drum, etc.)
Level 3

Ferranti Atlas
MULTICS
Burroughs
  B 5000, B 5700
  B 6700, B 7700
RCA Spectra 70
IBM S/360/M67
Honeywell Series 60 Level 64

Mapping Function
Address Translation
Replacement Algorithm

IBM S370
  M 158
  M 168
Amdahl 470V/6
Honeywell
  Series 6000/#6180
  Series 60/#66/60, 66/80,
    68/80

MAIN STORAGE
Level 2

Mapping Function
Address Translation
Replacement Algorithm

IBM S370
  M 85
  M 195

Honeywell Series 6000
  6070, 6080

CACHE
Level 1

FIGURE 9.1-2   Some examples of two- and three-level virtual hierarchies.

as discussed in Section 9.12. Commercial systems have implemented all types of such two- and three-level hierarchies, and a few examples appear in Fig. 9.1-2.

It should be clear from the foregoing discussion that a memory hierarchy consists merely of two or more storage systems that supplement each other. A memory hierarchy does not have to be a virtual memory system, but virtual memory systems are memory hierarchies. This point should be clearly understood to avoid confusion, since there are many storage hierarchies that are not virtual systems. Another point of confusion centers around the relationship of time-sharing to virtual memory and the amount of hardware versus software needed for each. A time-shared system shares a CPU and its main memory among many users. In principle, it can be done entirely with software, without the need for a virtual store. In fact, the first operational time-shared system, the MIT Compatible Time-Shared System (CTSS)* used a nonvirtual memory hierarchy, and the entire system was implemented mainly in software. This system suffered from poor response

---

* The CTSS, circa 1963, used an IBM 7090, modified to include some memory protection and relocation hardware, but the time-sharing was done in software. The system did not have a virtual store addressing capability. Nevertheless it was a precursor of subsequent systems.

time and very limited memory addressing per user. For practical, efficient time-shared system of large size, a virtual memory is essential, as well as a balance between hardware and software implementation. Likewise, a virtual memory can be implemented strictly in software but a balance between hardware and software can produce a better system.

From a purely fundamental point of view, the one essential difference between a virtual memory system and a nonvirtual memory system is that the former allows the user to address memory in terms of an address space which is larger than the actual main memory address space. In other words, the user writes programs *as though* main memory was larger than it actually is. In nonvirtual memory systems, the user is limited in addressing to the actual (or alloted) size of main memory. To see how this difference affects the user, suppose we are writing a large problem in Fortran language and require the use of a large 3D matrix. Let us assume that we have available a main memory space of 64K' word capacity and that the matrix has dimensions $64 \times 64 \times 64 = 256K'$. In a virtual memory system, we could write a dimension statement for this problem as

DIMENSIONS (64, 64, 64)

and continue with the remainder of the instructions as if main memory could hold the entire problem. In a nonvirtual system, only some segment of the matrix—in particular, one-quarter at most—could be stored; thus our dimensions statement would become

DIMENSIONS (64, 64, 16)

Now the user has the job of segmenting the matrix into independent pieces as much as possible and providing necessary tests and transfer of data to ensure that correct data are available when needed. We could now argue that the problem could be avoided by running on a larger system with considerably more memory available. This is certainly true if the user can get a system large enough to be devoted to this problem alone. However large systems require multiprogramming to be efficient. Economics quite often force the computing center to limit the size of each user's allotted memory space to some fraction of the total, which means that in this system the overall storage allocation becomes even more complex. The virtual memory system takes care of these details for the user. Potential pitfalls in the use of a virtual memory system are detailed in Section 9.13.

Even though the idea of a virtual store was suggested as early as 1961 at Manchester University (Fotheringham, 1961), the implementation of a practical, efficient system required significant innovation both in hardware and knowledge of computer usage. Advances in monolithic semiconductor circuits and accumulated program statistics culminated in practical designs for cache and virtual memories in the late 1960s. An efficient multiprogram-med system required less innovation, hence was a first step. In addition to the fundamental difference in addressing, the major practical differences between a virtual system and a nonvirtual system are in terms of the extra hardware used to achieve a feasible system for the former. A brief history of the evolution of virtual memory systems is given below.

In essence, we can categorize memory hierarchies as a means to bridge the technology gaps with architecture rather than with better hardware alone. The implementation of a hierarchy does involve additional cost, but the increase in cost for the resulting performance improvement represents an attractive tradeoff. How far this architectural bridge can be extended is an interesting and important question. As large-scale integrated circuit mem-ories decrease in cost and increase in both density and speed, the trend is likely to shift back toward larger main memory. However the two laws governing computer expansion will continue to exert pressures for more storage and speed, perhaps with larger functional gaps and more complex hierarchies.

It is important to distinguish between a virtual *memory* system and a virtual *computing* system. The latter is much more complex and requires consideration of the entire computer architecture, which is beyond our purpose. The virtual memory is just one subsystem within the overall com-puting system, and we are concerned mainly with the former. We assume that a processor logical address for a word or byte has been formed, and we proceed to describe the manner in which this address is used by the virtual memory subsystem. We will demonstrate that virtual systems work because of the natural clustering of data. In Section 9.9 the Multics virtual system is briefly compared to the IBM virtual system to show that the virtual memory subsystems are nearly identical, even though the virtual processor address formation and symbolic segmentation referencing are basically different.

9.1.2   Evolution of Virtual Memory Systems

The Ferranti Atlas of early 1960 vintage was one of the first computers to incorporate the concepts of a paged one-level store (Kilburn et al., 1962). The system used pages of a fixed size and was designed to allow many dif-ferent programs to be held simultaneously in the store. As detailed in Section 9.9.1, however, the full capacity of the CPU logical address could not be used simultaneously by many programs; instead, full addressing capacity of 20 bits to logically address 1M' words of storage was divided among all programs. Hence if any one user required 1M' words of storage, only that program could be run in the machine. This limitation was a result of the failure to provide a means for additional address bits to identify the user (i.e., no user ID register: see Section 9.3). In other words, the total running job stream could use the full CPU logical addressing capacity only for the number of users it could accommodate at that moment. This represents a one-level store, since the 16K' core main memory was addressed with the full 20 bit CPU logical address as if it contained all 1M' words of the total core and drum. This was not a multiprogrammed virtual memory as commonly used today; this system did not transfer control to a second program whenever a page fault was encountered. Thus although several programs, if small enough, could be stored in the primary memory simultaneously, the CPU remained unproductive during page transfer, and this represented a serious limitation. An experienced programmer having sole use of primary storage could often minimize page transfer by proper organization and segmentation. However this requires considerable effort and is undesirable. One alternative is to use a prediction program based on past page usage. This can be of some value, particularly in long problems. Another alternative is to transfer the CPU to a second program for which pages are currently in primary storage. Thus in the early 1960s, the utility of multiprogramming and the one-level store became evident.

The next major step was to permit multiple users, with switching between users whenever the CPU became idle for long periods (e.g., during a page miss or other I/O operation). One of the first such systems, the Burroughs B5000, provided a multiprogrammed, one-level store but used a variable page size called a segment.

To understand the reason for the change from a fixed page to variable segment size as well as the subsequent evolution of virtual systems, it is necessary to digress briefly to the concept of problem segmentation. In the early 1960s there was considerable concern about the "natural" page or segment size of any given problem. Experience with the earlier, simple hierarchies in which program segments were overlaid into main memory indicated that such segments were always of variable length. It seemed that the size of the natural unit should be allowed to vary for optimum results. Hence the Burroughs B5000 provided for a variable segment size. Continued concern for the segmentation question led the original Multics system to provide for page sizes of either 64 or 1024 words/page, at the choice of the programmer, but this was later dropped to a fixed page size. Experience has shown that in general, the segmentation problem is not as serious as expected, provided many pages of a given user can be in primary storage at one time. Thus fixed page sizes can on the average give very large hit ratios. Some problem have low hit ratios, no doubt at least partly attributable to the problem of segmentation.

Irrespective of the segmentation problem, the importance of swapping information in a multiprogrammed, one-level store was well recognized and received considerable attention in the early and mid-1960s. By 1963 Univac was swapping between drums and main memory, but considerable user involvement was required in the segmentation process, even though operating systems handled most of the allocation process. Up to this time, systems relied mostly on software to perform the swapping rather than hardware. Furthermore, with the exception of the B5000, the initial segmentation and allocation process was not fully automatic.

By 1965 the CDC 3300 had automated the memory allocation processes and fixed the size of pages. By the mid-1960s the concept of a total virtual memory had been implemented in two experimental time-shared systems the Multics* system and the IBM 44/44X. The former became the commercial Honeywell Multics system, and the latter was a precursor to the IBM 360 model 67 (Section 9.9 discusses both these). Both commercial systems use a fixed page size but allow a user to have many pages, which essentially represents a variable segment size. Though not labeled a virtual memory machine, the model 67 was in fact a virtual memory, time-shared system and precursor to the IBM virtual memory systems. The first commercial system to be sold as a virtual memory system was the RCA Spectra 70 series of 1970 vintage. The IBM virtual memory system was introduced commercially as such in 1972.

In large virtual systems (see Section 9.9) pages are of fixed sizes and grouped together in segments. The address translation proceeds by first identifying the segment in which a desired page is located, then the page slot within that segment. This process of grouping pages into segments has little to do with the above-mentioned segmentation problem; it is done mainly to reduce the amount of main memory consumed by the translation tables and to facilitate global sharing of supervisory programs.

9.2 THE I/O PROBLEM AND STORAGE ARCHITECTURE

Nonrandom access storage systems furnish large storage capabilities at low cost, but with a relatively slow access time compared to main memory. The large capacity at low cost and reasonable data rates have long been attractive features of such storage systems and have greatly influenced the overall computer systems architecture. Memory hierarchies are used as well as complex software systems simply because in many cases, a more nearly optimal system can be obtained by combining various technologies to take

---

* The original MULTICS (MULTiplexed Information and Computing Service) began as a joint research project at MIT with sponsorship by Project MAC at MIT, Bell Laboratories, General Electric, and the Advanced Research Project Agency of the Department of Defense (Carbato and Vyssotsky, 1965; Daley and Dennis, 1968).

advantage of each technology's strength and to circumvent its weakness by architectural design. For example, the low cost of disk technology makes it attractive for use as a backup store to main memory. However when a computing system is implemented in the most elementary way, as in Fig. 1.1-1, the overall operation tends to be unbalanced and inefficient for optimum processing of problems. The CPU, which is the fastest and most expensive portion, would remain idle a large percentage of the time, whereas the backing storage, which is the slowest and least expensive, would tend to be used a larger percentage of the time. Under such circumstances, the system is said to be "I/O bound," meaning that the overall speed is determined by the input/output equipment, which is assumed to be the backing store for our discussion. This is very similar to the situation described in Sections 1.2 and 9.1 with respect to the Eniac processing speed being determined by the punched card writing and reading rate.

A considerable improvement in performance can be obtained but at the expensive of a more complex architecture. We now consider a simple system to see that an I/O problem indeed exists; then we proceed to investigate ways of alleviating the difficulty. More specifically, we see that a CPU coupled to a typical disk storage system can result in poor CPU utilization efficiency when operating on one task. The CPU efficiency can be improved by interleaving many tasks, but this requires additional hardware—namely, an I/O processor and a more complex storage architecture than that in Fig. 1.1-1. This leads us to the concept of multiprogramming and, further, to virtual memory systems in which the I/O processor plays a key role. We deal with multiprogramming to the extent that it influences the storage architecture. Virtual memory is discussed in detail in the remainder of this chapter.

To understand the I/O problem, consider the simplified example in Section 1.6 in which segments are overlaid into main memory with the critical relations expressed by (1.6-7) to (1.6-13). We demonstrated that the disk access time gave poor CPU utilization, that is, (1.6-11). A slight improvement was obtained by increasing the segment size from multiple 16K byte segments to one segment equal to the full memory size as shown by (1.6-13). This eliminates many of the disk accesses but then the total transfer time becomes a limiting factor.

To achieve better CPU utilization for this system, the wait time T_w must be reduced. Improving hardware speed is one obvious approach, but a very expensive one. The question is, How can wait time be reduced by architecture rather than better hardware alone? The answer is, By providing more than one segment in main memory and allowing the CPU to continue with a second segment while the first is being replaced. The CPU can then run at nearly 100% efficiency. However there are two problems. First, some arithmetic-logic capability is necessary to find the desired segment on disk that represents the access time portion of T_w in (1.6-9). Second, once the segment is found, the data transfer requires use of main memory; hence during the transfer process, the CPU must wait. These two problems are circumvented as follows. During the access time portion of T_w, a special purpose I/O processor can be supplied to do the necessary arithmetic-logic functions. In principle, under the proper architecture this can free the CPU for the entire T_{access} time. This still leaves the $T_{transfer}$ time. The CPU can remain busy for a large portion of the transfer time because the data from a disk are transferred to main memory in units of one or more bytes, requiring one memory cycle time to write or read, and the bytes are separated by many memory cycle times. In other words, the data comprise small pieces of information separated by large time periods of no activity. The CPU can have access to main memory during the inactive periods. For example, in the above-mentioned case the data rate is 2.5M bits/sec. As the data come off the disk, they are stored in a register or buffer memory in the I/O processor until a full byte or full word is available, then are transferred as a full byte or word with all bits in parallel. Hence the data rate seen by main memory would be approximately 0.31M bytes/sec, or a repetition rate of about 3.2 μsec/byte if

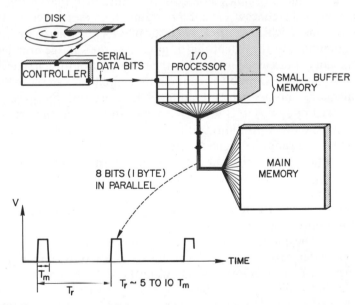

FIGURE 9.2-1 Schematic of data transfer between disk, I/O processor, and main memory, showing long time intervals between data pulses.

single bytes are transferred.* This is illustrated in Fig. 9.2-1 where T_m is the main memory access time (read or write) and T_r is the data repetition time for the disk in seconds per byte. The actual time required in the storage of the byte once it is available in the register of the I/O processor, is the memory access time. A typical memory access time for such a large system is 0.3 μsec and a 0.5 μsec cycle time as assumed earlier. The actual transfer delay is thus about 0.3 μsec, or less than the memory cycle time, which indicates that one byte can be stored easily when ready. An architectural question of some importance is that of priority for main memory references. Since the disk access is a slow process, once the desired segment is located it has priority over the CPU for access to main memory. Otherwise, additional access time must be tolerated, and this is undesirable.

The I/O processor contains a small buffer memory to allow for any slack encountered by its independent, hence asynchronous, operation with respect to the CPU. This buffer must transfer bytes to main memory about once every 3.2 μsec, or a delay between completion of the first and initiation of last cycle of about $3.2 - 0.3 = 2.9$ μsec. This is between 5 and 6 main memory cycle times. If data is transferred in 2 or 4 byte units, the delay between data is that much longer. The CPU can then make references to main memory during these long waiting periods and for this case, approximately one memory cycle out of six is stolen by the I/O process for data transfer. The I/O processor is a key element in practical virtual memory systems—without it, the virtual memory could not work very efficiently.

If the data transfer rate were increased significantly, let us say that now one byte of data is available every main memory cycle time, the CPU would not have access to main memory during the block transfer and the average efficiency would decrease. This raises an interesting question about the effect of data rate on overall system efficiency which we do not attempt to answer. It should be pointed out only that statistically, the cycle stealing is sometimes done when the CPU does not need a memory reference. The CPU may be busy on a complex computation that requires a time equal to several main memory cycles. On an average basis, this would tend to improve the overall CPU efficiency.

In a multiprogrammed or virtual system, an I/O instruction executed by the I/O processor and controller requires a certain number of instruction fetches from main memory. These references preempt the CPU and cause it to remain idle during that fetch cycle. On the average, however, such a fetch keeps the I/O processor and controller busy for a very long time, typically thousands of CPU cycles. In essence, therefore, the access time portion of the I/O execution is completely overlapped with the CPU operation. The

---

* Some large systems transfer many bytes or full words into main memory on one memory cycle.

I/O processor thus steals cycles both during the secondary storage access time as well as on the data transfer time. The effectiveness of the overlapping functions depends to a large extent on the speed of the CPU versus that of the I/O hardware.

Transferring of control from one user to another may require execution of tens to hundreds of control and bookkeeping instructions; thus the time saved by overlapping may be too small to justify the additional complexity. The amount of overlapping varies greatly among commercial machines— generally the smaller systems have little or no overlapping and large systems have considerable. The foregoing outline of the I/O problem has demonstrated the need for multiprogramming. It should be clear that the I/O processor has the job of circumventing the wait time T_w, (1.6-9). Since T_w has two components, its two main functions are

1. To find the desired segments or block with little interruption of the CPU.
2. To transfer data to main memory with as little interruption of CPU as possible.

Both functions are aimed specifically at freeing the CPU from rudimentary details, hence allowing it to perform the job it is designed for: processing of the program. The I/O processor can be incorporated into the system in many forms. In one common system used in the IBM 360/370 series, the I/O processor takes the form of a channel (Fig. 9.2-2). In principle, the data transfer to or from main memory is accomplished by the cycle stealing procedure just described. During the "finding" or access cycle, the channel makes use of I/O instructions that are stored in main memory. These instructions are fetched on a cycle stealing basis just as with the data transfer. Since instructions are needed very infrequently, very few cycles are priority stolen from the CPU, and only a small decrease in CPU efficiency results. Once again, the CPU may not need a reference to main memory simultaneously with the I/O processor; thus no loss in efficiency occurs under such conditions. The channel contains a very small buffer memory for assembling or disassembling data between main memory and secondary storage, as described previously.

Another method for implementing the I/O processor is that used by CDC in the 6000 and 7000 series systems (Fig. 9.2-3). The I/O processor is somewhat different than that above. The required I/O functions are performed by the 10 peripheral and control processors called Peripheral Processing Units (PPU), which act both as a system control computer and I/O processor. These PPUs contain a 4K' word, 60 bit/word, random access memory and can operate independently and simultaneously as a stored program computer. Thus unlike the channels of Fig. 9.2-2, the PPUs do not usually require references to main memory during an I/O access because the instructions

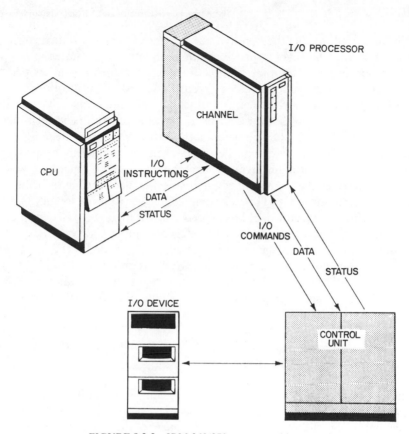

FIGURE 9.2-2 IBM 360/370 storage architecture.

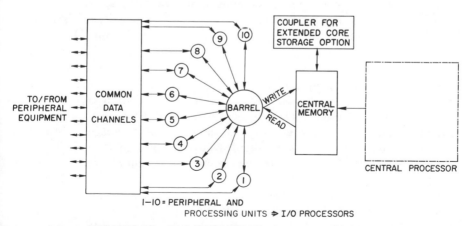

FIGURE 9.2-3 CDC 6000 and 7000 series storage architecture.

can be stored within their individual memories. During data transfer to main memory, however, some form of cycle stealing is necessary. These PPUs do not solve complex arithmetic-logic problems but rather perform all the rudimentary functions for efficient CPU and I/O utilization.

We can now summarize the I/O problem as resulting from the key position of the main memory as the reservoir of all data and the need for different functions, CPU and I/O, to reference this store. The above techniques for improving CPU efficiency can be made even more efficient by providing parallel segments of main memory, each having its own functional address register, decoders, sense amplifiers, and so on, hence capable of being truly accessed simultaneously. This is known as interleaving of memory (see Sec. 4.14) and requires additional high speed control logic. Such techniques are often used in the high performance models of commercial systems.

Our examples of storage architecture are not intended to be descriptive, nor complete; rather, the fundamental problems and fundamental solutions are sketched. The details of the entire storage hierarchy are intimately related to the total system architecture, which is beyond the scope of this book.

9.3   FUNDAMENTAL REQUIREMENTS OF TWO–LEVEL VIRTUAL MEMORY HIERARCHIES

The primary goal of a virtual memory system is to combine two storage systems that have widely different capacities, speeds, and costs, such that the combined system has very nearly the speed of the smaller, faster memory but the cost and apparent storage capacity of the more inexpensive and slower memory. The storage capacity of the faster, smaller system is thus virtually extended by proper interconnection with the larger store. For the main memory–disk virtual system, this extension of capacity implies a very important characteristic; namely, each user separately must be able to address the virtual memory in terms of the total size of the permissible system logical address, irrespective of the actual capacity of the smaller memory. The value of such a scheme can be appreciated by recalling that in any computer, the CPU can only fetch or store information through main memory. In early systems, when a program exceeded the size of main memory, the user had to provide the storage allocation. This was relatively easy because the program was simply divided into independent "segments" that were replaced or "overlaid" in main memory in a sequential fashion. Furthermore, the user was the sole user of the system, and users were familiar both with the problem (which allowed easier segmentation) and with the computer (which permitted easier storage allocation).

As CPU, main memory, and storage become larger and are shared among many programs simultaneously, the problems of memory allocation grow in complexity, requiring increasing amounts of a user's time. In addition, it may be desirable to run a given program on a similar system with different memory and storage capacity, or new memory and storage may be added to an existing machine. The memory addressing problem, if tailored to a specific implementation, could conceivably require substantial rewriting of a program, a very undesirable situation. Thus we would like a system that is flexible, independent of the physical storage attached to the machine at any one time, and independent of other users sharing the system. Implementing these features involves many concepts such as paging, hit ratio, and address translation. For now, we give a general summary and overview of a two-level virtual hierarchy, pointing out the minimum fundamental functions required. Conceptual implementation of these necessary functions as well as performance trade-offs are detailed in subsequent sections, along with practical implementation of these functions in commercial systems.

Except where noted, the following discussion is carried out in terms of a *multiuser main memory–disk virtual system, but it applies equally well to the cache–main memory virtual store* (Section 9.10). Single user virtual systems, as employed on some small computers, are a limiting case of the more general case treated here.

The goals of a virtual system can be achieved to a significant degree only as a result of the fortuitous fact that for most processing, the references to memory tend to be highly localized or to cluster in small groups. In other words, after a given word from a given location in main memory has been processed, the subsequently needed memory word most often is located nearby. A workable system is obtained by operating on small pieces of information stored in main memory. These pieces, called pages, are portions of the total program and often contain both the program instructions and the alphanumeric data.* Pages tend to have an optimal or natural size that can be determined from program statistics (Section 9.4). Both main memory and secondary storage are divided into pages of equal size and equal to the natural length. Main memory normally contains several pages for each of several users. When the CPU is operating on a given page, a substantial number of operations can be performed, since many references are localized within that page.

The processor logical address, which specifies the maximum directly addressable secondary storage, is much larger than the main memory address length. Hence we need to be able to translate the program logical address into the correct page and correct word within that page. If a memory reference is not localized within a given page but rather within a second page, the system

---

* Multics (Section 9.9) uses separate pages for data and instructions.

proceeds with little difficulty as long as the second page is also within main memory. If the second page is not in main memory, the required page is transferred into main memory as needed; this is called demand paging, or in some cases the page is transferred in advance by special look-ahead operations. Demand paging is more commonly used. Assuming that main memory is already full, the subsequent operations necessitate a replacement algorithm to determine which page is to be removed, a mapping function to determine where it is to be relocated on secondary storage, and means of keeping track of its new location. Also the location of the desired page in secondary storage must be determined. Since page replacement is a time-consuming operation, either the CPU transfers operation to a different user's program and continues processing, or it sits idle while the transfer is performed. This is a design option set by the desired system cost-performance. Once a page is transferred to main memory, many words within that page will be used more than once, such as in looping operations. Thus one rather slow transfer of information subsequently results in many fast accesses to that information, with a net gain resulting from the clustering of memory references.*

Assuming that memory references do cluster into natural page sizes of reasonable length, it can be deduced from the previous discussion that the fundamental, minimum functions necessary for a virtual memory system are as follows:

1. Page mapping function (Section 9.5).
2. Address translation (Section 9.6).
   a. Word addressing within a page.
   b. Page addressing within both primary and secondary storage.
3. Page replacement algorithm (Section 9.7).

In large, multiprogrammed systems, a number of additional practical functions are needed to produce a feasible, efficient system. Some important practical requirements in a multiuser system are as follows:

a. I/O processor and technique for efficient page relocations.
b. Storage protection.
c. Sharing of pages.

When a required page is not in primary storage, the I/O processor finds and transfers the required page, allowing the CPU to transfer to a different user and continue processing. These overlapping functions combined with cycle stealing for data transfer (Section 9.2) greatly improve the CPU utiliza-

---

* In this case "memory references" means both program instructions and the actual alphanumeric data processed.

tion. Yet even without this, some advantage in efficiency over a nonvirtual system can result because of the clustering of memory references,* but the main advantage would be the virtual addressing capability. This is the situation in some small, single user virtual system. In large, multiuser virtual systems, speed and system efficiency are important as well as virtual addressing capability.

The storage protection function ensures that any given page of memory is not inadvertently changed or removed, nor accessed by unauthorized users. In multiuser systems, sharing of pages that contain, for instance, the supervisory program, is highly desirable to conserve memory space. In data based systems, sharing of data between users with proper access rights becomes a fundamental necessity, but this represents a more complex system than that being considered here. In a simple, two-level, multiuser virtual hierarchy, the latter three optional features are of practical importance but are not fundamentally necessary—a workable, but perhaps inefficient system can be envisioned without them. The advantages of an I/O processor, detailed in Section 9.2, are valid here as well. Sharing of pages is a complex issue that is not considered.

To better understand how the fundamental requirements interact, we now discuss a large, multiuser virtual system consisting of a disk as secondary storage and main memory as primary storage. We consider only a multiple virtual address space system: a single virtual address space is fundamentally no different and is just a simpler, limiting case.† The total logical address that addresses secondary storage consists of N_s bits, of which u bits are the user identification bits. These N_s bits can be contained in one or several registers within the CPU—typically, several are used. Each page is divided into 2^{N_r} words or bytes, where N_r represents the lowest order address bits (Fig. 9.3-1). The total number of pages in the virtual disk storage is thus 2^{N_v}, where

$$N_v = N_s - N_r \qquad (9.3\text{-}1)$$

Since the number of users U must be

$$U = 2^u \qquad (9.3\text{-}2)$$

---

* The main advantage is the saving in multiple access times. A nonvirtual system with improper memory segmentation may require numerous accesses to the disk for the same number of words processed, whereas a virtual system may use only one or a few accesses. The clustering of subsequent memory references to pages already present eliminates a large number of disk accesses but not the data transfer time.

† In practical terms, a single virtual space system does not have a separate user ID register (Fig. 9.5-2b and Fig. 9.8-2). Rather, the u bits are contained within N_t' so each user has a virtual address space which is smaller than the total CPU address N, but this can still be larger than the actual main memory address n_p.

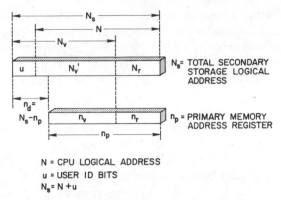

N = CPU LOGICAL ADDRESS
u = USER ID BITS
N_s = N + u

FIGURE 9.3-1   Definitions of address bits in primary and secondary addresses.

each user has a total virtual storage capacity of

$$\text{pages/user} = 2^{N_v'} \tag{9.3-3}$$

where $N_v' = N_v - u = N_s - u - N_r$, as shown schematically in Fig. 9.3-1. This is equivalent to N address bits per user, where N is the standard address length of the CPU as given by column 7 of Table 1.1-1. For instance, on the IBM systems 360/370, $N = 24$ bits and the additional user address bits u are contained in a special register (see Section 9.9). Primary storage is addressed by n_p bits, where

$$n_p < N_s \tag{9.3-4}$$

Hence it can hold only 2^{n_p} words, which is normally considerably less than 2^{N_s}. Since pages are of fixed size,

$$n_v = n_p - n_r \tag{9.3-6}$$

The CPU can reference pages through main memory only. Since in principle all 2^{N_v} pages must eventually be referenced by the CPU, the page slots in main memory must be shared by many virtual pages, at different times, of course. The mapping of this large number of virtual pages into a smaller number of page slots is performed by the mapping function (Section 9.5) as indicated schematically in Fig. 9.3-2.

The addressing of such a system is considerably more complex than for an ordinary memory. Each of the N_s bit combinations represents a unique word in the virtual disk store therefore all these bits *must* be used to address main memory. However the main memory address register can only hold n_p, giving a deficiency of

$$n_d = N_s - n_p \text{ bits} \tag{9.3-7}$$

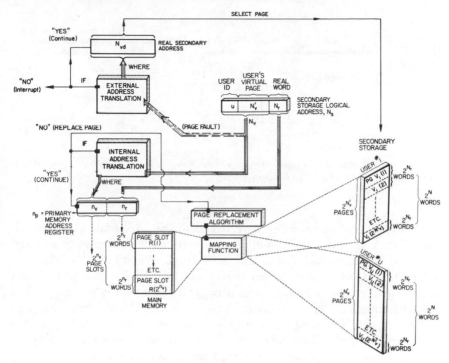

FIGURE 9.3-2 Schematic of basic functional requirements in multiuser virtual memory system, showing information flow during translation of virtual address to primary memory address.

as in Fig. 9.3-1. These deficient bits must be used in addressing main memory, hence this number of bits (but not necessarily these bit positions) *must be decoded externally*. The words or bytes within a page are addressed by the lowest order address bits, denoted as N_r in Fig. 9.3-1. These bits are real and convert directly to n_r in the primary address register (Fig. 9.3-1 or 9.3-2).* Since many virtual pages can occupy that same page slot, the remaining N_v bits must be used to indicate IF and WHERE the desired page resides in main memory. The various parts of the address translation are shown in Fig. 9.3-3. When the IF part produces a "yes," the address residing in the primary address register is used. When a "no" answer is obtained from the IF part, that page does not reside in main memory and a page relocation is necessary. The address that appears in the primary address register is aborted,

---

* These bits may be added to the contents of an index or base register but nevertheless are converted directly to the real address.

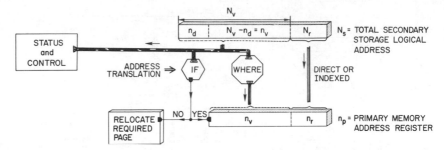

FIGURE 9.3-3 Schematic of translation of virtual logical address N_s into primary address showing IF, WHERE, and DIRECT components.

and now the N_s bits must be converted to the disk (secondary) address in Fig. 9.3-2. A separate external address translation function must be invoked which, as before, provides an IF and a WHERE. When the IF is "yes," the WHERE address is valid. When the IF is "no," that virtual page is not present in the secondary store and a program interrupt is generated. The WHERE function converts the virtual page address N_v into a real disk page address N_{vd}. In principle N_{vd} represents the same number of bits as N_v; hence any of the 2^{N_v} pages of any user can be accessed in secondary storage. Since all words of a page are transferred, the real address bits N_r are incremented by either hardware or software from zero to N_r, and the translation must be concerned only with the page address bits N_v as shown.

When main memory is full, it is necessary to remove one page before a new one can be entered. The page replacement algorithm keeps track of page usage in main memory and decides which page is expendable on request for a new page not present. If this expendable page has been modified, it is transferred back to disk, and only afterward can the new page be transferred. These three fundamental requirements are represented in block diagram form in Fig. 9.3-2 with only some lines of communication and control included. In actual implementation, these functions do not necessarily divide into convenient, separate pieces but often are closely interleaved. The address translation function has two major, separate components: to convert N_s into n_p if that page is resident in main memory; or, when a page fault is obtained, to convert N_s into a disk address. Each of these translations can be done in several fundamental ways, as we see later. The integration of these functions into a system can take various forms as detailed in Sections 9.8 through 9.11. In large multiprogrammed systems, additional status and control functions are often included to indicate whether pages have been changed, to control each user's access rights and sharing of pages, and to implement other practical concerns.

In summary, we can state that the basic functions of Fig. 9.3-2 are necessary and sufficient to make a virtual memory work in a logical sense. From a practical point of view, however, data clustering is needed to make the system efficient. If references to primary storage physical locations occurred in a purely random fashion, page swapping between secondary and primary storage would occur very frequently, greatly reducing the overall system efficiency. Fortunately references to memory locations do not occur at random but cluster into groups called pages. The clustering is not precise, hence page size varies with the miss ratio required, size of primary storage, and other factors. This subject is covered in detail in Section 9.4. Thus the functions in Fig. 9.3-2 are those required to make virtual addressing logically feasible; overlaid on these is the phenomenon of data clustering, which makes the virtual memory economically feasible.

9.4 DATA CLUSTERING, PAGING, AND HIT RATIO

As was mentioned briefly in Section 9.1, early commercial virtual memory systems were dominated by the use of *segments* of *variable* size. This approach evolved because in the early storage hierarchies, where program segments were overlaid into main memory, the segments always appeared in widely varying sizes. In fact, the natural length varied with the problem as well as with the programmer. Thus it seemed natural for a virtual system to allow for variation if efficient operation was to be obtained. Later, however, this notion proved to be incorrect. Though the natural segment length does indeed vary, allowing for this in any memory allocation procedure leads to gross inefficiencies. A number of small, fixed size pages can approximate any segment, and since the memory allocation procedure is much simpler, considerable improvement in overall efficiency can be obtained. The fundamental problem with segmentation is that it requires contiguous words in primary storage and the segments may be of varying size.* A request for transfer of a segment into primary memory requires locating an empty region of the proper size. The empty regions may not singly be large enough, even though their sum may be more than sufficient. Since they are not contiguous, however, they cannot be used, and on a statistical basis, many regions of primary storage may remain unused. In a paged system with fixed page sizes, transferring a page only requires finding or creating an empty page slot in primary storage. This is considerably easier than finding or creating

---

* Contiguous words are required just as for a page in Section 9.3, since the word within a segment is obtained by catenating the lower order real address bits to the higher order segment address bits.

contiguous segments of varying size and is one of the important reasons for the widespread usage of paging techniques. We do not attempt to prove that paging is superior to segmentation, rather, we implicitly assume this in what follows. Denning (1970) gives an excellent review of the past work, both analytical and simulation results, demonstrating the general superiority of paging.

Considerable work has been done in the literature to derive mathematical relationships for various aspects of virtual memory systems (Franaszek and Wagner, 1974; Ingargiola and Korsh, 1974; Mitra, 1974). Unfortunately most such analyses are based on rather severe, oversimplifying assumptions. As such, the results provide valuable insights but are often of little help in design of virtual systems. For actual design, the measurement and simulation techniques based on analysis of actual job streams have proved to be much more useful (Belady, 1966; Gibson, 1967; Mattson, et al., 1970; Saltzer, 1974; Boyre, 1974). We make use primarily of the latter rather than analytical techniques for understanding the design tradeoffs.

Paged memory hierarchies are useful because over a long period, memory references in real programs are not random but cluster into natural block or page sizes. The clustering of memory references occurs both for the data that are processed and for the program instructions that do the processing. In the following discussions, the clustering of these two is lumped together unless specifically stated otherwise. We shall use typical job streams that contain a large number of different individual problems, hence different I/B ratios (Sec. 1.5), ensuring that average, representative values are automatically included in the results.

Page size is a very important parameter because it affects the number of page relocations that must be made and the length of time required to replace each page. Unfortunately, the effects are in the opposite direction: a large page size, for instance, includes more memory references, but at the same time takes longer to relocate and allows fewer pages in primary storage. All these factors affect the system efficiency. Since the relocation time can be greatly varied by the overall system design, we ignore it for the moment. We wish to determine whether there is a natural page size and if so, the appropriate value or range of values.

It is self-evident that memory references for any given problem must always cluster within some set, however large. The worst case will be the set containing the total data for the problem (e.g., all instructions, matrices, and constants needed for an engineering calculation). This worst case set is often too large, consuming large portions of primary storage. The real significance of data clustering is that the natural size of a set, called a page, is considerably smaller than the entire problem. In other words, all problems can be segmented into smaller pages, and these pages can be processed as a

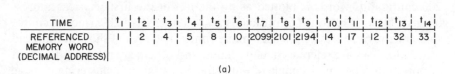

TIME	t_1	t_2	t_3	t_4	t_5	t_6	t_7	t_8	t_9	t_{10}	t_{11}	t_{12}	t_{13}	t_{14}
REFERENCED MEMORY WORD (DECIMAL ADDRESS)	1	2	4	5	8	10	2099	2101	2194	14	17	12	32	33

(a)

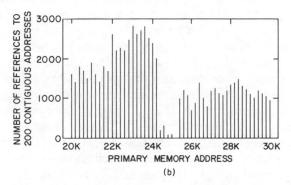

(b)

FIGURE 9.4-1 (*a*) Hypothetical example of memory reference trace. (*b*) Trace pattern of memory references for a typical Fortran analysis program running on an XDS Sigma 5 (medium-sized computer). After Meade, (1972).

unit with only occasional need to reference data in other pages not currently in primary storage. The natural or optimum size of pages cannot be derived from first principles, it results instead from simulation of typical job streams processed on assumed memory hierarchies. To understand the concept of clustering, let us look at what happens in a hypothetical program on consecutive memory references. The program and data are laid out linearly in the main memory (i.e., in contiguous physical memory words). If we trace the physical word address of memory references as a function of time, these addresses might resemble Fig. 9.4-1*a*. The references first tend to remain in one small area of memory, then jump to another area, typically far away, where they remain for awhile, then jump again, often back to the first localized area as shown. If there was no clustering of memory references, the successive references in Fig. 9.4-1*a* would essentially be random addresses. Fortunately this is not the case. Even though the successive references can vary significantly as a function of time, over a long period the references tend to cluster into relatively small groups. This can be seen more clearly by plotting the total number of references to some small region of contiguous words as a function of the physical address, over a very long period—say, the total running time of the program. Such a case is illustrated in Fig. 9.4-1*b* for a typical Fortran program. The total number of references to a small region of

200 contiguous words is plotted as a function of the first physical address of this 200 word region. The ordinate can be larger than 200, since of course some memory addresses are used many times. The results show that indeed some addresses are referenced many times, and others are referenced seldom or not at all. The small sample of data suggests a natural clustering or page size of roughly 4K addresses.* However, additional data are required before we can specify the optimum page size, and it is expedient to introduce the concept of hit ratio below. Before proceeding it should be pointed out that in essence, Fig. 9.4-1a presents memory references as a function of time for a large address space, whereas Fig. 9.4-1b presents the memory references as a function of memory space for a long time period. They are complementary functions representing the same data, the former being the temporal and the latter the spatial representation. The clustering in space provides the natural page size, whereas the time distribution of successive references determines the number of pages that must be resident in primary storage to reduce page faults. The number of pages that can be resident is given by the word capacity of primary storage divided by the page size. Hence both are important and both are included in what follows.

Hit ratio H_R is a useful concept for determining optimum page size. It represents the average amount of data† clustering to be expected for a given problem set. Specifically, it indicates the amount of data clustering within a given page size and simultaneously the amount of clustering among pages for a given primary memory size. In the following, the hit ratio indicates the total number of times a referenced word is found anywhere within primary storage divided by the total number of references to primary storage or, in fractional form

$$H_R = \frac{\text{references found in primary memory}}{\text{total memory references}} \tag{9.4-1}$$

The value varies with time, and an average over a long time or long problem set is used as the indication of average data clustering.

If an addressing pattern such as that in Fig. 9.4-1a is random, we would expect the probability of finding one of 2^{N_s} words in a group of 2^{n_p} possible locations to be the ratio of these two. This probability is the hit ratio, and it is the word capacity of primary storage divided by the capacity of secondary storage, or

$$H_R \bigg|_{\substack{\text{random} \\ \text{addressing}}} = \frac{2^{n_p}}{2^{N_s}} = \frac{1}{2^{n_d}} \tag{9.4-2}$$

---

* Fortunately the 200 word regions are significantly smaller than this natural clustering size to make the data meaningful. If this natural page size were, say, 100 words, the ordinate would have to be plotted in terms of number of references to, say, 10 contiguous words.

† Data = alphanumeric data plus instructions.

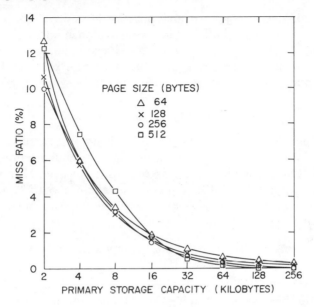

FIGURE 9.4-2 Miss ratio versus primary storage capacity for various page sizes in a typical Fortran job stream: total number of access in job stream = 8,804,286; total number of instructions = 6,624,606. LRU replacement algorithm, fully associative mapping function. After Lin and Mattson (1972).

For any reasonable paged system, the capacity of secondary must be at least 10 times that of primary storage, usually much larger. If the addressing is random, the best possible hit ratio in such a case is 0.1 or 10%, which is totally unworkable. The addressing pattern must be considerably more ordered than random if paging is to work efficiently.

Figure 9.4-2 gives an example of another type of analysis used to determine whether data cluster and if so, the optimum page size. A large problem set consisting of a Fortran job stream is essentially laid out linearly, then divided into pages of equal size. The pages are transferred into main memory as memory references are made to bytes within that page (demand paging). If data do cluster, subsequent references are made more often to that page or others already in main memory. If data do not cluster, many misses or transfers of new pages are required. The problems are processed sequentially, and pages are replaced using the least recently used (LRU) algorithm under a fully associative mapping function. The simulation then looks at each memory reference and determines whether it is present; if not, the LRU page is assumed to be replaced with the required page and subsequent references are analyzed. The entire job stream is processed this way.* The total number of references to memory, both instructions and alphanumeric data references, are counted. The total number of misses is also counted, and dividing by the number of memory references gives the average miss ratio for the assumed page size and primary storage size. The miss ratio, which is one minus the hit ratio, or

$$M_R = 1 - H_R \qquad (9.4\text{-}3)$$

is plotted as a function of primary store capacity for several values of page size as shown. The total program, which in this simulation represents the effective size of secondary storage, is 6.6M words (or bytes). From Fig. 9.4-2, at a primary capacity of 16K bytes, the miss ratio is about 2%, or a 98% hit ratio. If the address patterns were purely random, we would expect from (9.4-1) a hit ratio of

$$H_R\Big|_{\text{random}} = \frac{16K}{6.6M} = 2.4 \times 10^{-3} \qquad (9.4\text{-}4)$$

or 0.24% hit ratio. Obviously, a much better value is obtained, indicating that data do indeed cluster. For a given page size, the miss ratio decreases or improves as the capacity of primary storage increases. This is exactly as would be expected. The improvement is quite large at small capacities but nearly levels off at larger capacities. For example, a large improvement is obtained by increasing the capacity from 2K to 32K bytes, but an additional 32K bytes results in a much smaller improvement. This indicates that 32K bytes is a reasonable optimum for cost/performance *if* the corresponding miss ratio of about 1% is adequate for overall system performance. This is usually the case for cache systems; hence 16K to 32K' byte primary storage capacity is typical. A smaller miss ratio is needed for virtual memory, hence larger primary storage is required (in the range of 256K' bytes or more). Another less easily predicted conclusion from Fig. 9.4-2 is that for primary storage capacity below 16K bytes, as the page size increases from 64 to 128 bytes (e.g., at a primary capacity of 8K bytes), the miss ratio decreases, as expected. But further increases in page size to 512 bytes results in an increasing miss ratio. This comes about because fewer pages are possible in

---

* All results presented in this chapter for hit ratios and data clustering are valid for continuous single program models only unless otherwise specified. Multiprogramming in a general sense is not included; in other words, when a miss occurs, the simulated execution does *not* transfer to a new user, even though the second user may have pages resident in primary storage. If such general multiprogramming was permitted, the model would become much more complex. It would have to include more parameters such as the number of users simultaneously resident in primary storage, the number of pages per user, priority for transfer back to previous programs after a page swap, and others. This general multiprogramming case has not been satisfactorily modeled.

the primary store as the page size increases, hence the occasional reference another page will find that page not present. If the number of pages is allowed to increase by increasing primary storage capacity, this effect disappears, the crossover point being approximately between 16K and 32K bytes primary capacity, as shown.

For virtual memory systems, a rather low miss ratio is required, and the linear scale of Fig. 9.4-2 is not adequate to see the dependence on page size. The miss ratio on a log log scale for a Fortran job stream and a very different, inventory job stream appear in Fig. 9.4-3a and b, respectively. The broken line at a 0.02% miss ratio represents the approximate value needed for virtual memory. For values of miss ratio below 1%, these curves reveal that the miss ratio decreases as page size is increased up to roughly 4K' or 16K' but begins to increase again. This is the same effect noted previously, except page and storage capacity are shifted to large values and miss ratio is shifted to smaller values as would be expected. Thus again some optimum

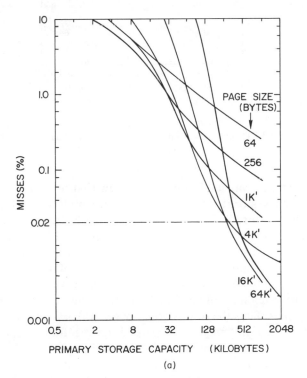

FIGURE 9.4-3 (*a*) Miss ratio versus primary storage capacity for various page sizes and Fortran job stream; LRU replacement algorithm and fully associative mapping. Courtesy R. Mattson.

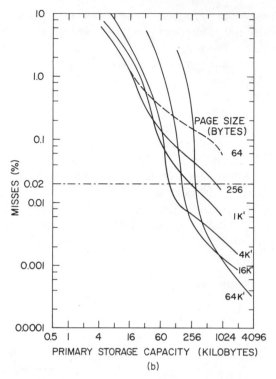

FIGURE 9.4-3 (*b*) Miss ratio versus primary storage capacity for various page sizes and inventory job stream; LRU replacement algorithm and fully associative mapping. Courtesy R. Mattson.

range of page size is evident. These figures show that to achieve a miss ratio of 0.02%, primary storage capacities of approximately 256K and 128K, respectively, are required. If we assume our total job stream to be a mixture of these, a minimum of about 256K would be required. Further examination also shows that page sizes roughly in the range of 1K to 4K are reasonably optimum values for values of miss ratio in the range of 0.02%.

It should be pointed out these results merely show the statistical distribution of memory references and are totally independent of any storage access and transfer times. Thus the results are very general, based only on an LRU replacement algorithm, fully associative mapping function, and typical specified job streams all operating under demand paging.

Liptay (1968) has also shown that clustering of data is not random. For instance, in a paged cache system the hit ratio for a given job stream was found by simulation analysis to be 96.8%, whereas if the memory references were entirely random, the hit ratio would be less than 1%.

In all the paging statistics given previously, the alphanumeric data and instructions are intermixed within any given block or page. It is to be expected that instructions for a program will tend to cluster much more than the alphanumeric data, since many instructions are sequential or looping, with occasional branching. We naturally wonder whether this really is true, and if so, to what extent. The variations between instruction and data address patterns were measured for 20 programs and approximately 50M addresses executed on an IBM 7040 computer (36 bit words) (Scherr, 1966). The results, plotted on linear and semilog scales in Figs. 9.4-4 and 9.4-5, clearly indicate that instructions do cluster more than alphanumeric data. Even though the alphanumeric data clustering probability is lower than that for instructions, this effect is counterbalanced by the fact that I/B, the instructions executed per byte of data processed by a CPU, is generally larger than unity (Section 1.5). On the average, more references are made to instructions; thus the overall probability is often closer to that for instructions.

In Figs. 9.4-4 and 9.5-5, the high probability, nearly unity, for successive instructions to be within the same page results because instructions are normally executed from successive memory locations. This is shown more clearly in Fig. 9.4-6, which gives the probability distribution for the distances between successive addresses for both the instruction and the data stream (note that the instruction stream reaches a probability of 0.71 for a distance of 1 where "1" means the next location). The finite probability for reference to a word a considerable distance away, such as 80 words on the abscissa in Fig. 9.4-6, is equivalent to the occasional reference to a word (page) located

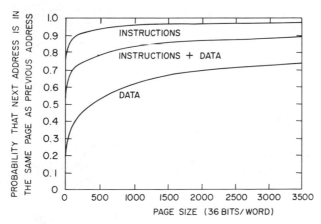

FIGURE 9.4-4 Page hit ratio versus page size for data and instructions separately, on linear scale. After Scherr (1966).

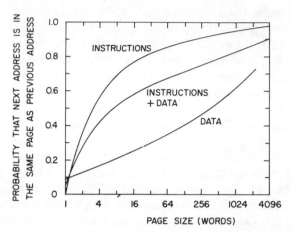

FIGURE 9.4-5 Page hit ratio versus page size for data and instructions separately, on semilog scale. After Scherr (1966).

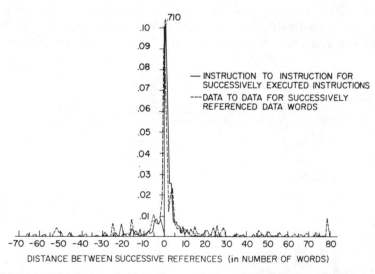

FIGURE 9.4-6 Distribution of address distances for instructions and data. After Scherr (1966).

far away such as that illustrated in Fig. 9.4-1*a*. Of course, the distributions vary in detail for different programs and different systems but the same general trends are encountered.

Pages per Program in Primary Storage

In the execution of any program, there are usually at least four areas of activity—one instruction area, two areas for source data (operands), and one area for sink data (answers). Thus a minimum of four pages would seem to be desirable for each user. However programs generally have instructions and data intermixed; in addition, branching instructions can increase this minimum page requirement. Thus it would be desirable to know, particularly in a multiprogrammed system, how many pages should be allotted to a given user. Figure 9.4-7 presents the miss ratio as a function of the number of pages

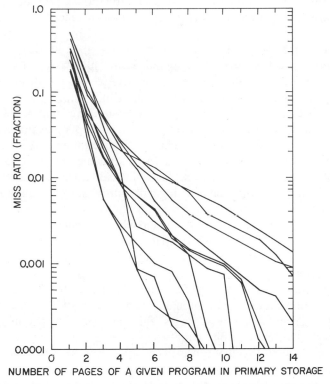

FIGURE 9.4-7 Miss ratio versus number of pages of a given program in primary storage; page size = 1024 words; total program size = 32 pages; various curves are for different user programs, each of 32 pages total size; LRU replacement algorithm. After Scherr (1966).

present in primary storage for many different user programs. Each program is a maximum of 32 pages total size, each page containing 1024 words. The results for the particular set of programs indicate that relatively few pages can give a rather small miss ratio. Four pages result in about a 1 % miss ratio, whereas 10 pages can reduce this by 2 orders of magnitude. The conclusion is that relatively few pages of a user's program are required to achieve reasonable miss ratios.

9.5 MAPPING FUNCTIONS

The secondary or virtual store contains a large number of pages that must be mapped or compressed into a smaller number of page slots in primary storage. The mapping function, requirement 1 in Section 9.3, specifies how this mapping is to be done. We consider the various mapping techniques in their general, fundamental form and derive relationships that are useful latter. The mapping function has a very significant effect on the address translation.

In practice, mapping functions are considered in four distinct groups (Conti, 1969): direct, sector, set associative, and fully associative. Fundamentally, they form a continuum of set associative organizations, with the direct and fully associative being two extremes and sectoring a special case.

A point of confusion often arises in understanding mapping functions because the mapping functions are only logical concepts that impart overall organization to the page mapping schemes. A given mapping function can be implemented in different ways and when implemented, it becomes part of the address translation function. These logical concepts can be used to visualize the mapping of logical to logical addresses, or logical address to physical address. The precise meaning of this and its consequences are discussed later in this section. First we deal with the general forms of logical mapping functions, assuming that the page slot allocations and relationships to follow are done in terms of *logical* structure *without* necessarily requiring the same *physical* structure.

Following the nomenclature in Section 9.3 and Figs. 9.3-1 through 9.3-3, secondary store contains a maximum of 2^{N_v} pages, each of 2^{N_r} words, whereas primary storage contains only 2^{n_v} pages of the same size. The primary address register has a deficiency of bits equal to n_d given by (9.3-7) as in Fig. 9.3-1. Since $2^{n_v} \ll 2^{N_v}$ as in Fig. 9.5-1, it is necessary to specify how this compression or mapping is to be done. Any page slot in primary storage must hold many different virtual pages, but at different times of course. The actual number of virtual pages that a logical page slot must accommodate varies with the mapping function; the minimum number, however, is the total

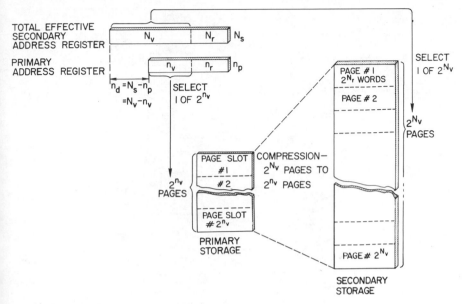

FIGURE 9.5-1   Compression of secondary pages into primary page slots with associated address bits.

page capacity of secondary divided by the total page capacity of primary storage or

$$\frac{\text{minimum number of pages}}{\text{logical page slot}} = \frac{2^{N_v}}{2^{n_v}} = 2^{N_v - n_v} = 2^{n_d} \qquad (9.5\text{-}1)$$

Thus the minimum number is determined by the deficient bits n_d. The maximum number is the total page capacity of secondary storage, or 2^{N_v}. These two cases represent the extremes of direct and associative mapping, respectively. Between these two limiting cases are any number of possibilities. In a more general form, we can allow a virtual page from secondary storage to reside in any of S page slots in primary storage as in Fig. 9.5-2a. These S page slots form a set, and the mapping is the general form of set associative. There are obviously 2^{n_v} total slots; hence the number of possible sets in primary storage is

$$Q = \frac{2^{n_v}}{S} = \frac{2^{n_v}}{2^s} = 2^{n_v - s} = 2^q \text{ sets} \qquad (9.5\text{-}2)$$

where

$$q = n_v - s \qquad (9.5\text{-}3)$$

$$S = 2^s \qquad (9.5\text{-}4)$$

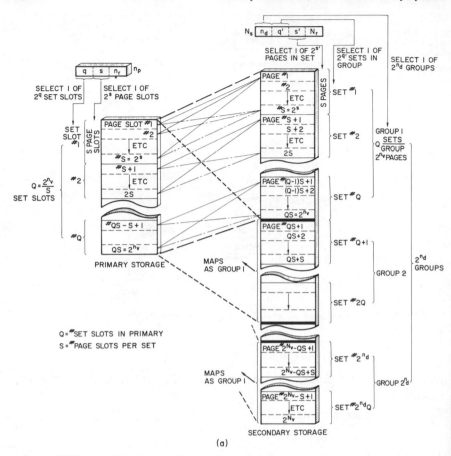

FIGURE 9.5-2 (a) General format for mapping secondary to primary storage.

But there are 2^{N_v} virtual pages that must be accommodated in 2^{n_v} page slots. The easiest way to visualize how this might be done is to think of secondary storage as being logically divided into groups of pages, each group of length equal to that of primary storage or 2^{n_v} page slots. Each group contains Q sets and each set contains S pages. Each set slot in primary storage must be shared by the Qth set in secondary storage. Thus set slot 1 is shared by sets 1, $1 + Q, \ldots, 2^{n_d}$. Likewise set slot Q in shared by sets $Q, 2Q, 3Q, \ldots, 2^{n_d}Q$. Pages within a set are associatively mapped into any of the S page slots. All virtual pages are thus assigned to one and only one logical set and can be located in any one of S specific page slots within that set. Sets from different groups can be intermixed within primary storage; therefore not all sets from one given group need be simultaneously resident in primary storage. We

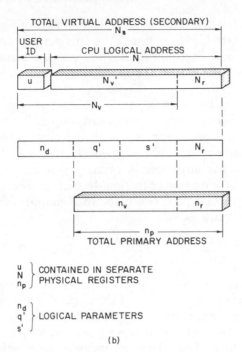

TOTAL VIRTUAL ADDRESS (SECONDARY)

USER ID

CPU LOGICAL ADDRESS

u | N_v' | N_r

N_v

n_d | q' | s' | N_r

n_v | n_r

n_p

TOTAL PRIMARY ADDRESS

$\left.\begin{matrix} u \\ N \\ n_p \end{matrix}\right\}$ CONTAINED IN SEPARATE PHYSICAL REGISTERS

$\left.\begin{matrix} n_d \\ q' \\ s' \end{matrix}\right\}$ LOGICAL PARAMETERS

(b)

FIGURE 9.5-2 (b) Relationship of physical and logical address bit parameters.

may have, for instance, sets 1 from several different groups resident in primary storage, which means that all these virtual pages would have the same q address bits but different n_d address bits.

One reason for such a seemingly complex allocation of pages is that knowledge of which logical set and group a page must occupy constitutes *additional addressing information* that is used by the address translation function. The total number of virtual pages that can possibly reside at different times in any given slot in primary storage is the total number of virtual pages 2^{N_v} divided by the number of sets Q, or

$$\frac{\text{virtual pages}}{\text{logical page slot}} = \frac{2^{N_v}}{Q} = \frac{2^{N_v}}{2^q} = 2^{N_v - q} \qquad (9.5\text{-}5)$$

But from (9.5-3), $q = n_v - s$; thus substitution gives

$$\frac{\text{possible virtual pages}}{\text{logical page slot}} = 2^{N_v - (n_v - s)} = 2^{n_d + s} \qquad (9.5\text{-}6)$$

$$= S2^{n_d} \qquad (9.5\text{-}7)$$

The logical level of organization in secondary storage of Fig. 9.5-2a starting from the lowest to the highest is thus 2^{N_r} words per page, $S = 2^s$ pages/set, $Q = 2^q$ sets/group, and 2^{n_d} groups total. The analogous hierarchy in primary storage is 2^{n_r} words/page, $S = 2^s$ page slots/set, and Q set slots/primary storage.

When the physical locations of sets in primary storage are fixed to be equivalent to the logical locations, the word "logical" can be replaced by "physical" in all the above expressions. In the more general case, logical and physical allocations are not equivalent. In the most flexible case, any virtual page can reside anywhere in primary storage, irrespective of the logical structure of the mapping function. In such a case, the total possible virtual pages per physical page slot is the total number of possible virtual pages. Thus for the general case,

$$\frac{\text{possible virtual pages}}{\text{physical page slot}} = 2^{N_v} = 2^{n_d+s+q} \tag{9.5-8}$$

These relationships are important in the address translation process. The smaller the number of slots S per set, or the larger Q, the fewer logical places a page can reside and the easier it will be to find. Likewise larger values of S or smaller Q allow more possible slots per virtual page, and the more difficult the page will be to find. Thus one factor in the selection of a mapping function is the effect on the address translation.

Also important in the choice of a mapping function is the primary slot contention problem. In any mapping scheme, all the virtual pages required for a given problem can, statistically, reside in the same set, and the number of required pages might exceed the size of that set. Thus contention problems between two or more pages for unavailable slots can result in a large miss ratio for that problem, which is undesirable. The probability of contention problems, of course, varies with the number of page slots per set S.

The various distinct types of mapping function can be obtained by varying the value of S. Fully associative mapping results when S is its maximum value of 2^{n_v} and Q is its minimum value of 1. Direct mapping is just the opposite, resulting when S is its minimum value of 1 or $s = 0$ and $Q = 2^{n_v}$. Set associative occurs for any values of S and Q between these extremes. Sector mapping is just a special case of fully associative mapping with the page enlarged to encompass many pages, called sectors. Thus it is apparent that the address parameters q and s are logical entities that can be selected by the designer. They can be taken from the physical address registers, and the value of each is determined by the arrangement of the physical wires connecting the registers. The relationship between the various physical and logical address bits is shown in Fig. 9.5-2b. Each of the mapping functions is now considered separately.

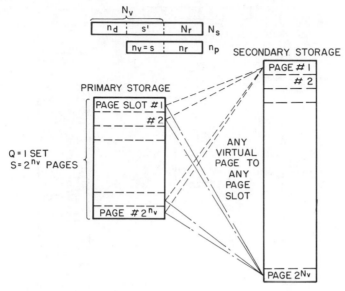

FIGURE 9.5-3 Schematic of fully associative mapping: $S = 2^{n_v}$ page slots/set; $s = n_r$, $Q = 1, q = 0$.

9.5.1 Fully Associative Mapping: $S = 2^{n_v}, Q = 1, s = n_v, q = 0$

If we allow S to become its maximum value of 2^{n_v}, there can only be one set in primary storage (i.e., $Q = 1$). Under these circumstances, any virtual page can be mapped logically into any page slot, and the mapping becomes fully associative (Fig. 9.5-3). This mapping is the most general and provides the minimum probability for page slot contention problems. Two virtual pages can contend for a page slot only when the pages required simultaneously for a given problem exceeds 2^{n_v}, which is most unlikely. Hence fully associative mapping provides the largest hit ratio for a given problem on a given virtual system and is the most desired mapping function. However an associative type of compare is required in the address translation (Section 9.6), making this the most difficult mapping function to implement.

9.5.2 Direct Mapping: $S = 1, Q = 2^{n_v}, s = 0, q = n_v$

One way to completely avoid associative searching and greatly simplify the address translation is to let $S = 1$, giving only one page slot per set. This is referred to as direct mapping, illustrated in Fig. 9.5-4. Any given page in secondary storage can reside logically only in a specific page slot in primary storage. Using the rules previously described, the first logical page slot in

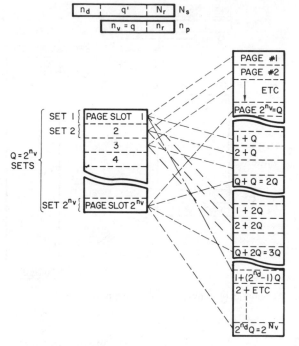

FIGURE 9.5-4 Schematic of direct mapping; $S = 1$ page slot/set; $Q = 2^{n_v}$ sets, $s = 0$, $q = n_v$.

primary storage is assigned to hold virtual page 1, or $1 + Q, 1 + 2Q, \ldots,$ up to page $1 + (2^{n_d} - 1)2^{n_v}$. Likewise, the second page slot is assigned virtual pages 2, $2 + Q$, $2 + 2Q$, and so on, as shown, where $Q = 2^{n_v}$. When the logical and physical allocations are identical, primary storage will physically contain the pages as shown.

A serious disadvantage of direct mapping is the high probability of primary slot contention. For example, suppose a problem is being processed using arrays or matrices. If each array is in a separate page with array A_{ijk} in page 1 and array M_{ijk} in page $1 + Q$, a problem of the form

$$\sum C_1 A_{ijk} + C_2 M_{ijk} = F_{ijk} \qquad (9.5\text{-}9)$$

would require a transfer of one of the arrays for every evaluation of F_{ijk}, since both arrays are needed for each point. But only one of these arrays can be present in primary storage at any time, giving a low hit ratio and very inefficient operation. It could be argued that the data could, or should, be organized so that this does not happen. This is possible in principle, but it

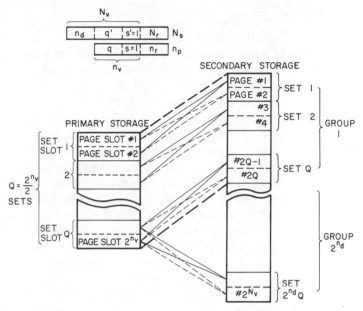

FIGURE 9.5-5 Schematic of set associative mapping showing 2 page slots/set: $S = 2$, $s = 1$, $Q = 2^{n_v}/2$, $q = n_v - 1$.

is not always known beforehand how the data will be used. Even when known, such organization presents many formidable problems to the system allocation of storage, requiring "hand tuning" for efficient operation. Therefore direct mapping of the secondary to primary logical address space is never used.

9.5.3 Set Associative Mapping

In fully associative mapping, the slot contention problem is minimized but the address translation problem is maximized. Direct mapping does just the opposite; contention problems are maximized and the address translation problem is minimized. Set associative mapping represents a compromise between these two. The general form is that of Fig. 9.5-2a. Some typical values are $S = 2$ or 4 page slots per set. The case for $S = 2$ is presented in Fig. 9.5-5. A virtual page can now reside in either of two logical page slots in primary storage. Hence the contention problem arising with direct mapping in solving (9.5-9) is eliminated. However other contention problems can and do arise. Larger values for S are desirable, when possible. A case for $S = 4$ is described in Section 9.11.2.

9.5.4 Sector Mapping

Sector mapping is a special case of fully associative mapping. In fact, if we ignore the labeling of what constitutes a page, the two are fundamentally identical. In practice there are some differences arising from the way the words are divided and decoded.

Sector mapping can be approached in two ways. The simplest method is to consider that the pages in Fig. 9.5-3 are increased in size to encompass many previous pages. If we wish to maintain our definition of a page (i.e., the number of words that is approximately the natural block size), we can just redefine the groupings. Instead of larger pages, we now define a sector to consist of several pages (Fig. 9.5-6). Both primary and secondary storage are broken into sectors of Z pages, and sectors are associatively mapped into primary storage. Obviously a sector of several natural pages has now taken the place of a single page in the fully associative mapping. All the previous rules pertaining to pages now apply to sectors. Note, however, that for a given physical implementation, the value of S, the number of page slots per set, takes on a slightly modified meaning and is reduced by the factor of $1/Z$. In other words, the number of associative compares is now $2^{n_v}/Z$, since only the presence or absence of the sector is required. In practice, this has considerable merit to the extent that the number of sectors can be quite reasonable (e.g., 16); thus if tags are used for sector identification, the tags can be kept in a small associative memory that is very fast and not excessively expensive.

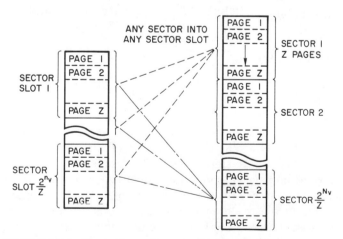

FIGURE 9.5-6   General form of sector mapping with Z pages per sector.

This sector technique using tags has been used with some modifications in the IBM system 360 model 85 cache. The essential idea remains the same— namely, to reduce the size of associative compare hardware while giving the flexibility of an associative mapping. The difficulty with this scheme is that Z must be reasonably large (16 or more), thus the number of sectors in primary storage becomes too small, resulting in a lower average hit ratio.

9.5.5 Logical versus Physical Address Space of Primary Storage

The mapping functions have been discussed in terms of secondary to primary logical address space, as previously indicated. The logical mapping represents the relationship between the symbolic addresses of page slots and can be done independently of any physical address mapping. The descriptions and figures require some conceptual representation of the primary page slots, and these might give the *appearance* of being the actual physical locations. Although this can indeed be the case, it need not be, and in general is not. The confusion between logical and physical mapping comes about because in our minds, we can picture page slots into which virtual pages may be placed, and they appear to have some physical relationship to other page slots. We can quickly address any specified page slot by visual inspection, and we tend to overlook the fact that we have performed a complex address translation function. Yet such a visual search is a sequential associative addressing function. In a computer, the same or other addressing operations can be performed but must be specifically implemented in hardware, just as our visual search is implemented with our eyes and the associative functions of the brain. Thus in our minds, the mapping function appears as though it were mapping secondary store to the physical primary page slots. But when we implement the mapping in the computer, we have removed the associative function provided by the human brain and must supply it in some other manner. This is then the primary logical to physical mapping, which is an essential part of the overall mapping function.

To understand the fundamentally important difference between logical versus physical address and mapping, let us consider the problem of mapping a deck of ordinary playing cards into a set of boxes. For simplicity, we assume that there are only four boxes into which cards can be placed. Also, since an ordinary deck of 52 cards is not a power of 2, we use only the highest 32 cards, from aces to sevens. The cards essentially represent the secondary virtual pages, and the boxes are the primary store page slots. The exact physical address of each box is in the item of importance ultimately, and this has not yet been specified. Let us "logically" label the boxes in some random fashion a, b, c, d by attaching tags (Fig. 9.5-7). The mapping is assumed to be set associative with $s = 1$, which means that a given card can

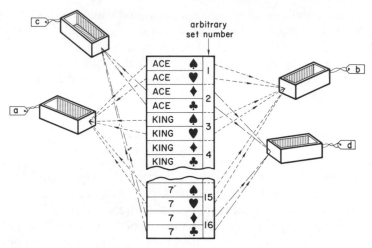

FIGURE 9.5-7   Logical mapping of cards into boxes for set associative mapping with $s = 1$ and four primary storage boxes.

reside in only one of two specifically labeled boxes as shown. For simplicity, we arrange the deck with the highest value card on top (ace of spades) and the lowest card on the bottom (seven of clubs). Since logical mapping is totally independent of physical address, it makes no difference which cards are mapped into which "logical" boxes, as long as we are consistent and obey the mapping rules. Thus we arrange the logical mapping so that the first set, consisting of the aces of spades and hearts, can reside only in the boxes tagged a and b; the second set, consisting of the aces of diamonds and clubs into boxes c and d; set 3, consisting of the kings of spades and hearts into boxes tagged a and b, and so on, similar to that in Fig. 9.5-2a. This information about how cards are mapped must be stored *somewhere*. In this very simple case, we may be able to remenber the mapping, so it is stored in our brains. As a rule, however, the mapping is too complex to remember, therefore let us store this information on a sheet of paper (second, third, and fourth columns of Fig. 9.5-8a). To completely understand the mapping function and the kind of information that is required, we must attempt to find various cards in boxes, which invokes some address translation operations. However, we do these only in a very general way without specifying the actual implementation. Section 9.6 demonstrates the various ways in which the address translation function can be implemented in terms of the mapping information.

Continuing with the example, we specify that only one card may reside in a box at any one time and start moving the cards in random fashion into

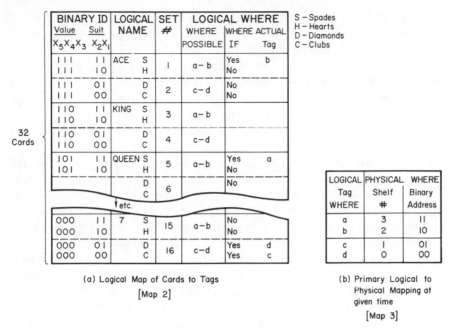

(a) Logical Map of Cards to Tags

[Map 2]

(b) Primary Logical to Physical Mapping at given time

[Map 3]

FIGURE 9.5-8 Mapping information for cards in boxes.

and out of the boxes. At any given instant of time, the four boxes contain four cards. We know from the mapping function which cards may be in which boxes, assuming no mistakes in the swapping process. Suppose that we wish to know IF and WHERE the ace of spades is residing in one of the boxes; a quick check on Fig. 9.5-8a shows that it is useless to look into boxes c and d. Hence we need to associatively search only boxes a and b. If this associative search fails to provide a match, the IF is a "no" and the WHERE is irrelevant. A "yes" match supplies the IF and WHERE directly. Only two associative searches are needed because the boxes are logically tagged and the tags are visible on the boxes. Suppose we remove the tags from the boxes so that the required mapping information is contained only on the piece of paper of Fig. 9.5-8. Since the boxes are identical, it may be difficult determining which two boxes to search for the ace of spades. But *we remember* that box a is on the lower left and box b on the upper right; thus we might search these boxes. However we have made a very important assumption, namely, that there is a "direct" relationship between the logical tags and physical location of the boxes; that is, the logical to physical mapping of the boxes (primary) is direct. If this relationship is true, our search is valid.

Suppose, however, that we rearranged the boxes in some random fashion as we swapped cards. Now with the logical tags on the piece of paper only, there is no way to find the physical location of the ace of spades except by a completely associative search of all four boxes. If we had provided some mapping of the logical tags to physical location of the boxes, only two associative searches would be needed to locate the ace of spades. For instance, suppose we keep the boxes on four shelves and specify that boxes a and b are always on the top two shelves and c and d are always on the bottom two shelves. Now there is no need to search the bottom two shelves, which makes the search simpler. This additional information about where the boxes physically reside must be stored somewhere (e.g., in the primary logical to physical mapping of Fig. 9.5-8b). There are various techniques for implementing this mapping, but then it becomes part of the address translation. The essential point is that in the most general sense, the secondary to primary mapping function is a logical map. When the physical position of the boxes is specified by the use of tags stored directly on the boxes, the logical map is directly converted into a physical map. When the tags are stored separately from the associated boxes, an indirect conversion to the physical location of each box is required. Both cases of directly or separately stored tags involve the use of an additional mapping of the logical tag to physical location of the box, the former represents direct mapping and the latter a form of associative mapping. In either case, this logical to physical map is a fundamental requirement.

The case of finding IF and WHERE the ace of spades might be in the boxes requires a minimum of two associative searches plus the second, third, and fourth columns of Fig. 9.5-8a and the map of Fig. 9.5-8b. It is possible to avoid associative searches completely by storing more information within the mapping tables. Suppose we provide a fifth column in Fig. 9.5-8a called "WHERE ACTUAL," specifying IF and WHERE any card actually resides logically within a box. Thus the ace of spades and three other cards have a "yes" for IF and a logical box location WHERE each is. The boxes logical to physical translation must make use of Fig. 9.5-8b as before. Thus the location of the ace of spades requires direct addressing only: a reference to its binary address, shown as 111-11 in Fig. 9.5-8a, yields "yes," "tag b" for IF and WHERE from the last column; an access to tag b in Fig. 9.5-8b yields shelf 2 (note that any of the four shelves just as easily could have been indicated here). The price we pay for the elimination of associative searches is the need for more stored mapping information.

In a completely analogous manner, we can show that the initial orientation of the entire deck of cards as in Fig. 9.5-7 is a logical orientation, and the initial selection of a physical card from the deck (secondary) before being placed in a box requires a mapping of the secondary logical to secondary

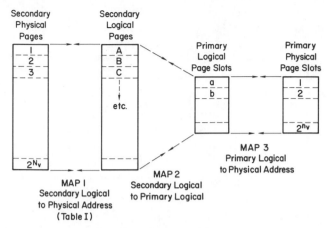

FIGURE 9.5-9 Schematic of logical and physical address spaces showing three fundamental maps required for a two-level virtual memory hierarchy.

physical location. In other words, we picture the logical orientation of the cards as in Fig. 9.5-7, but given a shuffled deck, we would need a logical to physical mapping to find the ace of spades, and so on. Thus we can conclude that any two-level virtual hierarchy requires three mapping functions. One map is required for each level to map that level's logical to physical space, and one map is required between levels. Figure 9.5-9 shows these maps schematically for a disk–main memory type of two-level hierarchy. Map 1 is generally provided by Table I discussed in Section 9.8. In a cache–main memory type of two-level hierarchy without a disk–main hierarchy, there are no pages in the main memory that are visible to the user. The CPU (secondary) logical address is converted into a physical main memory address by the compiler, assembler, link editor, and so on; thus Map 1 in Fig. 9.5-9 is essentially a direct mapping in such a case. The internal memory physical pages are mapped into the logical cache pages with an analogous Map 2, and likewise the cache logical to physical mapping with an analogous Map 3.

In a three-level hierarchy, containing a disk–main virtual store and a main–cache hierarchy, the cache is paged out of main memory just as in the the two-level hierarchy. However additional mappings are obviously required. One logical to physical map for each level and one map between each level results in a minimum of five maps for this case. The disk and main memory mappings would be as indicated in Fig. 9.5-9, with disk being the secondary, the main memory the primary, and the total CPU logical address the equivalent to the "secondary logical pages." When a cache is inserted into

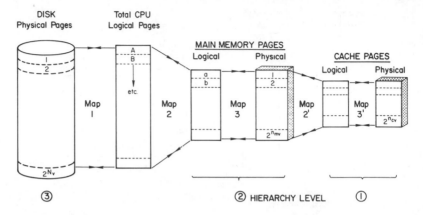

FIGURE 9.5-10 Schematic of logical and physical address space showing various maps required for a typical three-level virtual memory hierarchy.

this system, its position in the mapping scheme must be determined. Fundamentally, the logical cache pages can be mapped into the cache starting from the CPU logical pages, from the main memory logical pages, or from main real (physical) pages. However since the CPU logical pages are so much more numerous, and since they must be mapped into the main memory logical space anyway, it is advantageous to start either with the main logical or physical pages. For various practical reasons, the latter are often used (see Section 9.12). The schematic of the various maps for such a case appears in Fig. 9.5-10. In all systems, Maps 2, 2′, 3, and 3′ are implemented as an integral part of the address translation function discussed in Section 9.6. All three maps can take on any of the possible forms discussed previously from direct to fully associative. The degree of associativity of one does not affect the associativity of the others, since each is completely independent.

Some of the important conclusions about mapping of physical secondary pages to physical primary pages in a two-level hierarchy can be summarized as follows.

1. Three mapping functions are a fundamental requirement.
2. Contention problems for primary page slots are determined only by the secondary logical to primary logical mapping function and become less severe as the degree of associativity 2^s increases.
3. The mapping of primary logical to physical address has no bearing on the page slot contention problem; more generally, all three maps are independent of each other in principle.

9.6 ADDRESS TRANSLATION FOR A TWO–LEVEL VIRTUAL HIERARCHY

To understand virtual memory addressing, familiarity with the concepts and mapping functions discussed in Section 9.5 is imperative.

The functions performed by the address translation were outlined in Section 9.3. The N_s bits must be converted into an IF and WHERE real address. As shown in Fig. 9.3-3, N_r is directly translated, hence only the virtual page address N_v need be considered. When the desired page happens to be resident in primary storage, the IF translation produces a "yes" and the correct, real n_v must be provided by the WHERE translation. This is essentially an implementation of Maps 2 and 3 of Fig. 9.5-9. When the desired page happens not to be resident in primary storage, the IF produces a "no" and the real address of that page in secondary storage must be found. This is an implementation of Map 1 of Fig. 9.5-9. In a two-level hierarchy, the conversion of N_v into n_v when the desired page happens to be resident (i.e., IF = "yes") becomes the critical factor in the overall speed of address translation. If the entire process is to run at an effectively fast cycle time, this part of the translation should not introduce excessively large delays. We concentrate mainly on this, the most important part of the translation function, and its associated Maps 2 and 3 of Fig. 9.5-9. We consider the various fundamental schemes in considerable detail and derive important tradeoffs and relationships.

9.6.1 Translation of Logical Address to Primary Storage Address

Irrespective of the mapping function used, the address translator must decode all N_v bits of the secondary storage logical address. Only a WHERE function is performed in ordinary nonvirtual decoding, since in such cases each logical address has the same length as the primary memory address register and uniquely specifies a memory word. In virtual address decoding, the WHERE function is more complex and the additional IF function must be performed. More generally, ordinary nonvirtual decoding could be thought of as virtual decoding with the IF functions always set in the "yes" state. However the given nonvirtual address will always be unique and real, which allows for a simple implementation, since a one-to-one correspondence exists between the address and the physical location. In virtual addressing, this correspondence is lost. As indicated in the general mapping form of Fig. 9.5-2a, a given page slot in primary storage can contain different pages at different times. Although the virtual page address N_v uniquely specifies the virtual page in secondary storage, N_v by itself is not sufficient to specify

IF and WHERE that page resides in primary storage. Thus *additional information* must be stored in some manner to tell how the mapping is performed, and this constitutes the mapping function. The *manner* in which this information is stored and *used* constitutes the address translation function. A mapping function is only a conceptual, logical view of how page slots are to be shared, and when implemented, it becomes part of the address translation function. Clearly these two must work closely together. As previously indicated, we must implement both Maps 2 and 3 of Fig. 9.5-9— the secondary to primary logical address map and the primary logical to physical address map. The address translation must provide the IF and WHERE for both maps. However the logical IF is easily converted into a physical IF (e.g., by the hard-wired "Yes/No" control line on the primary memory address register as in Fig. 9.3-2). There are numerous ways of implementing this conversion, but it is relatively straightforward, and we concentrate here on the fundamentals of the address translation function to provide the logical IF, logical WHERE, and physical WHERE. The exact form of the address translation function varies in a continuous manner from a pure table requiring look-up for each request, to a simple associative directory, assuming a general form of mapping as in Fig. 9.5-2*a*. With such a mapping function, some form of association must be established between the real and the virtual page, irrespective of the method of address translation. The table form of translation provides this association by storing the real location of every virtual page, hence requires considerable storage. The associative directory provides this association very directly but requires a great deal of associative logic. Between these two methods lies a continuum of translation techniques requiring varying amounts of storage and associative logic, as might be expected. In fact this represents the fundamental tradeoffs in the choice of an address translation function; the table look-up is relatively slow because the table is stored in primary memory and requires additional memory access. The directory is small, thus can be fast, but it is expensive because of the necessary associative hardware.

The example of placing cards in boxes in Section 9.5 did not specify the details of implementing the mapping function because it is carried out by the address translation function. To see the range of possible schemes, let us continue with the "cards in boxes" example and consider two possible approaches, representing the end points of a continuum. After the example, we investigate address translation in its general form and derive important relationships.

Section 9.5 partially described these two cases of a table and an associative directory, but without the details and some remaining important considerations. We already know that certain mapping information must be stored somewhere, the exact amount varying with the address translation scheme chosen. Let us store this information in a general random access memory called the "tag store" and see how much and what information it must actually contain. We arbitrarily define a table scheme as one for which no associative compares are needed and a directory as one for which associative compares are needed. If we are to avoid associative compares and use direct decoding instead, some form of Fig. 9.5-8a and b must be stored. We initially assume set associative mapping for both Maps 2 and 3. The tag store will have to contain at least one tag in the form of a table entry or word for each card. If we use a 5 bit address $X_5, \ldots, X_1$ for each of the 32 cards, the logical name of each is replaced by an address of the tag store: hence the column labeled "Logical name" in Fig. 9.5-8a is unnecessary. To determine IF and WHERE a given card resides, the last column must be included. In addition, the information of Map 3, Fig. 9.5-8b, must somehow be incorporated. Note that the last column of Fig. 9.5-8a contains the logical tag for each of the four boxes and is redundant with the first column of Fig. 9.5-8b. Hence the physical WHERE of Map 3 can be included directly within the last column of Fig. 9.5-8a in place of the logical WHERE tag. This greatly simplifies both mapping information and address translation. Furthermore, since each of the four cards resident in a box now has the physical box location (i.e., shelf address) stored with its entry in the tag store, this address can be any of the four shelves within invoking any difficulties. Hence the box logical to physical mapping can be fully associative as easily as set associative, so the former is chosen. This does not necessarily have an effect on the secondary to primary logical Map 2. If the latter is set associative, we do *not* need to know where it possibly can reside for address translation because its address is already given by the physical WHERE. To swap a new card into a box, however, we would have to specify which logical boxes are permitted. But this is totally unnecessary: if the address translation does not need to know the set, we may as well make this mapping fully associative and eliminate the complexity of mapping and replacement: Thus columns 3 and 4 of Fig. 9.5-8a are unnecessary, leaving only the first column contained in the address decoding network of the tag store and the last column as the actual stored information. The IF function can be done with a one-bit logical operation called a flag, and the WHERE function must be able to specify at least one of 2^{n_v} pages in primary storage, which requires n_v bits, or 2 in this case. The general form of this table (Fig. 9.6-1) represents that actually used, with some modification, in virtual memory systems as detailed in Section 9.9. The logical flag "IF." is shown converted to a physical IF by a direct enable input to the primary address decoder.

The associative directory can be approached in many different ways. If we study the table of Fig. 9.5-8a, we note that most of the entries contain "no" for the IF function. In fact, only four cards can ever be resident in a box;

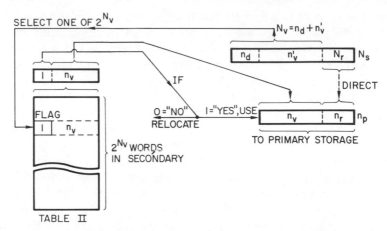

FIGURE 9.6-1   Table address translation showing fully associative mapping for Maps 2 and 3.

thus it is necessary to store information about these four boxes only, which greatly reduces the size of the tag store. In other words, instead of storing information about each card, most of which is "no," we store information only about each box. The difficulty is that many different cards can reside in any given box, and although the required storage is reduced, the process of address translation becomes more complex.

We assume a fully associative mapping, giving $s = n_v = 2$. The tag store must now contain only one entry or word per box to implement Map 2. Since we do not know a priori the identity of the card in any box, this must be stored in the tag store word, which requires 5 bits of $X_5, \ldots, X_1$. This is equivalent to N_v or $n_d + n_v$ bits, as is evident from Fig. 9.3-3 and 9.5-2b. To implement Map 3, we can do as previously with the table and store the real physical address of the box as part of the tag store word. The tag store then becomes a fully associatively addressed directory (Fig. 9.6-2). The 5 bit ID of each of the cards resident in a box would be stored in the N_v portion of each word. An associative match on each of these produces one "match" condition that is equivalent to IF = "yes," and the physical WHERE address of that box is the n_v portion of that match word. For instance, if we want to test for the ace of spades whose ID is 11111, each word of the tag store is matched against this ID. The second word in Fig. 9.6-2 will give a match, and the n_v portion indicates shelf 2 (binary 10), as originally indicated in Fig. 9.5-8. Thus Maps 2 and 3 are both contained in the directory, and both are fully associative in this example. The tag store is much smaller than previously with the table scheme, but now it must perform associative selection capabilities, which is more difficult.

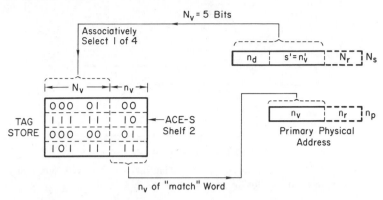

FIGURE 9.6-2   Fully associative tag store (directory) for address translation.

We now consider the address translation in its general form to see the "continuum" of schemes and subtle tradeoffs. Some profound conclusions that become evident are summarized later. For the general case, we assume the mapping to be the general set associative form of Fig. 9.5-2a. In our two specific examples of "cards in boxes," we saw that the amount and character of the additional stored information could vary considerably, depending on the implementation of the mapping function. Therefore let us assume that the required information is stored as 2^e logical entries or words of as yet unspecified length, in some undefined tag store. These entries contain all tags and other information needed to implement Maps 2 and 3, as well as the address translation function. Let us first determine the bounds on the number of such logical entries, the amount of information that must be stored in each, and the various ways in which this information can be used to determine IF (logical) and WHERE (logical and physical) the real page exists in primary storage. We let e be some fraction of the total secondary virtual page bits as in Fig. 9.6-3. where the maximum value is $e \leq N_v$. The minimum value for e can be deduced easily. Since there are 2^{n_v} page slots in primary storage, it is necessary to store some information concerning at least each of these slots with one logical entry per page slot. Thus e must be at least as large as n_v, and the bounds on e are

$$N_v \geq e \geq n_v \qquad (9.6\text{-}1)$$

Obviously the two previous cases of "cards in boxes" were the ends points $e = N_v$ for the table and $e = n_v$ for the directory. Let us now consider the various possible cases for some general value of e between the bounds of (9.6-1). First note that the associativity of the secondary logical to primary logical mapping functions, specified by s, can vary independent of e, that is,

$$n_v \le e \le N_v$$

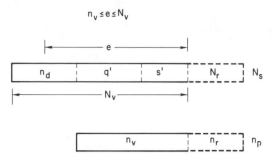

FIGURE 9.6-3 Relationship of tag store addressing bits e to the secondary and primary page-addressing bits N_r and n_r, for the general case.

any degree of associativity can be translated by any value of e satisfying (9.6-1). This is fundamentally true for the logical mapping, but the method of implementation forces certain relationships between e and s in terms of the number of bits that must be associatively compared. For the general case with $e < N_v$, the number of stored logical entries is *less* than one per virtual page by the amount $2^{N_v - e}$. To find IF and WHERE a given N_v address is resident in primary storage, this "unstored" information of length $N_v - e$ bits must be stored in each logical entry. In addition, for a given mapping of associativity 2^s, a required page might possibly reside in any of these 2^s slots of a set. Hence s bits must also be stored in each logical entry of the tag store to assist in the logical IF and WHERE determination. Completing the search therefore requires

$$\text{number of associative compares} = 2^s \qquad (9.6\text{-}2)$$

$$\text{number of bits/compare} = N_v - e + s \qquad (9.6\text{-}3)$$

These fundamental requirements are valid irrespective of the primary logical to physical mapping or the remaining implementation. These associative compares provide only the logical IF and WHERE, the former signaled by a "yes/no" match condition. This can be easily converted to a physical IF by using a simple logic gate to activate or deactivate the primary address register as in Fig. 9.3-2. Other techniques are possible, but we assume the method just described in subsequent cases.

The primary logical to physical mapping (Map 3) can be done as previously, by storing the real address of length n_v bits within each of the 2^e entries. As before, this makes Map 3 fully associative without affecting the overall address translation, irrespective of the value of s used in Map 2. We do not have to make Map 3 fully associative: if a set associative map of associativity $S_2 = 2^{s_2}$ is used, only $n_v - s_2$ bits need be stored in this portion of the tag store. Since this seldom saves many bits and greatly complicates the system, a fully associative Map 3 storing n_v bits is typically used. A direct map could also be used, which would require no stored bits but only a direct *enable* or similar function on a page of a semiconductor chip (see Section 9.13). A direct map 3 becomes very important in one special case of a fully associative Map 2 as discussed later.

Now we have a tag store consisting of 2^e entries or words, each storing $N_v - e + s$ bits, which are associatively compared to provide the logical IF and WHERE for Map 2, and each contains also from 0 to n_v bits for Map 3 depending on the associativity of the latter. The general scheme is given in Fig. 9.6-4a, assuming that Map 3 is fully associative and Map 2 is of associativity 2^s. Since at least 2^s entries must be associatively addressed, 2^{e-s} can be directly addressed. The address translation procedure would be as follows. For a given virtual page address N_v, the higher order bits $e - s = n_d - (N_v - e) + q'$ are used to directly address one of the possible sets in the tag store; only 2^q of these can have valid entries, since there are only 2^q sets in primary storage. Comparison of the $N_v - e + s$ bits stored within each of the 2^s entries of the directly selected set with the same bit positions from N_v produces a "yes" or "no" match. If "yes," the n_v from the matched

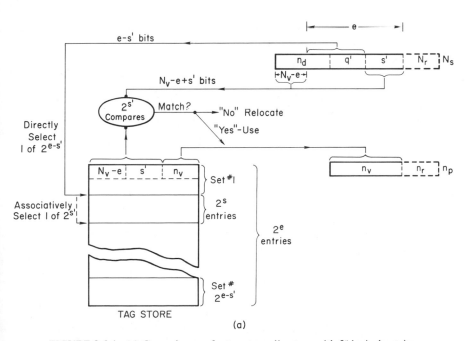

FIGURE 9.6-4 (*a*) General case of a tag store directory with 2^e logical entries.

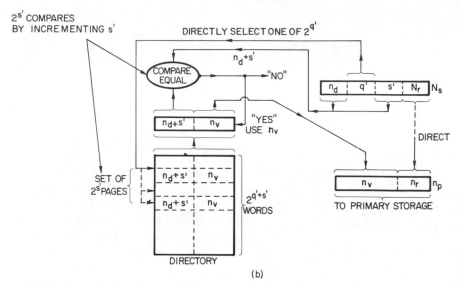

FIGURE 9.6-4 (*b*) Example of minimum tag store directory implementing a set associative Map 2 and fully associative Map 3 showing 2^s sequential compares.

entry provides the real WHERE address for the primary store address register as shown. In this case, the tag store must be accessed first to find the real n_v and subsequently the primary store is accessed using $n_v + n_r$ to obtained the desired byte or word. A specific example for $e = n_v$, set associative Map 2 and fully associative Map 3 appears in Fig. 9.6-4*b*.

A fundamental relationship of considerable importance is the total number of *possible* pages in secondary storage that share the *same* logical set in the tag store. This is simply the total number of secondary pages divided by the number of logical sets in the tag store, or

$$\text{secondary pages sharing each tag store set} = \frac{2^{N_v}}{2^{e-s}} = 2^{N_v - e + s} \quad (9.6\text{-}4)$$

This relation is used later to obtain a number of important conclusions about the tag store.

9.6.2 Special Cases of the Tag Store

We should be able to obtain previous examples of the table and fully associative directory from this general scheme by letting e take on the values N_v and n_v, respectively. Let us try these to see some important consequences.

CASE 1

When $e = N_v$ and $s > 0$, the tag store contains 2^{N_v} entries. Following the general operation already given, a search requires a direct decoding to one out of 2^{e-s} or 2^{N_v-s} entries, and 2^s associative compares on $N_v - e + s = s$ bits. The result of a correct match must produce n_v bits for the real page address, assuming Map 3 to be fully associative.

Equation 9.6-4 indicates that the total number of possible secondary pages sharing the same logical set in the tag store is 2^s pages. But since this is also the maximum number of logical page slots in a set, any number of pages of any mix can be accommodated simultaneously in the tag store. Hence the logical mapping is fully associative for any value of s in this special case. Let us choose $s = 0$, to permit the number of associative compares to reduce to $2^0 = 1$, and the number of bits to be compared to reduce to zero. This results in a direct decoding to one of 2^{N_v} or the entire table, storage of n_v real address bits, and one associative compare over zero bits. The latter represents the degenerate case of merely specifying whether that page is resident. It could be done by performing a logical check on whether an n_v address is present. It is simpler to provide a one-bit logical flag; hence we have reduced the tag store to the previous table scheme.

CASE 2

When $e = n_v$ and $s > 0$, the tag store contains 2^{n_v} entries. A search requires a direct selection of one of $2^{e-s} = 2^{n_v-s}$, 2^s associative compares on $N_v - n_v + s = n_d + s$ bits, and a match must produce the real n_v bits. This is a specific case of a set associative directory such as that in Fig. 9.6-4b. If we let $s = n_v$, the direct selection of one of 2^{n_v-s} reduces to zero and 2^{n_v} associative compares are required on $n_d + s = n_d + n_v = N_v$ bits. This is the fully associative directory previously discussed.

A fundamental conclusion of profound consequences is that the associativity of the secondary to primary logical mapping, Map 2, provided by a general tag store, hence the required number of associative compares, is fixed at 2^s for all values of e except for the special case of the table where $e = N_v$. The fundamental reason for this follows very directly from (9.6-4) and results from contention problems for *logical* page slots. Even when the real primary store is not full, contention problems can arise because the pages required *simultaneously might happen* to be all from the *same logical set*, and the *number required* might be greater than 2^s. For instance, for any tag store with $N_v - e \geq 1$ or $e \leq N_v - 1$, the number of secondary pages sharing a logical set, given by (9.6-4), is obviously greater than 2^s. But by chance, this larger number could be needed simultaneously in that logical set, whereas only 2^s can be accommodated within the tag store (i.e., the degree of associativity is 2^s). Hence a new contention problem may arise within the tag store even though the primary store has empty page slots. Set associative mapping, therefore, introduces a second kind of contention problem, one for tag store space, in addition to the ordinary contention arising because the primary store is smaller than secondary storage. We did not have this contention problem in the special case of $e = N_v$ because as previously discussed, the maximum number of secondary pages sharing a logical set is 2^s, which exactly equals that which can be accommodated. Hence except for the special case, the associativity of the general tag store with 2^e entries is determined only by s.

The above conclusion raises the question, What properties of the address translation are affected by changing e? As the number of entries e varies, only the number of bits that must be associatively decoded varies as

$$N_v - e + s \tag{9.6-5}$$

As e increases, the number of bits associatively compared decreases, and vice versa, Thus we merely trade the number of tag store entries for word size and associative bits compared. The minimum number of bits required in any tag store scheme is just the number of logical entries times the number of bits per entry. These various expressions and other important relations are summarized in Fig. 9.6-5 for the general case, the table, and the minimum sized directory. The table can require considerably more storage than the minimum directory. The ratio of total storage capacity for these two (from Fig. 9.6-5, assuming Map 3 to be fully associative) is

$$\text{bit capacity} \; \frac{\text{table}}{\text{directory}} = \frac{(1 + n_v)2^{N_v}}{(n_d + s + n_v)2^{n_v}} = \frac{1 + n_v}{N_v + s} 2^{n_d} \tag{9.6-6}$$

Some typical values might be

$$N_v = 18, \qquad n_v = 6, \qquad s = 2 \,(q = 4), \qquad n_d = 12$$

Substitution of these into (9.6-6) gives the ratio as $0.35 \times 2^{12} = 1434$, a substantial difference showing the value of the minimum directory. However we have said little about the hardware characteristics of the tag store for each case. Typically for the table implementation, the tag store uses primary (main) memory, since only random access addressing is required and the table can become quite large. A fundamental requirement of this table is that the entries be logically contiguous, since successive binary values of N_v refer to successive logical entries in the table. Thus even if many entries are blank, they *cannot* be removed from the table to make the table shorter.* The table

---

* Except for the rare case that all entires above a certain binary address are blank or the user requests a smaller total number of pages, which automatically makes the table smaller.

TAG STORE Description	NUMBER LOGICAL ENTRIES	NUMBER ENTRIES DECODED Directly	Assoc.	NUMBER BITS COMPARED ASSOCIATIVELY	MINIMUM NUMBER BITS PER ENTRY Map 2	Map 3	MINIMUM STORAGE CAPACITY #
A. General TAG STORE	2^e *	2^{e-s}	2^s	$N_v - e + s$	$N_v - e + s$	0 to n_v	$(N_v - e + s + n_v)2^e$
B. Minimum TAG STORE ($e = n_v$)	2^{n_v} *	$2^{n_v-s} = 2^q$	2^s	$n_d + s$	$n_d + s$	0 to n_v	$(N_v + s)2^{n_v}$
C. TABLE ($e = N_v$)	2^{N_v}	2^{N_v}	0	0	1	0 to n_v	$(1 + n_v)2^{N_v}$

* Can be 2^{e-s} physical words – see section 9.12
\# Assuming Map 3 = n_v & excluding control bits

FIGURE 9.6-5 Comparison of tag store characteristics for different implementations.

must contain one entry for each possible logical (virtual) page. A method for reducing the amount of this table that must be stored in primary memory is described in Section 9.8, and examples are given in Section 9.9. For the minimum directory implementation, the tag store is usually a separate random access memory because of the required associative compares. Further discussions concerning the various design considerations are given in Sections 9.8 and 9.10.

It is clear that the choice of mapping function has a significant effect on the method of address translation. This effect can be linked to a telephone directory in which names are listed in various ways. If we assume that no two names are identical, a purely alphabetical listing is like direct mapping: there is one and only one possible logical position for each unique name, and it is easily found. If the listing is purely random or has no structure, this is comparable to fully associative mapping and requires the capability for an associative search on every name, to be able to find the final phone number. Set associative mapping would be analogous to listing together all names say, starting with A, then all those starting with B, etc., but no order within the A's or B's, etc. Hence the number of associative searches equals the number of names under the letter of interest, which is identical to the number S of possible logical names per set.

In all the above examples we have emphasized the use of fully associative mapping for the primary logical to physical Map 3, even though in principle, direct or set associative mapping can be used. The reason is practical in that a direct or set associative Map 3 would involve additional complexity in the actual page swapping and would greatly limit the ability to incorporate operating systems and memory expansion. Thus a fully associative Map 3 is most desirable. A very special and important case arises in which this Map 3 has the appearance of being fully associative even though it is a direct mapping, in fact can be a hard-wired direct mapping. This situation occurs when the secondary to primary logical mapping (Map 2) is fully associative; that is, $s = \quad$, in such a case, *any* virtual page can reside in *any* logical page slot. If a direct Map 3 is used, logical and physical page slots become identical. Now, any virtual page can reside in any physical page slot as desired, and Map 3 has no effect on this capability. This principle is discussed more fully in Section 9.13 with example.

Some important conclusions about address translation are as follows.

1. The address translation function cannot be implemented without including the mapping function for both Maps 2 and 3.
2. Translation schemes form a continuum of tag stores of varying number of entries e, with the table and minimum directory at the two extremes for e equal to N_v and n_v, respectively.
3. Any secondary to primary logical mapping with associativity of degree 2^s must perform 2^s associative compares on $N_v - e + s$ bits: a special case occurs for $e = N_v$, which yields a table of any degree of associativity.
4. Increasing the number of entries e in the tag store only reduces the number of bits that must be associatively compared; it does not change the required number of such compares.
5. Implementation of the logical to physical IF function is very simple.
6. Implementation of the primary logical to physical WHERE map is much easier than the secondary logical to primary logical WHERE map, and the former can typically be fully associative as easily as any other mapping.
7. When the secondary logical to primary logical mapping function is fully associative, the primary logical to physical map can be direct while giving the appearance of being fully associative in the sense that complete freedom is provided for the physical location of any page in the primary store. This is a special case.

Fundamentally, the address translation function is required only to perform the IF and WHERE translation of virtual to real pages. In practical systems it is also desirable to provide a certain amount of "status and control" information. For instance, if no changes (i.e., no writing) have been made within a given page, it can be erased when it is to be swapped out of primary memory. In addition, storage protection in the form of access rights can be implemented within the address translation function if desired. Additional information stored within the previous necessary logical entries of the tag store can control access and sharing of pages among various users. Examples are given in Section 9.9. When the address translation is accomplished with a directory, the need for speed dictates that the information for the replacement algorithm be contained within the logical entries or an equivalent hardware scheme (see Section 9.7). Thus the various schemes for storing the additional information for address translation sometimes contain status and control information in addition to the IF and WHERE information.

9.7 REPLACEMENT ALGORITHMS AND IMPLEMENTATION

Replacement algorithms can be placed arbitrarily into two broad categories: (a) algorithms that *do not* use historical information to determine which page to remove from primary, and (b) algorithms that *do* use historical information for replacement.

The first category does not require storing any information about page referencing, hence essentially includes random or near-random replacement algorithms. The second category requires storage of some kind of information about page referencing, depending on the exact nature of the algorithm. This represents the bulk of algorithms—first in, first out (FIFO), least recently used (LRU), least frequency used (LFU), and so on. The implementation of the first type—say, a near-random replacement—is simple in principle, requiring only a pseudo-random number generator. The second type requires additional storage hardware and logic processing functions, both of which can vary considerably depending on the exact nature of the algorithm and sometimes are quite complex.

Intuitively it would seem that if data clustering (Section 9.4) occurs, page replacement should be based on some history of page usage. This generally seems to be the case, but there are many exceptions wherein a random replacement can give a better hit ratio. Unfortunately, the best algorithm cannot be derived from first principles but must be obtained from simulation of actual job streams as was done in Section 9.4. Vavious studies (Belady, 1966) have resulted in the conclusion that no one best algorithm exists; rather, certain algorithms are best for particular classes of problems and worse for other classes. As a result, disk–main memory virtual systems use a "not recently used" type of algorithm that is an approximation to the LRU algorithm. This can be implemented in many ways. Intuitively it seems reasonable to suppose that the more historical bits that are maintained about page usage, the better would be the choice of page to be replaced. However this requires more stored information and updating, which is expensive and time-consuming. Hence a tradeoff is necessary. In the selection of a page for replacement, one would expect that if a page has not been referenced over a certain time period, it is less likely to be needed next than pages that have been referenced. Hence a reference bit R for a certain time period is necessary. But before selecting a page for removal, it must be recognized that if a page has not been modified (i.e., has not been written into), it need not be written back onto disk but simply can be overlaid (i.e., erased). If it has been modified, however, it *must* be placed back on the disk before erasure. Since this requires considerably more time than just overlaying, a second status bit is also stored with the previous R "reference" bit. The second bit M specifies whether the page has been modified while residing in main. A page that has not been modified is more eligible for replacement than one that has been modified. In addition, locking bits are often used to protect storage when a page is undergoing swapping, or for other reasons, which we ignore for now.

In principle, the replacement algorithm can be implemented with the R and M bits alone. Whenever a page is referenced, its associated R bit is automatically set to "1"; likewise, M is set to "1" when that page is modified. Eligibility for replacement then goes as "not modified and not referenced," "not modified but referenced," and so on. The time period over which the "not referenced" criterion exists requires some consideration. The M bit is not affected because once modified, a page must be so indicated for the entire time it is resident in main memory. The time period over which the R bit is evaluated can be a fixed or variable period.

Theoretically we do not have to evaluate pages for replacement until a page fault occurs in main memory. At this time, we can scan all pages for replacement, select one, and reset all R bits to zero, indicating a new time period. We may introduce additional historical bits H, to indicate the number of such successive scan intervals over which each page was not referenced. One historical H bit would allow indication of usage during the previous scan interval, two bits over four intervals, and so on. For such a case at scan time, any page with $R = 0$ would have the "unreferenced interval" H bits incremented by binary "1" and R would remain unchanged. If R were "1," indicating "referenced," the H bits would be turned off and likewise R would be turned off. A large binary value for the H bits would indicate a large number of successive intervals over which that page was not used. Of course the opposite polarity could also be used. Eligibility of pages for replacement is then modified to include these H bits, pages with a large binary value of successive "not referenced" intervals (large H) being more eligible than those with smaller values. The scan interval in this case would be variable, since it is initiated by a page fault. This scanning can also be done periodically during fixed intervals. For various practical reasons, the latter scheme is often used in large commercial systems. There are, of course, numerous possible variations of this procedure as well as other replacement procedures. The cost/performance tradeoffs vary with the system as well as the manufacturer, hence the details can differ substantially. This type of algorithm is often referred to as an approximation to the LRU algorithm, but it is a gross approximation at best. It really replaces pages *not* recently used in a somewhat random fashion according to the simple referenced/modified priority scheme. Considerable logical processing is required, but much less than for even slightly more complex algorithms. The implementation can be in hardware or software, but more of the latter is common.

In the cache–main memory type of virtual system, which typically uses set associative mapping, a required page that must be brought into the cache can go only into a fixed logical set. Hence a page must be removed from *that* logical set. Typically an LRU-type algorithm for each set is stored and processed with separate hardware. This is basically the technique used on the IBM 195 and 168.

Of the various types of algorithm in use, the LRU has intuitive appeal as an average technique over a large job stream, despite many exceptions. Since a pure LRU over a large number of pages is rather difficult to implement, some approximation of the type described earlier is used in main–disk virtual memories. However the mapping of a cache paged out of main memory is typically set associative (see Sections 9.10 and 9.11) with very few page slots per set. An LRU algorithm is typically implemented in hardware for each set of the cache. The following discussion considers some of the fundamental aspects of implementing a pure LRU in a general case.

9.7.1 LRU Algorithm Implementation

To implement any general ordering type of algorithm, some means must be provided within the system for keeping track of each page usage with respect to all other pages. In other words, all pages must be continually ordered among themselves for each new page reference. This calls for two fundamental pieces of information: (*A*) the address of the pages within a given ranking order, and (*B*) the relative order or ranking of page usage among themselves. In conjunction with these two pieces of information, two fundamental operations are necessary:

A'. Search Rank for Address. Search usage information and produce address of page with required ranking.

B'. Update the Usage Information. Enter new page slot usage into the ranking after each page reference.

These operations can be implemented with the use of associative or nonassociative functions.

9.7.2 LRU via Associative Functions

In general, there are two basic ways to implement an associative ordering algorithm. We can store the address of the pages within a stack of registers

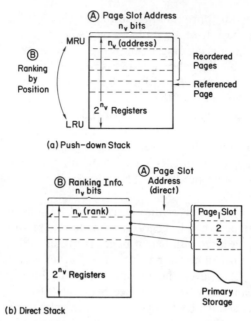

FIGURE 9.7-1   Two fundamental schemes for implementing LRU replacement algorithms by way of the associative function.

and perform the ordering by the arrangement of the stack (i.e., order from top to bottom of the stack via a push-down (or up) stack) Fig. 9.7-1a. An alternative is to store the ordering within a stack of registers and allow each register to have a direct, one-to-one correspondence to each page slot in primary storage. For instance, the top of the stack contains ranking (usage) information for page slot 1, and the bottom register contains the ranking for page slot 2^{n_v} (Fig. 9.7-1b). Thus for the very general implementation, we can store the page slot address in registers and perform the ranking externally by ordering the registers from top to bottom (push-down stack) or, alternatively, we can store the ranking within the register, allowing the page address to be determined externally by the physical correspondence to page slots. If an ordered stack* is used as in Fig. 9.7-1a, the bottom (or top) of the stack contains the identity of the least recently used page and the top contains the most recently used page. Under these circumstances, B is determined by the physical ordering of the stack and requires no extra information. In such a case, A, the identity of the pages within the stack, requires a number

_____

* The stack can be a list in main memory or special hardware registers.

of bits given by

$$\text{identity bits/page slot} = \log_2 p = n_v \qquad (9.7\text{-}1)$$

where p is the number of pages requiring ordering. The stack would have $p = 2^{n_v}$ entries each of the length given. The fundamental operation A' of finding the LRU page is very simple and requires only reading the address from the bottom entry. However, operation B' is not so simple. A new reference to any page within the stack, except the most recently used page, involves considerable logical reordering of the stack. For instance, the ranking or actual register corresponding to the referenced page must first be found, and thus requires some kind of associative compare, either serial by register or all in parallel. After the correct ranking position is found and the register position stored, this page slot address must be moved to the top register (MRU), and all registers from the top, down to the previous register position of the referenced page, must be pushed down by one ranking position.

In the alternative scheme of Fig. 9.7-1b, the situation is not much better. We still need 2^{n_v} registers, one for each page slot, and n_v bits per register, to be able to rank these from 1 to 2^{n_v}. Note that the same *number* of bits is stored in both schemes, but the information is different (an address in the first case and a ranking order in the second). The operation of entering new ranking or usage information (i.e., B') is very easy for the referenced page—it now becomes the highest rank (i.e., MRU). However reordering these pages between the previous MRU and the previous ranking of the referenced page becomes quite complex. An associative search must be made on each entry to see whether it requires reordering; if so, it is lowered by one. The operation of finding a page slot to be replaced (i.e., A') also requires an associative search to determine which of the registers contain the desired ranking position (e.g., LRU rank).

9.7.3   LRU via Nonassociative Functions

The above method of implementing the LRU algorithm are only two fundamental ways that require associative compare capabilities. These associative techniques minimize the number of additional bits required for large numbers of pages, but the hardware becomes expensive and slow. It is possible to eliminate the need for associative compares, but for large numbers of pages, the additional stored information becomes large. Let us first study the basic technique, then compare the additional hardware required versus that in the previous associative schemes.

In the nonassociative scheme, each page is paired with every other page. If there are p pages to be ordered, the total number of pairs of pages is p pages for the first one of the pair and $p - 1$ for the second, or a total of

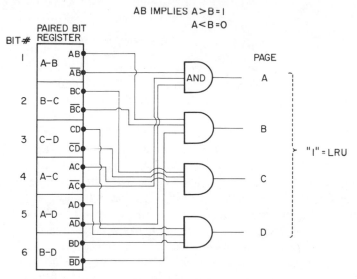

FIGURE 9.7-2   Nonassociative implementation of LRU algorithm with pairwise inequality bits.

$p(p - 1)$ pairs. However there are many duplicates, since pairs such as AB are identical to BA. Hence the number of distinct pairs is half the value just given, or

$$\text{number of distinct pairs} = \frac{p(p - 1)}{2} \qquad (9.7\text{-}2)$$

where p = total number of pages.

One ranking bit is stored in separate hardware for each pair. The bit is, say, "1" if A is more recently used than B and "0" if A is less recently used than B. The total number of such stored ranking bits is thus equal to the number of pairs of (9.7-2). The general idea for the ranking is simply that these bits form a pair-wise inequality that uniquely specifies the LRU page. For instance, if we have three pages and we know $A > B, B < C$, and $A > C$, we can deduce that B is the lowest entry. The question now is, How can we implement this in nonassociative hardware? It is actually quite simple. Each page has one AND logic gate associated with it (Fig. 9.7-2) for the example with four pages. Each AND receives an input from a "pair bit" that has that page for one of its pairs. For instance, page A must have an input from the pair bits A–B, A–C, and A–D. Similarly page B must have an input from pair bits A–B, B–C, B–D, and so on. Thus the fan-in must be $p - 1$. If we specify that the AND gate with an output signal indicates the LRU or lowest ranking page, we must connect either the pair-bit or its complement, depending on which page in the pair, being more recently used, gives a "1" output. For the pairing in Fig. 9.7-2, if $A > B = 1, A < B = 0, B > C = 1, B < C = 0$, and so on, the complements must be used on pages for which that page is the higher ranking in the pair as shown. Obviously searching for the LRU page is trivial compared to the associative case. The LRU page is always specified by the AND gate that is "on."

Let us now determine the number of stored pair-bits required for this nonassociative scheme for a system that has, say, 256 pages, all of which are ordered. From (9.7-2), the additional storage required is

$$\text{pair-bits} = \frac{256(255)}{2} = 32,640 \text{ bits}$$

In addition, 256 AND gates each with an equivalent logic tree fan-in of 255 are required. For the associative scheme, (9.7-1) indicates that the total number of stored bits is only

$$\text{total associative bits} = p \log_2 p$$

$$= 256(8) = 2048 \text{ bits}$$

This is more than 15 times less than the nonassociative scheme but requires associative hardware. If one uses set associative mapping, only the LRU within each set must be maintained. For instance, for a four way associative set (i.e., $s = 2$), only 6 bits/set are required as in Fig. 9.7-2. Such a scheme is actually used on the IBM model 195 cache (Section 9.11.2). Other schemes are possible for reducing the total number of stored bits, but the logic can become complex. For instance, it is possible to store one string of bits specifying the entire ranking of all pages relative to one another. For p pages, there are a maximum of p factorial combinations or rankings relative to one another. The number of bits required to specify any one relative ranking of all pages is $\log_2 p!$. This can be substantially less than that for the previous cases. The scheme takes on the form of a decoding tree in which one logical combination must be decoded from the given bit stream. For large p, the logic operations become complex for searching (decoding) and, especially, for updating after a reference.

There are, of course, many possible ways to implement replacement algorithms, but all require additional hardware and time. In addition, the updating after a page reference, which must be performed by the storage control unit, can become quite complex even in the scheme of Fig. 9.7-2. The IBM 370 models 195 and 165 cache memories use the latter type of set LRU implementation, whereas the model 168 cache uses a stored address type of stack register similar in principle to that of Fig. 9.7-1a.

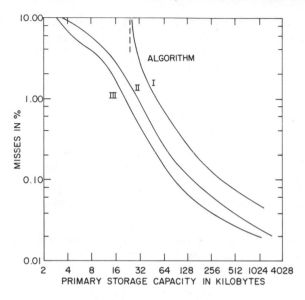

FIGURE 9.7-3   Percentage of misses versus primary storage capacity for various algorithms, showing hypothetical general cases.

9.7.4   Effect of Replacement Algorithm on Hit Ratio

The variation in hit ratio for different replacement algorithms is a matter of fundamental importance. Since it is a function of many variables, we give some general trends* and demonstrate a basic technique for circumventing the problem.

If the miss ratio is plotted as a function of primary storage capacity for a fixed page size, a curve similar to one of those in Fig. 9.4-2 is obtained for any replacement algorithm. The miss ratio must obviously approach 100% as primary storage capacity approaches zero, and it must approach zero as primary capacity approaches the total capacity required by the problem or job stream. If we consider these curves as applied to specific users in the job stream, the primary capacity axis becomes a measure of the number of pages allotted to that user. If we were to plot similar curves for different replacement algorithms, the results might be something like the hypothetical curves of Fig. 9.7-3. All show a general improvement with increasing storage capacity. For a specific user, one of the algorithms (e.g., I in Fig. 9.7-3) might require a certain minimum number of pages to achieve any reasonable miss

* See Belady (1966) for discussions and performance of various algorithms relative to the optimum for specific cases.

ratio, because of the nature of the problem. This could arise under the conditions described by the example in Section 9.14 or similar cases. If the allotted pages were in this "minimum" neighborhood on the horizontal axis, a different replacement algorithm could give a much improved miss ratio. If the algorithm is fixed, as is usually the case, an improvement can also be obtained by increasing the number of pages or primary bytes allotted to that user. Unfortunately in a given multiprogrammed system, this reduces the number of pages available to other users. Thus while the hit ratio may be improved for the first user, the overall system hit ratio and through-put may degenerate. Theoretically, dynamic fine tuning of the system hit ratio is possible but is usually too complex to be feasible.

9.7.5 Working Set Replacement Algorithm

Denning (1962) attempts to dynamically assign the number of page slots of primary storage allotted to a given user in terms of past history. The working set for a given user is defined as the set of pages that are referenced in a given period of time. In other words, referring to Fig. 9.4-1a and assuming that the address references refer to pages rather than words, the working set would be the total number of different pages appearing in the trace for a single user over some specified number of time intervals, usually referred to as the window size. The longer the time period, the larger the working set and hit ratio for a given user, but the poorer the hit ratio will be for another user. If the time period is too small, a very poor hit ratio will result. The major problem is then determining the correct value of the time period. Additional fundamental statistics are required to ascertain whether the optimum time period is substantially smaller than the problem running time to be useful. Also needed is information on variations between problem sizes and problem types.

9.8 VIRTUAL MEMORY SYSTEM DESIGN CONSIDERATIONS

Using the previous sections, let us now consider the conceptual design of a virtual memory system consisting of main memory and a disk-like backing store. Remember that the primary goal is to bridge the capacity gap between main memory and disk. However the overall speed must be reasonable, or the primary goal is of little value.

The system is assumed to be identical to that of Fig. 9.3-2, consisting of $U = 2^u$ users, each with a virtual store of 2^{N_v} pages or 2^N words as shown.

Each of the three fundamental requirements must be implemented with the design consideration in mind. The choice of page size and replacement algorithm depends on problem statistics and is not amenable to any analysis from first principles. The results of Section 9.4 indicate that the LRU algorithm can give adequate miss ratios. However the LRU algorithm is difficult to implement, and an approximation to LRU is commonly used.

The required miss ratio for a given system can be determined only by simulation. In a large system, a miss causes transfer of control of the CPU to a new user whose pages are in primary storage. The transfer of control may require tens, hundreds, or thousands of CPU execution cycles. Although time-consuming, it nevertheless introduces much less delay than the page access and relocation time. However, maintaining a high CPU utilization requires a small miss ratio—in the range of 0.02% or less. To achieve this ratio, the results of Section 9.4 indicate that page sizes of 1K' to 4K' bytes, with a minimum of 256K' bytes of useful primary storage, are required for the job streams and parameters used. The actual values change for different job streams, but the difference is not orders of magnitude. These parameters represent typical values that are adequate for many cases. The two address translation functions of Fig. 9.3-2 (external and internal) can be implemented separately; thus the type of tag store to be used must be decided for each. The external translation, which converts N_s into a real disk address, is required only on a page fault in main memory. This occurs rather rarely, and when encountered, the CPU transfers to a different user already resident in main memory. Thus speed is not a major concern, and this translation can be implemented economically with a table, called Table I as in Fig. 9.8-1. This table contains a maximum of 2^{N_v} contiguous entries, one for each virtual page. A software algorithm uses the N_v address to access the table. Each

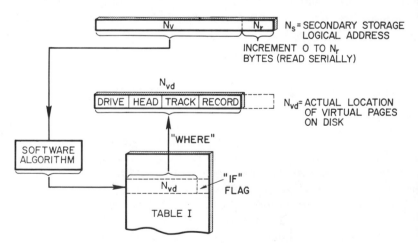

FIGURE 9.8-1   Translation of logical address N_s to actual disk page address using Table I.

entry contains an IF flag, the actual WHERE address, and any other desired control functions. Such an implementation automatically makes Map 1 in Fig. 9.5-10 fully associative. Since Table I potentially can be very large, it is normally stored on disk and transferred into main memory when a user is entered. In principle, Table I can remain on disk (located, e.g., as the first file on the first disk, etc.). This would conserve main memory space but at the expense of a sequential search of the disk via the I/O processor. The latter is slow but would be feasible if sufficient time were available between page faults. Since this is not usually the case, Table I would have to be entered when needed.

The internal translation, which converts N_s into n_p, is required on every memory reference; hence speed is of vital concern. In addition, maximum flexibility in physical page location within main memory is necessary, making a fully associative Map 3 in Fig. 9.5-10 essential. The need for speed suggests the use of a fast, minimum tag store (directory) with a fully associative Map 3 and set associative Map 2 in Fig. 9.5-10. However this directory would need 2^{n_v} logical entries, and the associativity would have to be rather large for a good hit ratio. In other words, the directory would be large and would have to perform many associative compares, which would make the directory slow and very expensive. The use of a table translation scheme stored in main memory would be relatively inexpensive and would provide fully associative mapping. However every CPU reference to main memory would require a minimum of two or more main memory cycles, which is a severe speed penalty. To circumvent this dilemma, large commercial systems typically compromise, storing a few of the most recently used pages in a very small partial directory for speed, while using a table as backup. Examples are given in Sections 9.9 and 9.12. The partial directory is usually quite straightforward and need not be detailed here. The table translation, however, becomes somewhat complex because of practical considerations.

Table Translation: Design Considerations

In principle, the table translation of the virtual address N_s into a real address in main memory can be accomplished with a single table. This table (referred to as Table II) is fundamentally as shown in Fig. 9.6-1, although this represents a very general means of address translation. For a virtual memory system as outlined in Section 9.3 and specifically in Fig. 9.3-2, one important requirement that does not appear in the scheme of Fig. 9.6-1 is the means each user employs to address the memory in terms of the full CPU logical address N. To see this, the reader should study Fig. 9.5-2b, which gives a complete identification of all address bits used previously. The total virtual or secondary store logical address N_s consists of the processor logical address N, and the user ID bits u. In other words, $N_s = u + N$. Not only must each

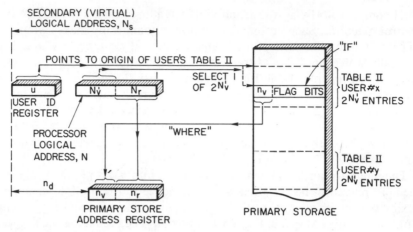

FIGURE 9.8-2   Translation of virtual address N_s into real, primary store address using single table for each user.

user be able to address main memory as if it consisted of 2^N words, but the system must contain the capability to be transferred from one user to another when a page fault is encountered. The simplest way to achieve this is shown in Fig. 9.8-2. The user ID bits are contained in a separate register. These bits give the real, origin address of that user's Table II in main memory. The virtual address part of the CPU logical address, namely, N'_v, then increments to one of the entries in the table. This entry contains a minimum of n_v plus one flag bit as specified in Fig. 9.6-5, where $n_v = q + s$. Thus the higher order bits

$$u + N'_v = n_d + q + s' \tag{9.8-1}$$

do indeed point to the table as shown in Fig. 9.6-1. Each entry in the table must contain the higher order address bits n_v for *each page* of that user. Since each user must be able to use the full CPU logical address length, each user has $2^{N'_v}$ pages as in Fig. 9.3-2. Thus Table II must contain $2^{N'_v}$ entries for each user. In the implementation in Fig. 9.8-2, when the processor transfers to a new user, the ID bits are changed in the user ID register and then point to user y, for instance. Thus each user current on the system must have a Table II stored in main memory. The following analysis reveals that it is generally not possible to store Table II as a single table; hence it is divided into smaller parts. Nevertheless, the concept of address translation using tables is identical in principle to that achieved with a single table as shown. If Table I is stored in main memory for the active users, it can be addressed in a manner very similar to that used for Table II.

To see why a large table and only a partial tag directory is used for the internal address translation as well as why Table II is divided into parts, let us make the approximate calculation of the additional storage capacity and number of associative compares required for a full-sized directory and table translation. This requires some estimates of the values of various parameters. If a virtual memory is to be effective, the total external storage should be considerably larger than main memory by a factor of 1000 or more. We will assume a minimum value of

$$2^{N_s} \geq 1024 \times 2^{n_p} \quad \text{or} \quad N_s \geq \log_2 1024 + n_p = 10 + n_p$$

Using the definition of n_d given by (9.3-7), we have

$$n_d = N_s - n_p \geq 10 \text{ bits}$$

For further parameters of the system, let us assume that $n_r = 10$ bits (i.e., 1K' words/page) and main memory has the minimum size of 256K' words or $n_p = 18$ bits. Since $N_s = n_p + n_d$, the number of secondary storage address bits is $N_s = 18 + 10 = 28$ bits (this in somewhat on the low side). We further assume that the mapping is fully associative or $q = 0, s = n_v = n_p - n_r = 8$, and that each user can have $2^{12} = 4096$ pages maximum.

The various parameters are thus

$$n_p = n_v + n_r = 8 + 10 = 18$$

$$s = n_v - 8 \qquad q = 0 \qquad n_d = 10 \qquad u = 6$$

$$N_s = n_d + n_p = 10 + 18 = 28$$

$$N_v = n_v + n_d = 18 \qquad N_v' = 12$$

From Fig. 9.6-5, the minimum storage capacity for full translation for all $2^6 = 64$ users is

Directory Storage

$$2^{n_v} = 2^8 = 256 \text{ words}$$

$$n_d + 2s = 10 + 16 = 26 \text{ bits/word}$$

Table II Storage

$$2^{N_v} = 2^{18} = 256\text{K}' \text{ words}$$

$$1 + s = 9 \text{ bits/word}$$

The table storage requires a 100% increase in addressable words or entries at a minimum of 2 bytes/entry, assuming 8 bits/byte. Note that a similar storage capacity would be required for Table I if it is all stored in main memory. The full directory requires one-thousandth as many addressable

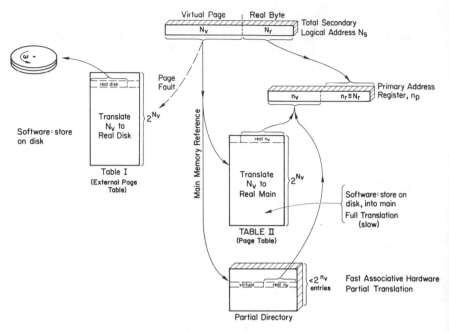

FIGURE 9.8-3   Address translation on typical virtual memory system using tables and partial directory.

words as the main memory, with a minimum of 4 bytes/entry. The latter thus seems more reasonable except that $2^s = 256$ associative compares are required, whereas the table needs no associative compares. Both methods appear to be rather expensive, and the designer is faced with a dilema that is solved by the use of both, as previously indicated. This solution is shown schematically in Fig. 9.8-3 for typical commercial systems. A CPU reference to main memory initiates the address translation simultaneously to the small, fast, partial directory and to the slow Table II. Since the partial directory contains only a few (e.g., 8 or 16) of the most recently referenced pages, a page may be in main memory but without an entry in the partial directory. If the latter is true, the translation proceeds by way of Table II. The real and virtual addresses of the page are then entered in the partial directory, since it is most likely to be referenced next. If the required page already was present in the partial directory, the Table II access would be aborted. When the required page is not resident in main memory, a page fault occurs. Then Table I must be accessed to obtain the real address as discussed in Section 9.3.

For the partial directory scheme to be effect, it must have a high hit ratio. A small hit ratio would require excessive translations via Table II in main memory, which would seriously deteriorate system speed. The partial directory must contain enough entries to achieve a high hit ratio, thus it is an important design parameter.

The above analysis assumed that all 64 users used the maximum number of virtual pages and all 64 tables were stored in main memory. Two serious objections are first, few users actually use the full virtual memory size, second, in the normal course of operation, programs are completed and new users must be entered. Thus it would be desirable to make these tables pageable just like other data, to permit relocation as required and also to provide a means for acquiring a variable table length. For the most general case, a pageable table (Table I or II) requires a table hierarchy and automatically provides a means for variable table length. The need for a table hierarchy can easily be understood as follows. In general, the maximum size of Table II for any given user can be much larger than one main memory page slot. If Table II is divided into many such page sizes, *physically* each page can reside in any real main memory page slot, but *logically* the table must be contiguous. Thus some means is necessary to associate the logical contiguity with the random physical locations. This can be done with a small, additional table that maintains a listing of the real origin of any portion (page) of Table II. If this additional small table exceeds a page slot size, there must be another level of this table hierarchy. The number of levels required in this table hierarchy for accommodating a single *logical* Table II for each user can be deduced from a knowledge of the page slot size of 2^{n_r} bytes or words, the maximum number of virtual pages per user of 2^{N_v}, and the necessary number of bytes or words per table entry B_e. Let us assume for simplicity that B_e can be expressed as a power of 2, or $B_e = 2^{n_e}$. A page slot then holds a number of table entries given by

$$\text{number of table entries per page slot} = \frac{2^{N_r}}{B_e} = 2^{N_r - n_e} \qquad (9.8\text{-}1)$$

In effect, the table entries in this page slot are addressed by $N_r - n_e$ address bits. If we assume that any additional levels in this table hierarchy also require B_e bytes or words per entry, the number of levels can be determined by the number of groups of $N_r - n_e$ address bits required in the total virtual address per user N_v'. Thus the number of levels in this table hierarchy is the higher integer value of the ratio of total table address bits divided by the effective address bits per page slot, or

$$\text{number of levels in page table hierarchy} = \left\lceil \frac{N_v'}{N_r - n_e} \right\rceil \qquad (9.8\text{-}2)$$

Obviously a one-level table results when $N'_v \leq N_r - n_e$. In the previous example we had $N'_v = 12$, $N_r = 10$, and $n_e = 1$. Substituting these into (9.8-2) gives

$$\text{number of levels} = \left\lceil \frac{12}{9} \right\rceil = 2$$

Thus our one long contiguous logical table of Fig. 9.8-2 for each user would require another level to contain the origin of the various pageable parts of the actual table. The next section indicates that the virtual address space and page sizes result in the need for a two-level table in IBM 360/370 virtual system and a three-level table in Multics.

If the external page table, Table I, is stored and paged into main memory, it must be handled in a manner analogous to that given. The number of bytes or words per entry may be different as a result of additional information which is conveniently stored in these tables.

It should be clearly understood that these translation tables are not fundamentally necessary. The address translation can be done in hardware with a tag store. Most commercial virtual memory systems use such tables created by software and paged into main memory because they provide a flexible, economical scheme. In addition to address translation, these tables can provide such other functions as the control of access rights and sharing of pages among users. These multiple functions are often incorporated into the table because of convenience and economy. Fundamentally, they can also be done in other ways with hardware or software. The details of such subjects require a consideration of the overall architecture of a virtual computing system that is beyond the scope of this chapter.

The replacement algorithm typically used in virtual memory systems is some form of a "not recently used" algorithm discussed in Section 9.7. The page usage and control information can be stored in hardware/software-created tables, or both; typically combinations of both are necessary. The various commercial and supervisory systems offer wide variations in details, but not in principle.

Current virtual memory systems tend to implement considerable amounts of the necessary functions in software for economy. However this has created enormous supervisory programs and tables that not only are complex, but consume ever-increasing amounts of main memory. It can be shown that all these functions can be implemented in associative-type hardware either in a separate array or on-chip as in Section 9.13, while still providing overall system flexibility and fine-tuning capability. This hardware would be highly desirable if sufficiently inexpensive and reasonably fast. Eventually the new high density, low cost FET may take over more and more of these functions.

9.9 EXAMPLES OF VIRTUAL MEMORY SYSTEMS

Examples of a few large virtual memory systems are included here.

9.9.1 Ferranti Altas

One of the early paged virtual memories, the Ferranti Atlas, used a 98,304 word magnetic drum secondary store paged into 16K' core primary store.* The total logical address length, N_s was 20 bits, allowing a maximum of 1M' words for all users. This was the total size of secondary storage permitted on the system, and it was all addressed randomly by the 20 bit logical address. Hence there was only one mode of addressing, and the system represented the first operating example of a one-level store. Secondary storage was divided into 2048 pages of 512 words/page. Thus the logical address consists of 9 lower order real bits and 11 higher order virtual bits (i.e., $N_r = 9$, $N_v = 11$, as in Fig. 9.9-1. Main memory (primary) thus contained a maximum of only 32 page slots, which requires a higher order address length of $n_v = 5$ bits. Hence the address translation must convert the 11 bits of N_v into an IF (yes/no) command and a 5 bit page slot address specifying WHERE the desired page is in core. This is accomplished by a tag directory. Each of the 32 page slots in primary store is assigned one register or word of the directory. The 11 bit virtual address tag N_v of the correct page stored in each primary slot is maintained in the directory.† For translating a given logical address, the 11 N_v bits are associatively compared with the 11 bits of all 32 tags in the directory. If no match is found, a relocate cycle is initiated. If a match is found, the register (i.e., page slot number) of the directory is flagged, and its address, expressed as 5 bits binary, is used as the higher order bits n_v of the primary store address register as shown. The 9 real bits complete the 14-bit address required to select one of 16K' words in primary storage. When a miss occurs, location of the desired page on the drum is accomplished by use of a page directory (i.e., Table I of Section 9.8). This table stores the 11 bit logical page address and the associated correct drum address. The 11 bit logical address of each page is scanned sequentially until the correct drum address is found. Subsequently that address is used to read the desired page into primary storage. This tag directory is similar to the cache directory used in the IBM model 85 in that the binary address of the entry in the tag directory serves as the higher order address bits of the primary address register. In other words, since there is a one-to-one correspondence between the position of the tag in the directory and the position of the page (or sector in model 85) in the primary store, in essence Map 3 (Fig. 9.5-9) is direct.

---

* In addition, there was approximately 4M words of tape storage for I/O.
† A twelfth bit for storage protect is also stored in the directory.

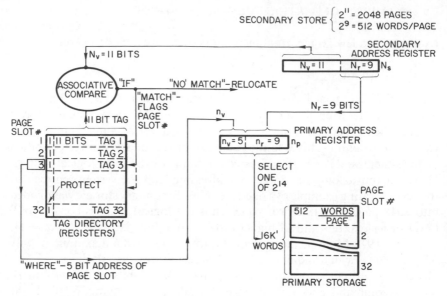

FIGURE 9.9-1   Schematic of virtual paging scheme on Ferranti Atlas.

To determine which page to remove from core to make room for a new page, the Atlas system used a learning program, part of which is similar to the LRU algorithm. Each of the 32 page slots in primary storage has associated with it a "use" bit stored in a separate register. Hence there are a total of 32 "use" bits. A given bit is set to "1" whenever a word from the current page in that slot is used. The learning program reads these bits destructively, setting them to "0" but storing them in a new list in a subsidiary memory (private store). These "use" bits are read every time 1024 instructions have been executed as determined by an instruction counter.* These bits are added to the subsidiary store list, then used by the program to update two sets of times also stored in the subsidiary memory. These times consist of 32 values for t and 32 values for T, one of each for each page slot in primary storage. The value of t is the length of time† since the current page in that page slot was last used; T is the length of time of the last previous period of inactivity of that same page. A page is then removed from primary store based on three simple tests in the following order of priority: remove

---

* This is not real time, since I/O interrupts can cause real time to be any value.
† Time measured in 1024 instruction intervals.

the page that has

1. $t > T + 1$.
2. Maximum value of $(T - t)$ with $t \neq 0$.
3. Maximum value of T with all $t = 0$.

The first rule selects the page that has been out of use for the longest time, hence is equivalent to LRU except that in this case it is possible for no page to qualify. Rule 2 ignore pages in current use ($t = 0$) and selects the page that will not be needed by the program for the longest time. If the first two rules fail, rule 3 ensures that one page will be selected and also that if this page is immediately required again, T becomes 0 and the same mistake will not be repeated on the next page replacement.

When a page is relocated back to the drum, a means is also provided to store the value of T so that when this page is once again called to primary storage, the value of T is set in the subsidiary memory.

The Atlas was not multiprogrammed in the sense that program control was not transferred when a page miss occurred. Nevertheless, it was partitioned such that output from a previously completed program or input for a new program could share main memory during idle cycles (e.g., page misses) of a third program that was being processed.

This machine thus represents a one-level store of a very simple type. One limitation is the small number of page slots. Also, and more serious, is the maximum of 1M' logical words to be divided among all programs if there are several programs resident at one time. It is more desirable to allow each user to have the full 20 bit addressing capability of the system and to multiprogram the entire logical address space. However this could not be done because there was no user ID register, hence no "u" bits as in Fig. 9.3-2. This feature evolved in later systems.

9.9.2   IBM System 360/370 Virtual Memory Fundamentals

The IBM virtual memory systems implement the various requirements of Section 9.3 in a manner very similar to that outlined in Section 9.8 in the following way:*

1. *Page Mapping Function.* This is fully associative both from disk† to main memory and from main memory back to disk.
2a. *Word Addressing.* Pages consist of from 1K' to 4K' bytes, depending on model.

---

* This section is not intended to be a full description of IBM systems; it merely indicates how the fundamentals are implemented.

† In some systems the secondary store may be drums, disks, or a combination.

2b. *Page Address Translation*. This makes use of a partial tag directory and table schemes to capitalize on the strengths of each while minimizing the respective weaknesses. The tables make use of a Table I and Table II as described in Section 9.8, and both are implemented entirely in software.

3. *Page Replacement Algorithm*: An approximation to the LRU algorithm is implemented in various ways, depending on the system.

a. *I/O Processor*. This function is provided by the channel coupled to the control units as explained in Section 9.2. The channel is a basic part of system 360 and 370 architecture, with or without virtual storage.

b. *Storage Protection*. This is provided in the form of keys associated with each $4K'$ word module of main memory. The modules and keys are assigned by the operating system and only protect supervisory programs from unauthorized usage. They do not protect users from each other and are required irrespective of the virtual memory.

c. *Sharing of Pages*. Global sharing of supervisory programs is implemented by way of Table II.

We now cover the address translation in more detail with particular reference to the system 360 model 67, although the basic concepts pervade the 360/370 virtual systems. The CPU logical address is 24 bits, (32 bit version available on 360/M67). This provides a virtual store of $2^{24} = 16M'$ bytes/user. The user ID bits in Fig. 9.8-2 are maintained in a separate 32 bit register as shown.

The maximum value of n_p is 24 bits, which would allow $16M'$ bytes of main memory. However n_p is generally much smaller but has a lower limit for each system (e.g., for the model 67, $18 \le n_p < 24$). Some typical parameters for a system might be as follows.

Since fully associative mapping is used,

$$s = n_v \le 12 \qquad q' \equiv q = 0 \qquad s' \equiv N_v' = 12$$
$$s' \ne s \text{ except in special case of } s = \text{maximum value}$$
$$n_p = 18 \qquad \text{or} \qquad 256K' \text{ byte main memory}$$
$$n_v = n_p - n_r = 6 \text{ bits}$$
$$N_r \equiv n_r = 10 \text{ to } 12 \text{ bits} \qquad \text{or} \qquad 1K' \text{ to } 4K' \text{ bytes/page}$$
$$N = 24 \text{ defined by system } 360/370 \text{ architecture}$$

In principle, the address translation function is implemented exactly as as shown in Fig. 9.8-3. To allow a relatively large number of page references to be done fast, only 8 of the most recently used pages are kept in a partial directory, as illustrated in Fig. 9.9-2 for the model 67. This associative directory compares all the s' (i.e., N_v') bits to determine a match; hence u bits are

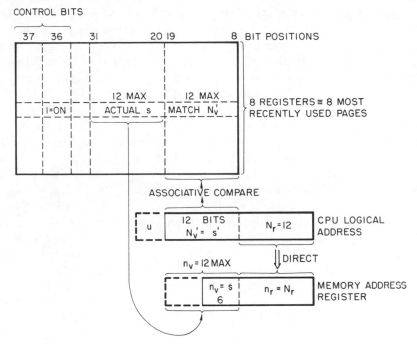

FIGURE 9.9-2 IBM 360, model 67, address translation, using small partial directory for the eight most recently used pages.

unaccounted for. These bits *must* be decoded or an invalid page could be referenced by the s bits found in a matching word. These u bits are taken care of by the use of control bits 36 and 37 of the associative register. Whenever a specific user is first given control of the CPU, these two control bits are set to "0" in all words of the register, meaning none of the pages is valid. The given user must first reference pages through the tables, after which time the associative register is loaded with the virtual address $N'_v = s'$ and the correct value of s for that page of that user as shown. This correct value for s is obtained from the page table, to be described shortly. When a page address is loaded in the register, the control bits 36 and 37 are both set to "1" to indicate a valid page for that user. A user must reference eight different pages through the tables before the partial directory is full. When all entries are full, such that all bits 37 equal "1," they are all set equal to "0" and bit 36 of all is still "1." A subsequent reference to an already present page will reset bit 37 to "1" for that page. Thus bit 36 indicates the presence of a valid page, whereas bit 37 indicates usage. In essence, then, bit 36 is the control bit that indirectly decodes the u bits while bit 37 is used as a means for replacing entries. For instance, if a page reference is found to not exist in the directory, the first entry with bit 37 equal to "0" is replaced by the currently demanded page. Note that this does *not* constitute the page-swapping algorithm from secondary disk to main memory, rather, only replacement within the directory. This small directory does *not* perform a full address translation as would the directory of Fig. 9.6-4a or b. The currently demanded page may be in main memory (in the table described below) but not in the directory. If the CPU control switches between users too frequently, of course, the partial directory is of little value. Hence a high hit ratio is desired.

The main memory obviously holds more than eight pages. If the desired page is not one of those contained in the partial directory, the IF and WHERE are determined from a Table II much as that shown in Figs. 9.6-1 and 9.8-2. Actually the table search is initiated simultaneously with the partial directory as in Fig. 9.8-3. Table I and II can each be organized as one list as described in Section 9.8. However the need for pageability requires a multilevel table hierarchy. The number of levels is given by (9.8-2). For the current case, the real page address N_r can be from 10 to 12 bits, the number of virtual pages per user N'_v from 14 to 12, respectively, and $n_e = 1$ (2 bytes/table entry). Substituting these into (9.8-2) gives for IBM 360/370 table hierarchy

$$\text{number of Levels} = \left\lceil \frac{14}{10-1} \right\rceil \quad \text{to} \quad \left\lceil \frac{12}{12-1} \right\rceil$$

$$= 2$$

This two-level table hierarchy is organized as follows. Referring to Fig. 9.9-3, assuming $N_r = 12$ bits, the N'_v bits of the CPU logical address are divided into a 4 bit segment and an 8 bit page portion as shown to form a segment table and multiple page tables. Each user can have up to $2^4 = 16$ segments, with each segment having $2^8 = 256$ pages for a total of 4K' pages per user as required. Each of the 16 segments of the segment table contains the origin address of one page table for that user.

The address translation by way of this table hierarchy proceeds as follows. The user ID register contains the 24 bit address of the origin of a given user's segment table in main memory. The 4 bit portion of the CPU logical address represents the lower order address bits and indicates how deep the desired word is within the table. The so-located word contains a length portion, a page table origin address, and a control bit. The control bit indicates whether the required segment of pages is actually present. The length portion is compared with the 8 bit page portion of the CPU logical word only to save time. The comparison is done very fast in CPU hardware and tells whether the page table is large enough to possibly hold the page identification bits.

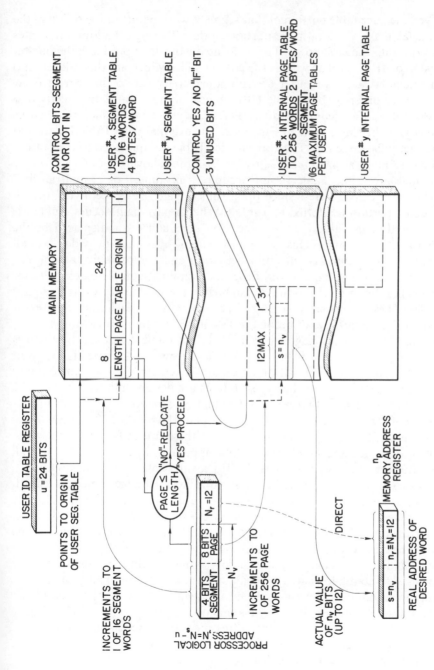

FIGURE 9.9-3 IBM 360/370 virtual memory showing address translation using segment and page tables.

613

If yes, the page table portion of that segment word points to the origin of the page table and the 8 bit page portion of the CPU logical address indicates how far into the table to go. The so-located word then produces the one-bit yes/no or IF control as well as the correct s bits, which are then placed into the memory address register for subsequent reference to the correct page. The lower order N_r bits in the CPU logical address translate directly into the n_r bits of the memory address register, hence the table hierarchy works exactly as the single table in Fig. 9.8-2. The external page Table I is treated in exactly the same way. For convenience Table I is appended to the bottom of each "internal page table" in Fig. 9.9-3 (not shown). Note that for the example given, the Table II slot occupies a maximum of 256 entries at 2 bytes/entry or 512 bytes. Since the assumed page size is $4K'$ bytes, the remaining portion is allotted to Table I. When a page fault occurs, Table I is addressed as in Table II except the 8 bit page address is displaced by the appropriate amount. This seemingly complex system provides overall flexibility in virtual system implementation and compatibility among different models. The supervisory program is granted complete flexibility for control of the primary storage consumed by the various segments and page tables. These tables may be stored permanently for each current user or swapped dynamically as needed. IBM 360/370 batch processing systems generally load the full page tables, both Tables I and II, at the time a user is made active in the CPU. In time-shared systems, when a user is in a wait state his complete Table II, or only part, may be removed from primary storage if necessary. All these possibilities are design options that must be evaluated in terms of the actual system and type of job stream environment. Different types of virtual supervisory system, IBM CP67, VS1, VS2, MVS, TSS, as well as Multics and others handle these tradeoffs in different ways. There does not appear to be one best approach. In any case, the overall architecture of a hierarchy for Table II provides considerable flexibility.

A two-level table also facilitates global sharing of pages among users, although other techniques may be used. Two users may share a page by having the "page table origin" portion of each user's segment table contain the same information, hence pointing to the same page table in main memory. Sharing could be done with a one-level address table but becomes unwieldy.

A fundamental characteristic of this system is that the segment table consists of contiguous words in main memory. Consequently, if a user's storage requirement overflows from one segment into another, the higher order segment address bits are incremented by one to allow addressing of the next segment. In other words, addressing between segments is continuous. One disadvantage is that the user is limited to a finite number of segments, namely, 16 maximum in this case.

Since all references to main memory must proceed by way of the memory address registers, the pointers form the user's ID register pointing to a segment table, the segment table word pointing to a page table, and page table pointing to actual page must be correctly loaded and aligned in the memory address register. This requires some control logic but is rather straightforward in principle and is not considered further. The replacement algorithm is essentially the "not recently used" algorithm described in Section 9.7 and is primarily software implemented. The various supervisory programs use varying number of historical H bits, called unreferenced internal count (e.g., VS1 uses 1 bit; MVS uses 8 bits). Storage protection makes use of a storage key that is associated with each 2048 byte block of main memory. Each program is assigned a protection key that is stored as part of the status word, or in a separate array. A memory reference into any specific block of main memory is permitted only if the user's protection key matches the storage key, or if the former is zero. These keys only protect the supervisory programs from unauthorized access.

9.9.3 Honeywell Multics Virtual Memory (645 Processor)

The intention behind the original Multics was to allow a user to program any problem with essentially an infinite number of segments. The system has evolved over the years, taking on various forms. In one form, the Honeywell Multics (Multics, 1972; Organick, 1972) allows a user to program up to 2^{18} segments with 2^{18} words/segment. In other words, the processor effective logical address is 36 bits long and each user may program as if a main memory of 2^{36} bits were available. But the main memory address register can contain a maximum of 24 bits and the real main memory may be smaller than this (e.g., 2^{18} words, or 18 bits effective main memory address register as in the previous example). Thus it is necessary to translate these 36 logical address bits plus a user ID into a real address of 18 to 24 bits specifying WHERE the required word might be and IF it does in fact reside there. This address translation function, assuming the logical address to be already available, is performed in a manner very similar to that in Figs. 9.8-2 and 9.8-3 but with some practical differences in detail. Memory and storage are divided into pages of fixed length (1024 words). The 10 lower order address bits of the logical address are real; hence as in all previous cases, these bits address one of the words in a page. This leaves $N'_v = 36 - 10 = 26$ bits/user for addressing pages. Since the table used for address translation must be pageable, a multilevel table hierarchy is required. Since $N_r = 10$ and $N'_v = 26$ bits, assuming $n_e = 1$ bit (2 bytes/table entry), the number of levels for Multics, from (9.8-2), is

$$\text{number of Level 9} = \left\lceil \frac{26}{10 - 1} \right\rceil = 3$$

Obviously the larger virtual address has resulted in a more complex table hierarchy. The Multics address translation (Fig. 9.9-4) is implemented as follows. The origin of each user's first table is contained in the so-called descriptor base register, which is the user ID register described previously. This register contains the real core address of the first table for address translation and a field L_1 which specifies the length of the descriptor segment table in main memory. The processor logical address consists of two major components $s + i$, each of 18 bits for 36 bits total. This logical address is divided into four components, namely

$$s + i = s_x + s_y + i_x + i_y$$

These are used in conjunction with the descriptor base register (user ID) as follows. Referring to Fig. 9.9-4, the length bits L_1 of the descriptor base register are compared with the s bits to determine whether the first set of segment tables is long enough to contain the desired information.* If "yes," the u bits are catenated to the s_x bits to give the origin address of the page table PT_1 of the descriptor segment.† A flag bit F indicates presence or absence of the desired entry; $F = $ ON indicates "not present." This flag provides one part of the "IF" translation function. If the flag is off, the contents of this word provide the origin address of the page of the descriptor segment table P_1, and the s_y bits increment to the correct entry in that page. The entry in this table contains the origin address of the page table, a length L_2, which specifies the length of the segment, an access field ACC, which specifies the access rights of this segment, and a flag bit F as before. The ACC field provides storage protection at the segment level. The second flag bit provides further "IF" translation. Assuming that the F bit does not generate a fault, the binary value of the L_2 bits is compared with the i bits to determine if the next table PT_2 is long enough to contain the desired information, as before. If L_2 is less than i, a miss is generated. If L_2 is greater than i, the ACC field is compared with the operation code of the instruction to determine whether the specified operation is permitted. If "yes," the origin field points to the page table origin and the i_x bits select one of 256 words in the page table PT_2. This page table likewise specifies the true higher order address bits of the required page; the 10 lower order address bits i_y, which are real and equivalent to N_r previously defined, give the correct word. The last two address bit fields constitute the final memory address as shown in n_p.

This table translation works in principle just as that described in Section 9.8 and previously except for details of the control bits and number of components into which the CPU logical address is divided. Because of the large

---

* These tables need not be filled.
† The nomenclature is that used by the Multics system.

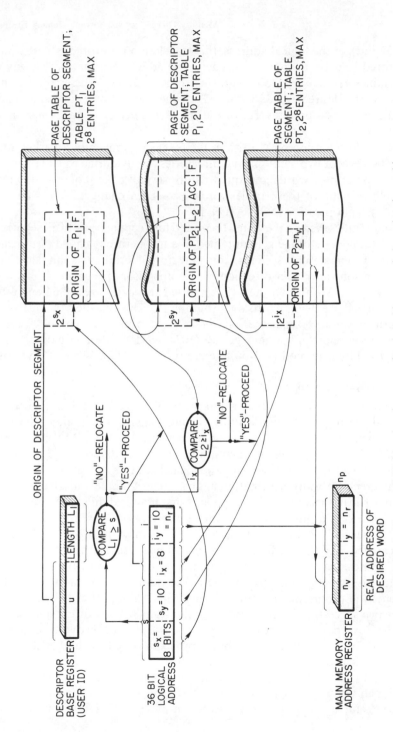

FIGURE 9.9-4 Honeywell Multics virtual memory showing address translation using three tables.

617

size (36 bits), of the logical address, this translation uses three tables; which are stored in main memory as needed. The address translation by way of these tables can be very slow, requiring three memory accesses plus a final access to the desired word. To speed up the translation process, a small, partial directory stores several of the most recently used pages just as in Fig. 9.8-3.

The implementation of Multics in the 6000 series machines works much as the 645 except two small partial directories are used (one to store several segment descriptor words and one to store several page table words); also the field formats of these table words have been changed somewhat for more efficient operation (MULTICS, 1972).

In the Multics system, the Table I required for keeping track of all segments on the secondary storage is maintained in a file hierarchy called *directories*. As with other similar systems, this directory hierarchy is implemented entirely in software under direction of the supervisory program.

The original Multics on the 645 supported two page sizes of 64 and 1024 words, the choice being left to the programmer. This reflected the historical concern of variable segmentation versus fixed page size. The 6000 series processors support only one page size (1024 words), although page size can be changed by field modification to any power of 2 from 64 to 4096 words.

9.9.4 Comparison of IBM and Multics Virtual Systems

We have already seen that the virtual memory address translation is nearly identical for the IBM and Multics virtual systems. The major difference comes about from the use of symbolic segment referencing in Multics, whereas IBM systems use linear segmentation. This basic difference gives rise to rather different ways of generating the logical address within the processor. The difference in address formation has some effect on the underlying virtual memory subsystems but only results in some practical differences in details such as the organization and amount of information stored in the various tables (essentially Table I and Table II), the manner in which these tables are searched, and the method of sharing and protecting segments.

In Multics, the symbolic segment names are converted by the supervisory system to segment numbers—namely, the address s—in a manner that prevents the programmer from knowing what value of s will be assigned. Hence two successively referenced symbolic segments do not get successive s numbers except in rare coincidences. Such a scheme provides complete generality of segment names within a procedure segment and is desirable from a logical point of view. Howerver it can lead to practical problems. Suppose, for instance, that a large problem is being executed which requires more than one segment (i.e., more than 2^{18} pages). In particular, suppose two segments are required. An instruction in segment 1 may branch to a word in segment 2 and then wish to come back. The programmer knows that in his program (virtual space) this required word is a certain number of memory references from the branch instruction. In logical memory space, however, since the branch must cross the segment boundary, the actual number of memory references cannot be known to the programmer before-hand. This is true because the linkage mechanism assigns the two segments noncontiguous locations in the descriptor segment table. Hence the program-mer cannot use a simple indexing scheme to cross the segment boundaries but rather must use a more complex method of indirect addressing. In the IBM systems, during execution time, each user's segments are loaded contig-uously in his separate segment table, ensuring that the boundaries between segments are contiguous: that is, the logical address of the last page of the first segment C is contiguous with the logical address of the first page of the second segment $C + 1$. Thus segment boundaries can be crossed with simple indexing.* It can be seen that this segment linkage difference is completely independent of the virtual memory subsystem. In fact, this difference comes about mainly from the method of compilation (or assembling) and loading of the source program. In the IBM systems, segments are assigned specific numbers and predetermined positions in the user's segment table. Con-secutive segments are loaded into consecutive positions, hence are linearly related. In Multics a position in the segment table (descriptor segment)—that is, a value for s in Fig. 9.9-4—is not assigned until execution time; there-fore the positions of segments in the table are not related in any way. These types of segmentation are known as linear (IBM) and symbolic (Multics).

In a nutshell we can say that the Multics and IBM virtual memory systems differ mainly in the way the general logical address is formed, with Multics maintaining symbolic segment representation and IBM using linear segmen-tation. The virtual address translation, mapping, paging, and replacement display practical rather than fundamental differences.

9.10 CACHE MEMORY SYSTEM DESIGN CONSIDERATIONS

A cache memory system represents a type of memory hierarchy that attempts to bridge the CPU–main memory speed gap by the use of a very small, high speed random access memory whose cost per bit is roughly 10 times that of main memory [see (1.3-1)] but whose total cost is relatively small because of the small size.

The cache–main memory hierarchy is really a virtual hierarchy of a limited variety, since the CPU now can reference stored data only through the cache,

---

* This continuity across segment boundaries exists only for the logical addresses. The real physical address is seldom continuous but is of no concern.

and main memory assumes the role of secondary storage. The only difference is that here the secondary store is directly addressable out of the main memory address register, whereas when secondary storage is a disk, a completely different accessing method must be initiated by way of the I/O processor and controller. Otherwise, the same concepts are used for both and the same fundamental problems arise. However the method of implementation is usually different because of the high speed demanded by the entire cache–main memory hierarchy. Thus this hierarchy usually has the addressing, paging, and other extra requirements implemented in special hardware, whereas a multiuser virtual memory is usually implemented by a combination of hardware and software features.

To understand the detailed organizational aspects of cache, it is essential to keep in mind that the primary requirement is speed, particularly the access and cycle time to a given page. Thus we have a demand for high speed both in the basic cycle time of the cache and in the address translation function. Speed is also of some concern in the page replacement function for moving pages out of and into the cache. One can imagine that the use of special logic control function similar to the I/O processor in Section 9.2 could be used to free the CPU during a page replacement. In other words, the time required for page replacement could be overlapped with CPU operation by cycle stealing during contention references or by available open periods for memory references due to the problem statistics (e.g., "multiply" may require 3 to 10 or more CPU cycles between memory references). Unfortunately, transferring control to another user's page requires a considerable amount of processing in itself, which can be greater than the time the CPU remains idle during a page transfer. This is true only when the speed difference between cache and main memory is not too large, when a wide data path between the two can be achieved, or both. Section 9.4 indicated that a page size of about 64 bytes is adequate for cache. The data bus width can be 8 or 16 bytes per memory reference; if the latter, only four main memory cycle times are interleaved to achieve the page relocation. This can greatly speed up the system.

The remainder of this section explains how the need for speed influences the organization of the address translation. Before proceeding, the reader should be thoroughly familiar with the general operation of virtual memory of Section 9.3, especially the fundamentals of mapping and address translation of Sections 9.5 and 9.6. We make use of the fundamental system diagram of Fig. 9.3-2. The only difference is that secondary storage is now main memory, the cache being primary storage. We can use the same notations and definitions for address bits as previously.

As before, the lower order bits $N_r = n_r$ are real. The problem is to translate the higher order N_v bits to specify IF the desired page is present in the cache and if so WHERE. Both these should be done on one memory cycle if at all possible. This eliminates the use of a table (Fig. 9.6-1) for translating the $n_d + s'$ bits of N_v, leaving only tag directory schemes. Again, because of the need for versatility in physical page location, Map 3 of Fig. 9.5-9 should be fully associative, suggesting the tag store schemes of Fig. 9.6-4. We assume a minimum directory with $e = n_v$. For Map 2 of Fig. 9.5-9, S compares are required, and since S depends on the mapping function, this is a major decision. Direct mapping with $S = 1$ or $s = 0$ is unworkable because of page slot contention problems. Fully associative mapping would have to be done with an associative memory, which is not only expensive but would be slower than a random access memory. Hence a set associative mapping seems more feasible. The value of S must be chosen such that a page or word access can be done in one cycle. This seems to be contradictory because S associative compares must be made simultaneously, which implies at least a partially associative memory. In other words, we must make S compares in one cycle. How can this be done without an associative directory? Non-associative memory requires that the compares be made external to the array. Simultaneous compares require that all S tags be available on one directory fetch. Together these requirements mean that a physical word must be composed of S logical words, each logical word with its own tag as in Fig. 9.10-1. Each physical word of the directory is thus composed of S logical words. Obviously while there are only 2^q physical words, there are still $2^{q+s} = 2^{n_v}$ logical words, as required in Fig. 9.6-5. A set is now specified by one physical word of the directory, and when one such word is selected by the q' address bit of the logical address, all S tags appear in the directory output buffer register. Since we do not know which if any of the logical words is correct, S compares are still required, as shown. These can be done simultaneously, and when a "yes" is obtained, the correct page origin address in cache is immediately available. Thus retrieval of the desired word requires one access to the page directory and one access to the cache itself. If no match gives a "yes" answer, the required page is not present and a relocate cycle is immediately initiated. This entire system is identical in principle to that of Fig. 9.6-4 except for the use of several logical words per physical word, which allows several simultaneous external compares. The compare functions can be implemented in high speed CPU register technology, hence introduce very small additional delay.

One might ask, Why not make the tag directory contain more entries? Why not let $e = N_v$, reducing the number of associatively compared bits to s (see Fig. 9.6-5)? This can be done in principle, but since primary storage only contains $2^q = Q$ set slots, there would be a considerable number of wasted entries in the table. Only 2^q entries could contain useful information at any one time, the others being essentially blank. Since directories are expensive, it is desirable to reduce the size as much as possible by removing

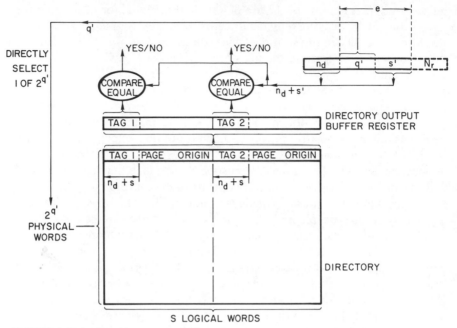

FIGURE 9.10-1 Tag directory decoding using multiple logical words per physical word for high speed with $e = n_r$ and set associative Map 2.

unnecessary, unused entries, which is achieved by reducing the value of e. For example, assuming $q' = n_d = 7$ bits (e.g., Fig. 9.11-2), if we use a directory with $e = N_v$, this requires $2^{14} = 16K'$ physical words. Each word must be capable of storing $2^s(s' + n_v)$ bits, but most entries will be empty at any one time. The scheme of Fig. 9.10-1 (or Fig. 9.11-2) with $e = n_v$ obviously is smaller because normally it will be full, representing only the information part of the 16K' directory.

The need for speed in a cache hierarchy, coupled with only about one order of magnitude difference in speed and cost of cache versus main memory, raises two other important design considerations: "store-through" and "load-through." In store-through, whenever a change is made in a page residing in the cache, the same change is made in that page as it resides in main memory. Thus when a page is to be removed from cache, it can be simply erased instead of recopied into main memory. Since statistically only some bytes are changed, store-through can be more efficient and is often employed in practical systems. Load-through allows the data from main memory, as they are being paged into the cache, to be available simultaneously to the CPU without waiting for a full transfer and cache read cycle.

In essence, scratch-pad memories (Section 9.1) operate as a cachelike virtual memory system except the page is only one word long. The primary store or scratch pad is very much smaller than secondary storage, hence the addressing of the scratch pad requires both an IF and a WHERE function similar to those described in Section 9.3. As originally conceived, scratch pads were very small (in the range of 256 words), to introduce only small additional costs.

9.11 EXAMPLES OF CACHE MEMORY SYSTEMS

Early computing systems such as the Univac 1110 used fast scratch-pad memories to bridge the CPU–main memory speed gap as pointed out in Section 9.1. The first computer to incorporate a complete system using paged cache was the IBM 360/85.

9.11.1 IBM 360/85* Cache

To achieve flexibility and high hit ratios, associative mapping is desirable. However fully associative mapping requires a large number of associative compares. A cache must be accessed at high speed, necessitating an associative memory for address translation. Since this is expensive, the model 85 uses sector mapping as a compromise between these conflicting demands. Main memory and the cache are divided into sectors of 16 blocks/sector. Each block, which is almost equivalent to our previously defined page, consists of 64 bytes/block. Hence each sector consists of 1024 bytes (Fig. 9.11-1). Blocks or pages are mapped in sequential order within all sectors. Hence the location of any byte in a sector is fixed so that the 10 lower order address bits are real. In essence, the six lowest order bits specify one of 64 bytes within a block and the next four bits represent one of 16 blocks within that sector.

When a miss occurs requiring data transfer from main memory to cache, only the desired block is transferred. If all 16 blocks of a sector were transferred, additional, unnecessary delays and degradation in performance would result. The tag directory is a small associative memory built of CPU register technology for speed.

For a given logical address, the 14 high order bits uniquely specify the sector in main memory. Since there are only 16 sectors in the cache, these 14 bits must be decoded into an IF and WHERE function. This is accomplished with the tag directory in the following way. An associative compare is performed on all 16 tags of the directory. If no match occurs, a relocate

---

* There is no disk–main but only a main–cache virtual memory. For a more complete description of this system and the cache, see *IBM* (1968).

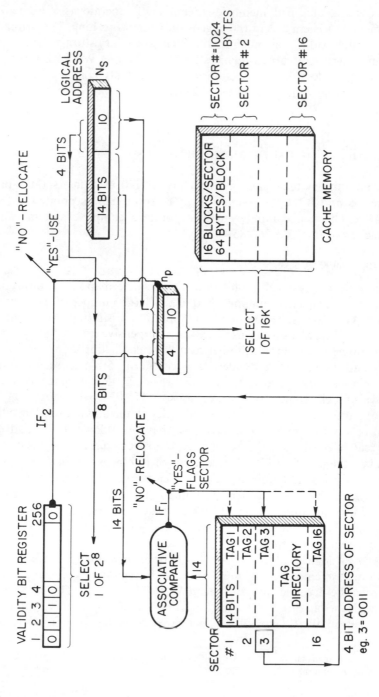

FIGURE 9.11-1 Cache organization and address translation on IBM 360/370 model 85.

624

cycle is initiated. If a match occurs, the IF determination is "yes" for that sector (but not necessarily for the required block). This represents the first part of the IF translation, indicated as IF_1 in Fig. 9.11-1. The number of the physical word of the directory for which the match occurs specifies the physical origin in cache of that sector. This number, in binary form, represents the four higher order address bits of the cache, the 10 lower order bits are real as shown. Since not all blocks of a sector need be present at one time, a further translation step is necessary to determine IF the required block is present. This is done by storing a "validity" bit for each block in cache, hence requires 256 such bits. Each validity bit, normally "0," is set to "1" when a block is placed in the cache and reset to "0" when a sector is reassigned. The remaining IF translation (IF_2 in Fig. 9.11-1) is then accomplished by testing the proper bit for the specified block: "1" = yes, "0" = no. Thus two processor cycles are required to fetch a given byte from the cache. The first cycle simultaneously searches the tag directory and the validity bits to determine IF and WHERE the data are in the cache. The second cycle fetches the data out of the address specified by the first cycle in combination with the real address bits. These validity bits are stored in CPU logic registers. Selection of the correct bit is done by using the four bits decoded from the tag directory plus the four higher order bits of the 10 real bits of N_s as in Fig. 9.11-1.

When a miss occurs, the least recently used sector is replaced. This is determined by a logical stack that maintains a logical ordering of sectors in terms of usage. When a sector is referenced, its number is moved to the top of the stack. Hence the bottom of the stack always specifies the least recently used sector. This logical stack, like the validity bits, is implemented entirely in CPU logic hardware. The model 85 cache uses both store-through and load-through to increase overall speed.

The bus width for transfer of data from main memory to cache is 16 bytes in parallel because the physical words of main memory are 8 bytes long, and two units are paired to give and effective word size of 16 bytes or 128 bits. Since a block is 64 bytes, four main memory words are required. Each of these is stored automatically in four separate memory modules, which can be separately accessed (i.e., four-way interleaved at time intervals equal to the cache time). Hence transfer time is approximately one main memory access time plus four cache times or about $0.880 + 4(0.080) = 1.2$ μsec.

Performance studies (Liptay, 1968) on 19 job streams of about 250,000 instructions each and simulated on the model 85 cache gave a hit ratio of from 92 to 99 %, with a mean of 96.8 %. Though adequate in many cases, the sector mapping did not provide the high hit ratios desired for such large systems. The difficulty is that when a miss occurs and the required block belongs to a sector not present in the cache, an entire sector must be removed.

This means that up to 16 blocks are removed, and even though being the least recently used sector, one of these 16 removed blocks has a high probability of being referenced subsequently. Nevertheless this system demonstrated the power and utility of the cache concept. The subsequent IBM models 360/195, 370/158, and 370/168 use set associative mapping for their cache–main memory hierarchies.

9.11.2   IBM System 360 Model 195 Cache*

This cache memory consists of a random access array using the organization of Fig. 4.9-5. The cycle time of the array itself is 54 nsec, which equals the basic processor clock cycle time. Pages are 64 bytes long, since this length is more optimum, as previously described. The cache capacity is 32K' bytes, or 512 pages maximum. Main memory is 1M' to 4M' bytes of core storage with 756 nsec cycle time. A physical word consists of 8 bytes; thus one access to a physical word every 756 nsec produces 8 logical words or 8 bytes. The mapping function is set associative with four page slots per set.

As indicated in Section 9.10, two design factors are especially important. First, it is desirable to perform a memory reference with only one access time to the cache, plus a minimum of other delays for address translation and data transfer. Second, when a miss occurs, it is desirable to have a fast page transfer from main memory to cache, to minimize any possible subsequent delays. Considerable concurrency exists in this system by way of pipeline processing, as well as up to 10 instructions simultaneously in various stages of decoding and execution. Thus one cannot easily specify exactly what happens on, say, a miss, without analyzing an entire instruction stream, yet fast page transfer is desirable on an average basis. The first criterion results in the use of a tag directory and associative compares for address translation.

The second criterion is fulfilled because the main memory is at least eight-way interleaved,† so that each of the eight modules can be accessed separately. In this way the 8 physical words of 8 bytes each, which equals one page, can be transferred into the cache at the cycle time of the cache. If the main memory were not interleaved, 8 cycles of 756 nsec each would be required to transfer one page, an intolerably long time.

To allow fast address translation without consuming large amounts of additional storage for the translation, the address translation is done exactly as shown in Fig. 9.10-1 but with $S = 4$ pages/set, hence 4 logical words per physical word. The directory (Fig. 9.11-2) contains 128 physical words, with each word storing four tags of length $n_d + s'$ and the correct $s + q$ bits

---

* There is no disk–main but only a main–cache virtual memory.
† 2M' and 4M' byte versions are 16-way interleaved.

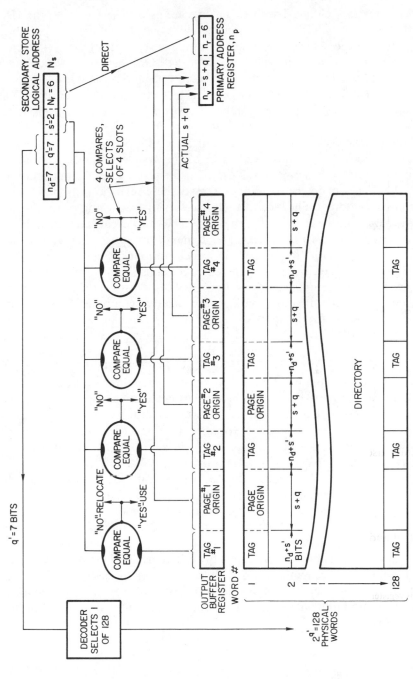

FIGURE 9.11-2 Tag directory system for IBM model 195 showing various components for address translation of N_s to n_p with set associative mapping.

627

associated with each tag. The virtual q' bits are used to select one of the 128 words, which is read into the output buffer register, yielding four possible locations. Four logical compares are simultaneously made of the $n_d + s'$ bits of the virtual address with each of the four tags. Only one of these can give an equal or "yes," which then gates the correct page location bits $s + q$ into the primary address register. Since the n_r bits are real, the translation is complete. If none of the four compares gives a "yes," a page transfer is initiated.

Although the cycle time of the cache array itself is 54 nsec and equals the processor clock cycle time, a full cycle of the system requires three such cycles for a total access time of 162 nsec. The first cycle gates the information from the processor to the directory, accesses the directory, and obtains the correct page address. The second cycle accesses the cache and produces the required word in the cache buffer register.* The third cycle gates the data to the proper section of the processor as required for processing. Hence the data became available for use by the processor only after three machine cycles. Since any page origin $(s + q)$ can be contained in the directory, pages can reside anywhere in the cache so Map 3′ of Fig. 9.5-10 is fully associative.

Even though the directory performs associative compares, it is not an associative memory in the strict sense. The directory is a high speed, random access memory with only one word accessed at a time. The associative logic is external to the array. It would be desirable to have a fully associative directory, which would allow fully associative mapping, since better overall paging efficiency could be obtained. Associative mapping requires a smaller cache for a given miss ratio objective than set associative mapping. Furthermore, the fully associative design is less sensitive to the particular job stream being processed, since it tends to optimize itself into the map most appropriate for the job. Fully associative design is more expensive, however, as well as slower for typical cache designs (Meade, 1971).

The replacement algorithm is the LRU procedure previously discussed. Since a page can reside in only one of four possible page slots, the least recently used page of each set must be tracked. In any design using LRU replacement, the order of all elements relative to one another in terms of usage must be stored. For four elements or four pages per set, there are four factorial or 24 possible combinations of relative usage. This requires 5 bits minimum plus an occupancy control bit, giving a 6 bit usage control function for each of the 128 sets. These are stored in special hardware with separate control and updating algorithms. Two other important features used in the model 195 to increase the overall speed are store-through and load-through. Store-through merely ensures that when a change is made in the cache, it is

---

* This register is contained in the buffer storage control unit.

simultaneously made in main memory. Thus when a miss occurs and the cache is full, the least recently used page within the proper set can be erased without having to write possible changes back into main memory. Load-through arranges the order of page data transfer when a miss occurs. It ensures that the referenced 8 byte word of the desired page is retrieved first and simultaneously provided to the processor and cache. The remaining bytes are then transferred, furnishing the necessary information to the processor with minimum delay.

The operation of the cache is hardware controlled by a storage control unit and is not program addressable. The user addresses main memory as usual, and the cache operation is transparent to the user. The user's logical address is equivalent to a main memory or in this case a secondary storage address. Table I, needed in Section 9.8 for keeping track of virtual pages on the disk or in this case in main memory, is unnecessary because this information is contained within the user's program.

Performance evaluation of the model 195 cache (Murphey and Wade, 1970) using 17 job segments indicates that the effective cycle time of the hierarchy is about 162 nsec, with occasional increases to 175 nsec. The 17 segment job stream contained a mixture of commercial processing and moderate amounts of decimal arithmetic, scientific, engineering, and systems-type processing (sorting, assembling, compile, link edit). The average hit ratio for the buffer during simulated processing of these 17 segments was 99.6%. Smaller hit ratios give quite adequate performance.

9.11.3 CDC 7600 Memory Hierarchy (Cyber 70 Model 76)

Although the operation of the memory hierarchy in the CDC 7600 system is quite different in detail from that of the cache concept, it serves the same purpose—to speed up the effective or apparent cycle time of a large, slow main memory with a smaller, faster memory. This hierarchy has certain aspects similar to the older scratch-pad concept and certain concepts similar to the cache, hence it could be classified as an alternative to both. This system is not a paged virtual system in the fundamental sense for several reasons. (a) The operation of the hierarchy is *not* transparent to the user, in fact must be programmed in detail (i.e., no automatic address translation nor relocation hardware). (b) The number of words that are block transferred between secondary and primary storage can vary at the discretion of the programmer (i.e., pages are not of fixed size). Because of these differences, greater involvement is required from the programmer, but more freedom is also provided for fine tuning the system to individual problems. This freedom is often useful in scientific problems for which this system was specifically designed.

The memory hierarchy within the central procesing unit consists basically of a large core memory (LCM), which is the secondary store in this hierarchy. This memory has a maximum capacity of 512K' words of 64 bits/word.* The complete read/write cycle requires 64 CPU clock cycles of 27.5 nsec each (see Table 1.1-1) or 1.75 μsec. This memory is backed by a small core memory (SCM) with a maximum capacity of 64K' words × 65 bits/word.† This smaller primary store has a read/write cycle time of 10 CPU clock periods or 0.275 μsec and an access time of 4 clock periods or 0.110 μsec. This is considerably slower than the CPU clock period but is compensated by interleaving of modules. The SCM is organized logically into a maximum of 32 independent modules or banks. Since the read/write cycle time is a maximum of 10 clock pulses, 10 banks can be in operation at one time. Under ideal conditions with data that can be perfectly interleaved, the effective cycle time is thus one-tenth that of any module; that is, the successively operating banks deliver one memory reference on successive clock pulses. Hence an effective access rate of 27.5 nsec is obtained under ideal conditions. In random addressing, far fewer banks, typically only four, are in operation, giving a longer effective cycle time of the primary store.‡

In operation, block transfers of data from the large secondary store to the small primary store require that the program specify the length of the block and the beginning address in both stores. Each of these three parameters is placed in separate CPU registers,§ thus acting as base registers for simplifying subsequent word addressing during programming. The 60 bit words are read and copied from consecutive addresses at the rate of one word per CPU clock period. All other activity is stopped during this data transfer except for I/O word requests, which can proceed simultaneously. Exactly the same circumstances exist when data are transferred in the reverse direction, from the smaller memory back to the larger store. Thus it is apparent that the operation of the primary store is not transparent to the user and in fact must be programmed in detail.

The architecture of this entire system is very different from that of previously described systems. The central processor is augmented by 10 peripheral processing units, each with its own memory of 4096 words × 12 bits (plus one parity bit) per word. These peripheral processors act both as I/O controllers and as local computers as described in Section 9.2. This architecture represents one approach to the problem of speeding up the entire

---

* This is a 60 bit word plus 4 parity bits.
† This is a 60 bit word plus 5 parity bits.
‡ This is quite different from the cache, which has a basic read/write cycle time equal to one CPU cycle time.
§ The total block length is obtained by adding an 18 bit field from the instruction for BLOCK COPY to the register containing the block length.

computational process. Increasing the effective speed of main memory is one important aspect of this larger problem.

9.12   VIRTUAL MEMORY SYSTEMS WITH CACHE: THREE–LEVEL HIERARCHY

The foregoing discussions and examples have dealt with systems that had either a disk–main memory *or* a cache-type of virtual store. In large multi-programmed systems, it is often desirable to combine both features for better efficiency and versatility. Since the overall operation of such systems becomes very involved with the overall computer architecture, we consider only a few basic ideas pertinent to operation of the various storage levels. Assume a three-level hierarchy in which the main memory is paged out of a disk and the cache is paged out of main memory. To maintain consistency with previous definitions but to provide a distinction between various level, we define the various address bits as follows. Referring to Fig. 9.5-2b, we let n_m and n_c represent the total address register capacities of main and cache, respectively, with $n_m > n_c$; N_s and N remain as previously, but now we have

$$\text{main} \qquad n_m = n_{mv} + n_{mr} \qquad (9.12a\text{-}1)$$

$$\text{cache} \qquad n_c = n_{cv} + n_{cr} \qquad (9.12a\text{-}2)$$

where n_{mv} and n_{cv} are the page address bits and n_{mr} and n_{cr} are the real byte reference bits. Section 9.4 stated that page sizes for disk to main should be in the range of 1K′ to 4K′ bytes, whereas 32 to 64 bytes is more reasonable for cache.* So the real address bits using the nomenclature just given would be

$$N_r = n_{mr} \sim 10 \text{ to } 12 \text{ bits}$$

$$n_{mr} > n_{cr} \sim 5 \text{ to } 6 \text{ bits}$$

In principle this presents no problem and need not change the translation scheme. We are normally given a total logical address $N_s = u + N$, and ideally this byte should reside in the cache as well as main memory. Thus it is necessary only to translate all the N_s bits into n_c with an IF and WHERE part. This can be the same as that described in Sections 9.10 and 9.11 for translation from main to cache, except for some practical differences. First, N_s is so much larger than n_c that the directory becomes large and expensive. The major question is, Can it be simplified?

---

* In IBM manuals cache pages are called "blocks." Also, main memory page slots are called "frames"; the term "page slot" refers only to those on disk.

Before answering this, let us analyze the operation of the three-level hierarchy more closely. If we decode N_s into n_c by the use of a directory, ideally the IF part of the translation will be "yes" (i.e., a hit). However, when a "miss" occurs it is necessary to determine IF and WHERE this N_s address resides in main memory. Since the processing *cannot transfer to a new user on a miss to the cache, it is most desirable to initiate* the address translation of N_s to main memory *simultaneously* with that to the cache. A hit to the cache can then abort the main memory decoding, and a miss will provide faster fetching from main. So far, this requires nothing different from the previous separate pieces of the hierarchy. The translation of the total logical address to main memory physical address can be done as in Section 9.8 or 9.9, using a Table II assisted by a small partial directory. The simultaneous translation of the same logical address to the cache physical address can be done with a full directory as in Section 9.10 or 9.11. Since such a three-level hierarchy is useful only on rather large systems, both the partial and full directories begin to require large amounts of (expensive) storage capacity. Thus ways to reduce these amounts are desirable and are possible, since the two stages of translation of N_s to n_m and n_c have in common certain elements that can be used to advantage. As a result, the address translation for such three-level hierarchies appears to be more complex, though in principle it is simpler. We shall try to show this, then relate to an example using a large system, the IBM 370/168 virtual memory system with a cache. Theoretically, the partial directory could be expanded to perform a full translation of N_v into the real n_{mv} with no change in the three-level translation scheme.

Let us continue with the idea of the two stages of decoding to main and cache simultaneously, using a partial directory to be called a translation lookaside buffer (TLB) for the former and a full directory to be called buffer address array (BAA) for the latter. The former TLB must decode the N_v page address to give an IF equal "yes" or "no," and a WHERE, in terms of the real main page address bits n_{mv}. The BAA must take $N_v + N_r - n_{cr}$ bits and convert these into n_{cv} bits for WHERE and a yes/no for IF. Note from Figs. 9.6-2 and 9.6-5 that the number of bits that must be stored and associatively compared in the minimum tag store directory increases with the size of N_v. But we really need not separately translate $N_v + N_r - n_{cr}$ bits in the BAA for the following reason. If a portion of a page is in the cache, it must be somewhere in main memory, with an entry either in the TLB or in Table II. *Such being the case, it is necessary only to translate the real value of n_{mv}, which is already available from the TLB or Table II, into the real cache address.* This is the first fundamental principle of such a three-level hierarchy, and it greatly reduces the number of bits that must be associatively compared in the BAA.

Another general principle, mentioned now and described in the example later, is as follows. There are different page sizes in main memory and cache; however even though the cache pages, which are called *blocks* or *lines*, must be in contiguous memory locations in main memory, they may be set associatively mapped into cache. This permits a simple translation of the bits $N_r - n_{cr}$.

We now examine the IBM 370/168, primarily to see how the address translation is implemented in terms of the fundamentals presented in this chapter.* No attempt is made to be complete: rather simplification of such systems into fundamental principles can greatly assist in achieving an overall understanding. As always, there are two general, fundamental problems in address translation that cannot be avoided but only designed around. First, as the size and versatility of the virtual store increases, maintaining overall efficiency tends to increase the number of associative compares and the number of bits that are associatively compared; second, these increases make the translation slower and/or more expensive. Hence the general design approach is to minimize both factors. These problems should be kept in mind in the following example.

IBM 370/168

For a large multiprogrammed system with a fully associative disk–main memory mapping function, it is desirable to make the partial directory, which assists Table II, larger than the eight entries of Fig. 9.9-2, to improve the hit ratio and to accommodate several user's pages. However if a full directory were used, the large number of associative compares of $2^{n_{mv}}$, and the large number of bits compared associatively (namely, $N_v - n_{mv}$) would make this impractical. The model 168 circumvents these two problems while providing an effectively large partial directory (TLB) in the following way. The large value of $N_v - n_{mv}$ (i.e., n_d or $N_s - n_m$) is reduced *inside the CPU* by reducing the large user ID address to a 3 bit STO ID. The large number of associative compares is reduced by combining the N'_v bits with the STO ID, using a hash decoding that produces an address to directly address the TLB directory for WHERE and requiring only one associative compare (on four fields) for IF.

More specifically, the principles of the model 168 are as follows. The total size of N_v, which equals $u + N'_v$ bits, is rather large, representing many *possible* logical pages for many users. Of this possible size, only a small fraction will ever be used at any one time by the current users resident in the system. Thus it would seem desirable and expedient to reduce the potentially large size of N_v to a more manageable size. The model 168 accomplishes this in two steps. In the first step the logical user ID, consisting of u bits

---

* Additional details can be obtained from manuals [IBM].

representing millions of potential users ($u \geq 24$ bits), is reduced to a more manageable size. The full user logical IDs of only the six CPU-active users are stored in a STO address array consisting of six registers of u bits each. Associated with each register is a 3 bit STO ID. Thus the u bits are reduced to 3 bits represented by one of the addresses of the STO array as in Fig. 9.12-1. When a transfer to a second user is performed, an associative search of the array produces the 3 bit active STO ID of that user, if a match occurs. If no match occurs, the new user is entered, assigned one of the six possible STO ID values, and the TLB directory must be cleared of all such IDs that referred to the removed user. In the second step, the active STO ID is combined with the higher order N'_v bits of the CPU logical address in a hash decoder to produce a smaller address to directly select the TLB as shown. The hashed address need not be unique either for the current user nor among various users. In other words, the nature of hash decoding can produce the same TLB entry address for different users, or for different logical pages of the same user.

This nonunique hash address problem is circumvented by the use of a one-step associative compare as follows. The direct selection of one of 64 TLB entries yields six data fields; two fields are different STO ID bits (plus storage protect keys) for two different users who happen to hash code to the same entry, or alternatively are the same STO ID. Similarly, two fields contain the same, or alternatively different logical addresses $N - n_{mv}$ that happen also to code to the same entry. An associative comparison on these four fields is required to select one of the correct "real n_{mv}" address bits, very much like the directory scheme of Fig. 9.11-2. In this case, however, a "yes" match must be obtained simultaneously on both the STO ID and the corresponding logical page address, to permit use of one of the real n_{mv} addresses.

In this implementation the TLB allows only for two-way redundancy in the hash coding, which usually is sufficient. If greater redundancy occurs by chance in the hash decoding, no match is obtained in some cases and the translation must proceed by way of Table II. Incidentally, since hash decoder is also used to initially store a user's entry in the TLB, once established, a given logical address for that user will always decode to the same TLB entry. The primary purpose of this hashing procedure is to randomize virtual page allocations within the TLB so fundamentally, hashing is not necessary. The actual hash decoder is relatively simple. The large CPU virtual address and STO ID bit positions are merely arranged into six columns and added. No carry is used between columns but only the absolute value, giving the 6 bit TLB entry address. Obviously the above translation scheme has reduced the number of bits to be compared associatively through the use of the STO stack array and has reduced the number of associative compares by the use of hash decoding and providing only for two-way redundancy. This TLB and

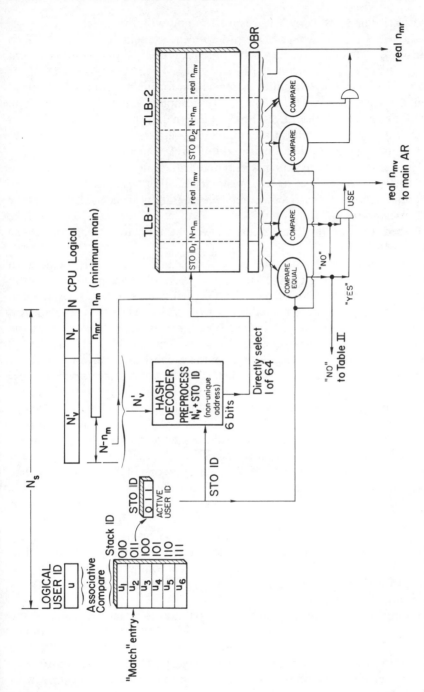

FIGURE 9.12-1 Translation of virtual address to real main memory address via hash decoder and partial directory (TLB) on IBM 370/168.

635

associated logic has many features in common with the directories of Figs. 9.6-4b and 9.11-2. However it should be clearly understood that the TLB holds only a small percentage of the more recently used pages of the current active users similar to the model 67 directory of Fig. 9.9-2. As such, it does *not* perform the complete address translation for main memory. A Table II similar to that of Fig. 9.6-1 performs the complete address translation and serves as backup to the TLB. On the other hand, the cache directory, described below, must perform a complete address translation, which it does in a manner similar to that illustrated in Figs. 9.6-4b and 9.11-2.

The cache address decoding is initiated at the same time as the decoding of the main address. In effect, we must decode all of N_s into n_c. However the first fundamental principle of a three-level hierarchy specifies that the cache may use the real n_{mv} address bits instead of N_v. Since these bits must be produced anyway, they might just as well be used to simplify the cache translation function.

The decoding of the cache is done with a tag store that is identical in principle to that of Figs. 9.10-1 and 9.11-2 except for some minor changes in detail. We now show how all the total logical address bits N_s are decoded in conjunction with a tag store directory or BAA to yield the cache address n_c. The cache blocks (pages) are 32 bytes, giving real bits of $n_{cr} = 5$; the mapping is eight-way set associative, thus $s' = 3$ bits. Referring to Fig. 9.12-2, the five lower order bits of N_r are real in the cache, hence convert directly to n_{cr} as shown. The remaining six higher order bits of N_r, labeled q', are real in main memory, hence must be in contiguous addresses there. In the cache storage array, however, the corresponding blocks can belong to different virtual pages. Thus these six q' bits may also be real in the cache address, but the actual page to which each address belongs must be determined. Hence these q' bits go directly into the cache address register, but they also must be used in decoding the s' bits by selecting one of $2^{q'}$ in the BAA. The s' bits of the cache logical address plus the deficient bits are decoded exactly as in Fig. 9.11-2 except that these bits are first converted into the real main virtual page address n_{mv} as in Fig. 9.12-1. Then these bits are used to do the eight-way associative compares on the real $n_d + s'$ bits in the BAA as shown. Since the real bits of the main memory address are used to select the set in the BAA directory, as well as for the associative compare, the mapping goes from physical main to logical cache as in Fig. 9.5-10 rather than from logical main to logical cache.

A simpler way to understand this translation is to merely think of the entire process as being identical to that of Fig. 9.11-2, but with two minor changes. First, the $n_d + s'$ bits are preprocessed because of the interaction with main memory. Second, rather than making Map 3' of Fig. 9.5-10 fully associative, which requires $s + q$ bits, we may make it *set associative* with

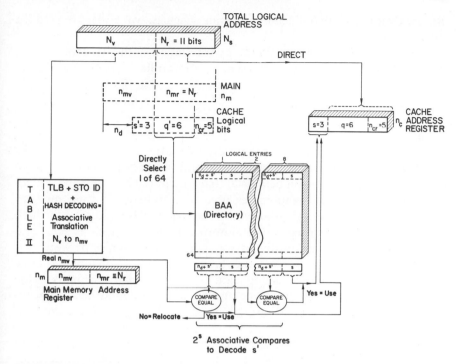

FIGURE 9.12-2 Translation of real main memory address to real cache address via a directory (BAA) on IBM 370/168.

no difficulties. Hence we do *not* store q bits within the page origin of the directory as is done in Fig. 9.11-2, but rather only the s bits; the q bits are obtained directly from N_s. Hence the model 168 cache uses a tag store directory with set associative Maps 2' and 3 and real main memory address bits for the associative compare bits $n_d + s'$.

Note that in addressing the cache, a minimum of two cycles is required as previously (Fig. 9.11-2). The first cycle interrogates the TLB and BAA simultaneously to obtain the real cache s bits; the second cycle then accesses the cache itself. If only read operations were required from the cache, it would be possible to do this in approximately one cycle by accessing a full set in the cache (i.e., all possible s bit locations) simultaneously with the interrogation of the directory. The directory would then specify which, if any, of 2^s cache pages is correct. The latter logical operation can be done very fast; hence the entire access is performed in one cache cycle. For writing, however, we must first determine the correct s bits, then write into the cache on a second cycle.

Rather than having two different accessing schemes, two cycles are used for all accesses.

In principle, the three-level hierarchy translation of the Amdahl 470 V/6 works as just described, although there are some differences in details.

9.13   ASSOCIATIVE MEMORY APPLICATIONS IN VIRTUAL MEMORY HIERARCHIES

It was pointed out in Section 9.5 that fully associative mapping of the blocks between primary and secondary storage provides a system that is less sensitive to the particular job stream being run than any of the other mapping functions. Fully associative mapping is used in commercial virtual memory systems, but the address translation is done with tables because of the high cost of associative type hardware. However the table scheme is slow, and cache systems use set associative mapping as a compromise between cost and speed. In this section we assume that fully associative mapping is used, and we investigate the various applications of an associative memory in the address translation function. The complexity and speed of associative memory, which determine the cost, are discussed in Chapter 4 and are not considered here.

Section 9.6 presented the fundamental ways in which address translation could be carried out, and these should be understood before proceeding. Referring to Fig. 9.3-1, when pages of fixed size are used, the maximum number of bits that require decoding is $N_v = N_s - N_r$, where N_r are the real bits. Since $n_r = N_r$, primary storage contains 2^{n_r} directly addressed words within each page, but each of the 2^{n_v} pages must be indirectly addressed (e.g., with an associative memory). It is easily deduced from this that we would not use a totally associative memory for primary unless n_r were very small (e.g., 0 or 1). However n_r is generally from 6 to 12 bits; thus an associative primary memory would be uneconomical and slow. In other words, the n_r bits need not be decoded associatively, and doing this becomes increasingly wasteful as n_r increases. Thus the first general conclusion is that *it is fundamentally unnecessary to make primary storage entirely associative.*

The next question is, Where and how might associative memory be useful? There are two basic choices: use a fully associative directory or use a hybrid associative primary memory. The former is no different from the directories previously discussed, except with $s = n_v$, 2^{n_v} associative compares are required for each page reference. In addition, when a match is found, the real s bits must be transferred to the primary address register for a subsequent reference to the desired page (Fig. 9.13-1). The storing and transfer of the s bits provides a fully associative Map 3 (Fig. 9.5-9) as discussed in Section 9.6. Recall, however, that when Map 2 is fully associative, Map 3 can be a direct

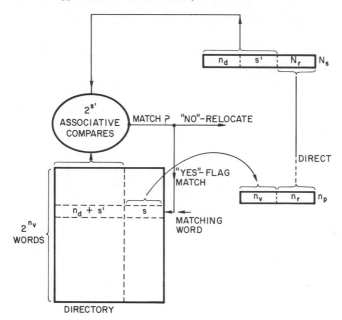

FIGURE 9.13-1   Fully associative directory using $n_d + 2s$ bits/word; $s = n_r$.

mapping and still provide the appearance of a fully associative map. The directory can have hard-wired direct enable lines to primary pages in place of transferring the s bits, thus eliminating the second access. This is one of the principles used in the hybrid primary store. Rather than fabricating a separate directory, the associative functions can be placed close to the proper pages, as in Fig. 9.13-2. Large-scale integration allows either of these schemes to be implemented with a number of possible configuration. Let us consider some of the advantages and disadvantages of each approach. Assume for simplicity that fully decoded $2\frac{1}{2}$D semiconductor chips, similar to those of Fig. 4.9-4, are available, and each chip contains a full page of 2^{n_r} bytes or words. The real address bits must then be broken into two parts n_{r1} and n_{r2} as in Fig. 9.13-2—one part to select one of $2^{n_{r1}}$ word lines and the other part to select one of $2^{n_{r2}}$ segments of bit/sense lines, each segment of b bits as in Fig. 4.9-4. As detailed in Section 4.9, these address bits are paralleled to all chips, hence require an additional chip selection, which is provided by the ENABLE input to the chip decoder as shown. The ENABLE input permits a very simple implementation of the associative translation function. Along with the other devices, each chip has a separate register fabricated that performs a single compare on all N_v bits, and this compare is done simultaneously on all chips. Only one chip can have a match, and this match

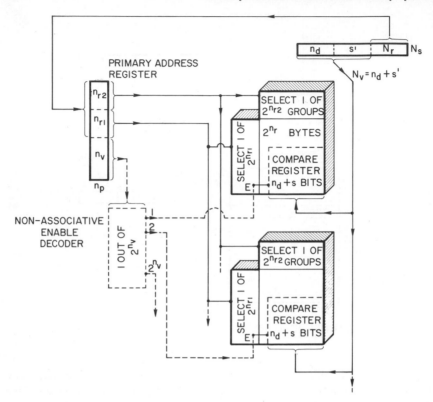

FIGURE 9.13-2   Hybrid primary store with on-chip associative address translation.

produces an immediate ENABLE signal on the chip decoder as shown. It is *not* necessary in this case to first provide the s bits in the primary address register for ENABLE decoding, as would be required in the scheme of Fig. 9.13-1, since this is actually done directly. Of course nonassociative decoding of the n_v or s bits in the primary address register would still be done by a separate decoder and a separate input to the same ENABLE function on each chip* (dashed lines in Fig. 9.13-2). Hence only one access to the primary store is needed, and if the on-chip compare register is fast, the entire translation could be fast. The decoding of the real n_r bits for the word and bit/sense line of each chip can be performed simultaneously with the associative decoding of the N_v chip selection bits. One serious disadvantage of this on-chip hybrid scheme is that an additional N_v pin connections must be made to

---

* The two inputs to the ENABLE terminal would be ORed together.

every chip.* The identical scheme can be implemented with off-chip associative compares and direct Enable signals to each page, and only one additional pin per chip is required.

The direct page ENABLE signal necessary in the above scheme can be obtained from an associative memory array that provides $\bar{F}$ type flags as detailed in Section 4.12. A simple inverter NOR gate with $\bar{F}$ as input for each page would provide the ENABLE signal immediately. Note that if Map 3 were fully associative as in Fig. 9.13-1, rather than direct with a direct ENABLE as previously, an associative memory array such as that described in Section 4.12, which performs the compare functions internal to the array, would require two cycles to fetch the real n_v page address. The first cycle would provide the match flag and the second cycle would read the match word to obtain n_v. This second cycle can be avoided only by doing the compare functions external to the array as in Figs. 9.10-1 and 9.11-2. This still necessitates a subsequent decoding of the n_v bits in the primary address register, and both requirements are avoid by the direct ENABLE implementation for Map 3 as in Fig. 9.13-2.

The page usage and control information required for each page could also be included in the on-chip associative register, which uses the same direct page ENABLE line. Such a scheme would have considerable advantages.

9.14 POTENTIAL PITFALLS IN PROGRAMMING VIRTUAL MEMORY SYSTEMS

Even though virtual systems can relieve the user of much detailed programming, there are potential pitfalls which can sometimes seriously degrade the problem solution. We wish to show by example that the programming is not always optimized, and in some cases the user must pay close attention to data organization. Generally the key problem is to minimize the number of page swaps—in other words, to maximize the hit ratio required for problem solution. The following case demonstrates that the number of page swaps can depend critically on the organization of arrays and the method of iterating or looping the array elements.

Let us assume that an engineering problem to be solved involves three-dimensional arrays. A virtual memory system is available having the following characteristics.

---

* We would also need some method of signaling that no match has occurred on any chip to initiate a relocate cycle. Conceivably this could be done on the existing sense lines, but an additional pin might be needed.

1. Demand paging. "LRU" page replacement algorithm.
2. Page size = 2048 words, 40 bits/word.
3. Maximum allotment of 8 pages of physical main memory per user (i.e., 16,384 words/user).
4. Virtual memory on disk (any size).

The problem requires evaluation of the function.

$$F_2 = \sum_{\text{all } I, J, K} (C_1 A_{IJK} + C_2 A_{IJK}^2)$$

The 3D array A_{IJK} is organized as follows. Each element A_{IJK} occupies one word; I varies from 1 to 2048, J varies from 1 to 4, and K from 1 to 2. The pages are made up of segmented listings of the array elements, starting page 1 with $A_{111}, A_{211}, A_{311}, \ldots, A_{2048,1,1}$; page 2 with $A_{112}, A_{212}, A_{312}$, and so on, through page 8, with $A_{142}, A_{2,4,2}, \ldots, A_{2048,4,2}$. The pages may be placed in any manner on one disk surface.

Let us first do this problem by looping or iterating on subscript K with I and J constant, then J, and finally I. A Fortran program that would accomplish this is as follows:

```
    DIMENSIONS A(2048, 4, 2).
    COMMENT—ARRAY A OCCUPIES 8 PAGES.
    F1 = 0.
    DO 2 I = 1, 2048.
    DO 2 J = 1, 4.
    DO 2 K = 1, 2.
1   F1 = C1 × A_IJK + C2 × (A_IJK)².
2   F2 = F2 + F1.
    COMMENT—F2 SUMS F1 OVER ALL ARRAY ELEMENTS.
    PRINT F2.
    COMMENT—PROGRAM AND ANSWER REQUIRES 1000
    WORDS MAXIMUM.
```

Note. In this Fortran program, K loop is done first, then J, then I.

Let us now determine the number of page swaps executed. We will see that considerable page swapping is required because of poor data organization. Significant improvement will be seen to be possible by simply rearranging the order of I, J, and K within the DO loops, or by reorganizing the arrays.

One page is required for the program and work space to hold constants and intermediate results in the calculations. Thus there are only seven pages available to hold alphanumeric data. Page numbers are determined by the JK subscripts only since each page contains all I from 1 to 2048 words. The page numbers and corresponding J K subscripts are listed in Table 9.14-1.

TABLE 9.14-1   Page Numbers and Corresponding Subscript Designations

Page Number	J	K
1	1	1
2	1	2
3	2	1
4	2	2
5	3	1
6	3	2
7	4	1
8	4	2

The program first increments K from 1 to 2 with $J = 1$ and $I = 1$, which requires pages 1 and 2. Next J is incremented progressively from 1 to 4, requiring pages 3, 4, 5, 6, 7, and 8. Since only seven pages can be present at one time, and these are assumed to be already loaded, page 1, the least recently used, is removed and page 8 is transferred in. Next I is incremented to 2 and the interactions on J and K are repeated. This requires pages 1 through 8 successively. But page 1 is out and page 2 is the least recently used. Thus page 2 is replaced by page 1. But 2 is needed next, and 3 is now the least recently used. Therefore another swap of 3 with 2 takes place. The process continues, requiring a total of seven page swaps. As the end, the pages are back in the original order, and when I is incremented to 3, only one page swap is required. On $I = 4$, however, again seven page swaps are required. Hence when I is an even number, seven page swaps are required, whereas when I is an odd number ,only one swap is needed. Thus a total of 1024 + $(7 \times 1024) = 8K'$ swaps are needed, a rather formidable amount.

The situations can be greatly improved simply by reversing the order of the DO loops to

DO 2 $K = 1, 2$
DO 2 $J = 1, 4$
DO 2 $I = 1, 2048$

Now all 2048 interations on a total page are performed before incrementing to a new page. After the seventh page is complete, page 8 must be swapped in as before, but only one page swap is required for the entire program.

Clearly the ordering of page references can be very important. Of course the problem could be eliminated by allotting more pages per user, but this is not always possible, and the programmer must be aware of these limitations.

References

Abbas, S., J. Ayling, C. Gifford, R. Gladu, T. Kewi, and W. Taren, "A Balanced Capacitor Read-Only Storage," *IBM J. Res. Dev.*, **12** (1968), 307.

Agusta, B., "A 64 Bit Planar Double-Diffused Monolithic Memory Chip," *Proc. IEEE International Solid State Circuits Conference*, February 1969.

Ahern, G., Y. Dishon, and R. Snively, "Design Innovations of the IBM 3830 and 2835 Storage Control Units," *IBM J. Res. Dev.*, January 1972, p. 11.

Anderson, H. L., et al., "LAMPF Data-Acquisition System," Los Alamos Scientific Laboratory, Los Alamos, N.M., Technical Report LA-4504-MS, August 1970.

Anderson, J. R., "Ferroelectric Storage Elements for Digital Computers and Switching Systems," *Electr. Eng.*, **72** (1952), 916.

Arking, A., "Processing of TIROS Cloud Cover Pictures on a Digital Computer," in F. Gruenberger (Ed.), *Computer Graphics*, Thompson Book Co., 1967, p. 137.

Ayling, J. K., and R. D. Moore, "Main Monolithic Memory," *IEEE J. Solid State Circuits*, **56-6**, No. 5 (October 1971), p. 276.

Ayling, J. K., and R. B. Moore, "A High Performance Monolithic Store," *Proc. IEEE International Solid State Circuits Conference*, February 1969, pp. 36 ff.

Bahr, K., "The Magnetoresistor, A Very Simple Solid-State Transducer," *EDN/EEE*, Jan. 15, 1972, p. 36.

Bajorek, C. H., and D. A. Thompson, "Permanent Magnet Films for Biasing of Magnetoresistive Transducers," *IEEE Trans. Magn.*, **MAG-11**, No. 5 (September 1975), 1209.

Barrett, W. A., F. B. Humphrey, J. A. Ruff, and H. L. Stadler, "A Card-Changeable Permanent-Magnetic-Twistor Memory of Large Capacity," *IRE Trans.* **EC-10**, No. 3 (1961), 451.

Bate, G., and J. Alstad, "A Critical Review of Magnetic Recording Materials," *IEEE Trans. Magn.*, **MAG-5**, No. 4 (December 1969), 821.

Beam, W. R., *Electronics of Solids*, McGraw-Hill, New York, 1965, p. 572.

Belady, L. A., "A Study of Replacement Algorithms for Virtual Storage Computers," *IBM Syst. J.*, **5**, No. 2 (1975), p. 89.

Berger, H., and S. Wudmann, "The Bipolar LSI Breakthrough, Part 1," *Electronics*, September 4, 1975, p. 89.

Berkowitz, A. E., W. J. Schuele, and P. J. Flanders, "Influence of Crystallite Size on Magnetic Properties of Acicular γ-Fe_2O_3 Particles," *J. Appl. Phys.*, **39**, No. 1 (February 1, 1968), 1261.

Bethe, H. A., "Introduction," in S. Fernback and A. H. Taub (Eds.), *Computers and Their Role in the Physical Sciences*, Gordon & Breach, New York, 1970.

Bobeck, A. H., "A New Storage Element Suitable for Large-sized Memory Arrays—The Twistor," *Bell Syst. Tech. J.*, **36** (November 1975), 1319.

Bobeck, A. H., A. J. Perneski, and J. P. Reekstin, "Some Properties of an Anisotropic Thin-Film Waffle Iron Memory Cell," *J. Appl. Phys.*, **37**, No. 3 (March 1, 1966), 1357.

Bonyhard, P., A. Davies, and B. Middleton, "A Theory of Digital Magnetic Recording on Metallic Films," *IEEE Trans. Magn.*, **MAG-2**, No. 1 (March 1966), 1.

Bouknight, W. J., S. A. Denenberg, D. E. McIntyre, J. M. Randall, A. H. Sameh, and D. L. Slotnick, "The Illiac IV System," *Proc. IEEE*, **60**, No. 4 (April 1972), 369.

Bourne, H., T. Kusuda, and C.-H. Lin, "Wall Streaming, Creeping, and a New Parade Motion in NiFe Films Excited by Hard Axis Pulses," *IEEE Trans. Magn.*, **MAG-4**, No. 3 (September 1968), 440.

Boyre, J., "Execution Characteristics of Programs in a Page-on-Demand System," *Commun. ACM*, **17**, No. 4 (April 1974), 192.

Bozorth, R. M., and D. M. Chapin, "Demagnetizing Factors of Rods," *J. Appl. Phys.*, **13** (May 1974), p. 321.

Bozorth, R. M., *Ferromagnetism*, Van Nostrand, New York, 1951.

Bradley, E. M., "Properties of Magnetic Films for Memory Systems," *J. Appl. Phys.*, Suppl. to Vol. 33, No. 3 (March 1962), 1056.

Brainerd, J. G., and T. K. Sharpless, "The ENIAC," *Electr. Eng.*, **67** (February 1948), 163.

Brennemann, A. E., J. McNichol, and D. Seraphim, "Delay Time for Switching In-Line Cryotrons," *Proc. IEEE*, July 1963, p. 1009.

Brooks, F. P., "Mass Memory in Computer Systems," *IEEE Trans. Magn.*, **MAG-5**, No. 3 (September 1969), 638.

Brown, D., R. Eibsen, and C. Thorn, "Channel and Direct Access Device Architecture," *IBM Syst. J.*, **11**, No. 3 (1972), 186.

Brown, W. J., *Magnetostatic Principles in Ferromagnetism*, Amsterdam, North Holland, 1962.

Brownlow, J., and K. Grebe, "Miniature Ferrite Cores," *J. Appl. Phys.*, **38**, No. 3 (March 1, 1967), 1190.

Buchholz, W., "The System Design of the IBM Type 701 Computer," *Proc. IRE*, October 1953, p. 1262.

Buchholz, W., *Planning A Computer System*, McGraw-Hill, New York, 1962, p. 209.

Buchholz, W., "File Organization and Addressing," *IBM Syst. J.*, **2** (June 1963), p. 86.

Buck, D. A., "The Cryotron, A Superconducting Computer Component," *Proc. IRE*, **44** (April 1956), 482.

Camenzind, H. R., "A Guide to Integrated Circuit Technology," *Electro-technology*, February 1968, p. 49.

Carbato, F. J., and V. A. Vyssotsky, "Introduction and Overview of the MULTICS System," *AFIPS Conf. Proc.*, **27** Part 1 (1965), 185.

Carr, W., and J. Mize, *MOS/LSI Design and Application*, McGraw-Hill, New York, 1972.

Chang, H., "Coupled-Film Memory Elements," *J. Appl. Phys.*, **38**, No. 3 (March 1, 1967), 1203.

Chapman, D. W., "A Study of the Writing and Reading Process in Digital Magnetic Recording," IBM Technical Report 02.205, April 25, 1962.

Cherry, W., and J. Gittleman, *Proceedings of a Symposium on Superconductor Technology for Computing Systems*, OTS Document 161763, ONR, 1960, p. 75.

Christopherson, W. A., "Matrix Switch and Drive System for a Low-Cost Magnetic Core Memory," *IRE Trans. Electron. Comput.*, June 1961, 238.

Chynoweth, W., J. Jordan, and W. Kayser, "Pedro—A Transducer-per-Track Recording System with Batch-Fabricated Magnetic Film Read/Write Transducers," *Honeywell Comput. J.*, **7**, No. 2 (1973), 103.

References

647

Chynoweth, W., and W. Kayser, "Thin-Film Inductive Recording Heads," *AIP Conf. Proc.*, No. 24 (1974 Conference on Magnetism and Magnetic Materials), 1975, p. 534.

Clementi, E., J. Mehl, and W. van Niessen, "Study of the Electronic Structure of Molecules, XII. Hydrogen Bridges in the Guanine-Cytosine Pair and the Dimeric Form of Formic Acid," *J. Chem. Phys.*, **54**, No. 2 (January 15, 1971), 508.

Codd, E. F., "A Relational Model of Data for Large Shared Data Banks," *Commun. ACM*, **13**, No. 6 (June 1970), 377.

Computer Decisions, December 1974, p. 52.

Comrie, L. J., "On the Construction of Tables by Interpolation," *Monthly Notices, Royal Astronomical Society*, April 1928.

Comrie, L. J., "The Applications of the Hollerith Tabulating Machine to Brown's Tables of the Moon," *Monthly Notices, Royal Astronomical Society*, May 1932.

Constantine, G., Jr. "A Load-Sharing Matrix Switch," *IBM J. Res. Dev.*, July 1958, 205.

Conti, C. J., "Concepts for Buffer Storage," *IEEE Comput. Group News*, March 1969, p. 9.

Conti, C. J., D. Gibson, and S. Pitkowsky, "Structural Aspects of System 360 Model 85," *IBM Syst. J.*, **7**, No. 1 (1968), 2.

Cummins, S., "Switching Behavior of Ferroelectric $Bi_4Ti_3O_{12}$," *J. Appl. Phys.*, **36**, No. 6 (June 1965), 1958.

Cushman, R., "Spinel May Make MOS Faster than T^2L," *EDN/EEE*, January 15, 1971, p. 35.

Cushman, R. H., "Can EE Systems Engineering Solve World Problems?" *EDN/EEE*, September 1, 1971, p. 46.

Daley, R. C., and J. B. Dennis, "Virtual Memory, Processes, and Sharing in MULTICS," *Commun. ACM*, **11**, No. 5 (May 1968), 306.

Damron, S., J. Lucas, J. Miller, E. Salbu, and M. Wildmann, "A Random Access Terabit Magnetic Memory," *AFIPS Conf. Proc.*, **33**, Part 2 *Fall Joint Computer Conference* (1968), p. 1381.

Damron, S. S., and E. K. Kietz, "Exceptionally High-Density Data Recording," *Modern Data*, December 1968, p. 28.

Davis, E. M., W. E. Harding, R. S. Schwartz, and J. J. Corning, "Solid Logic Technology: Versatile, High Performance Microelectronics," *IBM J. Res. Dev.*, **8** (April 1964), p. 102.

DeBuske, J. J., J. Janik, and B. H. Simons, "A Card Changeable Nondestructive Readout Twistor Store," *Proc. Western Joint Computer Conference*, San Francisco, March 3–5, 1959, IRE, N.Y., p. 41.

Dekker, A., *Solid State Physics*, Prentice-Hall, Englewood Cliffs, N.J., 1957, Ch. 8.

Dennard, R. H., "Field Effect Transistor Memory," U.S. Patent No. 3,387,286, issued June 4, 1968.

Denning, P. J., "Working Set Model for Program Behavior," *Commun. ACM*, **11**, No. 5 (May 1968), 323.

Denning, P. J., "Virtual Memory," *Comput. Surveys*, **2**, No. 3 (September 1970), 153.

Dietrich, W., "Partial Switching Processes in Thin Magnetic Films," *IBM J. Res. Dev.*, July 1962, p. 368.

Dietrich, W., W. Proebster, and P. Wolf, "Nanosecond Switching in Thin Magnetic Films," *IBM J. Res. Dev.*, April 1960, p. 189.

Dussine, R., "Evolution of ROM in Computers," *Honeywell Comput. J.*, **5**, No. 2 (1971), 79.

Eccles, W. H., and F. W. Jordan, "A Trigger Relay Utilizing Three-Electrode Thermonic Vacuum Tubes," *Radio Rev.*, Dublin, **1** (1919), 143.

Eckert, J. P., "A Survey of Digital Computer Memory Systems," *Proc. IRE*, October 1953, p. 1402.

Eckert, J. P., J. Weiner, H. Welsh, and H. Mitchell, "The UNIVAC System," *Proc. AIEE–IRE Joint Computer Conference*, December 1951 (publ. AIEE February 1952), p. 6.

Eckert, W. J., "Punched Card Methods in Scientific Calculations," *T. J. Watson Astronomical Computing Bureau*, Columbia University, New York, January 1940.

EDN/EEE, "FAMOS Electrically Programmable ROM," April 1971, p. 20.

EDN/EEE, "Capacitors Make Efficient ROM," December 15, 1971, p. CH5.

EDN/EEE, "Floppy Disks Begin to Enter the Mini-Mass-Memory Arena," April 15, 1972, p. 16.

Electronics, March 29, 1973, p. 51.

Elfant, R., "Direct Observation of Rotational Switching in Polycrystalline Ferrite Materials," *J. Appl. Phys.*, **34**, No. 4, Part 2 (April 1963), 1112.

Elrod, T. H., "The CDC 7600 and Scope 76," *Datamation*, April 1970, p. 80.

Elson, M., *Data Structures*, SRA, Palo Alto, Calif., 1975.

Farber, A. S. and E. S. Schlig, "A Novel High-Performance Bipolar Monolithic Memory Cell," *IEEE J. Solid State Circuits*, **SC-7**, No. 4 (August 1972), 297.

Fatuzzo, E., and W. J. Merz, "Switching Mechanism in Triglycine Sulfate and Other Ferro-electrics," *Phys. Rev.*, **116** (1959), 61.

Fernbach, S., and A. H. Taub (Eds.), *Computers and Their Role in the Physical Sciences*, Gordon & Breach, New York, 1970.

Forrester, J. W., "Data Storage in Three Dimensions," *Project Whirlwind*, Report No. M-70, MIT Servomechanisms Laboratory, Cambridge, Mass., April 29, 1947.

Forrester, J. W., "Digital Information Storage in Three Dimensions Using Magnetic Cores," *J. Appl. Phys.*, **22** (1951), 44.

Fotheringham, J., "Dynamic Storage Allocation in the Atlas Computer, Including an Auto-matic Use of Backing Store," *Commun. ACM*, **4**, No. 10 (October 1961), 435.

Fraher, J. J., "Bulk Storage Requirements at the Social Security Administration," *IEEE Trans. Magn.*, **MAG-7**, No. 4 (December 1971), 833.

Franaszek, P. A., "Sequence-State Methods for Run-Length-Limited Coding," *IBM J. Res. Dev.*, **14**, No. 4 (1970), 376.

Franaszek, P. A., and T. J. Wagner, "Some Distribution-free Aspects of Paging Algorithm Performance," *J. ACM*, **21**, No. 1 (January 1974), 31.

Freeman, D. N., and J. R. Ragland, "The Response Efficiency Tradeoff in a Multiple-University System," *Datamation*, March 1970, p. 112.

Freiser, M., and P. Marcus, "A Survey of Some Physical Limitations on Computer Elements," *IEEE Trans. Magn.*, **MAG-5**, No. 2 (June 1969), 82.

Frizzell, C., "Engineering Design of the IBM Type 701 Computer," *Proc. IRE*, October 1953, p. 1275.

Frost, C. R., "IBM Plug-to-Plug Peripheral Devices," *Datamation*, October 15, 1970, p. 24.

Gabor, A., "Adaptive Coding for Self-Clocking Recording," *IEEE Trans. Electr. Comput.*, **EC-16** (1967), p. 866.

Gater, H. R., J. D. McKinney, and W. D. North, "Bipolar LSI for Main Memory," *IEEE International Solid State Circuits Conference Digest*, February 1971, p. 78.

Geller, S. B., "Erasing Myths About Magnetic Media," *Datamation*, March 1976, p. 67.

Giaever, I., and K. Megerle, "Study of Superconductors by Electron Tunneling," *Phys. Rev.*, **122** (1961), 1101.

Gibson, D. L., "Considerations in Block-Oriented Systems Design," *AFIPS Conf. Proc.*, **30** (1967), 75.

Gibson, D. L., "Simulation in Computer Design," *Proc. 1970 CERN Summer School on Computing and Data Processing*, Varenna, Italy, published February 1971, p. 59.

Gilligan, T. J., "$2\frac{1}{2}$D High Speed Memory Systems—Past, Present, Future," *IEEE Trans. Electr. Comput.*, **EC-15**, No. 4 (August 1966) 475.

Goldstine, H. H., "Early Electronic Computers," in S. Fernback and A. H. Taub (Eds.), *Computers and Their Role in the Physical Sciences*, Gordon & Breach, New York, 1970.

Goldstine, H. H., *The Computer from Pascal to von Neumann*, Princeton University Press, Princeton, N.J., 1972.

Goldstine, H. H., and A. Goldstine, "The Electronic Numerical Integrator and Computer," *Math. Tables Aids Comput.*, **2** (July 1946), 97.

Greenblatt, S., "360/370 Compatible Peripherals: Part I. Tape, Disk, Main Memory," *Modern Data*, August 1972, p. 46.

Greenwald, S., R. C. Haueter, and S. N. Alexander, "SEAC," *Proc. IRE*, **41** (October 1953), 1300.

Gyorgy, E. M., "Magnetization Reversal in Nonmetallic Ferromagnets," in G. T. Rado and H. Suhl (Eds.), *Magnetism*, Vol. III, Academic Press, New York, 1963.

Haering, R. R., A. M. Toxen, P. B. Miller, W. P. Dumke, and B. W. Kington, "Magneto-optic Studies on the Continuous Sheet Memory," *Solid State Electronics*, Vol. 6, Pergamon Press, New York, 1963, p. 365.

Hamilton, F. E., and E. C. Kubic, "The IBM Magnetic Drum Calculator Type 650," *J. ACM*, **1** (1954), 13.

Hamilton, W., and D. Nance, "System Analysis of Urban Transportation," in *Computers and Computation* (Readings from *Scientific American*), Freeman, San Francisco, 1971, p. 183.

Hanlon, A. G., "Content Addressable and Associative Memory Systems: A Survey," *IEEE Trans. Electr. Comput.*, **EC-15**, No. 4 (August 1966), 509.

Harding, P., "What is 2 Wire $2\frac{1}{2}$D?" *EDN/EEE*, November 15, 1971, p. CH-16.

Haskell, J. W., "Design of a Printed Card-Capacitor Read-Only Store," *IBM J. Res. Dev.*, **10**, No. 2 (1966), 142.

Heller, L. G., D. Spampinato, and Y. Yao, "High Sensitivity Charge-Transfer Sense Amplifier," *International Solid State Circuits Conference Digest of Technical Papers*, February 1975, p. 112.

Hemel, A., "Making Small ROM's Do Math Quickly, Cheaply, and Easily," *Electronics*, **43**, No. 10 (May 11, 1970), 104.

Herrell, D., "Femtojoule Josephson Tunneling Logic Gates," *IEEE J. Solid State Circuits*, **SC-4**, No. 5 (October 1974), 277.

Hoagland, A. S., *Digital Magnetic Recording*, Wiley, New York, 1963.

Hoagland, A. S., "Mass Storage Revisited," Fall Joint Computer Conference, *AFIPS Conf. Proc.*, **31** (1967), 255.

Hoagland, A. S., "Mass Storage—Past, Present and Future," *AFIPS Conf. Proc.*, **41** (FJCC 1972), 985.

Hogan, C. L., "Types of Integrated Circuits," *IEEE Spectrum*, June 1964, p. 63.

Hoper, J. H., and W. Kayser, "High-Speed Creep Effects in Magnetic Films," *IEEE Trans. Magn.*, **MAG-4**, No. 4 (December 1968), 669.

Hopkins, A., "Eelectronic Navigator Charts Man's Path to the Moon," *Electronics*, January 9, 1967, p. 109.

Hunt, R. R., "A Magnetoresistive Readout Transducer," *IEEE Trans. Magn.*, **MAG-7**, No. 1 (March 1971), 150.

Huskey, H. D., R. Thorensen, B. F. Ambrosio, and E. C. Yowell, "The SWAC—Design Features and Operation Experience," *Proc. IRE*, **41** (October 1953), 1294.

IBM, *IBM J. Res. Dev.*, **18**, No. 6 (November 1974): special issue on magnetic recording.

IBM, IBM Maintenance Library, "*Model 168 Theory of Operation/Diagrams Manual*, Vol. 1," Sy22-6931-1, 1973; "Model 168 Functional Characteristics," GA22-7010-2, 1974.

IBM, *IBM Syst. J.*, "Structural Aspects of System 360 Model 85," **7**, No. 1 (1968). I, "General Organization," C. Conti, D. Gibson, and S. Pitkowsky. II, "The Cache," J. Liptay. III, "Extension to Floating-Point Architecture," A. Padegs.

Ingargiola, G., and J. Korsh, "Finding Optimal Demand Paging Algorithms," *J. ACM*, **21**, No. 1 (January 1974), 40.

Integrated Circuit Engineering, by staff of Integrated Circuit Engineering Corp., Boston Technical Publishers, 1966.

Jona, F., and G. Shirane, *Ferroelectric Crystals*, Macmillan, New York, 1962.

Jones, R. and E. Bittmann, "The B8500 Microsecond Thin Film Memory," *Proc. Fall Joint Comput. Conf.*, 1967, 347.

Josephson, B. D., "Possible New Effects in Superconductive Tunneling," *Phys. Letters*, **1** (July 1962), 251.

Josephson, B. D., "Coupled Superconductors," *Rev. Mod. Phys.*, **36** (January 1964), 216.

Josephson, B. D., "Supercurrents Through Barriers," *Adv. Phys.*, **14** (October 1965), 419.

Karlquist, O., "Calculation of the Magnetic Field in the Ferromagnetic Layer of a Magnetic Drum," *Trans. Royal Inst. Tech.* (Stockholm), No. 86 (1954), 3.

Kasahara, A., "Computer Simulations of Global Calculations of the Earth's Atmosphere," in S. Fernback and A. H. Taub (Eds.), *Computers and Their Role in the Physical Sciences*, Gordon & Breach, New York, 1970.

Katz, B., *Nerve Muscle, and Synapse*, McGraw-Hill, New York, 1966.

Keyes, R., "Physical Problems and Limits in Computer Logic," *IEEE Spectrum*, May 1969, p. 36.

Keyes, R., "Physical Problems of Small Structures in Electronics," *Proc. IEEE*, **60**, No. 9 (September 1972), 1055.

Keyes, R. W., E. P. Harris, and K. L. Konnerth, "The Role of Low Temperature in the Operation of Logic Circuitry," *Proc. IEEE*, **58**, No. 12 (December 1970), 1914.

Kilburn, T., G. C. Tootill, D. B. G. Edwards, and B. W. Pollard, "Digital Computers at Manchester University," *Proc. IEE* (London), **100** (1953), 487.

Kilburn, T., D. Edwards, M. Lanigan, and F. Summer, "One-Level Storage System," *IRE Trans. Electr. Comput.*, April 1962, p. 223.

Kilby, J. S., "Invention of the Integrated Circuit," *IEEE Trans. Electron. Devices*, **ED-23**, No. 7 (July 1976), 648: special issue on history of important tube and semiconductor devices.

Kirkpatrick, J. T., "Information Retrieval: United Airlines Operations System," *IEEE Trans. Magn.*, **MAG-7**, No. 4 (December 1971), 835.

Kittel, C., *Introduction to Solid State Physics*, 2nd Ed., Wiley, New York, 1956, p. 446 or Ch. 8.

Knight, K. E., "Changes in Computer Performance," *Datamation*, September 1966; p. 40; "Evolving Computer Performance 1963–67," *Datamation*, January 1968, p. 31.

Knuth, D. E., *The Art of Computer Programming*, Vol. 3. Addison-Wesley, Reading, Mass., 1973.

Kolsky, H. G., "Some Computer Aspects of Meteorology," *IBM J. Res. Dev.*, **11** (1967), 584.

Kvamme, F., "Standard Read Only Memories Simplify Complex Logic Design," *Electronics*, **43**, No. 1 (January 5, 1970), 88.

Lake, J. A., "Low Cost Core Memories Don't Have to be Slow and Bulky," *EDN/EEE*, April 15, 1972, p. CH. 14.

Landauer, R., "Irreversibility and Heat Generation in the Computing Process," *IBM J. Res. Dev.*, July 1961, p. 183.

Landauer, R., "Fluctuations in Bistable Tunnel Diode Circuits," *J. Appl. Phys.*, **33**, No. 7 (July 1962), 2209.

Laska, R. M., "The World Model Controversy: Will Mankind Survive?" *Computer Decisions*, April 1972, p. 24.

Lefkovitz, D., *File Structures for On-Line Systems*, Hayden, N.J., 1969.

Lewin, M. H., "A Survey of Read-Only Memories," *1965 Fall Joint Comp. Conf. AFIPS Proc.*, **27**, Part 1, p. 775.

Lin, Y. S., and R. L. Mattson, "Cost-Performance Evaluation of Memory Hierarchies," *IEEE Trans. Magn.*, **MAG-8**, No. 3 (September 1972), 390.

Lindsay, P., and D. Norman, *Human Information Processing*, Academic Press, 1972, Chs. 8–10.

Liniger, W., and S. Schmidt, "Transient Magnetic and Electric Fields Above a Conducting Ground Plane of Arbitrary Thickness," *IEEE Trans. Magn.*, **MAG-2**, No. 4 (December 1966), 727.

Liptay, J. S., "Structural Aspects of the System/360 Model 85, II. The Cache," *IBM Syst. J.*, **7**, No. 1 (1968), 19.

Looney, D. H., "A Twistor Matrix Memory for Semipermanent Information," *Proc. Western Joint Computer Conference*, San Francisco, March 3–5, 1959, p. 36.

Luecke, G., J. Mize, and W. Carr, *Semiconductor Memory Design and Application*, McGraw-Hill, New York, 1973.

Luisi, J., "Silicon on Sapphire Brings New Life to Read-Only Units," *Electronics*, February 17, 1969, p. 115.

Lum, V. Y., P. S. T. Yuen, and M. Dodd, "Key-to-Address Transform Techniques: A Fundamental Performance Study on Large Existing Files," *Commun. ACM*, **14**, No. 4 (April 1971), 228.

Levy, S., "The Last Decade of Computer Development," *Computer Design*, May 1968, p. 73.

Lovell, C. A., "Continuous Electrical Computation," *Bell Lab. Record*, **25** (1947), 114.

Mallach, E. G., "Emulation: a Survey," *Honeywell Comput. J.*, **6**, No. 4 (1972), 287.

Martin, T. C., "Counting a Nation by Electricity," *Electr. Eng.*, **12**, No. 184 (November 11, 1891), 521.

Masson, S., and S. Minn, "Preparation of Ferroelectric Thin Films of Barium Titanate by Vacuum Evaporation," *J. Phys. Soc. Japan*, **28**, Supplement, *Ferroelectricity* (1970), 421.

Mathias, J., and G. Fedde, "Plated-Wire Technology: A Critical Review," *IEEE Trans. Magn.*, **MAG-5**, No. 4 (December 1969), 728.

Matick, R. E., "Magnetic Fields Associated with Thin Nickel-Iron Films," *J. Appl. Phys.*, **35**, No. 11 (November 1964), 3331.

Matick, R., P. Pleshko, C. Sie, and L. Terman, "A High Speed Read-Only Store Using Thick Magnetic Films," *IBM J. Res. Dev.*, **10**, No. 4 (July 1966), 333.

Matick, R. E., "Transmission Line Pulse Transformers—Theory and Application," *Proc. IEEE*, **56**, No. 1 (January 1968), 47.

Matick, R. E., *Transmission Lines for Digital and Communication Networks*, McGraw-Hill, New York, 1969.

Matick, R. E., "Review of Current Proposed Technologies for Mass Storage Systems," *Proc. IEEE*, **60**, No. 3 (March 1972), 266.

Matick, R. E., "Memory and Storage," in H. Stone (Ed.), *Introduction to Computer Architecture*, SRA, Palo Alto, Calif., 1975.

Matisoo, J., "The Tunneling Cryotron, A Superconductive Logic Element Based on Electron Tunneling," *Proc. IEEE*, **55** (February 1967), 172.

Mattson, R. L., J. Gecsei., D. R. Slutz, and I. I. Traiger, "Evaluation Techniques for Storage Hierarchies," *IBM Syst. J.*, **9**, No. 2 (1970), 78.

Meade, R. M., "How a Cache Memory Enhances a Computer's Performance," *Electronics*, January 17, 1972, p. 58.

Meier, D. A., "Millimicrosecond Magnetic Switching and Storage Element," *J. Appl. Phys.*, **30S** (April 1959), 459.

Merwin, R. E., "The IBM 705 EDPM Memory System," *IRE Trans. Electron. Comput.*, **EC-5**, No. 4 (December 1956), 219.

Merz, W., "Switching Time in Ferroelectric BaTiO$_3$ and Its Dependence on Crystal Thickness," *J. Appl. Phys.*, **27** (1956), 938.

Methfessel, S., S. Middlehoek, and H. Thomas, "Nucleation Processes in Thin Permalloy Films," *J. Appl. Phys.*, Supplement to Vol. 32, No. 3 (March 1961a), 295S.

Methfessel, S., S. Middlehoek, and H. Thomas, "Partial Rotation in Permalloy Films," *J. Appl. Phys.*, **32**, No. 10 (October 1961b), 1959.

Middlehoek, S., "Ferromagnetic Domains in Thin Ni-Fe Films," Doctoral Thesis, Drukkerij Wed. G. Van Soest N.V., Amsterdam, 1961.

Middlehoek, S., "Static Reversal Processes in Thin Ni-Fe Films," *IBM J. Res. Dev.*, October 1962, p. 394.

Miller, G. A., *The Psychology of Communication*, Pelican Books, 1967.

Mitra, D., "Some Aspects of Hierarchical Memory Systems," *J. ACM.* **21**, No. 1 (January 1974), 54.

Modern Data, "Removable-Disk Memories" (IBM-compatible), December 1968, p. 48; "Disk and Drum Memories" (non-IBM-compatible disk), February 1969, p. 48; Disk and Drum Memories (continued)," May 1969, p. 42; "Disk and Drum Drives, Part 1—IBM 2311 and 2314 Compatible Disk-Pack," January 1971, p. 58; "Disk and Drum Drives, Part 2—Large Scale Drives," February 1971, p. 68; "Disk and Drum Drives, Part 3—Medium and Small-Scale Drives," March 1971, p. 56; "Removable Disk Cartridge Drives," January 1976, p. 36.

Morgan, W. L., "Bibliography of Digital Magnetic Circuits and Materials," *IRE Trans. Electron. Comput.*, **EC-8**, June, 1959, 148.

MULTICS Technical Papers, Honeywell Information Systems, Order No. AG95, New York, June 1972.

Murphey, J. O., and R. W. Wade, "The IBM 360/195," *Datamation*, April, 1970, p. 72.

Murphy, W. J., "Magnetic Tape Systems: Part 1, Cassette, Cartridge, and Small Tape Transports," *Modern Data*, 1971, p. 32.

Murray, B. C., and M. E. Davis, "Space Photography and the Exploration of Mars," *Appl. Opt.*, **9** (June 1970), 1278.

Néel, L., "Remarques sur la Théorie des Propriétés Magnetiques des Couches Minces et des Grains Fins," *J. Phys. Radium*, March 1956, p. 250.

Newhouse, V. L., *Applied Superconductivity*, Wiley, New York, 1964.

Nisenoff, N., "Hardware for Information Processing Systems: Today and in the Future," *Proc. IEEE*, **54**, No. 12 (December 1966), 1820.

Olson, A. L., and E. J. Torok, "Magnetization Creep in Thin Nickel-Iron Films," *J. Appl. Phys.*, **36**, No. 3, Part 2 (March 1965), 1058.

Olson, C. D., and A. V. Pohm, "Flux Reversal in Thin Films of 82 percent Ni, 18 percent Fe," *J. Appl. Phys.*, **29**, No. 3 (March 1958), 274.

Organick, E. I., *The Multics System*, MIT Press, Cambridge, Mass., 1972.

Osborn, J. A., "Demagnetizing Factors of the General Ellipsoid," *Phys. Rev.*, **67**, Nos. 11, 12 (June 1945), 351.

Pear, C. B., *Magnetic Recording in Science and Industry*, Reinhold, New York, 1967, p. 33.

Pohm, A., and R. Zingg, "Magnetic Film Memory Systems," *IEEE Trans. Mag.*, **MAG-4**, No. 2 (June 1968), 146.

Pomerene, J. H., "Historical Perspectives on Computers—Components," *Proc. Fall Joint Computer Conference, AFIPS Conf. Proc.*, **41**, Part 2 (1972), p. 977.

Potter, R. I., "Analysis of Saturation Magnetic Recording Based on Arctangent Magnetization Transitions," *J. Appl. Phys.*, **41**, No. 4 (March 1970), 1647.

Potter, R. I., R. Schmulian, and K. Hartman, "Fringe Field and Readback Voltage Computations for Finite Pole-Tip Length Recording Heads," *IEEE Trans. Magn.*, **MAG-7**, No. 3 (September 1971), 689.

Potter, R. I., and R. Schmulian, "Self-Consistently Computed Magnetization Patterns in Thin Magnetic Recording Media," *IEEE Trans. Magn.*, **MAG-7**, No. 4 (December 1971), 873.

Proc. IEEE, Microelectronics issue, **52**, No. 12 (December 1964).

Pugh, E. M., "Magnetic Films of Nickel-Iron," in G. Hass (Ed.), *Physics of Thin Films*, Academic Press, New York, 1963, p. 327.

Pulvari, C., and W. Kuebler, "Polarization Reversal in Tri-Glycine Fluoberyllate and Tri-Glycine Sulfate Single Crystals," *J. Appl. Phys.*, **29** (1958), 1742.

Rabinow, J., "The Notched-Disk Memory," *Electr. Eng.*, August 1952, p. 745.

Raffel, J., et al., "Magnetic Film Memory Design," *Proc. IEEE*, January 1961, 155.

Rajchman, J. A., "Static Magnetic Matrix Memory and Switching Circuits," *RCA Rev.*, **13** (June 1952), 183.

Rajchman, J. A., "A Myriabit Magnetic-Core Matrix Memory," *Proc. IRE*, **41** (October 1953), 1407.

Randell, B. (Ed.), *The Origins of Digital Computers: Selected Papers*, Springer-Verlag, Berlin, 1973.

Reisman, A., "Germanium ICs Point the Way Towards Picosecond Computers," *Electronics*, March 3, 1969, p. 88.

Richardson, L. F., *Weather Prediction by Numerical Process*, Cambridge University Press, London, 1922 (reprinted by Dover).

Romankiw, L. T., and P. Simon, "Batch Fabrication of Thin Film Magnetic Recording Heads; A Literature Review and Process Description for Vertical Single Turn Heads," *IEEE Trans. Magn.*, **MAG-11**, No. 1, January 1975, p. 50.

Rosen, S., "Electronic Computers: A Historical Survey," *Comput. Surveys*, **1**, No. 1 (March 1969), 7.

Rosenkrantz, G., "National Archives Mass Storage Requirements 1975 to 1980," *IEEE Trans. Magn.*, **MAG-7**, No. 7 (December 1971), 843.

Russel, L. A., et al., "Ferrite Memory Systems," *IEEE Trans. Magn.*, **MAG-4**, No. 2 (June 1968), 140.

Saltzer, J., "A Simple Linear Model of Demand Paging Performance," *Commun. ACM*, **17**, No. 4 (April 1974), 181.

Scherr, A. L., "Analysis of Computer Memory Performance," American Statistical Association Conference, session on Probability and Statistics in the Design of Computer Systems, Los Angeles, August 18, 1966.

Schwartz, S., and S. Klein, "Read-Only Memory Control Logic," *Honeywell Comp. J.*, **2**, No. 1 (1968), 25.

Sebestyen, L. G., *Digital Magnetic Tape Recording for Computer Applications*, Chapman and Hall, London, 1973.

Sharpe, W. F., *The Economics of Computers*, Columbia University Press, New York, 1969, p. 297.

Shevel, W. L., "Millimicrosecond Switching Properties of Ferrite Computer Elements," *J. Appl. Phys.*, **30S**, No. 4 (April 1959), 475.

Shirane, G., F. Jona, and R. Pepinsky, "Some Aspects of Ferroelectricity," *Proc. IRE*, December 1955, p. 1738.

Smith, C. V., *Electronic Digital Computers*, McGraw-Hill, New York, 1959.

Smith, D. O., "Anisotropy in Permalloy Films," *J. Appl. Phys.*, **30**, No. 4 (April 1959), 264S.

Smith, D. O., "Anisotropy in Nickel-Iron Films," *J. Appl. Phys.*, **32**, No. 3 (March 1961), 70S.

Smith, D. O., M. S. Cohen, and G. P. Weiss, "Oblique-Incidence Anisotropy in Evaporated Permalloy Films," *J. Appl. Phys.*, **31**, No. 10 (October 1960), 1755.

Speliotis, D. E., "Magnetic Recording Materials," *J. Appl. Phys.*, **38**, No. 3 (March 1967), 1209.

Sproull, R. L., *Modern Physics*, Wiley, New York, 1956, p. 127.

Stein, K., and E. Feldkeller, "Wall Streaming in Ferromagnetic Thin Films," *J. Appl. Phys.*, **38**, No. 11 (October 1967), 4401.

Stifler, W. W. (Ed.), *High Speed Computing Devices*, Engineering Research Associates Staff, McGraw-Hill, New York, 1950.

Stoner, E. C., "The Demagnetizing Factors for Ellipsoids," *Phil. Mag.*, **36**, No. 263 (December 1945), 803.

Stoner, E. C., and E. P. Wohlfarth, "A Mechanism of Magnetic Hystersis in Heterogeneous Alloys," *Phil. Trans. Royal Soc. London*, Ser. A240 (1948), 599.

Swanson, J. A., "Physical vs. Logical Coupling in Memory Systems," *IBM J. Res. Dev.*, **4** (July 1960), 305.

Takei, H., and S. Chiba, "Vacancy Ordering in Epitaxially-Grown Single Crystals of Fe_2O_3," *J. Phys. Soc. Japan*, **21** (1966), 1255.

Tang, D. T., "Run Length Limited Codes," *IEEE International Symposium on Information Theory*, Ellenville, N.Y., 1969.

Taub, D. M., "A Short Review of Read-Only Memories," *Proc. IEE* (London), **110**, No. 1 (January 1963a), 157.

Taub, D. M., "Analysis of Sneak Paths and Sense Line Distortion in an Improved Capacitor Read Only Memory," *Proc. IEEE*, November 1963b, 1554.

Taub, D. M., and B. W. Kington, "The Design of Transformer (Dimond ring) Real-Only Stores," *IBM J. Res. Dev.*, September 1964, p. 443.

Taylor, G., "Utilization of t^* Partial Switching Properties of Ferroelectrics in Memory Devices," *IEEE Trans. Electr. Comput.*, **EC-14**, No. 6 (December 1965), 881.

Thompson, D. A., "Magnetoresistive Transducers in High-Density Magnetic Recording," *AIP Conf. Proc.*, No. 24 (1974 Conference on Magnetism and Magnetic Materials), 1975, p. 528.

Tiller, C., and G. Clark, "Coercive Force vs. Thickness for Thin Films of Nickel-Iron," *Phys. Rev.*, **110**, No. 2 (April 1958), 583.

Tomkins, S., and S. Messick (Eds.), *Computer Simulation of Personality*, Wiley, New York, 1963.

Tricbwasser, S., "Ferroelectric Materials," in *Modern Materials*, Vol. 3, H. Hausner (Ed.), Academic Press, New York, 1962.

Tucker, J. H., "Simulation of Slave Memories," Technical Memorandum 66/1, University Mathematics Laboratory, Cambridge, March 1966.

Tucker, S. G., "Microprogram Control for System/360," *IBM Syst. J.*, **6**, No. 4 (1967), 222.

Vadasz, L. L., A. S. Grove, T. A. Rowe, and G. E. Moore, "Silicon-Gate Technology," *IEEE Spectrum*, October 1969, p. 28.

von Hippel, A., R. G. Breckenridge, F. G. Chesley, and L. Tisza, "High Dielectric Constant Ceramics," *Ind. Eng. Chem.*, **38** (November 1946), 1097.

von Neumann, J. H., *The Computer and the Brain*, Yale University Press, New Haven, Conn., 1958.

Wallace, R. J., "Reproduction of Magnetically Recorded Signals," *Bell Syst. Tech. J.*, **30** (October 1951), 1162.

Warner, R. M. (Ed.), *Integrated Circuits—Design Principles and Fabrication*, McGraw-Hill, New York, 1965.

Weik, Martin H., "A Survey of Domestic Electronic Digital Computing Systems," Report No. 971, Ballistic Research Laboratory Aberdeen Proving Ground, Maryland, December 1955; "A Second Survey of Domestic Electronic Digital Computing Systems," Report No. 1010, June 1957; "A Third Survey of Domestic Electronic Digital Computing Systems," Report No. 1115 March 1961; "A Fourth Survey of Domestic Electronic Digital Computing Systems," Report No. 1227 January 1964.

Whalen, L. R., and H. Leilich, "Ferrite Memory Systems," *IEEE Trans. Magn.*, **MAG-4**, No. 2 (June 1968), 134.

Wieder, H., "Ferroelectric Polarization Reversal in Rochelle Salt," *Phys. Rev.*, **110** (1958), 29.

Wilkes, M. V., "Slave Memories and Dynamic Storage Allocation," *IRE Trans. Electr. Comput.*, April 1965, p. 270.

Wilkes, M. V., and W. Renwick, "The EDSAC, An Electronic Calculating Machine," *J. Sci. Instrum.*, **26** (December 1949), 385.

Wilkes, M. V., and J. B. Stringer, "Microprogramming and the Design of the Control Circuits in an Electronic Digital Computer," *Proc. Cambridge Phil. Soc.*, **49**, Part 2 (1953) 230.

Wilkes, M. V., W. Renwick, and D. J. Wheeler, "The Design of the Control Unit of an Electronic Digital Computer," *Proc. IEE*, **105-B**, No. 20 (1958), 121.

Williams, F. C., and T. Kilburn, "A Storage System for Use With Binary-Digital Computing Machines," *Proc. IEE (London)*, **46**, No. 3 (March 1949), 81.

Winbrow, J. H., "A Large Scale Interactive Administrative System," *IBM Syst. J.*, **10**, No. 4 (1971), 260.

Worlton, W. J., "Bulk Storage Requirements in Large Scale Scientific Calculations," *IEEE Trans. Magn.*, **MAG-7**, No. 4 (December 1971), 830.

Yeh, A. C., "An Application of Statistical Methodology in the Study of System Performance," Conference on Statistical Methods for the Evaluation of Computing System Performance, Brown University, Providence, R.I., November 22–23, 1971.

Additional References

Chang, H., and G. C. Feth, "Bibliography of Thin Magnetic Films," *IEEE Trans. Commun. Electron.*, **83**, No. 75 (November 1964), 706.

Chang, H., and Y. S. Lin, "Bibliography of Thin Magnetic Films (1963–1967)," *IEEE Trans. Magn.*, **MAG-3**, No. 4 (December 1967), 633.

Gray, H. J., *High Speed Digital Memories and Circuits*, Addison-Wesley, Reading, Mass., 1976.

Magnetic Materials Digest: Literature of 1962, M. H. Francombe and A. J. Heeger (Eds.), M. W. Lads, New York, 1963.

Mee, C. D., *The Physics of Magnetic Recording*, North Holland, Amsterdam, 1968.

Newhouse, V. L. (Ed.), *Applied Superconductivity*, Academic Press, New York, 1975.

Prutton, M., *Thin Ferromagnetic Films*, Butterworths, London, 1964.

Shiers, G., *Bibliography of the History of Electronics*, Scarecrow Press, Metuchen, N.J., 1972.

Solymar, L., *Superconductive Tunneling and Applications*, Wiley, New York, 1972.

Soohoo, R. F., *Magnetic Thin Films*, Harper & Row, New York, 1965.

Index